MONEY, INFORMATION AND UNCERTAINTY

MONEY, INFORMATION AND UNCERTAINTY

C. A. E. GOODHART

BOOKS
10 East 53d St. New York 10022
(a division of Harper & Row Publishers, Inc.)

First published 1975 by
The Macmillan Press Ltd
London and Basingstoke

Published in the U.S.A. 1975 by
HARPER & ROW PUBLISHERS, INC.
BARNES & NOBLE IMPORT DIVISION

ISBN 0–06–492492–0

Printed in Great Britain

Contents

Preface and Introduction

In recent years there has been a spreading movement among economists to re-examine and to explore the fundamental insights into the working of the real economy which Keynes expressed so vividly. These are, shortly, that the world is filled with uncertainty, that actions are based on insecure expectations, that accurate information is at a premium, and that mistakes are constantly being made, so that our system lurches from one short-term period of disequilibrium to another.

This view of the central message of Keynes's work, maintained by Shackle over many years, revivified by Leijonhufvud and further advanced in recent years by economists such as Alchian and Clower, leads on to the interpretation of the role of money as an informational device made necessary by the enfolding uncertainties of a complex economy. This approach, of course, stands in clear contrast to the construction of general equilibrium systems (à la Walras) in which it is often hard to see what necessary functions money plays at all. So, conceptually, the main theme of this book is the critical importance of uncertainty for understanding the working of the monetary system.

The increasing appreciation of the validity of Keynes's emphasis on the importance of uncertainty, expectations and information costs has, however, been accompanied by a continuing criticism of several of the analytical moulds into which Keynesian theory was simplified and subsequently rigidified. Pre-eminent among these formulations is the *IS/LM* model initially constructed by Hicks. And there are certain other parts of Keynesian analysis which have remained in their simplified moulds, for example the analysis of the determination of the money supply in terms of a multiplier relationship between the monetary base and the money stock. Indeed, one touchstone of areas in macro-economics where analysis has failed to advance has been those that rely on mechanical multiplier relationships between aggregates, rather than relate adjustments to behavioural responses to changes in market signals, usually in the form of shifts in relative prices. In the field of monetary economics the greatest steps forward in this latter direction have been taken by Tobin and the Yale school, particularly in their development of the analysis of portfolio adjustment. Analytically, portfolio adjustment is the main descriptive tool used in the following chapters to examine the working of the monetary system.

In any case, these and many other developments that have taken place in recent years have led to a growing divergence between the substance of current research work appearing in the journals and the contents of many of the existing textbooks. Therefore, there appeared to be something of a gap to be filled by an intermediate textbook which could cover the space between the contents of existing introductory textbooks and the state of current theoretical analysis. What is meant by the term 'intermediate' is that it is assumed that all readers already have a firm grounding in standard Keynesian macro-economic analysis, in particular the *IS/LM* paradigm, and also have had at least an introductory course in money and banking. It is primarily intended for undergraduates in their final year and graduate students who are specialising in monetary economics.

The objective of the book is to advance as far as practically possible into the conceptual framework that lies behind recent analytical developments in monetary economics. In that respect it enters into some fairly complicated fields. On the other hand, it includes virtually no mathematical or econometric analysis, so it requires very little in the way of prior technical skill from the reader. This is partly intended, in order to encourage readers to find out what current monetary economics is all about without slogging through thickets of equations, and partly imposed by my own technical limitations.

The structure of the book is fairly simple and straightforward. It begins in Chapter 1 with a consideration of the role of money in the economy; it goes on in Chapters 2 and 3 with an examination of the demand for money; Chapters 6–8 are devoted to a study of the supply of money and the role of banks and other financial intermediaries; then in Chapters 9–11 we explore the transmission mechanism whereby monetary disturbances work through upon the economy; this leads on in Chapters 12 and 13 to a review of monetary policy; finally in Chapters 14 and 15 we turn to an examination of inter-regional and then international adjustment and of the role of money in that process. There are, however, two chapters, Chapter 4 on the term structure of interest rates and Chapter 5 on the financial behaviour of companies, that fit rather awkwardly into this structure. The reasons for including these chapters at this point, which are perhaps not compelling, were that in Chapter 3 on Macro-Economic Analysis of the Demand for Money, the question of the appropriate degree of aggregation for the purpose of economic analysis was raised. In my view the main issues in the analysis of the term structure of interest rates can, and indeed should, be seen as a dispute about the appropriate extent of aggregation over assets; so it seemed to follow on here. Having based the analysis in Chapter 4 on this theme, the appropriate extent of aggregation over assets, it seemed proper to go on in Chapter 5 to examine the degree of aggregation over groups of participants in the economy, and this led on to a consideration of the role of firms, and then to the particular effects of financial factors upon their behaviour.

Within the framework of this general structure, and in most sub-sections, I have normally tended to start with the micro-economic aspects of the subject at hand, dealing with these on a fairly abstract theoretical level. Then we move on towards the macro-economic, practical and even policy-oriented areas of the subject. In this context I have consciously pointed out in several places the political forces and constraints that bear on monetary economics. Our subject has been rightly called 'political economy', and those who choose to leave out the politics in the pursuit of rigour, or the avoidance of value judgements, or whatever, are to my mind losing too much that is important for the relevance and the immediacy of the subject.

Writing a textbook, mainly consisting of interpretations of the work of others, is a humble, even a humbling, task. Yet perhaps readers should be warned that at certain points the analysis presented here is individualistic, and does not represent an attempt merely to reproduce and to interpret the accepted work of leading monetary economists. In particular Chapters 6–8 on the determination of the stock of money and the working of the financial system, with its concentration on the portfolio adjustment approach and its rejection of multiplier analysis, is out of sympathy with the mainstream of current work in this field.

Moreover, even when one is trying to do no more than to extract the central elements of accepted analysis, one's selection process, deciding what is important and what is not, is inevitably biased by one's views and background experience. Here I hope that my own background of working, both as an academic economist and as an adviser in government and in the Bank of England, has helped to give some grasp of which areas of theoretical analysis have a practical relevance, and which do not.

I have learnt much during my work in the Bank. Nevertheless the views, and errors, expressed in this book are very much my own, and no one should attribute anything here to a Bank view, if indeed such a stable, monolithic entity can ever be truly said to exist. This book was written, though, in time which the Bank allowed me to take away from my regular duties, and for this I am very grateful. In this respect I have a special debt of gratitude to Leslie Dicks-Mireaux who arranged that this could be possible.

There would have been many more errors and quirky views contained in this book but for the great help which I received from colleagues and friends in the course of its preparation. Among those whose comments and criticisms on earlier drafts of the book were particularly helpful, I should like to mention Bill Allen, Andrew Bain, Peter Burman, Vicky Chick, Tony Coleby, Andrew Crockett, David Laidler, Kit McMahon, Robin Marris, Rainer Masera, Allan Meltzer, Marcus Miller, Steve Nickell, Bill Poole, Lionel Price, David Sheppard, Case Sprenkle, Michael Thornton, Geof Willetts, John Williamson and Geof Wood. I should, perhaps, add that often the most helpful and trenchant comments and criticisms came from those who do not share my viewpoint on monetary economics.

In addition I had much needed mathematical support from Peter Burman, Mike Clements and David Williams. The figures were drawn under the kindly aegis of Miss Crosby. Graham Hacche looked out the data for Appendix 3B. The main weight of typing, and retyping, the drafts in their various stages fell upon Gill Brewster, with support from Val Carter and Christine Stokes. I am very grateful to them all.

But perhaps the main burden falls upon an author's family, who ceased in this case to see much of me at weekends for over a year. To them I can only apologise for selfishly pursuing the urge to write this book.

C. A. E. G.

1

The Role of Money

SUMMARY

In Section A it is argued that the need for money as a means of payment is caused by the existence of uncertainty. A distinction is drawn between the narrower concept of a means of payment and the broader concept of a medium of exchange. A medium of exchange, but not a means of payment, would be needed even in an economy where everyone was certain of future events. In Section B the lack of personal information on the credit standing of the prospective purchaser is put forward as the main uncertainty that forces us to use a means of payment, rather than rely on credit arrangements. Once forced into using a means of payment, the use of money is much more efficient than barter in a market context, though the range of transactions which do not pass through markets at all but are internalised in social groups is often under-estimated. In order to serve as a means of payment, an object should embody sufficient information to make it generally acceptable without detailed and costly investigation. As is shown in Section C, fiat currency can serve this purpose since its value is based on the power of the state. This power enables the authorities to enjoy seignorage, the margin between the nominal value of the notes and coin issued and the costs of their production. Since these production costs are very low, the authorities could in theory issue sufficient fiat money to buy up any additional quantities of goods and assets required. They are held in check in practice by the political unpopularity of the ensuing inflation. The existence of a gap between the real costs of issuing financial liabilities and their value makes it worthwhile for intermediaries (banks) to bid for deposits of currency by offering attractive substitute assets. During the nineteenth century transfers between current accounts (demand deposits) of banks became accepted as final payment, and so these deposits should also be included in the definition of money, as argued in Section D. But the instrument that sets the payment transmission process in motion, the cheque payment, does not contain full information about the payer's credit standing, etc., so that the transfer process contains more credit elements than in the case of cash payment.

A. Certainty and Uncertainty

Money can be and has been defined in many ways. For statistical purposes the stock of money is often defined in terms of certain clearly distinguishable, but analytically arbitrary,[1] institutional dividing lines; for example, the stock of money is often defined as including the sight or short-notice liabilities, notes and coin and deposits of a short maturity, of certain sectors in the economy, usually the Central Bank and the banking sector.

---

[1] Among the statistical issues which require decision in order to reach a definition of the money stock are the following: What is a bank? What is a deposit? Are the sight and short-term liabilities of public-sector institutions, such as the Post Office and Local Authorities, to be included in the money stock? Are non-resident holdings of domestic money balances to be included, or resident holdings of foreign money balances?

Alternatively the choice of assets[1] to be included in the definition of money may be taken on pragmatic and empirical grounds. For example, money might be defined as that set of liquid financial assets which has both a close correlation with the development of the economy, and which is potentially subject to the control of the authorities. Attention then becomes focused on the fluctuations of that set of assets giving the clearest indications of the development of the economy and of the authorities' efforts to influence that development.

But if we are to understand why the stock of money may vary with economic conditions, why it is held at all, then it is necessary to begin by enquiring what functions money fulfils. Thus the primary definition of money, from which the other definitions emerge, is functional. What role does money play?

There are a number of functions which money is traditionally seen as having. The most important is that it acts as a specialised means of payment. Final payment is made whenever a seller of a good, or service, or another asset, receives something of equal value from the purchaser, which leaves the seller with no further claim on the buyer. Money is the asset which specialises in this role, being used generally for the settlement of transactions. As such it must, by definition, be a store of value and, in general, it proves most efficient to treat the means of payment as the unit of account.[2]

Yet another approach to the definition of money is to examine the cross-elasticities of demand and supply between monetary and other assets. This is the normal method that an economist would use to define a particular commodity, or industry, and has the advantage of combining aspects of both the pragmatic and the functional approaches. Only if a definition is chosen where these cross-elasticities are low will there be a close correlation between the growth of the money stock so defined and of the economy, and will this growth be subject to the control of the authorities. Otherwise the process of substitution, either on the demand or the supply side, would weaken the empirical links between movements in the stock of money and in money incomes.

However, if one probes further to ask why there should be a low cross-elasticity of demand between money and other assets,[3] it is ultimately necessary to revert to enquiring what special, necessary functions money carries out. Money, in fact, carries out several general functions, serving as a store of value, unit of account, means of payment, etc., and many specialised functions;[4] for example, only certain coins can be used to operate a pay telephone box. The most important general function is, however, to serve as a means of payment.

---

[1] In common parlance money is sometimes used as a generic term to cover all financial assets. Thus the term, 'he is rolling in money,' does not usually mean that the man keeps a lot of banknotes in his bedroom, but that he is wealthy. In some cases people drawing up home-made wills fell foul of this difference in terminology, since a will leaving 'all my money to my dearest nephew' would provide him with Aunt's cash balances only, while the securities, not being mentioned, would be gobbled up by the State. Although, following Humpty-Dumpty (in *Alice through the Looking-Glass*, chap. 6), a word can mean whatever you want it to mean, it is often more important to know what it will mean to other people.

[2] That it is not necessary, but efficient, to treat the means of payment as the unit of account can be observed easily by examining the habit of certain conservative professions of expressing their bills in 'guineas,' an obsolete coin. A guinea is not a means of payment, so the receipt of such bills requires the recipients to undertake some tiresome arithmetic to work out how much to pay.

Even so the value of the guinea is at least fixed in terms of the means of payment. Worse problems occur when alternative means of payment may vary in relative value amongst themselves, for example fluctuations between gold and silver in a bi-metallic system.

[3] The cross-elasticity of the supply of money and other assets is considered in chaps 6–8.

[4] Cars and trains serve the same transportation function and for some purposes we might want to define a 'transportation services' good. But for other purposes we will want to distinguish between cars and trains. The same argument can be applied to money. We define it above as providing a 'means of payment' service, but for some purposes we may want to distinguish currency and demand deposits with banks.

It is important to note that the functional definition of money as 'a means of payment' is different from, and narrower than, the concept of an asset as 'a medium of exchange'.[1] A medium of exchange includes those assets, or claims, whose transfer to the seller will commonly allow a sale to proceed. The distinction is that when the seller receives a medium of exchange, which is not a means of payment, in return for his sale, he will feel that he still has a valid claim for future payment against the buyer, or even more generally against some other group on whom the buyer has provided him with a claim. As Professor Shackle insisted, 'Payment is in some sense final.' Many, perhaps even most, transactions are, however, carried out on a credit basis, trade credit, or a personal charge account at the store. Such credit does represent a medium of exchange, but not a means of payment.

This distinction is important because the conditions that will require a medium of exchange are more general and wider than those that will generate a means of payment. It is, therefore, possible to specify the functions of a means of payment in an economy rather more precisely. In fact, a medium of exchange will be desirable in any economy with a time dimension. Because of differences between people in tastes, endowments, etc., exchanges will occur. Because of the existence of time, these deals will not all take the form of contemporaneous exchanges of goods or services, i.e. barter. So the process of exchange must involve the extension of credits and debits, i.e. there will be a medium of exchange through which current goods will be exchanged for future claims to payment.[2] But in a world of certainty, without transactions costs, there is no reason why the ultimate payment need be made in the form of a specialised means of payment. Person A could sell goods to person B at time 1, confident in the knowledge that his claim on goods in return will be met by a transfer from person C at time $t + n$, while B may extinguish his debt by selling services at some other time to some other person.

In such a world of certainty the whole time path of the economy is effectively determined at the outset with both present and all future markets cleared at known relative prices. No one can default on an obligation, or purchase goods and services which over the course of time exceed the value of the goods and services which he can proffer in return, through the employment of his initial endowment of physical and human capital (plus transfer payments). Under these circumstances everyone knows to whom to send his products and where to pick up his own consumable goods in return. As Professor Meltzer noted, in a discussion on the subject of 'Is there an optimal money supply?', that '... in the economy under discussion all market exchange ratios are known, all price changes are correctly foreseen and the only service of money is to serve as an inventory. In the economy, why can't the inventory gap be closed by holding verbal promises to pay, produced whenever they are required without any trips to the bank?'[3]

So the main function of money, defined as a specialised means of payment, is to meet and alleviate problems of exchange under conditions of uncertainty, for otherwise a generalised claim on future goods would suffice. In a world of certainty market exchange ratios (i.e. relative prices) are fixed at the very outset of the system, in period one. From then on activities, production, consumption, proceed along pre-arranged lines. Whenever all market activity can be collapsed in this way into the initial period, there will be no need for money. Such a condition is, of course, unrealistic. Nevertheless perfect certainty is not the

---

[1] This distinction has been emphasised by Professor Shackle, for example, in his comments on Professor Clower's paper at the Sheffield seminar on money in 1970, reported in *Monetary Theory and Monetary Policy in the 1970s, Proceedings of the 1970 Sheffield Money Seminar*, ed. G. Clayton, J. C. Gilbert, and R. Sedgwick (Oxford University Press, 1971) pp. 32–4.

[2] These claims will bear an interest rate dependent on the real forces of time preference and time productivity, even in a world of complete certainty. For an excellent, thorough, but difficult analysis of interest rates under conditions of certainty, see J. Hirshleifer, *Investment, Interest and Capital* (Prentice-Hall, Englewood Cliffs, N.J., 1970) pt. I.

[3] *The Journal of Finance*, vol. XXV, no. 2 (May 1970) p. 452.

only state in which all market activity could, in theory, be simultaneously arranged in the initial period. If marketing transactions were costless (and required no time to complete), then in principle it would be possible for the members of the economy to prepare themselves for *all* possible uncertain outcomes by exchanging claims on contingent commodities (i.e. a claim for x units of good y if state of the world z should occur).[1] Transactors can, in these circumstances, arrange their affairs to take into account all possibilities at the outset. Exactly as in the case of a certainty economy, all market decisions, all relative prices (for each possible path of the economy) could be fixed in the first period.[2] Although consumption and production take place over time, all planning and decisions on the allocation of resources, all market activity, could still be collapsed into the first period. Whichever path the economy took, depending on uncertain developments such as weather, health, technology, etc., the pattern of transfers of resources and goods could have been pre-determined. Such an economy can be described as having a certainty-equivalent form.[3] In such an economy, presumably, no money would be needed because people would know in advance, for each possible path of the economy, what transfers of goods and services would take place, and also that such transfers would satisfy the conditions that, ultimately, everyone had obtained equal value in goods and services for those that he had sold.

Yet the assumption of a world of uncertainty without transactions costs is so strained that it soon runs into practical difficulties.[4] For example, what happens if some of the transactors are dishonest? Perhaps it would be possible to cope with this by widening the set of states of the world still further to encompass the various subjective probabilities of each of the other various transactors honouring his contracts.[5] But there are in any case, even without worrying about honesty in dealing, a virtually infinite number of possible states of the world in any future period, let alone sequence of periods, and to establish a complete set of contingent prices – and transfers at such prices – for all goods and services in all such states is clearly impossible. It would take for ever. Time is a scarce resource also, and the use of time represents an opportunity cost.

It is also arguable that it is superfluous to specify both uncertainty and transactions costs as necessary conditions for the existence of money,[6] since uncertainty will entail

---

[1] See F. H. Hahn's paper 'On the Foundations of Monetary Theory,' in *Essays in Modern Economics*, ed. M. Parkin (Longman, London, 1973) pp. 230–42.

[2] If marketing processes were costless, presumably it would be possible to arrange for tatonnement, recontracting marketing arrangements which would allow this. In practice, of course, marketing involves participants having to make commitments, either simultaneously or sequentially, which cannot be recontracted. This will, in general, prevent all marketing decisions being taken in the first period.

[3] An excellent analysis of several aspects of an economy of this type is provided by J. Hirshleifer, *Investment, Interest and Capital*, pt II.

[4] Even though in this context we are not including among transactions costs those transportation expenses that must be incurred, even in a certainty world, in shipping goods from A to B.

[5] Though this might lead, perhaps, to the re-introduction of 'money' into an economy of this form if, for example, all commodities were subject to physical decay and some transactors were regarded as more trustworthy than others. Then, under conditions of subjective uncertainty over honesty, it might be of general benefit to arrange for payment in the liabilities of the trustworthy transactor.

[6] These conditions of uncertainty and transactions costs are, it may be interesting to note, exactly the same as R. H. Coase regarded as required to establish a rationale for the existence of firms, see his paper on, 'The Nature of the Firm,' *Economica*, New Series, vol. IV (November 1937) pp. 386–405, reprinted in *Readings in Price Theory*, American Economic Association Series (Allen & Unwin, London, 1953) pp. 331–51. Otherwise the functions of a firm, essentially the organisation and combination of factors of production for the provision of certain goods and services, could have been undertaken through the market mechanism.

transactions costs.[1] Certainly transactions costs mainly, if not entirely, reflect the cost of obtaining information (i.e. of reducing uncertainty). Costs are involved in learning the demand and supply schedules for tradeable goods of others in the economy, and in discovering the prices bid and offered. Setting up physical markets, which in itself involves a resources cost, is a means of trying to reduce such search costs. Once a seller has made a sale he will need information, either on the honesty and worth of the purchaser – should the purchaser offer deferred payment – or on the value and characteristics of the asset or good offered in exchange, which of course leads on directly to the specialised role of money as a device for simply providing the requisite information necessary to consummate an exchange.

Despite its patent unreality, the abandonment of a certainty, or a certainty-equivalent, economy as the main paradigm of the system causes serious difficulty for economic analysis. Most of the studies of market behaviour, of price determination, of equilibrium, of Pareto optimal conditions, have been undertaken within the context of a system[2] which can be collapsed into one period, in an important sense in a timeless system. The rigorous analysis of an economy in which market decisions under incomplete information take place in sequence – described as a 'sequence economy' in the growing literature – is only now beginning and is proving to be rather complex.[3]

In the meantime much of the analysis of the micro-foundations of the economic system, choice-theoretic analysis of the determination of equilibrium prices in markets consisting of transactors with differing tastes and endowments, continues to be done on the basis of systems of certainty or certainty-equivalence, with the resulting tendency for equilibria to be achieved. Yet in such systems there is no role for money. Money is an asset whose very existence depends on uncertainty, transactions costs and the possibility of disequilibria. No wonder economists such as Clower express doubts whether the theoretical foundations of monetary policy have yet been firmly established.[4]

B. Money, Information and Markets

In a world of certainty there is no need for the physical existence of markets or for money. So uncertainty, a condition which would also seem to imply the existence of transactions costs, is a necessary condition for a monetary system, defined as one which generally uses some specialised means of payment to implement exchanges. Is uncertainty also a sufficient condition to require a monetary system?

The answer is probably not, if the roles of the various participants in the social system can be established with sufficient overall direction and coherence. There are usually, for example, no monetary transactions within a monastery. To take a somewhat wider example,

---

[1] If, as suggested, transactions costs are a function of uncertainty, it is not entirely logical to investigate systems of uncertainty without transactions costs or of certainty with transactions costs. Yet there has been some academic interest in such hypothetical situations, especially in the case of uncertainty without transactions costs. Studies of the other situation, where there are transactions costs but no uncertainty, are less common; indeed it does seem to represent an even more artificial and less interesting framework. Nevertheless, some analyses of an economy of this kind have also been attempted, for example, by D. A. Starrett in a paper on 'Inefficiency and the Demand for "Money" in a Sequence Economy,' *The Review of Economic Studies*, vol. XL (4), no. 124 (October 1973) pp. 437–48.

[2] Basically the Walrasian system, as extended and developed by Arrow and Debreu.

[3] Most of this work, by such authors as Hahn, Radner, Starr and Ostroy is very mathematical in form. Students might, however, read Hahn's paper 'On the Foundations of Monetary Theory,' in *Essays in Modern Economics*, to get a flavour of the work under way in this field, which could become of increasing importance to our understanding of the fundamental basis of economics.

[4] R. W. Clower has written several papers which touch on this general subject. Among them, see 'Theoretical Foundations of Monetary Policy,' from *Monetary Theory and Policy in the 1970s*.

once a contract has been agreed between employer and employee, the employer can, within the terms of that contract, direct the employee to allocate his labour services first on this project, then on that. No money passes hands in the often long intervals between pay-days. The price mechanism is *not* being used to ensure that the worker is so employed at every moment of the working day as to equate his marginal revenue product with his wage.[1] If the system of employment works in a fashion that causes the price mechanism to be in abeyance for most of the time over a large range of economic activity (e.g. university professors do not get paid per lecture, nor professional footballers per tackle – indeed, there is much imprecision about the marginal productivity of workers), one can easily enough conceive of a system in which the price mechanism is not used at all and the allocation of goods and resources is by central direction. Then no money would be required.

In a system where the role of each participant is laid down by agreement and/or by custom, for example the family, the commune, religious communities, transactions between individuals will not take the form of exchanges of stores of value. It would represent an inefficient way of achieving the goals of the group, as any allocative benefits of a monetary system would be outweighed by the extra marketing and transactions costs in these cases. Indeed, considering the very large range of our activities in any day, all of which in principle could be organised through the price mechanism and involve monetary transfers, it is remarkable what a very large proportion are internalised in social groups such as the firm,[2] or the family, or even informal groups of friends.

Nevertheless, the complete suppression of the price mechanism, and the allocation of goods and resources by direction, somehow organised internally, would require a more authoritarian society than most people would desire, particularly since the difficulty of maintaining harmony in any group beyond some small size is notorious. Therefore, in any such system the wishes of some of its members would tend to be over-ridden. These problems imply that in the majority of those cases which involve relationships between large numbers of participants, economic transactions must be seen to be to the personal advantage of each individual, rather than adding to the social welfare of the group.[3]

Many economists, seeking to explain the existence of money, consider that the development of a monetary economy results from the availability of transaction economies in a marketing context.[4] This is certainly an important element in the story, but it is not the

---

[1] See Coase, 'The Nature of the Firm,' and also A. A. Alchian and H. Demsetz, 'Production, Information Costs and Economic Organisation,' *American Economic Review*, vol. LXII, no. 5 (December 1972) pp. 777–95, for a discussion of this point.

[2] Oliver Williamson noted in his paper on 'Managerial Discretion, Organisation Form, and the Multi-division Hypothesis,' included as Chapter 11 in *The Corporate Economy*, ed. R. Marris and A. Wood (Macmillan, London, 1971), that 'Internal resource allocation can be regarded both as a market substitute and an internal control technique.' As the unitary firm expands, however, the internal information network becomes overloaded with resulting control loss. In order to cope with this, firms tend to develop multi-divisional forms which make more use of the price mechanism and monetary transfers to allocate resources between divisions. Allocation of resources between the constituent quasi-firms of the multi-divisional firm is based on objective financial results separately calculated rather than on subjective information on relative productivity, as in the case of the unitary firm.

[3] It is partly a question of perception. The distribution of welfare in a competitive system is arbitrary, without ethical content, and certainly violates the wishes of some of the members. But it has the advantage of not requiring conscious agreement, and seems to distribute welfare by act of God rather than of authority, whereas in an uncertain, decentralised and complex world it is very hard to obtain an altruistic consensus.

[4] For example, cf. Clower, 'Theoretical Foundations of Monetary Policy,' op. cit. p. 20; K. Brunner, *A Survey of Selected Issues in Monetary Theory*, Reprint no. 2 of the Research Project in Monetary Theory and Monetary Policy at the University of Konstanz (University of Konstanz, 1971) pp. 7–13; J. Niehans, 'Money in a Static Theory of Optimal Payments Arrangements,' *Journal of Money, Credit and Banking*, vol. 1, no. 4 (November 1969) pp. 706–26.

initial key, since it already assumes the existence of a market economy. And, although virtually all economies do include both markets and money, it remains true that most activities are internalised within social groups rather than organised through markets. The analysis of such non-market transactions, and the determinants of which transactions shall be internalised and which arranged through the price mechanism has on the whole been ignored by economists. Moreover, as all social scientists, except economists, understand, the role of money and markets is primarily to do with the nature and form of social relationships.

Given, however, a system in which exchange transactions take place between individuals, each seeking to maximise his own personal welfare – though each may obtain utility or lose it through seeing others better off, through benevolence or envy – the question then becomes how can each individual assess when a transaction will be to his advantage? This is largely a matter of the adequacy of information. If you have no information about the behaviour of the opposite number to a transaction, e.g. a casual purchaser at your stall, then the risk that he would abscond or default, if he does not pay on the spot, is high. The only way to minimise risk sufficiently to enable a transaction to go forward to the benefit of both is to exchange physical stores of value.[1] If, however, the seller has more information about the buyer, e.g. a local farmer comes to buy at the stall, so that there is both information on his balance-sheet position and sanctions against default[2] (e.g. by informing all the other traders), then the seller may be prepared to exchange his goods for credit, involving, perhaps, an interest payment. The debtor will, however, still have to extinguish this debt in due course by the transfer to the creditor of a store of value acting as a means of payment.

If market information improves still further, so that there is complete, or virtually complete, information on the standing and behaviour of all the participants, then there is no need even for bilateral clearing of debits and credits.[3] Instead we have returned to a certainty world, in which transactions will give rise to credit and debit balances which can be settled multilaterally without the need for a monetary asset as a means of payment. The extent to which transactions in any economy are settled by exchanges of stores of value, or by bilateral credit arrangements, or by multilateral credit arrangements (non-monetary sub-systems), depends on the availability of information on the parties to each transaction. The proportion of transactions settled through monetary exchanges will, however, rise with the growing complexity and dispersion of the economy, because of the

---

[1] 'One way or another, we must see to it that nobody can get something for nothing.' J. Niehans, op. cit. p. 707. Also see the section on 'Trust, Rationality and Noncooperative Solutions' in M. Shubik's paper on 'Commodity Money, Oligopoly, Credit and Bankruptcy in a General Equilibrium Model,' *Western Economic Journal*, vol. XI, no. 1 (March 1973) pp. 36–7. He notes that 'As the general equilibrium model of the economy is nonstrategic [i.e. participants do not have trading strategies], it is natural for a modeler to implicitly ignore the problem of how strangers in a market economy can trade together efficiently and more or less impersonally with a minimal need for trust. When the economy is modeled as a non-cooperative game, this problem must be faced. If individuals trust only cash and there is no banking system, then although it is highly likely that optimality in trade cannot be attained without credit, at least all trades that are made are made for immediate value received by both parties.'

[2] On this point see the important paper by J. M. Ostroy on 'The Informational Efficiency of Monetary Exchange,' *The American Economic Review*, vol. LXIII, no. 4 (September 1973) pp. 597–610. Ostroy's key point is that 'Sellers, by requiring payment in money, are guaranteeing a steady flow of information such that the monetary authority, and it alone, is able to monitor trading behaviour.' In this case the monetary authority can provide sanctions against failure to maintain overall budgetary balance.

[3] Thus the degree to which 'the bilateral balance requirement' holds, c.f. Niehans, op. cit. is a function of information. With little information it holds both by transaction and time. As information increases the time constraint will be loosed. With full information, the requirement will cease to hold at all.

greater likelihood of *not* having adequate information on the behaviour of the counter-party to the transaction, and will decline with the development of methods to increase the information available about the participants. Seen in this light credit cards are, of course, an information-augmenting device. Reductions in the use of money, as a means of payment, depend on increases in personal information.[1]

If, however, the extent of personal information on the credit standing of the prospective purchaser is not adequate, transactions will only take place on the basis of a physical exchange of stores of value. When one good is exchanged for another, say apples for haircuts, the nature of the transaction – the transactions technology to use a jargon term – is called barter. It is sometimes said that barter requires a joint coincidence of wants and endow-ments,[2] finding a person with apples wanting a haircut meeting up with a barber who is feeling that he might appreciate an apple. Certainly there would normally be little likelihood of finding such a joint coincidence of wants, even when the process is facilitated by the development of markets which provide an occasion for all prospective buyers and sellers to assemble in one place. Indeed, the search costs involved in overcoming the need for a joint coincidence of wants are so considerable that barter rarely takes that form.[3] Instead, one or other of the parties to the deal will take in exchange a good which he does not want himself with a view to subsequent resale, with the intention of moving towards his desired position through a chain of sales and purchases.

It is, therefore, possible to overcome the double coincidence of wants if one of the parties to the deal will accept in payment some good that he does not directly want. But why should he do so? He is still left holding a good, which he wants to sell, and with wants, which he should like to satisfy, and he still faces uncertainty whether, and on what conditions, he can market his new good.

One answer is that there are some goods which have a broader and more stable market than others. If a person is offered salt, or corn, or cows in payment for some sale, he is more likely to find a wide group of transactors, offering a large variety of products, wishing to buy this product at a reasonably stable price, than if he was offered a fishing rod, or roses, or a bowl of goldfish. Thus there will be a tendency for people to move towards the general use of one or more goods (assets) as a common means of payment, in order to avoid the inefficiencies of barter, in a system where uncertainty requires the use of means of payment.

Following the illuminating analysis of Professor Brunner[4] such inefficiency derives mainly from two sources. First the length of the transaction chain necessary to complete

---

[1] David Peretz, 'Thirty-five Years of Change for the Financial System,' *Futures*, vol. 3, no. 4 (December 1971) pp. 349–56 has noted (p. 353) that 'Cash is basically a decentralised information system; possession of cash is an indicator of entitlement to resources to the holder, and to those who sell to him; but cash itself provides no means of centralising (and then analysing) information about all holders and all transactions.'

[2] 'The well-known problem of a barter economy reflects the necessity for a double coincidence of wants before any exchange can take place and the resulting high search costs which this implies. A problem which has not received as much attention is that a barter economy also involves the necessity for a double coincidence of timing of transactions.' M. Perlman, 'The Roles of Money in an Economy and the Optimum Quantity of Money,' *Economica*, vol. xxxviii, no. 151 (August 1971) p. 234.

[3] Except, perhaps, among schoolboys swapping treasures. Even then it is noticeable how some frequently used, standardised treasure, such as marbles or football cards, becomes the common basis for exchange and valuation, and, moreover, is prized for its use in exchange. Even if my son already has a Leeds United picture, he will welcome another for its swap value.

[4] In *A Survey of Selected Issues in Monetary Theory*, pp. 7–19. Also see the article on 'The Uses of Money: Money in the Theory of an Exchange Economy,' *American Economic Review*, vol. lxi (December 1971) pp. 784–805, by Brunner and Meltzer, where they develop their ideas further. This is, in my view, by far the best article on the uses and nature of money to be found in the literature.

the desired exchange (of good A for good X) will commonly be elongated by barter (in order to overcome the double coincidence of wants and time in a barter context), and secondly each link in the chain involves uncertainty. Assume a chain of the form A B C i X. When making each step the participant has to assess the quality and value of the good offered in exchange. In this case to get from A to X the participant either has to bear considerable risk or obtain a good deal of information (on the characteristics and marketing prospects) on goods B, C and i. If then a good can be found which embodies desirable informational qualities, there will be a tendency to use it as the counterpart of all trades both to reduce the length of the transactions chain and to limit the extent of uncertainty involved at each step.

There are two main pieces of information which people need to learn about goods if they are to accept them as a step in their transactions chain.[1] First, has the object got satisfactory physical characteristics? Think of the difficulties of using cars or furniture as money! Secondly, is there a good market for the object where it can be swapped on? It will be easiest to use as money some object whose precise physical attributes do not require continuous and skilled checking (otherwise each transaction will necessitate the cost and time involved in checking out the state of the means of payment as well as the object being sold), and whose acceptance is guaranteed.

C. What makes Currency Serve as Money?

There have been two common forms of answer adopted by societies to the problem of finding some standard means of payment, embodying sufficient information to make it generally acceptable without detailed physical checking. The first has been to use objects of varying intrinsic use-value – sometimes very little – which also symbolise some esteemed abstract value, often status, prestige, power. If your standing in the group is determined by the number of cows, pigs or cowrie shells you possess, rather than the precise physical state of these objects, then they can be accepted in payment irrespective of minor physical differences between them, so long as they count recognisably as a member of the set possessing the desired quality. The second has been to have some external authority provide the information on the monetary object, by stamping it or marking it in a manner that signifies information to potential users about the characteristics of the object.

There has long been a debate between those who argued that the use of currency was based essentially on its symbolism of the *power* of the issuing authority (Cartalists), i.e. that currency becomes money because the coins are struck with the insignia of majesty, not

---

[1] Niehans has shown that, under certain assumed conditions, some commodities with relatively low transactions costs may emerge 'automatically' as means of payment, as a result of optimisation processes to minimise transactions costs. 'The adoption of money requires neither law nor convention, nor can it be attributed to an "invention"; it is simply the effect of market forces.'

In my view, however, Niehans's commodity, which becomes used as a means of payment, is not *initially* to be described as money, any more than any other commodity. After a period during which it has been used as a means of payment, this process will, however, alter the information about its characteristics, in particular the existence of good markets where it can be swapped on. This accretion of information will result in falling transaction costs for this commodity, and turn it into a general 'means of payment,' *money*. Thus the development of money by this route should be seen as a dynamic process, not settled by relative transactions costs at a point of time.

In practice, however, the main transactions costs would seem to be related to information costs. So exogenous factors affecting such information (the role of the State, religion, custom, conventions, etc.) are likely to be as, or more, potent than physical characteristics in determining what is used as money. On this point see Niehans's 'Money in a Static Theory of Optimal Payments Arrangements,' *Journal of Money, Credit and Banking* (November 1969), and also a further development of a similar approach in 'Money and Barter in General Equilibrium with Transactions Costs,' *American Economic Review* (December 1971) pp. 773–83.

because they happen to be made of gold, silver or copper, and those who argued that the value of currency depended on the intrinsic value of the metal, with the role of the authorities (e.g. minting) restricted to the nevertheless vital function of providing the necessary information[1] on the characteristics of the metal in the currency (Metallists). The substitution of fiat, paper money, for metallic coin as the main component of currency in the last 200 years provides strong support for the Cartalist view that the monetary essence of currency can rest upon the power of the issuer and not upon the intrinsic value of the object so used.[2]

But if it is the stamp of authority rather than their metallic content that makes coins money, why then did the kingdoms of earlier years cast their more valuable coins out of precious metals, gold and silver, thus seemingly reducing their seignorage, i.e. the difference between the value of the resources which could be obtained in exchange for the coin and the cost of its production? If the value of coins was derived, *ab initio*, from the fiat of the government that the coin should be accepted as being worth a certain sum, why not then make the coins out of the cheapest material possible, thus maximising the seignorage?[3] There are a number of reasons for this. First there was, and indeed remains, the problem of discouraging counterfeiting. If the techniques for stamping the emblem of power on to currency are crude and easily copied, then it will be necessary to reduce the profits of counterfeiting (by reducing the seignorage) and to raise the penalties in order to prevent this.

Second, the power of the earlier kingdoms was quite limited, both absolutely in their own areas and geographically. If the coins had little intrinsic value they could not be used in trade across the borders of the kingdom; Gresham's law would come into operation. The population would tend to hold and to hoard the foreign coin of greater intrinsic value and would use the local coin for paying taxes, thus returning them to the authorities. And if the authorities sought to re-issue them at an exchange rate *vis-à-vis* goods that was different from their exchange rate in foreign trade, the population would become resentful at being exploited. Finally, the localised nature of the early economies meant that the bulk of transactions in them could be undertaken without much use of money, owing to good local information, and such trade as went on was often with participants in neighbouring principalities or areas of power. Under such circumstances it would be difficult to induce the population to hold and to use the local currency, especially if the power of the authorities was considered to be of possibly short duration. In order to increase the attractions and to lower the risk of money holding, the early authorities had to give a proportionately high intrinsic value to their coins. In short, they could not gain much seignorage because they did not have much power.

One of the problems before the authorities in such early states was the percentage seignorage to be incorporated in the currency. An increase in this percentage – often described as 'debasing the currency' – would bring in a higher return per unit in circulation but would, on the other hand, lead to an increasing unwillingness among the community to hold the currency, and to a growing preference for substitutes.

---

[1] Precious metals in an unworked state have only been used as a means of payment in exchanges under very special circumstances – e.g. in the various gold rushes in California and Klondike – and, even then, the picture, immortalised, for example, in film by Charlie Chaplin, of merchants and bar tenders weighing and checking the gold dust before accepting it in payment, suggests that payment in unworked precious metals has more in common with barter than with a monetary payment.

[2] There are definite overtones of this debate in the current concern for the reform of the international monetary system. There are those who would seek to base the international monetary system upon some object, gold, with characteristics that make it a suitable monetary object, and those who recognise that, *au fond*, the establishment of an international monetary system must be based on the realities of international power.

[3] Coins could hardly ever become worth less than their intrinsic metallic value, for otherwise they would be melted down for their metallic content; but they are frequently worth much more.

As the power of the state increased, and with the technical developments of printing providing more protection against forgers, so it became possible for the authorities to lower the intrinsic metallic value and to raise the seignorage obtained from the issue of currency.[1] The use of such state-issued fiat currency was supported by several factors. First, the state levies taxes and can insist that these be paid in state-issued money. This ensures that such fiat currency will have some value. The larger is the ratio of tax payments to total income the more important this becomes as a reason for employing the same money in private transactions. Second, state-issued fiat money typically has superior character-istics, especially with respect to risk, to the notes of small, private institutions; for example, wild-cat banking in the United States was so called because only a wild cat could find its way to the issuing bank to redeem their issued notes in legal tender. Third, the authorities could place legal barriers against the use of currency substitutes, e.g. through the definition of legal tender and prohibition on the holding by private citizens of potential substitutes such as foreign currencies and gold. This gave them an even stronger monopoly position.

The choice of the form, design, range of denominations, etc., of the currency is taken by the authorities with the convenience of the public in mind, i.e. with the hope and intention that they will wish to use and to hold the currency provided, along with other considerations such as the prevention of counterfeit and the reduction of production costs. But the question of varying the seignorage by changing the physical form of the currency, into forms with more or less 'intrinsic use value,' no longer enters as one of the main arguments considered by the authorities in their decisions on the type of currency to provide. Nevertheless, the issue of the appropriate seignorage on currency still carries on under a new guise in the debate on whether to provide a rate of return on currency holdings, say in the form of an interest payment. This question has received most urgent attention in the international sphere, where attention has been focused on the question of what inducements need to be offered, given the division of power between nations, to make recipients keen to accept and to hold international paper money (S.D.R.s). But even within individual countries there has recently been considerable academic attention[2] given to the question of whether the authorities could and should pay interest on currency. This subject will be treated in more detail subsequently in Chapter 13, and so is not pursued further here.

Given that the authorities can use their power to impart a fiat value on a virtually costless piece of paper, the question – a serious one – then needs to be asked why the authorities do not use their power to buy up everything in sight for their own benefit. The answer to this comes in two parts, the first being more of a technical qualification while the second is more fundamental. First, the issue of currency by the government, for the object of buying up goods and assets, will raise prices (as supply constraints are encountered), and the increase of prices will normally lead to expectations of further inflation (the role of monetary expansion in causing inflation is discussed further in Chapter 11). If people hold currency during periods of inflation, the real value of that currency will be declining.

---

[1] Interestingly enough a similar sort of development may be taking place on the international front, with the attempt to replace, or at least to supplement, gold with S.D.R.s. Analogy with the history of the development of local currencies would, however, suggest that the extent of seignorage which the issuing organisation can achieve from the issue of currency of any form is strictly pro-portional to its political power. If an organisation has little political power, then the intrinsic attraction, perhaps in the form of interest payment on its currency, has to be equivalent to that obtainable on other assets in order to ensure that it is held. The 'link' proposal, whereby S.D.R.s would be provided to the less-developed countries, represents a most interesting innovation, an attempt to provide the seignorage from currency issue to a group with need but not power. It is hard to think of an analogy in domestic national policies, except perhaps in the old English custom of issuing Maundy money, distributed to certain specific needy groups.

[2] Initially stimulated by M. Friedman's paper on 'The Optimum Quantity of Money,' reprinted in *The Optimum Quantity of Money and Other Essays* (Aldine, Chicago, 1969).

So the expectation of inflation should cause people to wish to hold less currency. Moreover, the loss inevitably involved during major inflations, either in holding currency or in undertaking transactions more frequently in order to divest oneself of unwanted currency, will make the use of currency in transactions as a means of payment increasingly expensive. Despite the monopoly power of the authorities, people would turn to other forms of means of payment, e.g. foreign currencies.[1] Because the use of an object as a means of payment depends on information and familiarity with its characteristics, such a move towards an alternative would tend to cumulate over time. Although one can imagine the government printing sufficient money to buy up all the goods and assets in the economy at present prices, prices in terms of this currency would adjust so fast to the attempt to do so that the authorities would not succeed. Given the relationship between the demand for currency and the expected rate of inflation, there will be some rate of monetary expansion which would maximise steady-state government revenue.[2] Any faster constant rate of monetary expansion would cause a proportionately faster rate of inflation, given the disinclination of people to hold money under such conditions, and thus lower real government revenues.

Thus the first point is that the rate of monetary expansion that would maximise the steady-state ability of the authorities to extract resources from the rest of the economy is bounded by the ability of the public to economise on money holdings, and find money substitutes as inflation takes hold. The more fundamental reason, however, why the authorities do not behave in this way is that their power is limited by the consent of the governed, and that for the most part their own objectives include the welfare and happiness of the general public. Given that inflation is disliked (the question of the costs and benefits to the economy of differing rates of inflation is discussed further in Chapter 13), the issue of additional money to obtain command over resources, leading to a faster rate of inflation, involves a political cost. The authorities have various ways of obtaining command over real resources, expropriation, taxes, bond issues and the issue of currency. They have to balance the benefits (to themselves and/or to society in general) of diverting resources to public use against the (political and economic) costs of the various methods of doing so.

Professor Ahmad has pointed out that the process of optimisation requires that the marginal disutility to the authorities of all forms of obtaining command over real resources should be equal at the margin. Thus he writes, 'To be in equilibrium the governments' negative marginal return from the issue of bonds must equal the negative marginal return (imputed) from the issue of money'.[3] What Professor Ahmad failed to recognise, however, is that his calculus is basically political rather than economic. Assuming a democracy, this approach would suggest that the authorities would be in equilibrium when the marginal

---

[1] Though people are reluctant to change their accustomed means of payment as inflation takes hold, partly owing to the inconvenience involved, partly to 'lingering confidence in its future value.' P. Cagan's study of seven hyperinflations showed that in no case did the flight from money accelerate sufficiently to make price increases self-generating, see 'The Monetary Dynamics of Hyperinflation,' in *Studies in the Quantity Theory of Money*, ed. M. Friedman (University of Chicago Press, 1956) pp. 25–117, esp. p. 88.

[2] A number of economists have now begun to consider the question of the 'optimal' behaviour of the authorities in deciding on the volume of currency to issue. For example, in his thesis, as described in the abstract of his doctoral dissertation, reported in the *Journal of Finance*, vol. XXVI, no. 3 (June 1971) pp. 786–7, R. J. Barro 'extends the model by viewing inflation as a vehicle for generating government revenue. The earlier results on demand for money are used to derive the rate of monetary expansion which maximises steady-state government revenue. If the government presses the rate of monetary expansion beyond this "optimal" rate, steady-state revenues decline.' In a similar vein see M. Friedman's article on 'Government Revenue from Inflation,' in *Journal of Political Economy*, vol. 79, no. 4 (July/August 1971) pp. 846–56, and note the references (p. 856) to previous articles on this subject.

[3] S. Ahmad, 'Is Money Net Wealth?', *Oxford Economic Papers*, vol. 22, no. 3 (November 1970) pp. 357–61.

addition to votes arising out of additional public expenditures was equal to the marginal cost in votes of each alternative form of obtaining resources to finance that revenue. In the light of the political unpopularity of inflation[1] – and of the earlier dodge of debasing the currency – the rate of monetary expansion which maximises government revenue is not likely to lead to a 'steady state', politically speaking. Thus, in their own political interests, which depend directly or indirectly on the pleasure of the public, the authorities are led to restrict the issue of fiat money at a point where the market value of assets, which could be bought with the currency, still far exceeds the marginal cost of producing the notes and coin.

D. Bank Deposits, Cheque Payments and the Definition of Money

In view of this gap between the marginal cost of production of fiat money, and the market value of assets which can be bought with it, there would seem to be a clear profit to be gained by producing a money substitute, albeit at a higher real cost, which people would be prepared to hold instead of State-issued fiat currency. An asset which could be transformed easily, at a known constant exchange ratio, on demand, and without much cost into legal tender currency would serve as a very close substitute, even though it was not backed by the power of the state. As is well known from the early history of banking, the precursors of modern bankers, money-lenders, goldsmiths, etc.,[2] discovered that they could virtually guarantee ready transformation (convertibility) back into gold, or legal tender fiat currency, of such currency placed with them, while only holding a relatively small proportion of currency reserves against their own note and deposit liabilities. So long as confidence in their ability to maintain convertibility continued, only a small proportion of their customers would be likely to want to withdraw their deposits or to redeem their notes on any one day, so only a relatively small reserve requirement would be needed to meet the occasional excesses of withdrawals over new deposits. The remainder of the currency which they attracted could be lent out to customers, thus gaining a return on the margin between the yield on the assets purchased and the various costs of inducing people to deposit their currency with them.

In the earlier part of the nineteenth century banks, both in the United Kingdom and in the United States, customarily issued note as well as deposit liabilities. In the course of the nineteenth century, however, the ability of ordinary commercial banks to issue their own bank-notes was first restricted, for example by Peel's Bank Charter Act of 1844, and then progressively abolished.[3] There is no indication from the historical records that this was motivated by a desire on the part of the authorities to increase their revenue from seignorage by monopolising the issue of currency, though the issue was unlikely to arise in any case under gold-standard conditions. Instead, the main objective was to strengthen the power of the Central Bank to control monetary conditions within the economy. So long as private bank-notes could be freely substituted for state (or Central Bank) issued currency, the Central Bank would have difficulty in restraining monetary expansion during booms, and holders of both the note and deposit liabilities of private banks would be the more

---

[1] This political unpopularity, however, probably occurs most strongly in response to an unexpected change in the rate of inflation away from the norm, so the authorities may have some slight leeway to change the rate of monetary expansion, and inflation, gradually over some long period without incurring general public resentment.

[2] The occupational origins of the early bankers were, however, quite diverse, see for example R. Cameron, *Banking in the Early Stages of Industrialisation* (Oxford University Press, London, 1967), chap. 2, 'England,' which also gives references to more detailed sources of information on the occupations of these early bankers.

[3] A few vestiges remain. The Scottish banks, for instance, issue their own notes in place of, but equivalently backed by, Bank of England notes.

likely to be injured by defaults when the boom broke. The solution to this problem was to prohibit commercial banks from competing freely with the Central Bank in the provision of notes, and to require them to hold a (prudential) reserve of currency and deposits with the Central Bank against their deposit liabilities. These bank-deposit liabilities are close substitutes for currency in many, or most, circumstances, but by this means the Central Bank enhanced its power to control the growth of such substitutes.

Not only can a deposit with a bank be readily and quickly converted back into currency, into legal tender, but also keeping a deposit with a bank has certain advantages in the form of safe-keeping, convenience, attendant book-keeping services, etc. People, therefore, came to accept that the transfer of a credit to their current account at a bank represented a satisfactory final payment. The willingness to accept a transfer to one's account with a bank as a means of payment depends, however, not only on the characteristics of that account, i.e. safe, convertible, etc., but also on the costs and ease of making such transfers. So, in addition to offering safe-keeping, interest payments, financial advice, etc., to depositors, the banks have operated a payments transmission service to facilitate such transfers. The costs involved in this process are very sizeable,[1] but the provision of adequate transmission facilities, thereby enabling bank customers to make payments[2] by drawing cheques on their banks, plays an integral role in maintaining the attraction of holding and using bank deposits as a means of payment.

Even so, the transfer of credit through the banking system will not always be acceptable as a method of payment. There is the well-known pub sign, 'We have an agreement with our bank. We do not cash cheques, they do not sell beer.' People without bank accounts may stipulate payment in cash, since the transfer costs of cashing a cheque may be relatively high for them. Moreover, the means of payments is the actual transfer on the banks' books, but the medium of exchange at the time of the sale (the transaction) takes the form of writing out a cheque, an order to the bank to make this transfer.

It is sometimes overlooked that handing over a signed cheque to the seller of a good does *not* complete the payment; it is not a means of final payment, in the sense that handing over currency or the transfer of other goods (barter) does represent a means of payment. A cheque merely represents an order to a third party, the banker, to complete the final payment to the creditor. The process of payment through the banking system, put into motion by drawing the cheque, therefore involves several credit relationships, requiring the establishment of a state of personal trust dependent on adequate information. This is not the case with payment by barter or, perhaps, with currency, whose value, though, does reside in the public's confidence in the continuing power of the issuing authority.

In the case of cheque transfers there are two main inherent credit relationships. First, the seller (creditor) has to trust that the buyer (debtor) has sufficient credit with the third party, the banker, so that the cheque will be honoured by him. It does not matter how large your current account may be in fact; if the shopkeeper should come to the conclusion that you look a shifty, untrustworthy character, he may not feel able to afford the risk of ad-

---

[1] The cost incurred by the British banking system in providing a money transmission service in 1971 was possibly of the order of £350 million per annum.

[2] There are so many transactions in which either currency or a cheque can be used that clearly demand deposits and currency will be very close substitutes overall. Thus the price ratio of a cheque for £10 and £10 in currency hardly ever deviates from unity, though it can do so: cheques passed at a discount, for example, in the United States in the aftermath of the 1907 banking crisis. Now the price ratio between currency and a range of other fixed nominal value assets, e.g. certain forms of public sector non-marketable debt, building-society deposits, etc., is also fixed at unity. Yet there is less substitution between those assets and currency than between demand deposits and currency. This is because of the greater transfer costs involved in using those other assets to make or to receive payment. It is, therefore, the provision of adequate transmission facilities, as well as the fixed price ratio, that makes demand deposits a substitute means of payment alongside currency.

vancing you credit by selling you merchandise in exchange for a cheque which may not be met. Nevertheless, shopkeepers and other traders are loath to lose profitable business owing to worries of the risk involved in accepting cheque payment from strangers. The natural solution is to try to invent means of reducing the uncertainty (increasing the informational content) for the seller. This is, perhaps, the main function of the credit card. It allows bank deposits to be used in place of currency in circumstances where the seller has little information about the purchaser.

One factor that may well have been conducive to the development of deposit banking, and to the use of cheques as a medium of exchange, particularly in England, was the existence of a well-defined class system. A class system implies the existence of a set of easily observable signals distinguishing one group from another (speech, dress, etc.). There has been generally a fairly high correlation between class status and wealth (credit worthiness). Thus the class system could be used, at zero marginal private cost, to provide the necessary personal information to the seller whether there was a high risk, or not, involved in taking a cheque in payment.

In order to accept payment by cheque, the crucial information which the seller needs is whether the bank, to whom the order is addressed, will honour the payment order.[1] This does not depend solely on the state of the payer's current account credit balance. As Professor Shackle has noted, 'I cannot write a cheque on my deposit account, but I can write one on my current account which, even if that account is empty, will be honoured if covered by my deposit balance.'[2] In addition, 'A man can just as well make a payment by increasing his overdraft (if he has his banker's permission to do so) as by reducing a credit balance.'[3]

Even if the drawer of the cheque is completely sure of the value of payment orders which the banker will honour (and he often may not be), the payee does not possess this information. Unlike the transfer of currency, or barter, the payee is, in a sense, extending credit to the payer until the cheque has been cleared.[4] Indeed, the distinction between accepting a cheque and accepting trade credit is not entirely clear-cut. Both involve the extension of credit until final payment is completed.

Moreover, the extension of credit by the payee to the payer, until the payer's cheque is honoured by the bank, is not the only credit relationship involved in the transfer process. Both payer and payee have to trust that the bank will honour its obligation to make the payment.[5] If the bank should fail, or close for some other reason, both drawer and payee[6]

---

[1] Moreover, the experience of the Irish bank strikes, during which the banks were shut for several months, suggests that the inability of a bank to honour such an order immediately, in this case because of physical constraints, will not prevent the use of cheques as a medium of exchange, so long as the payee is confident that the payer, or some intermediary endorser, will in due course be able, if required, to make payment in legal tender. There is a very interesting unpublished paper on this episode by A. E. Murphy on 'The Nature of Money – with Particular Reference to the Irish Bank Closure' (mimeo: Trinity College Dublin, 1972).

[2] Discussion of Clower's paper on the 'Theoretical Foundations of Monetary Policy,' in *Monetary Theory and Monetary Policy in the 1970s*, p. 33.

[3] Ibid. p. 33.

[4] In practice the payee's account will be credited with the value of the cheque paid in while in transit. This reduces the cost to the payee of the extension of credit to the payer, but so long as there remains a finite probability of the cheque bouncing – i.e. until it is finally cleared – the process still essentially involves an extension of credit.

[5] In order to lessen the risks involved in using the banking system, banks need to maintain asset portfolios and adopt behavioural patterns (e.g. paying for deposit insurance, accepting the rules of the game as laid down by the authorities, etc.), which will be seen to reduce their chances of being forced into defaulting on their obligations.

[6] The payee will still have a valid claim on the drawer, but the latter may no longer have the funds to meet that claim if his bank has closed its doors.

stand to lose. So in the payment process, set in motion by making out the cheque, the payee has to trust the payer, and both have to trust the bank. Since none of the parties, including the bank, has complete information on the behaviour of the others, this will involve some risk. And in some cases the risk may seem so considerable that cheques will not be acceptable.

The use of cheques, as a medium of exchange, to operate the payment for a transaction by transfers within the banking system does, therefore, involve certain credit relationships which are virtually absent when currency is used in payment. This qualitative distinction has aroused, at different times, three separable but related questions about the monetary role of bank deposits. First, cheques may sometimes be declined as a medium of exchange, either because the payee does not want to accept payment in the form of a transfer to his credit within the banking system, or because the payee does not trust that acceptance of the cheque will, in fact, provide the stated credit transfer. On these grounds, particularly before the banking system is fully mature and established, it may be argued that bank current-account deposits do not count as money at all.[1]

Second, since the acceptance of cheques is akin to the acceptance of trade credit, in that both involve some extension of credit, it has been argued that a bank balance, which is in a sense an immediately available unused credit facility, is fulfilling basically the same function as any other source of unused credit, which could be used as a medium of exchange. On this argument the definition of 'money' would have to be widely extended to cover overdraft facilities, trade credit facilities and loan facilities from all sources.[2]

Third, a bank customer does not have to hold a positive current account (demand deposit) balance in order to have his order to complete the payment honoured by his bank. Payment may be made from unused overdraft facilities[3] or by a semi-automatic transfer from time deposits. The means to complete the requisite payment may be established by holding time deposits or by having access to unused overdraft facilities in a bank. On these grounds it may be argued that the definition of money, while not encompassing all credit facilities, should at least include all bank deposits and, perhaps, unused overdraft facilities with banks.

The first question is pragmatic. It is certainly true that under some conditions payment by cheque may be refused, but then under other conditions payment by cheque may be much preferred to payment in currency. You will not be allowed to pay your taxes by dumping a lorry-load of pennies in the front lobby of the Inland Revenue. There are dangers,

---

[1] In the nineteenth century this was a subject of considerable dispute being, for example, one element in the celebrated debate between the Currency and the Banking Schools in the United Kingdom. On this point see D. Laidler's paper on 'Thomas Tooke on Monetary Reform,' from *Essays in Honour of Lord Robbins*, ed. M. Peston and B. Corry (Weidenfeld & Nicolson, London, 1972) pp. 168–86, especially pp. 172–7.

[2] This argument is favoured by Laffer in his article, 'Trade Credit and the Money Market,' *Journal of Political Economy*, vol. 78 (March/April 1970) pp. 239–67. He argues that 'the empirical counterpart of the classical concept of money must include unutilised trade credit available along with demand deposits and currency.' Clower also agrees that trade credit should be included in the definitions of money, c.f. 'Theoretical Foundations of Monetary Policy,' in *Monetary Theory and Monetary Policy in the 1970s*, p. 18.

[3] Examination of the variations in bank 'float' suggest that in the United Kingdom, where reliance on overdrafts is widespread, about 60 per cent of items in transit will result in a reduction in gross deposits and about 40 per cent will lead to an increase in advances. The proportions are, however, not very clearly determined. In other countries, where overdrafts are less used, a higher proportion of payments will be made from deposit balances. Again the English class system provides free personal information to bankers which enables them to take a more flexible attitude towards overdrafts. Lacking this, the U.S. banks are much more rigid in their operations; hence the earlier appearance of credit cards in the United States.

of loss or theft, in carrying high-value notes, so most large transactions (at least those that are legal) are carried out by preference through cheque payments. Even by the end of the nineteenth century the greater bulk of total transfers, in value terms, passed through the banking system.[1] People in fact do generally accept that a credit transfer to their current account with banks represents final payment, and that makes current accounts a means of payment. If people widely accepted transfers to their accounts with other financial intermediaries, such as building societies, as a form of final payment, this would make such accounts serve *de facto* as money.

The second issue is based on a confusion between the general need for instruments to serve as a medium of exchange and the more specialised role of money as a means of payment. There is, indeed, no fundamental difference between accepting a cheque or accepting any other form of credit as a medium of exchange allowing the transaction to take place. The fundamental difference occurs later, when the transmission process initiated by drawing the instrument has been completed. When the current accounts of the payer and payee have been respectively debited and credited by their banks, the payment is completed; nothing further needs to be done. When trade credits and debits are written in the books, or when loans have been negotiated to finance the original payment, an obligation remains to be settled; the process is not completed.[2]

Similarly, the argument that unused bank overdraft facilities serve as a means of payment fails on the same grounds.[3] If A owes B money, but gets C to pay B, then A has merely substituted a debt to C for a debt to B. At some stage the debt has to be paid off. B may regard the transfer as completed, but it is not, since A has yet to make the final payment. Whether C, who steps in to finance A's payment to B, is a person, a bank, or some other financial intermediary is irrelevant.

A much more difficult question is whether to include time deposits with banks, along with current accounts, in the definition of money. Although the process may be somewhat costly and time consuming, holders of time deposits can use these to make payments. The transfer of funds from A to B by debiting A's time deposit and crediting B's current account will complete the payment for both A and B.[4] There would seem no very strong basis on theoretical grounds for excluding time deposits from the definition of money. The issue should, perhaps, be again decided on pragmatic grounds. If the turnover of current accounts is much higher than that of time deposits, one could conclude that there is a real difference in the usage of these assets as a means of payment. The degree to which the various types

---

[1] See the survey by D. Kinley reported in 'Credit – Currency and Population,' *Journal of Political Economy*, vol. 10, no. 1 (December 1901) pp. 72–93.

[2] For a somewhat similar approach to the definition of money, see W. T. Newlyn, *The Theory of Money* (Clarendon Press, Oxford, 1962), especially chap. 1 on 'Definitions and Classifications,' and also his paper on 'The Supply of Money and its Control,' *The Economic Journal*, vol. LXXIV (June 1964) pp. 327–46, especially pp. 334–9. However, in addition to the above condition that the transfer of the asset must complete the payment for the payer and payee, Newlyn also requires 'the consequential adjustments in the financial system [to] have a zero sum.' This seems unnecessarily restrictive; as noted in a subsequent footnote shifts in the composition in which the public prefer to hold their money balances will cause adjustments in the financial system. See the criticism of Newlyn's approach by M. Friedman and A. J. Schwartz in their paper on 'The Definition of Money,' *Journal of Money, Credit and Banking*, vol. 1, no. 1 (February 1969) pp. 1–14.

[3] In addition there is the practical, operational problem of obtaining adequate estimates of the total of unused credit facilities. It is dubious whether this is possible even in principle. Attempts by Laffer, op. cit. to do so were remarkable for their heroism.

[4] The banks' balance sheet position will have altered. But it will also alter, and more drastically, if A pays B by cheque and B draws the money out of the bank in cash. A shift in the composition in which the public holds their money balances between cash, current accounts, and time deposits may have major consequences for the financial system, but this fact is hardly relevant to the question of what assets serve as means of payment.

of deposit serve as money could be calculated approximately by the figures for relative turnover.[1] Unfortunately, in the United Kingdom such data are not available, but in Holland monetary assets are indeed classified on the basis of their relative turnover. Even though it might be possible to construct a theoretically preferable monetary series, with assets entering weighted by their relative turnover, this would inevitably seem an artificial and complex concept. In the meantime it is probably best to think of the total of currency and bank-demand deposits as an operationally useful approximation to the total means of payment in the economy, on the grounds that most surveys show a very much higher turnover for current accounts than for time deposits.

---

[1] D. Laidler addresses the same question, whether time deposits should be counted as part of the money stock, in his paper on 'The Definition of Money,' *Journal of Money, Credit and Banking*, vol. 1, no. 3 (August 1969) pp. 508–25. Laidler agrees that the test should be empirical and pragmatic. My preferred test, however, is to examine whether time deposits do serve as a means of payment; his preferred test is to examine whether current accounts and time deposits appear to be close substitutes in econometric studies of demand for money functions. The two approaches are quite closely related (i.e. if time deposits are not used as a means of payment they are less likely to be a close substitute for current accounts), but they might give somewhat differing results.

2

Micro-Economic Foundations of the Demand for Money

SUMMARY

At the individual, or micro, level demand for money balances will be a function (i) of the differential between the perceived yield on money and on other assets; (ii) of the costs of transferring between money and other assets; (iii) of the price uncertainty of assets; and (iv) of the expected pattern of expenditures and receipts. In practice, analysis of the demand for money as a function of all these variables simultaneously has proven difficult to handle, and so the analysis has been artificially segmented into two main parts. First, consideration of asset-price uncertainty is suppressed and the 'transactions' demand for money is studied, involving minimisation of the costs of undertaking expenditures. Then the 'speculative' demand for money is analysed, specifically incorporating asset-price uncertainty, but usually involving drastic simplifying assumptions about transfer costs and/or the time pattern of expenditures. This dichotomy is not valid; nevertheless the tradition of examining these two aspects of the demand for money separately is followed here, since this approach has been so common that the development, and literature, of the subject cannot be appreciated otherwise.

We concentrate on the inventory-theoretic analysis of the transactions demand for money, starting with Baumol's simplified initial model – which largely abstracts from uncertainty – but moving on to the more complex but more realistic models, developed for example by Orr, in which there is uncertainty about the future flow of cash payments. Once such uncertainty is introduced it is difficult to distinguish the 'transactions' from the 'precautionary' motives for holding money. This first section then ends with a short summary of the attack made on this approach by Sprenkle. He claims, on empirical grounds, that the money holdings of companies, for example, are far larger than can be explained by the inventory theory, and on practical grounds that these models have overlooked many of the important institutional features of the monetary system.

In the second section we begin with a restatement of Tobin's classic analysis of 'Liquidity Preference as Behaviour towards Risk' within a system with one safe and one risky asset in a single period context, an analysis which is compared and contrasted with Keynes's analysis of the speculative demand for money. The approach is then extended to deal with the more general situation where the investor is confronted with an assortment of risky assets, touching here on modern portfolio analysis. Finally, some of the problems of moving from a single period to a multi-period analysis are presented, though hardly solved.

A. The Transactions Demand for Money

Because of uncertainty, especially owing to a lack of personal information as a result of which A cannot be sure of B's creditworthiness and vice versa, there will be a demand for some instrument which will obviate the need either for such personal information or for barter in the course of exchange transactions, and will thereby serve as a specialised means of payment. In the previous chapter, Section C, we saw how a government can issue monetary instruments of this kind in the form of liabilities upon itself – even at a zero interest rate. Although the government can command, or delegate – say to the Central Bank – monopoly control over the issue of legal tender within its own demesne, financial intermediaries (banks) can provide liabilities which will act as close substitutes for legal tender, i.e. as monetary liabilities fulfilling the function of a means of payment. But banks can only make their liabilities into close substitutes for currency by ensuring the maintenance of convertibility between their deposit liabilities and legal tender and also by providing certain payment transmission facilities that enhance the attractiveness of cheque payment.

The maintenance of sufficient reserves of legal tender to ensure instantaneous convertibility and the provision of payment transmission services are expensive. It therefore follows that private-sector financial intermediaries will have to offer a lower rate of interest on demand deposits than on liabilities which are not immediately exchangeable at a fixed rate into a legal tender (e.g. marketable assets), or which are only exchangeable into legal tender at a fixed rate after a period of notice or on an appointed date. In the latter case there would be certain penalties, or transactions costs, incurred should the asset holder attempt to switch back into legal tender, or into demand deposits, before the due date. Thus there can be a whole spectrum of interest rates on private-sector liabilities; the intermediary is able to offer a higher rate on those assets which it is not committed to redeem at short notice into monetary liabilities at a fixed rate and which have a lower frequency of withdrawal, since it can then deploy its earning assets in a higher yielding portfolio and provide fewer transmission services; the investor, in turn, will demand a higher mean expected yield to make up for the additional risk of variations in the nominal price of marketable assets and/or the extra transaction costs of switching between non-monetary financial assets and money.

Likewise, the public sector can also issue a range of marketable debt, not exchangeable at a fixed rate into legal tender, and non-marketable fixed-price debt, the convertibility of which into means of payment is limited by institutional constraints or by transactions costs. Despite its ability to gain command over real resources by issuing zero-interest fiat money, the authorities may prefer to issue higher interest debt for that purpose, because the effect on the economy (and thus on their own popularity), especially the consequences for price inflation, may be preferable. Although the power of the government, which supports the value of its fiat currency, also stands behind its other debt, the characteristics of such debt, e.g. asset-price uncertainty,[1] limitations or costs on convertibility, prevent bonds and savings certificates being used as a means of payment, in exact analogy to the reasons why the bonds or savings certificates issued by banks (or other intermediaries) will not normally be used as a means of payment.

When analysing the development of the economy as a whole, at the macro level, it is reasonable to assume that the authorities are influencing the overall supplies of various forms of public-sector debt in their monetary and debt management operations: if this is so, it is interest differentials (given transaction costs and asset-price uncertainties) that adjust to clear the market. At the individual, or *micro level*, the pattern of relative interest rates appears instead as a market parameter inducing the individual person or company to adjust the proportions (to their total wealth) in which they wish to hold their assets. So

---

[1] It is not the uncertainty about the money price of marketable securities, whether in the form of public or private-sector debt, that is of greatest importance, for this is only the reciprocal of the 'security price of money, which is equally uncertain. It is rather the fact that the money price of a bundle of goods, and assets, tends to be relatively sticky, whereas the 'security prices of goods' are less so. During periods of volatility in general price levels, however, e.g. during hyperinflations, other assets, e.g. foreign currencies, real assets, may be found to provide more value security, and may become used as substitutes for domestic money.

at this level the analysis becomes turned around to express the micro-level demand for money as a function (i) of the observed interest-rate differential between the yield for money on the one hand and on other assets; (ii) of the transfer costs between money and these other assets; (iii) of the price uncertainty on other assets; and (iv) of the expected pattern of expenditures and receipts requiring the use of means of payment.

Analysis of the individual, micro-level demand for money function has traditionally (following Keynes's exposition) been, somewhat artificially, segmented. First, the third argument above, asset-price uncertainty, is suppressed, eliminated from the analysis, so that the demand for money is treated as a function of interest differentials (i), transfer costs (ii) and the pattern of payments (iv). This is generally termed the transactions demand for money, the demand that would still occur even if there was no asset-price uncertainty. The next stage is to reformulate the analysis to include asset-price uncertainty (iii) as an argument, but dropping transfer costs (ii) from the analysis. This is usually described as the speculative demand for money, the demand that would still occur even if transfer costs were relatively unimportant.

It is inappropriate, as noted also in the next chapter, to regard the overall demand for money as the simple arithmetical sum of these two separated components of the demand for money, the transactions and speculative motives.[1] Nevertheless, despite the invalidity of attempting to distinguish, at the aggregate macro level, between balances held for transactions and for speculative purposes, a complication which has not deterred generations of economists from trying to draw this distinction in applied, empirical work,[2] this distinction between the two motives has been so widely followed, and presumably fruitful, in the literature, especially at the micro level, that it would be very difficult to comprehend analytical developments in this area without following the same dichotomy.[3] Accordingly, in the remainder of this section we shall review the analysis of the transactions demand for money, abstracting from asset-price uncertainty, and pass on to the analysis of the speculative demand for money in the second section.

One feature that is common to the analysis of both the transactions and the speculative demand for money is that the (subjective probability distribution of the expected) timing pattern of expenditures and receipts on goods and services is usually taken as given, an external parameter in the light of which the individual adjusts his desired money balances (in part by varying the timing pattern of his transfers between money holdings and other financial assets). This is not strictly accurate. Individuals will have some flexibility in adjusting the timing of their own expenditures, for example by altering their shopping habits, though the periodicity of income payments is usually institutionally fixed in the short run. Firms can, however, vary the timing of their expenditures on bought-in materials and components, even if not on labour.

---

[1] Balances held for one motive may also go to satisfy the need to hold money for the other purpose. On this point see M. Friedman, 'The Quantity Theory of Money – A Restatement,' clause 14, from *Studies in the Quantity Theory of Money*, ed. M. Friedman (University of Chicago Press, 1956).

[2] See, for example, J. Tobin's early work on 'Liquidity Preference and Monetary Policy,' *Review of Economics and Statistics*, vol. 21 (May 1947) pp. 124–31, and M. Bronfenbrenner and T. Mayer, 'Liquidity Functions in the American Economy,' *Econometrica*, vol. 28 (October 1960) pp. 810–34. These studies were the ones noted by H. G. Johnson in his majestic review article on 'Monetary Theory and Policy,' *American Economic Review*, vol. 52 (June 1962) pp. 335–84 and reproduced as chap. 1 in *Monetary Theory and Policy*, ed. R. S. Thorn (Random House, New York, 1966).

[3] Nevertheless, the dichotomy remains invalid. This is one of the loose ends of the subject that remains to be tidied up. It would seem, however, that the complexity of handling a formal model which incorporates asset-price uncertainty, uncertainty over the timing and size of future expenditures and receipts, and transfer costs, all at the same time, has been too much to be tackled effectively yet.

So if the opportunity cost of holding money rather than other assets, in the form of interest foregone, is high, but the transfer costs of switching between money and assets are also considerable, people could react by altering their expenditure habits. Examples can be observed during periods of hyperinflation, when income recipients try to accelerate their expenditures immediately after their receipt of incomes, to avoid holding depreciating money balances.[1] During more normal times, however, it is generally assumed that the (expected) pattern of expenditures and receipts is set by institutional custom and habit and relatively insensitive to those fluctuations in interest rates and transfer costs that occur in normal conditions. There have, in any case, been very few empirical studies of the interaction of payment habits and of the demand for money[2] to changes in financial conditions, except for crisis periods such as hyperinflations and breakdowns of the payments system, e.g. periods of bank closures in the United States in 1907[3] and in 1933. This treatment of the pattern of payments as a parameter determining the demand for money balances rather than as a jointly determined variable is thus usually defended on the grounds that it is largely institutionally determined.

With the (expected) pattern of expenditures given, and abstracting from asset-price uncertainty, individuals might be expected to wish to hold that amount of money that enables them to make these payments with the minimum cost. There is an opportunity cost in interest forgone from holding low-yielding money rather than alternative higher-yielding assets and this has to be balanced by the cost of switching between these assets and money, to provide the cash when it is needed to make payments, in order to find that system of cash management that minimises costs.

Conceptually the problem is simple. In practice, the mathematical solution of the cost-minimisation problem can become quite complex. For example, the optimal cash-management system, which minimises costs, appears to be quite sensitive to the form of the transfer costs between money and higher-yielding assets, whether these are fixed per transfer or some function of the size of the transfer. The problem, moreover, becomes considerably more complex when the realistic assumption is made that future payment (and receipt) patterns are not known for sure but have instead some subjective probability distribution. The search for cost-minimising cash-management policies under a range of alternative assumptions about the functional form of transfer costs and payments patterns has developed into a field for the use of mathematical operations research techniques[4] which have an undoubted intellectual appeal in themselves but have, perhaps, only a limited interest to the more general monetary theorist.

This general approach to the analysis of the transactions demand for money is often described as the inventory theory of the (transactions) demand for money, because of its similarity to the more general analysis of the demand for inventories which had been developed previously. Baumol[5] constructed the first monetary model along these lines. The

---

[1] See R. J. Barro, 'Inflation, the Payments Period, and the Demand for Money,' *Journal of Political Economy*, vol. 78, no. 6 (November/December 1970) pp. 1228–63.

[2] Some recent theoretical studies of the optimum quantity of money have, however, incorporated explicit consideration of the costs of exchanges between goods (and services) and money into their analysis, c.f. M. Perlman, 'The Roles of Money in an Economy and the Optimum Quantity of Money,' *Economica* (August 1971) and E. Feige and M. Parkin, 'The Optimal Quantity of Money, Bonds, Commodity Inventories, and Capital,' *The American Economic Review*, vol. LXI, no. 3, pt 1 (June 1971) pp. 335–49.

[3] For example, A. P. Andrew, 'Substitutes for Cash in the Panic of 1907,' *The Quarterly Journal of Economics*, vol. 22, no. 4 (August 1908) pp. 497–516.

[4] See, for example, D. Orr, *Cash Management and the Demand for Money* (Praeger, New York, 1970).

[5] W. J. Baumol, 'The Transactions Demand for Cash: An Inventory Theoretic Approach,' *Quarterly Journal of Economics*, vol. 66 (November 1952) pp. 545–56.

particular features of his model include a known stream of expenditures, amounting to T in a given period, which have to be paid for in cash. This is obtained by withdrawals from assets, bearing a constant known interest rate i, at a fixed cost per withdrawal of b.[1] If the individual withdraws M each time his balance reaches zero, his average money balance will be $M/2$ and brokerage costs bT/M, so total costs in a given period amount to

$$C = \frac{bT}{M} + \frac{iM}{2}$$

The objective is to minimise C, and the value of M (the size of withdrawal and therefore the average money balance $M/2$) which achieves this can be found by calculus (setting the derivative of the above with respect to M equal to zero). This reveals that the optimal withdrawal size (twice the average balance) is given by

$$M^* = \sqrt{\frac{2bT}{i}}$$

So in this situation the individual should desire to hold money in relation to the square root of the value of transactions: the elasticities of demand for money with respect to real expenditures[2] and interest rates are respectively $+$ and $-\frac{1}{2}$. The time path of the money balance in this case follows a saw-tooth pattern as shown in Fig. 2.1.

An immediate extension of this model is to consider the case where the steady expenditures are financed, not out of an inexhaustible stock of earning assets, but from periodic receipts (income payments), where expenditures are treated as exhausting income.[3] Let

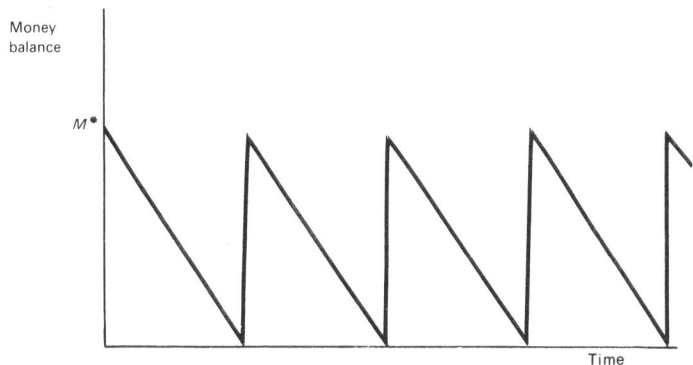

Fig. 2.1

---

[1] The conditions of this model, including a known pattern of expenditure, known asset prices, etc., abstract from all those facets of uncertainty, which give money its essential role as a means of payment, as argued in Chap. 1. Given the artificial nature of its basic assumptions, this particular model can hardly be expected to throw much light on behaviour in the real world. It is none the less worth studying, because it has an important place in the development, and literature, of the subject. Subsequently other economists, as will be seen, have extended this approach, relaxing the assumptions of known expenditure patterns, etc., and replacing them with uncertain, stochastic expectations.

[2] Note, however, that a once-for-all doubling of all prices would also presumably double transactions costs, b, but would leave i unchanged, assuming that expectations were for prices to remain constant at their new level – so that the demand for money would double following a once-for-all doubling of prices.

[3] Any interest receipts may be assumed to be paid over with income at the start of each subsequent period.

the income payment be Y, and let the cost of transfers be a linear function of the sum withdrawn (or invested) with a constant, fixed element and a proportional element, so that

$$D = b + km$$

where D is the transfers cost, b the fixed element, k the proportional element and m the sum transferred. Then the individual has the choice between holding his receipts all in cash form while awaiting expenditures, which would involve an interest penalty of $iY/2$, or of investing some of the cash at the start in higher-yielding assets (e.g. bonds) and drawing this down over the rest of the period. If he invests and then replenishes his cash balances by $n - 1$ equal sales, so that his total transfers amount to n (one purchase followed by $n - 1$ sales), his total costs would amount to

$$C = \frac{iY}{2n} + nb + 2kY\left(\frac{n - 1}{n}\right)$$

The third term includes the ratio $n - 1/n$, since at the start of the period $1/n$ of the income receipts will be held in cash for immediate expenditures. Again the procedure is to find the value of n that minimises C; n can equal zero,[1] but not 1 – which would represent a purchase without a subsequent sale – and has to be an integer. In the simple case where $k = 0$, and assuming that the values of b and i are such as to make any investment worthwhile, the optimal number of transactions is given by the expression

$$n^* = \sqrt{\frac{iY}{2b}}$$

and the average cash balance

$$M^* = \sqrt{\frac{bY}{2i}}$$

so that the previous elasticities with respect to (real) incomes and interest rates still hold.

Even while maintaining the restrictive assumption of a known future path of incomes and expenditures, a considerable range of variations can be played on this general theme. The form of the transfer-cost functions can be varied and the costs of investing and withdrawing funds distinguished separately. In particular, it should be noted that the value of the elasticities obtained by Baumol do depend on the particular assumptions of his model. As Professor Orr notes, 'A proper choice of departure from the Baumol model can generate elasticity predictions that differ significantly from his.'[2] There is no inherent square-root law built into the transactions demand for money.

The conditions, indeed, that must hold if *any* temporary investment of the periodic income is to be advantageous are quite severe. Reverting to the previous example, with $k = 0$, Professor Orr shows that with an annual interest rate (i) of 6 per cent, and fixed costs per transaction (b) of \$2,[3] it would require a monthly salary of about \$1600 in order for

---

[1] If $n = 0$, the above formula for C does not apply. Instead $C = (iY/2)$ as stated earlier.

[2] Orr, op. cit. p. 47. Also see the paper by K. Brunner and A. Meltzer, 'Economies of Scale in Cash Balances Reconsidered,' *Quarterly Journal of Economics*, vol. LXXXI (August 1967) pp. 422–36. In this article the authors argue that plausible values for the parameters of the model, e.g. for the transfer-cost functions, would result in a unitary value for the income elasticity of demand for money.

[3] Two dollars may seem rather a high charge for switching out of demand deposits into, say, a savings account or an account with some other intermediary. And so it probably is in terms of purely pecuniary costs. But there are other costs in terms of time and effort involved, and these may well appear to rise with increasing affluence. Most of us may always stay below the point at which temporary investment of a monthly salary would seem worthwhile.

it to be economical for the individual to engage in any temporary purchase and resale.[1] If it is not economical to do so, the average balance becomes simply $Y/2$, involving a (nominal) income elasticity of unity (with respect to both incomes and prices) and an interest elasticity of zero.

The general circumstances of this kind of model, involving regular, predictable sequences of incomes and expenditures is probably most nearly met in the household sector. Yet here transactions costs would seem to make cash management unrewarding except for the very rich; so for this sector the model implies income elasticities near unity and interest elasticities near zero, rather than $\pm\frac{1}{2}$ per cent. Firms on the other hand are more often in a position to command balances of a size that will make cash management profitable, despite transactions costs. It is, however, very dubious whether a model involving certainty of the timing of payments is appropriate to any examination of the cash-management problem of firms.

Models, which allow for some uncertainty in the future pattern of cash payments[2] tend, however, to be considerably more complex. Optimal cash-management procedures in certain specified conditions of uncertainty over the timing of payments have been formally analysed by Orr[3] and Miller.[4] Orr's basic model has the following conditions:

(i) There are two assets available, zero-yielding money and interest-bearing assets (bonds) which have a yield of n per £ per day.

(ii) A transfer between the two assets involves a fixed cost per transfer, unrelated to the size of transfer, of g. These transfers can be put through instantaneously.

(iii) Cash balances cannot go below zero. There are no overdraft facilities (or alternatively these are always more expensive to use as a method of replenishing cash balances than sales of interest-bearing assets).

(iv) Cash flows are completely stochastic, and 'behave as if generated by a stationary Gaussian random walk'. In setting out his basic model Orr assumes that in any short period (t) (e.g. 1 hour) there is a 50 per cent probability, p ($p = 0.5$), of the balance rising by £m and an equal probability, $q = 1 - p$ ($q = 0.5$), of it falling by £m.[5] With t periods in a day, over an interval of x days, the distribution of changes in the cash balance will be binomial with mean

$$\mu_x = xtm(p - q) = 0$$

and variance

$$\sigma_x^2 = 4xtpqm^2 = xtm^2$$

---

[1] Orr, op. cit. p. 136. Sprenkle has pointed out that the frequency of income receipts over the planning interval will also be important in determining whether it is profitable to undertake switches between money and bonds, see his paper on 'The Uselessness of Transactions Demand Models,' *The Journal of Finance*, vol. XXIV, no. 5 (December 1969) pp. 838–41. The higher the frequency of receipts, i.e. the less that they are bunched, with a given total income, the less will be the return from switches between money and other short-term securities.

[2] Some economists would describe cash held to meet possible uncertain fluctuations in payments flows as being required for 'precautionary' rather than transactions purposes. In conditions when payments flows are not known for sure, it is hard to make any clear distinction between transactions and precautionary motives.

[3] *Cash Management and the Demand for Money*, see especially chap. III.

[4] M. H. Miller and D. Orr, 'A Model of the Demand for Money by Firms,' *Quarterly Journal of Economics*, vol. LXXX, no. 3 (August 1966) pp. 413–35, and 'The Demand for Money by Firms: Extensions of Analytic Results,' *The Journal of Finance*, vol. 23, no. 5 (December 1968) pp. 735–59.

[5] Orr extends his model in chap. IV to deal with cases of drift, where $p \neq q \neq 0.5$, that is where the individual (person or firm) is systematically gaining or losing money over some time interval. He argues that his basic model can be used successfully, 'so long as systematic movements in the cash flow persist over a time interval that is long compared to the mean elapsed time between transfers to adjust the cash balance,' op. cit. p. 73.

Since there are costs involved in making a transfer between cash and interest-bearing assets, the cash manager will not make continuous transfers, but will wait until the cash balance reaches its lower permissible limit (zero, given instantaneous transactions between cash and other assets) or an upper permissible limit, determined by the relative expense of transfers compared with the interest yield forgone on cash. If the cash balance reaches one of these limits, the cash manager then has to choose at what level within these limits to restore the balance. The problem for the cash manager is to select an upper bound, h, and a return point, z, so that the costs of managing the balance (which can be described as

$$E(c) = gP(T) + nE(M)$$

where $E(c)$ are the expected costs, $P(T)$ the probability of transfers and $E(M)$ the expected average cash balance), are minimised.

The solution to this can be found mathematically,[1] to give an optimal return point

$$z^* = \left(\frac{3gm^2t}{4n}\right)^{1/3}$$

and an optimal upper bound, $h^* = 3z^*$, so that the average balance becomes

$$\overline{M} = \frac{4}{3}\left(\frac{3gm^2t}{4n}\right)^{1/3}$$

Policies of this kind give rise to a time path of cash balances that will look somewhat like that shown in Fig. 2.2.

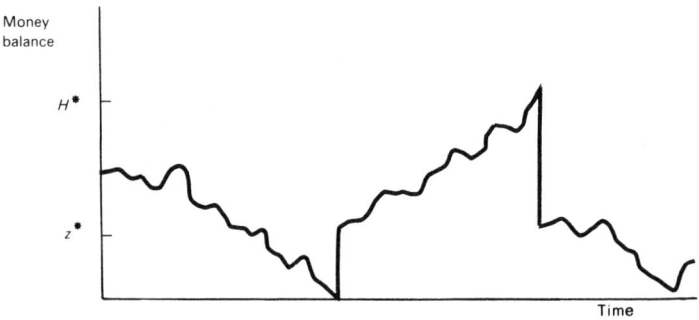

FIG. 2.2

An immediate point of interest is why the return point is not halfway between the bounds, but only one-third of the way to the upper bound. The basic reason for this is that the expected transfer cost is a symmetric function of the distance of the return point from the bounds, while the interest forgone is an increasing function of the average size of balance, see Fig. 2.3.[2]

As with the simpler fixed-payments Baumol model, the demand for money depends on relative transfer and interest costs. The most interesting feature of this model with uncertain payments is that the demand for money is related not to the *level* of transactions but to the *variance* of transactions, m^2t. What then would this model[3] predict about the income

---

[1] Orr, op. cit. pp. 58–63.
[2] See Orr, op. cit. Fig. VIII, p. 63.
[3] The model is, however, constructed at the micro, individual level. There could be serious aggregation problems involved in trying to draw conclusions about macro-economic behaviour from the working of this micro-economic model.

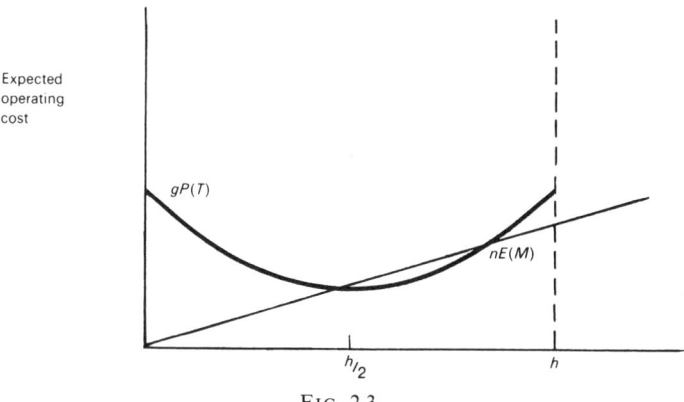

FIG. 2.3

elasticity of demand for money? This would depend how increases in incomes brought about changes in the frequency of transactions, t, as compared with the average size m. If the size remained constant as incomes rose, but the frequency increased, the elasticity would be as low as 1/3, the same absolute value as the predicted negative interest elasticity of demand. If transactions frequency remained constant, but the size of all transactions increased pro rata with incomes, then the income elasticity would be 2/3.

Indeed, the possible range for the income elasticity in this model is even greater. The ineluctable limits on time, together with the growing demands on that time that will be made as opportunities rise with incomes, mean that increasing efforts will be made to economise on time-consuming activities as the economy grows more affluent. So the number of separate transactions,[1] e.g. shopping trips, may even fall as incomes rise, leading to a rise in the average value of individual transactions proportionately larger than the increase in incomes and expenditures.

The actual mathematical formulae for h^* and z^* shown above depend on the postulated assumptions of the model. The form of the optimal cash-management policy in practice will be a function of the actual probability distribution of cash flows, the particular form of transactions costs between assets and money, the costs of delaying payments, the time taken during asset transactions, etc. Any manager of large cash balances would be well advised to call in specialist operations-research advice to help tailor a policy to meet his own individual requirements. For example, the policy of restoring cash balances to a return point $z = \frac{1}{3}h$ after it reaches one of the bounds $(0, h)$ is a consequence of the assumption of fixed, lumpy

---

[1] Exchanges between money and alternative financial assets are also time consuming. So the opportunity costs of brokerage, of transfers, will rise with incomes. If this is not specifically allowed for, it could lead to an upwards bias in the long-run estimates of the income elasticity, see for example, M. S. Khan, 'A Note on the Secular Behaviour of Velocity within the Context of the Inventory-Theoretic Model of Demand for Money,' *The Manchester School Journal*, no. 2 (June 1973) pp. 207–13. By an interesting coincidence exactly the same point was made at virtually the same moment by D. S. Dutton and W. P. Gramm in their paper on 'Transactions Costs, the Wage Rate and the Demand for Money,' *The American Economic Review*, vol. LXIII, no. 4 (September 1973) pp. 652–65. And a further exposition of the same general point was provided by E. Karni, 'The Transactions Demand for Cash: Incorporation of the Value of Time into the Inventory Approach,' *Journal of Political Economy*, vol. 81, no. 5 (September/October 1973) pp. 1216–25. Finally, on this point, see R. J. Barro and A. M. Santomero, 'Household Money Holdings and The Demand Deposit Rate,' *Journal of Money, Credit and Banking*, vol. 4, no. 2 (May 1972) pp. 397–413, especially pp. 406–11.

transfer costs. If transfer costs were proportional to the size of transfers, with no fixed element, then the optimal procedure would be to restore the cash balance to the bound which it had passed (assuming instantaneous transactions) but no further.[1] If transfer costs were some combination of fixed and proportional costs, then it would be preferable to restore cash balances after hitting the lower bound to a point, l, and after hitting the upper bound to a point, u, where $h - u > l - 0$, and the length $u - l$ depends on the relative weights of fixed and proportional transfer costs. The probability distribution of the cash balance occupying a value between 0 and h would then look as shown in Fig. 2.4.[2]

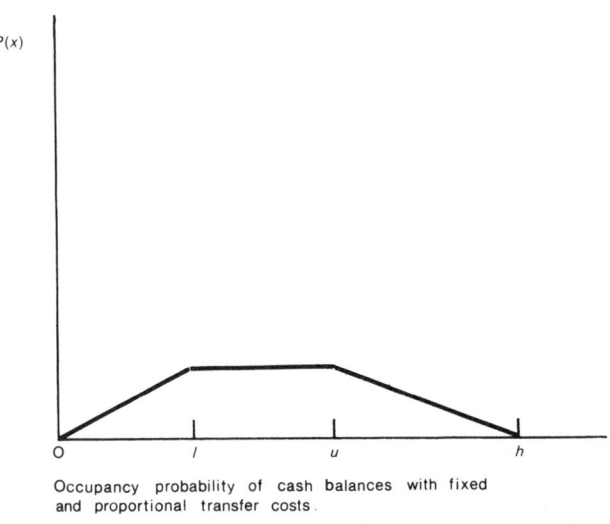

$P(x)$

O l u h

Occupancy probability of cash balances with fixed and proportional transfer costs.

FIG. 2.4

Precautionary balances are held to protect the individual (company or person) against uncertain fluctuations in the timing of receipts and expenditures. It is, therefore, natural that such balances should be a function of the expected variance, rather than the level, of cash flows. Companies[3] and individuals with very erratic cash flows, such as art dealers, car dealers and bookmakers, will tend to have relatively large cash balances. It is, however, likely to be difficult to observe systematic changes in the variance of cash flows from macro-economic aggregate data. As incomes rise, the variance of cash flows may either rise or fall depending on the effect of increasing affluence on transaction frequency. Depending on the relationship between rising incomes and the variance of cash flows, this model would allow for quite a wide range of income elasticities of demand for money, ranging from quite low

---

[1] In this case the optimal upper limit (H), assuming that all the other initial assumptions hold, would be given by the formula

$$H + 1 = \left(\frac{2dm^2t}{n}\right)^{1/2}$$

where d is the transfer cost per £ transferred. The average balance is simply $H/2$, Orr, op. cit. p. 104.

[2] Orr, op. cit. Fig. XII, p. 108.

[3] If large companies can, however, forecast future variations in cash flows, they should normally find it worthwhile to take steps to employ any sizeable prospective cash balances in the money market. For large firms the appropriate determinant of the size of cash balances should then be the standard error in *forecasting* the variations in cash flows, rather than the *actual* variance of such flows. I am grateful to Professor C. Sprenkle for pointing this out to me.

values of $\frac{1}{3}$ up towards unity. Furthermore, the assumption of instantaneous transfers between cash and other assets only holds at the limit. If it takes time to obtain additional balances, or if extra speed involves extra cost, there will need to be a further layer of cash to enable payments to be carried out as and when desired. There will always remain a risk that money will not be available – or only on exorbitant terms – to carry out some unforeseen large purchasing opportunity. Perhaps as investors become wealthier, they become prepared to forgo more interest receipts in order to avoid such risks. So besides a positive income elasticity of demand for money for transactions purposes, there could be a positive wealth elasticity also on this account.

Although the 'inventory theory' of the transactions demand for money has been developed in a most impressive manner, with the help of accomplished mathematical techniques, there have been criticisms that the theory fails to account for the observed data of money holdings, particularly of balances held by large firms, and also that its adherents have overlooked, or ignored, some key institutional features of the banking system, lacunae which may invalidate much of the usefulness of these models for explaining the real world.[1] Thus Sprenkle finds that the percentage of the actual cash balances held by large firms that can be explained by the simple Baumol model is miniscule (of the order of $2\frac{1}{2}$ per cent of the total)[2] and notes that other research[3] shows that State and Local Governments in the United States also appear to hold far larger money balances than the Baumol model would suggest.

The standard versions of the 'inventory theory' imply that cash balances must be maintained above zero at all times. In fact, the state of bank customers' cash balances is not continuously observed throughout each business day, but is monitored only at the close of business on each day. This means that operational constraints on the management of their balances, in the form of, say, maintaining a minimum, non-zero balance at the bank, only apply to a firm's closing balance. So long as firms, or other institutions with access to large amounts of liquid assets, can make day-to-day money-market loans at the end of business on each day, they should never hold in their closing bank balances more than the minimum size for which such short-term market loans can be profitably arranged. In so far as this minimum size of loan is mainly dependent on institutional arrangements in the financial market, the income elasticity of demand for transactions balances by large firms (with sufficient access to funds to enter the short-term money market on a regular basis) should be zero and the interest elasticity very low (in absolute terms), nearer 0 than -0.5.[4]

What then explains the observed data of 'close of business' money holdings of large firms? The standard versions of the 'inventory theory' usually incorporate the implicit assumption that each bank customer, person, firm, or institution, will have only one centralised bank balance. This is not the case for large firms and institutions. For several reasons, e.g. ease and security of handling currency, local autonomy, increasing speed of collections and disbursements, large firms and institutions will tend to have a number of bank balances in conjunction with their major centres for cash payments (e.g. at factories) or receipts (e.g. at sales outlets). Optimal cash management will require that balances be

---

[1] The main proponent of this contrary view is Professor C. Sprenkle, c.f. his papers on, 'The Uselessness of Transactions Demand Models,' *Journal of Finance*, vol. XXIV, no. 5 (December 1969) pp. 835–47; *Effects of Large Firm and Bank Behavior on the Demand for Money of Large Firms* (American Bankers Association, mimeo, 1971); 'On the Observed Transactions Demand for Money,' *The Manchester School of Economic and Social Studies*, no. 3 (September 1972) pp. 261–7.

[2] 'The Uselessness of Transactions Demand Models,' pp. 843–7.

[3] J. Richard Aronson, 'The Idle Cash Balances of State and Local Governments: An Economic Problem of National Concern,' *Journal of Finance*, vol. XXIII, no. 3 (June 1968) pp. 499–508.

[4] 'Thus for large firms the rather striking result is that the demand for money depends neither on income nor on interest rates, but is simply a constant depending on the minimal overnight trading unit,' Sprenkle, 'On the Observed Transactions Demand for Money,' op. cit. p. 265.

remitted to the centralised head-office account when the return to be made from the use of the funds by the financial manager at head office outweighs the transfer costs, subject to any operational constraints on each balance, for example that (close of business) balances shall not fall below zero. Uncertainty over the flow of receipts and disbursements, the variance of the cash flow, may require a sizeable balance to be maintained in each account if there are any difficulties or delays involved in replenishing the balance, to ensure that it meets the required greater-than-zero constraints. If, however, there are (automatic) over-draft facilities available for each separate account, then this constraint also is relaxed. The mean expected cash balance which the firm plans to maintain in each account (and around which the actual observed balance will vary), should then be a function of the differential between the overdraft rate(s) being charged and the rate available on funds remitted to head office, or otherwise employed.

Such decentralisation of cash management with a resulting multiplication of separate bank accounts, especially in view of the likelihood that many of these separate balances may be too small to make careful cash management worthwhile, can explain some part of the larger observed money balances. Sprenkle, however, claims that such factors are still insufficient to explain a large part of corporate money holdings, at least in the United States where his evidence shows that the ratio of these balances (cash plus demand deposits) to turnover is several times higher than in the United Kingdom. He argues that the main reason for such large balances in the United States is the tradition there of holding compensating balances with banks partly as a form of payment for banking services.[1] In short, Sprenkle argues that the standard versions of the 'inventory theory' overlook several of the crucial institutional features of the monetary system, and thus fail to provide an adequate explanation of actual behaviour. Certainly his criticisms of currently accepted theory have considerable force.

B. Asset Price Uncertainty and the Speculative Demand for Money

As noted in the previous section, borrowers can offer a higher mean expected yield on their liabilities if they are not committed to redeeming these on demand at a fixed money value, since this gives them the freedom in turn to invest in a higher yielding but riskier portfolio of assets. Equally lenders, at least those investors exhibiting normal risk aversion, will require a premium, a positive differential in rates, in order to induce them to hold riskier assets (see also Chapter 4 on this subject). Thus asset-price uncertainty is one determinant of the yield differential between capital-certain assets such as money, and risky assets, whose nominal value in the market place may vary. Put the other way round, with the yield differentials given, such uncertainty is one of the factors determining the relative pro-portions of 'safe' and risky assets which each investor will want to hold in his own portfolio. Having abstracted from such uncertainty in the previous section, in order to concentrate upon the analysis of the transactions demand for money, the objective in this section is to examine how such asset-price uncertainty affects the portfolio distribution between risky and safe assets, and within the set of safe assets how it affects, in particular, the demand for money.

For there is, at least in all financially developed countries, quite a wide assortment of alternative 'safe', capital-certain assets, besides money, available for investors to hold. There are even some assets, e.g. national savings bonds, which are certain in the sense that both the interest payment and the capital value on that asset are fixed over their complete life. A somewhat larger group of assets, including most forms of deposits with financial

---

[1] For a discussion of the role, rationale and development of compensating balances, see D. Hodgman, *Commercial Bank Loan and Investment Policy* (University of Illinois Bureau of Economic and Business Research, 1963).

intermediaries, have fixed, certain capital values, but their interest payments can be varied from time to time as in the case, for example, of the rate payable on time deposits at banks; there will be uncertainty about the prospective fluctuations in such rates. There would, however, be no cost to the investor in failing to predict these variations, so long as he was able to observe them and to respond by adjusting his holdings from one asset to another quickly and without expense. If information is sparse, say because the investor is going to be out of the country, or if it is costly and time-consuming to shift from one capital-certain asset to another, the investor might diversify his holdings even among capital-certain assets to reduce the resultant risks of variations in rates. But these potential costs to the investor, resulting from unforeseen changes in the interest offered on capital-certain assets, arise from frictions and costs in the adjustment process. All funds invested in such assets would be placed in the currently highest-yielding form but for the presence of transactions costs.[1] We may describe all such capital-certain assets, diversification among which depends on the balance between transfer costs and yield differentials, as 'safe' assets.

Moreover, when the length of time over which it is intended to hold financial assets, before their realisation to provide funds to purchase goods and services or to give to some-one else, i.e. the holding period, is known for sure, it will generally prove possible to find a marketable asset which matures towards the end of that period. This will then be a quasi-safe asset since its capital value when required will be certain. However, there will still be uncertainty over the rates at which the periodic coupon payments of interest may be reinvested in the intervening period, and any attempt to switch out of the asset before redemption, say because some other safe asset was offering a higher yield, would expose the investor to capital risk of having to sell at a depressed market value.

So there is generally a selection of safe, or quasi-safe assets, whose nominal return till the end of the holding period is virtually certain, which an investor can choose. The choice within the set of safe assets will depend on the balance between transactions costs and yields, along the lines already examined. Transactions costs, however, become relatively less important, compared with prospective yields, the longer the intended holding period. So investors requiring a temporary safe haven for funds, say for a week or so, will tend to keep them in cash, current accounts. If the holding period is to be a month or more, de-pending on the size of the funds, the interest rate offered and the transactions costs, it may pay the investor to place such funds in time deposits, certificates of deposit, etc. As the holding period lengthens, the range of assets that can be treated as safe widens and, with transactions costs becoming a lesser consideration, short-dated marketable assets, Treasury bills and short-dated government bonds will become receptacles for investors seeking to avoid asset-price uncertainty.

Given known holding period(s),[2] the certain yields over these period(s) and the schedule of transactions costs, the choice of assets within the set of safe assets can, therefore, be treated as an extension of the analysis in the previous section. The next question is what determines the division of the portfolio between the set of safe assets with virtually certain returns and the set of risky assets, where the return over the holding period is uncertain, in particular because their capital values will change in line with uncertain future changes in market yields. To simplify the analysis, consider the case of one safe asset, which may or may not be money and therefore may or may not have a positive nominal return during the period, and one risky asset.

---

[1] See the paper by M. Parkin, with R. Barrett and M. Gray, 'The Demand for Financial Assets by the Personal Sector of the U.K. Economy,' Proceedings of the London Business School Con-ference of June 1972 on Modelling the U.K. Economy (forthcoming). Also see Parkin and Gray on 'Portfolio Diversification as Optimal Precautionary Behaviour,' chap. 12 in *Theory of Demand: Real and Monetary*, by M. Morishima *et al.* (Clarendon Press, Oxford, 1973).

[2] Though, in reality, the length of the holding period(s) will also be uncertain.

The return from this risky asset will not be exactly predictable, but each investor can imagine a subjective probability distribution of its likely return.[1] Following Tobin,[2] we shall assume that the investor concentrates his attention on the first two moments of this distribution, the mean and standard deviation, and ignores higher moments, skewness, etc. One can try to justify this assumption, either on the grounds that the subjective probability distribution of returns is completely described by the first two moments, as in the case of the normal distribution, or that the investor's utility function takes a form, quadratic over the relevant range, which depends only on the level and variance of incomes (returns). Whether justification on these grounds is actually possible has been the subject of some advanced theoretical disputation.[3] In any case both assumptions seem unrealistic. There is virtually always a non-zero possibility of default on any asset, but, except on such assets as lottery tickets and premium bonds, virtually no chance of some equally large prize. Thus many assets, e.g. bonds, could have a negatively-skewed distribution, while others, e.g. equities, may exhibit positive skewness. Furthermore, the prevalence of behaviour such as gambling, which suggests some enjoyment of risk among individuals who in most other respects appear to be risk averters, for example in taking out insurance policies, makes the assumption that the utility of income (or wealth) can be described by some simple quadratic linear function, such as $U(Y) = (1 + b)Y + bY^2$ (where $0 < b < 1$ for a risk seeker, and $-1 < b < 0$ for a risk averter), doubtful.[4] None the less the assumption that investors concentrate only on the mean and variance of expected returns from their asset portfolio can be regarded as a helpful and fruitful simplification for analytical purposes, which does not seem to be seriously misleading in the various applications to which it has been put.

With two assets, the first a safe asset with zero variance and the second a risky asset, one can plot how the mean expected return and variance of the portfolio changes as the

---

[1] This is a standard assumption and would appear rational. Yet Shackle has queried whether expectations are really formed in this manner, see for example, *Expectation in Economics* (Cambridge University Press, 1952): one should not, perhaps, overlook the time and effort involved in trying to construct a subjective – and admittedly fallible – probability distribution.

[2] 'Liquidity Preference as Behaviour Towards Risk,' *Review of Economic Studies*, vol. 25 (February 1958) pp. 65–86.

[3] See the series of articles in the *Review of Economic Studies* on this issue, e.g. the articles by K. Borch, M. S. Feldstein and J. Tobin in vol. 36 (1) no. 105 (January 1969) pp. 1–15 and by P. A. Samuelson in vol. 37 (4) no. 112 (October 1970) pp. 537–42.

[4] An individual who has a declining marginal utility of income with a utility function that is concave downwards, as shown in Fig. 2.5 below, will be a risk averter. Given the chance to play a fair game with a 50 per cent chance of obtaining an income of $X + 1$ or $X - 1$, he will always prefer a certain return of X.

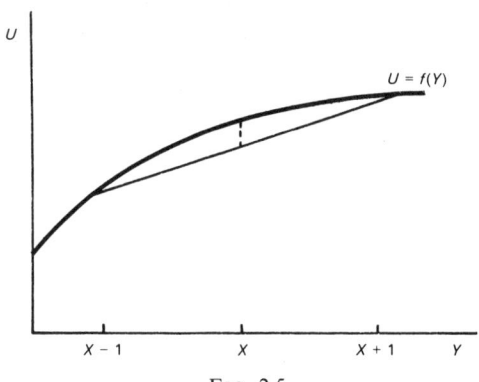

FIG. 2.5

proportion of the total portfolio invested in the risky asset is increased. In Fig. 2.6 the assumption is made that the mean expected return on the risky asset is higher than that on the safe asset. Otherwise no risk averters would hold the risky asset, and unless there were a sizeable number of risk lovers in the system buying the risky asset, its price would have to fall until its return rose sufficiently to attract risk averters into holding the asset.

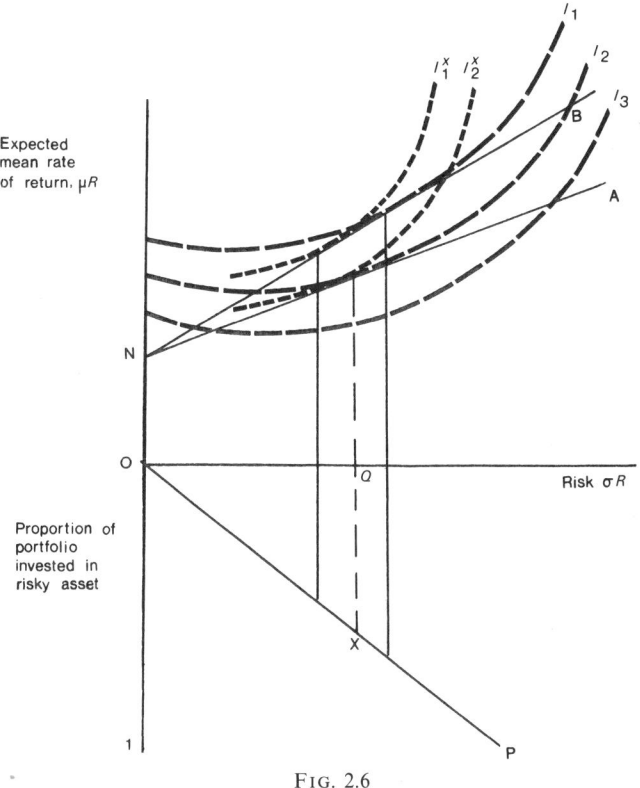

FIG. 2.6

Given his preferences he should insure, but not gamble, especially not in the usual situation where the odds are loaded against the punter since the organiser of the game, e.g. the bookie, will take his rake-off before distributing the winnings. In practice, however, gambling amongst most risk averters is restricted to wagering fairly small proportionate sums in relation to their overall wealth. This suggests that even those with a declining marginal utility of income may find that a limited, controlled risk adds utility, a certain savour, to an otherwise humdrum life. Furthermore, such gambling frequently takes the form of gambles offering a very small proportionate chance of fabulous wins, e.g. football pools, lotteries, premium bonds. It may be, as Professor Shackle would contend, that the dramatic nature of successes in such games (and indeed the dramatic nature of certain disasters, e.g. air crashes, fire, premature death of the breadwinner) makes one tend to focus so much on these outcomes that the subjective probability distribution is distorted out of true. Alternatively, such positively-skew gambles may provide utility in themselves by allowing us to dream about what might be, while insurance against negatively-skewed disaster situations enables us to avoid the morbid worries about them that their dramatic intensity would otherwise cause. Furthermore, S. C. Tsiang in his paper on 'The Rationale of the Mean-Standard Deviation Analysis, Skewness Preference, and the Demand for Money,' *The American Economic Review*, vol. LXII, no. 3 (June 1972) pp. 354–71, argues (p. 359) that skewness preference . . . is certainly not necessarily a mark of an inveterate gambler, but a common trait of a risk-avert person with decreasing or constant absolute risk-aversion.

The available combinations of risk and return are shown lying along the line NA. The point on this line where the investor arrives depends on the proportionate division of his portfolio into holdings of the safe and risky asset respectively, traced out along the schedule OP. The investor will select that combination which offers the most utility, i.e. that point on the line NA touching the highest indifference curve. In Fig. 2.6 the dashed indifference curves, $I_1 - I_3$, are drawn concave upwards, which implies that the investor requires a continuously increasing incentive in mean expected return to take on additional risk, i.e. that he is a risk averter.[1] As depicted, the investor will reach the optimum portfolio balance at Q, with OX of his portfolio in the risky asset and XP in the safe asset.

If the expected mean return increases, say because of a growing expectation of some capital gain on the risky asset, then the risk–return combination line will shift upwards from NA to NB, as shown in Fig. 2.6. With the indifference curves, as shown by the longer dashed lines (I_1–I_3), this rise in expected yields causes the investor to raise the proportion of his portfolio in the risky asset: the shape of the indifference curves might, however, be such, as marked by the shorter dashed curves, I_1^x–I_2^x, that he would reduce the proportion held in risky assets.[2] In this case the 'income effect' of a rise in yields, leading the investor to seek an increase in his security from risk as conditions allow improved risk–return combinations to be achieved, outweighs the 'substitution effect', as the mean expected rate on the risky asset rises relative to the rate on the safe asset. As the expected yield on the risky asset declines, relative to the yield on the safe asset, the theory implies an increasing (negative) interest elasticity of demand for the safe asset as the yield differential approaches zero, but there does remain some ambiguity about the sign of the relationship between the demand

---

[1] If the investor was a risk lover or a plunger, who required a diminishing incentive in extra mean expected return to take on additional risk, i.e. with indifference curves which were concave downwards, he would not distribute his portfolio between the two assets but would plunge all his funds in one or the other asset, depending on the slope of the risk–return combination available and the shape of his indifference curve. In Fig. 2.7, if the risk–return combination was NA1, the plunger would hold all his assets in the safe asset; with combination NA2, he would place them all in the risky asset.

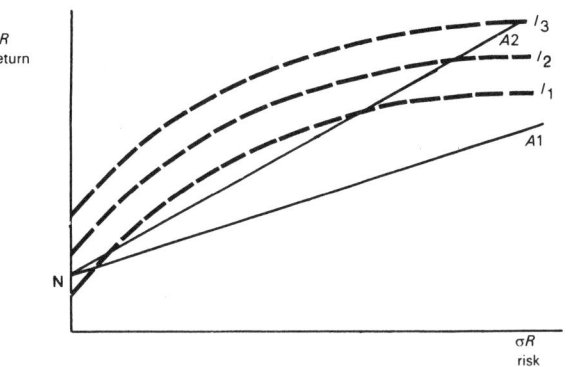

FIG. 2.7

Risk assumption on this scale, placing all one's funds into one asset or the other is, however, rarely seen, and may be regarded as a pathological phenomenon. Absolute risk preference, where the indifference curves slope downwards and all funds are placed in the riskier asset (as long as it provides an equal or larger mean expected return), is even rarer.

[2] Though it is doubtful whether the extreme risk aversion represented by such steeply rising indifference curves is plausible, see on this subject Tsiang, op. cit., pp. 362–8.

for the safe asset and relative yields, in circumstances when the expected yield on the risky asset rises sharply above the yield on the safe asset.

The great advantage of Tobin's reformulation of the theory of liquidity preference is that he linked it firmly to uncertainty about future asset prices,[1] and thus provided a rationale for portfolio diversification, beyond the existence of transactions costs (which are in turn basically a function of another form of uncertainty). In previous Keynesian analysis of liquidity preference, and of the speculative demand for money, investors were treated as holding completely confident expectations of the future yield on the risky asset. Each investor would then hold all his assets either in the risky asset or in the safe asset depending on which offered more, so there was no explanation of portfolio diversification at the individual level. The existence of a downward sloping aggregate liquidity-preference schedule relating the demand for the safe asset (money) to the yield differential between the risky and the safe asset (with the rate on money being zero) depended on differing expectations between investors (all confidently held!) and an assumption that investors would generally expect some 'normal' rate of return to be re-established on risky assets. These two assumptions together imply that a fall in interest rates on the risky asset below the 'normal' level would induce a growing proportion of investors to expect confidently a future rise in rates, and thus capital losses on holding risky assets, and so switch all their funds into the safe asset. Apart from the obvious inconsistency in the assumption of confident expectations in circumstances where most predictions would always be off target, this analysis rested on a particular assumption about the generation of expectations of future prices in this market. There was no good theoretical reason for expectations to be regressive in this manner; Keynes did not extend the same assumption about expectations to other markets, e.g. the goods and labour markets;[2] in practice monetary authorities tend to be more concerned with the possibility of extrapolative expectations in financial markets, i.e. price movements feeding on themselves and becoming excessively volatile. Finally, market views of what constitutes a 'normal' level of rates presumably depend on past experience, so that the existence of fixed views on the likely normal level must be a short-term phenomenon, though perhaps long enough for practical, policy purposes.

Tobin's reformulation allowed a much more general and plausible interpretation of the theory of liquidity preference. Portfolio diversification was given a justification at the individual level. This diversification is consistent with differing investors holding a range of expectations of future mean yields on the risky asset.[3] Moreover, the holding of safe

---

[1] One could argue, with Shackle and P. Davidson, that Tobin has merely replaced the implausible assumption that investors act as if certain of the future level of prices and rates of return on risky assets with an almost equally implausible assumption that they act as if certain of the future probability distribution of returns. It is, perhaps, a matter of judgement how much closer to reality Tobin's reformulation takes the analysis, and a subject for further study to discover whether some alternative assumptions can be found which approximate more closely to market behaviour.

[2] If people expected pre-depression price and wage levels to be 'normal' levels, to which they would return, expenditures and the demand for labour should respond directly to reductions in money wages and prices, even if nominal interest rates were sustained by the liquidity preference of investors.

[3] The range is not, however, unbounded. Unless there is considerable risk preference in the community the yield on the risky asset cannot fall below the yield on the safe asset. At the other end of the spectrum Tsiang, op. cit. pp. 368–70, has shown that, given the limitation upon the upward slope of the indifference curves (less than 45°) which theory suggests, it will be worthwhile to replace zero-yielding cash completely by further holdings of the risky asset, so long as the expected return on the risky asset is greater than the standard deviation of that yield. The existence of such assets, and Tsiang argues that 'there must be a host of assets in modern financial markets, e.g. savings deposits and Treasury bills, that would satisfy these requirements,' 'would eliminate all demand for cash for the portfolio balance purpose.'

assets, other than for 'transactions purposes', does not depend on some people confidently expecting future falls in risky asset prices.[1]

Furthermore this approach, based on the assessment of portfolios in terms of their mean-variance configuration, can be – and has been – extended from analysis of the selection of a portfolio consisting of one safe asset and one risky asset, to the much broader analysis of portfolio choice where the investor is confronted with a range of risky assets (and possibly, but not necessarily, a safe asset as well). Consider the case where the investor can choose to distribute some funds between two risky assets, X and Y. In situation 1, let there be two possible outcomes (states of nature). If outcome (i) occurs, X pays £6 and Y pays £3; if outcome (ii) occurs, X pays £0 and Y pays £1. The mean expected value of X is £3, of Y £2, the standard deviation of X, defined as $\sqrt{(1/n)(x - \bar{x})^2}$, is £3, of Y is £1. If all the portfolio is held in asset Y, then the risk–return combination is that shown at point A in Fig. 2.8. If the portfolio is held entirely in asset X, the risk–return combination obtained is plotted at point B.

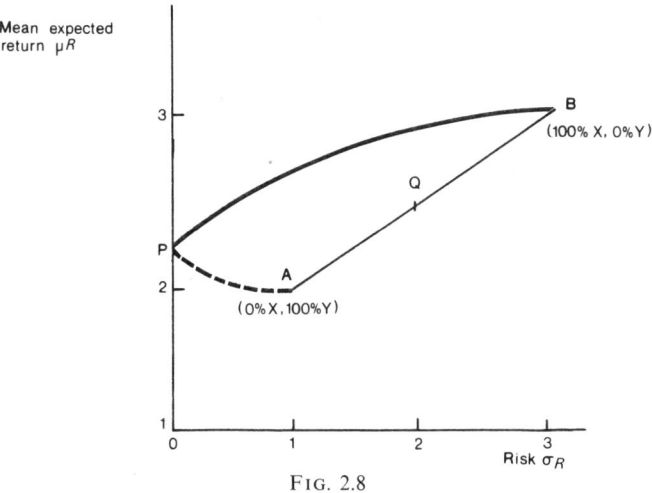

F IG. 2.8

The out-turns for X and Y have perfect positive correlation,[2] of +1, since they vary exactly together. If the investor then decides to hold 50 per cent of his assets in X and 50 per cent in Y, the expected mean value of his portfolio will be £2.50, and the standard deviation will be £2: the mean and standard deviation of this combination lies, at point Q,

---

[1] Indeed, the more common assumption now in portfolio analysis is to treat all individuals as having identical subjective expectations. This can be, certainly, a useful simplifying assumption for analytic purposes, but is hardly a reasonable representation of the real world and may be seriously misleading in some respects. See, for example, the comments of J. Stiglitz, 'Some Aspects of the Pure Theory of Corporate Finance: Bankruptcies and Take-overs,' *The Bell Journal of Economics and Management Science*, vol. 3, no. 2 (Autumn 1972) pp. 458–82, especially p. 459.

[2] Defined as

$$r_{xy} = \frac{\text{Covariance}}{\sigma_x, \sigma_y}(xy) = \frac{1}{n}\frac{\sum (x - \bar{x})(y - \bar{y})}{\sqrt{\frac{1}{n}(x - \bar{x})^2}\sqrt{\frac{1}{n}(y - \bar{y})^2}}$$

In this case

$$\frac{3}{3x1} = +1$$

half-way along a straight line joining A and B. All portfolios of X and Y in differing pro-portions will exhibit risk–return combinations lying along this line.[1]

In case 2, the mean and variance of X and Y remain as above, but in outcome (i) X pays £6 and Y pays £1, while in outcome (ii) X pays £0 and Y pays £3. In these circumstances with perfect negative correlation, of -1, a particular combination of X and Y can be chosen, in this case with 1/4 of the portfolio in X and 3/4 in Y, which will provide a mean return at £2.25, which is higher than the mean expected return on holdings of Y, with absolute certainty whatever the outcome. In this case the opportunities[2] open to the in-vestor lie along the line APB. Obviously the segment PB is preferable in all respects to the segment AP since it is possible to find points along PB which have a higher mean expected return with a similar variance, in comparison with the points on AP. The segment PB may, therefore, be entitled the efficient frontier of the portfolio, since it dominates all other available combinations.

Next take a situation where asset X, say, pays £3, £4, £4 and £5 when possible outcomes (i)–(iv) occur respectively, while asset Y pays £2, £1.50, £2.50 and £2 in the same outcomes. The respective means and standard deviations are £4 and £0.71 for X and £2 and £0.35 for Y. The covariance between the two assets, and thus the correlation also, has been constructed to be zero. In this case also it is possible to reduce the overall variance of the portfolio by a policy of diversification, at the same time as raising the mean expected return above the level, £2, obtainable when all the assets are invested in Y. Thus if half of the available funds are invested in X and half in Y, the mean return on the portfolio is £3 and the standard deviation is £0.39; if 2/3 of the funds are placed in Y and 1/3 in X, the mean return and standard deviation are £2.66 and £0.33 respectively. The available combinations, the line APB, are traced out in Fig. 2.9 (see p. 38). The minimum variance at point P[3] is £0.32 with 4/5 of the portfolio invested in asset Y, and mean return £2.40.

Clearly diversification is an effective method of reducing risk, so long as the risky assets exhibit low or negative covariances (and correlations). Consider, for example, a situation where the investor can divide his funds equally between n assets, which have zero covariance. In this case the mean return will be $1/n (\mu_1 + \cdots + \mu_n)$, and the variance of his portfolio will be $1/n^2(\sigma_1^2 + \cdots + \sigma_1^2)$. As n becomes large, the variance of this portfolio drops towards zero. So if one could find sufficient risky assets whose outcomes were nevertheless independent, with zero covariance, it would be possible to combine them to obtain a virtually riskless portfolio. In practice this cannot be achieved. There tends to be a systematic risk, with general positive covariances, among all risky assets. All assets represent, directly or indirectly, claims upon future economic resources, so that forces that affect the future development of the economy are likely to impinge in a similar fashion over wide groups of risky assets. Imagine an entrepreneur who wanted to take advantage

---

[1] With a portfolio consisting of asset X with mean expected return μ_x and variance σ_x^2, and asset Y with mean μ_y and variance σ_y^2, the formulae for obtaining the mean and variance of the overall portfolio in a combination in which asset X takes up a fraction of the portfolio h and asset Y, $1 - h$, are as follows

$$Z = hX + (1 - h)Y$$
$$\mu_z = E(Z) = h\mu_x + (1 - h)\mu_y$$
$$\sigma_z^2 = \text{var}(Z) = h^2\sigma_x^2 + (1 - h)^2\sigma_y^2 + 2h(1 - h)r\sigma_x\sigma_y$$

where r is the correlation between X and Y.

[2] The opportunity loci for two asset portfolios are hyperbolas, except in special cases, e.g. where $r = +1$ or when σ_x or σ_y is zero, when the loci degenerate into straight lines. See J. Tobin, 'The Theory of Portfolio Selection', chap. 1 in *The Theory of Interest Rates*, ed. F. Hahn and F. Brechling (Macmillan, London, 1965) pp. 29–30.

[3] The formulae for finding the variance of the minimum-risk portfolio and the shares of the two assets in this are given by Tobin, op. cit. pp. 29–30.

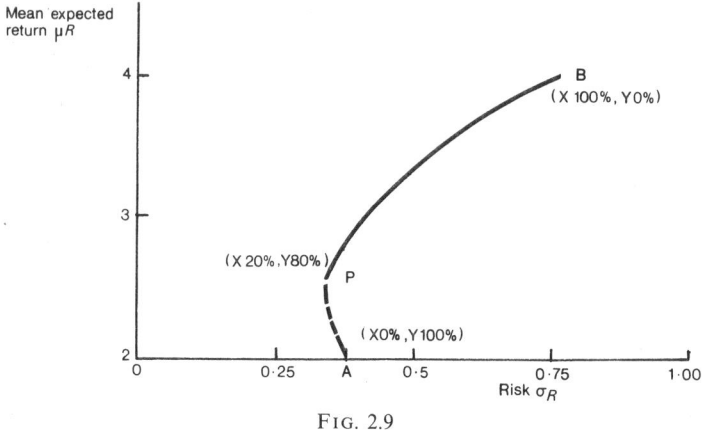

FIG. 2.9

of the demand for diversification and offered to the public an asset with the characteristics that its market value went up when market interest rates rose, and vice versa. How could he invest his funds so as to remain solvent during periods when interest rates rise? He could only do so by levying a charge for this insurance against market risks,[1] offering such a low return that a combination of this asset with other risky assets would offer no greater return with the same variance as already existing 'safe' assets.

When the investor was considering selecting between one safe and one risky asset, the attributes of the risky asset which were relevant to this decision, under the particular assumptions set out previously, were the expected mean return and variance of the asset. When the investor is considering adding a risky asset to a portfolio containing other risky assets the critical issue is how much the addition of a unit of the risky asset will add to the overall return and risk of the portfolio as a whole.[2] The various combinations of risky assets, which the investor could hold, will then provide a set of possible configurations for risk and return for the whole portfolio, which can be depicted by the shaded area in Fig. 2.10. The upper envelope of this set, the line joining P and R, gives the efficient frontier of portfolio combinations dominating all the other options. Drawing in the indifference curves for a risk averter, assuming that only risky assets may be held, the investor will choose portfolio S. However, there is no good reason why the investor should not be able to invest also in a

---

[1] Such events as increases in market interest rates do not have a well defined actuarial probability. It would, therefore, be even more difficult for a private-sector intermediary to offer insurance against them at rates that could allow the intermediary an acceptable risk–return configuration on his own business.

An entrepreneur might, however, consider inviting subscriptions to an intermediary set up to borrow long and lend short. An intermediary run in this way would have exhibited a considerable growth in equity value over the last two decades. I am indebted to A. D. Crockett for this suggestion.

[2] The marginal impact of the jth asset on the standard deviation of the market portfolio (consisting of an investment in every asset outstanding in proportion to its total value) is proportional to the covariance between the returns on the jth asset and the market portfolio. Thus

$$\frac{\partial \sigma(R_m)}{\partial X_j} = \frac{\text{cov}(R_j, R_m)}{\sigma(R_m)}$$

where R_m represents the expected return on the market portfolio, $\sigma(R_m)$ the standard deviation of that return and X_j the weight which asset j receives in the market portfolio. See M. C. Jensen, 'Capital Markets: Theory and Evidence,' *The Bell Journal of Economics and Management Science*, vol. 3, no. 2 (autumn 1972) pp. 357–98, especially pp. 362–3, and E. F. Fama, 'Risk, Return, and Equilibrium,' *Journal of Political Economy*, vol. 79, no. 1 (January/February 1971) pp. 30–55.

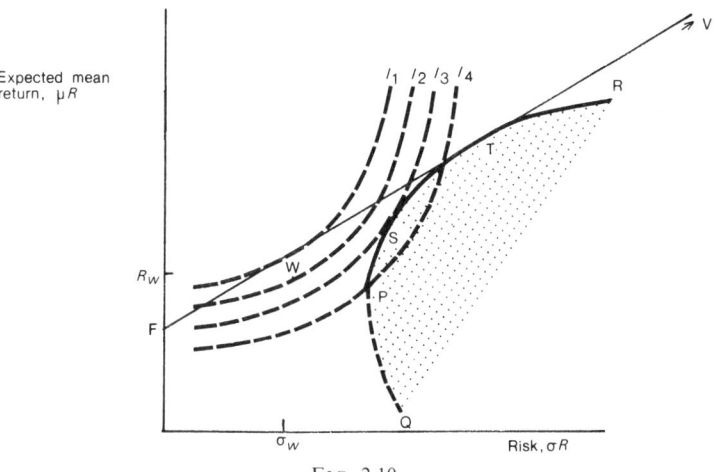

FIG. 2.10

safe asset and so, analogously to the previous case of one safe and one risky asset, one can assume that the investor can choose some combination of a safe asset and a portfolio of risky assets. Clearly the combinations offering the greatest potential utility must be of the safe asset and of market portfolio T, where T is the point at which the line from F (the point showing the available yield on the risk-free asset) tangentially touches the envelope enclosing the opportunity set of portfolios of risky assets. If the investor can also borrow, as well as lend, at the riskless rate of interest, the line FT can be extended onwards, indefinitely, towards V.[1] In this example the investor will achieve his greatest possible utility at point W, with a combination of the safe asset and the portfolio of risky assets offering the expected yield R_w and the subjective standard deviation (risk) of outcomes σ_w.

If all investors have identical expectations, and assuming that the outstanding quantities of all the risky assets are given, then the prices on such assets must shift until each investor holds all the available assets in proportion to their outstanding quantities in his own preferred portfolio, at T. Abstracting from complications caused by taxes, limited marketability of some assets, etc., these assumptions allow one to specify the equilibrium expected return on any asset. This will be greater than the risk-free rate by the extent of a premium which is the product of the general market risk premium per unit of risk (measured by the slope of the line FTV), multiplied by the actual addition to risk that the addition of this asset to the portfolio (in exchange for an equivalent amount of the market portfolio) brings about (which is basically a function of the covariance of the returns on this asset with those on the whole market portfolio).[2]

---

[1] This implies that a plunger might try to borrow at the riskless rate of interest enough to buy up all the risky assets in the system. In practice a number of factors would prevent this. Differing expectations within the economy would lead to prices being forced against him (higher prices on the risky assets, rising borrowing rates). Even though the borrowing would be covered by the collateral of the risky assets, the lenders would become increasingly chary of lending to this plunger as the possibility of his becoming bankrupt increased.

[2] The formula is

$$E(R_j) = R_F + \frac{(E(R_M) - R_F)}{(R_M)} \cdot \frac{\mathrm{cov}(R_j, R_M)}{\sigma(R_M)},$$

where R_F is the riskless rate of interest and R_j is the return on the jth asset; $E(R_j)$ is the expected return on the jth asset. See Jensen, op. cit. pp. 358–63.

This analysis has a wide range of practical applications. For example, so long as the assumptions on which the analysis is based hold true, it can be used in a normative manner to suggest how an efficient portfolio should be selected. It can also be used in a positive way to observe whether relative yields on differing assets have varied as the theory would suggest, a process which inevitably involves further extensions and revisions of the basic theory in order to account for the empirically observed discrepancies between actual market conditions and those predicted by the theory. Indeed, an expanding literature on this subject has appeared in the last few years.[1] To pursue this fascinating, but quite complicated, subject further at this juncture would, however, take us too far from the main theme of this chapter, the relationship between various aspects of uncertainty and the demand for money.

The analysis, moreover, has been conducted so far in terms of a single period of unspecified length. There are, in practice, two main temporal dimensions affecting the investor. The first is the length of his holding period, up till the moment when he needs to realise his assets. The second may be described as the length of his planning period. It is expensive in time and effort to reach investment decisions; in particular the acquisition of information about the probabilities of return and risk on different assets can be a very costly business. But as time goes by, the underlying conditions change and the basis on which the previous portfolio decision was made will become increasingly out of date, so that losses will be made by not using such information as could be obtained to readjust the portfolio. Thus the length of time between periodic portfolio reviews – the planning period – will be a function of such factors as the speed with which new information appears, the cost of assembling and interpreting information, the costs of executive time, transfer costs, etc., with the optimal period being that which minimises a cost function consisting of the costs of decision-making on the one hand and of losing opportunities by delaying decisions on the other.

Evidently the holding period must be at least as long as the planning period if any asset besides cash is to be held; if the holding period is shorter, because the costs of portfolio rearrangement (transfer costs) are relatively large, all the funds to meet the very short-term holding-period requirement will be kept in cash. Usually, however, the holding period will be considerably longer than the planning period. Indeed the divergence may be very great. A large pension fund may have an average holding period of several decades, but with its advantages of access to the market, to market-related information, etc. (i.e. enjoying certain economies of scale), may consider it worthwhile to review its portfolio daily.

There is, however, a set of circumstances in which the portfolio decision may be largely independent of the length of the holding period, so that the portfolio decision can be analysed purely in terms of each single separate planning period, abstracting from the fact that there will be many planning periods within the holding period. This is the case when asset returns are regarded by the investor as both statistically independent and stationary over time.[2] Statistical independence requires that the return on the ith asset in period t is not correlated with the return on either this ith asset or any other asset in any previous period. Stationarity over time requires that the probability distributions are believed to be governed by the same underlying laws at all present and future points of time.

These assumptions virtually allow one to chop up the longer holding period into separate independent planning periods. If the investor chooses a desired portfolio in period 1, and differing rates of appreciation among the assets held change the proportions of assets in that portfolio, then he should restore the desired portfolio distribution in the

---

[1] Consult, for example, the list of references given by Jensen, op. cit.
[2] See Tobin, 'The Theory of Portfolio Selection,' chap. 1 in *The Theory of Interest Rates*, pp. 42–7.

subsequent period. The investor should choose such a 'stationary sequence'.[1] If you organise your portfolio to give you the best combinations of risk and return in the short run under these circumstances, it should also do so in the longer run. The conditions that asset returns should be statistically independent and stationary over time perhaps hold most closely in the equity market. This would suggest that the appropriate horizon for equity investment might be the relatively short planning period, but that the general proportions, between different asset groups, in which the fund is held should be kept fairly constant over time. These precepts differ markedly from much investment advice which often stresses the advantages of the long-term quality (or growth prospects, or whatever) of certain shares, or sets of shares, and occasionally advocates major portfolio shifts from one group of securities to another.

In the case, however, of portfolios containing dated bonds, the conditions that allow the portfolio decision to follow a stationary sequence in consecutive periods cease to hold. If the actual returns on a dated bond of n year's life are lower than expected in some planning period, its price at the end of that period must have fallen below its expected level. Since it is a dated bond, this fall in price will entail a larger, certain subsequent appreciation in value between that time and its eventual redemption. This inverse relationship between returns in one period and in subsequent periods on a bond allow the investor to select a bond with a maturity equal to his holding period, the nominal return on which is subject only to the uncertainty of the rates at which the intermediate periodic coupon payments can be re-invested.

The question then becomes how to make use of the available information on the statistical interdependence of returns over time in order to construct the optimal multi-period investment strategy. This is a complex matter. Although it is no doubt possible to specify the parameters of some hypothetical system in such a way as to solve the problem for that restricted model, no general paradigm for optimising behaviour in such circumstances, which are the common experience in reality, has yet been developed. Possibly the best procedure, then, is to consider the actual investment practices of such institutions as life insurance companies, who have to cope with these problems. With actuarial calculations of life expectancies, their expected holding periods are, indeed, virtually known with certainty. They can, therefore, tailor the maturity of their assets closely to that of their liabilities and obtain a virtually safe, hedged portfolio with a return considerably above that available on short-dated liquid assets.

---

[1] For an example and attempted proof that a stationary sequence can always be found with the same expectation of return and lower risk over n planning periods than a variable sequence, see Tobin, ibid, pp. 43–7. Even under these circumstances, however, the length of the holding period does affect the portfolio distribution decision in one way because the n period expectation of risk is a positive function of the common one (planning) period mean expected return and the number of (planning) periods in the holding period, as well as of the individual one-period risks. The higher the average expected return, the greater the possible dispersion of results in the long run. Thus the investor with a long holding period faced with the same initial opportunity set as an investor with a one-period horizon and with the same utility functions may nevertheless select a different portfolio.

Tobin's proof has, however, been challenged by Guy Stevens in his paper 'On Tobin's Multi-period Portfolio Theorem,' *Review of Economic Studies*, vol. xxxix, no. 120 (October 1972) pp. 461–8. In this paper Stevens shows that for certain functional relationships between risk and expected return in each individual planning period a stationary sequence will *not* always provide the lowest risk consonant with a given expected rate of return over a multi-period horizon. He also notes that Tobin's approach must imply 'an implicit constraint that portfolio decisions are to be taken simultaneously at a given time.' Otherwise changes in the initial wealth at the start of each new planning period, depending on the variable returns obtained in all preceding periods, would lead to re-adjustments in portfolios. 'The optimal portfolio in the last period, n, is a function of the risk–return locus for period n, but also of the investor's level of wealth at the beginning of that period. This wealth level is determined by the actual *outcomes* of portfolio decisions in earlier periods, and cannot be known until after earlier portfolios are chosen.'

In a sense this long period, quasi-safe return becomes the equivalent of the risk-free rate in the shorter planning-period decisions. Portfolio sequences have to offer an expectation of at least as high a nominal return over the long period, in order to compensate for any additional assumption of risk. Thus an investor with a long holding period might be persuaded to shift into money, but only if he expected a temporary fall in asset prices sufficient to enable him to switch back into marketable assets at a price low enough to raise the long-period return from the sequence of portfolios sufficiently high above the safe, hedged return, to recompense for the additional uncertainty incurred. It would be inefficient to buy and hold a safe asset which yielded less than the highest available quasi-safe return, but it might be advantageous to consider temporary investment in such an asset as one stage on a relatively risky, but potentially higher-yielding sequence.

Investors will not usually have just one holding period to consider. Assets will be held against several future contingencies occurring on different dates. It may be a convenient fiction to imagine investors dividing their wealth into as many separate portfolios as there are separate expected realisation dates. This would, however, exaggerate the costs of portfolio management (including transfer costs if any economies of scale were available), while combining the various portfolios relating to each separate future requirement might allow the investor to obtain an improved overall risk/return opportunity set.

In general, with the availability of dated bonds providing statistical interdependence over time, one would expect to see the minimum-risk portfolio consisting of some combination of bonds, with maturities roughly equal to the various holding-period requirements, plus equities, since the long-run correlation between capital goods' values and consumer goods' prices should provide equity holders with some protection against unpredictable changes in price levels. Apart from direct transactions purposes, i.e. for very short holding periods, it is difficult to see money balances playing much part in asset portfolios as a hedge against asset-price uncertainty. Unless planning periods are very short, money (cash plus demand deposits) will usually be dominated as a safe asset by some other asset (even when the liquid asset is being held temporarily as one part of a relatively risky sequence of portfolios by the investor with a longer holding period). And some of those investors who do have very short planning periods, particularly professional investment managers, will be dealing with such large sums that any economies of scale in transfer costs will enable them to make a better return by holding their funds in other very short-dated, money-market assets rather than in money balances.

This examination of the micro-economic determinants of the demand for money leaves us, however, with an awkward conclusion. This is that it is not easy to explain or to account at the individual level for the amount of money balances held. Companies, and other corporate bodies such as local authorities, appear to hold much larger balances than inventory–theoretic transactions demand models show to be optimal. And money should be dominated by other interest-paying capital-certain assets in the role of providing a safe asset in portfolios. We explained in Chapter 1 why money would be demanded and held, but further micro-economic analysis in this chapter suggests that there is, perhaps, something of a puzzle still to explain why such large balances are held.

3

Macro-Economic Analysis of the Demand for Money

SUMMARY

The factors which would determine the demand for money at the micro, individual level – it was argued in Chapter 2 – were largely expectational considerations of the future level and variance of cash flows, of asset prices, etc. It is difficult to find quantitative counterparts, at least at the macro-economic level, of such behavioural factors. The tendency has been to turn instead for the study of behaviour at the aggregate level to a rather more generalised, simpler theory of asset demand, relating the demand for each asset to total wealth (as the budget constraint), relative interest rates and other variables, such as the level of incomes, which affect the demand for the specific services of the various assets. This gives a demand for money function of the form

$$M_d = f(Y, r_i, W)$$

However, wealth is the capitalisation of present and future incomes, so the above explanatory variables are not fully independent. The normal procedure is to omit either W or Y from the estimating equation. Much of the controversy between 'monetarists' and 'Keynesians' (or 'fiscalists') has focused on the particular form of the demand for money function, whether it was stable and predictable, and whether the interest elasticity of demand for money (determining the response of holders of money balances to changes in yields on alternative liquid financial assets) was high or low. The question of the (real) income elasticity of demand for money, though of interest in itself, has engendered less heat, since no crucial point of theory rests on this issue. Monetarists take the view that the demand for money function is relatively stable and predictable, and the interest elasticity of demand for money relatively low (at least in comparison with the interest elasticity of demand for goods); Keynesians argue the opposite. The result of putting these hypotheses to empirical test is, as usual, something of a compromise. On the whole demand for money functions have been quite stable, but the interest elasticity of demand for money is highly significant.

Many of the issues in this field seem, therefore, capable of resolution, in principle, by empirical investigation, by positive appeals to the facts. Most of these exercises have, however, taken the form of running alternative single equations, relating aggregate money balances as the dependent variable against a set of explanatory variables, to explore which version fits best. A selection of statistical results from these exercises is presented in Appendix B. In Appendix A, however, it is argued that the single-equation studies provide in some respects a less satisfactory format for studying asset demands than a simultaneous analysis of portfolio adjustments among all assets. The framework of such a model is exhibited, partly as a guide to explain the techniques used in the growing number of econometric portfolio studies, and partly in preparation for the heuristic use of portfolio-adjustment models in subsequent chapters.

In the previous chapter it was argued that there are two main reasons why people hold money balances. First, in its role as a specialist means of payment, people want to hold money balances against known, or possible, future transaction requirements, even though there might be a higher certain yield on some other alternative asset. For money and an alternative asset with a higher, certain yield to coexist, there must be costs involved in transfers into, or out of, the other asset. This leads on to the general conclusion that the demand for such transaction balances will be a function of the probability distribution of cash payments, the level of the 'certain' yield on the alternative asset, and the transfer costs of switching between that asset and money.

Second, money is itself an asset with a certain yield – at least in nominal terms. People want to hold safe assets even with a lower, even zero, mean expected yield, in conjunction with their portfolio of risky assets, in order to obtain a preferred combination of risk and return. However, it was noted that there is a range of alternative safe, or quasi-safe, assets, so that demand deposits would certainly, and time deposits (and certificates of deposits) would often, be dominated by other safe assets offering higher, but equally certain yields, except over short planning periods when transactions costs become a relatively more important consideration.

It is thus possible to distinguish between the transactions (or exchange uncertainty) motive to holding money and the speculative (or asset-price uncertainty) motive. This does not, however, imply that the overall demand for money of an investor is an additive function of these distinct functions. Money balances held, say, as a safe asset over short planning periods to achieve the optimal risk/return configuration for the asset portfolio will also be available for use if some unforeseen expenditure opportunity should crop up. If individuals facing relatively high transfer costs, or very variable cash flows, feel the need to hold large money balances, their asset portfolio will then include on this account a large proportion of low-yielding safe assets, so that the choice of asset holding over the remainder of the portfolio will be influenced by that fact.

One can draw an analogy, for example, with the demand for jewellery, which provides some services of beautiful adornment and some conspicuous status-enhancing services. Jewellery is also an asset which may rise or fall in value over time, and there is an expected probability distribution of monetary return on holding jewellery. In some circumstances, e.g. of severe political instability, jewellery may be a safer asset, in terms of the probability distribution of real returns, than money. Jewellery, therefore, has a profile of characteristics which endow it with a range of services to its holder. It would not, however, be a sensible procedure to estimate the demand for jewellery by analysing the demand for each service separately, and then adding them up together. These various services are provided *jointly*. If more jewellery is held as a good investment, it will also be available as a potential adornment.

In analysing the demand for the joint services of jewellery, one would consider a range of factors bearing on the demand for such services, such as the longer-run shifts in institutional and social factors (e.g. the custom of giving engagement rings, and various social prescriptions on personal adornment and conspicuous status symbols), and shorter-run changes in the probability distribution of risk and return from holding jewellery. But the analysis would cover the demand for jewellery as a single asset, not for the separate individual services of jewellery. In the same vein the various services for money are, in the main, provided jointly. It is not, therefore, appropriate to seek to identify, say, the transactions demand for money apart from the speculative demand and then add the separate functional relationships together in order to obtain an aggregate demand function.

A study of the various services provided by money balances, as undertaken in the previous chapter, should, however, give a firmer basis for deciding which variables are likely to affect the aggregate demand for money. Factors which have been already mentioned as likely to affect desired money balances include the extent and nature of transfer costs, the availability of alternative 'safe' assets, the length of planning and holding periods, expectations and uncertainty about the pace of future inflation, the level of wealth, the level and variance of income and expenditure flows, and expectations about the relative yields to be obtained on money balances and alternative assets.

Some of these factors are likely to change only relatively slowly over the longer term. Thus transfer costs are largely determined by the technology of the payments transmission mechanism. The pattern of expenditure and income flows is constrained over the short run by social customs (e.g. the weekly wage packet, the monthly salary cheque) which inhibit flexibility in adjusting the form and frequency of cash flows to changing circumstances.[1] Our statistical records are so short and insufficient, and so many variables move together over the long run, that it is very difficult to distinguish the effects of the several longer-run factors upon the velocity of money. These include technological improvements in the payments transmission mechanism, the increasing availability of alternative 'safe' liquid assets, changes in the structural characteristics of the economy (e.g. urbanisation), and increases in income and wealth.[2]

Moreover, some of the variables influencing the demand for money balances can only be measured with difficulty, if at all. Transfer costs will vary between individuals, and companies, depending on their precise situation, and are not well documented. Feelings of uncertainty about future events are by their nature hard to capture in statistical form. The portfolio choice depends on the relative real yields that are *expected* to hold on money and alternative assets over some *unknown future* planning period.

Faced with the problem of trying to provide some empirical, factual clothing to the corpus of theory, the tendency has been to use observable, objective, *ex post* data as proxies for subjective, *ex ante* expectations, wherever possible, and to despatch those variables which have no obvious *ex post* quantitative counterpart, such as transactions costs and uncertainty, to that statistical limbo of being represented by a constant, a trend term or some other 'dummy' variable in the usual regression analysis. Thus the most common form of demand for money function which is tested empirically relates aggregate money holding (sometimes deflated by a price index and some measure of population on to a per capita real balance basis) to nominal incomes (again often deflated into real terms by a price index, or divided into real and price components) and to the current market rate of interest (the yield to redemption on a marketable asset) on one or more assets which are taken as an alternative holding to money. Despite the emphasis on uncertainty, on the variance of the probability distribution of expected returns or of cash flows, on the unknown length of holding period, in the theoretical analysis of the demand for money it is extremely difficult to incorporate such subjective, *ex ante* elements in any statistical tests,[3] and they are

---

[1] In the longer run, however, payment periods and practices will adjust to the costs of holding and transferring money. 'Surely, the increase in the average cash balance over the past century in this country that has occurred for other reasons has been a factor producing a lengthening of pay periods and not the other way around.' Quotation from Friedman's, 'The Quantity Theory of Money – A Restatement,' chap. 1 in *Studies in The Quantity Theory of Money*, ed. M. Friedman, from clause 11.

[2] Some economists, for example Garvy and Blyn, *The Velocity of Money* (Federal Reserve Bank of New York, New York, 1969), have emphasised the role of technological advances in money transmission and cash management techniques in affecting the demand for money; others, for example Gurley and Shaw, *Money in a Theory of Finance* (The Brookings Institution, Washington, 1960) chap. VI, and the authors of the Radcliffe Report, *Committee on the Working of the Monetary System, Report*, Cmnd. 827 (H.M.S.O., London, 1959), chap. IV and para. 392, have stressed the growing availability of alternative liquid assets; others, for example Friedman and Schwartz, *A Monetary History of the United States, 1867–1960*, National Bureau of Economic Research (Princeton University Press, Princeton, 1963), chap. 12 especially, have argued that increases in income have been the main determinant of long-run trends in the velocity of money.

[3] Moreover, these factors influence the demand for money balances at the individual, micro level. There are aggregation problems to be faced in the process of deriving an aggregate, macroeconomic relationship from the multitude of micro-level functions, a problem noted, for example, by D. Laidler in his review of Orr's, 'Cash Management and the Demand for Money,' *Economica*, vol. 39, no. 156 (November 1972) pp. 452–4.

virtually universally excluded from consideration in the macro-economic empirical work.

Even when data can be found to serve as proxies for expectational variables that actually influence individual behaviour, the approximation may in practice be subject to considerable error. In particular the *ex post* yields on alternative assets, or the calculated yields to maturity, may often be a poor guide to actual expectations of yield over the individual's planning period. If a rise in market interest rates only induces a small reduction in money balances, how can one distinguish between the hypothesis that the interest elasticity of demand for money is low and the hypothesis that the rise in market rates has led to a much smaller increase in the expected yield on that asset over the planning period, perhaps because market rates are expected to rise (and prices to fall)[1] yet further in future periods? Only if the planning period and the maturity of the marketable asset – the assumed alternative investment to money – should be the same will the yield to maturity become identical with the expected yield.

If behaviour depends on expectational variables which cannot be observed at all clearly, then empirical exercises using available *ex post* statistics will only provide very broad brush tests of the theoretical hypotheses. This is a limitation inherent in the nature of the subject. Moreover, from a practical policy point of view it may not really matter that the relationship between the dependent variable, here money balances, and the explanatory variables is based on an unobservable mixture of a relationship between the included *ex post* statistics and the relevant *ex ante* expectational variables and a second relationship between the expectational variables and the dependent variable. So long as the observed, statistical relationship is stable and predictable, it can be used as the basis for policy.[2]

---

[1] Current asset prices should fully reflect the market's expectations about the future; otherwise the structure of current prices would allow opportunities for profitable speculation by rational investors. Nevertheless, future expected short rates do not have to be the same as current actual short rates. There is no good reason why some change in information should not cause revisions to expectations of future rates as large as, or greater than, the change in current short rates. The postulate that markets make rational and efficient use of information does not imply that market prices can never be expected to change from their current values, at least according to Sargent. In his paper on 'Rational Expectations and the Term Structure of Interest Rates,' *Journal of Money, Credit and Banking*, vol. IV, no. 1 (February 1972) pp. 74–97, Sargent tests two hypotheses about the behaviour of the term structure of interest rates. 'The first hypothesis is the "expectations hypothesis," which states that forward rates of interest are forced into equality with the short rates that investors expect to prevail in subsequent periods. The second hypothesis is that the expectations of investors are rational in the sense of John F. Muth ('Rational Expectations and the Theory of Price Movements,' *Econometrica*, vol. 29, July 1961, pp. 315–35). By this we mean that investors' expectations are equivalent with the optimal forecasts of statistical theory for a certain specified class of statistical models' (p. 74). Subsequently (p. 85) Sargent notes that these two hypotheses 'do not imply things that are commonly thought to be their implications. Thus, they do not imply that the spot one-period rate, R_t, follows a random walk, which would mean that $R_t - R_{t-1}$ is serially uncorrelated. They do not imply that the j-period spot rate follows a random walk for any finite j. Moreover, the "fair game" property built into the model clearly does not mean that spot rates cannot be described by a stable stochastic difference equation.' Sargent does, however, note that there is disagreement about the implications of the efficient market hypothesis, and quotes other authors, e.g. Granger and Rees, who have presented contrary views.

[2] This approach to economics, often termed 'positive,' can, however, lead to an excessive emphasis on searching for statistical regularities between numerical series: there is then a tendency for theoretical analysis of the inter-relationships involved to be accorded less importance than the attainment of satisfactory statistical properties (e.g. goodness of fit, no autocorrelation in the residuals from the fitted equation, stability of the coefficients when fitted over sub-periods): the concept of causation can come to be treated more as a statistical function of the timing between movements in time series than as a behavioural phenomenon. Moreover, the facility with which computers can calculate the relationship between data series, enhanced by the use of flexible lag

(*Footnote* [2] *continued on p. 47*)

Mainly because of the need to make do with the limited observable data available, the theory of the demand for money, which was set out in the previous chapter at the micro level largely in terms of uncertainty and transactions costs, thus undergoes a transformation at the macro level. The functional forms which are examined in the macro-level empirical exercises usually do not include such factors directly at all. How far, then, these macro-level, aggregative statistical studies can be regarded as a test of, or compatible with, the underlying micro-level theoretical hypotheses is debatable. It is, however, necessary for practical, policy purposes to estimate such macro-economic functions. Even if the functional forms which can be estimated from the data do not correspond very closely to the micro-economic theoretical rationale for money holding, it is possible for theory to provide some guidance both on the (statistically available) variables that are likely to influence the demand for money and on the values of the coefficients of such variables that would accord with theory.

Alternatively, it is possible to regard the usual form in which the demand for money function is estimated as deriving from a rather more generalised, simple theory of asset demand (see Appendix A, pp. 55–62). In this the demand for any asset is estimated as a function of wealth, acting as the budget constraint, of the relative expected monetary return, or yield, on the asset relative to that available on alternative assets, and of variables which affect the demand for the specific services of the asset, other than its monetary return. In the case of money, which provides specific services in its role as a means of payment, the level of income acts as a broad proxy both for the level of transactions, and perhaps also for the variance of cash flows. Other forms of uncertainty and transactions costs are treated as constant (or incorporated into a time trend), and thus omitted from specific analysis.

The general form of the asset-demand function that results from this approach is

$$M_d = f(Y, r_i, W)$$

where M_d is the demand for money, Y the level of income, r_i the observed monetary yield on the ith asset, and W represents total (non-human)[1] wealth. The monetary yield on money, narrowly defined as currency and demand deposits at banks, is normally taken to be

---

functions which allow for a search over a wide range to find the best fitting timing relationship between series, has considerably raised the likelihood of finding spurious statistical regularities between such ill-assorted variables as, say, the average hours of sunshine per day in Glasgow and the rate of growth of real Gross National Product in Canada over the subsequent three years, or the production of motor cars in the United Kingdom and the level of the Dow Jones index in Wall Street seven years hence. There will be, however, a natural reluctance to extrapolate any past statistical regularity into the future unless the relationship can be given a reasonable' explanation. Thus theory not only suggests where the empirical researcher might start to look for regularities, from among the vast set of all available data series, but also provides some check of plausibility on the statistical findings.

---

[1] Human capital cannot be bought and sold in a market in the same way as non-human capital. If the present value of one's human capital rises, e.g. because one's particular skill comes into greater demand, one cannot sell part of it in order to buy financial or real assets and thus maintain a desired portfolio distribution. One can, however, borrow against one's expected higher future income to effect that same diversification. But the uncertainty about future income streams, and the cost to the lender of obtaining an informed view of these likely future income streams, raises the cost of borrowing against future incomes earned from human capital. So the imperfections (basically of information) in the capital market are likely to introduce a differing response in asset holding to changes in human and non-human wealth.

zero,[1] so that variations in the monetary yield on other assets also provide a measure of variations in the relative yield as compared with monetary balances.[2]

In practice this relationship is usually simplified even further by omitting W, the wealth term. Wealth can be defined as the capitalisation of current and future income streams. The functional form above, however, includes a variable representing income streams, and a yield (r_i), a capitalisation rate applicable to some asset over some holding period. There is, therefore, likely to be considerable multi-collinearity between the variables Y and r on the one hand and W on the other; indeed the three variables are not independent of one another. Moreover, in most countries wealth data are either unavailable or include a generous proportion of uncertain estimation, informed guesswork; for example, data on the market value of real property, land and houses, can only be described as rickety. In the United Kingdom the time series for wealth is trend dominated, and the apparent variations of the data around the trend are hardly reliable. The income and interest rate series are at least more accurately measured, even if they do not necessarily closely approximate to the underlying factors (e.g. the level and variance of cash flows; the level, variance and co-variances of expected yields over the relevant planning periods) which determine the demand for money.

Furthermore, the wealth elasticity of demand for money, when narrowly defined, should be very low. Since money does not bear a competitive rate of interest, the objective is to minimise the opportunity costs involved in holding money for transactions purposes – subject to the level of transfer costs. Thus if wealth should be higher, but the volume of incomes (transactions) and the yield on alternative assets – and the level of transfer costs – were unchanged, then exactly the same volume of money holdings would be demanded. The wealth elasticity of transactions balances should be zero. So long as planning periods are not extremely short, some other capital-certain asset is likely to dominate zero interest-bearing money as a 'safe' asset in portfolios. Therefore the volume of 'narrow' money balances held for such 'speculative' purposes is likely to be very small anyhow. It is possible,

---

[1] In the United States regulations prevent any explicit payment of interest on demand deposits. In the United Kingdom until 1971 the clearing bank cartel maintained an agreement not to pay interest on current accounts. But there is no essential reason why banks should not make such interest payments, especially in inflationary conditions; indeed in Chap. 13 it is argued that it would be desirable if such payments were made. Even though explicit payments of interest on demand deposits may be prevented, the banks can still compete for current-account funds by varying the additional banking services offered (book-keeping, investment advice, loan facilities, etc.) or the charges for banking services (e.g. for operating the payment-transmission system) in the light of the (average) balance maintained. It is not, therefore, strictly accurate to treat the monetary yield on means of payment as zero, and some studies have incorporated an attempt to take account of this, especially the various cross-section studies of the demand for money in the United States, mostly using data from the separate states. See, for example, Feige's book on *The Demand for Liquid Assets: A Temporal Cross Section Analysis* (Prentice-Hall, Englewood Cliffs, N.J., 1964); B. C. Cohen, 'The Demand for Money by Ownership Category,' *National Banking Review*, vol. 4, no. 3 (March 1967) pp. 317–36; T. H. Lee, 'Substitutability of Non-Bank Intermediary Liabilities for Money: The Empirical Evidence,' *The Journal of Finance*, vol. XXI, no. 3 (September 1966) pp. 441–57. These studies use data of service charges on demand deposits as a proxy for the (negative) rate of interest on such deposits. This procedure is not without its drawbacks, as noted by Laidler in his paper on 'The Definition of Money,' *Journal of Money, Credit and Banking* (August 1969) p. 522. Finally on this subject see R. J. Barro and A. M. Santomero, 'Household Money Holdings and The Demand Deposit Rate,' *Journal of Money, Credit and Banking*, vol. 4, no. 2 (May 1972) pp. 397–413.

[2] When the alternative asset has a fixed nominal capital value the comparison between monetary yields over the appropriate period will also provide an estimate of relative real yields since inflation will affect the purchasing power of both assets equally. If, however, real assets, as well as financial assets with fixed nominal values, are substitutes for money, the expected rate of inflation should enter the demand for money function as a separate argument since it will affect the expected relative yield on real assets *vis-à-vis* money holdings.

however, that the volume of money held for precautionary purposes, to prevent the risk of unforeseen expenditure opportunities slipping away, responds positively to changes in wealth. Nevertheless, taken all in all, the micro-level analysis suggests that narrowly-defined money balances should not be very responsive to changes in wealth, certainly much less than to changes in income, interest rates or transfer costs.

The same conclusion does not hold, however, with respect to interest-bearing time deposits or certificates of deposits (C.D.s) issued by banks, which are generally included in broader definitions of the money stock. So long as the banks are not prevented by regulation (Regulation Q in the United States, for example) or by cartel agreement, they will presumably pay a competitive interest rate on time deposits and C.D.s. Indeed banks should be in an extremely strong position to compete for funds, which investors want to place in 'safe' assets, since their joint role in providing a means of payment offers some attractions to investors, e.g. ease and low cost of transfer into a means of payment, economy in management, which other intermediaries or other assets, e.g. National Savings, cannot match. There is no reason to believe that time deposits or C.D.s need be dominated by other capital-certain assets as repositories for that part of their wealth which investors wish to keep in relatively safe form.[1]

Partly because of the difficulty of measuring wealth, the demand for money function in the economy is usually expressed as a function only of incomes (Y) and interest rates on alternative assets (r_i). Movements in nominal incomes are, however, usually divided into two separate components, changes in the price level (P) and in real output (y) respectively, on the grounds that there is reason to believe that the demand for money balances might respond differently depending on which of these components of nominal income varies. With given nominal interest rates a uniform rise in all prices, including transfer costs, should theoretically lead to an exactly proportional increase in desired money balances, i.e. money holding should be homogeneous of degree one in prices.[2] Unless there is some form of money illusion, investors should be concerned to achieve their desired level of real money balances. This consideration has led some economists to relate the real level of money balances, M/P, to real output, y, and relative interest rates. This is probably not the correct procedure. In the first place the homogeneity of money balances with respect to prices is an hypothesis, albeit a strong one, which still needs testing. In practice, however, this hypothesis does usually receive support in empirical tests (see Appendix B, pp. 62–5). Rather more important, demand for money functions, certainly when estimated with quarterly data, usually are shown to involve lagged reactions to changes in the explanatory variables. These lags represent adjustment costs, delays in recognition of changing circumstances, etc. But taking M/P as the dependent variable usually involves the implicit assumption that the response of money balances to price changes is instantaneous, whereas responses to output changes and to changing interest rates are distributed over time.

Changes in real incomes (y) are not so likely to have an equi-proportionate effect on the demand for money. As real incomes per capita rise, transfer costs should not rise at the same rate, unless the technical progress responsible for the rise in real incomes has completely by-passed the payment-transmission mechanism. In reality, many of the most dramatic technical advances of recent decades have been in the field of data handling, the key technology in the payments process; the relative costs of making transfers should thus have declined compared with the average cost of goods and services in recent decades. Moreover, as incomes rise more companies (and wealthy individuals) will pass the point

---

[1] Moreover security, like convenience, may well be something of a luxury. As people get richer, they may be prepared to give up relatively more expected yield in order to be sure of retaining what they already possess. Fat cats are relatively more defensive than hungry cats. If so, the wealth elasticity of interest-bearing deposits could be greater than unity. In any case if (non-human) wealth was higher, but incomes, interest rates, etc., remained unchanged, one would expect investors to place part of this additional wealth with banks, in time deposits or C.D.s.

[2] C.f. Orr, *Cash Management and the Demand for Money*, p. 197.

that makes it worthwhile for them to pay closer attention to cash management. With increasing transactions, as incomes rise, the law of large numbers should lead to economies of scale in cash management, so one would expect that the income elasticity of demand for money for transactions purposes would be less than unity, though this effect may be offset to some extent by greater affluence reducing the frequency with which people will find it 'convenient' to make transactions, whether between assets and money or goods and money.[1] This desired reduction in the frequency of transactions could raise both transactions and precautionary money balances, in the latter case because the reduction in the frequency of transaction will raise the variance of the cash flow. Even so, it seems difficult to believe that this effect would be sufficient to outweigh the available economies of scale in cash management as real incomes increase, so that the income elasticity of demand for money should be less than unity.

The various econometric studies of the demand for money, at least those undertaken using post-1945 data, virtually all show a lower income elasticity of demand for a narrow definition of money than for a broad definition including time deposits. Moreover, the estimates of the income elasticity of demand for money (even on a long-run basis after allowance for lagged responses), narrowly defined, are frequently lower than unity, implying some economies of scale. Estimates of the (long-run) income elasticity of demand for money, more broadly defined, on the other hand are frequently well in excess of unity (see Appendix B). There is, however, no convincing reason why the *income* elasticity of time deposits or certificates of deposit should be so high; indeed why should it be higher than the income elasticity of demand deposits? If wealth and interest rates were constant, while transactions and incomes in real terms were higher, there would presumably be a greater demand for time deposits as a second-line precautionary balance, but it is not immediately obvious why this second-line precautionary balance should show a greater elasticity than demand deposits. The greater likelihood is that the estimated higher *income* elasticity of time deposits really is a reflection of a much higher *wealth* elasticity, and that the basic income elasticities of both monetary definitions are less than unity.

There have been controversies in the literature over the likely size of the income elasticity of demand, and over the associated question of the factors responsible for the long-period trends in the income velocity of money. Insistence that the income elasticity of demand for money is greater than unity[2] is hard, though not impossible, to reconcile with the basic micro-level theories about why people hold money – as distinct from the more reasonable argument that the wealth elasticity of 'safe' assets, especially those interest-bearing assets which dominate non-interest-bearing money balances, may be greater than unity. Nevertheless, no crucial point of macro-economic theory rests on this issue. And monetary policy can be equally effective whether the income elasticity of demand for money is greater or less than unity, so long as the functional relationship is stable and predictable.

In contrast, the issue of the elasticity of demand for money balances in response to changes in yields on other assets has been a focal point for dispute between major schools of macro-economic theorists, between 'Keynesians' and 'Monetarists.' The main area of contention is whether money balances are particularly close substitutes, i.e. have a high interest elasticity, with a subset of alternative liquid financial assets, or whether money is a widely generalised substitute for all other assets, including real assets, goods, and so a close substitute with no single one of them. As discussed further in Chapter 9 on the transmission mechanism, there is widespread agreement that monetary policy works by causing changes in asset yields, thus inducing a divergence between the calculated present value of real assets and their cost of construction. But if money balances were a particularly close substitute for some subset of other financial assets, the implication would be that a monetary

---

[1] One of the distinguishing features of a rich society is how much less time is devoted to shopping, at least by those members of the society who have anything much else to do.

[2] As Friedman has maintained, for example in his paper on 'The Demand for Money: Some Theoretical and Empirical Results,' *Journal of Political Economy*, vol. 67 (August 1959) pp. 327–51.

disturbance would have its initial effect in altering the yields, interest rates, on these assets, without much, or any, direct effect in changing the yields and prices of other assets, e.g. real assets, which were less good substitutes. So the effect on real demand would depend on the initial change in yields on such financial assets being transmitted in turn, via purchases of somewhat less liquid assets, further along the liquidity spectrum. 'The effect of a change in the money supply is seen to be like a ripple passing along the range of financial assets, diminishing in amplitude and in predictability as it proceeds farther away from the initial disturbance. This "ripple" eventually reaches to the long end of the financial market, causing a change in yields, which will bring about a divergence between the cost of capital and the return on capital.'[1]

The ultimate effect upon the demand for real assets is, on this view, regarded as the final stage of a chain of responses to relative price adjustments, working outwards from money via substitute financial assets. The extent of this effect will depend on the relative elasticity of the response of financial interest rates to the initial monetary disturbance, and of the response of the demand for goods and assets to changes in those rates. Furthermore, reasons have been suggested why in some circumstances the transmission of monetary stimuli along the chain might be prevented or retarded. The classic example is to be found in the supposed possibility of a 'liquidity trap,' a spectre raised by Keynes, which has been reformulated by Leijonhufvud[2] in terms of possible difficulties in forcing long rates in some cases to respond to movements in short rates that have been generated by monetary operations (see further Chapter 10). More generally the length of this chain, and the flexibility of the links along the way, would reduce the stability and predictability of the relationship between money incomes and the money stock.

On the other hand monetarists believe that money is not a close substitute just for a small range of paper financial assets. Instead money is thought to be an asset with certain unique characteristics, which cause it to be a substitute, not for any one small class of assets, but more generally for all assets alike, real or financial. Thus 'the crucial issue that corresponds to the distinction between the "credit" [Keynesian] and "monetary" [monetarist] effects of monetary policy is not whether changes in the stock of money operate through interest rates but rather the range of interest rates considered. On the "credit" view, monetary policy impinges on a narrow and well-defined range of capital assets and a correspondingly narrow range of associated expenditures . . . . On the "monetary" view monetary policy impinges on a much broader range of capital assets and correspondingly broader range of associated expenditures.'[3]

In simple terms this means that if someone feels himself to be short of money balances he is just as likely to adjust to his equilibrium position by forgoing some planned expenditure on goods or services as by selling some financial asset. In this case the interest elasticity of demand for money with respect to any one asset, or particular group of assets, is likely to be low, because money is no more, or less, a substitute for that asset – real or financial – than for any other. If the interest elasticity of demand for money is very low

$$\left(\frac{dM}{di} \simeq 0 \right)$$

then the macro-economic demand function for money is further reduced to the simple form, $M_d = f(Y)$. The implication of this is simple, that a monetary disturbance causing a

[1] C. Goodhart and A. Crockett, 'The Importance of Money,' *Bank of England Quarterly Bulletin*, vol. 10, no. 2 (June 1970) pp. 159–98, quotation from p. 161.

[2] *On Keynesian Economics and the Economics of Keynes* (Oxford University Press, New York, 1968); see, on this subject, chaps iv:5, v:3 and vi:2.

[3] Friedman and Meiselman, 'The Relative Stability of Monetary Velocity and the Investment Multiplier in the United States, 1897–1958', Research Study Two in *Stabilisation Policies*, a series of research studies prepared by E. Cary Brown and others for the Commission on Money and Credit (Prentice-Hall, Englewood Cliffs, N.J., 1964) p. 217. This passage provides an excellent statement of the theoretical basis of the minetarist viewpoint.

disequilibrium between the supply of money (M_s) – assumed to be given and fixed by the authorities, but see further Chapter 8 – and the demand for money (M_d), must lead to an adjustment in nominal incomes[1] until equilibrium is restored.[2,3] Moreover, if the impact of monetary changes on the demand for real assets occurs by direct substitution, and not via a whole chain of substitution links involving a specified subset of financial assets (such as bonds and equities), then the effect of monetary policy on the demand for

---

[1] The division of this change in nominal incomes into its components of changes in real incomes and changes in the price level is considered further in Chapters 10 and 11.

[2] Moreover, if the demand for money is a function of a lagged distribution of incomes, e.g. $M_{dt} = f(Y_t, Y_{t-1}, ..., Y_{t-n})$, with all coefficients taking positive values (as would be expected), then the initial change in Y following a monetary disturbance, i.e. a change in M_s, will be greater than the long-run, steady-state response. Furthermore, the subsequent path of incomes may well be cyclical, depending on the coefficients on the current and lagged income terms. Indeed it is easily possible to imagine a plausible set of values for the coefficients in the demand for money function that would cause the system to lose stability, to explode after a monetary disturbance.

Consider, for example, demand or money functions taking the values

(i) $M_{dt} = 0.7Y_t + 0.2Y_{t-1} + 0.1Y_{t-2}$

(ii) $M_{dt} = 0.2Y_t + 0.6Y_{t-1} + 0.2Y_{t-2}$

If, then, M_s increases by one unit, the subsequent path of Y_t in the two cases would be:

	time period						
	1	2	3	4	5	6	7
(i)	1·43	1·02	0·93	1·02	1·00	1·00	1·00
(ii)	5·00	−10·00	30·00	−75·00	200·00	−520·00	1365·00

For a more extended analysis of this subject see A. Walters's paper, 'Professor Friedman on the Demand for Money,' *Journal of Political Economy*, vol. 73, no. 5 (October 1965) pp. 545–51.

[3] Each individual member of the private sector will treat the expected level of expenditures and the yields on alternative assets as parameters, and adjust his money balances to these in accordance with his demand for money function. At the macro-economic aggregate level, however, the authorities can, in principle, set the level of the money stock and force subsequent adjustments in interest rates and money incomes upon the economy. In this case the appropriate, single-equation relationship to estimate statistically would not be a macro-economic demand for money function, but a relationship linking movements in interest rates and/or money incomes, as the dependent variable, to current and past movements in the money stock; on this point see C. Sims, 'Money, Income, and Causality,' *The American Economic Review*, vol. 62, no. 4 (September 1972) pp. 540–52. This concern that the structure of the empirically estimated relationship should accord with the direction of causality, i.e. whether the aggregate money stock should enter as a dependent or independent variable, does not itself have any bearing on the wider issues separating Keynesians and monetarists. Keynesians would not deny that the authorities could, in principle, control the money stock, but they would in such circumstances expect the direction of causation to run first through induced changes in interest rates on a subset of financial assets, and only subsequently to changes in money incomes. Thus, if the money stock was being autonomously controlled by the authorities, a Keynesian would tend to estimate a relationship with interest rates as the dependent variable, while monetarists would go straight to a money multiplier, relating changes in money incomes to current and past changes in the money stock.

Even though it does not cast light directly on the controversy between monetarists and Keynesians, the question whether the money stock is, in fact, autonomously determined by the authorities (so that estimating demand for money functions becomes inappropriate), is of much interest in itself. This is further considered in Chap. 6, Sec. C, and Chap. 8. To anticipate these latter passages, the authorities, both in the United Kingdom and in most other industrialised countries, at least until recently, have mostly operated to control *interest rates*, and this does make the money stock endogenous, and a demand for money function, with money as the dependent variable, appropriate.

assets and goods can *not* be approximately measured by the relative interest elasticities of the demand for money and for assets respectively (nor alternatively in terms of the relative slopes of the *IS* and *LM* curves).

Clearly, therefore, the extent of substitution between money and other assets is of crucial importance in determining the role of money within the economy. Again one's attitudes to this matter will be influenced both by *a priori* theoretical arguments and by the econometric findings. In my own opinion the *a priori* arguments give somewhat more support to the Keynesian than to the monetarist position. The monetarists argue that money can be distinguished from all other assets by its unique characteristics. Indeed, money does have certain special attributes as an asset, but then all assets have their own particular mix of characteristics; building society deposits, unit-trust units, insurance policies, equities, houses, cars, factories, etc., have their own particular attractions. Moreover, time deposits, or certificates of deposits held with banks, are species of a rather broad genus of interest-bearing, liquid, capital-certain assets, including in the United Kingdom deposits with building societies, finance companies, local authorities and national savings. There are a number of alternative capital-certain 'temporary abodes of purchasing power.' Indeed, one could even claim on institutional grounds that time deposits had more close substitutes than many other types of asset. 'In a highly developed financial system (such as the United Kingdom system) . . . , there are many highly liquid assets which are close substitutes for money, as good to hold and only inferior when the actual moment for a payment arrives.'[1]

If there was only one 'safe' asset available, money, then portfolio theory, as set out in Chapter 2, would suggest that the quantity of money held would depend on its own rate relative to the return and risk on the market portfolio of all risky assets, which would in turn be a function of the rates on all risky assets available and the covariances between them. In such circumstances the elasticity of the demand for money to changes in the yield on any one other asset, assuming that each asset formed a fairly small proportion of the total portfolio, would indeed be low. But this is not the situation in fact. There are a number of capital-certain assets, competing for inclusion in the investor's holding of safe assets, and the degree of substitution between them should be relatively high.

The special characteristics of money stand out in greater clarity when money is narrowly defined as a means of payment. Other assets have not usurped money's role in providing a means of payment.[2] Nevertheless, the inventory theories, described in Chapter 2, suggest that the demand for money in its special role as a means of payment will not be insensitive to relative interest rates, though the interest elasticity of demand implied by such theory is well below unity, in the range from 0 to -0.5. This, however, still leaves open the question whether the elasticity is higher with respect to some subset of liquid financial assets than to the generality of assets, real and financial. Switches between money and other assets, in order to minimise the costs of cash management, will naturally take place with those other assets where transfer costs are lowest, for example bank time deposits, local authority call money, etc. This would suggest intuitively that the demand for money, narrowly defined, should be most sensitive to interest rates on such liquid, alternative assets and less sensitive, if at all, to interest rates on other riskier, illiquid assets with high transfer costs and imperfect markets.[3]

---

[1] *Radcliffe Report*, para. 392.

[2] The set of assets which is acceptable as payment for transactions is not, however, immutable over time; it has changed in the past and could do so again in the future. If people should find it economically advantageous to accept, and to proffer, other financial claims in payment for transactions, then the set of assets which is to be described as money will alter.

[3] See the paper by M. Parkin, with R. Barrett and M. Gray, 'The Demand for Financial Assets by the Personal Sector of the U.K. Economy,' Proceedings of the London Business School Conference of June 1972 on Modelling the U.K. Economy (forthcoming).

In his study on *Cash Management and the Demand for Money*[1] Daniel Orr has challenged this widespread view. Assume a three-asset world, cash, some alternative, 'safe', liquid asset, and an earning, risky asset (say the market portfolio). Then if transfer costs between assets are fixed (lumpy in Orr's phrase) irrespective of the size of transfer, 'the two accounts, cash and shorts [the alternative liquid asset], may in effect be managed independently of each other without significant departure from optimality.' In this case 'the relevant interest measure [for cash management] is the "long" or "cost of capital" rate.' When transfer costs are proportional to the size of the transfer, however, which is the more normal case, 'the decision rule parameters for [managing] the shorts account and the cash account are interdependent,' and in this case, 'cash will be sensitive to both interest rates.' This analysis[2] is, as Orr notes, of major interest since it gives, almost for the first time, some theoretical substance to the argument that the demand for money, at least narrowly defined, might be a general function of yields on longer, earning assets rather than a function of yields on other liquid short-term assets.

The *a priori* arguments would, therefore, suggest that bank *time deposits* should be relatively close substitutes with other capital-certain, interest-bearing assets. The interest elasticity of demand for demand deposits and currency might be expected to be considerably less, and the question of which interest rates are relevant for cash management decisions has been re-opened by Orr after years in which the consensus view had been that the yields on alternative liquid assets would be the appropriate measure.

A considerable volume of empirical work has been undertaken to examine the evidence provided by the available data[3] on the interest elasticity of the demand for money. These studies have fortunately been summarised, in Appendix 1 of the article on 'The Importance of Money' in the *Bank of England Quarterly Bulletin* (June 1970) and in Laidler's study of *The Demand for Money*.[4] The general conclusion of these surveys is that the interest elasticity of demand for money is highly significant, taking values that correspond reasonably closely to those that would be predicted on the basis of the micro-level behavioural theories, i.e. around -0.5. The results would seem to contradict the expectations of more extreme Keynesians, who may have supposed that the availability of alternative liquid assets as substitutes for money would have removed 'any limit to the velocity of circulation.'[5] Equally they undermine the extreme version of the quantity theory, namely that there is a fixed short-term link between the stock of money and money incomes. Thus studies of the demand for money function, having conceded a role for interest rates on financial assets in determining the demand for money, do not show the extreme results that would be consistent with monetary policy having only a very slight effect (a very large interest elasticity) or an all-important impact (very low interest elasticities) in determining nominal incomes. The issue of the strength of monetary policy thus remains open, and is considered further in Chapter 9.

There is also the question whether it is possible to discern a subset of short-dated, liquid assets, which are closer substitutes for money than other longer-dated, riskier assets. The evidence is not clear-cut, partly because all interest rates tend to move together. Moreover, rates on short-dated assets tend to fluctuate more widely than yields on longer-

---

[1] Chap. 6.

[2] Unfortunately I am not able to provide an intuitively acceptable, simple résumé of Orr's analysis, based as it is largely on mathematical working.

[3] It is worth recalling that such data often take the form of the observed yields to maturity on Treasury bills or marketable bonds, or presently estimated earnings or dividend yields on equities, or current running yields on capital-certain assets, none of which are necessarily equivalent to the expected yield on holding such assets over the relevant planning period(s).

[4] *The Demand for Money: Theories and Evidence* (International Textbook Company, Scranton, 1970) especially chap. 8.

[5] *Radcliffe Report*, paras 391, 392.

dated assets; so the statistics usually show a larger estimated interest elasticity of demand for money on long bonds than on shorter-dated bills and bonds. The relative size of the coefficients provides, therefore, no test as to whether the demand for money responds more closely to variations in short rates than in long rates. Attempts to discriminate statistically between the use of short-term and longer-term assets in the demand-for-money equation, in terms of providing the best overall fit, of stability over differing periods and over different specifications of the estimating equation, have usually suggested that alternative short-dated assets do better.

Overall the empirical results leave the standard neo-Keynesian analysis of the demand for money, in terms of money incomes and yields on alternative financial assets, relatively unshaken. The relationships seem more stable, the income elasticities somewhat higher, and the interest elasticities rather lower, than many Keynesians might have imagined. Nevertheless, the econometric studies of the demand for money have not required any radical reassessment of prior theory.

APPENDIX A

Money in the Asset Portfolio

Many of the issues discussed in the course of Chapter 3 appear capable of resolution by empirical examination, e.g. whether the demand for money function is stable and predictable, whether the interest elasticity of demand for money is low or high. Most of the empirical exercises to examine these issues have taken the form of running a single equation relating the stock of money, as the dependent variable, to various alternative series of interest rates, nominal incomes, real output, price indices, wealth, etc., as explanatory variables. The purpose of this appendix is to suggest that stronger empirical tests of these hypotheses, about the form of the demand for money function, might be achieved by giving explicit recognition to the fact that money balances represent one asset among many within the total asset portfolio: by examining the simultaneous response of sets of assets, including money balances, to disturbances, it is possible to impose and to test additional constraints upon the values that the coefficients in the system should take. Given the difficulty of discerning clearly from econometric exercises between alternative hypotheses in a system where most variables tend to move together and the available time series are quite short,[1] procedures that allow more searching empirical tests to be undertaken have attractions.

In practice, empirical studies of the simultaneous determination of the demand for the various component assets within an overall portfolio are a fairly recent innovation. There are a number of difficulties, for example, in obtaining accurate and complete balance-sheet data, while manipulating the resulting system of equations is considerably more complicated than is the case with a single-equation approach. Furthermore, the initial studies of this kind have not yielded empirical results that have really been significantly different from, or superior to, those obtained by single-equation exercises. Nevertheless it is, in principle, preferable to examine financial developments within the context of a complete portfolio-adjustment model, rather than in single, individual equations. Moreover, even though there may be few examples yet of empirically valuable studies using this approach.

---

[1] One aspect of this problem may be illustrated by reference to the difficulty of distinguishing, for example, between different versions of the consumption function. In their paper, for instance, on 'Short-run Consumption Functions for the U.K., 1955–66', chap. 3 in *The Econometric Study of the United Kingdom*, ed. K. Hilton and D. Heathfield (Macmillan, London, 1970), K. Hilton and D. Crossfield set out a number of alternative variants of this function, the majority of which have R^2 values above 0·995.

it can be applied as a heuristic framework, for example in simulation exercises, to describe how systems will adjust to disturbances. Indeed this is done later in Chapters 6 and 7, where we seek to explain how the financial system as a whole responds to disturbances. In this respect this appendix lays out some of the formal groundwork for the portfolio-adjustment models which are used in later chapters.

Within the context of a portfolio-adjustment model changes in money balances held must be explicitly inter-related with movements in other assets in the portfolio. Total wealth has to be held in one of the available forms of assets (liabilities, i.e. borrowed funds, may be treated as negative assets). If the response of demand for asset i with respect to wealth, i.e. the amount of asset i people wish to add to their portfolio as wealth increases, is comparatively large, then the response of all other assets, taken together, has to be smaller in order to ensure that the increase in all assets demanded as wealth increases is constrained exactly to equal that increase in wealth. In short the sum of the coefficients relating the demand for all the individual assets with respect to wealth must sum to unity.

With a given value of wealth, if the movement of some explanatory variable, say the level of nominal incomes or of interest rates, causes an increase in demand for asset i, then the demand for the sum of all other assets must fall by a like amount, in order to maintain the balance-sheet identity, that the sum of assets held must equal the total value of wealth. That is to say, the sum of the coefficients on other explanatory variables (the level of wealth remaining given) must sum to zero. Thus if the demand for money increases with the level of incomes, wealth being held fixed, then the demand for other assets, taken as a group, must fall equivalently in order to accommodate the increased demand for money. These constraints must hold as a matter of accounting identity.

These systems of asset equations can be set out quite simply. Consider an n asset model. Each asset $(A_1, \ldots, A_n)$ has its own (expected) yield; r_i being the yield on the ith asset. For the moment we will assume that variations in r_j, or in other explanatory variables – in this case we take the level of incomes, Y, as a representative example – leave wealth unaffected. Then we may set out each separate equation as follows

$$A_1 - a_1 r_1 + a_2 r_2, \ldots, a_i r_i, \ldots, a_n r_n + a_w W + a_y Y \tag{1}$$

$$A_2 = b_1 r_1 + b_2 r_2, \ldots, b_i r_i, \ldots, b_n r_n + b_w W + b_y Y \tag{2}$$

$$\vdots \qquad\qquad\qquad\qquad\qquad\qquad\qquad\qquad \vdots$$

$$A_n = n_1 r_1 + n_2 r_2, \ldots, n_i r_i, \ldots, n_n r_n + n_w W + n_y Y \tag{n}$$

where the a_s, b_s and n_s are coefficients relating the demand for that asset to the various explanatory variables. To reduce the number of different symbols this can be rewritten

$$A_1 = a_{11} r_1 + a_{12} r_2, \ldots, a_{1i} r_i, \ldots, a_{1n} r_n + a_{1w} W + a_{1y} Y \tag{1}$$

$$A_2 = a_{21} r_1 + a_{22} r_2, \ldots, a_{2i} r_i, \ldots, a_{2n} r_n + a_{2w} W + a_{2y} Y \tag{2}$$

$$\vdots \qquad\qquad\qquad\qquad\qquad\qquad\qquad\qquad \vdots$$

$$A_n = a_{n1} r_1 + a_{n2} r_2, \ldots, a_{ni} r_i, \ldots, a_{nn} r_n + a_{nw} W + a_{ny} Y \tag{n}$$

For further ease of handling this same set of equations can be depicted in matrix form as below

	r_1	$r_2, \ldots, r_i, \ldots, r_n$	W	Y
A_1	a_{11}	$a_{12}, \ldots, a_{1i}, \ldots, a_{1n}$	a_{1w}	a_{1y}
A_2	a_{21}	$a_{22}, \ldots, a_{2i}, \ldots, a_{2n}$	a_{2w}	a_{2y}
$\vdots$	$\vdots$			
A_n	a_{n1}	$a_{n2}, \ldots, a_{ni}, \ldots, a_{nn}$	a_{nw}	a_{ny}

According then to the accounting identities, given the assumption that changes in r_i and Y leave wealth unaffected, the sum of the coefficients in columns 1 to n and column Y must equal zero while the sum of the coefficients in column W must equal unity, thus ensuring that the accounting identity that wealth is the sum total of all the assets held is satisfied.

Apart from the assumption of linearity, which may not be justified, one shortcoming of this simplified system, as set out, is that it implies that the absolute response in the demand for the various assets to a change in some interest rate(s) is the same irrespective of the level of wealth. In practice the response of assets to changes in interest rates is likely to vary proportionately with the level of wealth. Thus if an increase of 1 per cent in the yield on asset i, with all other yields remaining constant, led to an increase in demand for that asset of £X when wealth was £Y, when wealth rises to $2Y$ one would expect the increase to a similar change in relative yields to be around $2X$. In order to adjust for changes in the scale of the portfolio, each equation could be deflated by total wealth (W), giving a relationship in which the proportion of wealth held in each asset, Ai/W, is determined by interest rates, a constant (aW/W) and the ratio of income to wealth Y/W. Alternatively, the interest-rate variables, $r_1, \ldots, r_n$, could be multiplied by W, thus making them proportionately larger as W increases. So long, however, as the scale of the system remains relatively constant, the bother of taking account of scale effects by deflating (or grossing up) by a scale variable, which introduces non-linearities into the system and thus adds to computational difficulties, may outweigh the benefits of obtaining a more accurate estimate of the working of the system. In future examples of systems of this general form, in subsequent chapters, we shall for simplicity ignore such scale problems, leaving the system as shown in the previous matrix.

In so far as changes in (expected) yields on assets do not cause changes in (subjectively perceived) incomes and wealth, their effect will be limited to causing a substitution between assets in the portfolio, as the relative return on alternative holdings vary. Since this substitution effect depends on relative returns, an increase of X per cent in the yield on all assets, leaving the differentials between asset yields unchanged, should not change the proportions in which asset holders wish to distribute their portfolio between the various assets (incomes and wealth being assumed fixed). This, then, implies that the sum of the coefficients 1 to n in each row should equal zero, so long as variations in the interest-rate variables only induce a substitution effect upon the portfolio. Otherwise an equal increase of X per cent to each interest rate, leaving the relative differentials unchanged, would result in a shift in portfolios. Furthermore, limiting the analysis to substitution effects, the flow of funds into asset i as the yield on asset j falls should theoretically be exactly the same as the flow out of asset j as the yield on asset i rises, at least in the long run when the adjustment process, which may differ from case to case, is completed. So the coefficients on interest rates in the matrix, when income and wealth effects are eliminated, should take the relationship $a_{ij} = a_{ji}$. This effect (known in standard price theory as the Slutsky effect) requires the sub-matrix of interest-rate coefficients to be symmetrical, with both columns and rows adding to zero, coefficients $a_{ij} = a_{ji}$, so that the elements below the main diagonal form a mirror image of the elements above, as in the example below

	r_1	r_2	r_3
A_1	$+14$	-6	-8
A_2	-6	$+8$	-2
A_3	-8	-2	$+10$

In this example the response of the investor to an increase in the yield on any asset is to hold a larger proportion of it in his portfolio. Thus the coefficients of the response of the demand for each asset to a change in its own yield, the values $+14$, $+8$, $+10$ lying along the main diagonal, are positive. Indeed, in any situation where only substitution effects are being considered this must be so, since an improvement in the relative yield on asset i must lead to substitution in favour of that asset[1] (even if income or wealth effects may lead to shifts out of that asset).

It is not, however, necessary that all of the off-diagonal elements should be negative. One could have a symmetric matrix of the form, say

	r_1	r_2	r_3
A_1	+12	−6	−6
A_2	−6	+5	+1
A_3	−6	+1	+5

This implies that an increase in the yield of asset 3 will raise the demand for asset 2, and vice versa. This would occur when assets 2 and 3 were complements: a negative off-diagonal relationship would suggest that the assets were substitutes.

It is rather hard to think of convincing examples of assets likely to be complements in portfolios, unlike the ease with which simple examples can be found in consumer theory, e.g. bacon and eggs. There may be cases where the covariance between two assets is relatively low or even negative, so that the increase in the share of a portfolio taken by one of the assets, as the expected yield on it rises, leads to a stronger demand for the other asset as a complement to give the portfolio a better risk/return shape. Depending on the investor's preferences between risk and return, an increase in the overall yield on a portfolio of risky assets could lead to a shift into a 'safe' asset, out of some risky assets. Thus some safe assets could be complementary with certain risky assets. But, as noted previously in Chapter 2, money – at least when narrowly defined – is liable to be dominated as a receptacle for 'speculative' balances by other, higher-yielding safe assets.[2]

In general, the normal relationship in an individual's portfolio between assets, including money, is that of substitution, with cases of complementarity rare; findings of statistically significant positive relationships between the demand for asset i and the level of interest

---

[1] An increase in the own rate on a liability, borrowed funds, will cause the desired volume of such borrowing to fall, i.e. to take an absolutely smaller negative value in the portfolio, to move in a positive direction. The treatment of liabilities within the system is thus consistent with that of assets.

[2] Some economists have emphasised the role of money in facilitating the activities of production and distribution, and this has led them to suggest 'putting money into the production function' in their models. See, for example, the paper by D. Levhari and D. Patinkin, 'The Role of Money in a Simple Growth Model,' *The American Economic Review*, vol. 58, no. 4 (September 1968) pp. 713–53, especially section III on 'Money as a Producers' Good,' pp. 737–48. A few empirical studies have also adopted this departure, for example A. Sinai and H. Stokes, 'Real Money Balances: An Omitted Variable from the Production Function?,' *The Review of Economics and Statistics*, vol. 54, no. 3 (August 1972) pp. 290–6.

At first glance this approach might be expected to reveal possible complementarity of money balances with other factors of production, e.g. real capital. When the expected yield on real capital rises, leading to an expansion in the stock of real assets, one might, perhaps, envisage a complementary rise in money balances. Money balances, however, are not used in the actual physical production process in the same way as machines or labour. Rather, money balances are held, to an extent depending on such factors as transfer costs, etc., mainly to facilitate payments. With the expected pattern of cash flows given, variations in the quantity of real capital should have little effect on the services provided to businesses by holding money, though in so far as additional holdings of real capital raise the risk of a firm's balance sheet position, there may be some demand for additional liquidity. On the other hand the rise in yields, that presumably prompted the increased demand for real capital, increases the extent of the yield foregone by holding money balances. On balance it is my expectation that money would be a substitute, albeit not perhaps a close one, for all the other assets included in a production function.

rate j usually represent a warning sign, throwing doubt on the validity of the results, since it is rare to see such findings supported by any institutional or other external evidence to suggest why that relationship might be expected to be complementary. And the assumption will be made in the simulation studies of portfolio adjustment, in Chapters 6 and 7, that the form of the relationship between all the assets in the portfolio of any single investor[1] is one of substitution, i.e. that all off-diagonal elements in such matrices showing the substitution effect of interest-rate movements are negative.

In practice, of course, it is not so easy to isolate and to concentrate upon substitution effects arising from changes in interest rates. Changes in yields on marketable assets have direct effects on the prices of such assets, and therefore on the current market value of an investor's wealth. So changes in interest rates on marketable assets will alter the level of wealth via capital gains and losses, and this alteration in wealth levels will, given relative yields, cause a redistribution of asset holdings in response to the wealth elasticity of demand for assets. Changes in rates paid on capital-certain assets will not change the level of existing wealth, but they will alter income flows, which in turn may influence the desired portfolio distribution. Thus changes in interest rates will entail income/wealth effects, in addition to substitution effects.

The calculation of the expected relative yield, over the chosen planning period, on a marketable asset depends on the periodic payments of interest or dividends, and the expected capital gain (loss) at the end of the period. This is a function of expectations of *future* levels of yields. This raises a problem of how to capture, to observe, mean expected yields on marketable assets when the planning period, itself unobservable and no doubt variable, is not equal to the maturity of the asset. Moreover, the possibility of changes in wealth, as interest rates vary, raises the problem of how to incorporate uncertainty, the expected variance and covariance of returns on the assets, into the analysis. Commonly in applied, empirical studies, these problems are ducked, by treating the observable yield to maturity on each asset as a proxy for the mean expected yield, and by treating uncertainty as constant. There have, however, been some attempts, e.g. by taking a distributed lag on past rate levels as, perhaps, some guide to future expected rate levels, to provide a better proxy for mean expected yields.[2] There have also been attempts to use past data of asset-price variance to give a proxy for expectations of the relative variance on each asset.[3] These efforts to incorporate expectations, of the mean and variance of future returns on available assets, into the model have been, perforce, rough and ready.

---

[1] It does not follow that within the economy as a whole the relationship between all assets would then also be invariably one of substitution, because the interaction of two or more groups of investors in differing situations could lead to apparent complementarity. Suppose, for example, that rates offered on bank time deposits were varied. Then private-sector holdings of bonds, say, would go down when deposit rates rose, as people shifted out of bonds into bank deposits, but bank holdings of bonds would rise, in line with their larger portfolio, and could conceivably rise by more than the non-bank public's holdings of bonds fell.

[2] For example in his paper on 'Discount House Portfolio and Debt Selection,' *The Review of Economic Studies*, vol. 37 (4), no. 112 (October 1970) pp. 469–97, M. Parkin reported, p. 480, that 'alternative methods of proxying the expected interest rates which were tried were (i) first- and second-order autoregressive forecasting schemes, (ii) adaptive expectations and (iii) actual interest rates lagged up to one and a half quarters and led up to half a quarter . . . . There was little to choose between the quarter end rates and rates led by half a quarter. . . . The implication of this would seem to be that the Discount Houses are very good at forecasting and do much better than an autoregressive or adaptive expectations scheme would approximate.'

[3] See, for example, W. White, 'The Term Structure of Interest Rates – A Cross-Section Test of a Mean-Variance Model,' in *Issues in Monetary Economics* (forthcoming); F. Modigliani and F. Cotula, 'An Empirical Analysis of Financial Flows and the Composition of the Financial Wealth of the Economy,' *Banca Nazionale del Lavoro* (forthcoming).

Some of these problems, e.g. of coping with uncertainty and expectations, can be alleviated by concentrating on investors' selections among the set of capital-certain assets. Indeed, several of the initial empirical exercises to estimate investors' portfolio responses have limited their scope to studies of sets of capital-certain assets,[1] including various monetary assets.

The total effect of changes in interest rates on the distribution of assets is, therefore, some amalgam of substitution, income and wealth effects. Even so, it can be desirable, especially because of the attractive features of the matrix of substitution effects, e.g. symmetry, to try to examine these effects separately. In the examples of portfolio adjustment in future chapters this will be done by separately specifying these various effects. For this purpose the level of wealth at any point of time, W_t, can be divided, as an accounting identity, into three parts, being initial wealth at the end of the previous period, W_{t-1}, capital gains (or losses), CG_t, which is a function of interest-rate changes, $CG_t = f(dr_i)$, and savings, S, which may also be a function of interest rates, as well as of disposable incomes. The level of wealth can be decomposed into its components to show the various factors accounting for its current level, as follows

$$W_t = W_{t-1} + CG_t + S_t$$

where

$$CG_t = f(dr_i) \quad \text{and} \quad S_t = f(Y, r_i)$$

This separation is intended to allow a clearer distinction between the pure substitution effects of changes in interest rates, and their income/wealth effects. Furthermore, it may be that the *initial* portfolio distribution among assets of an addition to wealth from new savings, or from capital gains, might differ from the long-run desired distribution of existing wealth. That is, in a matrix of the form below

	$r_1, r_2, \ldots, r_n$	W_{t-1}	CG_t	S_t	Y_t
A_1	$a_{11}, \ldots, a_{1n}$	a_{1w}	a_{1g}	a_{1s}	a_{1y}
A_2					
$\vdots$	$\vdots \qquad \vdots$	$\vdots$	$\vdots$	$\vdots$	$\vdots$
A_n	$a_{n1}, \ldots, a_{nn}$	a_{nw}	a_{ng}	a_{ns}	a_{ny}

the sums of coefficients in columns W_{t-1}, CG_t and S_t must all equal unity, but a_{iw} need not necessarily equal a_{ig} or a_{is}.

Differences of this kind between the initial and long-run responses are caused by various lags in the process of adjustment. For example, savings initially accrue in monetary form, and capital gains in a raised value of those particular assets whose price has risen. It may take time for such increases in wealth in a particular form to be redistributed among other assets. On the other hand any reshuffling of existing portfolios of assets involves transaction and information/decision costs, while the placement of new savings avoids prior asset sales, and regular savings flows may lead to shorter planning periods. It is often

---

[1] Among these are the paper by J. Townend, 'Substitution among Capital-Certain Assets in the Personal Sector of the U.K. Economy, 1963–71,' presented at the European Meeting of the Econometric Society in Budapest in September 1972, and summarised in *The Bank of England Quarterly Bulletin*, vol. 12, no. 4 (December 1972) pp. 509–11; the paper by E. Gramlich and J. Kalchbrenner, 'A Constrained Estimation Approach to the Demand for Liquid Assets,' presented at the Federal Reserve Committee on Financial Analysis (April 1969) (mimeo); the paper by M. Parkin, with R. Barrett and M. Gray, 'The Demand for Financial Assets by the Personal Sector of the U.K. Economy,' Proceedings of the London Business School Conference on Modelling the U.K. Economy (forthcoming).

claimed that the redistribution of many institutional portfolios (e.g. of some insurance companies) is a gradual process determined largely by shifts in the investment pattern of new savings, with little or no switching of existing holdings. So the response of asset demand to some change in external circumstances, for example a change in relative yields, could depend jointly on that change and the ratio of new savings to existing wealth.

Indeed, financial systems do seem to be characterised by quite long lag adjustments, whether because of slow recognition of changing conditions, long planning periods, high transfer and information costs, or whatever. Certainly, models based on quarterly data cannot overlook the likelihood of lagged responses. But the need to cope with lag responses often causes considerable data-handling problems in estimating portfolio responses over sets of assets. In single equations a number of flexible methods of handling lag distributions have been developed, but in portfolio-adjustment models there will be constraints applying to the coefficients of the lagged variables, derived from the inter-relationships between the variables, in the same way as constraints apply to the coefficients on current variables. For example, given the value of W_t, if the demand for asset i is a positive function of W_{t-n}, the sum of the coefficients on other assets with respect to W_{t-n} must have an equal negative value. The treatment of lag adjustments in such models, therefore, tends either to lead to an unwieldy expansion of the scale of the model or to some compromise with the maintenance of the appropriate constraints.

Even without lagged explanatory variables, the size of the matrix after inclusion of all the many variables, in addition to relative yields and wealth, which may affect investors' asset demands, such as some variable to represent expectations of price inflation, can be overly large. The most crushing obstacle to working with such systems is, however, that in most countries the basic balance-sheet data are not available, and when available may only be of limited accuracy and cover short time periods.[1] A greater number of countries, such as the United Kingdom, which do not have a complete, coherent set of balance-sheet data, do possess complete flow-of-funds data. There is always a hope that it may be possible to use flow-of-funds data, showing asset transactions, to provide a proxy for a balance-sheet adjustment model. However, basic theory is clear that investors should be concerned with the changing values of their assets, while the flow of funds measure only one aspect of such changing values, omitting entirely capital gains (losses) and other non-market transfers, e.g. arising from debentures issued with stock-conversion options.[2]

There are, in my opinion, considerable advantages in using a coherent system of asset-demand (and supply) equations, with the inter-relationships spelled out, as an expository device to explore how portfolios adjust to disturbances, and this will be done in some subsequent chapters. Nevertheless, the shortage of satisfactory data and the complications involved in the simultaneous estimation of large systems of equations have prevented any large-scale development of empirical work on financial systems along these lines, and it has really only been in the last few years that any has been undertaken.[3] It is doubtful, moreover,

---

[1] Another serious problem is that most observed interest rates tend to move closely together. The resulting multi-collinearity makes it difficult to observe clearly how the system responds to disturbances.

[2] For a somewhat differing view, in which the value of flow of funds data *vis-à-vis* balance-sheet data is given a higher rating, see A. D. Bain's article on 'Flow of Funds Analysis: A Survey,' *The Economic Journal*, vol. 83, no. 332 (December 1973) pp. 1055–93.

[3] In the United Kingdom M. Parkin has taken the leading part in the development of such studies. In addition to his papers on the Discount Houses and Personal Sector, which have already been noted, he has published papers on 'The Portfolio Behaviour of Commercial Banks,' in *The Econometric Study of the U.K. Economy*, and on 'The Portfolio and Interest Rate Behaviour of Building Societies,' in *The Manchester School of Economic and Social Studies* (December 1972). He has also studied portfolio adjustment among other groups in the U.K. banking sector, e.g. the Scottish and Northern Irish banks, and is currently working on portfolio-adjustment studies of certain sectors in Australia.

whether such empirical work to date has achieved much (beyond giving confirmation of the expected existence of significant substitutions between assets in response to changing interest differentials) that has given any more illumination than, or challenged the results of, the single-equation studies.

While there are advantages, at least heuristic ones, in setting out the inter-relationships between the individual asset equations in a formal system, it should not be forgotten that macro-economic systems of asset-demand equations will share the structural deficiencies of the individual equations. In these equations there is usually no explicit role for uncertainty except in so far as it is relegated into the constant terms, say, reflecting normal yield differentials. The relationship between the *ex post* variables actually employed and the *ex ante* subjective expectations that shape behaviour is tenuous to say the least. The possible difficulties of aggregating over disparate groups are frequently brushed aside.

APPENDIX B

Some Statistical Results of Econometric Studies of Demand for Money Functions

A selection of statistical results obtained from empirical studies of demand for money functions is provided in Table 3.1 (pp. 64–5).[1] As far as possible representative equations have been chosen from the work of each author, though often other equations give somewhat different coefficients. Table 3.1 sets out the income and price elasticities obtained; as noted in the main text a summary of the estimated values of the interest elasticity of the demand for money is to be found in Laidler's study on *The Demand for Money* (chap. 8) and in the article on 'The Importance of Money' in the *Bank of England Quarterly Bulletin* (June 1970) (Appendix I, pp. 188–9).

References for Table 3.1

[1] M. Bronfenbrenner and T. Mayer, 'Liquidity Functions in the American Economy,' *Econometrica*, vol. 28, no. 4 (October 1960) pp. 810–34.

[2] A. H. Meltzer, 'The Demand for Money: The Evidence from the Time Series,' *The Journal of Political Economy*, vol. 71, no. 3 (June 1963) pp. 219–46.

[3] K. Brunner and A. H. Meltzer, 'Some Further Investigations of Demand and Supply Functions for Money,' *The Journal of Finance*, vol. 19, no. 2 (May 1964) pp. 240–83.

[4] R. L. Teigen, 'Demand and Supply Functions for Money in the United States: Some Structural Estimates,' *Econometrica*, vol. 32, no. 4 (October 1964) pp. 476–509.

[5] H. R. Heller, 'The Demand for Money: The Evidence from the Short-Run Data,' *The Quarterly Journal of Economics*, vol. 79, no. 2 (May 1965) pp. 291–303.

[6] G. C. Chow, 'On the Long-Run and Short-Run Demand for Money,' *The Journal of Political Economy*, vol. 74, no. 2 (April 1966) pp. 111–31.

[7] D. Laidler, 'The Rate of Interest and the Demand for Money – Some Empirical Evidence,' *The Journal of Political Economy*, vol. 74, no. 6 (December 1966) pp. 543–55.

[8] T. H. Lee, 'Alternative Interest Rates and the Demand for Money: The Empirical Evidence,' *The American Economic Review*, vol. 57, no. 5 (December 1967) pp. 1168–81.

[9] A. A. Shapiro, 'Inflation, Lags and the Demand for Money,' *International Economic Review*, vol. 14, no. 1 (February 1973) pp. 81–96.

[10] M. Friedman, 'The Demand for Money: Some Theoretical and Empirical Results,' *The Journal of Political Economy*, vol. 67, no. 4 (August 1959) pp. 327–51.

[11] B. Motley, 'A Demand for Money Function for the Household Sector – Some Preliminary Findings,' *The Journal of Finance*, vol. 22, no. 3 (September 1967) pp. 405–18.

---

[1] I am very grateful to Mr G. Hacche, who undertook the work of collecting and compiling the data shown here.

[12] D. E. W. Laidler, 'The Influence of Money on Economic Activity – A Survey of Some Current Problems,' in G. Clayton, J. C. Gilbert, and R. Sedgwick, *Monetary Theory and Monetary Policy in the 1970s* (Oxford University Press, London, 1971) pp. 75–135.

[13] D. Fisher, 'The Demand for Money in Britain: Quarterly Results 1951 to 1967,' *The Manchester School of Economic and Social Studies*, vol. 36, no. 4 (December 1968) pp. 329–44.

[14] C. A. E. Goodhart and A. D. Crockett, 'The Importance of Money,' *Bank of England Quarterly Bulletin*, vol. 10, no. 2 (June 1970) pp. 159–98 (Appendix II).

[15] L. D. D. Price, 'The Demand for Money in the United Kingdom: A Further Investigation,' *Bank of England Quarterly Bulletin*, vol. 12, no. 1 (March 1972) pp. 43–55 (Appendix).

[16] N. J. Kavanagh and A. A. Walters, 'Demand for Money in the U.K., 1877–1961: Some Preliminary Findings,' *Bulletin of the Oxford University Institute of Economics and Statistics*, vol. 28, no. 2 (May 1966) pp. 93–116.

[17] D. Laidler and J. M. Parkin, 'The Demand for Money in the United Kingdom, 1955–67: Preliminary Estimates,' *The Manchester School of Economic and Social Studies*, vol. 38, no. 3 (September 1970) pp. 187–208.

TABLE 3.1

Author	Data used	Income variable	Income elasticity	Price elasticity
A. U.S. data: Narrow[1] money				
Bronfenbrenner & Mayer [1]	Annual: 1919–56	Private sector G.N.P. (real)	1·299 (13·49)	1*
Meltzer [2]	Annual: 1900–58	N.N.P. (real)	1·05 (25·6)	1*
	Annual: 1900–58	{ N.N.P. (real) { Real wealth	0·13 (1·4) } 0·97 (9·5) }	1*
Brunner & Meltzer [3]	Annual: 1930–59	Real wealth[3]	1·516 (6·37)	0·804 (4·32)
Teigen [4]	Annual: 1924–41	G.N.P. (nominal)	0·844 (15·92)	..
	Quarterly: 1946 IV–1959 IV	G.N.P. (nominal)	0·476 (23·8)	..
Heller [5]	Quarterly: 1947–58	G.N.P. (nominal)	0·900 (12·0)	..
Chow [6]	Annual: 1897–1958	'Permanent' N.N.P. (nominal)	1·055 (105·5)	..
	Annual: 1897–1958	'Permanent' N.N.P. (real)	1·054 (16·5)	1·057 (12·9)
Laidler [7]	Annual: 1919–60	'Permanent' N.N.P. (real)	1·526 (29·92)	1*
	Annual: 1919–60[4]	'Permanent' N.N.P. (real)	0·953 (4·06)	1*
Lee [8]	Annual: 1951–65	'Permanent' N.N.P. (real)	0·535 (6·18)	1*
Shapiro [9]	Quarterly: 1950 IV–1970 II	G.N.P. (real)	0·9[2]	1*
B. U.S. data: Broad[1] money				
Friedman [10]	1870–1954, smoothed over cycles	N.N.P. (real)	1·8	1*
Meltzer [2]	Annual: 1900–58	{ N.N.P. (real) { Real wealth	0·13 (1·4) } 1·18 (12·4) }	1*
Brunner & Meltzer [3]	Annual: 1930–59	Real wealth[3]	1·427 (6·88)	0·771 (4·76)
Heller [5]	Quarterly: 1947–58	G.N.P. (nominal)	1·431 (16·45)	..
Laidler [7]	Annual: 1892–1960	'Permanent' N.N.P. (real)	1·394 (63·36)	1*
	Annual: 1892–1960[4]	'Permanent' N.N.P. (real)	1·216 (7·33)	1*
Lee [8]	Annual: 1951–65	'Permanent' N.N.P. (real)	0·928 (12·3)	1*
Motley [11]	Annual: 1920–65 (households only)	'Permanent' P.D.I. (real)	1·26[2]	1*
Laidler [12]	Annual: 1900–65	N.N.P. (real)	1·195 (26·56)	1*
	Annual: 1900–65	'Permanent' N.N.P. (real)	1·229 (13·97)	1·020 (17·29)
Shapiro [9]	Quarterly: 1950 IV–70 II	G.N.P. (real)	1·5[2]	1*

TABLE 3.1   *(continued)*

Author	Data used	Income variable	Income elasticity	Price elasticity
Shapiro [9] (cont.)	Quarterly: 1950 IV–70 II	G.N.P. (real)	2·5^2 (time deposits only)	1*

C. U.K. data: Narrow[1] money

Fisher [13]	Quarterly: 1955 I–67 II	P.D.I. (nominal)	0·656^2	. .
Goodhart & Crockett [14]	Quarterly: 1955 III–69 III	G.D.P. (nominal)	1·25^2	. .
	Quarterly: 1955 III–69 III	G.D.P. (real)	0·55^2	1*
Price [15]	Quarterly: 1956 I–69 IV	G.D.P. (real)	0·42^2	1·79^2

D. U.K. data: Broad[1] money

Kavanagh & Walters [16]	Annual: 1880–1961	G.N.P. (nominal)	1·149 (54·71)	. .
Fisher [13]	Quarterly: 1955 I–67 II	P.D.I. (nominal)	0·743^2	. .
Goodhart & Crockett [14]	Quarterly: 1955 III–69 III	G.D.P. (nominal)	1·09^2	. .
	1955 III–69 III	G.D.P. (real)	0·67^2	1*
	Quarterly: 1963 II–69 III	G.D.P. (nominal)	1·41^2	. .
	1963 II–69 III	G.D.P. (real)	2·64^2	1*
Laidler & Parkin [17]	Quarterly: 1955 III–67 IV	G.D.P. (real)	0·680^2	1*
Laidler [12]	Annual: 1900–65	N.N.P. (real)	0·631 (12·13)	1*
	Annual: 1900–65	'Permanent' N.N.P. (real)	0·515 (4·77)	1·188 (18·86)
Price [15]	Quarterly: 1956 I–69 IV	G.D.P. (real)	0·55^2	1·94^2
	Quarterly: 1964 I–70 IV	G.D.P. (real)	1·69^2	1·03^2

Notes

Figures in brackets are the *t*-statistics of the respective elasticities.

. ., price elasticity not estimated; nominal income variable used.

*, constrained to unity.

[1] The 'narrow' definition of money is usually currency plus demand deposits: 'broad' money includes time deposits.

[2] Long-run elasticity, from an equation containing lags; no *t*-statistic is given, as its meaning would be ambiguous.

[3] Wealth elasticity, quoted where no income variable was used.

[4] Equation estimated in first differences.

N.N.P., Net National Product.

G.N.P., Gross National Product.

P.D.I., Personal Disposable Income.

G.D.P., Gross Domestic Product.

'Permanent' income is estimated as a distributed lag on current and past incomes, generally as a proxy for the subjective, longer-run 'normal' level of incomes.

4

The Term Structure of Interest Rates

SUMMARY

In order to estimate the demand for assets within the context of a portfolio adjustment model – as described in Chapter 3, Appendix A – it is necessary to reduce the size of the model to manageable proportions. This is achieved by aggregation over assets which are close substitutes, where relative variations in supply will have little impact on prices. It is exactly such issues, whether long-dated bonds are close substitutes for short bonds, whether variations in the relative supply of bonds will affect the pattern of bond prices, that lie at the heart of arguments about the determination of the term structure of interest rates. It is, perhaps, unfortunate that analysis of the term structure often begins in a certainty context, since then all assets are virtually perfect substitutes by definition, though the mechanics of the relationship between present bond rates, implicit forward rates and forward bond prices can be set out more easily in such circumstances.

If investors were risk-neutral and held similar expectations then the introduction of uncertainty would not alter the term structure greatly. Both assumptions are, however, implausible. It is, therefore, necessary to take account of risk aversion among investors with differing holding periods and expectations. The attempt to do so by adding a constant liquidity premium into an equation otherwise based on risk-neutral behaviour (i.e. assuming that the sole objective is to maximise the mean expected return) is unsatisfactory. The risk involved in adding a bond of differing maturity to the portfolio is not theoretically a constant, but depends on several factors, such as the expected variance and covariances of the bond, the investor's holding period, etc.

If investors exhibit risk aversion, short bonds should not be very close substitutes for long bonds; some economists, in particular Culbertson, have gone so far as to argue on such grounds that the market will be segmented. On the other hand bonds of adjacent maturities are likely to be very close substitutes, though less so at the short end of the market. The interesting question then is how quickly, if at all, does the degree of substitution fade as the distance along the maturity spectrum increases.

Such a question can only be answered by examining the data. In the appendix to this chapter a number of the major empirical studies are surveyed. Much of the renewed interest in this subject can be traced to Meiselman's reformulation of the expectations hypothesis, in terms of systematic revisions to expected future short-term rates in the light of errors in forecasting the current short rate. One criticism of this approach is that all such revisions are based on errors in forecasting only the current short rate. Masera has tried to generalise this approach by allowing errors in forecasting each rate to influence future expectations of that rate, but this more general approach may not be able to distinguish so sharply between 'structural' and 'expectational' factors. Both studies rely on obtaining observations of implicit forward rates from calculated yield curves, and the tests of their hypotheses may be affected by the method used to construct such curves.

The studies undertaken by Modigliani, with Sutch and Shiller, get away from the use of constructed yield curves by regressing actual long rates on past and present short rates.

Apart from the fact that the chain principle of forecasting adopted is no stronger than its weakest intermediate link, recent theoretical work on rational efficient markets and empirical analysis of interest-rate time series have thrown doubt on the existence of causal links between long rates and past short rates. The final approach surveyed, developed by White and Burman, starts from the proposition that no investor feels capable of making sensible forecasts beyond some near-by horizon. Given such ignorance, investors are assumed to make an extremely simple assumption (of constant rates) about conditions beyond the horizon, and on that basis to arrange their portfolio to achieve the optimal risk/return combination in the period up to the horizon.

All these empirical exercises produced quite good statistical fits. There is no doubt that expectations play a major role in determining the term structure, though exactly how these expectations are formed and revised remains uncertain. More surprising, in view of the prevalence of risk aversion, has been the general failure of empirical studies to reveal clear signs of supply factors influencing the pattern of rates, though a number of reasons can be adduced in partial explanation for this.

There are in any developed economy very many different assets, real and financial. The question when, and under what circumstances, it is appropriate to aggregate certain of these assets into sets forms a link between the subject matter of the previous chapter and the theory of the term structure of interest rates. In order to study the process of portfolio adjustment, as described in the previous chapter, especially in Appendix A, it is necessary to limit the size of the exercise to manageable proportions by aggregating the numerous assets into a smaller number of groups.

How does one choose which assets to group together into larger aggregates? The process of aggregation should reduce the system into a model of more manageable proportions, but has the result of obscuring some of the inter-relationships one wishes to examine. The objective is to aggregate in such a way as to minimise the loss in explanatory power obtained in exchange for greater simplicity.

In particular, the process of aggregation prevents any explicit consideration of the effect of variations in the relative supplies of the aggregated elements which leaves the aggregate supply unaffected. Thus aggregation will not be appropriate when variations in the relative supplies of the individual elements have any significant effect on the variables, or problem, under consideration. This, of course, implies that the appropriate degree of aggregation depends on the problem at hand. If your interest is planning the production schedule for the future issue of bank-notes, the analysis of the problem would hardly be advanced by aggregating over all denominations of notes. If, however, your concern was the growth of the national economy, the substitution of more £10 notes for £5 notes, leaving the overall note issue unchanged in value terms, is unlikely to affect any crucial variable in the system.

In general, the greater the degree of substitutability between any two items the less information will be lost by treating them as an aggregate. If two items are very close substitutes, then a shift in relative supplies will only require a very small shift in relative prices to restore equilibrium. If relative prices are virtually unchanged, the effect on the rest of the economy of the shifts in relative supplies within the aggregate is likely to be minimal. In such circumstances aggregation over these items would normally be appropriate.

In many ways the nub of the major issues in dispute in the analysis of the term structure of interest rates resides in the question whether it is appropriate to aggregate over all Central Government (or public-sector) bonds. The questions whether investors regard bonds of differing maturities as close substitutes; whether the bond market is segmented, with separate demand (and supply) schedules for bonds of different maturities; whether shifts in the relative supply of bonds of different maturities alter the term structure, are all essentially raising the issue whether it is appropriate to aggregate short and long bonds[1] (with otherwise similar characteristics).

Government bonds are, in normal circumstances, free of default risk. They do bear different coupons, and sometimes have unusual call provisions, but their main character- istics are basically similar, *except* that the various outstanding bonds differ in their term till maturity. Is this difference of sufficient importance that one should treat short-dated and long-dated bonds separately in any analysis of financial adjustment within the economy, or would a sale by the authorities of short bonds balanced by a purchase of longs, to the same value say, with no net effect on the money stock, leave the economy relatively un- affected?

At first sight it may look entirely implausible to regard long-dated bonds, or perpetuities, as close substitutes for short-dated bonds. But it is always possible for an investor to hold a series of short bonds rather than a long bond over some long holding period, or to hold a long bond for a short time and then sell it rather than hold a short bond (to maturity). If people should have very firm *expectations* about the future returns available on short bonds, and the future prices at which they can sell long bonds, then investors will choose that sequence of bond holding that will maximise their expected holding-period return. If all investors have similar expectations, their portfolio adjustment will drive bond prices to levels at which the total return (interest plus expected capital gain or loss) for each sequence of bond holdings will be expected to be the same over any given period. If, then, more of bond i is supplied, and less of bond j, in these circumstances where all investors have uniform, very sure expectations, it will only take a minimal increase in the current market yield of bond i and fall in that of bond j to make investors switch from bond j to bond i. In such circumstances shifts in the relative supplies of the various bonds will have hardly any effect on relative prices and aggregation in, for example, a study of general portfolio adjustment would be appropriate.

Indeed, in an economy without any uncertainty, one can aggregate over *all* assets. All assets must have the same certain return over a given period[2] irrespective of their super- ficial characteristics. All assets would be perfect substitutes; there would be only one kind of financial asset. With a certain future, the return to be obtained on holding bonds (or any other asset) over an n-year period would have to be identical whether a bond with a life of n years was held to maturity, or whether a sequence of shorter bonds was held with the proceeds being re-invested, or whether a longer bond was held to be sold after n years. If they were not identical, a sure arbitrage profit could be made by simultaneously purchas- ing the asset with a higher yield and selling the asset with the lower yield. Assume that the sequence of buying two one-year bonds is known to give a higher return than holding a two-year bond. Then all holders of two-year bonds should sell them and re-invest in one- year bonds – in the sure knowledge of the coming yield on next year's one-year bond – until the returns over the two-year holding period are driven into equality. In this circum- stance a visitor from Mars could deduce from the present term structure of rates exactly what everyone foresaw with certainty for future short rates of interest, and for future asset prices on all existing bonds at future dates. Thus the expected future short rates would

---

[1] See A. Leijonhufvud, *On Keynesian Economics and the Economics of Keynes*, especially sect. III, 'The Aggregative Structure of Alternative Models.'

[2] This certain return could, however, vary as the length of the holding period varies, depending on foreseen variations in real economic conditions, such as thrift, investment opportunities, harvests, etc. An investor with a short holding period cannot take advantage of, say, higher certain future short-term rates beyond that period, since he would have to borrow funds at these future higher rates to finance his investment. In this certain economy the certain return (on all assets, long or short) over n years may differ from the return obtainable over q years ($n \neq q$), but the investor in each case will be indifferent whether he holds sequences of short or long assets to obtain the certain return.

be those making the return on a sequence of short holdings exactly equal to the return on long holdings. Abstracting from the complication of periodic coupon payments, which require re-investment at the future expected rates, i.e. treating all bonds as pure discount bonds (the return from which arises entirely from the discount from their final maturity value at which they are sold), the expected yields will be equal when

$$(1 + R_k)^k (1 + {}_{t+k}r_n)^n = (1 + R_{k+n})^{k+n}$$

where R is the rate offered currently (spot), the subscript R_{k+n} meaning that this rate is offered over a period of length $k + n$; r is the expected future rate, r_n is a future rate over n periods, and ${}_{t+k}r_n$ is a future n-period rate which is expected to occur $t + k$ periods from now. By means of this equation, in a world of certainty one could deduce all future expected short rates from the current structure of spot rates, e.g.

$$(1 + {}_{t+1}r_1) = \frac{(1 + R_2)^2}{(1 + R_1)}$$

Thus the one-year rate expected to rule next year can be deduced from the current two-year and one-year spot rates. Equally, the expected n-year forward rate on a bond of maturity $n + 1$ can be obtained by a similar calculation, e.g.

$$(1 + {}_{t+1}r_n)^n = \frac{(1 + R_{n+1})^{n+1}}{(1 + R_1)}$$

and it follows, of course, that certainty of future forward rates also implies certainty of future asset prices.[1]

If investors were subject to uncertainty, but ignored such uncertainty – i.e. they were risk neutral – they would still take any arbitrage opportunities that seemed to offer an expected positive return, irrespective of the risk involved. If one abstracts from such imperfections and practical problems as transactions costs, brokerage margins between borrowing and lending rates, restrictions on short sales, differential tax considerations, etc., any such investor would attempt to eliminate any differential between expected returns on alternative sequences of bond holdings over any period by borrowing (making short sales of) that sequence of asset(s) with the lower expected rate to invest in the asset sequence with the higher expected return *without limit*.

This follows irrespective of the holding period of the investor.[2] If the return over n years from holding a long bond is greater than that from holding a sequence of short bonds, the investor with a holding period of k years ($n > k$) can still buy the n-year bond and arrange to borrow on short bonds from k till n to finance his holding if that course promises an arbitrage profit.[3]

---

[1] For a thorough analysis of the relationship between models based on expectations of future rates and those based on expectations of future asset prices, see D. Luckett, 'Multi-Period Expectations and the Term Structure of Interest Rates,' *Quarterly Journal of Economics*, vol. 81, no. 2 (May 1967) pp. 321–9, and B. G. Malkiel, *The Term Structure of Interest Rates* (Princeton University Press, 1966), especially chap. 3.

[2] This implies that the holding periods of each investor are exogenously given, say by their prospective income and expenditure plans. In principle, of course, such plans – and therefore intended holding periods – would be influenced by the available yields on assets. As is discussed further in Chapter 9, the propensity to save out of incomes does not, in practice, respond sensitively to changes in yields. We shall, therefore, disregard the point that holding periods and interest rates are jointly determined, as a complication of secondary importance in fact, and treat these holding periods as pre-determined.

[3] But even if arbitrage did equalise the expected returns for each investor on all sequences of holdings over any given period, the equilibrium expected holding-period returns could still differ between investors depending on the length of their respective holding periods.

The characteristics of a market consisting of, or dominated by, risk-neutral investors with identical expectations would be very similar to those that would hold under conditions of certainty. The implicit forward rates that can be calculated, using the previous formula, from the current spot rates would represent the mean expected future rates, rather than the future certain rates. The assumption that all, or a dominating proportion, of investors have identical expectations is, of course, extreme. There are, however, some difficulties inherent in envisaging a system dominated by risk-neutral investors with differing expectations. What would happen if there were inconsistent expectations, for example with A seeing an arbitrage opportunity over an n-year horizon in selling longs to buy a sequence of shorts, while B believes that a return can be made from arbitrage in the opposite direction. This difference of opinion must be a reflection of disparate views about some future short rate. If there was a market in future short-term loans,[1] risk-neutral A would be prepared, say, to contract to borrow an infinite volume of future short-term loans at the going rate, expecting to be able to re-lend them at a higher rate, while risk-neutral B would be prepared to make future contracts to provide an infinite volume, expecting to be able to borrow then to finance the loans at a lower rate. Both would be prepared to extend their future obligations without limit, so long as they were not prevented by some external constraints.

The problem of accommodating inconsistent expectations among risk-neutral investors can be overcome by making the pragmatic assumption that there are certain costs of dealing, or certain other limitations on an investor's operations, e.g. restrictions on short sales, so that investors may see prospective arbitrage opportunities, but not be in a position to take full advantage of them. In this case each investor, depending on the limitations on his own operations, will have to concentrate his own holdings in that asset (and liability) sequence which offers the highest expected return over his own holding period. Because of the spread of expectations, risk-neutral investors with limited access to resources would concentrate their holdings in those bonds offering the highest subjectively-expected returns: so the issue of additional bonds of maturity length M would require some additional investors to switch their individual funds into that bond; this can only be done if more investors come to believe that holding bond M offers the highest expected return.

If the spot rate on bond M, i.e. R_m, rises relative to the spot rate on other bonds, R_i, then, *ceteris paribus*,[2] holding bond M will offer a relatively higher return compared

---

[1] That is a market where one could contract to borrow, or to lend, money at some negotiated rate for some specified time period to be taken up at some future date. Some future markets of this kind do exist, for example the futures market in certificates of deposit in London. Such markets should not be seen only as vehicles for speculation; they can also be used for hedging. For instance, a banker's customer may arrange to draw upon his facility in three months' time (to finance, say, an investment project), and the existence of a futures C.D. market will allow the banker to hedge his position in advance.

[2] The main *ceteris paribus* condition, of course, is that the change in current spot rates should not affect future expected short rates (and also future expected asset prices). With risk-neutral investors, the equilibrium condition between spot rates, given expectations of future rates, $\bar{r}_i$, is given by the relationship

$$(1 + {}_{t+k}\bar{r}_n)^n = \frac{(1 + R_m)^m}{(1 + R_k)^k} ; \qquad m = k + n$$

If $\bar{r}_i$ remain constant, a rise in R_m relative to R_k must induce purchases of bond M. But, if the change in R_m should cause some revision of expected $\bar{r}_i$, it would be possible for $\bar{r}_i$ to change in such a way that a rise in spot rates, R_m, could have no effect, or even a perverse effect, on the demand for bond M. The question of the relationship between changes in current spot rates and expected future short rates is taken up further later in this chapter. For the moment, however, let us accept that variations in relative spot rates would be needed, and would suffice, to restore equilibrium after a shift in the proportions of different stocks outstanding in a market dominated by risk-neutral investors, with limited access to borrowed funds (at the default free-lending rate), with a spread of differing expectations.

with other alternative sequences of bond holdings in investors' opinions. Thus to obtain holders for a larger issue of bond *M*, its price must fall relative to the market, in a series of steps whose length depends on the wealth (and access to borrowed funds) of each additional risk-neutral investor attracted into holding this bond, as illustrated in Fig. 4.1.

The range of investors' expectations has been empirically studied through surveys and questionnaires by Malkiel and White.[1] These studies show the range to be quite wide. Nevertheless, there were no very strong *a priori* reasons to dismiss the *possibility* of closely similar expectations among investors in the market. Indeed, professional investors largely receive the same information and communicate frequently with each other. One could, perhaps, reasonably expect that the relative rate adjustments needed on this account to restore equilibrium, as the supply of bonds of different maturities varied, might be very slight, i.e. that the demand schedule in Fig. 4.1 might be virtually horizontal. In this case the assumption that all investors were alike could possibly be regarded as a useful, simplifying approximation, except that the assumption is apparently belied by the empirical evidence.

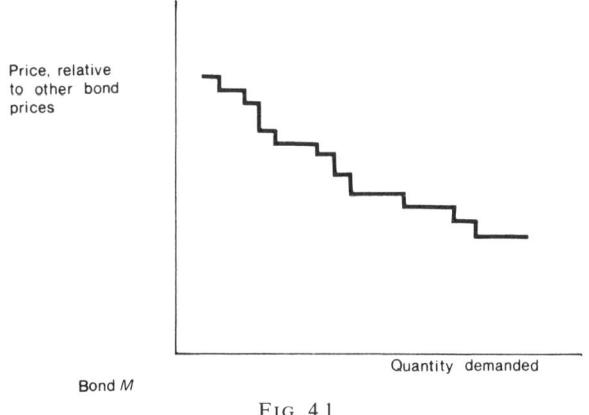

FIG. 4.1

On the other hand the proposition that there are a sufficient number of risk-neutral investors to dominate the determination of market prices does seem contrary to 'common sense', i.e. that potent mixture of intuition and casual empiricism. As noted previously, the idea that many investors would accept unlimited additional uncertainty to raise the mean expected return by a minute amount appears psychologically absurd. Nor does one commonly observe – indeed never does one observe with institutional investors, who often dominate financial markets – individual portfolio behaviour that would be consistent with risk neutrality, such as concentration of funds in that asset, or group of assets, offering the highest mean expected return, plus maximum possible borrowing (up to the point where the cost of borrowing equals the mean expected return on the preferred asset(s)) in order to add further to such holdings.

If, on such grounds, pure risk neutrality is dismissed as implausible, it simply will not do to seek to capture risk aversion by adding some constant premium (a 'liquidity premium') to otherwise risk-neutral behaviour. This has been a common practice in the literature; for example, in Hicks's analysis, 'forward short-term rates are biased estimates

[1] See W. R. White, 'Expectations, Investment and the U.K. Gilt-Edged Market – Some Evidence from Market Participants,' *The Manchester School of Economic and Social Studies* no. 4 (December 1971) pp. 293–314, and B. Malkiel and E. Kane, 'The Term Structure of Interest Rates: An Analysis of a Survey of Interest-Rate Expectations,' *The Review of Economics and Statistics*, vol. 49, no. 3 (August 1967) pp. 343–55.

of expected future spot rates . . . , the bias being a risk premium. . . . It is commonly assumed that risk premia increase monotonically at a decreasing rate with term to maturity.'[1] But if the *raison d'être* of the risk premium is risk aversion, then the premium cannot theoretically be a constant. It must itself be a function of such factors as the expected variance and co-variance with other assets of each bond, of the relationship between the supply of the various bonds and the number of investors with holding periods of a similar duration, i.e. of factors which influence the perceived risks of holding the differing bonds. In particular, the risk premia should, in theory, be a function of the relative supplies of the differing bonds.

The additional risk involved in any switch in the maturity distribution of an investor's bond portfolio will be a function of his own particular intended holding period(s) and cannot be ascertained without some indication of that; and investors have differing holding periods. If an investor with a long holding period holds a long bond he can be sure of its nominal value on maturity, and the income risk that he suffers from uncertainty about the rate at which he can re-invest any intermediary dividends – if the bond is not a pure discount bond – will be less than if he held short bonds and was re-investing both the capital and interest. On the other hand possible variations in expectations[2] of price inflation will lead to an increase in the risk (to the investor with a long holding period) of holding long bonds, because he could not retain the flexibility of switching between bonds and, say, real assets without considering premature sales, and thus run a capital risk on his long bonds. So a switch in the portfolio from shorter to longer bonds may, or may not, represent a reduction in risk for investors with long holding periods. For investors with short holding periods the avoidance of risk, whether of varying nominal or real returns, will be achieved by holding short rather than long bonds.

In any case, given risk aversion, investors would have to be tempted out of holding 'quasi-safe' assets, of a length approximately coincident to their holding period, by an offer of higher rates, to offset the assumption of additional risk. Depending on the degree of risk aversion, one would expect that relative rates on a given supply of stocks of differing maturities would be influenced by the distribution of holding periods among investors. At any time, if the supply of long-dated bonds was proportionately large relative to the frequency of investors with long holding periods, then the rate on long bonds would have to be higher relative to short rates to tempt risk-averse investors out of their safe shorter bonds. Indeed the basis for the introduction of liquidity premia was largely a belief in the existence of some such constitutional or congenital weakness of this kind in the long end of the market.[3] Nevertheless, this 'premium' cannot be treated as a constant; nor is it necessarily positive. Its size should depend on the ratio of the proportionate supply (from a given total supply of bonds) of bonds of a particular maturity to the proportion of investors with roughly that holding period.

How large would these risk premia have to be to tempt investors to switch? The answer to this question was set out, theoretically, in Chapter 2, Section B. The margin between the yield on the 'safe' or 'quasi-safe' asset and on a riskier asset should depend on the risk premium (a function of the investor's risk aversion) multiplied by a factor measuring the extra risk incurred by adding that particular asset to the overall portfolio. If most market operators are characterised by a considerable degree of risk aversion, the premium

---

[1] Consult R. S. Masera, *The Term Structure of Interest Rates* (Clarendon Press, Oxford, 1972) chap. 1, 'A Brief Survey of the Literature on the Term Structure,' sect. 1.6, 'The Hicksian Risk-Premium Model.'

[2] Note that 'in principle there ought to be different rates of expected inflation, according to the period of time over which the expectation is entertained,' R. Masera, 'Properties of a Monetarist Model for Economic Stabilization: Comment on Andersen,' from Proceedings of the First Konstanzer Seminar, Supplement to *Kredit und Kapital*, ed. K. Brunner (Duncker & Humblot, Berlin, 1972) pp. 127–36.

[3] See R. Masera, op. cit. appendix to chap. 1, and pp. 18–19.

required for them to shift from a roughly matching portfolio, with assets approximately equal in maturity[1] to liabilities or to expected contingent requirements, would have to be large. Nor is there much to be gained in the way of risk avoidance by diversifying the bond portfolio: in practice spot rates (and prices) of bonds tend to move quite closely together. With a high covariance between movements in spot rates (and prices) of bonds, the risk in holding differing bonds mainly depends on their own individual expected variance of return over the planned holding period.

So, assuming that the distribution of holding periods among all investors (weighted by funds available for investment) remains relatively constant in the short run,[2] variations in the proportions of bonds of different maturities supplied *ought* to cause fluctuations in relative yields in order to restore equilibrium. There are, therefore, two good reasons – differences in expectations, and risk aversion among investors with differing holding periods – why one *should* expect relative rates to be sensitive to changes in the balance between the supply of bonds of various maturities. In so far as these factors operate, the pure expectational theories of the term structure, relating the implicit forward rates (or implicit forward prices) that can be calculated from current spot rates entirely and directly to expectations about mean future expected rates (and/or future expected asset prices), with or without the addition of a constant term, should be deficient. When there is strong risk aversion, bonds of widely differing maturities will not be close substitutes. Aggregation in portfolio studies, over all such bonds irrespective of maturity, would then be inappropriate. Instead, investors should be regarded as having separate demand functions, possibly containing quite different arguments, for bonds of different maturities.

Some economists, for example Culbertson, have emphasised the extent of segmentation within the bond market that may occur from risk aversion among investors with disparate holding periods. Complete segmentation, however, implies extreme risk aversion, i.e. that investors would not be prepared to accept even a small additional risk in exchange for a large improvement in the mean expected rate of return. This sounds as, or more, implausible – and just as contrary to casual observation of normal behaviour – as the view that investors are completely indifferent to risk.

Moreover, the additional risk assumed when an investor with an n-year holding period shifts from holding a bond with a maturity of n years to one of $n + 1$ or $n - 1$ years is not very large, especially when n is already quite large. Adjacent bonds within the maturity

---

[1] The concept of maturity is not entirely straightforward for bonds which provide regular interest payments. When such coupon payments occur, each bond can be thought of as providing a whole set of separate payments at different maturities. In such cases, the 'duration' of the bond, which represents a weighted average of the maturities of the individual payments, with the weights normally being taken as the present value of the future payments, is a more appropriate statistic than its date of maturity. A bond with a larger coupon but a similar final maturity to another will have a shorter duration. See F. Macaulay, *Some Theoretical Problems Suggested by the Movements of Interest Rates, Bond Yields and Stock Prices in the United States since 1856*, publication no. 33, National Bureau of Economic Research (New York, 1938) chap. 2, and Masera, *The Term Structure of Interest Rates*, chap. 1, pp. 4–6.

[2] This assumption can be challenged. Cyclical variations in incomes and savings may cause considerable fluctuations in the relative flow of funds into differing savings media, particularly as between discretionary and contractual savings forms (e.g. insurance and pension funds). Funds deposited with life insurance companies are likely to be re-invested in longer-dated assets by the intermediary than funds deposited with savings banks. Thus variations in relative interest rates over the cycle could reflect cyclical fluctuations in the strength of supply, and of demand, of funds by risk-averse borrowers and lenders with very strong preferences for borrowing (lending) in each particular maturity segment. For arguments along these lines, see the work of J. M. Culbertson, e.g. 'The Term Structure of Interest Rates,' *Quarterly Journal of Economics*, vol. LXXI (November 1957), and 'The Interest Rate Structure: Towards Completion of the Classical System,' from *The Theory of Interest Rates*, ed. Hahn and Brechling (Macmillan, London, 1965) chap. 10.

spectrum should be relatively close substitutes and the prices on such bonds should move closely in concert. The degree, however, to which the prices on bonds move together, in response to a *similar* rate change on all maturities, depends on the maturities of the bonds. For a given change in rates, the potential price fluctuations for long-term bonds are roughly similar over a wide range of maturities, but the price fluctuations in short-term bonds will depend sensitively on the exact length of life. 'Hence, bonds of longer maturities, which are mathematically almost equivalent securities in terms of price responsiveness to changes in the level of interest rates, may plausibly be expected to be close substitutes whose yields would consequently be very similar. Conversely, in the short and intermediate range of the maturity spectrum, the extension of maturity even for a few years implies considerably different price risks and opportunities for capital gains.'[1]

Those factors causing a reassessment of current spot-bond rates and, by the same token, of forward implicit rates and forward implicit asset prices, factors such as changes in the pace of inflation, in political stability, in investment opportunities, in the state of the balance of payments, in monetary policy, would mostly seem likely to persist over a period of time, sometimes undergoing a permanent step change, sometimes a cyclical swing. Therefore the likelihood of a situation developing in which variations in expected forward short rates would be uncorrelated must be extremely low. The more variations in forward expected rates are positively correlated, the greater will be the covariance in spot-asset price movements.

Thus, unless there is a quite extraordinary degree of risk aversion in the bond market, asset prices especially at the longer end of the market and redemption yields on bonds of adjacent maturities are virtually bound to move closely together. This degree of substitution over any short range within the maturity spectrum implies that there should be continuous price adjustment throughout overlapping small segments over the whole spectrum, except perhaps at the very short end of the market, and that there would be little loss in aggregation over any narrow range; it does *not* imply that it is possible to aggregate over the whole spectrum. Thus, given risk aversion, a shift in the supply of long- relative to short-dated assets may have little effect on price relativities between two adjacent bonds but could, in principle, cause a large swing in relative rates at the extremes of the spectrum.

Most recent empirical analysis, following Meiselman[2] or Modigliani and Sutch,[3] has tended to concentrate on the relationship between rate movements at the very short end of the market, e.g. in Treasury bill rates, and changes in rates throughout the rest of the market, with the presumed line of causation running uni-directionally from changes in short rates through to changes in longer rates. There are several reasons for this. First, several of the studies, implicitly or explicitly, treat the holding period as equal in length to the maturity of the short asset. The yield on this asset then fixes the certain yield on the 'safe' asset against which prospective combinations of risk and return on the other bonds must be compared. Second, the rate on this short bond, or bill, is treated as determined largely by the actions of the monetary authorities, but in any case by economic factors, e.g. the rate of growth of the money stock relative to the rate of growth of prices and incomes. Given that this one rate is thus exogenously fixed, and that all other rates are linked to it via the pattern of expectations, the whole term structure then becomes a function of monetary policy in the broad sense.

---

[1] B. G. Malkiel, op. cit. p. 59, but see all of chap. 3.

[2] D. Meiselman, *The Term Structure of Interest Rates* (Prentice-Hall, Englewood Cliffs, N.J., 1962).

[3] F. Modigliani and R. C. Sutch, 'Innovations in Interest Rate Policy,' *The American Economic Review*, vol. 56, no. 2 (May 1966), papers and proceedings of the 78th A.E.A. meeting, pp. 178–97, and 'Debt Management and the Term Structure of Interest Rates: An Empirical Analysis of Recent Experience,' *Journal of Political Economy*, vol. 75 (1967) pp. 569–89, and F. Modigliani and R. J. Shiller, 'Inflation, Rational Expectations and the Term Structure of Interest Rates,' *Economica*, vol. XL, no. 157 (February 1973) pp. 12–42.

The implication is that other factors which might be expected to influence the pattern of rates directly, e.g. changes in rates on other assets such as real capital, which might be thought to be fairly close substitutes for bonds of similar maturities[1] or open-market operations by the authorities in longer-dated bonds, do not do so, except to the extent that they have some direct effect on the pattern of expectations. Rather, such factors are held to affect the term structure *indirectly* by altering the rates of growth of money incomes or of the money stock, and thus the bill rate. On such grounds expectation theorists have often advocated a monetary policy of 'Bills Only'[2] as more direct and effective than operations in longer bonds, where the market in the United States is anyhow less broad (so that the market's response to large-scale operations by the authorities would be less stable and less predictable).

To be sure, this is challenged by those who believe that risk aversion among investors with differing holding periods and differences in expectations are factors capable, in principle at least, of limiting the extent of substitution between bonds with far-apart maturities. On this latter view systematic disturbances to the pattern of relative rates and prices can be introduced at any point in the spectrum – not just at the short end – by a number of other factors, e.g. variations in rates on a range of other assets which might be substitutes for bonds of different maturities, such as real capital and equities at the long end and capital-certain assets, foreign Treasury bills, etc. at the short end. Adjustment to disturbances in rates can then travel in both directions, from long to short as well as vice-versa, through substitution between bonds of adjacent maturities.

Since there is not much doubt that bonds of adjacent maturities will be close substitutes[3] in portfolios except, perhaps, at the very short end of the market, movements in spot rates over any narrow range of maturities are likely to accord reasonably well with the expectations hypothesis. The interesting question is how rapidly, if at all, does the degree of substitution fade as one moves further along the spectrum. The association between movements in four- and six-year rates may be close, but is there also a close link between movements in four-year rates and twenty-year rates? Can one find other variables which also systematically affect this latter relationship,[4] such as changes in rates on other assets or shifts in the relative supplies of bonds? Are there any signs of breaks in the links of substitution along the spectrum, dividing the bond market into discernible segments?

---

[1] On this point see, in particular, A. Leijonhufvud, *On Keynesian Economics and the Economics of Keynes*, section III, 'The Aggregative Structure of Alternative Models,' pp. 111–87; this includes such statements as, 'In the Liquidity Preference theory, physical stores of value with a low rate of turnover are not good substitutes for those with a high rate of turnover, nor are long bonds good substitutes for short bonds. Obviously, then, short bonds cannot be close substitutes for long-lived capital goods,' and 'Keynes' assumption of a high elasticity of substitution between bonds and capital goods must consist of streams of approximately the same duration.' Quotations from p. 171.

[2] A short summary of the arguments involved in this issue and references to the extensive literature on the subject can be found in Masera, *The Term Structure of Interest Rates*, chap. 7, 'Short-run Implications of the Model,' pp. 195–204.

[3] Unless institutional intervention by the authorities prevents this. In the United Kingdom, for example, the authorities have designated certain short-term assets as reserve or liquid assets, which the banks have to maintain against their liabilities, while other, fairly comparable short-term assets have not been so designated. The result has been that any pressure by the authorities on the reserve-asset base of the banks causes a marked divergence between the rates on reserve assets which fall (or rise less) relative to the rates on non-reserve assets. Differing tax provisions can also lower the elasticity of substitution between bonds of similar maturities.

[4] The existence of other significant variables affecting the relationship between short rates and long rates is not, however, necessarily a refutation of the expectations hypothesis, since any variable which systematically affects the pattern of future expectations could shift the yield curve (in this theory) without involving any current adjustment in short rates. Nevertheless, if a range of other variables were shown to affect the shape of the term structure, the explanatory power of the pure expectations hypothesis and the ability to discriminate between it and other explanations of the term structure, involving some segmentation, would be reduced.

On such questions there is little alternative but to appeal to the facts. It is not the intention here to reproduce the empirical findings in any detail; nevertheless, the form and specification of the various econometric studies, most of them based on some version of the expectations theory, are of interest, and a short résumé of a number of the key studies is included in Appendix A (pp. 77–85). When there are a number of empirical studies, each specified in different ways using data from different countries over various time periods, it becomes difficult to assess the results. Nevertheless, given the possible strength of factors that might be expected to weaken the links of substitution between the short and long ends of the bond market, the extent to which expectational theories, mainly along the lines pioneered by Meiselman and Modigliani, have explained movements in the rate structure has been impressive and even surprising.

On the basis of their results it would be extremely difficult to deny that expectational factors play a major role in determining the term structure of interest rates. It is, however, much harder to establish beyond doubt that such expectations of future mean rates (and/or of future prices) of bonds are the *only* factors determining the shape of the yield curve.

Almost more surprising than the relative success of the pure expectational theories in explaining the term structure of rates has been the difficulty experienced by research workers in this field in finding evidence that shifts in the relative supply of different kinds of bond, or rates on other assets that might be substitutes for bonds of different maturities, or the degree of risk (as measured by the variance) on particular bonds, has had much effect on relative rates in the market.[1] One suggestion that has sometimes been advanced, in partial explanation of this negative finding, is that changes in relative rates between long and short bonds might cause compensating changes in the supply of bonds in the market, tending to restore the previous balance. 'The monetary authorities and private issuers are influenced by the structure of interest rates in determining what maturity of security to issue. Since the direction of causation works both ways, it is not appropriate to posit that changes in the relative supply of debt instruments cause changes in the relationship between short- and long-term interest rates. ... Since the supplies of debt instruments depend on a fairly complicated set of relationships ... it is not surprising that the specification of an identifiable supply equation has thus far proved elusive.'[2]

In the United States, where most of these empirical studies have been made, the volume of private-sector debt in a form closely similar to public-sector debt is relatively large and the available data on such debt are 'extremely crude'.[3] Thus it is possible that observed variations in the outstanding maturities of public-sector debt in the United States have been a most inadequate proxy for variations in total supplies of differing maturities of relatively default-free debt. Indeed, if companies were risk-neutral (and all had similar expectations) any variation in relative yields away from the pattern determined by their expectations of future mean rates would cause a readjustment from the supply side sufficient to force market prices into line with expectations, irrespective of the behaviour of possibly more risk-averse investors.

In practice, however, one would expect companies to be just as risk averse as individuals, or more so (see the further discussion of this in Chapter 5). If so, it would require an even

---

[1] See, for example, Malkiel, *The Term Structure of Interest Rates*, chap. 8; Modigliani and Sutch, 'Innovations in Interest Rate Policy,' *The American Economic Review* (May 1966) especially p. 191; W. R. White, 'The Term Structure of Interest Rates – A Cross-Section Test of a Mean-Variance Model,' a paper presented at the Bournemouth Money Study Group Conference (February 1972) proceedings to be published by the Oxford University Press, under the title *Issues in Monetary Economics*, ed. R. Nobay and H. Johnson; W. Nordhaus and H. Wallich, 'Alternatives for Debt Management' (especially Table 2), a paper given at the Federal Reserve Bank of Boston Conference on 'Issues in Federal Debt Management' (June 1973).

[2] Malkiel, op. cit. p. 225.

[3] Ibid. p. 222.

larger incentive in terms of relative expected returns to get companies to shift their pre-ferred pattern of financing. Moreover, the transactions costs of new debenture issues are relatively large, so that it is often cheaper for companies to stick to established channels of finance.[1]

Furthermore in the United Kingdom, as contrasted with the United States, the size of the market for public-sector debt overshadows the market in company debentures.[2] Operations by the authorities in public-sector debt here largely determine variations in the maturity structure of the whole outstanding debt. Of course, one of the authorities' con-cerns is to minimise the cost of the National Debt to the Exchequer, so that the issue of new stock in the various maturity ranges will not be entirely independent of the ruling rate structure. But the authorities have usually maintained tap stocks on offer regularly at the relatively short and relatively long end of the market (the market for medium-term issues in the range five to fifteen years being regarded as constitutionally weaker), and the keenness of the authorities to make sales of such virtually continuous taps has, in the main, been influenced by more pressing factors than a desire to minimise expected interest costs over time to the Treasury. Thus conditions for examining the effect of changes in the supply of debt of various maturities upon the shape of the yield curve seem more propitious in the United Kingdom than in the United States. Nevertheless, there is little evidence of any more obvious effect of changes in supply conditions upon the pattern of relative rates in the United Kingdom than in the United States. A study of the effect of such supply factors underway in the Bank of England has so far produced mainly negative conclusions.

All told, the evidence to date in favour of close substitution between bonds, irrespective of differences in maturity, on the basis of expectations of mean rates of return, and against segmentation, owing to the existence of risk-averse investors with differing holding-periods and diverse expectations, seems surprisingly strong.

APPENDIX A

Some Empirical Studies of the Term Structure of Interest Rates

Early studies of the expectations hypothesis compared the implicit forward rates, which can be calculated from the pattern of current spot rates, with the actual rates that later occurred in the market, i.e. they compared $_{t+k}r_{n,t}$ with $R_{n,t+k}$. These studies generally showed that the predictive power of the implicit forward rates was quite weak.[3] This was not, however, a conclusive test of the expectations theory, since it remained possible for the

---

[1] For example, in 1970–2 in the United Kingdom there seemed to be a considerable rate advan-tage for companies offering debentures with a ten-year life in place of the customary twenty-five-to thirty-year debenture. In the event few companies took advantage of this apparent opportunity since there was not such a broad market in medium-term company debentures, so that the extra transactions costs nullified the rate advantages.

[2] The figures are as follows:
U.K. debt quoted on London Stock Exchange, nominal value, £ million

	Outstanding stock		New issues (gross cash raised)		
	Central govt	Company sector	Central govt		Company sector
March 1965	16,648	2500*	1968	681	304
March 1970	21,569	5502	1969	766	425
			1970	1635	270

  * Estimated.

[3] See the studies quoted by Masera, op. cit. p. 16, footnote 21.

current structure of rates and asset prices to be determined entirely by current expectations, even if these expectations should subsequently be proved erroneous.[1]

In his study on *The Term Structure of Interest Rates*,[2] Meiselman brilliantly developed the expectations hypothesis, side-stepping the complications inherent in comparing inferred expectations with future outcomes, by reformulating it in terms of a systematic process of revising expectations. He put forward the hypothesis that expected future short-term rates would be systematically revised on the basis of errors made in forecasting the current short-term rate: '*changes* in, rather than *levels* of interest rates can be related to factors which systematically cause *revisions of expectations*.'[3] On this basis he constructed an error-learning model of the form (using the notation already introduced on p. 69)

$$_{t+n}r_{1,t} - {}_{t+n}r_{1,t-1} = f_n(R_{1,t} - {}_tr_{1,t-1}) \qquad n = 1, 2, \ldots$$

where $R_{1,t} - {}_tr_{1,t-1}$ is the error (E) between last period's forecast of the current one-year rate and its actual value, and $_{t+n}r_{1,t} - {}_{t+n}r_{1,t-1}$ is the revision to the one-year implicit forward rate occurring at $t + n$ between last period and now. One contentious point is worth noting, that revisions to all forward rates are the result of errors only in forecasting the shortest rate, not in any errors of prediction elsewhere in the market.

He tested a linear version of this relationship against the data, of the form

$$_{t+n}r_{1,t} - {}_{t+n}r_{1,t-1} = a + bE_t + u$$

where u is a stochastic error term. If 'a' was non-zero it would imply that forward implicit rates changed over time, even if there was no 'error' in forecasting current short rates, and this might be taken as evidence for the existence of liquidity premia.[4] However, the converse, that 'a' = 0 would show that there were no such premia, did not hold, as was shown by Kessel and Wood.[5] Since the one-year forward implicit short rate $_tr_{1,t-1}$ could itself incorporate a liquidity premium, the calculated 'error' could be partially a true 'error' and partially represent the unwinding of a liquidity premium. In practice, most empirical studies using Meiselman's approach have found that 'a' is not significantly different from zero. These studies have also shown that the value of 'b' usually varies between 1 and 0, dropping towards 0 (as does also the value of the correlation coefficient) as n rises.

One may next ask whether revising expectations in the manner hypothesised by Meiselman is an optimal method of forecasting, whether 'investors' expectations are equivalent with the optimal forecasts of statistical theory for a certain specified class of statistical models'.[6] If the expectations theory is to hold, and all available information is to be used efficiently, it must not be possible to predict that an implicit forward rate will itself be

---

[1] If the errors could, however, be shown to be systematic and not just random, it would throw doubt on the expectations hypothesis, since rational investors should use past experience to eliminate systematic errors from forward predictions: the market expectation of any relevant variable should represent the best forecast that could be made of that variable, on the basis of all the information available at the time of the forecast. See J. F. Muth, 'Rational Expectations and the Theory of Price Movements,' *Econometrica*, vol. 29 (1961) pp. 315–35.

[2] Prentice-Hall, Englewood Cliffs, N.J., 1962.

[3] Meiselman, op. cit. p. 18.

[4] Predictable, systematic changes in forward rates would not, however, be consistent with a rational, efficient market. See T. Sargent, 'Rational Expectations and the Term Structure of Interest Rates,' *Journal of Money, Credit and Banking*, vol. 4, no. 1 (February 1972) pp. 74–97, especially p. 77.

[5] R. Kessel, *The Cyclical Behavior of the Term Structure of Interest Rates*, Occasional Paper 91, N.B.E.R. (New York, 1965) pp. 16ff. and J. Wood, 'Expectations, Errors, and the Term Structure of Interest Rates,' *Journal of Political Economy*, vol. 71, no. 2 (April 1963).

[6] Sargent, op. cit. p. 74

changing in a systematic manner over time.[1] Sargent shows that 'Meiselman's equations are implied when things are restricted a bit more than they need to be [to satisfy the above condition]'.[2] However, his empirical tests suggest that the values of b actually found are too low to be fully consistent with the expectations hypothesis in an efficient market.[3] And his conclusion on the basis of his several tests is that, 'The evidence ... implies that it is difficult to maintain both that *only* expectations determine the yield curve *and* that expectations are rational in the sense of efficiently incorporating available information'.[4]

Since implicit forward rates are all derived from present spot rates, the error-learning model can be restated in terms of a difference of a function of spot rates at time t and a function of spot rates at time $t - 1$.[5] There might, therefore, be a danger that the positive correlations observed from Meiselman's model could simply be a function of the tendency of spot rates to move in concert rather than a confirmation of his specific hypothesis about the formation of expectations. This possibility may be tested by comparing Meiselman's model with a simpler model of the form

$$\Delta_{t+n}r_{1,t} = f(\Delta_t R_{1,t})$$

i.e. that the current change in the calculated implicit one-year rate, expected to rule in $t + n$ years, is a function of the actual change in current one-year rates.

---

[1] This implies that forward rates must follow a martingale; a sequence

$$\{x_t, x_{t+1}, x_{t+2}, \ldots\}$$

is said to follow a martingale if

$$E(x_{t+1}/x_t, x_{t-1}, x_{t-2}, \ldots) = x_t;$$

the above requirement thus implies that

$$\{_{t+j}r_t, {}_{t+j}r_{t+1}, \ldots, {}_{t+j}r_{t+j-1}, R_{t+j}\}$$

follows a martingale. See Sargent, ibid. pp. 75–6.

[2] Ibid. p. 75 and section II, pp. 76–85.

[3] Ibid. p. 93, 'It has also been noted that Durand's one-year spot rates seem to be adequately approximated by a first-order autoregressive process. Thus for the period 1905–54, the following regression was obtained by the method of least squares:

$$R_t = 0 \cdot 2073 + 0 \cdot 9278 R_{t-1}$$
$$(0 \cdot 1995) \quad (0 \cdot 0544)$$

$$R_A^2 = 0 \cdot 8554$$

Including additional lagged Rs resulted in a drop in the adjusted R^2.

'... If the above equation is accepted as an adequate description of spot rates, then under the hypothesis of rational expectations $\hat{B}_1$ ought to have an expected value of about 0·93. Meiselman's estimate is only 0·703. ... The difference between them should be taken seriously.'

[4] Ibid. p. 94.

[5] From the relationship

$$(1 + {}_{t+n}r_{1,t}) = \frac{(1 + R_{n+1,t})^{n+1}}{(1 + R_{n,t})^n}$$

the error-learning model can be rearranged as

$$\left[\left\{ \frac{(1 + R_{n+1,t})^{n+1}}{(1 + R_{n,t})^n} - 1 \right\} - \left\{ \frac{(1 + R_{n+2,t-1})^{n+2}}{(1 + R_{n+1,t-1})^{n+1}} - 1 \right\} \right] = f_n \left[R_{1,t} - \left\{ \frac{(1 + R_{2,t-1})^2}{(1 + R_{1,t-1})} - 1 \right\} \right]$$

See Masera, op. cit. p. 133.

The contrast with Meiselman's model can be seen by noting that

$$\Delta_t R_{1,t} \neq R_{1,t} -_{t,} r_{1,t-1}$$

that is, the actual change from year to year in the one-year rate is not equal to the 'forecasting error' (E_t).

This latter model is usually described as an 'inertia' model: it implies simply that all rates tend to move together. When the two alternative models are directly compared, e.g. by Masera,[1] Meiselman's model usually gives a better fit, which suggests that his particular expectational hypothesis has some real predictive power in comparison with the null hypothesis that all rates tend, for whatever reasons, to move together.

A serious complication in testing any model which seeks to examine the relationship between implicit forward rates and actual market developments is that, in practice, implicit forward rates can only rarely be deduced directly from actual spot market rates and prices. There are often gaps in the maturity spectrum between adjacent bonds. Some bonds have peculiar call provisions. More important still, bonds generally bear differing coupon rates. This would in any case complicate rate and price comparisons, but these difficulties are often exacerbated by tax conditions, whose impost may vary both between interest income and realised capital gain and between different kinds of investor in the market.

The result has been that empirical studies using this kind of approach have tended to have two parts: first, a continuous yield curve is estimated from the scatter of actual market rates, and second, the test of the hypothesis is carried out on the estimated yield curve. As illustration, Fig. 4.2 shows the actual scatter of yields to redemption on government bonds and the yield curve calculated[2] by the Bank of England on 29 December 1972. Unfortunately the results of this second test are not independent of the methods employed to obtain the yield curve.[3] In general, construction of yield curves by freehand or by fitting some low-order polynomial curve imposes a continuous, smooth curve upon the scatter of rate observations. But the imposition of such a smooth curve of itself implies a continuous regular process of adjustment and substitution along the spectrum. Thus any test of the expectations hypothesis, however subtle in formulation, based on an artificially constructed yield curve rather than the raw data, must be suspect of serious favourable bias.

Indeed, this whole approach of constructing an *ad hoc* smoothed yield curve from the raw data and then applying a complex hypothesis to it is dubious. The need, instead, is to devise a term-structure model that will incorporate, *inter alia*, coupon and tax effects in order to explain the raw data. Then, having tested the whole model against the raw data,

---

[1] Masera, op. cit. pp. 131–5.

[2] This curve shows the yield that would have to be offered on a new stock at each maturity which was to be sold at par. When interest rates have been rising the par yield curve will lie above the yields on existing redeemable stocks, since their yield to maturity includes a sizeable capital appreciation which is taxed on more favourable terms than interest income.

For an account of the method used to fit this curve, see the paper by J. P. Burman and W. R. White, 'Yield Curves for Gilt-edged Stocks,' *Bank of England Quarterly Bulletin*, vol. 12, no. 4 (December 1972) pp. 467–86; and by J. P. Burman, 'Yield Curves for Gilt-edged Stocks: Further Investigation,' *Bank of England Quarterly Bulletin*, vol. 13, no. 3 (September 1973) pp. 315–26.

[3] For example, economists found very different results when applying Meiselman's model to U.K. data depending on the method employed to fit yield curves. The more angular interpolations used by J. Grant gave worse fitting results than the technique (of multiple regression) used by D. Fisher or the freehand curves adopted by A. Buse; see their various articles on this subject in *Economica*, as follows: Grant, 'Meiselman on the Structure of Interest Rates: A British Test,' vol. 31, no. 121 (February 1964) pp. 51–71; Fisher, 'The Structure of Interest Rates: A Comment' – Grant, 'A Reply,' vol. 31, no. 124 (November 1964) pp. 412–22; Fisher, 'Expectations, The Term Structure of Interest Rates, and Recent British Experience,' vol. 33, no. 131 (August 1966) pp. 319–29; Buse, 'The Structure of Interest Rates and Recent British Experience: A Comment' – Fisher, 'Reply,' vol. 34, no. 135 (August 1967) pp. 298–313.

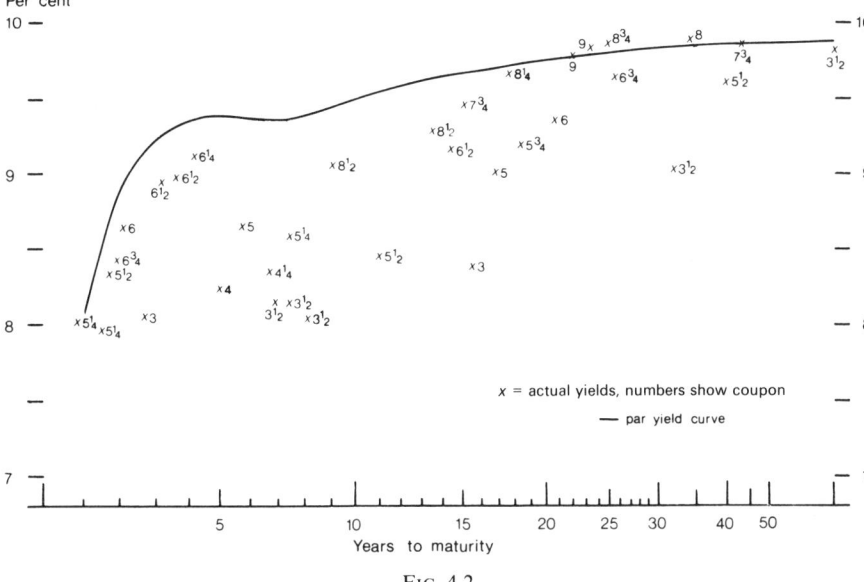

FIG. 4.2

a yield curve could be derived that predicts the differences in yield between maturities required to take account of expectations and risk, but abstracts from coupon and tax effects. This can be done: a yield curve obtained in this manner is currently published by the Bank of England,[1] showing the yield that would need to be offered on a newly issued bond priced at par, if it was to be in line with the market.

Despite the probably favourable bias imparted by testing the expectations hypothesis against an artificially smoothed yield curve, in some studies Meiselman's model has not provided a very good fit, with the values of 'b' and of the correlation coefficients declining rapidly as n increases.[2]

Masera attributes this relatively poor fit, at least in the Italian case, to the restrictive assumption that all revisions to future expectations are based on the 'error' in forecasting only the current short rate. Each investor, in a world of uncertainty, even though he may not be risk averse, must be aware that his own ability to forecast future short rates with any accuracy into the dim, distant future is so slight as to make the exercise hardly worth the effort involved. Investors, therefore, will have to make up their minds about short-term future price movements on long-term bonds, independently of unpredictable movements in long-term forward short rates. This suggests that an error-learning process might involve a revision of expectations of the rate (price) of each bond in response to previous errors in forecasting *its own* rate (price). Masera, therefore, tests a model of the form[3]

$$_{t+1}R^e_{n,t} - {_{t+1}}R^e_{n,t-1} = a_n + b_n(R_{n,t} - {_t}R^e_{n,t-1}) + u_{n,t} \qquad n = 1, 2, \ldots$$

[1] See the paper by J. P. Burman and W. R. White, 'Yield Curves for Gilt-edged Stocks,' *Bank of England Quarterly Bulletin*, vol. 12, no. 4 (December 1972) pp. 467–86.

[2] For example, in Masera's study of the Italian experience in *The Term Structure of Interest Rates*, pp. 131–5.

[3] Masera, op. cit. p. 167.

where R_n^e is the expected n-year rate. Masera's model incorporates, therefore, a combination of the expectations model with the amendment suggested by Malkiel and Luckett[1] that the relevant expectations relate to short-term future changes in rates (prices) on long bonds, rather than to long-term future changes in short rates.

Although Masera may well be right that Meiselman's assumption about the process of revising expectations – on the basis of 'errors' in forecasting the current short rate – is too restrictive, his alternative model also provides a less stringent test than Meiselman's of the expectations hypothesis. In Masera's model an n-year rate, say to be concrete a twenty-year rate, is determined by the current one-year rate and the nineteen-year rate expected to hold next year, which in turn has been revised in the light of the previous year's error in forecasting the current nineteen-year rate. So the forecasts for each future bond price (for each long-term rate expected to hold next year) appear to depend on errors in forecasting the previous movements in only that one price (long-term rate) in the latest period. The links between the revisions to the forecasts for the prices (rates) on the various bonds of differing maturities appear much weaker than in Meiselman's model. The possible degree of independence in the movement of prices of bonds of differing maturities, which Masera's model appears to allow, seems hardly consistent with the emphasis on the close substitution between bonds of all maturities inherent in the expectations hypothesis.

Suppose, for example, that the relative supply of short and long bonds altered, or that rates on assets which were substitutes for long bonds changed, thus causing longer rates to rise while short rates remained unchanged. Previous forecasts of long rates, e.g. for the nineteen-year rate, would presumably be found to be underpredictions, so forecasts of future long rates would be revised upwards. Masera's model would probably fit the actuals quite well, even though the systematic factor causing the change could be described as a structural rather than an expectational phenomenon. In short, Masera's model is too general; it is likely to give a good fit in most cases irrespective of differences in the underlying behavioural characteristics determining the shape of the term structure; in particular it is doubtful whether it can discriminate sharply between 'expectational' and 'structural' explanations of the determination of the term structure.

Masera rejected Meiselman's assumption that all expectations were revised in the light of errors in forecasting the short-term rate, but retained his empirical method of basing his study of revisions in expectations on the implicit forward rates calculated from the constructed yield curves. Modigliani, with Sutch and Shiller, did the reverse, retaining the assumption that expectations of long rates were revised in the light of changes in present, and past, short rates, but abandoning the use of calculated implicit forward rates. In some part Modigliani has, therefore, been able to get away from reliance on artificially constructed yield curves, implicit forward rates, *et hoc genus omne*, by concentrating only on the relationship between two actual points on the yield curve, a short rate and a long rate, and abstracting from all intermediate rates.

Modigliani, however, retains the traditional expectational hypothesis that long rates are a function of expected future short rates, plus a constant term or liquidity premium, depending on the 'preferred habitat' of investors, and believes that these expectations are generated from present and past short rates by a combination of extrapolative and regressive responses. A relationship of this kind for predicting long rates should, however, be able to predict all intermediate rates as well, or better, since the strength of this chain principle of forecasting[2] can be no stronger than its weakest link. Until it is demonstrated

---

[1] Malkiel, *The Term Structure of Interest Rates*, especially chap. 3; Luckett, 'Multi-Period Expectations and the Term Structure of Interest Rates,' *Quarterly Journal of Economics* (May 1967).

[2] See Modigliani and Shiller, 'Inflation, Rational Expectations and the Term Structure of Interest Rates,' *Economica* (February 1973) p. 14.

that his model can also explain all intermediate rates,[1] one should remain sceptical of the explanatory power of a regression linking a single short rate with a single long rate to illuminate the underlying behaviour that determines the shape of the whole term structure.

Given that all interest rates do tend to move together for whatever reason, and that the use of flexible lag operators allows the research worker to test a very wide range of relationships to find the best statistical fit between series, it is not surprising to find a high correlation in such an exercise, though the stability of Modigliani's relationships outside the fitted period has been impressive. On the other hand his equations, like many others in this field, have suffered from autocorrelation of the residuals and Modigliani now claims that this is mainly due to the omission of a significant variable, in this case the expected rate of inflation.[2] This is plausible, but it does complicate and obscure the theoretical simplicity of the pure expectations theory. Apart from the difficulty of untangling the inter-relationships between inflation, current and past short rates, and expected future rates, it allows one to query why all sorts of other economic forces, such as balance-of-payments fears, changes in rates on other assets, etc., might not also have an independent effect on future expectations beyond their effect on current and past short rates.

Moreover, this observed autocorrelation could be a sign that the supposed significance of some of the coefficients in the regression could be exaggerated. Hamburger[3] claims that, when the regression is run with transformed variables to eliminate the autocorrelation, the coefficients on past short rates become insignificant. He argues, furthermore, that in a rational efficient market one should not be able to predict near-future changes in long rates (in bond prices) from past movements in short rates since use of this knowledge would provide the smart investor with capital gains from switching; in a rational efficient market all such opportunities should be competed away. Indeed, a number of recent empirical studies on the relationship between interest-rate series have suggested that, after the series have been appropriately transformed to eliminate their autoregressive properties, the only really strong relationship between them is synchronous with little sign of significant lag relationships.[4]

One weakness common to all the expectational theories relating movements in long rates to expectations of future short rates is that they imply that investors act as if they formulate specific views about future short rates *n* years into the future. As introspection informs us, uncertainty about the future is so dense that attempts to forecast movements in short rates more than, say, five years into the future are simply not worth the effort. Yet the implication of the approach, as used by Modigliani and many others, is that an investor buying consols must work out for himself mean expected short rates, 'every day from today until Kingdom come'.[5]

---

[1] Moreover, observation of periods when the yield curve has not been monotonically increasing or declining, e.g. when there have been 'humps' in the middle ranges, suggests that a statistical relationship of this kind between two distant points on the yield curve may on occasions not give a good fit to intermediary points.

[2] Modigliani and Shiller, op. cit. sect. II, pp. 19–28.

[3] See his paper on 'Expectations, Long-Term Interest Rates and Monetary Policy in the United Kingdom,' *Bank of England Quarterly Bulletin*, vol. 11, no. 3 (September 1971) pp. 354–71, especially p. 359; also M. Hamburger and E. Platt, 'The Expectations Hypothesis and the Efficiency of the Treasury Bill Market' (mimeo, Federal Reserve Bank of New York, 1973).

[4] See, for example, T. Cargill and R. Meyer, 'A Spectral Approach To Estimating the Distributed Lag Relationship Between Long- and Short-Term Interest Rates,' *International Economic Review*, vol. 13, no. 2 (June 1972) pp. 223–38. Also Sargent, op. cit. sect. III B, pp. 87–91, and V. Smith and R. Marcis, 'A Time Series Analysis of Post Accord Interest Rates,' *The Journal of Finance*, vol. 27, no. 3 (June 1972) pp. 589–606. These studies were done on U.S. data, but exactly similar results are also found in the United Kingdom, according to a study under way in the Bank of England.

[5] Joan Robinson, 'The Rate of Interest,' *Econometrica*, vol. 19 (1951) p. 102.

As already noted, a common response to this pertinent criticism has been to reformulate the expectational theory in terms of expectations of future short-term movements in bond prices, rather than of long-term movements in short rates. In conditions of certainty there is, of course, no real difference between these two alternatives; and even under conditions of uncertainty, the relationship between bond prices now may be largely a function of expected future rates, i.e. of the re-investment rates expected to rule in future years. What then is the basic difference between these alternative versions of the expectations theories? Essentially, I believe, it resides in the way the acceptance of uncertainty as a characteristic of the real world colours the view of theorists who adopt this approach, such as Malkiel, Luckett, Masera, W. R. White.

We have already seen that Masera argues that in these conditions revisions to forecasts of the future n-year rate predicted to occur next year will depend not just on errors in forecasting the one-year rate, but also on previous errors in forecasting the n-year rate itself. Malkiel suggests[1] that in conditions of uncertainty people will expect future interest-rate fluctuations to be bounded within some normal range which has existed in the past. Depending on the size of this range, this limits the extent to which changes in current short rates can lead to a revision of future expected short rates and bond prices. In effect, this constrains the Meiselman relationship between changes in current short rates and revisions to expectations of future short rates. As short rates rise, revisions to expectations of future short rates will pull long rates above the middle of the range for the normal (average) expected long rate, but as the actual long rate approaches the upper bounds, set by past experience, increases in current short rates should have increasingly less impact on future expected short rates (vice versa for falls in short rates). This relationship between short and long rates should really be non-linear, but Malkiel tests a linear approximation of the form, $L - S = a + b(L - L_A)$, where S is the short rate, L the long rate, and L_A is a moving average of past long rates, i.e. a proxy for the market's opinion of a 'normal' long rate. This suggests that the balance between extrapolative and regressive expectations arising from a *change* in current short rates may be affected by the relationship between the current *level* of short rates and previous historical levels of rates. It may be true, as a psychological norm, that the more people penetrate into the unknown the greater their regressive expectations for a return to the range of historical experience, but one would like to see confirmation from studies of other markets and other circumstances that the psychological foundations for this view were firmly based.

A more plausible, and intuitively attractive, constraint on forward short rates in the face of uncertainty has recently formed the centrepiece of the model of the term structure developed by W. R. White and J. P. Burman at the Bank of England. The starting-point of their analysis is the belief that investors do *not* have the information to make useful forecasts of rate movements beyond some horizon, and are fully aware of that plain fact. In this state of ignorance the simplest and best that they can do is to assume that future short rates beyond this horizon will be constant. This implies that the future yield curve would be horizontal – subject to possible liquidity premia – at the horizon, which fixes expected bond prices then. So long as the holding period is as long as, or longer than, the horizon, investors will, subject to possible risk aversion, adjust their holdings and thus alter current prices until the yield on all bonds between now and the horizon is equal. Thus the price of each bond is a function of the expected yield (and level of prices) expected at the horizon, the length of time from now till the horizon, the relative risk on each bond, the coupon on each bond, tax considerations, and the weight of differing kinds of investors

---

[1] Malkiel, op. cit. chaps 3 and 4.

[2] W. R. White, 'The Term Structure of Interest Rates – A Cross-Section Test of a Mean-Variance Model,' *Issues in Monetary Economics* (forthcoming), and Burman and White, 'Yield Curves for Gilt-edged Stocks,' *Bank of England Quarterly Bulletin* (December 1972).

in the market, who will place a different value on interest income and prospective capital gains, depending on their various tax positions. The raw data on the current price of each bond (excluding those with unusual call provisions) can then be used to calculate the values of these parameters which provide the best fit to the scatter of bond prices.

The advantages of this model are considerable. It is firmly based on a plausible interpretation of investor reactions to uncertainty. The model is fitted from the raw data, allowing coupon and tax effects to be directly estimated, so that the resulting yield curve is derived, not imposed. The model fitted the data comparatively well but empirical work with this model on U.K. data, however, showed that the fit could be considerably improved if the bond market was segmented into two parts, a long market consisting of bonds with over five years till maturity, for which a horizon of three to four years was found to be satisfactory, and a short market for bonds with a life between one and five years with a horizon of one year.[1] Apart from the resulting improvement to the fit, this division is of interest as providing one of the few statistical indications of segmentation in the bond market. Such segmentation is presumably largely owing to the existence of risk-averse investors with differing holding periods, but attempts to take risk factors into account directly did not prove very successful. The main problem was due to multicollinearity between future rates at the horizon and risk. Thus a low price on long bonds relative to short bonds could be equally well explained by expectations of higher future rates or by aversion to risk.

Besides this fact that the relative effects of certain of the factors influencing the term structure could not be clearly distinguished from each other, the parameters thrown up by estimating the best statistical fit to the raw data at each point of time remain, as yet, just numbers. Thus, using this technique one can estimate that the best fit at time t implies an expected yield of, say, x per cent at an horizon y years hence, but this still leaves the task of providing a theoretical justification for the levels and changes in the values of the statistically deduced parameters. The values obtained by statistical fitting may be 'plausible', but one would ideally prefer to see a more closely argued rationale for the values of, and the imposition of more *a priori* constraints on, the parameters; for example, by limiting the extent of change in their values from observation to observation, even at the expense of a less close fit.

In a sense White and Burman have reversed the basic assumptions of the traditional expectations theories. These latter assume, often implicitly, that the horizon over which the investor can make useful forecasts is infinite, while the normal holding period, in so far as risk aversion is considered at all, is taken to be quite short. White and Burman, instead, assume the forecasting horizon to be short and treat the average holding period as relatively long.

Investor behaviour under conditions of uncertainty cannot be deduced from abstract reasoning. The studies, reported here, do seem to show that expectations play a major part in determining the term structure – and supply factors a surprisingly minor role. But how these expectations are formed, over what future period they apply and how they are revised remain uncertain. Perhaps more light could be thrown on this issue by direct studies of investor behaviour than by examination of *ex post* market data.

---

[1] These segments are not well defined and local arbitrage ensures that the yield curve remains continuous (and differentiable); so, in practice, the short and long segments are spliced over the range four to eight years.

5

Some Aspects of Company Financial Behaviour

SUMMARY

In this chapter we begin by analysing the distinctive role of companies as that of organising factors of production in joint team processes. Many of these factors, particularly capital, are specific in form. This characteristic often makes the investment decision irreversible, and this affects the form of the investment function. In particular, expectations of future outcomes will be crucial. These subjective expectations may be very diverse, providing a further reason for firms to hold financial assets to finance investment when outsiders are unduly pessimistic.

We then, in Section B, turn to the question of the optimal structure for the firm's financial liabilities. This subject was thrown into contention by the conclusions of Modigliani and Miller that, under quite a wide range of conditions, the structure of liabilities did not matter. The two main requirements are that there should be no relative tax effects and no chance of bankruptcy. Following two papers by Stiglitz – this passage is not easy – we examine both these conditions, tax effects and bankruptcy effects, more closely. The latter, the possibility of bankruptcy is the more important and has a pervasive effect on firms' behaviour.

A. Information, Expectations and Company Behaviour

There are many participant members, taking several different institutional forms, e.g. firms, persons, partnerships, etc., in any economy. If we tried to specify the reactions of each of them, in order to examine the response of the economy as a whole to some disturbance, the scale of the analysis would become impossibly large. In the last chapter we noted that, in order to keep the analysis manageable, it was necessary to aggregate over groups of assets; similarly it is necessary to aggregate over certain groups of members in the economy. Again the objective is to do this in such a way that variations *within* the chosen aggregates are relatively unimportant compared with variations *between* them in determining the variables, here the development of the economy as a whole, under consideration.

From the start, in Chapter 1, we have emphasised the distinction between the government, more broadly the public sector, and the private sector.[1] Does it help, for the purpose of analysing the economy, to disaggregate the private sector any further? The answer to

---

[1] In particular the constraints on the economic actions of the government are quite different from those imposed on members of the private sector. Individuals and firms within the private sector are restrained by budget constraints; because of their power to issue legal tender, governments are not; instead they face political constraints. Moreover, the existence of a separate government provides the main basis for the subsequent division between 'domestic' and 'foreign' economies, for individual countries, or economies, are essentially those with independent governments.

this is not so clear: in many models it has not been thought necessary. On the other hand the national-income statistics, which presumably are arranged in order to reflect the crucial conceptual and practical distinctions within the economy, usually show further divisions within the private sector, in so far as the data allow, between the corporate[1] and the personal sectors.

This division between the corporate and the personal sectors raises two further questions. First, why do firms, as an institution, exist at all, and secondly, what are the critical behavioural differences between firms and persons that makes it worthwhile making this distinction for purposes of economic analysis? It is, perhaps, something of a digression to consider the raison d'être of firms, but the interesting point to note is the similarity between the theories of the institutional functions of both money and the firm, both being based on informational requirements under conditions of uncertainty.

It was pointed out by Coase[2] that the operations centralised within a firm could, in principle, all be undertaken through markets in a decentralised manner. He argued that the organisation of a firm allowed factors to be combined together in many circumstances more cheaply and more efficiently than via market transactions. Basically this is because the development of specialised information within the firm reduces the costs of internal organisation relative to the costs, which largely derive from imperfect information, of market transactions. This idea has now been extended and developed by Alchian and Demsetz,[3] who claim that the information most difficult to obtain through the market would be the measurement of the marginal productivity (and hence setting the appropriate payment) of individuals combining together in joint team production. Because it may be difficult and costly to meter the contribution to the joint product of each separate member of the team, each member would have an incentive to shirk, i.e. to substitute leisure for effort, since part of the cost in reduced output would fall on other members of the team. Each member of the team would be under the same incentive to shirk, but each would wish the other members of the team to be faced with the true rate of substitution between their output and leisure in calculating their payments. The solution to this problem is for one of the team to specialise in obtaining information on the actual performance of the various other members of the team so that greater productivity can be rewarded or shirking penalised.[4] This man, who selects, organises and monitors the team, is its manager.[5]

---

[1] Within the corporate sector banks and other financial intermediaries are, for some purposes, further distinguished and shown as separate sectors. Discussion of the role of these intermediaries appears in the following two chapters.

[2] R. H. Coase, 'The Nature of the Firm,' *Economica*, vol. IV (November 1937) pp. 386–405.

[3] 'Production, Information Costs, and Economic Organisation,' *American Economic Review*, vol. LXII, no. 5 (December 1972) pp. 777–95. A number of other economists in the field have also emphasised that the development and monitoring of internal information flows plays a crucial role in determining the structure of the firm. See, for example, R. Marris, 'Why Economics Needs a Theory of the Firm,' *The Economic Journal*, vol. 82, no. 325 (supplement) (March 1972) pp. 321–52, and O. Williamson, 'Managerial Discretion, Organisation Form, and the Multi-division Hypothesis,' in *The Corporate Economy*, ed. R. Marris and A. Wood, chap. 11.

[4] 'Managing, or examining, the ways to which inputs are used in team production is a method of metering the marginal productivity of individual inputs to the team's output,' Alchian and Demsetz, ibid. p. 782.

[5] Clearly the ability and efforts of the manager will be crucial in determining the success of the team as a whole. But how is he in turn going to be kept from shirking, since the resulting output losses would also partly fall on other members of the team? One way to give the manager an incentive to perform his function thoroughly is to offer him partial or complete 'title to the net earnings of the team, net of payments to other inputs,' Alchian and Demsetz, ibid. p. 782. The position of being the residual claimant to the net proceeds of the company's activities should normally suffice to ensure the best efforts of the manager. In practice, however, the growth in the size of companies, the desire among wealth owners to avoid risk by limiting their liability in any single enterprise and

(*Footnote* [5] *continued over*)

In theory a manager should be able to hire all his inputs, capital and land, as well as labour, and therefore ought to be able to operate with only a relatively small working capital to span the period between hiring the assorted factor inputs and receiving payment for the output. The most efficient size of capital units can, however, be extremely large, for example oil tankers, chemical plants, planes, steel plants, etc. So even an entrepreneur who intended to hire his capital equipment would in many industries nowadays have to have considerable command over wealth.

In the above list of forms of capital equipment, two are in practice regularly hired, tankers and planes, and two are hardly ever hired, chemical and steel plants. The main difference in this respect between steel plants and planes is that the former is more special-ised, specific to a particular place and to a particular form of production. A steel, or a chemical, plant cannot be easily transmuted into a form capable of producing some other product, nor can it be moved without vast expense. Once such capital is in place its resale value for any alternative occupation is very low; its value resides only in the expected future returns from its initial intended use. Unless a firm, which first installed hired capital in a specific form, should continue to renew the hiring contract, the beneficial owner of that capital would face a high probability of a serious loss in capital value. But if the agree-ment involves continuous renewal of the hiring agreement until the end of the working life of the equipment, this becomes tantamount to transfer of ownership, which would represent a simpler transaction than perpetual hiring.[1] It is, therefore, mainly the specific nature of installed capital that induces firms to become owners, rather than hirers, of most of their own capital.[2]

The main function of a corporate organisation, therefore, is to bring together factors of production, often possessing specific faculties,[3] for joint team production. Most produc-

---

by diversifying their assets, and the advantages inherent in selecting managers by ability rather than by the accidents of inheritance (advantages even for those fortunate enough to be born wealthy) has led in most cases to a divorce between management and ownership.

Management will then only have a partial share in the net earnings of the firm and may even be paid entirely in the form of a salary. In such cases there will be a need to search for other methods of monitoring the efficiency of the managers themselves. Of course in any large firm there will be a hierarchy of managers, each of whom will supervise his juniors in the pyramid, but the key question is who ensures satisfactory performance at the top of the pyramid. One solution is to have some kind of Board of Directors, or the equivalent, officially senior to the chief executive manager, whose sole real function is to satisfy themselves that the manager is performing adequately.

---

[1] Moreover, the operators of a firm (managers and owners) not only should have specialist information about the future of their industry, but having chosen voluntarily to stay in that industry are presumably relatively optimistic about it. Even if arrangements for the regular renewal of hiring could be satisfactorily negotiated, any potential hirer of capital, with less information and probably less optimism than the owners of the firm, would ask for a return, to protect himself from risk, at a rate that might be considerably in excess of that which the firm's operators would regard as justified. The critical factor is the difference in information and expectations. For a similar analysis in a somewhat different context see J. Stiglitz, 'Some Aspects of the Pure Theory of Corporate Finance: Bankruptcies and Take-overs,' Bell Journal of Economics and Management Science, vol. 3, no. 2 (autumn 1972) pp. 458–82.

[2] Alchian and Demsetz, ibid. pp. 791–3, however, emphasise another factor, whether 'depreci-ation or user cost is more cheaply detected when the owner can see its use than by only seeing the input before and after.' If so, 'there is a force towards owner use rather than renting.' Thus if a tenant is likely to allow land to deteriorate in a way that cannot be monitored, except at considerable expense, the rental rate must reflect such risks. Since a 'good' user of the land will not expect it to deteriorate under his care, there would be an incentive to ownership. This again turns on differences in the information available to the hirer and user.

[3] For example, particular skills acquired by labour through a learning process, often involving a significant investment in time and money.

tion in developed economies is organised in teams. Not all productive teams are, however, part of the corporate sector, as defined for national-income statistics. The institutional forms into which such teams are organised are various, e.g. partnerships and unincorporated business as well as incorporated firms. Although the form of the organisation may make some difference to the behaviour of the decision-makers (e.g. whether the manager is also the owner or is salaried), the important functional distinction is between the productive sector, organised into teams, and the personal sector, which supplies the labour and ultimately owns all the assets used in the productive sector. Thus there is no very important distinction to be drawn in principle between a private and an incorporated building firm, but a major difference between these firms and the individuals forming the teams in the firms.

The basic dichotomy is between the *personal* function of providing a flow of labour services, consuming the flow of goods and services, and holding financial claims to goods and services to bridge the gaps between incomes and expenditures, and the *productive* function of obtaining and organising factor inputs, financed in part by issuing financial liabilities, for the purpose of producing a flow of goods and services. The distinction in the national-income accounts between the company sector and persons is simply the best available statistical proxy to illustrate the division between the personal function and the productive function.[1] This distinction then allows for a separation to be made, in principle, between the personal function of deciding to add to wealth by saving[2] and the productive function of deciding to invest in real assets[3] in order to carry on production. It is to the determination of this investment decision, and to the effect of financial factors upon this, that we now turn; analysis of the effects of financial conditions on the savings decision is held over until the start of Chapter 9.

It was, we have argued, mainly the specific nature of equipment that made it more economical for firms to own, rather than to hire, real capital. By the same token, this makes investment decisions irreversible. If it were not, primarily, for this feature of irreversibility of investment decisions, the firm would need only to consider current conditions, the current level of demand and current factor prices, in determining its present investment decision. In other words the investment decision of the firm at any point of time could and would be myopic.[4] Assume that capital is infinitely malleable (or putty, to use the accepted jargon), so that it can be hired for a short period, say one week, and then handed back to the owner in malleable form to take on whatever new role the owner wants. How much investment, hiring of malleable capital, should the firm undertake? The answer is simple:

---

[1] It is not a very well or clearly drawn dividing line. Apart from the common inclusion of farmers, unincorporated businesses, etc., in the personal sector, any individual owning real assets can be regarded, *pro tanto*, as involved in the productive function, in the same way as companies. An individual who owns his own home can be thought of, quite reasonably, as having decided that there was an attractive profit to be made by buying a real asset (the house), which combined with current labour operations (cleaning by the wife) at rates of reward determined internally within the organisation, would produce an output of current housing services which could be sold (to himself) at an implicit price sufficiently high to make the productive exercise profitable. The services of real assets can be hired or rented, e.g. housing, consumer durables. Any individual choosing to buy rather than to rent has in a sense decided to engage in a productive process.

[2] Of course, in practice, much saving occurs as a result of managerial decisions to retain profits; but the manager is retaining funds on behalf of the owners of the funds, and if the owners do not like the effects of the manager's decisions they can choose to sell their ownership claims (which makes it cheaper for a take-over bidder, who believes that he can do better as manager/owner, to obtain command over the firm and change policy), or even try to replace the manager directly.

[3] The firm will also need to hold financial assets for transactions purposes and to retain greater flexibility in its operations. We discuss this issue again further on.

[4] See K. Arrow, 'Optimal Capital Policy, the Cost of Capital and Myopic Decision Rules,' *Annals of the Institute of Statistical Mathematics*, vol. 16, nos 1–2 (Tokyo, 1964).

so long as the firm can be sure of obtaining additional profits from the marginal investment sufficient to meet the pre-tax rate of interest, which it has to pay, it will add to the present value of the firm by undertaking that project.[1] Thus optimal investment (in the absence of uncertainty) requires that

$$\frac{\delta \pi t}{\delta K t} = r_t$$

i.e. the cost of capital is just the before-tax rate of interest.

The argument for this proposition has been nicely put by Stiglitz[2] as follows: 'Assume we have an optimal policy. If it is optimal, there can exist no perturbation of the policy which makes us better off. Consider the effect of an increase in the capital stock at time t, keeping the size of the capital stock at all other dates unchanged. This necessitates increasing I_{t-1} by a unit and reducing I_t by a unit. To do this, assume the firm increases its borrowing at time $t - 1$ by a unit. The incremental amount then that the firm can distribute to its shareholders (at time t) after paying interest on the loan and after taxes is

$$\left(\frac{\delta \pi t}{\delta K t} - r\right)(1 - Tc)$$

(where Tc is the corporate profits tax rate). No matter how the returns are distributed to shareholders – as dividends or capital gains – it is clearly profitable to undertake the investment if

$$\frac{\delta \pi t}{\delta K t} \geq r.'$$

If additional investment adds to profits over and above the interest charged it is worth doing, irrespective of the rate of corporate tax, so long as this is less than 100 per cent. On this basis Stiglitz criticises Jorgenson, and many others who have followed him, for introducing tax terms into the estimate of the cost of capital. 'In the absence of uncertainty, the corporate profits tax with the interest deductability provision is completely non-distortionary. It does not shift resources (at the margin) from the corporate to the non-corporate sector. It is an intra-marginal tax on the return to capital (or pure profits) in the corporate sector.'[3]

The analysis naturally becomes more complicated after allowing for the presence of uncertainty, but while the assumption of perfectly malleable capital is retained the gist of the results remains unaltered. So long as none of the possible uncertain (one-period) outcomes is bad enough to entail an inability to repay debt, i.e. when there is no likelihood of the firm going bankrupt, the relevant cost of capital to the firm will still be the before-tax rate of interest. When the fear of bankruptcy does constrain a firm's operations, the

---

[1] Like other simple answers it does depend on a number of implicit assumptions. Among these are (i) there is no (expected) change in the price of capital goods over the hiring period; (ii) the firm is not in a position where it has to pay out (a proportion of) additional earnings in taxable dividends; and (iii) the depreciation allowable against tax is exactly equal to the economic depreciation of the firm's capital. For a detailed analysis of these issues see M. A. King, 'Announcements of Tax Changes and Optimal Investment Behaviour,' presented to the European Meeting of the Econometric Society (mimeo, Budapest, September 1972).

[2] J. Stiglitz, 'Taxation, Corporate Financial Policy, and the Cost of Capital,' *Journal of Public Economics*, vol. 2, no. 1 (February 1973) pp. 1–34, quotation from pp. 25–6.

[3] Ibid. p. 26.

cost of capital may differ from the before-tax rate of interest, but Stiglitz argues that it may not differ greatly from (and could even be less than)[1] the before-tax rate of interest.

So, if capital was completely and perfectly malleable, capable of instantaneous adjustment at zero cost into any form,[2] the yield on capital would be brought into equality with the before-tax rate of interest. There would be no distinction between the marginal productivity of capital and the marginal efficiency of investment. The expected return on investment is the same as the extra return from an additional unit of capital now, since under these circumstances capital can be installed (new investment can be undertaken) instantaneously for infinitesimal periods of time.

The assumption, however, of completely malleable capital does not seem well founded in practical experience. The reality probably lies closer to the assumption that the installation of capital in a specific form is irreversible over its lifetime. In this case, the marginal productivity of capital, the return on an extra unit of capital at a single point of time, and the marginal efficiency of investment, the expected return on a unit of investment over its whole life, can diverge quite sharply. An excellent analysis of the investment decision facing firms in such a position, in a context of imperfect competition, has been presented by Nickell.[3] In his model demand, x, is a function of price and also varies over time (with the growth of the economy). There is no rationing, so that capacity (y) is always equal or greater than demand, i.e.

$$y_{(t)} - x(p(t), t) \geq 0$$

Capacity is a function of investment and of the rate of depreciation of existing capital, since labour – needed to work with capital in a fixed coefficients technology – has an infinite elasticity of supply at the going wage cost per unit of output (w), so that

$$y_t = \lambda I_{(t)} - \delta y_t$$

where δ is the rate of depreciation. Because of the irreversibility assumption existing capital cannot be sold at any reasonable price, so $I_{(t)} \geq 0$. The firm's objective will be to maximise net present value[4] subject to these constraints and the initial level of capacity (y_0).

The output which the firm chooses to produce determines the minimum level of capacity which the firm has to install. The firm can lower the required level of capacity, and thus of investment, by raising its price. The marginal cost to the firm of increasing capacity[5] would be

$$w + v \frac{\left(\delta + r - \dfrac{\dot{v}}{v}\right)}{\lambda}$$

---

[1] Ibid. pp. 27–32. If there are tax advantages to be obtained by retention rather than distribution of profits, and the firm does not have, or perhaps does not wish to exercise, the option of investing in financial assets (e.g. because it feels that it is not in, and does not know, the business of financial intermediation), then it may find it worthwhile to place retained profits in additional real assets at an expected yield even below that of the before-tax rate of interest.

[2] See J. P. Gould, 'Adjustment Costs in the Theory of Investment of the Firm,' *Review of Economic Studies*, vol. xxxv(1), no. 101 (January 1968) pp. 47–56.

[3] S. Nickell, 'On the Role of Expectations in the Pure Theory of Investment,' *The Review of Economic Studies*, vol. 41 (1), no. 125 (January 1974) pp. 1–19.

[4] This means that the firm will try to maximise the following expression

$$\int_0^\infty \varepsilon^{-a(t)}[(p(t) - w(t))x(p(t), t) - v(t)I(t)] \, dt$$

where v is the price of new capital goods and $\dot{a}(t) = r(t)$, where r is the current rate of interest.

[5] If all capital were perfectly malleable, the marginal cost of increasing capacity and of increasing output would be the same. When investment is irreversible, and spare capacity can develop, the two can obviously differ.

where v is the price of capital goods, so $\dot{v}/v$ shows the capital gain (loss) obtained on holding such assets, and r is the rate of interest. Because installed capital is irreversible, the marginal opportunity cost of additional *output* to the firm is lowered whenever a firm with malleable capital would be reducing its capital inputs, and will fall back to w when spare capacity develops. Setting marginal revenue equal to marginal opportunity cost implies that the firm will be earning less than the marginal costs of additional *capacity* during those periods when demand drops off so sharply that a firm with malleable capital would have a negative rate of gross investment. Nickell shows that the 'second best' optimality condition forced on the firm by the irreversibility of investment will be to plan, in the light of the future expected path of demand, to achieve equality over any cyclical fluctuation in demand between the integral of the discounted marginal costs of additional *capacity* and of the discounted marginal revenues, where the discount factor is the real rate of return adjusted for depreciation.

Assuming a cyclical path of demand, as shown in Fig. 5.1, where the rate of decline of demand outdistances the natural rate of depreciation of capital (δ) over the period t_0-t_1, to achieve the planned optimal path, with the marginal cost of capacity

$$w + v \, \frac{\left(\delta + r - \dfrac{\dot{v}}{v}\right)}{\lambda}$$

held constant throughout, marginal revenue must rise relative to the marginal cost of capacity in phase 1 over the period n_0-t_0. The locus of the price of output over the cycle is shown in Fig. 5.2. Marginal revenue, and price, rise relative to marginal capacity costs during phase 1, since investment is stopped before the peak in demand, forcing up prices in order to bring demand into line with the restricted capacity output. The marginal productivity of capital will apparently be rising relative to the cost of capital during this period. This will not induce investment, because supernormal profits during cyclical peaks will be necessary to balance unavoidable losses on installed capital during the troughs of the predicted demand cycle.

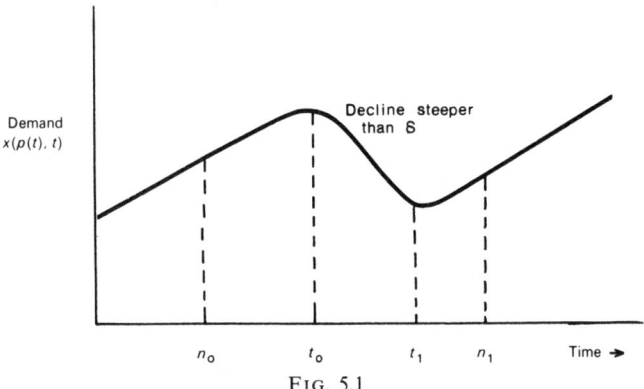

FIG. 5.1

Thus if businessmen forecast a downturn in demand in future the current yield on real capital may seem high without inducing much new investment. Profits and prices may be temporarily high, as businessmen try to meet extra demand without installing new capital, while the market value of real capital (equities) may be lowered by investors looking ahead to the next, forthcoming depression. Equally, as the upturn gets under way while the excess capacity is still being worked off, the yield on real capital may appear low, at a time when the marginal efficiency of investment is rising rapidly.

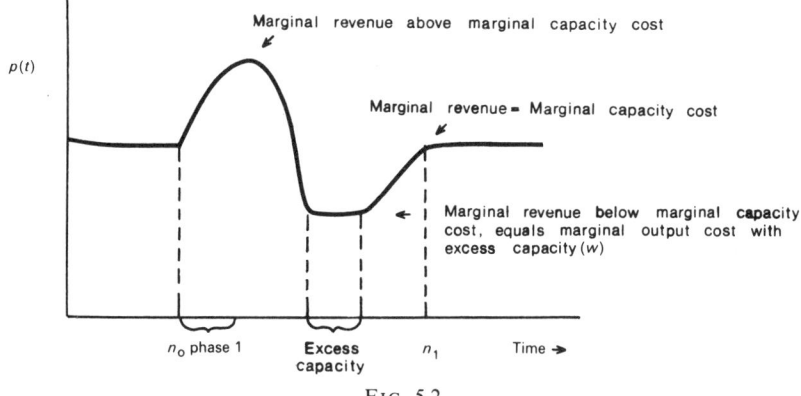

FIG. 5.2

As Nickell emphasises, in a model with specific, irreversible capital, expectations about the future course of demand are of paramount importance. 'A consistent thread which permeates all the results . . . is the crucial role of expectations as a factor in determining the level of investment in fixed capital. Reaction to government policy [e.g. in changing the level of interest rates], for example, depends crucially on when an upturn in demand is expected. On this factor will depend whether there is a reaction at all, and if there is a reaction, how long it will be delayed. Casual empiricism would tend to confirm this result, which goes a long way towards explaining why investment in fixed capital seems to react somewhat arbitrarily to government policy, in terms of both the size and the delay of the reaction.'[1]

In conditions of uncertainty, of limited access to partial information, such expectations about the future course of demand and the likely profitability of current investment will be highly subjective phenomena. Expectations of future outcomes are likely to be very diverse, depending on individual humours and varying access to such information as is available.[2] This diversity of expectations provides yet another reason for ordinary commercial firms to hold financial assets, besides those already mentioned, e.g. the need for precautionary balances to meet unforeseen swings in receipts and expenditures, already discussed in Chapter 2. If expectations are diverse, it could well happen that managers (or owners)[3] of a firm are more optimistic about prospects than outside investors.

The outcome may seem more assured to the entrepreneur than to his banker. The entrepreneur may feel that the appropriate rate of interest to finance such an assured prospect would be the riskless rate. The outside lender may take a more jaundiced view and require a higher rate on loans to offset the greater risks foreseen. If the business holds financial assets, it can use these to finance its investment at those times when it feels that outside lenders have adopted an unduly pessimistic view about the future outlook. At such times internal finance will appear cheaper than external finance. In this way the

---

[1] Ibid. p. 17.

[2] In practice, the extent of information on the possible investment opportunities open to a firm, which is available outside that firm, is usually quite slight. Certainly firm managers should have a much clearer idea of the expected distribution of future earnings from investment opportunities than outside investors. In view of the limited information available to the market, it is doubtful whether the stock-market prices of individual firms really closely reflect their managers' views of their appropriate price in the light of their own expectations about future earnings.

[3] Since owners/managers in any firm are, in a sense, self-selected they are likely to hold relatively confident expectations about their own prospects.

availability of financial assets provides firms with flexibility by allowing them to proceed with their plans, as may seem best to themselves, without necessarily having to convince outside lenders,[1] banks, insurance companies, stock-market investors, of the validity of their appreciation of future outcomes.

And, as will be seen in the next section, the existence of diverse views about future possible outcomes for the firm not only influences its asset structure, making the holding of financial assets more attractive, but also helps to determine the optimal structure of a firm's financial liabilities.

B. The Structure of Company Liabilities

If the future was certain, the present value of a firm could be calculated as the present discounted value of its future known earnings, π_t, so that $V = \int_0^\infty \varepsilon^{-\rho t} \pi_t \, dt$. This will obviously be the case whatever the liability structure of the firm;[2] when returns are fixed equities become equivalent to riskless bonds. But even where future returns are uncertain the value of a firm under some quite general conditions will be independent of the structure of its financial liabilities, so long as there is no chance of bankruptcy[3] and there are no relative tax effects depending on the financial structure of the firm, i.e. differing provisions for the taxation of company earnings, depending on whether these are paid out in interest (on debt), in dividends or retained in the firm.

When there is no chance of bankruptcy, and there are no such tax effects, the company's future expected earnings will be independent of its liability structure. Moreover, each investor should be able to offset the debt/equity ratio adopted by the firm by alterations in his own portfolio, 'homemade leverage.'[4] If a firm was too unlevered for the risk/return preferences of shareholders in the market, i.e. it had too low a debt/equity ratio, the price of its equity might be expected to fall. But if this dragged the market value of the firm below the present value of its expected future earnings as estimated by an investor, discounted at the rate relevant to the risk class of that particular industry which depends on the expected variance of earnings of firms in that line of business, then that investor should be able to make an expected profit, and obtain his desired risk/return combination by issuing his own personal debt to obtain funds to buy the shares. Since the expected returns on these shares must be, by assumption, high enough to avoid any risk of bankruptcy as the debt/equity ratio varies, the investor should be able to borrow at the riskless rate by pledging the shares as security. Ignoring transactions costs, the investor should be able to borrow

---

[1] Moreover, the exercise of obtaining funds from outside sources can entail sizeable transactions costs.

[2] If the rate of growth of earnings is greater than the rate of discount, then the present value is infinite. The economic implications of this mathematical result are of some interest. Since we observe that all firms have finite market values, we can presumably conclude either that people envisage some ultimate limits to growth and/or that uncertainty, mortality, etc., raise the rate at which we are prepared to discount future earnings.

[3] In my opinion to assume that bankruptcy is not possible, whatever the debt/equity ratio, is very strong and most implausible in practice. Take any firm whose capital consists virtually entirely of bonds. Then the absolute worst possible outcome must enable that firm with certainty to pay off all its debt obligations. No wonder the conclusions of such an assumption have a certainty equivalent form! In this guise one would be well advised to regard the no-bankruptcy case as an interesting theoretical construct, and treat the analysis of the situation when bankruptcy can occur as the general case.

[4] The importance of such 'homemade leverage' was first recognised and analysed by F. Modigliani and M. H. Miller in their path-breaking article on 'The Cost of Capital, Corporation Finance and the Theory of Investment,' *The American Economic Review*, vol. 48, no. 3 (June 1958) pp. 261–97.

in such a way as to obtain his own desired risk/return combination, and will continue to borrow and to invest until the present market value of the company is driven back into equality with his estimation of the present discounted value of its future earnings. Similarly, if the firm is so highly levered that the market lowers equity prices – from fear of excessive risk – to a level where the market value of the firm fell below the present value of its expected future earnings, then again the individual investor could expect to benefit by unlevering his own holdings through purchasing a combination of safe bonds and equities; by holding a portfolio of bonds and equities in the same proportions as they have been issued by the firm, the individual would obtain the same risk/return combination as if the firm had issued no debt at all. The possibility of homemade leverage thus allows each investor to obtain his own preferred risk/return combination independently of the debt structure of the firm, and thus on the assumptions posited makes the debt structure of the firm irrelevant to the determination of the present market value of the firm.

If everyone had similar expectations of the future potential earnings of the firm, and had similar risk/return preferences, then all investors would hold the shares in the company and would establish the same homemade debt/equity ratio, which could be entirely different from that adopted by the firm. If everyone had similar expectations of future company earnings, but different risk/return preferences, they would still all hold shares but with differing homemade debt/equity ratios. If there was a diversity of view about future company earnings, those who were relatively optimistic about the outcome for company A would hold that company's shares and determine its market value (so long as *everyone* still believed that no bankruptcy was possible, the optimists could still borrow at the riskless rate), and those who were relatively optimistic about company B would hold that company's shares and determine its market value.

This proposition, put forward by Modigliani and Miller,[1] that under some quite general circumstances the structure of a company's debt should not affect its market valuation, was both stimulating and challenging. In the following years there were a number of articles examining the limits of the context (i.e. the necessary assumptions) in which this held true.[2] Subsequently attention has turned rather to empirical testing of these hypotheses,[3] and to analysis of the effect of the tax code in determining the 'optimal' financial structure, so that for a given expected earnings stream the present net of tax value can be maximised,[4] and on the role and functions of bankruptcy as an institutional process.[5] It is to these latter subjects that we now turn. (Of the two subjects considered the role of bankruptcy is fundamentally more important and readers could without much loss skip pp. 96–8 on tax considerations.)

---

[1] 'The Cost of Capital, Corporation Finance and The Theory of Investment,' *The American Economic Review* (June 1958).

[2] See, among others, the articles by W. J. Baumol and B. G. Malkiel, 'The Firm's Optimal Debt–Equity Combination and the Cost of Capital,' *Quarterly Journal of Economics*, vol. 81, no. 4 (November 1967) pp. 547–78, and J. Stiglitz, 'A Re-examination of the Modigliani–Miller Theorem,' *The American Economic Review*, vol. 59, no. 5 (December 1969) pp. 784–93.

[3] For a recent example using U.K. data, see A. Glyn, 'The Stock Market Valuation of British Companies and the Cost of Capital, 1955–69,' *Oxford Economic Papers*, vol. 25, no. 2 (July 1973) pp. 213–40. Empirical studies using U.S. data can be found in many recent issues of *The Journal of Finance*, which publishes many articles on such topics. A complete reading list on empirical studies in this field would now be lengthy.

[4] Again *The Journal of Finance* remains the best source for articles in this area. See, for example, the paper by C. W. Haley on 'Taxes, the Cost of Capital, and the Firm's Investment Decision,' *The Journal of Finance*, vol. xxvi, no. 4 (September 1971) pp. 901–17, and its attached list of references to prior work. This is an increasingly large field with a considerable volume of both theoretical and applied work involved.

[5] For a general assessment of the current state of the art in this area, see Irwin Friend, 'Mythodology in Finance,' *The Journal of Finance*, vol. xxviii, no. 2 (May 1973) pp. 257–72.

The existence of tax regulations which impose differing rates of tax on company earnings depending on how these are allocated (to interest payments, dividends or retentions), clearly makes the present value of the company a function of its financial structure, since the different tax imposts make the expected stream of net of tax earnings a function of financial policy. In the United Kingdom and the United States, interest payments by companies are deductible against earnings for tax purposes. Profits, which are calculated net of interest cost and allowable depreciation, are then subject to corporation tax. The combination of corporation tax and subsequent taxation of dividends as income in the hands of their recipients may or may not, depending upon the offsets allowed under the code in force, discriminate against distributed earnings in favour of retained earnings. The extent of such discrimination has varied widely in recent years in the United Kingdom as the political parties have in turn introduced legislation to bring into effect the conditions which they felt to be more conducive to growth and efficiency.[1] Similarly, the situation with respect to the tax deductability of interest payments by *persons* has remained unsettled in recent years in the United Kingdom, with the position varying by the particular form of debt (e.g. building-society mortgage, hire-purchase debt, bank borrowing) and over time as legislation altered (e.g. the change in the Finance Act of 1972 to allow interest on personal bank borrowing to be tax deductible).

The question whether an investor should prefer a company which is mainly equity[2] or mainly debt-financed depends on the relevant tax rates, *including* the individual's own tax position, particularly in respect of the provisions for allowing interest on personal borrowing to be deductible against tax. If the individual's own tax rate is high, relative to the corporation-tax rate, and personal interest payments are allowable against tax, he could do best by financing his present consumption by borrowing against the security of his equity holdings, whose value will be increased by retained earnings. He can offset his interest payments against his (presumed) large other sources of income and can delay capital gains tax until the ultimate date of realisation. If, on the other hand, his own personal-tax rate is relatively low compared to the corporate-tax rate, and/or interest payments on his own borrowing are not tax deductible, the investor will be better placed if company debt is substituted for personal debt.

Stiglitz has noted that, 'There are basically three reasons that bond financing is not as attractive as the earlier literature would have suggested:

(1) A larger debt means less if the returns to capital can be taken in the form of capital gains, which are taxed at lower rates than interest income.
(2) Capital gains are taxed only upon realisation rather than upon accrual; even if capital gains and ordinary income were taxed at the same rate there would be an advantage to the use of equity.

---

[1] The main argument for discrimination in favour of retention was that it might increase total private-sector saving. The main argument against discrimination was that it might lead to an inefficient allocation of resources between companies. Neither argument is very compelling. Thus M. S. Feldstein, 'Tax Incentives, Corporate Saving and Capital Accumulation in the United States,' *Journal of Public Economics*, vol. 2, no. 2 (April 1973) pp. 159–71, has challenged the claim that such discrimination, at least in the long run, does lead to larger total private-sector saving. On the other hand much recent work on the functioning of the equity market leads one to doubt whether it is in possession of sufficient information to allocate resources efficiently. Thus I. M. D. Little with A. C. Rayner in their book on *Higgledy Piggledy Growth Again* (Blackwell, Oxford, 1966) conclude on p. 94 that 'The investor is not successful in spotting companies whose profitability will increase . . . the yield structure established by the market does not appear to perform a beneficial social service. It might as well be picked with a pin.'

[2] Equity finance should be understood here as including the retention of earnings as well as the issue of new shares on the market.

(3) Personal borrowing is a substitute for corporate borrowing, and interest payments on personal account are also tax deductible. Thus the return to a firm borrowing – as opposed to an individual borrowing on his own account – is not the savings in the corporate-profit tax, but only the difference between this and the savings which would have accrued to the individual if he had borrowed.'[1,2]

Thus there can be cases when the overall tax savings are greater if the individual borrows while the company's financial liabilities are largely in equity form, than if the company has a large debt and has to pay out its earnings in interest payments rather than retaining them,[3] despite the savings in corporate taxation. This might suggest that – so long as we can continue to abstract from consideration of bankruptcy – either an *all*-equity or an *all*-debt policy would be optimal, depending on relative tax rates and the clientele of shareholders which the managers of the firm were cultivating. There are, however, certain factors which operate to prevent such extreme financial policies being adopted.

While there may be certain tax advantages in a firm already having a financial structure consisting of equities, there are disadvantages in *raising* any additional funds needed for investment purposes, after retained earnings have been fully exploited, by going to shareholders for further equity issues. This is because the future taxation on payments by companies to shareholders – even if delayed until the realisation of capital gains – is not matched by any tax allowances on payments to companies by shareholders.

Accordingly, if the firm is not paying out any dividends, using all its retained earnings for investment, and financing the excess of investment over retained earnings by debt, an attempt to increase the equity by reducing the new-debt issue and increasing the

---

[1] J. E. Stiglitz, 'Taxation and Corporate Financial Policy,' *Journal of Public Economics*, vol. 2, no. 1 (February 1973) pp. 1–34, quotation from p. 7.

[2] The assumption that taxes on capital gains are lower than those on 'unearned' incomes, and are paid on realisation rather than accrual accords with usual practice. This need not always be so. Indeed, under the imputation system of taxation common in many European countries, it may benefit shareholders with a lower marginal rate of tax to have earnings paid out in dividends and additional issues of new equities made to finance investment. M. A. King has analysed the more general case, within a certainty context, in his paper on 'The Announcement of Tax Changes and Optimal Investment Behaviour,' delivered at the Econometric Society meeting at Budapest (mimeo, September 1972).

[3] Given the tax advantages which under most regimes have appertained to retaining net profits rather than paying them out in dividends, it is difficult to explain why many companies have continued to make such large dividend payments. Companies could instead use retained earnings to add to their financial assets or, if they were not allowed to do so by fiscal regulations, could find that the net of tax position would be improved by investing in real assets at an expected rate of return even below the riskless rate, rather than pay out additional dividends, see Stiglitz, ibid, p. 31.

One possibility is that for investors, with regular requirements for funds to meet expenditure commitments, the transactions costs of selling portions of their equity holdings are so great that they prefer dividend payments despite the extra tax cost. If, however, transactions costs really do loom so very large among so many investors, the argument that 'homemade leverage' can, in the no-tax, no-bankruptcy situation, make corporate financial policy irrelevant must also come under question.

Another suggestion that is sometimes made is that dividend changes represent a form of signalling, a provision of information, to investors by managers. If managers do not believe a rise in profits to be permanent, they will not raise dividends in line; if they do, they will. While casual empiricism suggests that dividend policy is used in this way, it still seems hard to regard this as the major function giving dividend payments their *raison d'être*. The tax position under most regimes is such as to make such signalling an expensive method of imparting information. Why can't the managers simply announce their expectations in their accompanying (annual) report? It is, perhaps, a matter of credibility. The public will remain sceptical until the managers put their money where their mouths are.

new equity issue will have disadvantageous tax effects; there will be no reduction in taxation on 'equity account' this period but an increase in corporate profits taxes paid in future periods because of the reduction in interest payments.[1]

Thus, even when tax rates are such as to make a high equity policy preferable, all new investment beyond that financed by retained earnings on the equity, whose initial value is given by the capitalisation of the value of the 'idea' of the firm, should be obtained from debt finance. In this case, the debt/equity ratio will vary over the life of the firm. While investment is taking place, debt will be rising though the value of equity will rise also as the date of the expected returns comes closer.

Initially, the presumption is that the debt rises faster than the equity, but then it rises more slowly. Eventually, the firm's profits exceed investment, so it starts repaying debt, the debt/equity ratio falls, and finally approaches zero at time T [the horizon].[2]

A firm must always start off with some equity, representing the capitalisation of the owners' initial idea. If the 'idea' had zero present value, there would be no point in undertaking the exercise. If tax rates were, however, such as to make a high-debt financial structure preferable, should the company not borrow in order to buy back this initial equity? In the first place, the tax regulations may not allow bonds to be issued for the retirement of shares or, at least, treat such payments as ordinary income. Even more important, however, the regular reduction in equity finance, and increase in the proportion of bond finance, must at some point conflict with the previously assumed condition that the minimum expected earnings of the firm are sufficient to meet its debt obligations. If the probability distribution of future expected earnings is very compact, i.e. the earnings pattern is nearly certain, the debt ratio could be high without incurring a risk of bankruptcy: indeed when earnings are certain all of a firm's liabilities are essentially in bond form irrespective of their nominal title. So for firms following a bond finance policy, subject to a no risk of bankruptcy constraint, 'the debt/equity ratio is a function . . . of the probability distribution of future prospects. If there were no risk, there would be no equity, but if there is a high variance to the returns, there may be a very low debt/equity ratio.'[3]

But why should firms want to restrict their activities by arranging their operations to avoid any risk of bankruptcy? Apart from the possible tax advantages inherent in raising the debt ratio, there may well be a number of projects with very attractive expected earnings streams, yet which entail a non-zero possibility of a sufficiently bad outcome to lead to an inability to meet even quite low debt obligations. Indeed, it may even be to the advantage of the shareholders in some circumstances to undertake a risky operation with a high probability of bankruptcy, even if this lowers the present value of the firm, because some of the loss, if the project is unsuccessful, falls on the bondholder while the shareholders obtain all the residual benefit of a successful outcome, after meeting the debt obligation.[4]

---

[1] Ibid. p. 7.

[2] Ibid. p. 18.

[3] Ibid. p. 22.

[4] Following the example given by Stiglitz, 'Some Aspects of the Pure Theory of Corporate Finance,' *The Bell Journal of Economics and Management Science* (autumn 1972) p. 460, consider the case of a firm with current assets of £100,000 in cash and outstanding debt in the form of pure discount bonds with a redemption value of £108,000. The current interest rate is 10 per cent. If the firm invests the cash at 10 per cent, it can pay off the debt and have £2000 over at the end of next year, whose present value is £1818. Alternatively, the firm may have the opportunity to invest in a project with two possible outcomes, a return of £125,000 with probability 0·25 and a return of £80,000 with probability 0·75. Clearly the expected present value of the firm as a whole is lower taking the risky investment than the safe investment. Yet the present value of the equity (£17,000 × 0·25 + 0 × 0·75/1·1 = £3864) is considerably higher if the risky project is chosen. As Stiglitz

(*Footnote* [4] *continued on p. 99*)

On the other hand, managers may be particularly keen to avert bankruptcy. A relatively large share of their own wealth is likely to be invested in their own firms, so that risk aversion should lead them to avoid projects involving a very large variance of outcome. It is also difficult in a world without repeated experiments to distinguish between bad luck and inefficiency.[1] It is, therefore, highly likely that bankruptcy will lead to the termination of their jobs, even if the company is reorganised and continues in operation after the onset of bankruptcy. Managers are thus akin to shareholders, rather than bondholders, in that they will tend to receive no further emoluments from the company if they lead it into bankruptcy, but in so far as their rewards are in salary form, they will not share commensurately with the shareholders if the outcome is successful. On all these counts the objectives of management are liable to make them more anxious to avoid bankruptcy than the shareholders might prefer, if they were privy to the same information as is available to managers.

Furthermore, the onset of bankruptcy is likely to entail very heavy costs. Because of the specific nature of capital, an attempt to meet the bondholders' claims by liquidation of the firm and sale of the assets will often fail to realise more than a small proportion of the value of the liabilities. On the other hand, an attempt by the bondholders (and the official receiver) to continue the operations of the firm, as a more hopeful way of ultimately satisfying their claims, runs into the difficulty that either they must make do with the existing management, whose previous failure provides *prima facie* evidence that they are below standard, or else they must hire new management. The new management, and indeed the official receiver in the interim, will lack the specialised information of the existing management. Thus while the change of management may improve the situation because the initial management was inefficient, it must provide a worse result than maintaining a good management which has built up from experience a private monopoly in relevant information.

So when the firm has a multiperiod life, the possibility of bankruptcy prior to the end of that life will itself affect the expected earnings stream of the company and thus its present value.[2] It is possible, however, to abstract from such considerations by examining a two-period model in which the firm invests in the first period and obtains returns in the second and then dissolves. Because of the short horizon management is not concerned with continuing employment and bankruptcy does not involve the liquidation or reorganisation of the firm. The future returns for the firm (and managers) do *not* depend in this case on the event of bankruptcy but only on the outcomes of given investment. In this circumstance

---

notes, ibid. p. 462, 'When there is a finite probability of bankruptcy, the rule of firm value maximisation is not equivalent to maximising the value of the equity.' He asserts that '. . . it is clearly the latter with which firms are concerned.' In my view, however, given the disadvantages of bankruptcy to managers, as noted above, it is *far from clear* which valuation managers will seek to maximise in such conditions. In fact we do observe relatively low levels of gearing (i.e. a low debt/equity ratio) in the United States and the United Kingdom (see *The Corporate Economy*, ed. R. Marris and A. Wood, appendix B) and this may be explained as reflecting the preferences of managers rather than those of shareholders. But in so far as managers did concern themselves mostly with the interests of stockholders, where these conflict with the interests of bondholders, it is clear, as the example shows, that this could result in productive inefficiency.

---

[1] A point stressed by several writers dealing with the theory of the firm, viz. R. Marris, 'Why Economics needs a Theory of the Firm,' *Economic Journal*, vol. 82, no. 325s (March 1972, supplement) pp. 321–52, especially pp. 328–32.

[2] This ignores the purely theoretical possibility of contracting for all possible future contingencies in markets at the outset, in a certainty equivalent world of the kind briefly noted in Chap. 1, Sect. A. In this system there would be as many securities as states of nature. It is difficult to see that bankruptcy as an institution would have any role in such a world, any more than money has.

Stiglitz shows that, so long as all investors, bondholders and shareholders, have the same expectations, the present value of the firm (ignoring taxes) is equal to the (common) expected value of the expected future outcome, discounted, when the investors are risk neutral, by the return on a safe asset, and that this value is independent of the debt/equity ratio.[1]

If investors have different expectations of the probability distribution of future outcomes the pessimists, who are likely to leave the shares in the company to the optimists,[2] may require a higher rate of interest on the risky bonds in the company (risky because of the possibility of bankruptcy) than the optimists believe that future prospects justify. Put alternatively, the optimists could not raise money indefinitely by borrowing on the security of the shares at the rate they believe to be appropriate in the light of their interpretation of the risks in the situation, because the lender will have less confidence that the earnings will be high enough to be sure of meeting their debt obligations.[3] When the expectations of investors diverge, then the present market value of the company will be a function of the debt/equity ratio. So long as the ratio is low enough to preclude the possibility of bankruptcy, even to more pessimistic lenders, then the market value of the company will be that set by the more optimistic expectations of the shareholders about the future expected earnings of the firm. Once the debt/equity ratio rises to the level where the divergence of expectations leads lenders (bondholders) to view the bonds as riskier than shareholders believe is the case, the shareholders will find themselves having to pay over the odds, in their own eyes, for debt finance and this will depress the market value of the company below their own valuation of the discounted future earnings stream.

So, even when the future outcomes themselves are not affected by the possibility of bankruptcy, differences in expectations between investors can make variations in the debt/equity ratio alter the market valuation of the firm. As a result attempts to maximise the present market value (or equity value) of the firm must involve a joint decision on both the optimal investment level and debt/equity ratio.[4]

For these reasons the financial policy of the firm should not be irrelevant. The market value of the firm may be expected to be a function of the debt/equity ratio as shown in Fig. 5.3, with the value rising initially as the company enjoys the tax advantages of a larger debt, but ultimately falling as the risks of bankruptcy rise.[5] Furthermore, within the total of debt, companies are likely to try to tailor the form and maturity of their outstanding debt to avoid bankruptcy. There will, therefore, be a modicum of 'segmentation' in the supply of company debt on to the market, in the sense that it would take quite a large shift in mean expected yields to tempt company treasurers from their preferred, safer habitat, involving a debt structure with a maturity related to the expected life and earnings of the company's capital assets. Companies investing in real assets will prefer to borrow in a form that corresponds with the nature of their assets. The less certain the outcome of their endeavour, the higher the ratio of equity to debt; the longer the average life of their equipment, the larger the proportion of long-term to short-term debt. Although company treasurers have a good deal of flexibility in the short run, delaying new issues, for example, until the stock market improves, the principle of matching assets and liabilities can lead to fairly rigid 'rules of thumb' of financial behaviour.

---

[1] Stiglitz, 'Some Aspects of the Pure Theory of Corporate Finance,' pp. 464–7.

[2] If all investors had similar expectations they would hold *pro rata* holdings of all securities.

[3] Once there is a possibility of bankruptcy, the possibilities of full homemade leverage cease. An investor buying a share in a levered company is not in the same position as an investor buying a share in a less-levered company on margin. If the firm should go bankrupt, his return in the first case is zero, but it is negative in the second. The investor could, perhaps, try to obtain some limited liability arrangements on his own borrowing, but the costs of this are presumably too great to make this feasible since such arrangements do not often occur in reality, see Stiglitz, ibid. p. 463.

[4] Ibid. pp. 467–71.

[5] As noted before, there is now a sizeable empirical literature on this controversial subject. The best source for articles on this subject is *The Journal of Finance*.

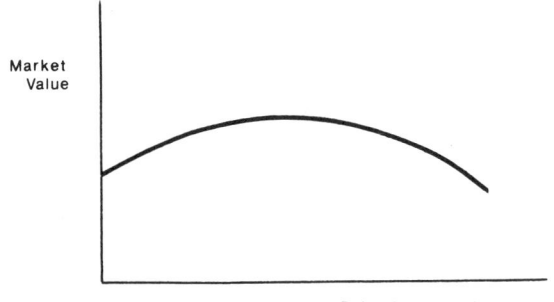

FIG. 5.3

Nevertheless, current interpretation of what represents prudent corporate financial behaviour can vary over time, partly in response to institutional changes that may allow access to additional markets for the issue of debt or alter the liquidity status of certain assets by providing some form of insurance against loss or a rediscounting facility, but also as confidence in growth and certainty of future cash flows and memories of previous financial crises wax and wane. Indeed, it is the thesis of Professor Minsky[1] that systematic shifts in the financial structure of companies have been, and still may yet prove to be, a significant factor contributing to major trade cycles. During booms growing confidence tempts companies to adopt a riskier financial structure with a top-heavy debt ratio and a shortening debt-maturity structure whose service requires a steady large cash flow. A faltering in demand can then push many companies to the brink of bankruptcy and over. Because bankruptcy is both a most costly process in itself, and because the event also immediately restricts the liquidity of the claims of creditors on the bankrupt company, this can set off a debt/deflation cycle. After this experience, of course, company treasurers revise their views of prudent behaviour, but the very conservatism of such resulting behaviour in the ensuing slump, combined with their doubts about the future expansion of demand, will make it harder for the authorities to reinvigorate the economy by the use of monetary policy. It was, according to Leijonhufvud, because of his doubts that Central Bankers would, or could, act with sufficient vigour to alter the thrust of monetary policy in the face of these swings in confidence that Keynes came to believe that the determined use of fiscal policy would be a necessary adjunct to counter-cyclical stabilisation.[2]

---

[1] Put especially clearly in his article on 'An Evaluation of Recent U.S. Monetary Policy. II Monetary Control and Economic Stability,' *The Bankers' Magazine*, vol. CCXIV, no. 1544 (November 1972) pp. 181–5. Also see his articles in *The Bankers' Magazine* in October and December 1972 and in February and March 1968.

[2] Leijonhufvud, *On Keynesian Economics and the Economics of Keynes*, especially the section on 'Keynes' Applied Theory: The Effectiveness of Monetary Policy,' pp. 401–16.

6

The Principles of Intermediation

SUMMARY

Intermediaries perform several functions. Firstly, they alleviate market imperfections caused by economies of scale in transactions in financial markets and in information gathering and portfolio management. Among intermediaries, whose main rationale is to be found in this role, are the various investment trusts, unit trusts, pension funds, etc. If it was not for such imperfections, everyone could in theory manage his own financial assets as well as a trust manager. Secondly, intermediaries provide insurance services: people dislike the prospect of accidents, such as fire, injury, burglary, and are quite prepared to accept a lower mean expected income (after payment of insurance premia) in order to insure against the risk of a severe reduction in living standards. These forms of financial intermediation need not involve much risk-taking by the intermediary. The intermediary, such as the unit trust, whose existence depends on economies of scale, can perform its functions at a profit while matching its assets with its liabilities: the insurance company can match its assets to the actuarial expectation of its contingent liabilities.

The third, and archetypal, type of financial intermediation, however, involves issuing liabilities of a kind preferred by lenders, accordingly at relatively low yields, and investing a proportion of the funds in higher-yielding earning assets of a form which borrowers prefer to issue. The intermediary attracts funds from the public by offering varying combinations of redemption terms, e.g. the date of its maturity, concomitant services, e.g. safe-keeping, and interest payments. If the intermediary offers very liquid liabilities, it will in general have to maintain a larger proportion of low-yielding reserves in its portfolio in order to honour its redemption obligations; so there will normally be an inverse relationship between the liquidity of the intermediary's liability and the rate of interest offered on it, an extreme example being the low yields offered on sight deposits.

A question raised here is why the public sector does not become a more active financial intermediary, since it is better placed than the private sector to bear the risks of an unmatched balance sheet; this is discussed again in Chapter 13.

Given the volume of deposits which an intermediary attracts, and the chances of future withdrawals of these deposits, an intermediary will divide its funds between alternative assets, e.g. cash reserves, bonds, advances, so as to obtain the preferred combination of risk and return. In practice, intermediaries do not act as price takers in all markets, but act as rate setters in loan markets, adjusting their rate-setting function in the light of rates on alternative assets and their own liquidity position.

If the rates which intermediaries can offer for deposits are fixed for them, say, by the fiat of the authorities, then their role in the determination of the volume of deposits is essentially passive. The volume of deposits then depends on the pattern of relative interest rates, the wealth of the public, and other factors – such as income levels – which affect the public's asset preferences. By their (monetary) operations the authorities can influence the preferred portfolio distribution (and wealth) of the public, and hence determine the volume of deposits. The analysis, however, becomes more interesting when intermediaries are free to vary their own deposit rates, since the determination of the total of deposits then depends directly upon their own responses as well as those of the public and of the authorities.

In setting their deposit rates, intermediaries will try to do so in such a way as to obtain their preferred combination of return and risk.

This analysis is illustrated by a simplified model, and numerical examples (simulations) are provided. The model, however, as initially set up, implies an instantaneous process of adjustment, taking place in all markets simultaneously. In practice there will not be sufficient information to allow this, so we end Section B by examining a more dynamic model in which a disturbance initially provokes adjustment only in the market in which it occurred.

Nevertheless, the process of portfolio adjustment, in response to changes in relative interest rates and in wealth, remains the same whether the system adjusts instantaneously or sequentially. In the final section this portfolio-adjustment approach to the determination of the volume of deposits is contrasted with the more common multiplier analysis. My objection to this latter is that, while the multiplier analysis is correct, indeed it is true by definition, it lacks the behavioural content of the portfolio-adjustment approach.

A. The Role of the Intermediary

Because of risk aversion, reinforced by the wish to avoid bankruptcy, there will be a tendency for private-sector borrowers to issue financial liabilities with a life till maturity related to the expected life of the investment to be financed, and in a form (e.g. equity or debt) which reflects to some extent the degree of uncertainty of the proposed investment project. The preferences of such borrowers may not match closely the 'preferred habitats' of personal-sector lenders. Because of their need to keep a sizeable proportion of their assets in liquid form for transactions and precautionary purposes, personal-sector lenders may exhibit a greater preference for shorter-dated assets in capital-certain form than private-sector borrowers would wish to provide, *ceteris paribus*. An excess supply of long-dated, relatively risky, private securities and an excess demand for short-dated, capital-certain, private-sector securities could, therefore, develop. This would lead, naturally, to a rise in yields on long-dated securities and a fall in yields on short-dated securities in order to tempt both lenders and borrowers out of their preferred habitats,[1] in order to restore equilibrium.[2] Certainly the yield curve has had an upward slope more often than not.

This disparity between the preferred habitats of private-sector lenders and borrowers need not, however, extend to the economy as a whole. The private-sector borrower wishes to tailor the time pattern of his liabilities to the expected profile of his returns from investment, in order largely to avoid the dangers of illiquidity and possible bankruptcy. But the government cannot go bankrupt, at least in a closed economy, nor need it worry about liquidity. It can pay off its maturing liabilities by issuing more legal-tender currency. In

---

[1] It is for some reason more common to think of variations in yield tempting lenders to depart from their preferred habitat, to take up a riskier portfolio, than it is to consider the possibility of borrowers also shifting from their preferred habitat. For example, Leijonhufvud, *On Keynesian Economics and the Economics of Keynes, passim*, e.g. pp. 202–3, 282–314, 354–85, 401–16, argues that Keynes believed that speculators with regressive expectations might prevent falls in short-term interest rates being translated to the long end of the bond market. But this (if true at all) would only be a serious barrier to the successful contra-cyclical use of monetary policy if borrowers for investment projects are also deterred by risk aversion, or by the same speculative (expectational) considerations, from financing their projects with shorter-dated liabilities.

[2] *Per contra*, the empirical studies on the term structure of interest rates, reported in Chap. 4, revealed very little evidence of such segmentation in markets and, instead, showed that the term structure could be reasonably well explained by one or other version of the expectations theory. Nevertheless, the general arguments for believing in some degree of segmentation in financial markets are so compelling that I feel disinclined to accept that empirical evidence at face value.

those cases when the currency is in some part a commodity money, e.g. with a gold or silver content, the government can raise the required commodities by taxation, or expropriation, in order to pay its liabilities. The limits to a government's domestic credit are political rather than economic; it can be overthrown but not bankrupted (see Chapter 1).

So the public sector can issue short-dated liabilities, based on its power to levy taxes, with an insouciance which cannot be matched by commercial firms. Thus the public sector is in a position to restore the balance between the demand and supply of assets of differing characteristics, either by issuing relatively more short, capital-certain assets to finance its own long-term capital expenditure, or even by acting directly as an intermediary, buying up long-dated private-sector securities with the proceeds obtained from issuing short-dated liabilities to the public. Even in countries where the role of the public sector is most narrowly limited, it still usually provides important intermediary services, in the sense that the issues of public-sector debt tend to alter the overall balance of debt outstanding more nearly in line with public preferences for assets to hold.

Such intermediation should reduce the margin between yields at the long and the short end. However, as noted in Chapter 1, the government will be deterred from issuing large quantities of currency, which as legal tender will be accepted at zero interest[1] by the public, for the purpose of reducing longer rates, by the fears of the likely inflationary consequences which could, *inter alia*, have perverse effects both on the level of nominal interest rates and even on the demand for official currency (if endemic inflation leads the public to seek currency substitutes). Nor have governments on the whole been very adventurous in tailoring the characteristics of their liabilities to suit the varying preferences of the public for differing combinations of return and risk, sticking for the main to standard kinds of fixed-interest debt.

Although in principle the public sector should be capable of providing full financial intermediary services within the economy, in practice it has not done so very extensively, and the provision of such services has been largely left to the private sector. The interplay of the preferences of lenders and borrowers, in the context of the information and transaction costs which they face, has led to the development of various distinguishable kinds of intermediary service by the private sector.

The first function of intermediation is to alleviate the market imperfections caused by economies of scale in transactions in financial markets and also in information gathering and portfolio management. Included among intermediaries, whose main rationale is to be found in this role, are the various investment trusts, unit trusts and also, perhaps, pension funds.[2] If it were not for the above imperfections, everyone could in theory manage his own accrued assets as well as a trust manager. In those cases when the main function of intermediaries is of this kind, overcoming market imperfections, it is not necessary for them, in order to show a profit, to adopt a risky position with the maturities of their assets not

---

[1] The question whether the authorities *ought* to offer interest payments on currency, were this to be a practicable proposition, will be examined in Chap. 13.

[2] The conditions under which pension funds operate also, in practice, provide a way of forcing most income recipients to save more than they otherwise would voluntarily do. The justification for imposing such forced saving, other than for purposes of allowing a higher level of investment expenditure at full employment, is that people may suffer from a form of myopia, in which they discount future consumption and value current material gratification to a greater extent than the actual uncertainties of life and death really warrant. It is possible that many people recognise their excessive susceptibility to current temptations and will actually be grateful for some compulsion in this respect. For example, many sign on for regular savings programmes, i.e. in Christmas clubs or with insurance schemes, in part as a method of self-control over the use of income. In an analogous vein I would go to the dentist only on crisis occasions if I had to book the day ahead, since the prospect of immediate discomfort would outweigh the known greater longer-term benefits. Therefore I arrange a booking some weeks ahead so that both the discomfort and the benefits of the visit are reasonably distant. Having booked the visit, inertia and shame force me to keep it.

matched to, and usually longer than, the maturities of their liabilities. The existence of transactions costs, and imperfect markets, makes some kinds of matching intermediation profitable. Economies of scale in both brokerage and management make it cheaper for the small investor in equities to acquire an adequately diversified holding by buying shares or units in investment funds than he can do by himself. The manager of such a fund runs the risk of having the inflow to his business decline, and his judgement questioned, if his portfolio does not perform comparatively well, and faces a risk common to all unit-trust managers of shifts in the public's demand for equities, but subject to observing proper, non-fraudulent business conduct he runs no risk of either illiquidity or insolvency.

Similarly, there will generally be considerable economies of scale in arranging loans to, or new issues for, businesses in large single units, rather than in many smaller portions. The size of such loans, or new issues, may well be beyond the ability of any one person, or even institution, to finance, at least without devoting an excessively large proportion of their portfolio to that one security, so that it may be desirable to divide the provision of the required finance among many investors. Intermediaries of varying kinds have the expertise, information and market advantages to specialise in 'splitting bulk' (as wholesalers and retailers do for commodities) in this way. The intermediary may, perhaps, do no more than introduce the lenders and borrowers to each other, a pure brokerage service. Or it might go further and hold the liability of the borrower on its books as an asset, or as a contingent asset (e.g. an acceptance), matched by a liability of an exactly equivalent form. In this case, however, the intermediary, despite maintaining a balanced portfolio, does run the danger of debtors defaulting. It is, however, the specialised knowledge of borrowers' creditworthiness that makes such intermediation profitable. Beyond that, of course, the intermediary may take advantage of yield differentials, caused in part by divergences in preferred habitats, to obtain a profit by raising money from lenders on cheaper terms than it on-lends to borrowers, but that takes us into consideration of another function of intermediation.

The second main type of service provided by intermediaries covers insurance. The natural hazards facing people often seem to have a probability distribution exhibiting considerable negative skewness. Thus the chances of early death, or fire, or burglary, or accident, etc., are quite remote, but when such accidents do occur they leave the unfortunate victim(s) much worse off. So the probability distribution of expected incomes in the face of such natural hazards may look rather like that shown in Fig. 6.1, where the tail on the left represents those suffering the occasional serious accidents of life. It is a recognised fact that most people dislike negative skewness, and are prepared to receive a lower mean expected income in order to offset the skewed distribution. This can, of course, be achieved by buying an insurance claim which will pay out in the event of one of these accidents

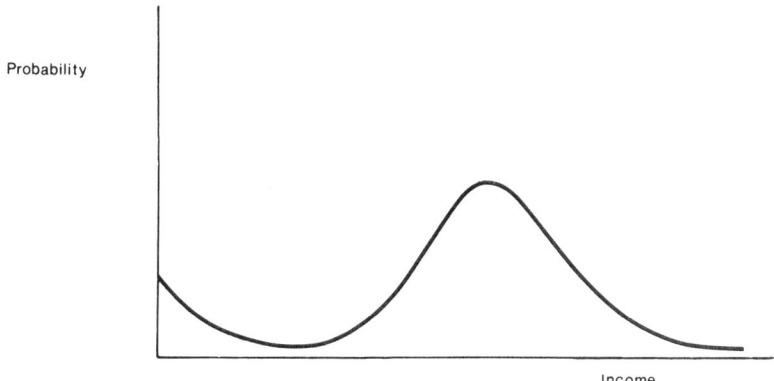

Probability

Income

FIG. 6.1

occurring. The premium that will have to be paid for such coverage will depend on the actuarial probability of such accidents, and also the extent to which the probabilities of occurrence can be actuarially established, the yield which the insurance company can obtain on the assets which it holds, the profit margins in the insurance business, etc. Even when the expected income distribution is not skewed, people may want to insure against falling into the lower tail of the income distribution. People will often accept a lower mean income, if by so doing they can reduce the variance (riskiness) of prospective outcomes.

Intermediaries providing insurance services can also do so perfectly well while continuing to maintain a matching portfolio, relating the form and maturity of their assets closely to the actuarial expectation of their liabilities. The expected variance of the calculated actuarial outcomes will, however, lead them to maintain certain additional precautionary balances among their assets. It should be, however, possible in principle to distinguish between the service of providing insurance and holding a matching portfolio against such contingent liabilities, and the services of intermediation between borrowers and lenders with differing preferred habitats, taking advantage of the resulting yield differentials. Insurance companies may undertake certain intermediary services of the latter kind, through the management of their asset portfolio, in addition to their main function.

Not only do people dislike negative skewness, but there are also some signs that they would prefer to be in a situation where they face a positively skew income probability distribution. A small chance of a large gain is worth having even if the purchase of this chance reduces the mean expected income very slightly. A gamble of this kind adds to the spice of life, whereas a gamble in the face of a negatively-skewed distribution raises fears because people are apt to exaggerate in their own minds the probabilities of dramatic events.[1] There is evidence, for example, that the demand for premium bonds is a function of the size of its largest prize rather than of its mean expected yield.[2] The football-pool organisations felt it necessary to vary their method of scoring drawn matches in order to lower the probability and thus raise the much publicised top prize for selecting a given number of (score) drawn matches. In this respect several kinds of gambling, which offer a very small chance of a large prize against a relatively small entry fee, represent a form of financial intermediation (state lotteries and premium bonds do so explicitly); this is the obverse of insurance, which for a relatively small entry fee will offset the material results of low-probability disasters.

Although intermediation of these kinds, based on specialist information or the provision of insurance, is important, the archetypal financial intermediary is one which makes its profits by issuing liabilities of a kind preferred by lenders, accordingly at relatively low yields, and invests a proportion of the funds obtained in higher-yielding assets of the form which borrowers prefer to issue. This is possible, in particular, because the intermediary services carried out by the public sector have not resulted in a closure of the margin between the yields on very short, slight liabilities and longer-dated liabilities. Thus the gap between the zero nominal yield on legal tender (it makes no difference for this purpose whether such currency is full commodity money, e.g. gold-based coinage, or fiat money with a zero production cost) and the positive yield on longer-dated assets makes it profitable for intermediaries to bid for cash until the marginal cost of attracting another unit equals the marginal return obtained from buying some other longer-dated asset.

So the third, and main, form of intermediation involves taking advantage of these

---

[1] The work of Professor G. L. S. Shackle is particularly interesting and stimulating on this whole subject; see his seminal book on *Expectation in Economics* (Cambridge University Press, 1949) and his response to the debate which that book caused in his subsequent book on *Uncertainty in Economics* (Cambridge University Press, 1955) pt 1.

[2] See the article by A. C. Rayner, 'Premium Bonds – The Effect of the Prize Structure,' *Bulletin of the Oxford University Institute of Economics and Statistics*, vol. 31, no. 4 (November 1969) pp. 303–11.

differing preferences of borrowers and lenders by issuing liabilities of a kind attractive to lenders at relatively low yields and using the money thereby obtained to lend to borrowers at higher yields. The intermediaries offer liabilities, often in a fixed value, capital-certain form, which possess certain advantages of security, yield and ancillary services such as book-keeping, financial advice, favoured access to loans, etc., which may suffice to attract lenders, leading them to substitute the liabilities of these intermediaries among the assets in their portfolio in place of other assets, public-sector debt, including currency, or other private-sector debt.

The purchaser of any asset, real or financial, must proffer, and the seller will anyhow demand, final settlement for the deal at some stage in a means of payment, money. If a financial intermediary makes its own liabilities more attractive to wealth holders, say by offering a higher rate of interest, so that wealth holders are induced to shift out of asset i into holding more of the intermediary's liabilities, the transition must take two stages, first a sale of asset i for money and then the deposit of such money with the preferred intermediary. A financial intermediary, even if it is a bank (some of) whose own liabilities serve as money, can always attract more monetary (cash) reserves to support its own liabilities, by bidding for them. An individual bank which makes its deposits more attractive will obtain a positive balance with other banks in the clearing house. This will not raise the cash reserves in the banking system as a whole, but the resulting increase in bank, and other private-sector, interest rates (when the reserve base is squeezed) relative to the yields on public-sector, and foreign, assets will lead people to shift out of these latter assets. If they then sell such assets back to the public sector, they will obtain monetary claims on the government (currency or deposits at the Central Bank – high-powered money), which will mainly end up deposited with the banks.

The banks' (the intermediaries') capacity to attract cash – by bidding for it – is not limited by their ability to get the public to substitute directly between bank deposits (financial-intermediary liabilities) and the currency (money) which they, the public, already hold. If the banks (the intermediaries) can induce the public, by offering better terms, to sell other assets for legal tender (for money) and subsequently place such currency (money) with themselves, then their reserves will rise just as much as if they had induced the public to switch directly out of currency (money). Of course, the banks' ability to obtain cash is conditioned on the authorities' willingness to accommodate the public's desire to switch out of other assets via currency into bank deposits at a price which makes the transfer still desirable. But under several common circumstances, for example when the government has fixed the exchange rate or is seeking to stabilise or peg interest rates, this will be the case for a range of assets such as foreign assets or public-sector debt, particularly those forms of public-sector debt such as national savings which have a fixed capital value or are shortly due to mature. Naturally, the corollary also holds that the authorities can act in such a way as to limit the access of the public to additional cash, except at unfavourable prices: even in the case of national savings, which can be redeemed at fixed values, in some cases virtually on demand, the authorities can respond – if they so desire – to any increase in the rates offered by intermediaries to depositors by raising the rate offered on national savings.

Just as sellers of an asset will insist on being paid in money, so equally purchasers of any asset will be concerned to establish the terms upon which they can subsequently realise that asset for money, that is whether the asset is marketable or not, whether the issuer has specified the terms on which he will be prepared to redeem the asset, e.g. at call, at short notice, after some specific maturity, and whether the issuer will be ready (albeit applying some penalty) to redeem on request before the due maturity. In order to attract lenders to deposit money with themselves, financial intermediaries have to compete for funds by offering attractive redemption terms, as one dimension of the set of incentives (including interest payments), which they offer to depositors.

In so far as they stand ready to redeem their own liabilities, the intermediaries will require monetary reserves to honour these obligations. Even the banks, (some of) whose own liabilities count as a means of payment, will require cash reserves against their monetary liabilities to meet outflows of cash. This will be in some small part to meet the possibility of an increased desire by the public for currency, but to a much greater extent to meet potential cash drains resulting from imbalances in inter-bank clearings or from net payments by the private sector to the public sector or to foreigners. Both of these latter sectors will have a limited willingness to build up and to hold claims on the domestic banking sector and will usually require their net claims on the banking sector to be settled in a manner involving a transfer of high-powered money (the monetary liabilities of the public sector).

The general public's use of currency forces the banks to hold additional till cash, but otherwise is *not* a crucial element in determining the need by banks for cash reserves. Indeed, the arrival of a cash-less society would leave the banks' requirement for reserves (other than in the form of till cash) relatively unaffected, since these are determined to a much greater extent (ignoring predictable seasonal and holiday variations in the public's currency demand) by the need to settle irregularities in inter-bank clearings and also net payment flows between the private sector on the one hand and the public and overseas sector on the other.

If everyone, including the public sector and foreigners, was prepared to accept the liability of *any* intermediary, whether it be bank, building society, or insurance company, as *final* settlement for any debt, then the deposits of that intermediary would become equivalent to legal tender for all practical purposes. Then such intermediaries could issue paper without having to offer any interest or other costly service, and with a virtually zero production cost they could expand their deposits indefinitely,[1] using the proceeds to buy up all other assets until inflation became so rampant that the public was induced to switch to other assets as a means of payment, or until their power to act in this way was restrained by political forces. The necessary constraint on the banking system (*a fortiori* on other financial intermediaries) is that some payments, which could perfectly well be settlements between the banking system and the authorities – in which the public plays no direct part – have to be made in cash, legal tender.

Thus all intermediaries, including banks, will have to maintain sufficient monetary reserves to honour their redemption obligations. These obligations depend on the specific redemption terms offered by the intermediary on its liabilities. In general the longer the maturity and/or the higher the penalty cost of early redemption, the less likely is an early drain of reserves from the intermediary; so the smaller reserve ratio need be held.[2] With deposits of a form that allow a larger proportion of the counterpart proceeds to be invested in earning assets, a profit can still be made even though a higher yield will have to be offered

---

[1] This subject was explored in a provocative, but in my view, confused way by B. Pesek and T. Saving in *Money, Wealth and Economic Theory* (Macmillan, New York, 1967); certainly readers of this book should also refer to some of the critical reviews, for example by H. G. Johnson, 'Inside Money, Outside Money, Income, Wealth, and Welfare in Monetary Theory,' *Journal of Money, Credit and Banking*, vol. 1, no. 1 (February 1969) pp. 30–45, especially pp. 31–7, and by A. L. Marty, 'Inside Money, Outside Money and the Wealth Effect,' ibid. pp. 101–11. At this stage in the analysis we are concerned with the determination of the volume of deposits; questions of wealth effects arising from the actions of banks and intermediaries, which were also raised by Pesek and Saving and discussed in these reviews, are considered later on in Chap. 10, Sect. B.

[2] Over medium-length periods, say of six months to one year, however, the need of the public to maintain an adequate holding of a means of payment to carry on normal expenditures and the relatively low interest elasticity of such means of payment may well make the longer-term stability of aggregate holdings of demand deposits greater than that of time deposits, so that the overall portfolio of assets held against current accounts can, perhaps, be more 'unbalanced' than the portfolio held against time deposits. Moreover in many countries, including the United States and the United Kingdom, banks generally refrain, whether by convention or by regulation, from offering any interest on current accounts. So, not only is the aggregate demand for such deposits

(*Footnote* [2] *continued on p. 109*)

to offset the attractions of deposits with shorter maturities and easier reconversion arrangements. So there can be a spectrum of capital-certain assets issued by intermediaries, with those offering deposits of longer maturities and with tougher penalty clauses having, in general, to proffer higher interest yields, and with those providing assets with more favourable redemption terms (which forces them to keep additional low-yielding monetary reserves to honour these obligations) giving lower interest payments.[1]

At the limit financial intermediaries can offer sight deposits, which can be redeemed in legal tender on demand without penalty. When a payee in some deal is satisfied with the reputations of both the payer and the intermediary to be ready and able to honour their commitment to pay legal tender if required, the payee will very often be prepared to accept payment by the transfer of a sight claim on the intermediary rather than in cash. The transmission of cash involves certain costs of transport and safe-keeping avoided by cheque transfer, and the latter also puts some of the book-keeping costs on the intermediary.

So, once their reputation (their 'name' in financial parlance) became established, there was a natural tendency for intermediaries offering sight deposits (essentially banks) to become involved in operating a payments transmission system. This process was cumulative, since the transmission services offered to holders of demand deposits increased the attractions of such assets. Something of a division has, therefore, developed between sight deposits with accompanying payments transmission services, and all other time, and notice, deposits offered by intermediaries, on which transmission services are only offered grudgingly, if at all. The willingness to offer sight deposits, and associated payments transmission

---

relatively insensitive to variations in yields on other assets, but the demand for deposits with each individual bank is not greatly affected by inter-bank competition. In contrast, the aggregate demand for time deposits is likely to be more strongly affected by variations in relative yields, and the demand for such deposits with any one bank will probably respond sensitively to inter-bank competition. So from a prudential point of view, one could make out a good case for applying a higher reserve ratio to time deposits, especially to large deposits obtained through the money market, than to demand deposits.

---

[1] Michael Parkin, in his paper with R. Barrett and M. Gray, 'The Demand for Financial Assets by the Personal Sector of the U.K. Economy,' Proceedings of the London Business School Conference of June 1972 on *Modelling the U.K. Economy* (forthcoming), has undertaken an empirical study of personal preferences among capital-certain assets using the assumption that, where there are two such assets with equal redemption costs, an individual will only hold that asset with the higher yield. It can then be shown that substitution will take place in portfolios consisting of capital-certain assets only between each asset and that asset with the immediately higher (or lower) redemption cost. Technically speaking, the asset-preference matrix (relating the demand for each asset to the yield offered on that and on alternative assets) becomes tridiagonal with all other elements equal to zero.

The above assumption can, however, be challenged. For example, if the interest payment is fixed for the whole life of the asset at the outset of the period, wealth holders with known commitments at approximately the date of maturity can avoid income risk by holding that asset even if its expected yield, having taken account of transfer costs, over the whole period is less than that of some shorter-dated asset. Even where the interest payment is variable, as for example on building society deposits, its variance may not be perfectly correlated with interest payments on other capital-certain assets so, where there are transactions costs involved in switching from one capital-certain asset to another, this lack of correlation between variations in yields could cause some additional portfolio diversification. Moreover, other ancillary attractions, such as geographical convenience, favoured access to certain kinds of loans, advisory services, etc., which differ between institutions, can serve to loosen the correlation between longer effective maturities and higher yields. Indeed, considerations of this general kind have to be adduced in order to explain the continued large holdings in the United Kingdom of deposits with the National Savings Bank (previously the Post Office Savings Bank) and Trustee Savings Banks on conditions no better than the building societies in respect to maturity and ease of redemption and offering in general far lower interest rates. Since these conditions have persisted over decades now, it is not easy to ascribe such holdings to slow adjustment.

services, which makes such deposits an acceptable means of payment, is one possible distinguishing mark between banks and other financial intermediaries. It is, however, not a very clear dividing line, since many well-established financial intermediaries, e.g. merchant banks, may consciously discourage their clients from using their services for effecting regular payment transactions and yet would regard themselves as proper banks. Conversely, certain savings institutions, such as the Trustee Savings Banks in the United Kingdom, which have not traditionally formed part of the banking sector are now offering depositors limited facilities for making cheque payments. And if the recommendations of the Hunt Commission are accepted in the United States, involving the removal of barriers between the different forms of financial intermediation, it may become increasingly difficult to define either the banking sector or the money supply there.

If the yield on longer-dated time deposits has, in general, to be higher than that on short-dated deposits, how must the yield on demand deposits compare with the fixed zero yield on currency? On the whole holding demand deposits is safer, easier and more convenient than holding cash, and a payment by cheque rather than through cash brings with it certain recording and book-keeping services, which is one reason why any slightly dubious transaction, which transactors like to keep 'off the record,' is normally settled in currency. For most purposes, therefore, demand deposits, at the same yield, are superior to cash in convenience. People would prefer to hold demand deposits even at some small negative rate of interest; that is, indeed, what they pay in bank charges. Bank charges, which represent in part a fee for the use of transmission services and in part a payment to the banks for safe-keeping and other services, allow the banks some leeway to discriminate between customers, depending on the size and activity of their respective balances.

To conclude, the first priority for any intermediary must be to attract money from the public, by providing liabilities with a combination of yield, conditions of payment, etc., that prove attractive to the public and yet allow the intermediary the prospect of a reasonable profit. Unless it can obtain money from the public in the first place, it can hardly take advantage of any specialised opportunities in lending.

B. Determinants of the Portfolio Composition and Size of Intermediaries

Given the redemption conditions on their liabilities, the intermediaries must organise their asset portfolios in such a way as to be able to honour these commitments, or else they will suffer penalties from failing to do so, which may be severe, i.e. enforced closure. So intermediaries will require an immediate monetary reserve (cash reserve in the case of banks), to an extent depending on the maturities and reconversion conditions of their liabilities and the probability of the reconversion options being exercised. If it were known exactly when customers would like to withdraw their money from the intermediary, the intermediary would be able to match the maturity of its assets to those of its liabilities. Only for very short periods, when the transactions costs of arranging intra-day lending might outweigh the return, would it be worth holding zero-yielding monetary reserves. The essential rationale for cash reserve holdings by intermediaries is primarily the uncertainty of withdrawals.[1]

There is a considerable opportunity cost in holding monetary reserves, since they provide only a very low yield in comparison with the higher return available on earning assets. Furthermore, the cost of not fulfilling the stated reconversion conditions is not always so very high; for example, the intermediary could ask the customer to wait a little

---

[1] On this see D. Orr and W. G. Mellon, 'Stochastic Reserve Losses and Expansion of Bank Credit,' *American Economic Review*, vol. 51 (September 1961) pp. 614–23, and W. Poole, 'Commercial Bank Reserve Management in a Stochastic Model: Implications for Monetary Policy,' *The Journal of Finance*, vol. 23, no. 5 (December 1968) pp. 769–91.

while it borrows cash from elsewhere or realises a security. In those cases where the cost in reputation, which will affect the probability distribution of the future inflow and with-drawal of money, of failing to live up to the letter of the reconversion conditions is felt to be overwhelming, the usual response, in practice, has been to establish prudential ratios, often sanctioned by common custom or codified by regulation, which will under virtually all conditions allow the reconversion clause to be satisfied, but which ratios in turn can themselves be breached at some positive, but finite, cost – often under terms which make the penalty for failure to abide by the required ratio cumulative. The proportion of cash held in the portfolio will be lower the less is the penalty for breaching the required ratio or for not complying with the arranged reconversion conditions, and also the easier and less expensive are the costs of borrowing, or realising securities, or attracting more money into their liabilities by offering better terms.

In order to economise on cash, one of the steps which intermediaries will take will be to maintain a second echelon of highly liquid short-dated assets, bearing a somewhat higher yield, which can be easily transformed into cash. There are likely to be periods of varying durations during which the average (mean) net inflow varies up or down. The public may choose for some reason to move its funds out of one intermediary into another. The economy may be in a boom, or a slump. There may be a shift in the public's preferences between different kinds of assets, e.g. because unforeseen variations in Stock Exchange prices cause people to review the relative advantages of unit trusts and investment funds, or because the publicised collapse of an institution has caused investors to re-assess the riskiness of all institutions of this kind. Although the net inflow, or net withdrawal, on any one day may be randomly distributed there may well be persistent trends in the net inflow into, or withdrawal from, institutions from one month to the next. It would be expensive to hold cash reserves against medium-term uncertainties of this nature. On the other hand the costs of borrowing or of bidding for further deposits, or of realising certain longer-term assets, could under unfavourable circumstances be excessive. To mitigate these medium-term uncertainties intermediaries are likely to want to hold assets of roughly equivalent maturities, thus reducing the possible costs of having to face prolonged bad periods. Indeed, intermediaries are likely to maintain a whole echelon of assets of differing maturities, depending on the maturities of the liabilities which they have issued and the uncertainties looming ahead.

The choice of the proportionate amount of each of these assets, ranging from completely liquid monetary balances with zero yield through the spectrum of assets to relatively illiquid, high-yielding loans, which intermediaries will select to hold, will depend on the same considerations of balancing risk and return outlined in Chapter 2. Thus the portfolio composition will depend on such factors as the subjective probability of net inflows or withdrawals of money, which in turn will be influenced by the maturity distribution of liabilities, and on the expected return and the expected variance and covariances of return on the available assets.

At this point it may be helpful to present a simplified, numerical example of the working and behaviour of an intermediary, and of the determinants of its holdings of assets and liabilities within a model of a complete system. This hypothetical intermediary is taken to hold cash as its monetary reserve, other government debt as its medium-term reserve asset and loans as its main earning asset. The subscript F refers to the intermediary, L and D are its loans and deposits respectively, both being capital-certain with fixed nominal values, and K stands for its capital and reserves. Intermediaries also hold other government debt (bonds) B, whose market value can vary, and monetary cash reserves C. The balance sheet of its assets and liabilities can then be set out, as an accounting identity

$$C_{Ft} + B_{Ft} + L_{Ft} = D_{Ft} + K_{Ft} \tag{1}$$

where B_{Ft}, for example, represents the market value of government bonds held by inter-mediary F at time t. The value of the intermediary's holdings of cash, bonds and loans must exactly equal its liabilities, deposits plus capital and reserves. Bonds in this model are marketable assets whose value varies in response to changes in interest rates. Since the deposits offered by the intermediary have a fixed nominal value, changes in the market value of the intermediary's existing holdings of bonds, whenever interest rates vary, must be reflected in an equal change in the value of its capital and reserves. This relationship may be approximated[1] by the following equation

$$K_{Ft} - K_{Ft-1} = r_{Bt-1} \cdot B_{Ft-1} \cdot \frac{1}{r_{Bt}} - B_{Ft-1} \tag{2}$$

which expresses the change in the intermediary's capital value as a function of the change in the value of its initial bond holdings (B_{Ft-1}) brought about by the change in interest rates on bonds (r_B) from $t-1$ to t.

Equations (1) and (2) above set out purely definitional accounting relationships. The next, more interesting step, is to examine the intermediary's *behaviour*. This depends on the structure of the system: that is which parameters the intermediary has to take as given, and which are the choice variables which the intermediary can vary in response to shifts in these external parameters. Until the asset preferences of the general public are explicitly treated, we cannot show how the volume of funds deposited with the intermediary is determined. This will be done shortly, but in the meantime the value of D, the intermediary's deposits, will be taken as given. Given, for the moment, the volume of its liabilities, deposits and capital, the intermediary's range of choice is restricted to asset management.

In its asset management the intermediary is generally assumed to be in the position of a price taker: that is to say that it has to accept the level of interest rates ruling in each asset market as an external datum. Given the risks (from the expected variances and covariances of return) on holding the various assets, and the prospective dangers of net withdrawals of funds, and assuming such risks to be constant, we can then write down the demand schedules of the intermediary for each asset as a function of the expected yields on those assets and the available volume of funds.

Following the approach set out in Chapter 3, Appendix A (pp. 55–62), each asset-demand equation is written in a simplified linear form[2] as

$$A_i = a_1 r_1, \dots, a_i r_i, \dots, a_n r_n + b_1 D + b_2 K$$

In this case with the intermediary holding three assets in its portfolio, the set of its demand functions can be put down in matrix form, as below,

	r_c	r_B	r_L	D	K
C_F	a_1	a_2	a_3	a_4	a_5
B_F	b_1	b_2	b_3	b_4	b_5
L_F	c_1	c_2	c_3	c_4	c_5

As described in Chapter 3, Appendix A, the sum of the coefficients of columns 4 and 5 must add to unity with all the coefficients ≥ 0, since the liabilities in the balance sheet

---

[1] The precise relationship depends, *inter alia*, on the actual maturity composition of the bond portfolio held by the intermediary. The total of capital and reserves will also be augmented by profit retentions. Later on in this section we do consider the factors affecting intermediaries' profits, but it seemed an unnecessary complication to incorporate retained profits into the formal model.

[2] We are again ignoring, for simplicity, and to avoid non-linearities in our examples, the complication that the absolute response in the demand of the intermediary for any asset to changes in relative interest rates should be adjusted for scale factors.

(D and K) must be matched by counterpart assets. The parameters, r_c, r_B and r_L represent the interest rates on cash, bonds and loans respectively, which the intermediary is assumed to take as given. Again as previously described, the sub-matrix

$$\begin{matrix} a_1, \ldots, a_3 \\ \vdots \qquad \vdots \\ c_1, \ldots, c_3 \end{matrix}$$

should be symmetrical with a positive main diagonal and all row and column sums equal to zero.[1]

Taking a numerical example with $r_c = 0$, $r_B = 4$, $r_L = 5$, $K = 600$ and $D = 2000$, and with an asset-adjustment matrix with the following coefficient values

	r_c	r_B	r_L	D_F	K_F
C_F	+40	−25	−15	+0·25	0
B_F	−25	+290	−265	+0·25	1·0
L_F	−15	−265	+280	+0·5	0

gives equilibrium values for the assets held in the portfolio of cash 325, bonds 935, loans 1340 ($325 + 935 + 1340 = 2600$). The relative sizes of the coefficients in this rate-response sub-matrix reflect, however, nothing more than my view that in this simulated system – at least over the range of values for which these linear relationships might be approximately true – the elasticity of substitution between bonds and loans is much higher than between (required) low-yielding cash reserves and either bonds or loans (though relatively higher with bonds than with loans).

Consider now the effect of a sudden fall of 1 per cent in bond rates, from 4 to 3 per cent from this starting position. This will raise the value of the intermediary's capital and reserves to 911, i.e. ($\frac{4}{3} \times 935 - 935 + 600$). With other rates and the volume of deposits unchanged, cash holdings would rise by 25 to 350 and the total of loans would rise by 265 to 1605, while the market value of bond holdings would also rise by 21, since the revaluation of existing holdings, raising the total value by 311, outweighs in this example the negative substitution effect of 290: assets and liabilities both rise by 311. In practice, of course, as will soon be demonstrated in a larger model, a sharp fall in bond rates is likely to be accompanied by a fall in other rates and by a rise in the level of deposits, which will cause further changes in the asset portfolio.

The above example of an intermediary's asset-management performance was based on the assumption that it acted as a price taker in all markets, treating all market yields as external parameters, data, to which it had to adjust. This need not generally be true: in some markets the intermediary may be in a position to act as a rate (price) setter, in which case the volume of such assets in the intermediary's portfolio will depend on how much of that asset others are prepared to supply to the intermediary at the selected rate. If, however, the total volume of the intermediary's funds are exogenously determined, then it must act as a price taker in at least one asset market, in order to ensure the maintenance of the balance-sheet identity between assets and liabilities.

In our example the intermediary must act as a price taker in deciding on its cash holdings, since the yield on cash is fixed at zero by the authorities and it will, most likely, regard itself

---

[1] A change in r_B will, indeed, have wealth effects as well as pure substitution effects, but for this exercise the wealth effect is captured via changes in the value of capital and reserves which, it is assumed, are held entirely in bond form. This leaves the sub-matrix to show only substitution effects. Income effects, e.g. working through changes in the level of bank profits, are similarly ignored at this stage.

as a price taker in the bond market. The authorities sometimes exert a dominating in-fluence over rates in the bond market, and in any case the market for government bonds and bills is, in the United Kingdom at least, so broad that single private-sector transactors in the market, even large financial institutions, are not likely to affect the ruling price significantly by their operations. The situation is, however, quite different with respect to the determination of the rate of interest charged by financial intermediaries on their loans. Loans from financial intermediaries to the private sector are not, generally speaking, traded in an open market, but are negotiated separately between individual borrower and lender. The lender quotes the conditions, e.g. collateral security, repayment arrangement and rates, on which he will provide the loan, and the borrower decides, after a modicum of haggling and shopping around for better terms, whether to take it or leave it. The rates to be charged are chosen by the intermediary. In situations of this kind, which are common to many forms of intermediation, the intermediary does not operate along a demand schedule deciding how many loans to take up from the market at its own volition at a given price (rate). Rather, the intermediary chooses the rate, and then provides loans to all acceptable customers at that rate.[1] This does *not* mean, however, that the rate will be insensitive to variations in the volume of loans obtained. Such variations affect the liquidity of the intermediary's asset portfolio, and changes in its liquidity position will in turn affect the rate which it will be prepared to offer.

The intermediary will set the rate which it will charge on loans, in relationship to the rates obtainable on other alternative assets which it could hold, and to the liquidity of its existing portfolio, so as to obtain a preferred combination of return and risk in the manage-ment of its portfolio.[2] In this case it has a rate-setting function for advances, rather than an asset-demand function. This relationship may take the general form

$$r_L = a_1 r_c + a_2 r_B + b_1 \frac{C_F}{D_F}$$

though with $r_c = 0$, we may simplify and linearise into the form

$$r_L = a r_B + b_1 C_F + b_2 D_F$$

With bonds providing an alternative, more liquid-earning asset, intermediaries will want to charge a higher rate on loans, so $a > 1$. As the intermediary becomes more liquid, it will wish to expand its holdings of the higher-yielding, but less liquid, earning asset, so $b_1 < 0$ and $b_2 > 0$.

If the intermediary is setting the rate on loans, then it cannot also choose their volume. So the total volume of funds which the intermediary is free to divide between those assets, cash and bonds in this case, where it acts as price taker becomes equal to $D_F + K_F - L_F$.[3]

The form of the intermediary's asset-demand functions for these two variables will

---

[1] In practice most intermediaries are not completely free to vary the rates which they charge, and rates are restrained by cartel arrangements of one kind or another, by political influence, or by fears of 'rate wars' under oligopolistic market conditions. In such circumstances an intermediary may have to take the rate on loans as approximately given and adjust its provision of loans, as conditions change, by rationing them more or less tightly to less-favoured customers. On this subject see D. M. Jaffee, *Credit Rationing and the Commercial Loan Market* (Wiley, New York, 1971).

[2] For an excellent analysis of the factors determining the rate-setting functions of banks for both loans and deposits see Mario Monti, 'A Theoretical Model of Bank Behaviour and its Impli-cations for Monetary Policy,' *L'Industria Revista di Economica Politica*, no. 2 (1971) pp. 165–91.

[3] On this, see W. R. White, 'Models of Deposit Bank Portfolio Behaviour,' part of the Proceed-ings of the London Business School Conference of June 1972 on *Modelling the U.K. Economy* (forthcoming).

change also, with r_L no longer entering as an argument (since r_L is no longer an external parameter, nor L_F a choice variable), and may be set out as follows

	r_c	r_B	D_F	K_F	L_F
C_F	a_1	a_2	a_3	a_4	a_5
B_F	b_1	b_2	b_3	b_4	b_5

If we specify, say, the demand function for cash in numerical form as, for example, $C_F = 50r_c - 50r_B + (D_F - L_F)$, then one can either treat the volume of bonds as determined as a residual, to satisfy the balance-sheet identity, or equivalently – and perhaps more satisfying – deduce from the constraints in the asset-demand matrix that in order to satisfy the accounting identities, $B_F = -50r_c + 50r_B + K_F$. With $r_c = 0$, $r_B = 4$, $D_F = 2000$, $K_F = 600$, $L_F = 1400$, then $B_F = 800$ and $C_F = 400$ ($800 + 400 = 2000 + 600 - 1400$).

The most that can be done in a study of the behaviour of an intermediary in isolation is to examine the determinants of its asset-demand functions and of its rate-setting function(s). In order to show the complete process of portfolio determination, it is necessary to explore the interplay between the intermediary (sector) and other sectors of the economy. For this purpose two other sectors have to be introduced, the public who hold the intermediaries' deposits and borrow their loans, and the government who have outstanding financial liabilities in the form of cash and bonds. In addition to holding the intermediaries' deposits and advances (treated in their accounts as a negative asset), the public in this simplified model also holds cash, bonds and real assets (K_p).[1] The public's balance sheet may be written down as

$$C_{pt} + B_{pt} + L_{pt} + D_{pt} + K_{pt} = W_{pt} \qquad (3)$$

With the market value of bonds varying (inversely) with the fluctuations in interest rates the public will, like the intermediaries, have capital gains (losses) on bonds as interest rates vary, which may again be approximately expressed by the relationship

$$CG_t = r_{Bt-1} \cdot B_{pt-1} \cdot \frac{1}{r_{Bt}} - B_{pt-1} \qquad (4)$$

where CG are capital gains. The wealth of the public can change in two further ways. First, they can invest in additional real capital (I); second, they can have a surplus $(+Q)$ in their current transactions with the government. By accounting identity $I + Q = S$, where S represents the public's current saving. In this exercise, however, we shall always take Q, the government deficit, as zero, so $S = I$. The volume of new investment in this case is assumed to be determined by a simple flow relationship in response to the levels of the alternative rates on real capital and bonds, so that

$$I_t = a_1 r_{Kt} + a_2 r_{Bt} \qquad (5)$$

where r_K is the yield on real capital and $a_1 > 0$, $a_2 < 0$. Ignoring for simplicity changes in the market value of existing real capital as r_K varies, this gives the definitional relationship

$$K_{pt} = I_t + K_{pt-1} \qquad (6)$$

---

[1] Among the real assets of the public should be included their equity in the intermediaries themselves. The market value of this equity may not, however, vary closely in line with the accounting value of the intermediaries' capital and reserves; so for this reason and for simplicity we shall ignore this further link between the intermediary sector and the public.

Since, by definition,

$$W_{pt} = CG_t + I_t + W_{pt-1} \tag{7}$$

equation (3) above can be rewritten as

$$C_{pt} + B_{pt} + L_{pt} + D_{pt} + K_{pt} = CG_t + I_t + W_{pt-1} \tag{8}$$

The advantage of this reformulation is that the public's preferred asset distribution may differ depending on whether it is choosing to redistribute existing wealth among assets (W_{pt-1}), or using new investment which goes to form additional real capital, or enjoying capital gains on its bonds.

In contrast to the case of intermediaries it seems reasonable to assume that the individual members of the private sector are always price takers. So, for the sector as a whole, assuming linearity (and taking risk factors as constant), the demand function by the private sector for each asset may be expressed as a linear function of the mean expected yields and the scale factors, W_{pt-1}, CG_t and I_t. This can again be set out in matrix form, with the subscript p showing that the functions relate to the personal sector, as follows

	r_c	r_B	r_L	r_D	r_K	W_{pt-1}	I_t	CG_t
C_p	a_1	a_2	a_3	a_4	a_5	a_6	a_7	a_8
B_p	b_1	b_2	b_3	b_4	b_5	b_6	b_7	b_8
L_p	c_1	c_2	c_3	c_4	c_5	c_6	c_7	c_8
D_p	d_1	d_2	d_3	d_4	d_5	d_6	d_7	d_8
K_p	e_1	e_2	e_3	e_4	e_5	e_6	e_7	e_8

where again the coefficients[1] on columns 6–8 must sum to unity, and the sub-matrix

$$\begin{matrix} a_1, \ldots, a_5 \\ \vdots \qquad \vdots \\ e_1, \ldots, e_5 \end{matrix}$$

should be symmetrical with positive main diagonal and with rows and columns summing to zero. The inclusion of intermediary assets and liabilities provides no obvious reason to expect complementarity between assets (liabilities), so presumably all off-diagonal elements would remain negative.

This leaves the final sector, the government sector. The value of government bonds outstanding ($B_t = B_{Ft} + B_{pt}$) will be increased either by a fiscal deficit (Q_t) (assumed to be financed in the first instance by bond sales), or by open-market sales of bonds for cash (OMO), or by changes in the market value of existing bonds. Putting these together gives the public-sector financing constraint

$$Q_t + OMO_t = B_t - B_{t-1} - CG_t - (K_{Ft} - K_{Ft-1}) \tag{9}$$

So the government, apart from setting the yield on currency at zero, and having (behind the scenes of this exercise) an influence on private-sector savings and investment by the form of its taxation policy, e.g. investment incentives, has two degrees of freedom. First, it can alter the size of its overall deficit (Q) (though for this exercise Q is held at zero throughout), and second, it has the power to set one monetary variable. Given Q it can either determine the outstanding value of bonds ($B = B_F + B_p$), with the total of cash becoming necessary

---

[1] The coefficient c_6 could, however, be negative, since in the range of values for which the linear approximation holds true the public will want to maintain some outstanding loans from the financial intermediary. Since this debt is treated as a negative asset, this could entail a negative coefficient on c_6. Similarly coefficient c_7 could well be negative.

to finance the government deficit and the bond rate being determined endogenously, or it can fix the total volume of cash ($C = C_F + C_p$), or the rate of interest on bonds, r_B. In a deterministic model of this kind it makes no difference whether the authorities select as their proximate target the level of cash (C), the volume of bond sales (OMO) or the bond rate of interest (r_B), in the sense that the choice of a value for one of these implies unique values for the other two variables. As noted later in Chapters 8 and 12, in an uncertain, stochastic system it can matter very much whether the authorities take interest rates or the cash base as their proximate target, but that is a complication to be dealt with later.

Before setting out the complete model there is, however, still one further matter that needs consideration. In the account of the system so far the yield on cash is assumed to be fixed by the authorities; the yields on bonds and on real capital are determined in the open market by the interplay of the demand for such assets with the supply of these (which is a function of past stocks plus in one case the authorities' financial operations and in the other the volume of new investment); the yield on advances may, depending on circumstances, either be set by the interplay of demand and supply of the public and the intermediaries, or be fixed by the intermediaries through a rate-setting function. But what determines the yield on deposits? In the case of some categories of deposit, e.g., certificates of deposit, the rate is set by an interplay of demand and supply in the market. But more commonly the rate is either fixed by the authorities, for example in the United States requiring that banks shall not offer interest payments on demand deposits and setting maximum interest rates on time deposits, or is set by the various intermediaries on the basis of some rate-fixing function. Thus there are four options,

(i) rate on deposits fixed by the authorities, loan-rate market determined,
(ii) rate on deposits fixed by the authorities, loan rate set by the intermediary,
(iii) rate on deposits set by the intermediary, loan-rate market determined,
(iv) both rates set by the intermediary.

We shall take option (i) as our basic system, but we shall also explore option (iv).[1]

It is now possible to set down the model of the complete system (with the intermediary assumed to be a price taker in all asset markets and the rate on intermediary deposits exogenously fixed, say by the authorities); in order to show how the system works, simulated numerical values will be given to the coefficients and the model solved to show the resulting values of all the variables within the system.

The Basic System

A. The Intermediary Sector

Behavioural equations

$$C_{FT} = 40r_{ct} - 25r_{Bt} - 15r_{Lt} + 0.25D_{Ft} \tag{10}$$

$$B_{Ft} = -25r_{ct} + 290r_{Bt} - 265r_{Lt} + 0.25D_{Ft} + K_{Ft} \tag{11}$$

$$L_{Ft} = -15r_{ct} - 265r_{Bt} + 280r_{Lt} + 0.5D_{Ft} \tag{11a}$$

Accounting identities

$$r_{Bt-1} \cdot B_{Ft-1} \cdot \frac{1}{r_{Bt}} - B_{Ft-1} = K_{Ft} - K_{Ft-1} \tag{12}$$

$$C_{Ft} + B_{Ft} + L_{Ft} = D_{Ft} + K_{Ft} \tag{13}$$

---

[1] There would have been no difficulties in exploring the other options also, but the extra insights to be obtained did not seem to justify extending the exercise further.

B. The Public

Behavioural equations

$$C_{pt} = 400r_{ct} - 100r_{Bt} - 50r_{Lt} - 200r_{Dt} - 50r_{Kt} + 0.22W_{pt-1} \qquad (14)$$

$$B_{pt} = -100r_{ct} + 1500r_{Bt} - 400r_{Lt} - 500r_{Dt} - 500r_{Kt}$$
$$+ 0.3W_{pt-1} + CG_t \qquad (15)$$

$$L_{pt} = -50r_{ct} - 400r_{Bt} + 1400r_{Lt} - 250r_{Dt} - 700r_{Kt} \qquad (16)$$

$$D_{pt} = -200r_{ct} - 500r_{Bt} - 250r_{Lt} + 1350r_{Dt} - 400r_{Kt}$$
$$+ 0.43W_{pt-1} \qquad (17)$$

$$K_{pt} = -50r_{ct} - 500r_{Bt} - 700r_{Lt} - 400r_{Dt} + 1650r_{Kt}$$
$$+ 0.05W_{pt-1} + I_t \qquad (17a)$$

$$I_t = -200r_{Bt} + 200r_{Kt} \qquad (18)$$

Accounting identities

$$C_{pt} + B_{pt} + L_{pt} + D_{pt} + K_{pt} = W_{pt-1} + CG_t + I_t \qquad (19)$$

$$r_{Bt-1} \cdot B_{pt-1} \cdot \frac{1}{r_{Bt}} - B_{pt-1} = CG_t \qquad (20)$$

$$K_{pt} = I_t + K_{pt-1} \qquad (21)$$

$$L_{Ft} = -L_{pt} \qquad (22)$$

$$D_{Ft} = D_{pt} \qquad (23)$$

C. Government Sector

Accounting identities

$$Q_t + \text{OMO}_t = B_t - B_{t-1} - CG_t - (K_{Ft} - K_{Ft-1}) \qquad (24)$$

$$B_t = B_{Ft} + B_{pt} \qquad (25)$$

$$C_t = C_{Ft} + C_{pt} \qquad (26)$$

Equations (11*a*) and (17*a*) are shown for the record, but given the balance-sheet identities (equations (13) and (19)) any one out of the set of behavioural relationships in the intermediary and private sectors (except equation (18)) can be deduced from the remainder and is, therefore, redundant (Walras's law). This leaves a system of seven behavioural equations and ten identities to solve seventeen unknowns; two interest rates, r_L, r_K, five intermediary-sector assets/liabilities, C_F, B_F, L_F, D_F, K_F, seven private-sector assets/liabilities, $C_p, B_p, L_p, D_p, K_p, I, CG$, and any three out of four public-sector variables, r_B, OMO, B or C (Q being zero throughout).

Given the starting conditions, that is the values at time $t - 1$, of $r_{Bt-1} = 4$, $B_{Ft-1} = 1000$, $K_{Ft-1} = 600$, $B_{pt-1} = 1600$, $K_{pt-1} = 7200$ and $W_{pt-1} = 10,000$, the system can be solved if values are chosen for r_c (equals 0), for r_D which is taken as fixed by the authorities at 3 per cent, and for r_B (or instead for C_t or for OMO$_t$ or for B_t). If $r_{Bt} = r_{Bt-1} = 4$, then there will be no changes in capital values, so it is perhaps easiest to take that as the base run. The result[1] is shown in Table 6.1.

---

[1] I am very grateful to I. M. Clements, who, with assistance from J. P. Burman, undertook these simulation exercises for me. The solution of this model was technically interesting since they found a method of obtaining an exact solution to a system containing mild non-linearities involving r_B.

TABLE 6.1

	Intermediaries	Public	Government	
Cash	311	558	869	
Bonds	971	1560	2531	OMO = −69
Loans	1252	−1252	—	loan rate = 4·80%
Deposits	1934	1934	—	
Capital Gain	0	0	—	
Investment	—	808	—	rate on capital = 8·04%
Net Worth	600	10,808	—	

This does not leave the system in a completely static equilibrium, because investment is continuing and wealth is growing. However, the purpose of this exercise is not to trace the dynamic properties of the economy as a whole; indeed, the real sector, and the investment function, is much too sketchily drawn in for that purpose. Rather the intention is to explore how, from a given starting point, the system would alter if the authorities varied their monetary policy. It can be checked that if the authorities set the total value of cash at 869 or OMO at −69 exactly the above conditions will be reproduced. In the footnote below[1] the tables illustrate how the system responds to variations in the monetary-control

[1]

(A) if $r_{Bt} = 3\%$ [$r_c = 0, r_D = 3$]

	Intermediaries	Public	Government	
Cash	613	745	1358	
Bonds	1544	1364	2908	OMO = −559
Loans	1757	−1757	—	loan rate = 3·79%
Deposits	2980	2980	—	
Capital Gain	333·3	533·3	—	
Investment	—	861	—	rate on capital = 7·31%
Net Worth	933·3	11,394	—	

(B) if $r_{Bt} = 4·5\%$ [$r_c = 0, r_D = 3$]

	Intermediaries	Public	Government	
Cash	161	464	625	
Bonds	740	1746	2486	OMO = 175
Loans	1000	−1000	—	loan rate = 5·31%
Deposits	1411	1411	—	
Capital Gain	−111	−178	—	
Investment	—	781	—	rate on capital = 8·40%
Net Worth	489	10,603	—	

(C) if cash C_t were raised by 200 to 1069 [$r_c = 0, r_D = 3$]

	Intermediaries	Public	Government	
Cash	435	634	Fixed at 1069	OMO = −269
Bonds	1183	1444	2627	bond rate = 3·59%
Loans	1458	−1458	—	loan rate = 4·39%
Deposits	2362	2362	—	
Capital Gain	113·9	182·3	—	
Investment	—	829·4	—	rate on capital = 7·74%
Net Worth	713·9	11,011·7	—	

(*Footnote* [1] *continued on p. 120*)

E.

instruments at time t, given the initial starting conditions at time $t - 1$: nothing very startling appears. When the authorities act in an expansive manner by lowering interest rates (or increasing the cash base, or undertaking open-market purchases) asset quantities rise and market-interest rates fall. It is not so much the particular numerical results that matter; indeed they are, in a sense, only the figment of my imagination, since they depend on arbitrarily-chosen numerical coefficients.[1] What is important is to grasp that the simultaneous determination of the value of *all* the endogenous assets, and rates, in the system depends on the interplay of the full set of sectoral behavioural functions, given the initial position and the policy actions taken by the authorities.

Two points are, perhaps, worth noting. First, the investment function in this model was constructed to be fairly sensitive to movements in the relative yields on capital[2] and bonds. Yet investment appears to respond only slightly to changes in monetary policy. This is because market forces allow a very much smaller change in the *relative* yield between rates on capital and rates on bonds as the latter is varied by the actions of the authorities. Thus investment may appear to respond much more to factors, such as improved expectations of future sales (see Chapter 5), that cause changes in r_K, while r_B is held fixed by the authorities, than to changes in r_B which induce changes in the same direction in r_K. This matter is discussed further in Chapter 9.

Secondly, in this version of the model the rate offered on deposits was held fixed (at 3 per cent): so variations in the bond rate, and in other market-determined rates as compared to the fixed deposit rate brought about relatively large swings in the volume of

(D) if cash C_t were lowered by 200 to 669 $[r_c = 0, r_D = 3]$				
	Intermediaries	**Public**	**Government**	
Cash	188	481	Fixed at 669	OMO = +131
Bonds	780	1710	2489	bond rate = 4·41%
Loans	1046	−1046	—	loan rate = 5·22%
Deposits	1506	1506	—	
Capital Gain	−93	−148	—	
Investment	—	786	—	rate on capital = 8·34%
Net Worth	507	10,638	—	

(E) if OMO reduced by 200 from base run $[r_c = 0, r_D = 3]$

Same as case (C) above

(F) if OMO increased by 200 from base run $[r_c = 0, r_D = 3]$

Same as case (D) above

[1] The practical complexities and the data limitations – particularly the lack of satisfactory balance-sheet data and the absence of proxy variables for expected mean yields on marketable assets – of adopting such a portfolio adjustment approach are so formidable that little applied work has been done to provide an empirical basis for models of this kind. Marcus Miller's thesis on the working of the U.K. financial system (unpublished Ph.D. thesis, Yale University) is one of the few examples known to me. So at this point of time it is only really possible to show solutions based on simulated systems with arbitrarily-chosen numbers (except that they must satisfy the appropriate constraints). The fact that it is difficult to provide this approach with an empirical coating does not diminish its conceptual validity.

[2] On the other hand changes in the market value of existing capital assets, which occur when yields on capital vary, are disregarded in this model. As discussed further in Chap. 9, the differential between the market value of existing real assets and the construction costs of new real assets is a potent determinant of the level of investment. To this extent this model omits entirely one important route whereby financial factors affect investment expenditures.

deposits in response to quite small changes in the authorities' policy instruments. With loan rate freely determined in the market, the variation in intermediary loans was less. As a result, therefore, of this rate fixity, the intermediary's reserve assets, cash and bonds, exhibited considerable volatility; in this version of the system, when r_B goes to 5 per cent, C_F goes down to zero. This does, indeed, illustrate one of the properties of the financial system, which is that rigidities in fixing rates (or a sharp change in relative rates) can bring about extreme fluctuations in flows of funds between different channels: on the other hand, so long as market rates can all vary relatively flexibly together, the authorities' action will have a more generalised impact with less disturbance to the pattern of intermediation.

This point can be further illustrated by taking a more extreme example in which not only is the rate on intermediaries' deposits held fixed at 3 per cent, but also the rate which they can charge on their advances is held fixed, at 5 per cent. With the rate on advances determined, a revised behavioural demand function for cash by the intermediary has to be introduced, taking the form here – as discussed previously –

$$C_F = 50r_c - 50r_B + (D_F - L_F) \tag{27}$$

This replaces equation (10) in the basic system, and equation (11) drops out of this variant. Since the behavioural form is different, the solution to the system when $r_B = 4$ also changes, as shown in case A in the footnote below.[1] In particular, the intermediary's demand for

---

1

(A) $r_B = 4 \ [r_c = 0, r_D = 3, r_L = 5]$

	Intermediaries	Public	Government
Cash	617	543	1160
Bonds	800	1439	2239
Loans	1034	−1034	—
Deposits	1851	1851	—
Capital Gains	0	0	—
Investment	—	824	— rate on capital = 8·12%
Net Worth	—	10,824	—

(B) $r_B = 3·5 \ [r_c = 0, r_D = 3, r_L = 5]$

	Intermediaries	Public	Government
Cash	1258	601	1860
Bonds	918	994	1912
Loans	728	−728	—
Deposits	2162	2162	—
Capital Gains	143	229	—
Investment	—	893	— rate on capital = 7·97%
Net Worth	743	11,122	—

(C) $r_B = 4·5 \ [r_c = 0, r_D = 3, r_L = 5]$

	Intermediaries	Public	Government
Cash	−25	486	461
Bonds	714	1936	2650
Loans	1340	−1340	—
Deposits	1541	1541	—
Capitals Gains	−111	−178	—
Investment	—	754	— rate on capital = 8·27%
Net Worth	489	10,576	—

cash function has been so changed that it obtains more reserves, when $r_B = 4$, than it held in the base run. But even this larger stock is hardly sufficient. When bond rates fall, relative to advances and deposit rates, the public wants to borrow much less, since advances have become comparatively expensive; so with deposits rising and advances falling, the intermediary becomes glutted with reserve assets (case B in footnote 1, p. 121). Equivalently when bond rates rise, relative to fixed advances and deposit rates, the intermediary's cash reserves become entirely exhausted (case C in footnote 1, p. 121).

The lesson to be drawn from this is that sharp changes in relative rates caused, say, by fixing certain rates while others are freely determined by market forces, are likely to cause considerable disturbances in the pattern of financial flows. Rather than absolutely fixing rates it is, therefore, more common to find intermediaries setting rates in relationship to rates on other assets in the market. The factors determining the rate to be charged by intermediaries on loans have already been discussed. At this point we turn to consider how intermediaries determine how much to offer on deposits.

In most cases there is no market place for the small funds which individuals can invest in financial intermediaries, though there have developed open markets, e.g. the C.D. (certificate of deposit) market, for large quantities of cash where prices are determined by the interplay of demand and supply. In the process of collecting great numbers of small sums of money from the general public, a typical function of intermediaries, the terms offered to depositors are generally set by the intermediaries, which then stand ready to take all the money offered to them at that rate. Intermediaries do not, therefore, have a demand function for deposits, deciding how much money to accept as the terms determined on some hypothetical, open market vary. Instead they set the terms, and then accept all the money deposited with them on such terms, though again it should be emphasised that the volume of funds deposited at this rate will, *ceteris paribus*, affect the liquidity of the intermediary's portfolio, and changes in the intermediary's liquidity will in turn influence its choice of rate.

There are, however, often severe constraints on the freedom of the individual intermediary to vary the rates which it offers in response to purely economic factors. Political regulation, or pressure, to control the rates offered on deposits or charged on loans is observed over a wide range of financial intermediaries, such as banks and building societies. The oligopolistic nature of many intermediaries, where economies of scale or official licensing cause barriers to entry, where the degree of substitution between the deposits (or the particular kind of loan, e.g. mortgage business) of the individual intermediaries is high, provides a natural breeding ground for cartel agreements on rates, fixing recommended rates, or relating common rates to some index of rates in the open market, so that competition between members of the group should not 'get out of hand'.

Although such extraneous factors often dominate rate fixing in reality, for the purpose of this exercise they will be set on one side. If the intermediary was completely free to respond to economic conditions, how would it set the rate to be offered to depositors? This will depend in large part on the return that can be made from extending the size of the portfolio. So the deposit rate offered will be higher the greater the yield on earning assets, and/or the more squeezed the intermediary is for reserve assets, so that the attraction of more funds would allow it to add to its reserve assets, and thus alleviate risk. The relationship in this case may be set down, as follows

$$r_D = b_1 + b_2 r_L + b_3 r_B + b_4 \frac{C_F}{D_F}$$

or in a simplified linear form

$$r_D = b_1 + b_2 r_L + b_3 r_B + b_4 C_F + b_5 D_F$$

where $b_2, b_3, b_5 > 0$ and $b_4 < 0$.

Giving simulated numerical values to the rate-setting relationships for deposits shown above, and for loans[1] discussed earlier, as follows

$$r_{Lt} = 1 \cdot 1 r_{Bt} - 0 \cdot 002 C_{Ft} + 0 \cdot 0004 D_{Ft}$$
$$r_{Dt} = 0 \cdot 35 r_{Bt} + 0 \cdot 3 r_{Lt} - 0 \cdot 002 C_{Ft} + 0 \cdot 0004 D_{Ft}$$

allows the model to be re-run with these rates, instead of being fixed, being determined by these rate-setting functions. With the intermediary's rates no longer fixed, but adjusted in line with other market rates, the volatility of financial flows between different assets and the severe pressures on the intermediary's cash position, that were observed in the previous exercise, now disappear. Instead, as shown below,[2] adjustment is much smoother; in

---

[1] Note that the rate offered on deposits does not enter as a factor determining the rate charged on loans. Given the overall size of the funds at the command of the intermediary, which does of course depend on the rates offered to depositors, the resulting choice for the intermediary then becomes one of distributing its resources optimally between the various potential assets which it can hold, and this depends not on the rates offered on deposits but on the yields, and risks involved, on alternative combinations of assets. On the other hand the rate that an intermediary can, and will under competitive conditions, offer for deposits will depend on the return that can be made from extending the size of the portfolio. On this point, see the article by Mario Monti, 'A Theoretical Model of Bank Behaviour and its Implications for Monetary Policy,' *L'Industria Revista di Economia Politica*, no. 2 (1971) pp. 165–91.

[2]

(A) $r_B = 4, r_c = 0$

	Intermediaries	Public	Government	Rates (per cent)
Cash	302	581	884	—
Bonds	800	1716	2516	—
Loans	1475	−1475	—	4·59
Deposits	1978	1978	—	2·96
Capital Gains	—	—	—	—
Investment	—	787	(rate on capital)	7·94
Net Worth	600	10,787	—	—

(B) $r_B = 3, r_c = 0$

	Intermediaries	Public	Government	Rates (per cent)
Cash	338	905	1243	—
Bonds	1083	1940	3023	—
Loans	1769	−1769	—	3·53
Deposits	2257	2257	—	2·33
Capital Gains	333	533	—	—
Investment	—	806	—	7·03
Net Worth	933	11,339	—	—

(C) $r_B = 5, r_c = 0$

	Intermediaries	Public	Government	Rates (per cent)
Cash	267	258	524	—
Bonds	650	1706	2356	—
Loans	1182	−1182	—	5·65
Deposits	1698	1698	—	3·59
Capital Gains	−200	−320	—	—
Investment	—	768	—	8·84
Net Worth	400	10,448	—	—

particular the cash ratio of the intermediary becomes much more stable, remaining very close to 15 per cent in all three simulated cases.

If the rate of interest which intermediaries can offer on deposits is externally fixed, for example by the fiat of the authorities, then – apart from offering inducements to depositors in other forms, e.g. better services of one kind or another – the intermediary has an essentially passive role in the determination of its stock of deposits. In such cases the level of deposits placed with the intermediary will depend on the private sector's wealth, factors such as the level of money incomes that will influence the public's asset preferences, and the pattern of interest rates. The authorities can control the volume of deposits placed with intermediaries by operating on these elements, e.g. on the pattern of interest rates. In a full information, deterministic model of the kind shown here the authorities can control the volume of deposits exactly by using their monetary instrument (whether it take the form of operating primarily through interest rates or through the cash base).

When an intermediary is passive in this sense, its freedom of manoeuvre is more or less limited to choosing to distribute a portfolio of a given size among various assets so as to achieve an optimal combination of return and risk. Portfolio selection was discussed in Chapter 2, and there is little to add to the analysis when the operator is an intermediary rather than an individual. An intermediary's behaviour, however, becomes more interesting when it is not purely passive, but adjusts the rates which it offers in line with market rates. Earlier it was simply asserted that the rates offered on deposits would rise in line with rates obtainable on earning assets and would vary inversely with liquidity. But this functional relationship derives in turn from the intermediary's wish to maximise a utility function which will include among its arguments the expected return on its assets, the expected variance of that return, the expected liquidity (safety) of the portfolio, and the expected variance of the liquidity position. In the very simplest case one might assume that the intermediary was a price taker in asset markets who expected the mean return, variance of that return, liquidity and variance of liquidity to remain constant as the asset portfolio expanded. In this instance one can draw up the perceived revenue function facing the intermediary, with average revenue equal to marginal revenue, as it expands its deposits. On the other hand, as the intermediary raises the rate offered to attract more depositors the average and marginal costs of funds will rise. As depicted in Fig. 6.2, the equilibrium level of deposits is OQ obtained at a cost of OA.

We can, however, go beyond such simple examples by using the model of the financial system already set up. Thus the level of the intermediary's earnings can be easily established from the equation

$$\pi = r_B \cdot B_F + r_L \cdot L_F - r_D \cdot D_F$$

while the liquidity position may be proxied by the cash ratio C_F/D_F. So the model can be used to simulate how the level of profits and liquidity might vary as the intermediary alters

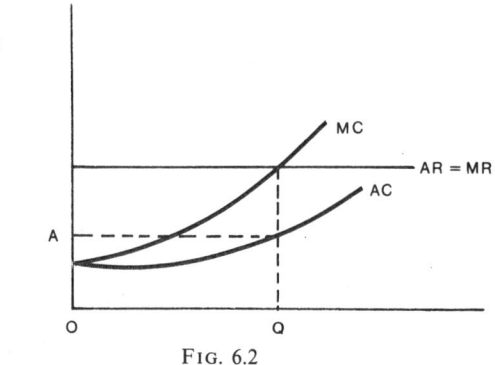

FIG. 6.2

its rate-setting function for deposits and, furthermore, how such profits and liquidity in turn fluctuate – for any given rate-setting function – in response to movements between easy and tight money policies. In short, it is possible to simulate a menu of outcomes, for profits and liquidity, achieved as differing rate-setting functions are adopted, and thereby show the options open to an intermediary. An example of this procedure is illustrated below.[1] In such circumstances, of course, the volume of deposits obtained by the intermed-

---

[1] We took as our basic case the version of the model where the intermediary sets both the deposit and loan rates. Holding the loan rate-setting function constant, we examined how profits, profit variability, cash ratio and cash ratio variability altered as the coefficients in the deposit rate-setting function were varied. This equation initially took the form

$$r_D = a_1 + a_2 r_B + a_3 r_L + a_4 C_F + a_5 D_F$$

where $a_1 = 0, a_2 = 0.35, a_3 = 0.3, a_4 = -0.002, a_5 = 0.0004$. We examined the effect of changing the value of a_1 and also of varying both a_2 and a_3 (together) up or down. In each case we obtained the resulting values for three values of r_B (3 per cent easy money, 4 per cent base run, 5 per cent tight money), and computed the average values and standard deviations of profits and of the cash ratio. A selection of the results is set down below.

Change in coefficients			Profit			Average profit	Standard deviation of profits	Cash ratio (per cent)			Average cash ratio (per cent)	Standard deviation (per cent)
a_1	a_2 and a_3	$3\%r_B$	$4\%r_B$	$5\%r_B$			$3\%r_B$	$4\%r_B$	$5\%r_B$		
0	0	42.19	41.08	38.25	40.51	2.029	14.98	15.29	15.70	15.32	0.36
0	−0.10	52.24	50.22	44.53	49.00	4.000	7.27	1.29	−12.68	−1.37	10.23
0	−0.05	47.97	47.02	43.55	46.18	2.325	11.78	10.16	7.53	9.83	2.14
+0.2	−0.05	50.72	48.83	44.44	47.99	3.223	9.29	6.78	2.46	6.18	3.46
0	−0.02	46.67	43.77	40.87	43.19	1.988	13.82	13.52	13.09	13.48	0.37
+0.2	−0.02	47.99	46.34	42.71	45.68	2.703	11.77	11.04	9.95	10.92	0.91
0	−0.01	43.46	42.47	39.64	41.86	1.982	14.42	14.45	14.48	14.45	0.03
+0.1	−0.01	45.28	43.96	40.79	43.34	2.309	13.50	13.37	13.19	13.35	0.15
−0.5	0	30.41	30.83	29.54	30.26	0.661	18.48	19.13	19.95	19.18	0.74
0	0	42.19	41.08	38.25	40.51	2.029	14.98	15.29	15.70	15.32	0.36
+0.1	0	44.10	42.69	39.56	42.12	2.326	14.11	14.30	14.56	14.32	0.22
+0.2	0	45.87	44.15	40.71	43.58	2.626	13.16	13.21	13.29	13.22	0.06
+0.5	0	50.30	47.66	43.31	47.09	3.532	9.74	9.18	8.36	9.09	0.69
0	+0.01	40.86	39.58	36.71	39.05	2.128	15.52	16.07	16.78	16.12	0.63
+0.3	+0.01	46.44	44.34	40.64	43.81	2.938	12.82	13.06	13.38	13.09	0.28
0	+0.10	26.62	21.93	16.15	21.57	5.244	19.23	21.00	22.88	21.03	1.83

The results showed that the average level of profits could be increased, as compared with the base run (when the initial values of the coefficients in the deposit rate-setting function were left unchanged), by increasing the constant or by decreasing the coefficients a_2 and a_3. In either case the improvement in the average level of profitability was generally accompanied by an increase in the variability of profits, by a fall in the average cash ratio and by an increase in the variability of the cash ratio. The trade-off, obtaining higher mean expected profits in return for increased risk, seemed rather more favourable when the constant term was increased than when the coefficients a_2 and a_3 were reduced. The particular numerical outcomes, however, are not important, since they depend entirely on the arbitrary numerical coefficients fed into the simulation. What is important is to see the kind of way in which the choice of rate-setting function will affect the outcomes and the risk/return combination available. Of course, in a real world setting businessmen cannot afford to undertake experiments of this kind. Nevertheless, on the basis of experience, market research, judgement, etc., they do have to make decisions about setting and varying price, and their subjective views about the effect of their decisions on the level of profits on the one hand and the risks involved on the other will be potent factors in determining such decisions.

An exactly similar exercise was also run (though not shown here) to explore the results of changing the loan-rate function, while holding the deposit rate-setting function constant. In this

(*Footnote* [1] *continued on p. 126*)

iary is in large part determined by its own actions and portfolio preferences.[1]

The process of the determination of the volume of intermediary deposits and loans is one of portfolio adjustment in response to shifts in relative interest rates, wealth and asset preferences. As will be argued further in Chapter 7 this is true for all financial intermediaries, whether banks or non-bank. The system can only be in equilibrium when *all* asset preferences are satisfied.

Given the asset-demand functions and the initial conditions, this simulation model shows the equilibrium values of the assets and rates, which satisfy all asset preferences. If all the participants in the system had perfect knowledge of all the functional relationships and all the initial conditions, then any disturbance to the system could lead to a simultaneous and instantaneous readjustment to the new equilibrium position. In reality they do not. A more likely course of events is that market adjustments occur sequentially. Some change, some disturbance in one market leads to an adjustment in that market. The receipts/payments for that asset in monetary form will, given prices in other markets, lead to sectoral money holdings becoming out of equilibrium; similarly the other asset markets will be out of equilibrium, since relative prices will have changed as a result of the initial disturbance. So at the next stage there will be a more general adjustment in other markets, which will cause a further change in relative prices, and lead on to successive adjustments, which if the system is stable – and if the process of adjustment itself does not affect the outcome, that is if there is no hysteresis – will ultimately converge to the same equilibrium values that would be achieved in a perfect information, simultaneous system.

So far the model has been presented as if full adjustment could indeed be obtained simultaneously and instantaneously. This is an implausible assumption. Instead we shall now assume that any disturbance initially affects only that market where it occurs, and then try to trace the path that the system follows in moving from one equilibrium position to another.[2] So in the final part of this section we shall turn shortly to a description, aided again by a numerical example, of the dynamic process of adjustment towards equilibrium following some disturbance. As an example of such a disturbance we shall take a monetary change by the authorities.

Working through this example, however, revealed that the financial system as set out in this model was not dynamically stable. The reason for this appeared to be the sensitivity of the intermediaries' rate-setting functions to *current* liquidity conditions. Thus a drain of cash from intermediaries at stage 1 would lead them to raise rates so much that they attracted large deposits (with reduced loans) at stage 2. This provided such large cash reserves that they then reduced their rates, below the initial level, at stage 3; and so on. In order to deal with this problem, we revised the form of the intermediaries' rate-setting

---

case it appeared that somewhat higher average profits could be obtained either by raising the coefficient on r_B slightly above $1 \cdot 1$ (reaching a maximum at about $1 \cdot 25$), or by adding a positive constant term, but only at the expense of incurring increased risks.

One possibly unsatisfactory feature of this model is that it shows intermediary profits generally rising during periods of easy money (and falling in periods of tight money), whereas in practice bank profits at any rate are higher during periods of tight money. This latter phenomenon, however, occurs in large part because the rate offered on their demand deposits is fixed at zero, so during periods of high interest rates the margin between the yield on their earning assets and the (average) cost of their funds increases. It is not so obvious whether those intermediaries who bid for all their deposits at market-related rates should do better or worse when interest rates generally rise.

---

[1] For a seminal analysis of the role of banks in the determination of the money stock, see J. Tobin, 'Commercial Banks as Creators of "Money",' chap. 22 in *Banking and Monetary Studies*, ed. D. Carson (Irwin, Homewood, Ill., 1963) pp. 408–19.

[2] This represents a change-over from analysis of comparative statics to dynamics. I am grateful to Vicki Chick for insisting that this be done.

functions, making the rates a function of the cash-reserve position in both the current and the previous period, as follows

$$r_{Lt} = 1 \cdot 1 r_{Bt} - 0 \cdot 001 C_{Ft} - 0 \cdot 001 C_{Ft-1} + 0 \cdot 0004 D_{Ft}$$
$$r_{Dt} = 0 \cdot 35 r_{Bt} + 0 \cdot 3 r_{Lt} - 0 \cdot 001 C_{Ft} - 0 \cdot 001 C_{Ft-1} + 0 \cdot 0004 D_{Ft}$$

The rationale for this might be that the intermediaries' cash-reserve position is so sensitive to random shocks that it would seem sensible for them to adapt fairly slowly and circumspectly to short-run variations in that position. Anyhow, as illustrated below, this revision did allow convergence to an equilibrium in the example chosen. We did not, however, pursue the question of the general stability characteristics of this model in response to other kinds of disturbances.

The disturbance, the response to which we did explore, was occasioned by the authorities' decision to bring the rate of interest on bonds down to a new lower level in a once-for-all step. Taking as the starting position the equilibrium values when the intermediary sets both deposit and loan rates and $r_B = 4$, gives the initial equilibrium values shown in Table 6.2. Now if the government raises the price at which it will buy bonds, dropping r_B to 3·5 per cent, the banks will want to sell twenty-five, given existing levels of deposits and loans, and the public will want to sell 750. So immediately after round 1, the position will be that shown in Table 6.3.

TABLE 6.2

	Intermediaries	Public	Government	Rates (per cent)
Cash	303	581	884	0
Bonds	800	1716	2516	4
Loans	1475	−1475	—	4·59
Deposits	1978	1978	—	2·96
Capital Gains	—	—	—	—
Investment	—	787	—	—
Capital	600	7987	—	7·94
Net Worth	600	10,787	—	—

TABLE 6.3

	Intermediaries	Public	Government	Rates (per cent)
Cash	328	1331	1658	0
Bonds	889	1211	2100	3·5
Loans	1475	−1475	—	4·59
Deposits	1978	1978	—	2·96
Capital Gains	114	245	—·	—
Investment	—	787	—	—
Capital	714	7987	—	7·94
Net Worth	714	11,032	—	—

Both the intermediaries and the public are now out of equilibrium, holding more cash than they desire and less of other assets. With bond rate falling and liquidity rising, the intermediaries will lower the rates which they charge on advances and offer on deposits. Given the coefficients in their rate-setting functions, the intermediaries will lower their loan rates by 0·58 per cent, i.e. (1·1 × 0·5 + 25 × 0·001), to 4·01 per cent and their deposit rates by 0·37 to 2·59 per cent.

If the authorities then hold bond rate at 3·5 per cent this fall in the rates on deposits and advances, together with the surplus cash position, will make the public wish to increase their holdings of bonds and capital (and to a lesser extent to add to their borrowings and to their deposit holdings). In order to equate the demand for capital with the existing stock, the yield on capital must fall, in this case to 7·45 per cent. Given this pattern of interest rates the public's asset position becomes as shown in Table 6.4.

TABLE 6.4

	Intermediaries	Public	Government	Rates (per cent)
Cash	240	759	999	0
Bonds	889	1871	2760	3·5
Loans	1649	−1649	—	4·01
Deposits	2064	2064	—	2·59
Capital Gains	114	245	—	—
Investment	—	790	—	—
Capital	714	7990	—	7·45
Net Worth	714	11,035	—	—

The public has bought 660 bonds back from the government at the fixed price, largely reversing their sales of 750 in the previous period (since rates on alternative assets have now fallen relative to bond rates); they have borrowed 174 more from the intermediaries, while depositing another 86 with them, thus obtaining 88 units of cash from them: overall, therefore, their cash position falls back to 759, i.e. (1331 − 660 + 88). The intermediaries' cash position falls by 88, the counterpart of the public's cash gain from them, since the intermediaries do not in this instance wish to alter their bond holdings.

This reduction in their cash holdings then places pressure on the intermediaries' liquidity position, who respond by raising their rates (to 4·11 per cent on loans and 2·72 per cent on deposits). This step causes a further adjustment in the system to the position shown in Table 6.5.

TABLE 6.5

	Intermediaries	Public	Government	Rates (per cent)
Cash	417	724	1141	0
Bonds	889	1729	2618	3·5
Loans	1592	−1592	—	4·11
Deposits	2184	2184	—	2·72
Capital Gains	114	245	—	—
Investment	—	804	—	—
Capital	714	8004	—	7·52
Net Worth	714	11,049	—	—

With their liquidity position now much more comfortable, the intermediaries will feel able to lower their rates again slightly (to 4·07 per cent on loans and to 2·66 per cent on deposits), in order to obtain a better configuration of assets, with more higher-yielding advances and somewhat fewer zero-yielding reserves. This further step takes the system to the position shown in Table 6.6.

By this juncture both the public and the banks have virtually reached their final equilibrium position, which is shown in Table 6.7.

If this assumption, that a disturbance in one market initially affects only that market, is valid, then the process of adjustment may well involve eddies and cycles. The instantaneous change in prices in this one market will subsequently feed through into other markets: so if prices in markets X are reduced by a disturbance, prices in competitive markets will be subsequently lowered. This will cause the initial extra demand for asset X

TABLE 6.6

	Intermediaries	Public	Government	Rates (per cent)
Cash	339	740	1079	0
Bonds	889	1791	2680	3·5
Loans	1611	−1611	—	4·07
Deposits	2125	2125	—	2·66
Capital Gains	114	245	—	—
Investment	—	798	—	—
Capital	714	7998	—	7·49
Net Worth	714	11,043	—	—

TABLE 6.7

	Intermediaries	Public	Government	Rates (per cent)
Cash	320	743	1063	0
Bonds	889	1806	2696	3·5
Loans	1622	−1622	—	4·06
Deposits	2117	2117	—	2·65
Capital Gains	114	245	—	—
Investment	—	797	—	7·48
Net Worth	714	11,042	—	—

(in response to its reduced price) to be partially reversed (i.e. people now want to sell asset X), as potential substitutes come to look relatively more attractive. If no one is willing to buy back asset X, its price must fall further. Under these circumstances the initial cash flow in the original market affected will normally be excessive if prices in that market are then held fixed, while the first-stage change in prices in that market will prove inadequate if the initial cash flow there is to be maintained unchanged.

So in a dynamic system of this sort the authorities' monetary operations may set up cyclical movements in bond sales if they operate with interest rates as their proximate objective, and cumulative movements in interest rates if they operate with the cash base as their proximate objective. Notwithstanding the complexities of the dynamic process of adjustment, the essential elements of the process whereby sectors alter their portfolios in response to shifts in relative prices and wealth remain, however, essentially unaltered whether the system adjusts instantaneously (comparative statics) or sequentially (dynamics).

C. Multiplier Analysis?

In the last section, the determination of the volume of liabilities (and of assets) of some 'representative' financial intermediary was examined and explained in terms of the interplay of the portfolio preferences of both the general public and the intermediary. Given the values of the exogenous variables, and those directly controlled by the authorities, the process involves continuous portfolio readjustment in the face of changing relative yields. This approach seems very different, at least superficially, from the multiplier analysis, the manner in which the determination of the liabilities of financial intermediaries, especially of the banks, is usually described.

There is, however, no real contradiction between the two. The (bank) multiplier analysis simply concentrates on a rather narrower set of behavioural responses, and treats the remaining aspects of the adjustment process as given, determined off-stage. Indeed, at the limit the multiplier analysis can be treated purely as an identity without any behavioural content at all. Thus the liquid financial assets held by the general public (L) can be defined as comprising two components, being respectively their holdings of the monetary liabilities of the government (C) and of the liabilities of the financial intermediaries (F). It is, therefore, possible to set down the identity

$$L = F + C$$

which must hold exactly by definition.

Similarly, it is possible to give a name, a description, to the sum of the monetary liabilities of the government sector held on the one hand by the general public (C) and on the other by the financial intermediaries as reserves (R). The title now commonly applied to this latter set of assets is 'high-powered money' (H). If the currency in the hands of the public was transferred by them to financial intermediaries in exchange for deposits, the intermediaries' cash reserves would rise equivalently, allowing and encouraging them (at the prevailing set of relative yields) to expand their lending – presumably, assuming a previous condition of equilibrium, by making loans more attractive to borrowers, say, by cutting the rates charged – and thus causing an increase in both their assets and their liabilities. The term 'high-powered' reflects the fact that financial intermediary deposits are some multiple of their reserve holdings, so that – assuming that the financial sector maintains fairly stable cash-reserve ratios – one would see a multiple increase in deposits accompanying an increase in cash reserves. The additional identity

$$H = R + C$$

can thus also be set down, which again must hold by definition.

By algebraic manipulation of these two identities it is possible to arrive at a third identity

$$L = H \frac{(1 + C/F)}{(R/F + C/F)}$$

describing the total holding of liquid financial assets in terms of the level of high-powered money and two ratios, R/F the financial intermediaries' cash reserve/deposit ratio, and C/F the general public's currency/deposit ratio. Since this relationship is also an identity, it always holds true by definition; changes in the public's holdings of liquid financial assets can, therefore, be expressed in terms of these three variables alone.

One of the several features distinguishing banks from other financial intermediaries, which has already been noted and will be taken up again in Chapter 7, is that other financial intermediaries hold their reserves mainly in the form of bank deposits, while banks hold their reserves in the form of the monetary liabilities of the government sector. A shift in the public's preferences between bank deposits and the liabilities of other financial intermediaries (OFI) could, therefore, alter the R/F ratio. One way of dealing with this potential cause of variation in the R/F ratio is to partition the financial sector into two parts, banks and OFI, and construct a multiplier for each separately.

Defining the money supply, M, as equal to deposits (D) plus currency in the hands of the public (including the OFI),[1] we can write

$$M = D + C$$

which together with the identity

$$H = R_b + C$$

---

[1] For a detailed note on various possible alternative definitions of the stock of money in the United Kingdom, see the *Bank of England Quarterly Bulletin*, vol. 10, no. 3 (September 1970) pp. 320–6.

where H is high-powered money, as before, R_b now represents bank reserves of high-powered money and C is currency holdings elsewhere in the private sector (including OFI), enables us to arrive at a third identity

$$M = \frac{H\left(1 + \dfrac{C}{D}\right)}{\left(\dfrac{R_b}{D} + \dfrac{C}{D}\right)}$$

describing the money stock in terms of the level of high-powered money and two ratios, R_b/D the banks' reserve/deposit ratio, and C/D the general public's currency/deposit ratio.[1] By an exactly similar process one can define the money stock M as consisting of two parts: M_p, that held by the private sector (exclusive of OFIs), and M_F, that held by the OFIs as reserves; and also define the general public's liquid financial assets (L) as equal to M_p, plus their holdings of the liabilities (OFI) of the non-bank financial intermediaries. Then from the two identities

$$M = M_p + M_F$$

and

$$L = M_p + \text{OFI}$$

we can construct the identity

$$L = \frac{M\left(1 + \dfrac{M_p}{\text{OFI}}\right)}{\left(\dfrac{M_p}{\text{OFI}} + \dfrac{M_F}{\text{OFI}}\right)}$$

Indeed, one can go on constructing further, bigger and more complex multiplier identities to take account of various distinctions between intermediaries and between liabilities.[2] These more complicated formulations, however, sacrifice the one great virtue of the multiplier approach, its simplicity, without obtaining equivalent benefits in the area of their greatest deficiency, their lack of behavioural content, for such multipliers generally do not illuminate the behavioural process whereby people and institutions adjust their overall portfolio to arrive at some general equilibrium. Yet to be able to express changes in the money stock, or in the total holdings of liquid financial assets, in terms of only three variables has considerable advantages of brevity and simplicity, though even these advantages may be lost in those circumstances where there is a plethora of differing kinds of banks or intermediaries, and of deposits, each involving separate reserve ratios.

---

[1] An array of slightly differing identities can be obtained from algebraic manipulation of the two basic identities. The differences between them have no analytical significance. See M. Friedman and A. J. Schwartz, *A Monetary History of the United States, 1867–1960*, National Bureau of Economic Research (Princeton University Press, 1963) especially Appendix B; and P. Cagan, *Determinants and Effects of Changes in the Stock of Money, 1875–1960*, National Bureau of Economic Research, Studies in Business Cycles, no. 13 (Columbia University Press, 1965) chaps 1 and 2 especially.

[2] For example, see A. N. McLeod, 'Credit Expansion in an Open Economy,' *The Economic Journal*, vol. 72, no. 287 (September 1962) pp. 611–40; K. Brunner and A. Meltzer, 'Some Further Investigations of Demand and Supply Functions for Money,' *The Journal of Finance*, vol. 19, no. 2, pt 1 (May 1964) pp. 240–83, especially 242–56; D. I. Fand, 'Some Implications of Money Supply Analysis,' *The American Economic Review*, vol. 57 (May 1967) pp. 380–400.

None the less the lack of any innate theoretical, or behavioural, content in the multiplier approach, *per se*,[1] may be realised more easily by noting that multiplier identities can be constructed over a virtually limitless range of cases. Take any aggregate, X, which can be decomposed into two parts, Y and Z, so that

$$X = Y + Z$$

then if the provision of Z is constrained by the identity

$$U = W + Z$$

one can construct the identity

$$X = U \frac{\left(1 + \dfrac{Z}{Y}\right)}{\left(\dfrac{W}{Y} + \dfrac{Z}{Y}\right)}$$

and various other mathematically-equivalent identities. Consider, for example, the potato multiplier of total personal expenditure, E. Personal expenditure is used for the purchase of potatoes (P_p), and of other goods and services (O), so that

$$E = P_p + O$$

The total production of potatoes (P) either is sold to persons (P_p) or goes to other uses (P_o), so that

$$P = P_p + P_o$$

then

$$E = P \frac{\left(1 + \dfrac{P_p}{O}\right)}{\left(\dfrac{P_o}{O} + \dfrac{P_p}{O}\right)}$$

In short, total personal expenditure is a multiple of the value of the production of potatoes, with the size of the multiplier depending on only *two* ratios, the ratio of expenditure on potatoes to expenditure on other goods and the ratio of sales of potatoes for uses other than personal consumption to other personal expenditure.

One can spread one's wings in the construction of exotic multipliers. Take, for example, the academic multiplier of total wealth. Let W represent total wealth, which is defined as comprised of human and non-human wealth, so that

$$W = W_N + W_H$$

Let $W_H/W = d$; let the value of human wealth be related to educational input (E); assume, for simplicity only, a linear relationship, so that

$$W_H = a + bE$$

---

[1] It is possible, of course, to add behavioural content by analysing the derivation of the elements in the identity in terms of the underlying behavioural relationships. But that leads back towards specifying the full structure of the system, as we did in Sect. B. If it is necessary to specify the structure of the system in order to understand why the multiplier works as it does, it is difficult to see what advantage is to be gained from using it as an analytical tool in the first place.

Let the ratio of expenditure on academic lecturers (A) to total education expenditures be g, i.e. $A/E = g$, then it follows that

$$W = \frac{a}{d} + \frac{b}{gd} A$$

Thus total wealth is some multiple of expenditure on academic lecturers, plus a term, a/d, which may in the short-run be taken as constant. Moreover, both g and d are between 0 and 1, since they relate a component of an aggregate to an aggregate, while we may presume that b is greater than unity, since education is widely regarded as a worthwhile investment for society. Therefore, total wealth is related to expenditure on academic lecturers by some very large multiplier. Apart from the simplifying assumption of the linear relationship between education expenditures and human wealth, and of the approximate short-term constancy of the a/d ratio, it is all true by definition.

These examples are intended to persuade readers either that it will be of enormous benefit to the nation to increase the salaries of academic lecturers multifold, or alternatively that the multiplier approach needs cautious handling if it is to be used as a basis for explaining something large, say national income, or the money stock, from movements in a much smaller component of that aggregate, say autonomous investment, or high-powered money, grossed up by some function which involves ratios connecting the small total to the large.[1] In order to use such an approach 'to explain' variations in the larger total – as contrasted with *describing* such movements, which definitional multipliers, however ridiculous, can always do – some further conditions are necessary.

The primary condition is that the ratios, linking the two variables, should be predictable, say a stable function of other variables which will also be predictable, under all prospective circumstances. Clearly if the ratios vary unpredictably, then information on the value of the small variable will not allow one to forecast how the large variable will change. But even if the ratios seem stable under one set of circumstances, they may not be so generally. Consider again the previous example of the academic multiplier of total wealth. It may be that the ratios in that example, b, g and d, have remained fairly stable over time, reflecting the preferences and structure of the system. If the authorities, however, should alter that system by doubling, or halving, expenditure on academic lecturers at a stroke, the values of the ratios would alter quite sharply so that the previous stability would be shattered. Obviously in this case the authorities cannot rely on the continued stability of this multiplier to vary total wealth by adjusting expenditure on academic lecturers.

If the ratios remain stable and predictable under all feasible states of the world, then if you know the value of the small variable, you will be able to predict with a high degree of confidence what the value of the large variable will be. In this sense, and this sense only, it is possible to say that variations in the small variable, say the high-powered money base, explain the variations in the large variable, say the money stock. It should be noted that this usage of the term 'explanation' does not depend on whether the small variable is being determined exogenously, say as a control variable by the authorities, or endogenously, when these are alternative possible states of the world. All that is necessary is that the

---

[1] The multiplier approach is, alas, used indiscriminately by all schools of macro-economic analysis. The Keynesian multiplier, relating changes in incomes to changes in autonomous expenditures, is of this genre. The theory of distribution developed by N. Kaldor, 'Alternative Theories of Distribution,' *Review of Economic Studies*, vol. 23 (1955) pp. 83–100 (reprinted in *Essays on Value and Distribution*, pp. 228–36) is essentially based on a definitional multiplier of this kind. Perhaps surprisingly, the money multiplier of the monetarists, see Chap. 9, Sect. C, relating movements in money incomes to current and prior changes in the money stock is not typical, since the money supply is not a component part of money incomes.

relationship should be predictable and stable in all possible states; indeed the bank multiplier will in some respects, perhaps, be most useful if the relationship remains unaltered whatever the state of the world, in our previous example whether the high-powered money base is, or is not, being fixed consciously by the authorities.

On the whole the bank multiplier, relating the money stock to the high-powered money base, is quite useful in the above manner.[1] As long as the probability distribution of deposit inflows and withdrawals, and the penalties resulting from a cash shortage, remain fairly constant,[2] the banks' reserve ratio is likely to remain a stable function of relative yields on alternative assets. Similarly, the public's desired currency/deposit ratio usually remains fairly constant over time, changing gradually in response to slow-moving institutional factors, and also perhaps to the relative yield attractions of holding deposits. It is possible, however, that if the authorities should suddenly change their system of monetary control, say by moving from a system in which they fixed interest rates in the market as their prime target to one in which they concentrated upon determining the monetary base, the subjective uncertainties – and penalties – facing the banks might change, resulting in possibly unforeseeable changes in their desired reserve ratios.[3] And if developments in the banking system should make the public revise their views of the safety of their deposits, the public's desired currency/deposit ratio could change very sharply, as in the United States in the 1930s. Nevertheless, as Friedman and Schwartz, and Cagan, have shown in the case of the United States, the relationships involved in the bank multiplier have remained fairly stable over a long run of years and during several different monetary regimes, e.g. gold standard with no Central Bank, Federal Reserve System in its differing phases of operation. So if you know what the change in the monetary base has been over some period, it is likely that you will be able to forecast what the change in the money stock will have been over the same period with reasonable accuracy, irrespective of the nature of the monetary regime or of changes in that regime. In this respect the bank multiplier has some useful explanatory content, as compared with the other examples of the potato multiplier or the academic multiplier, which have none.

Moreover, this ability to forecast the larger aggregate (e.g. the money stock) from movements in the smaller variable (e.g. the high-powered money base) requires only that a few ratios be predictable. If one instead looks at the wider canvas, at the complete portfolio adjustment of the sectors concerned, involving the interplay of all the asset preferences, the number of behavioural functions which have to be included in the analysis mounts up at a giddy speed. In the previous section the simplified portfolio adjustment model incorporated some forty coefficients. The multiplier approach, on the other hand, concentrates on the determination of one aggregate and eliminates analysis of a great proportion of the accompanying behaviour. Yet it achieves this extra simplicity, as compared with the more general approach, at a considerable cost in terms of information about the process at hand. Indeed, the informational content of the multiplier approach is remarkably slight.

Consider what the bank multiplier does *not* tell you. In the first place it provides no information on the factors which affect the determination of the high-powered monetary base. There is no *a priori* reason to believe that the authorities' intention is generally to control this variable; it may be endogenously determined. Indeed, historical experience would suggest that in the main the system has been such (e.g. the authorities' chief concern has been for the level of interest rates) that the monetary base has been determined endo-

---

[1] See, in particular, the work of Cagan, *Determinants and Effects of Changes in the Stock of Money, 1875–1960*.

[2] On this subject, see G. R. Morrison, *Liquidity Preferences of Commercial Banks* (University of Chicago Press, 1966).

[3] Changes in official reserve requirements will naturally alter the desired reserve ratio; but the response should be fairly predictable.

genously.[1] During such periods it does not take analysis much further forward to say that the money stock varied by x per cent because the high-powered money base altered by y per cent. This only evokes the question why the base changed.

Moreover, even when the authorities are giving priority to controlling monetary aggregates, the problems and operations involved in achieving such control are not indicated, or illustrated, by the bank multiplier. In particular, to start by assuming that the high-powered money base is given is to ignore virtually all the really interesting matters of concern to the monetary authorities. These issues are taken up at more length in Chapter 8.

Even more important from an analytical viewpoint, the multiplier approach gives little or no indication of the behavioural processes involved in the quantitative adjustments. The bank multiplier shows only that if you can observe the change in the monetary base between two occasions, and can predict the two relevant ratios, then you will be able to predict the change in the money stock with a high degree of confidence. This allows very little to be deduced about the process of adjustment. Indeed, most of the accounts of the dynamic process of adjustment which are derived from the multiplier approach are at best misleading and often wrong.

For example, the impression is still occasionally given that once some additional high-powered money is introduced into the system it cannot be expelled, and the system will have to adjust until all such extra reserves are held either as currency by the private sector or in bank reserves. This is wrong: every time the general public or the banks make a payment, by cheque or currency, to the government sector, the level of high-powered money falls.[2] Moreover, even when the process of monetary expansion involves the purchase of private-sector assets, financial or real, the transaction will involve certain shifts in relative yields, incomes and wealth that are likely to have some subsequent effect upon payments to the government sector. For example, increased expenditure on real assets is likely to cause – though admittedly after a rather long time lag – higher tax payments and – rather sooner – more imports; the purchase of equities, driving up the price-earnings ratio, apart from its effects on capital gains tax receipts, will alter relative yields in favour of public-sector debt and foreign assets. Of course the authorities, having undertaken an initial injection of additional reserves, say by an open-market operation, can try to offset subsequent portfolio adjustments whereby the initial injection would be cut back. They can lower taxes, lower yields offered on public-sector debt, lower the exchange rate. With a dynamic process of portfolio adjustment, requiring continual adjustments of yields and rates by the authorities in order to maintain any given level, or rate of growth, of the monetary aggregates, it is hard to see any virtue in treating the high-powered money base as given, even for expository purposes.

Furthermore, the usual description of the multiplier process suggests that an injection, or withdrawal, of cash reserves from the banks forces, in response, a quantitative change in

---

[1] 'Whereas everyone agrees that the monetary authority is capable of determining the money stock, we must nevertheless recognise that we live in the real world where there are lags and where the monetary authority apparently has never sought to control the absolute level of the nominal stock of money, opting instead to affect "credit conditions".' J. J. Klein, Discussion of Fand's paper on 'A Monetarist Model of the Monetary Process,' *The Journal of Finance*, vol. 25, no. 2 (May 1970) p. 322.

'However, concern over market interest-rate movements has been a major factor influencing Federal Reserve acquisition of Government debt over the last two decades.' K. Stewart, 'Government Debt, Money and Economic Activity,' *Federal Reserve Bank of St. Louis Review*, vol. 54, no. 1 (January 1972) p. 8.

Also see *The Sources and the Impact of Monetary Changes, an Empirical Study of Danish Experiences, 1951–68*, especially chap. 5, by N. Thygesen (Studies from the Copenhagen University Economic Institute, no. 17, Copenhagen, 1971).

[2] Unless the government sector keeps the proceeds with the domestic banks; even when this occurs it is usually only temporary.

the volume of their earning assets, irrespective of relative yields and rates. Except in so far as such rate movements affect the banks' demand for cash reserves, they appear to have to respond mechanically. The unstated implication of this analysis is that the banks are not trying to achieve any desired portfolio equilibrium. This is wrong: banks do *not* respond to a cash shortage by calling in loans on a large scale; it would not be good business to do so. Frequently their response is to change the rates offered, to raise rates on deposits and loans, rather than to make any large quantitative changes in their existing asset portfolio. The reduction in bank advances that follows a restrictive monetary policy – ignoring direct ceiling controls – will generally be due to a decline in *demand* for advances from the private sector as the banks are induced, by declining liquidity and rising bond rates, to raise rates on advances, rather than from a calling-in of existing advances by the banks.

The main conceptual criticism of the bank-multiplier approach, as indeed of multipliers generally, is that it obscures the behavioural process whereby people and institutions choose to apportion their wealth or income, presumably in some reasonably rational fashion, in the light of perceived circumstances. Multipliers may reveal the *result* of rational choice, but they do not illuminate that *process*. It was for this reason that in the previous section the analysis of the determination of the supply of financial liabilities (and/or of money) was described instead in terms of the interplay of the preference functions of the public and the intermediaries.

In the next chapter we turn to a subject that has already been hovering in the wings, to discuss the differences between banks and other financial intermediaries (OFIs) and whether these differences are such as to require a different framework of analysis for examining the determination of their respective totals of liabilities (and assets). Then in Chapter 8 we revert to a consideration of the role and operations of the monetary authorities. So far the authorities have simply been assumed to fix certain rates, say the rate on bonds, or certain quantities, and little or no consideration has been given to the constraints under which they operate, or the problems which they may face in trying to achieve desired financial objectives within the financial system. It is to these matters that we turn there.

7

Banks and Other Financial Intermediaries: Differences and Similarities

SUMMARY

Financial intermediation depends on adequate information. The information obtained in the process of one transaction can be used in another. Given economies of information of this kind, why are not all forms of financial intermediation provided by one single institution? In particular, since their operation of the payments mechanism gives them especially advantaged access to information, why do not the banks provide all financial services, e.g. insurance, housing mortgages, to their customers? In part the answer is that some differing kinds of intermediation require specialised information (e.g. actuarial skills, knowledge of the property market), so that there is less advantage to be gained by combining them all under one roof. In part the answer is that large, all-purpose banks can wield considerable market power, and so (political) steps may be taken to prevent the possible misuse of that power by restricting the range of business which the banks can undertake, and also to foster protected competitors in certain 'socially desirable' areas (e.g. the provision of saving outlets to the poor, housing finance). Lastly, the collapse of banks tends to have more serious effects than the failure of other financial intermediaries, since a bank closure virtually forces subsequent second-round asset sales by that bank's depositors to restore their money holdings. So banks are likely to be more tightly regulated, which will induce the separation of banking and non-banking activities.

Banks do, therefore, differ from other financial intermediaries in the kind of business which they do, and consequently in the form of their liabilities and the shape of their asset portfolio. The question at issue, however, is whether these differences are such that the processes whereby the totals of liabilities of the banks and of the other financial intermediaries (OFI) are determined are dissimilar. We examine three arguments suggesting that they might be. First, (some) bank liabilities are money. But, it is argued, banks need offer no inducements to people to hold additional money with them; they could, therefore, expand – if they were not directly controlled by the government – indefinitely. This is wrong. Current accounts (demand deposits) may serve as a means of payment, but they are not legal tender. Some payments, e.g. to the government, have to be made by transfers of legal tender. Banks have, therefore, got to attract reserves of legal tender from the public, by offering various costly inducements, just as OFIs have to attract monetary reserves.

Nevertheless, a cheque payment by a bank will be redeposited with the banking sector unless it involves a cash flow from the private sector to the public sector (or leads to larger cash holdings within the private sector), while a payment from an OFI will lead to an outflow of reserves from that institution if that cheque is used to add either to holdings of public-sector debt or to other private-sector assets. So the redeposit ratio of the banks may well be much higher than that of OFIs. This is true enough, but it is only a first-round, impact effect. The banks and the OFIs will react to these cash flows by varying the rates which they offer for loans and deposits. When full adjustment has been made to an initial disturbance, the final equilibrium will depend only on total wealth, the asset preferences of the public and interest differentials. The differing redeposit ratios affect the path to the final equilibrium, but not the equilibrium values themselves. In order to illustrate this, the model of the financial system described in Chapter 6 is extended in order to incorporate both a banking and an OFI sector, and some simulated numerical examples of the working of the model are presented. The deposits of both banks and OFIs are shown to be determined by a process of portfolio adjustment.

But if the banks cannot adjust the rates which they offer on advances and deposits because, say, these are constrained by regulation or convention, then they may not be able to take much active part in this adjustment process. If their actions are constrained in this way, their response to cash flows may, indeed, take on a rather mechanical form (as appears in elementary textbook descriptions of the banking multiplier). Thus the final argument for treating the process of determination of bank and OFI liabilities differently is that the banks may be more constrained (by external regulations) in their response to economic stimuli than OFIs. There is some truth in this. But it is not necessarily true, nor has it always been the case that banks have been more tightly controlled than all other financial intermediaries. And even when they do face such controls, bankers have been adept at finding ways around them, e.g. by offering other non-interest services.

In the previous chapter, Section A, the various functions which financial intermediaries perform were recounted, and the reasons why intermediaries issue liabilities with a range of characteristics were explained. But the question remains why, even with a range of proffered liabilities, there need be more than one institutional type of intermediary, offering all these intermediation services. Why should there be such a varied assortment of intermediaries, including distinct institutions such as banks, building societies (Savings and Loan Associations in the United States), finance houses, insurance companies, etc.?

In particular, the very act of carrying on business with a customer, whether as lender or borrower, increases the extent of information which both sides have of each other. This is especially true in the case of banks. Since the greater proportion of all the payments of their customers pass through their books, they ought to be in an excellent position to know whether it will be good business to extend loans to that customer. Similarly, even if to a lesser extent, the experience of a building society in taking deposits and offering mortgages to their clients should facilitate their ability to make a wide range of other personal loans and to undertake a wide range of additional customer services. One reason why an intermediary is likely to find any external constraint on the nature of its portfolio or business to be irksome is that the experience and information obtained in providing one kind of intermediation service can be used to develop another kind of service more cheaply. If there are indeed informational economies of this kind, i.e. that each contact lessens the cost of the information required to arrange some further financial transaction, why then are there so many different kinds of financial intermediary in existence? Since their role in operating the payments mechanism gives the banks especially favourable access to information, why do the banks not provide the complete gamut of financial services for their clients?

A partial answer is that there are limits to such informational economies, with differing kinds of intermediation requiring specialised forms of information. Insurance business requires specialised actuarial assistance and a judgement of risks of quite a differing nature from those familiar to bankers. Lending on the collateral of real property, especially in the case of mortgages, requires some specialised knowledge of the property in question, and of the likely market for that property. The information required to decide whether it will be good business to provide a short-term advance to a company can be in some respects rather different from that needed if an institution is considering buying equity in a company.

So a bank diversifying into the insurance business, or home mortgages, or leasing, might have to set up a specialised subsidiary to do such business. The economies still to be obtained, e.g. a more centralised control of the asset portfolio, could be rather sparse, and there could be disadvantages as the growing range of business covered either attenuated the specialised information of top management on each aspect of that business, or else led to an unwieldy expansion of the management structure, involving co-ordinating committees and such like.

Furthermore, the inherent market power of the banks, especially arising from their direct access to detailed information on their customers, has led on occasions to political demands to curb their strength and functions,[1] a political pressure which in some countries, for example the United States, has been reflected in legislation strictly limiting banking activities.[2] There is often concern whether information obtained in the provision of one form of intermediary service might not lead to a conflict of interest, or alternatively to an 'unfair' advantage, in the provision of some other financial service. The existence of 'economies of information' also raises the possibility that these could be exploited against the best interest of clients or of the economy to establish a monopoly position. This is one reason why there may be institutional barriers to the unbridled expansion of financial conglomerates.

Moreover, banks, whose current accounts, demand deposits, provide a medium of exchange (and a means of payment) for their customers, must by definition be holding a portfolio of assets which must all, except for cash reserves, have a longer maturity than their sight-deposit liabilities. They run on this account, perhaps, a greater risk of illiquidity than other financial institutions, the form of whose liabilities gives them more time to prepare their defences. Even though in ordinary times banks can rely on a quite stable (and relatively interest inelastic) volume base of current accounts, once a story circulates that a bank's liquidity could be imperilled, the resulting run could easily force the temporary closure of the bank even if it has been prudently and well managed.[3] Moreover, banks hold a large proportion of their customers' money balances, required for current transactions uses. A bank closure (failure), therefore, not only entails some possible loss of wealth, the extent of loss depending on the possibility of reorganisation and on the realisable value of the counterpart assets, but more immediately forces that bank's customers to realise other assets in order to replace the immediate loss of liquidity if ordinary day-to-day household and business expenditures are to be carried on.

This secondary response, the subsequent round of forced asset sales and/or borrowing under pressure, arising from a banking failure may be contrasted with the result of a failure of intermediaries with longer-dated liabilities, whose failure will generally derive from insolvency rather than illiquidity, since by definition they should have had time to realise marketable assets. In the latter instance, claimants on the failed company will have suffered some loss of wealth, and will lose the specific services provided, e.g. insurance,

---

[1] A good example is provided by the *Investigation of the Financial and Monetary Conditions in the United States*, before the House of Representatives' Subcommittee on Banking and Currency, under House Resolutions nos 429 and 504, 2 vols, 29 parts (Government Printing Office, Washington, 1912/13), otherwise known as the *Money Trust Investigation* or *Pujo Investigation*.

[2] For example, the Bank Holding Company Act of 1956, as amended by the Bank Holding Company Act of 1970, specifies the restricted conditions upon which a bank holding company may acquire interests in non-banking activities.

[3] For example, the banking crisis of 1907 in the United States was detonated by a run on the Knickerbocker Trust Company, which was in fact well managed and solvent, see chap. 4 on 'The 1907 Crisis' in C. Goodhart's, *The New York Money Market and the Finance of Trade, 1900–1913* (Harvard University Press, 1969). More recently, a collapse of confidence in some of the fringe banks in the United Kingdom in 1973, following the suspension of Cedar Holdings and London and County Securities, led to a large-scale withdrawal of market funds from all banks of a similar class, irrespective of their probity, solvency or management qualities.

but there will be less immediate pressure to sell other assets in a scramble to restore liquidity. Certainly the most infamous general financial crises and panics have been prominently associated with banking failures, for example Overend Gurney & Co. in 1866, The City of Glasgow Bank in 1878, even the averted failure of Barings in 1891 in the United Kingdom, the Credit-Anstalt in Austria in 1931, the Knickerbocker Trust Co. in New York in 1907 and the waves of banking failures in the United States from 1931 to 1933. In contrast it is harder to think of a general financial crisis resulting from a failure of a non-bank financial intermediary.[1] The failures of cut-price insurance companies, of unsavoury investment funds, etc., lead to severe losses of wealth and inconvenience to those unwary enough to be sucked in, but they do not – it seems from experience – spark off a cumulative process of asset realisation, withdrawal of funds from other intermediaries and deflation.

For this reason the authorities are likely to impose more stringent prudential requirements on the composition of bank-asset portfolios than on other intermediaries, since with banks the social, external costs of failure may well be much greater than the private costs of failure, whereas the gap between the social and private costs of failure is less marked for OFIs. Since the regulation of banking activities thus tends to be more cautious, in the frequency and extent of inspection, in constraints on the permissible asset portfolio, in capital requirements, than is the case with other forms of intermediation, there is bound to be some tendency to form separate subsidiaries for banking and other forms of intermediation even when a holding company is able to control both. Furthermore, legal and tax advantages may be given preferentially to certain kinds of intermediaries, e.g. mutually-owned institutions, or to businesses specialising in certain defined fields, e.g. building societies, and these distinctions also are likely to maintain a diversity among financial intermediaries.

So, besides the natural factors that may limit economies of scale and information as the coverage of a financial intermediary increases and so allows more scope for any advantages from specialisation to come into play, the authorities may also erect regulatory barriers to prevent banks from expanding into certain other lines of business and impose additional prudential requirements on them in order to lessen the danger of liquidity crises. The authorities' interventions have generally acted to increase the diversity of financial intermediaries, by limiting competition[2] from those institutions with the greatest opportunity for exploiting economies of information and by granting certain extra advantages to institutions specialising in particularly favoured fields, e.g. in the provision of intermediary services to the poor, in the provision of housing mortgages, etc.

The argument so far has not only suggested reasons for the continued existence of a diverse group of financial intermediaries, specialising in the provision of differing services, but has also pointed up some of the ways in which banks differ from other financial intermediaries. The banks operate the main payments transmission service in many countries. Their sight deposits are generally treated as a means of payment. Their position gives them great market strength in command over funds and in access to information, though it also leaves them liable to special risks. Because of the wider social consequences of such risks, the authorities have generally imposed more intensive regulations and controls on banks than on other intermediaries. Banks issue liabilities with particular properties, e.g. sight deposits, and offer their own special kinds of financial services, e.g. transmitting payments. In a valid sense banks can, therefore, be said to create bank deposits. But it is equally true to state that insurance companies create insurance contracts, that property unit trusts

---

[1] The failure of the Atlantic Acceptance Corporation in Canada in June 1965 caused widespread repercussions. In the next year there were fears for the viability of Savings and Loan Associations in the United States during the credit crunch of 1966. Financial crises originating outside the banking sector are certainly possible, but experience does seem to suggest that they are less serious.

[2] This subject is further discussed in Chap. 13.

create property bonds, that building societies create their own shares and deposits. If you should devise a new liability with characteristics of a kind attractive to the public, then you could be also said to have created that.

The real issue, in the debate whether a bank is or is not similar in kind to OFIs, is not over the question of whether a financial intermediary creates its own liability, since they all clearly do so, but over the limits upon such creation. There are those who argue that the expansion of bank deposits, because of the role of demand deposits as a means of payment, is not subject to the same constraints as the expansion of other intermediaries. This assertion, however, runs counter to the arguments set out earlier in Chapter 6, which may be restated as follows.

The amount of any asset which the private sector wishes to hold, given its wealth and the various characteristics of that asset, depends on the relative yields on that and on other assets. This will be as true for bank deposits as for any other asset. The volume of bank deposits which the public will hold will depend on the relative return on bank deposits *vis-à-vis* all other assets. Meanwhile the return, in the form of specific interest payments or services, which banks can offer to depositors will depend on the yields that the banks can obtain on their earning assets and their desire for liquidity. An expansion by the banks of their deposit liabilities, through the offer of higher interest payments or more services, will entail rising costs, while the counterpart increase in their assets may bring about a lesser rate of increase, or fall, in revenues, as the banks offer lower rates on advances or offer loans to less credit-worthy borrowers, in order to expand their earning assets. Given the exogenous and policy parameters of the system, there will be a stable equilibrium determinate volume of bank deposits. Exactly the same analysis holds true for all OFIs. In this sense the determination of bank deposits and of other intermediary liabilities is exactly similar.

What qualifications have to be made to this general proposition, if any, to take account of the special characteristics of bank deposits, and what are these crucial characteristics? The first critical issue is whether banks do need to offer a higher relative yield on deposits in order to get people to hold a larger proportion of their assets with the banking system. It may be a useful clarification to present a viewpoint on this matter contrary to the one above, set out in a quotation taken from Moore's *Introduction to the Theory of Finance*.[1]

He writes as follows: 'Section one considers the market supply and demand forces that in the absence of government regulation determine the volume of financial intermediation. Non-monetary intermediaries are considered first. The expansion of total assets and liabilities of different intermediary groups are shown to be constrained by the asset and debt preferences of surplus – and deficit – spending wealthowners. In competitive equilibrium the rate that an intermediary group charges borrowers exceeds the rate it pays to lenders by a premium just sufficient to cover the average costs of intermediation plus a normal rate of profit.' So far, so good; however he continues, 'The situation is formally similar for monetary intermediaries. But because their liabilities are readily acceptable as a means of payment, and so impose no constraint on the exercise of purchasing power, bank intermediaries unlike nonbanks need not increase the return paid on notes and deposits to induce wealthowners to increase their *nominal* lending to the banking system. ... Depending on the prevailing marginal return earned on tangible assets and the degree of price flexibility, this market-determined [that is without explicit government regulation] volume of monetary intermediation will not in general be consistent with general price level stability.'[2]

---

[1] B. J. Moore, *An Introduction to the Theory of Finance* (The Free Press, New York, 1968) chap. 7, pp. 185–6.

[2] B. Pesek and T. Saving present a similar analysis in their book on *Money, Wealth and Economic Theory* (Macmillan, New York, 1967).

In order to dissect the above quoted passage, it is necessary to distinguish between a means of payment which is legal tender and an asset which can be used as a means of payment but is not legal tender. Any intermediary, institution or individual, not only banks, whose liabilities were granted the status of legal tender could issue them without limit, until inflationary pressures caused the collapse of the political or monetary system, possibly of both together. If insurance-company paper became legal tender, it would instantly become, however unlikely in form, a means of payment and insurance companies could issue claims at zero interest rate, or cost, to an extent which would 'not in general be consistent with general price level stability.'

But without legal-tender status for their liabilities banks are forced to attract additional reserve assets to maintain a sufficient reserve base to support their own expansion. In order to obtain these extra reserve assets the banks will have to bid for them, which takes us back to our previous analysis. In this respect they are no different from other intermediaries. If the authorities set the rates at which they will exchange various assets, generally foreign-exchange or public-sector debt of one kind or another, for cash reserves, then the banks can obtain additional cash reserves by raising their deposit rate or offering improved services, causing people to switch out of public-sector debt, or foreign assets, into bank deposits. This process is limited by rising marginal costs and falling marginal revenues.

If the authorities try to limit the volume of cash reserves accruing to the banks, they will have to let rates on public-sector debt and foreign exchange adjust to prevent any inducement for the public to shift out of public-sector debt – or for there to be any currency flow across the exchanges – as the banks bid for funds.[1] The extent that banks will be prepared to push their bidding for funds will be mainly influenced by the strength of demand from the private sector for bank loans, as the rate on such loans rises in line with other market rates (with the banks at each stage trying to maintain an optimal portfolio distribution).

The banks are, therefore, competing with the public sector to attract the funds of the private sector; the size and rate of expansion of the banking system depends on the outcome of that competition. In turn the impetus for the banks to compete comes in large part from the opportunities to use those funds profitably, i.e. from the private-sector demand for loans. So long as bank deposits are not legal tender, and banks therefore need to attract reserve assets to support their deposit holdings, the banks are subject to the same general principles in the determination of the volume of their deposits as any other intermediary.

But even if this general principle be granted, that bank expansion will be limited in the same way as that of OFIs, by the rising cost (relative to the extra revenues generated) of attracting additional deposits, another distinction between the actual process of the determination of the volume of bank deposits on the one hand and of the liabilities of OFIs on the other is sometimes made. This is that banks can often pay for purchases of private-sector assets (though less so of public-sector assets) by writing up their own liabilities, whereas OFIs have to run down their reserves (usually of bank deposits rather than of cash). The ability of banks to pay in this manner will not, of course, be advantageous if the public then immediately withdraws cash reserves from the banks, by using the cheque payment to add to their currency holdings, or to make payments to the public sector, for taxes, to buy foreign exchange from the public sector's reserves, or to buy other public-sector debt. What matters to the banks, when they purchase earning assets, is the *redeposit* ratio, the proportion of their payment which will be redeposited with them. Equally, the loss of reserves suffered by the non-bank financial intermediaries, as they expand their earning assets, depends on the proportion of such payments that will be redeposited with them.

The volume of the banking sector's cash reserves will only be affected by flows of funds between the public sector and the private sector, as the members of the private

---

[1] And to offset those flows from personal-currency holdings to bank deposits which the authorities cannot prevent people from undertaking.

sector pay taxes, receive payments from the government, buy or sell public-sector debt or foreign exchange and add to, or run down, their cash holdings. Flows of funds within the private sector involving payments between two members of that sector, which do not involve any transactions with the public sector, will not alter the cash base of the banking system. Thus any purchase by the banks of earning assets from the private sector (e.g. by making loans) will lead to a redeposit of the means of payment, whether this was originally made in the form of cash or a cheque on the bank itself, except to the extent that the subsequent adjustment of portfolios leads to an outflow of funds from the private to the public sector, say as the public wishes to hold more currency itself or to buy more foreign exchange from the public sector's reserves, in order to buy foreign assets.

On the other hand the purchase of earning assets by non-bank financial intermediaries must be matched by an equivalent initial reduction in their reserve assets. Funds, money, will only be redeposited with non-bank financial intermediaries so long as these latter offer relatively attractive terms. So their ability to obtain and to hold reserves depends on their ability to make their liabilities competitively attractive in relation to all other assets whether public-sector or private-sector debt.

Banks' cash reserves are, therefore, immune from the effect of competition for funds within the private sector, so long as this does not affect the flow of funds between the public and the private sectors, whereas non-bank intermediaries' reserves will be directly affected by such competition. It might, therefore, be thought that the redeposit rate,[1] following on from an expansion of earnings assets, of the banks would be much higher than that of the non-bank financial intermediaries. Or to put the point in another way, the marginal cost curve of a bank might be much more elastic than for a non-bank financial intermediary, since any initial attraction of cash reserves by the banks (e.g. by offering a higher yield) will allow a multiple expansion of deposits as the bank payments – to add to their earning assets – lead to redeposits of these payments with the banking system, whereas the non-bank financial intermediary will have a lower redeposit rate and, therefore, a steeper marginal cost curve.

In my view this line of reasoning, which seeks to distinguish between the adjustment process of banks and non-bank financial intermediaries on the basis of differing redeposit ratios, is essentially wrong, and confuses impact effects with the ultimate achievement of equilibrium. The crux of the matter is that in equilibrium the public will only hold that volume of deposits, whether of banks or any other intermediary, consistent with its asset preferences, dependent on its overall wealth and relative interest rates. The growth in any intermediary's liabilities (from one equilibrium state to another) as it tries to make them more attractive depends on the interest elasticity of the public's demand for that asset, and the impact of the intermediary's actions on other interest rates, wealth, and other factors (such as incomes) influencing the relative demand for each asset. The redeposit ratio does not enter into the determination of these final equilibrium conditions, but instead influences the dynamic path of adjustment towards the final equilibrium.

At this point we shall again turn to our model of the financial system in order to try to illustrate these arguments with some simulated numerical examples. The model now has to be extended since there are in this case two sets of intermediaries within the system, the first being the banking sector which holds cash as its reserve asset, the second a non-bank intermediary holding bank deposits as reserves. The liability of this non-bank financial intermediary (F) provides a further asset with, no doubt, somewhat different characteristics for the public to hold, and the claims of this intermediary on the general public (L_F)

---

[1] For an analysis of the different positions of the banks and the non-bank financial intermediaries in terms of their relative redeposit ratios, see D. K. Sheppard and C. R. Barrett, 'Financial Credit Multipliers and the Availability of Funds,' *Economica*, vol. 32, no. 126 (May 1965) pp. 198–214.

may also have certain characteristics distinguishing them from bank loans (L_B). Again, in general, it seems nearer to reality to assume that the intermediary (say a building society, insurance company, finance house) is setting rates on its liabilities to, and claims on, the public, and then accepting all demands from the public at its chosen rate (until it is forced by the pressure of such demands on its liquidity position to change these rates), rather than that the intermediary treats such rates as market parameters. There are then in this system five assets (real capital, public-sector cash and bonds, bank and OFI deposits) and two liabilities (bank and OFI loans) held by the private sector in their portfolios: so the public's asset-preference matrix now has two more rows (the asset-demand functions for F_p and L_{FP} respectively) and two more columns (since there are two more interest rates r_F and r_{LF} for the public to take into consideration). The coefficients which will be used in the numerical simulations are shown in the footnote below.[1]

The behaviour of the banks in this extended system remains the same as that of the single intermediary in the simpler model in Chapter 6, with the banks setting both their loan and deposit rates. The rate-setting functions of the OFI will be similar in general form to that of the banks, with the loan rate depending on rates on alternative earning assets and their liquidity position, but different in detail; one reason for this is that they can obtain a positive return on their bank-deposit holdings. The coefficients selected for the rate setting functions of the non-bank intermediaries were as follows:

(i) Loan-rate setting function

$$r_{LF} = 1{\cdot}0r_B + 0{\cdot}4r_D - 0{\cdot}002D_F + 0{\cdot}0004F$$

where D_F are the bank deposits held by the non-bank intermediary as reserves;

(ii) Deposit-rate setting function

$$r_F = 0{\cdot}2r_B + 0{\cdot}2r_D + 0{\cdot}5r_{LF} - 0{\cdot}002D_F + 0{\cdot}0004F$$

(iii) Reserve-preference function (i.e. choosing whether to hold available liquid assets in the form of bonds or bank deposits)

$$D_F = -100r_B + 100r_D + F - L_F$$

Adding on the appropriate balance-sheet constraint for the OFI

$$D_{Ft} + B_{Ft} + L_{Ft} = F_t + K_{Ft}$$

(together with the relationship showing how changes in the market value of the OFI's bonds affect its capital values, and revising the identities to take account of the fact that bank deposits are now held by OFIs as well as by the public, and government bonds by OFIs as well as by banks and the public) then completes this extended model of the financial system. Given the initial conditions, and the value of the authorities' selected monetary instrument, this model can be solved to show the equilibrium values resulting. Some

1

	r_c	r_B	r_D	r_{LB}	r_F	r_{LF}	r_K	W_{pt-1}	CG	I
C_p	400	−75	−125	−25	−100	−25	−50	0·175	—	—
B_p	−75	2025	−500	−350	−400	−200	−500	0·22	1·0	—
D_p	−125	−500	1775	−200	−500	−150	−300	0·33	—	—
L_{Bp}	−25	−350	−200	1900	−125	−700	−500	—	—	—
F_p	−100	−400	−500	−125	1500	−75	−300	0·225	—	—
L_{Fp}	−25	−200	−150	−700	−75	1500	−350	—	—	—
K_p	−50	−500	−300	−500	−300	−350	2000	0·05	—	1·0

examples are shown in the footnote below,[1] with the authorities varying the rates on bonds. Again, of course, in this deterministic model it makes no difference whether the authorities operate via changing bond rates or changing the cash base; a 5 per cent bond rate implies a cash base of 1226, and a cash base of 1226 implies a bond rate of 5 per cent. These numerical results show nothing particularly startling, nor indeed were they meant to do so. As monetary expansion takes place, whether through an increase in the cash base or by a reduction in interest rates, asset quantities all rise (and interest rates fall) more or less proportionately together, leaving interest-rate relativities, asset ratios, etc., fairly constant. The banks' cash ratio, in this example, remains rather stable at about 23 per cent. One slightly odd result, arising from the particular set of arbitrary coefficients chosen,

---

[1] The initial conditions are: W_{Pt-1} 15,000, K_{Pt-1} 10,800, K_{Bt-1} 600, K_{Ft-1} 400, r_{Bt-1} 4 per cent; in the base run the authorities set r_{Bt} at 4 per cent again. The results are

(A)

	Banks	Intermediaries	Public	Government	Rates (per cent)
Cash	557	—	1062	1619	0
Bonds (at market value)	800	547	2234	3581	4
Bank Deposits	2410	580	1830	—	2·53
Bank Loans	1653	—	−1653	—	4·25
OFI Deposits	—	1480	1480	—	2·96
OFI Loans	—	753	−753	—	4·44
Investment	—	—	938	—	8·69 (rate on capital)
Capital Gains	0	0	0	—	—
Net Worth	600	400	15,938	—	—

(B) If the authorities set r_{Bt} at 3·0 per cent

	Banks	Intermediaries	Public	Government	Rates (per cent)
Cash	613	—	1398	2011	0
Bonds	1016	705	2690	4412	3
Bank Deposits	2683	529	2154	—	1·84
Bank Loans	1920	—	−1920	—	3·15
OFI Deposits	—	1616	1616	—	2·22
OFI Loans	—	971	−971	—	3·33
Investment	—	—	951	—	7·75
Capital Gains	267	190	767	—	—
Net Worth	867	590	16,718	—	—

(C) If the authorities set r_{Bt} at 5·0 per cent

	Banks	Intermediaries	Public	Government	Rates (per cent)
Cash	501	—	725	1226	0
Bonds	690	465	2085	3240	5
Bank Deposits	2137	631	1506	—	3·21
Bank Loans	1386	—	−1386	—	5·35
OFI Deposits	—	1344	1344	—	3·70
OFI Loans	—	534	−534	—	5·56
Investment	—	—	924	—	9·62
Capital Gains	−160	−114	−460	—	—
Net Worth	440	286	15,464	—	—

was that the reserve ratios maintained by both banks and OFIs in this model seemed to be considerably higher than found in reality. But this is really of no importance, and could have been remedied by choosing different coefficients. What matters is to see that the condition of equilibrium in financial markets requires that all asset preferences be satisfied; that models of such systems can be quite easily constructed to show that such equilibrium values are feasible; and to see how these equilibrium values alter as conditions change, for example as the authorities alter their control instrument(s).

Going a stage further, the profits of the OFI(s) can be calculated from the relationship, $r_D \cdot D_F + r_B \cdot B_F + r_{LF} \cdot L_F - r_F \cdot F = \pi_F$. So it is again possible to simulate how variations in the rate-setting functions of the OFI(s) would affect the level and variance of their own profits and reserve ratio (D_F/F); furthermore, such simulations show how the variations in the OFIs' rate-setting functions affect the banks' profits and size. There could be a possibility of an oligopolistic confrontation between groups of financial intermediaries organised into cartels. In that case each cartel would want to have some idea of the impact of its own decisions on the position of the other; some numerical examples are shown in the footnote below.[1] Again, of course, the resulting numbers are only the reflection of the arbitrary coefficients fed into the system. Nevertheless, the results illustrate that competition from the OFIs can have a varying effect upon the banks' position, depending on the circumstances. The table in the preceding footnote shows that, in this model, the OFIs are excessively liquid. If they then reduce their loan rate they can attract people into intermediary loans (partly out of bank loans), and shift their portfolios towards higher-yielding assets. As the demand for their assets grows, and their portfolio becomes less liquid, they will raise their deposit rates (with an unchanged deposit-setting *function*), again attracting funds partially from bank deposits. Although the margin between OFI deposit and lending rates narrows quite sharply (from 1·48 to 1·17 per cent), the gain in having a larger portfolio with a larger proportion of high-yielding assets outweighs it, and profits rise. *Per contra*, bank size, earning assets, and profits all decline. So in this case, when OFIs are competing for loan business with the banks, benefits accruing to the OFIs are largely at the expense of the banks.

There is, at least in this example, less cause for conflict between them in their competition for the public's deposits. As the OFI shifts its deposit rate upwards (leaving its loan-setting function unchanged) it attracts more deposits. Initially, given its loan-setting function, these are simply held in bank deposits, but this makes the OFI excessively liquid, so it will lower its loan rate (narrowing the margin between deposit and loan rates). In this case the ultimate equilibrium shape of the portfolio remains unchanged by the shift in the deposit rate, but the decline in the rate margin from 1·48 to 1·15 per cent more than offsets the beneficial effect of the larger portfolio. Meanwhile bank size (and profits) are hardly reduced,

---

[1] In the attached table, the equilibrium values that OFI and bank profits, deposits, reserve ratios, etc., would take if the authorities held bond rate at 4 per cent are calculated for varying versions of the OFIs' rate-setting functions. In this case the effect of introducing a constant (taking positive or negative values) into the rate-setting functions is examined.

| Value of Constant in OFI rate-setting functions: | | OFI Profit | OFI Deposits Outstanding | OFI Reserve Ratio (D_F/F) (per cent) | Bank Profit | Bank deposits held by | | | Bank Cash ratio |
Loan rate (per cent)	Deposit rate (per cent)					Public	OFI	Total	
0	0	26·19	1480	39·2	41·40	1830	580	2410	23·1
−0·4	0	26·52	1689	30·4	40·23	1775	513	2288	23·6
+0·4	0	24·35	1271	50·8	42·56	1886	646	2532	22·7
0	−0·4	27·01	1150	39·2	41·73	1972	451	2423	22·4
0	+0·4	23·42	1810	39·2	41·07	1688	709	2397	23·9

partly because a considerable proportion of bank deposits run off by the public remains held by the OFIs. This latter result, however, may well be mostly due to the implausibly high deposit-reserve ratio of OFIs incorporated in this model. In practice, OFIs in the United Kingdom hold only fairly exiguous working balances with banks, holding a larger proportion of their reserve assets in short-term government debt. In that case a transfer of funds by the public from bank deposits to OFIs will cause a somewhat larger drain of deposits from banks (though this will be partially staunched as they in turn raise their rates in competition). Nevertheless, it could be the case that upward shifts in OFI deposit rates could affect both banks and OFIs adversely, so that there could be a community of interest between them not to compete too vigorously for deposits.

This possible community of interest arises because the OFI can only attract funds out of the banks by raising its deposit rate, which serves to lower the margin between the interest rates on its loans and deposits. If, however, there is an autonomous shift in the public's preferences, at given rates, towards holding funds with the OFIs rather than with the banks, then the OFIs will benefit and the banks will lose, as shown in the numerical example below.[1]

To be sure, the differences in the asset and liability portfolios of the banks and the OFIs will have an effect upon the final equilibrium values of assets, interest rates, etc., within the system. But the determination of those equilibrium values in all cases depends on the same factors, both for banks and OFIs, e.g. the wealth and portfolio preferences of the public, the monetary actions of the authorities, and the responses, especially in altering the rates which they offer, of the financial intermediaries to changing liquidity pressures and profit opportunities.[2]

---

[1] Autonomous shifts in the public's preferences are proxied by changing the coefficients on W_{pt-1} (i.e. how the public prefers to distribute its wealth) in the public's asset-preference matrix. The first row of figures is the original base run: in each case the authorities hold bond rate at 4 per cent.

Coefficient on W_{pt-1} in equation for D_p	in equation for F_p	OFI Profit	OFI Deposits	OFI Reserve Ratio	Bank Profit	Bank Deposits Public	OFI	Total	Bank Cash ratio
0·33	0·225	26·19	1480	39·2	41·40	1830	580	2410	23·1
0·37	0·185	22·32	1169	38·5	43·48	2222	450	2672	23·6
0·29	0·265	30·91	1790	39·7	39·46	1438	710	2148	22·5

[2] The extended model, as before, describes the equilibrium values consistent with the given initial conditions. In the absence of full information, a new set of equilibrium values cannot be simultaneously and immediately achieved after a change in the initial conditions; but this model does not describe the process of adjustment in a limited information world. In the previous chapter this process was examined and illustrated with a numerical example. Analysis of the adjustment process becomes, however, even more complicated when the model is extended to include OFIs, and therefore involves interaction between the OFIs and the banks.

Again the model, as it stands, appears not to be dynamically stable. The main reason, as before, is that both the banks and the OFIs are presumed in their rate-setting functions to react only to the *current* values of their reserves and deposits, i.e. to their current liquidity position. But when they, either banks or OFIs, raise their rates, say in response to a fall in their current liquidity position, the impact effect on their reserves, with deposits rising and advances falling, is rather large. This is especially so in the case of OFIs; in particular their relatively low redeposit ratio ensures that any action by them to adjust their interest rates will have a considerable impact on their reserve position. In the above case, their reserves increase markedly in the second period, making the OFIs revise their rates down sharply, and so on.

Presumably, though, the OFIs will realise that, with a low redeposit ratio, adjustments in their rates relative to competitive rates elsewhere will have a sharp impact effect on their reserves. So their response to changes in their liquidity position is likely to be adaptive, in order to avoid instability. This kind of adaptive response may take the form of adjusting rates not just in response

(*Footnote* [2] *continued on p. 148*)

In these exercises to illustrate how the totals of bank deposits and OFI liabilities in the system are determined, both the banks and the OFIs were assumed to be equally free to adjust the rates offered on deposits and loans in order to achieve their preferred positions. This may not be the case. The rates which banks can offer on their deposits (and charge on their loans) may more often be subject to constraints, either from government regulation or oligopolistic cartel, than is the case with other intermediaries. So the determination of the volume of bank deposits may be less influenced by the attempts of banks to restore their desired portfolios, than is the case, say, with other financial intermediaries. A further reason, therefore, which is sometimes given for arguing that the process of determination of bank deposits is of a qualitatively different nature from that of OFI liabilities is that the banks are so trammelled with restrictions on their actions that they are not in a position to achieve their business objectives. Instead, it may be argued, they are often, or commonly, in a constrained disequilibrium position, in which the response to disturbances may seem mechanical rather than a form of portfolio adjustment.

If advances rates are fixed, particularly if they are fixed at some low level, the demand for advances may exceed the profit-maximising supply of advances. As a bank expands advances at the fixed rate it will incur an increasing administrative cost and its portfolio will become riskier. Moreover, a bank will first choose to make the safest advances, and/or those that promise to result in the most rewarding long-term customer relationship, so that the subjective yield to the bank will decline as it expands into 'the unsatisfied fringe of borrowers.' In Fig. 7.1, the marginal return to the bank of additional advances XX^1

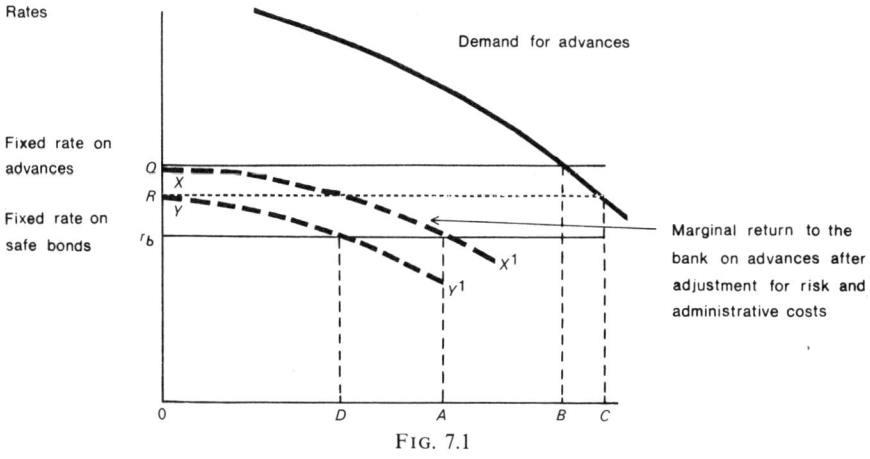

FIG. 7.1

to the current liquidity position and current cash flows but to the development of their liquidity position over several recent periods, i.e. by introducing lags into the rate-setting functions. Thus r_{F_t} and r_{LF_t} may be functions not only of D_{F_t} and F_t but also of $D_{F_{t-i}}$ and F_{t-i} ($i = 1, \ldots, n$). Once, however, this change is made the model becomes considerably more complex, and its dynamic properties become difficult to ascertain. Moreover, these properties depend on the coefficients involved, and in this model they are only arbitrarily chosen.

In a large system with several groups engaged in setting rates and prices interdependently, formal analysis of the adjustment process in a world with limited information and with sequential decision making is certainly difficult, and I offer no apologies for not proceeding further with it here. Nevertheless, I do contend that adjustment does occur within the financial system in the fashion described here by a process of adjusting asset holdings in response to relative interest rates, and adjusting rates to changes in asset holdings (e.g. to changes in the liquidity position and to expectations about future cash flows) and to changes in rates on other assets/liabilities.

(after adjustment for risk and costs) is shown as sloping downwards. The bank would like to provide 0*A* advances, i.e. up to the point where the marginal return on advances equals the marginal return on the safe asset, bonds. However, at the fixed rate the demand for advances, 0*B*, considerably exceeds the desired supply. Under these conditions the bank may either feel forced to accept a disequilibrium condition, or may try to ration advances by raising other non-interest barriers to borrowing, or seek round-about ways, e.g. compensating balances, to raise its return.

Under such circumstances the response of banks to easier financial conditions, larger cash reserves, lower bond rates, would be to reduce these non-interest rationing barriers to the 'unsatisfied fringe' so long as their loan rate remained (temporarily) sticky. Furthermore, variations in an externally fixed rate on advances, relative to the safe bond rate, could lead to the demand for advances moving in a different direction from the bank's desired supply. For example, in Fig. 7.1 a decline in the fixed advances rate from 0*Q* to 0*R*, relative to the constant bond rate, would cause the demand to rise to 0*C*, while the banks' desired supply falls to 0*D*. The pressure to ration increases; in such rationing, disequilibrium conditions, let alone more stringent circumstances of ceilings on bank advances, portfolio adjustment models will be less helpful.

And if the bank (or intermediary) is constrained to offer some fixed rate on deposits, it becomes impossible to vary that rate to achieve a desired equilibrium. If the demand for loans, say, rises, but the intermediary is restricted by interest-rate ceilings on deposits, it will not be able to bid for funds to meet that demand, and will have eventually to choke it off by rationing or by very high loan rates. Under these conditions the bank, or intermediary, has to employ such funds as are deposited with it at the given rate as best it can. Indeed, it is these circumstances where the banks' operations are externally constrained in this fashion that best fit the elementary textbook exposition of the multiplier process in which a bank receives a deposit of reserves, and then loans out a proportion of those reserves dependent only on its (fixed) reserve ratio. Of that loan a (fixed) proportion is redeposited, and so the process goes on, until a final multiple expansion is achieved. Relative prices, and yields, receive no mention. Such a process is inconsistent with unconstrained optimising portfolio adjustment, but it might come nearer the truth when the banking system suffers from external constraints over its adjustment process.

If, however, one seeks to differentiate between the process of the determination of the volume of bank and non-bank liabilities on the basis of greater external constraints over the rates which can be offered by banks to their customers,[1] there are two questions which need answering. The first is the empirical question whether it is generally true that banks are more constrained from rate competition than are other intermediaries, and the second, the more fundamental question, is whether limitation on the freedom to compete in the field of interest payments does not leave it open still to the banks to move towards equilibrium by competition in other dimensions, e.g. in the provision of services to their customers.

In the United Kingdom rates on current accounts were fixed at zero and on time deposits (at seven days' notice) in relation to Bank Rate by the clearing bank cartel for many decades.[2] In the United States rates on demand deposits have been fixed at zero, and the Federal Reserve Board sets, and from time to time alters, the maximum rate payable on various

---

[1] 'The differences [between commercial banks and other financial intermediaries] are more importantly related to the special reserve requirements and interest-rate ceilings to which banks are subject. Any other financial industry subject to the same kind of regulations would behave in much the same way,' J. Tobin, 'Commercial Banks as Creators of "Money",' *Banking and Monetary Studies*, p. 418.

[2] Agreements on rates can be traced back into the nineteenth century, though the agreements then covered only smaller parts of the country, see C. Goodhart, *The Business of Banking 1891–1914* (Weidenfeld & Nicolson, London, 1972) section II.

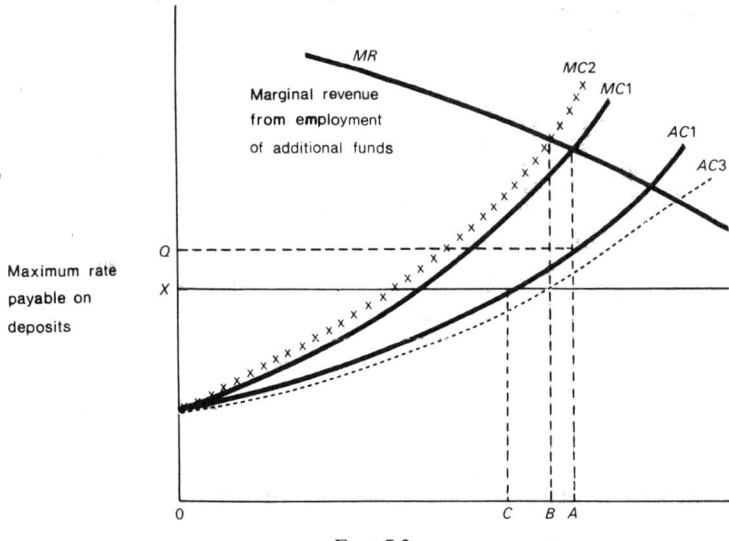

FIG. 7.2

categories of deposit account.[1] In 1971, however, the cartel in the United Kingdom was disbanded and the banks became free to set their own rates on current accounts, time deposits[2] and advances. One small bank has offered interest on retail-type current accounts, and should inflation continue to push up nominal interest rates its example could, perhaps, be followed.[3] Since 1971 banks in the United Kingdom have been at least as free to vary rates as, indeed in some ways more so than, the building societies, whose Association suggests recommended rates, and much more free of constraints than the Trustee Savings Banks. It is thus not necessarily true that banks' operations will be more cabined by external controls, and since 1971 in the United Kingdom it has not been true.

Even when banks are so restricted they are adept at finding ways around these restrictions. When faced with restrictions on the rates they could offer for deposits, the clearing banks in the United Kingdom set up subsidiaries which could bid in the open market for large funds; while in the United States banks bid for funds through the euro-dollar market and through holding companies in the commercial paper market. If the restriction is on

---

[1] 'Banks were prohibited by law [enacted after the waves of banking failures in 1931–3] or regulation from paying interest on demand deposits and from paying rates of interest on time deposits higher than those specified by the Board of Governors of the Federal Reserve System for member banks and by the FDIC for insured non-member banks,' M. Friedman and A. J. Schwartz, *A Monetary History of the United States 1867–1960*, a study by the National Bureau of Economic Research (Princeton University Press, 1963) p. 443.

[2] This freedom of action was not entirely without qualifications. In paragraph 15 of 'Competition and Credit Control,' a consultative document issued on 14 May 1971, and reprinted in *The Bank of England Quarterly Bulletin*, vol. 11, no. 2 (June 1971) pp. 189–93, it was stated that there might be a need to limit terms offered for savings deposits in order to protect savings banks and building societies from the full force of competition from the banks. Accordingly, when such competitive pressures were putting the building societies under strain in 1973, the banks were asked not to pay more than $9\frac{1}{2}$ per cent on deposits of under £10,000.

[3] By mid-summer 1973 the clearing banks had sharply increased the interest rate offered on average current account balances as an offset against bank charges, in one case from $2\frac{1}{2}$ to 5 per cent. But they still maintained their refusal to make any net interest payments to current account depositors, largely on grounds of tax complications.

deposit rates, bankers can try to devise a liability whose characteristics lie just outside the definition of a deposit. And, even if the authorities do contain rate competition, it is still open to banks to compete on services to attract the funds of the public. In Fig. 7.2 the authorities have fixed maximum deposit rates at X; with marginal and average cost curves as depicted ($MC1$ and $AC1$) this constraint on the maximum deposit rate payable keeps rates and total deposits below the profit-maximising level, at which the deposit rate would be $0Q$, with $0A$ deposits. Additional profits could be made, if only more funds could be attracted. The bank might, therefore, provide additional expensive services, for example gifts and beautiful free cheque books to new depositors, new branches in new buildings, etc., to attract more funds. The average *interest* cost of deposits will be reduced by this, since with additional services provided the public will now be willing to hold any given level of deposits at a somewhat lower interest rate; thus the average *interest* cost function falls from $AC1$ to $AC3$. However, *overall* marginal and average costs, including the costs of the additional services, will now rise to $MC2$ and $AC2$ (not shown in Fig. 7.2). At the new equilibrium ($MR = MC2$) the bank has offered just sufficient extra services to achieve its optimal position subject to the interest-rate constraint ($AC3 \leq X$). The new volume of deposits, $0B$, will be above the initial constrained position, $0C$, but below the unconstrained equilibrium, $0A$.

Constraints on the rates that banks, or any other financial intermediary, can offer may restrict and distort their response to disequilibrium conditions. Under such circumstances their ability to obtain their preferred portfolio may be limited, and their response to, say, reserve inflows or outflows, may appear mechanical. Yet even so the underlying process is one of general portfolio adjustment, subject to these constraints, in response to changes in relative interest rates, wealth, etc. It is not a mechanical process, even subject to these constraints, and it is basically exactly the same whether the intermediary is, or is not, a bank.

8

Controlling the Supply of Money: A Problem for the Authorities?

SUMMARY

When the public sector runs a deficit, say as a result of an expansionary budget, it has to find the requisite finance. This can be obtained either by non-monetary borrowing, domestically or externally, or by money creation. Although the monetary implications of fiscal actions may be taken into consideration, many other factors also enter the budget decision: so from the point of view of the monetary authorities, the size of the deficit to be financed is an external parameter which they have to accept. Moreover, several of the financing flows are outside the control of the monetary authorities; debt maturities are ineluctable, and in so far as rates and terms on the non-marketable savings instruments issued by the government are sticky, flows into and out of such instruments tend to vary perversely with the intended direction of monetary policy. Finally, and more important, open-market operations, to control monetary expansion, will cause interest-rate movements which, under a fixed exchange-rate system, can induce large-scale international capital flows which will to some extent offset and frustrate the domestic monetary actions.

The burden of controlling the pace of monetary expansion falls mainly on the authorities' open-market operations. In some circumstances this burden can seem insupportable. In particular, the authorities can rarely foretell with any confidence how the market will respond to their operations. Investors' demand for bonds is not just a simple function of current bond prices, but also depends on the expectations generated in an uncertain world. The existence of short-dated bonds, whose certain yield to redemption rises as interest rates rise, should provide, however, a fairly stable anchorage for the market, even when most investors work to short planning periods. Even so, uncertainty about the market's response and fear of large, erratic and unpredictable variations in interest rates make the authorities tentative in such operations.

Market response to the authorities' operations will depend in part on the strength of competition for money from the private sector. If borrowers from the banks are not deterred by higher rates, the banks will bid up in competition with the authorities and rates will spiral upwards. Faced with this situation, the authorities in the United Kingdom have often reacted by imposing direct controls on the banks. But it is extremely difficult to tell thereafter what proportion of the underlying demand for credit, the basic cause of the upwards pressure in rates, has been diverted to other channels and what proportion has been choked off. Even when the authorities are prepared to rely on general market instruments, rather than on direct controls, their ability to monitor developments and to bring about smooth adjustments is hindered by various lags in the system.

Most economic models take the money stock, or the high-powered money base, as given. This is not the way it appears to the authorities. To them the control of the pace of monetary expansion often involves a difficult struggle: four main factors determine how difficult this struggle will be:

(i) the size of the public-sector deficit;
(ii) the elasticity of substitution between foreign and domestic assets in an open economy, when exchange rates are fixed;
(iii) market reactions to the authorities' open-market operations; and
(iv) the interest elasticity of the demand for advances.

A. Government Finance[1]

It is true, by accounting identity, that changes in the money stock can be expressed in terms of changes in the high-powered money base in an algebraic formula that depends also on two ratios, the public's currency/deposit and the banks' reserve/deposit ratios (even though manipulation of such multipliers does not, we have argued, illuminate the behavioural process of adjustment). Moreover, movements in these two ratios are generally quite stable and predictable;[2] so a knowledge of movements in the high-powered money base should allow one to predict the movements in the money stock with some accuracy. This is so whether or not the authorities are concerned to control the rate of growth of the monetary base or the money stock. Furthermore, the high-powered money base, in most countries, more or less corresponds to the monetary liabilities of the Central Bank, consisting of notes and coin outstanding and deposits of the banks with the Central Bank. It would seem, on the face of it, as if any Central Bank should be in a position to control its own liabilities and thus the money stock. But even if the monetary authorities are pursuing some other objective, such as pegging rates on public-sector debt or on foreign exchange, which commits them to exchange cash for the asset whose rate is pegged and thus loosens their control over the monetary base, the ensuing growth in the volume of high-powered money will be related to the growth in the money stock.

For such reasons it is common, indeed customary, in monetary models to take the high-powered money base as exogenously given, determined off-stage, and then to relate the money stock to this base by a multiplier relationship, incorporating those behavioural responses affecting the two ratios involved. This approach, however, abstracts from *all* the main operational problems facing the authorities. It reveals nothing about the difficulties possibly confronting the authorities in achieving any desired level for the monetary base. It suggests by itself nothing of the implications for interest rates, markets and financial institutions of the authorities' choice of targets and market procedures. It gives no idea of the underlying forces with which the authorities may have to contend in controlling the money stock. Indeed, in making the initial assumption that the monetary base is under their control, all their operational problems are implicitly assumed to have been resolved.

Just as the algebra of the banking multiplier effectively obscures the underlying behavioural process of portfolio adjustment in response to relative prices, so the assumption of an exogenously-given monetary base effectively obscures consideration of the real

---

[1] Parts of this chapter are largely taken from my previous paper on 'Analysis of the Determination of the Stock of Money,' chap. 14 in *Essays in Modern Economics*, ed. M. Parkin, Proceedings of the Association of University Teachers of Economics, Aberystwyth, 1972 (Longman, London, 1973).

[2] Research into the variations in these ratios has been extensive in the United States, see for example P. Cagan, *Determinants and Effects of Changes in the Stock of Money, 1875–1960*, National Bureau of Economic Research, Studies in Business Cycles Number 13 (Columbia University Press, New York, 1965) especially chaps 4 and 5; also see his earlier work on *The Demand for Currency Relative to the Total Money Supply*, National Bureau of Economic Research, Occasional Paper 62 (New York, 1958). There has been much less research into this subject in the United Kingdom, largely because of much greater scepticism, especially among the authorities, of the usefulness of the multiplier paradigm as a framework for the study of the determination of the money stock.

problems facing the monetary authorities and their responses to such problems. So a first step is to abandon the assumption that the high-powered money base (H) is given. Instead we may start by proceeding to an examination of the factors determining the outstanding totals of all the various forms of government debt extant, including the cash liabilities of the public sector. In order to do this it is helpful to turn to yet another accounting identity, taken from the accounts of the flow of funds,[1] which describes how the financial deficit (or surplus) of each sector is financed by flows of funds through the various financial markets. In order that this accounting identity may be satisfied, it is necessary that a public-sector deficit, after taking account of certain financial transfers, e.g. import deposits, local authority loans for house-building, etc., must be financed by borrowing from other sectors, by issuing additional debt to them or by running down claims upon them, e.g. foreign-exchange reserves which represent claims on the overseas sector.

The provision of finance to the public sector occurs in a variety of ways.[2] For the purpose of this analysis such borrowing may be grouped into three components: finance which directly brings about an increase in high-powered money, ΔH; finance raised by other domestic borrowing; finance raised by receiving the domestic monetary counterpart of accommodating an external currency outflow. It may be useful to sub-divide this second item, the finance obtained by other domestic borrowing, into three separate components,

(i) the use of funds to repay maturing debt,
(ii) transactions (borrowing or repaying) in non-marketable debt, e.g. in the United Kingdom premium savings bonds, national savings certificates, etc., and
(iii) operations in marketable debt.

This accounting identity can then be set out as follows

$$PSD = OMO + NMD - MAT + ECF + \Delta H$$

where PSD is the public-sector deficit after taking account of various financial transfers such as import deposits, OMO represents the outcome of the authorities' operations in marketable debt, NMD represents the outcome of transactions in non-marketable debt, MAT shows the required use of funds to pay off maturing debt, ECF gives the total finance obtained from, or required for, accommodating external currency flows and ΔH represents the increase in the public sector's monetary liabilities, high-powered money.[3] This identity represents what Hansen terms the European type of public-sector budget constraint. In the U.S. form of this constraint the government finances itself entirely by selling debt in the market, and the Central Bank then decides how much of this debt to buy. As Hansen notes,[4] 'What can be done under one of these budget constraints can also be done under the other one,' but the '*automatic* responses are different under the two systems.' Rather than jump backwards and forwards between these alternative systems, we shall fix in the remainder of the chapter on the European-type budget constraint. Nevertheless, such differences can cause confusion, which can perhaps best be dispelled by reference to Hansen's paper on the subject.[4]

---

[1] Consult, for example, the regular 'Analysis of Financial Statistics' in each issue of the *Bank of England Quarterly Bulletin*.

[2] See, for example, columns 1–3 in Table L and also Table D in the Financial Analysis in the *Bank of England Quarterly Bulletin*, vol. 11, no. 4 (December 1971) pp. 472 and 460.

[3] Including for this purpose the increase in bankers' balances with the Bank of England Banking Department (counterbalanced by holdings of public-sector debt by the Department).

[4] B. Hansen, 'On the Effects of Fiscal and Monetary Policy: A Taxonomic Discussion,' *The American Economic Review*, vol. 63, no. 4 (September 1973) pp. 546–71. The importance of giving explicit recognition to the existence of the public-sector budget constraint was earlier noted by

(*Footnote* [4] *continued on p. 155*)

This ('European-type') accounting identity can equally well be reversed, to show the various financial flows accompanying any change in high-powered money, as follows

$$\Delta H = PSD - OMO - NMD + MAT - ECF$$

This identity at least points the analysis towards explicit consideration of those elements in the financial system which have traditionally been the main concern of the authorities (at least within 'European-type' systems), i.e. the size of the public-sector deficit, operations in public-sector marketable debt, the relative attractions of public-sector non-marketable debt, the weight of maturities to be financed, the impact on the foreign-exchange market – and on the reserve position – of a balance-of-payments deficit (or surplus).

Certain of these financial flows are, largely or entirely, outside the control of the monetary authorities. For example, the volume of maturities to be refinanced in any one year is ineluctably determined by prior contractual arrangements. The problem of refinancing maturities can be exaggerated, however, since holders, such as financial institutions, who are attempting to maintain a balanced portfolio can usually be tempted to switch regularly towards slightly longer-dated debt in order to maintain the desired balance of their portfolios. Even so, the occasion of a maturity reduces the transaction cost to holders of moving out of public-sector debt, and causes such holders, of necessity, to reconsider their investment plans. For such reasons maturities of debt issues of a kind bought previously in large quantities by less active portfolio managers, especially in the personal sector, can be expected to cause more serious refinancing problems to the authorities.

Although the monetary implications of any proposed fiscal change may be given some weight in the determination of fiscal policy, many other considerations of very different kinds also enter, and may well sway the judgement about the proper balance between expenditures and revenue of the public sector. To this extent variations in the size of the fiscal deficit must also be regarded as outside the control of the monetary authorities. Indeed variations in the size of the public-sector deficit may on occasions even hinder the intended thrust of monetary policy.[1]

Moreover, it is difficult to devise fiscal measures that can be frequently altered without involving considerable disturbance of one kind or another. It is therefore usual to alter tax rates and forward expenditure plans only once a year in the annual Budget. Even then lags intervene between the policy change and the resulting effect on monetary flows, so that the public-sector deficit in any given year may be conditioned as much by previous Budgets as by current fiscal changes. For all these reasons the monetary authorities cannot hope to vary the size of the public-sector deficit in the short run as a flexible instrument for the purpose of achieving some desired rate of growth in the monetary aggregates. This problem is seen in even more extreme forms in other countries where the executive face difficulties on occasions in obtaining legislative agreement to their fiscal proposals.

In principle it would be possible to envisage the authorities frequently varying the rates of interest offered on non-marketable debt for the purpose of inducing some desired level of flows into these instruments. In practice, however, in the United Kingdom rates on some

---

C. F. Christ, for example in his papers on 'A Short-Run Aggregate-Demand Model of the Interdependence and Effects of Monetary and Fiscal Policies with Keynesian and Classical Interest Elasticities,' *The American Economic Review*, vol. 57 (May 1967) papers and proceedings, pp. 434–43; and 'A Simple Macroeconomic Model with a Government Budget Restraint,' *Journal of Political Economy*, vol. 76, no. 1 (January/February 1968) pp. 53–67.

---

[1] Professor Tew, in his article on 'The Implications of Milton Friedman for Britain,' *The Banker*, vol. 119, no. 522 (August 1969) pp. 757–71, has termed the financing requirement which arises from the public-sector deficit and debt maturities, 'the flood.' In order to check the growth of the monetary aggregates, the authorities have to undertake the often extremely difficult task of damming this flood.

of these instruments have been notable rather for their constancy.[1] Thus in periods of monetary squeeze rates offered on non-marketable securities have generally tended to become less competitive. The result has been that flows of funds into national savings have tended to move inversely with fluctuations in market interest rates.[2]

The likelihood of capital inflows from abroad as domestic interest rates rise, thus altering the external currency flow to be financed (ECF), can form a further obstacle to the successful achievement of market operations intended to squeeze domestic liquidity. If such capital flows respond very sensitively, and in relatively large volume, to variations in financial conditions in any country, then under a regime of fixed exchange rates the autonomy of that country to undertake an independent financial policy is limited. On the other hand, in such conditions it becomes easier to achieve a desired level of international reserves by inducing large-scale capital movements.

Thus two of the monetary flows affecting the level of H (PSD and MAT) are to some considerable extent outside the control of the authorities, while another two (NMD and ECF) tend to respond perversely to interest-rate changes, in that an increase in domestic interest rates will tend to lead to cash flows from these sources causing increases in the high-powered money base. In addition, there could be some decline in the banks' desired reserve ratios as interest rates on earning assets rise relative to rates on reserves.

In order to achieve a desired level of H, or more usefully of M, the authorities have, therefore, to try to offset movements, which may on occasions be very large, in all these other flows[3] by inducing people to purchase, or if needs be to sell, marketable government debt. If these flows should require a very large amount of financing, then any attempt to restrict the rate of growth of the monetary aggregates imposes a severe pressure upon a Central Bank's operations in marketable debt.

B. Open-Market Operations

In the examples in the two previous chapters dealing with the adjustment process within the financial system, it was assumed that the authorities could regulate the rate of return on public-sector debt, in particular the yield on marketable bonds. Under conditions of

---

[1] For example, the rate of interest on Post Office Savings Bank ordinary accounts, retitled National Savings Bank ordinary accounts in 1969, remained constant at $2\frac{1}{2}$ per cent from the foundation of P.O.S.B. in 1861 by Gladstone until 1970 when Jenkins took steps to raise the rate offered.

[2] Evidence of this can be obtained from some simple regressions.

$$NMD_t = 18 \cdot 98 - 47 \cdot 98 dC_{t-1} - 31 \cdot 54 dC_{t-3} + 0 \cdot 594 NMD_{t-1}$$
$$\quad (18 \cdot 70) \qquad (22 \cdot 54) \qquad (0 \cdot 14)$$
$$\bar{R}^2 = 0 \cdot 56$$

$$NMD_t = 18 \cdot 58 - 65 \cdot 09 dBS_t - 34 \cdot 63 dBS_{t-1} + 0 \cdot 594 NMD_{t-1}$$
$$\quad (22 \cdot 19) \qquad (23 \cdot 74) \qquad (0 \cdot 12)$$
$$\bar{R}^2 = 0 \cdot 61$$

where NMD represents the inflow into non-marketable debt in £million (seasonally adjusted), dC is the change in consol rates and dBS the change in building society deposit rates, observed quarterly over the period 1963 $Q3$ to 1970 $Q4$.

[3] There is, however, some tendency towards negative covariation in these flows in the short run, i.e. they interact in a way that produces some partial compensation, which alleviates certain of the difficulties facing the authorities. A large foreign-exchange inflow usually encourages sales of gilts and also reduces company demand for bank credit. A big public-sector borrowing requirement implies a large private-sector surplus, which may induce large private-sector purchases of public-sector debt and, perhaps, lead to some reduction in the demand for advances. Moreover, a large public-sector borrowing requirement is more likely to coincide with an exchange outflow than with an inflow.

uncertainty, however, an investor can only be sure of the nominal yield on a marketable fixed-interest bond when he plans to hold that bond till maturity, and even then he will face uncertainty over the prospective real yield and whether his income/expenditure plans will develop as intended. Investors have to allocate their funds on the basis of their expectations of the real yield obtainable on the various available investments. Uncertainty about future developments usually deepens the further ahead in time one peers; for example, the dispersion of our subjective probability distribution for future rates of inflation is likely to be an increasing function of time. This is not, however, always the case: uncertainty about the future nominal capital value of a fixed-interest bond declines as it approaches maturity. But, apart from opportunities afforded to match assets against liabilities,[1] the uncertainty about the likely yield on an asset holding will tend to increase the longer the horizon to which the investor looks.

These considerations suggest that most investors should plan to review their asset holdings quite frequently, even though they may at each review compare the expected uncertain return over each relatively short planning period, i.e. the period between reviews, against the relatively safe nominal yield to be obtained on an asset with a maturity life equal to that of the contingent requirement for funds. So the return which investors are calculating, when deciding how to apportion their portfolio, will frequently be the expected return over quite a short planning period. The expected return on a marketable bond, with a life till maturity longer than this short planning period, includes the known nominal interest payment plus the uncertain capital gain or loss on the realisation of that bond at the end of the period. With a short planning period, a change in the running yield resulting from a fall in the price of purchasing the known interest payment(s) over that period will have a relatively small effect on the overall expected yield in comparison with any changes in expected capital gains or losses. So, under these circumstances, the market demand for an asset, following a change in its price, is likely to be strongly influenced by the effect of that change on expectations of the short-term future level of its price.

If a shift in the present price of an asset causes no revision to previous expectations of future price levels, then a decline in present prices will increase expected future capital gains from holding that asset. However, it is perfectly possible that expectations of future price levels might be lowered in line with a current price reduction, leaving the expected capital gain on the asset unaffected, or even lowered by more than the current change–i.e. when expectations are extrapolative.

Those reviewing their portfolios after such a change in the price of an asset, who have regressive expectations, expecting the price change to be reversed, will be tempted to buy that asset; those with extrapolative expectations will tend to sell, subject to inertia, transactions costs, etc. In a market with no transactions or information costs, so that reallocation of portfolios would occur continuously and instantaneously, equilibrium in the market for any asset would only be obtained when the sales of those expecting price falls in the next period were exactly balanced by the purchases of those expecting price rises. Even in a real-world approximation to such a perfect market, in financial markets where information is made available fairly cheaply and transactions costs are relatively low, the mean expectation of the price of each asset in the next period must be that it will be at nearly the same level as now, at least over short periods. Over longer periods there will be expected capital gains on, say, redeemable bonds selling at a discount, which expected capital gains will form part of their normal equilibrium prospective yield. In the very short run, however, any expected rise in the price of an asset would represent a very large yield

---

[1] These opportunities are greater for financial institutions, which can match assets against liabilities with both expressed in nominal-value terms, than for persons whose contingent liabilities, future expenditures greater than incomes, are in real terms and who are offered no asset offering a dated certain real yield.

at an annual rate, and would therefore induce portfolio switching into that asset. So if investors should think that the price of some asset in the next period will fall, they will sell that asset now, thus lowering its price.[1] Furthermore, if they expect its price to change in any future short period, say to fall between $t + n$ and $t + n + 1$, and there is a futures market, operators could sell the asset forward at time $t + n$ and repurchase at time $t + n + 1$, thus hoping to enjoy a capital gain.[2]

If asset markets are to show stability they cannot be dominated by investors with extrapolative expectations, since equilibrium will only occur when there is a balance between the pessimists and the optimists. But is there any theoretical reason why any, or all, asset markets need be stable? Apart from the empirical observation that asset markets do generally achieve equilibrium, usually without very large price fluctuations, why should expectations not be generally extrapolative? One reason, which may be advanced, to expect stability, is that certain aspects of the future can be foreseen with reasonable assurance, and this limits the potential instability of the system.

Consider, for example, a situation in the market for fixed-interest debt in which everyone had a planning period of one day, whereas the shortest available security, say a Treasury bill, had a longer life to maturity, say twenty days. If extrapolative expectations dominate and there is an initial fall in price, the expected return over the one-day planning period will continuously induce further sales, but the expected return from such transactions will be subject to *uncertainty* whether prices tomorrow will fall or not. As prices fall, the *certain* yield on holding a Treasury bill for twenty days will rise continuously. Assuming risk aversion, the ever-increasing certain yield on Treasury bills must outweigh at some point the uncertain subjective prospect of further falls in price. Moreover, people will realise that other people will be tempted by the rising certain yield on short-dated securities. So the very uncertainty of price expectations implies that prices of short-dated assets must be given a fairly stable anchorage by their certain redemption yields. Furthermore, if prices of

---

[1] If, in addition to behaving rationally by selling when there is an expectation of a further fall in price and buying when prices are expected to rise, the market is also efficient in its use of information, then there should be no significant correlation between past and current price changes, i.e. in a regression of the form

$$Ep_{t+1} - p_t = b(p_{t-n} - p_{t-n-1})$$

b should be insignificantly different from zero. Otherwise the market should use the available information to buy (sell) the asset now, changing p_t, until $Ep_{t+1} - p_t = 0$. This does appear to be the case in some financial markets, e.g. the stock market; see the various contributions to the book on *The Random Character of Stock Market Prices*, rev. ed., ed. P. Cootner (M.I.T. Press, Cambridge, Mass., 1967). The position in the gilts market is less clear. T. Sargent, 'Rational Expectations and the Term Structure of Interest Rates,' *Journal of Money, Credit and Banking* (February 1972) concluded (p. 94) that, 'The predictions of the random-walk version of the model are fairly decisively rejected by the data.' Also some preliminary work in the Bank of England on daily changes in gilts prices suggests that these have shown over the observation periods studied significant first-order autocorrelation.

[2] Taken to an extreme this might appear to suggest that no asset market would be in full equilibrium unless prices are expected to remain unchanged on balance for ever thereafter, which simple observation will show to be untrue. Rather, the expectation of capital gain (loss) on any asset over any future period, after taking account of transactions and information costs and also of the expected flow of dividend and interest payments, must not be such as to lead operators to borrow (lend) money over the same time period in order to buy (sell) that asset. This qualified statement is, of course, much weaker, and only implies that in a rational market intelligent operators will not allow fairly sure opportunities for profit to slip away, not that markets expect the price of IBM shares, or consols, or the $ exchange rate to remain constant for ever. A helpful analysis of exactly what are (and what are not) the implications of the hypotheses that rational investors are operating in an efficient market is provided by Sargent, op. cit. section II, pp. 76–85.

short-dated assets are relatively stable for this reason now they can, presumably, be expected to be relatively stable in future. If then future expected short rates are viewed as likely to stay relatively stable, arbitrage should ensure that prices of longer-dated assets will also exhibit a measure of stability.

Thus the prospect of a fall in bond prices, particularly if the fall is at the short end of the market, leading to a limitless collapse of the market is, in my view, chimerical. Nevertheless, this claim that the market will not exhibit complete instability, whatever the process by which expectations are generated, still allows considerable room for large-scale price fluctuations under certain circumstances, especially when there is a sudden change in conditions which scares and unnerves the market.

It is, therefore, not entirely reassuring to the authorities to believe that there will be some finite reduction in price on fixed-interest debt which will increase the demand for debt, to the extent necessary to achieve some given change in the monetary base, if they do not know what that required price change might be. In circumstances which seem to require additional debt sales, say because policy calls for some reduction in the rate of monetary expansion, uncertainty about the appetite of the market for debt might suggest that the authorities would be well advised to make their main efforts at the shorter end of the market where price and demand are supported by the certain short-term yields to maturity.

In any case it is the *uncertainty* about the response of the public to changes in the authorities' operations, rather than the possible sharp effect upon bond prices (and interest rates), that is really most disturbing. Even if their attempts to make small additional purchases (sales) should result in very large falls (rises) in yields on bonds, the authorities would be happier in undertaking open-market operations[1] so long as they knew what the market response was likely to be. The question whether erratic variations in interest rates[2] are as damaging to the economy as erratic variations in monetary quantities is deferred until Chapter 12. It remains, however, the case that the greater the instability of interest rates, in response to open-market operations designed to control the growth of the money stock, the greater the trepidation of the authorities in using this technique for that purpose.

If the market's response to changing conditions were determinate, totally predictable, it would not matter how the authorities' market operations were institutionally organised, that is to say whether they operated primarily on quantities or on prices. Thus if the demand function for debt instrument i was of the form

$$D_i = f(P_{it}, P_{it-1}, \ldots, P_{it-n})$$

where this functional relationship was known, fixed and exact, it would make no difference whatsoever whether the authorities fixed a certain level of sales (S^*) and allowed the current price P_{it}^* to be determined on the market, or fixed the price level at time t at P_i^* and accommodated the demand for debt that would occur at that price by sales of S^* of debt. The result is identical.

On the other hand, when the response of the market to changed conditions is unpredictable, it will make a considerable difference whether the authorities' operations are

---

[1] If the objective of policy was to reduce the rate of monetary expansion (assuming a closed economy), an increase in bond rates might do so by pushing up advances rates, and thus lowering the demand for bank loans, or more directly by cutting back the demand for real assets, and thus incomes and the demand for money, rather than by inducing any initial switch from private-sector debt into public-sector bonds.

[2] It is sometimes argued that private speculators could, and would, take over the job of stabilising bond rates if the authorities should withdraw from this function. There is some slight truth in this, but on my reading the record of the private speculator as a 'stabilising influence' has not been impressive. See further comment on this issue in Chap. 15 in the context of freely-floating exchange rates.

couched in terms of offers to buy or sell certain quantities of assets at prices to be determined in the market, or in terms of offers to buy or sell assets at certain prices with quantities to be determined in the market. In the first case asset prices will take the brunt of unforeseen fluctuations in preference functions; in the second case asset quantities, stocks, will be subject to greater uncertainty. The question of how to decide whether one would prefer a bit more price instability and less quantity instability, or vice versa, is a subject discussed further in Chapter 12.

In practice, the debt operations of the authorities in most countries usually represent something of a compromise between those who argue the case for less rate instability and those who call for less quantity instability. A system in which the central government finances its deficit itself by tender sales of marketable debt at whatever price it can get, and the Central Bank then, independently, chooses what total of debt to buy on the market to achieve the preferred money/bond asset quantity mix (i.e. with a U.S.-type public-sector budget constraint), would seem to be in the best position to minimise quantity instability. In reality, the possibility of severe price instability forces an erosion of the Central Bank's putative independence from concern with the prices obtained on bond sales. Bond sales, in countries where the institutional arrangements are of this kind, for example in the United States and Canada, are not made in a simple take-it-or-leave-it fashion. Instead, the markets will usually be carefully prepared in advance for the quantitative offer. Tenders will be underwritten, prices discussed with key people in the market, repurchase clauses arranged, 'even-keeling' undertaken, etc. One should not disregard the circumscribed nature of the authorities' quantitative operations, constraints which have the effect of reducing price instability at the cost of some increase in quantity instability.

On the other hand, countries such as the United Kingdom, where operations are carried out by fixing prices at which the authorities will sell (buy) certain fixed-interest securities on the market, would seem to minimise price instability at the expense of greater quantity instability. But in practice concern with avoiding price instability is likely to be tempered by worries about quantity instability. So the authorities are likely to vary their quoted prices more rapidly in response to undesired quantity responses from the market, and even to limit their willingness necessarily to quote prices at which they would unconditionally buy in stock from the public.[1] So, by the end of the story, whatever the initial institutional arrangements for market operations may have appeared, they are likely to be run in such a way as to achieve the desired compromise (trade off) between rate and quantity instability, a compromise largely reflecting the received economic wisdom of the day and, therefore, likely to be held at much the same point in different countries irrespective of their initial institutional framework.

C. Competition with the Private Sector

One of the reasons why it is difficult to foretell the initial response of the private sector to open-market operations undertaken by the authorities is that it depends on the strength of competition for money from the rest of the economy. If there is a strong demand for bank loans from the private sector, when banks' cash reserves are squeezed by open-market

---

[1] When the monetary authorities in the United Kingdom shifted the emphasis of policy towards paying greater attention to controlling the rate of growth of the monetary aggregates, one of the concomitant steps was to reduce the extent of intervention in the gilts market, and no longer necessarily to provide outright support for that market. See the various articles on 'Competition and Credit Control,' in the *Bank of England Quarterly Bulletin*, vol. 11 (1971) which have been brought together into a special offprint under that title.

operations, the banks are not going tamely to cut back on potential good business. They will be under pressure to raise the rate which they charge on advances, to restore portfolio equilibrium as rates on alternative assets (e.g. bonds) rise, and they will, then, bid for the funds necessary to provide the cash reserves to support creditworthy borrowers at this new higher rate by raising the yields which they offer to depositors. The competition from the banks for funds will diminish the yield differential in favour of public-sector debt, and therefore force the government to push rates on public-sector debt higher yet in order to restrain monetary expansion.[1]

The authorities sometimes react to such prospects of competition for funds between public-sector and private-sector borrowers via the banks by directly controlling the banks' ability to compete, either by quantitative ceilings on their loans to the private sector, by ceilings on the rates they can offer to depositors, or by ceilings on rates they can charge borrowers.[2] In all these cases, however, the limitation on the ability of the banks to compete leaves untouched the basic cause of the upwards pressure on rates, which is the competition for funds by the *ultimate* borrowers in the private and public sectors. In so far as the banks cannot avoid the controls, and their efforts to do so will of themselves involve cost and frictions, the demand by ultimate borrowers will be diverted to other intermediaries and through other routes, e.g. inter-company borrowing, avoiding intermediation altogether. The imposition of direct controls on banks forces the private sector away from achieving its preferred configuration of holdings of private-sector assets and liabilities. This may allow a given volume of public-sector debt to be sold on slightly more favourable terms (i.e. lower yields), as well as keeping down bank interest rates. On the other hand, other interest rates, in markets to which the excess demand has been diverted, will be higher. In addition, the rationing of bank loans by forcing excluded borrowers to look elsewhere to unfamiliar and generally higher-cost lenders, raising information and transactions costs, will lead to some cut back in the demand for borrowed funds from private-sector borrowers.[3]

The extent to which direct controls on banks lead to a diversion, as compared with a net reduction, in ultimate borrowing is, however, not known. The authorities have little idea of the overall effect of their actions when they introduce credit rationing, and the selection of this or that figure for, say, the maximum level of interest rates or the maximum expansion in loans to the private sector is an arbitrary process involving little or no economic justification.

The maintenance of ceiling controls, particularly when these are set in terms of some quantitative limit to the total volume of loans, cumulatively distorts the allocation of funds. It also becomes that much harder to use the rate of growth of the affected aggregates as an indicator, or monitoring device, of economic developments, particularly on occasions when the controls are introduced or relaxed. For example, after decades during which rates payable on bank time deposits had been fixed by the London clearing bankers in relation to Bank Rate and years during which bank loans to the private sector had been restrained by quantitative ceilings, in the autumn of 1971 the banks became free, and encouraged, to compete for business. To what extent did this change in the system account for the much more rapid expansion of bank deposits, relative to the growth of incomes, in

---

[1] 'The most probable outcome, in fact, is a tendency to a competitive spiralling of Treasury bill and temporary money interest rates as the markets compete for an inadequate supply of funds,' p. 31 of A. B. Cramp's, 'The Control of Bank Deposits,' *Lloyds Bank Review*, no. 86 (October 1967) pp. 16–35. In view of the subsequent problems of the U.K. authorities in controlling the pace of monetary expansion after the removal of ceilings on bank advances in 1971, Cramp's analysis appears not only correct but almost prophetic.

[2] These latter restrictions induce banks to cut back on such loans as other rates rise, in order to maintain overall portfolio equilibrium.

[3] 'A diffused difficulty of borrowing,' to use the term coined by Harrod and adopted in the *Radcliffe Report, The Committee on the Working of the Monetary System: Report*, para. 460.

1972 and in 1973 than in former years? Even with hindsight it is difficult to answer that question, and it was not possible to make an accurate guess in forecasting.

The extent that banks and other intermediaries will push up rates in competition with the public sector for funds depends largely on the interest elasticity of the demand for loans in the private sector. If borrowers are prepared to pay a higher rate, it will be worthwhile for intermediaries to bid more aggressively for funds to meet their requirements. With the growth of advances in the United Kingdom hedged around by ceiling controls for several years, interspersed with easier periods when the authorities contented themselves with the lighter touch of 'moral suasion', the time path of advances has been so disturbed by these extraneous factors that an accurate estimation of the ordinary economic determinants of bank lending to the private sector in this country has been made extremely difficult. This makes it the harder for the authorities to reckon how far they might have to push up interest rates in order to bring about some given reduction in the demand by the private sector for borrowing. Various empirical estimates of the demand for bank advances have been made in the United Kingdom,[1] but the range of uncertainty remains extensive.

The situation may be further complicated by lags in the response of demand for bank loans to changes in the rates charged. Arranging the financing of a project, even a simple exercise such as consumer-borrowing for the purchase of a car, requires a certain amount of time. The money will usually not be drawn till the negotiations, plans, etc., are almost completed. By this time a project will have developed a momentum of its own, and last-minute cancellation will be a step unpopular to both sides. So a rise in advances rates is, perhaps, more likely to have an effect in causing withdrawals and reconsiderations of plans, the financial arrangements for which are at a somewhat earlier stage of negotiation.

If the demand for advances is a *lagged* function of the rates charged, and there is some empirical evidence that such lagged responses are usual in monetary affairs,[2] then it becomes much more difficult to adjust financial conditions smoothly from one equilibrium situation to another without setting up cyclical eddies and instabilities. Consider, for example, a situation in which the demand for advances only responds very slightly to changes in interest rates in period 1, and then reacts much more strongly in period 2. Then if the authorities want to cut back advances steadily, they have to raise rates very sharply in period 1 (weak effect), since advances are mostly a function of the unchanged interest rates in the previous period. Then advances will go down so much in period 2, as people react to the higher rates in period 1, that in order to maintain a steady decline in advances, the authorities may have to cut rates below the initial starting level in period 2. In period 3 rates will have to rise even more to counteract the low rates in period 2, etc., etc.

This kind of model can clearly be given a formal algebraic representation, in which it appears in a difference, or differential, equation format, whose stability (or instability) depends on the coefficients and structure of the system. The sort of model discussed above could be represented as a simplified, linearised two-equation model, as follows

$$L_t = a_1 r_{Lt} + a_2 r_{Lt-1} + , \ldots, a_i r_{Lt-i}$$

The demand for loans is a function of current and previous rates charged on loans.

$$r_{Lt} = b_0 + b_1 r_{bt}$$

The banks set the rate for loans in line with the current market rates on government debt.

---

[1] For example, by W. E. Norton, 'Debt Management and Monetary Policy in the United Kingdom,' *Economic Journal*, vol. 79, no. 315 (September 1969) pp. 486–90.

[2] See, for example, J. Pierce and T. Thomson, 'Some Issues in Controlling the Stock of Money,' from *Controlling Monetary Aggregates II: The Implementation*, proceedings of a Conference held in September 1972, sponsored by the Federal Reserve Bank of Boston (Federal Reserve Bank of Boston, 1973) pp. 115–32, especially pp. 128–31.

The signs of all the 'a' coefficients are presumably negative, while $b_1 > 0$, so that if the authorities raise market rates with a single jump to a new level, which is then held, advances will decline in all periods towards a new lower equilibrium level. However, the rate of decline in each period may be very variable, depending on the values of the 'a' coefficients. If the authorities should wish to bring about a steady rate of change in the level of advances, they might not find themselves able to do this, even assuming full information on the coefficients, without imparting some variation, even possibly instability, into the time path of the instrument, in this example market rates (r_b). For example, assume that the demand for advances takes the following linear forms:

(i) $L_t = 10,000 - 700r_{Lt} - 200r_{Lt-1} - 100r_{Lt-2}$

(ii) $L_t = 10,000 - 200r_{Lt} - 600r_{Lt-1} - 200r_{Lt-2}$

and that the rate on bank loans is set by the banks at a constant mark-up over bond rate, so that $r_L = b_0 + r_b$. Then a once-for-all change in r_b, say an increase of 1 per cent, would lead to a similar reduction, after three periods, in bank advances of 1000 in both cases. But if the authorities desired a steady decrease in advances of 100 per period, the requisite time paths of r_b in cases (i) and (ii) would be as shown in Table 8.1.

TABLE 8.1

Change in r_b	Period								
	1	2	3	4	5	6	7	8	9
Case (i)	+0·14	+0·10	+0·09	+0·10	+0·10	+0·10	+0·10	+0·10	+0·10
Case (ii)	+0·50	−1·0	+3·0	−7·5	+20·0	−52·0	+136	−356	+934

Given lagged responses, the pursuit of steady adjustment in some objective variable(s) may bring with it, then, a danger of inducing instrument instability.[1] There were some signs of a situation of this kind developing in the United States in 1971. After a period of low interest rates at the end of 1970 and the beginning of 1971, the money stock was seen to be growing somewhat too fast towards the end of the first quarter. Interest rates were pushed up, but this seemed at this time to be having little effect in restraining the growth of the money stock, so there were – as may be imagined – calls for more vigorous action. Interest rates rose quite sharply from April until mid-August, but the rate of growth of the money stock did not subside much before August, when the President's new economic programme, incorporating a wage and price freeze and the promise of an incomes policy, was introduced. Initially, of course, this fall in the rate of monetary expansion was welcomed for its own sake, and it allowed the authorities to put in hand the pleasant task of lowering interest rates. But thereafter, in the fourth quarter, the rate of growth of the money stock stayed persistently more sluggish than expected at the time, and this led, naturally enough, to pressures for more vigorous stimulatory financial operations to restore the desired rate of monetary growth. No doubt there were many other factors bearing on monetary developments during the year, e.g. the adoption by President Nixon of his New Economic Policy in August 1971, but one interpretation of these events is that the time pattern of monetary growth was significantly affected by lagged responses to previous developments.

---

[1] See, for example, R. Holbrook, 'Optimal Economic Policy and the Problem of Instrument Instability,' *The American Economic Review*, vol. 62, no. 1 (March 1972) pp. 57–65. This general problem, instrument instability, is discussed further in Chapter 12, Section A, on 'Objectives and Instruments.' A paper in this field, of particular relevance to the issue of controlling the money supply, by D. Hester and D. Britto on 'Stability and Control of the Money Supply,' was presented by Hester at a meeting of the Money Study Group at the London School of Economics in 1973.

Thus, in a report on 'Open Market Operations and the Monetary and Credit Aggregates – 1971,'[1] A. Holmes and P. Meek concluded (p. 94) that

> Recent experience suggests that M_1 responds only slowly to the changes in nonborrowed reserves and the Federal funds rate initiated by System open market operations. To be sure, the decline in the Federal funds rate from October 1970 to February 1971 was followed by a more rapid growth of M_1 beginning in February. And the rise in the Federal funds rate from March to August was followed by a retardation of M_1's growth in August. But the lag in the response of M_1 appears rather long, perhaps on the order of four to six months, although independent shifts in the public's demand schedule[2] for M_1 during the period may well have distorted M_1's actual response to System operations.

Clearly the existence of such a lag, which also appeared in the econometric model of the monetary system using monthly data which was estimated by economists at the Federal Reserve Board,[3] might generate cycles, possibly explosive cycles, in interest rates if the authorities should persist in the attempt to maintain a fixed rate of growth in the money stock, month by month, come what may.

The likelihood of inducing unstable conditions in financial markets by holding to a policy of maintaining a stable rate of growth of the money stock might be increased if market operators became able to anticipate how the authorities were likely to react in each situation. Holmes and Meek noted[4] that trading banks, and no doubt other dealers, turned in 1971 to a more aggressive portfolio strategy with a shorter horizon. Whenever dealers saw any weakening in the rate of growth of M_1 below the supposed target of the authorities they might seek to buy Treasury bills and other short-term fixed-interest debt in the expectation that the Federal Reserve would have to drive market rates down further in order to restore the rate of growth of the money stock. Thus the onset of sluggishness in M_1 would cause a general strengthening in the demand for market debt, in anticipation of the Fed's reaction, and vice versa, when the expansion of the money stock was seen as pushing the Fed into a more restrictive posture. This kind of response, which commentators[5] have seen to recur on occasions subsequently, could exaggerate yet further the resulting fluctuations in market rates and make it even more difficult to maintain a steady pace of monetary expansion.

Institutional arrangements may further exacerbate such problems. Banks tend to relate the rates which they charge individual borrowers, depending on their various categories, to some notional prime rate, or base rate. This rate is a highly visible administered one, and much public comment is evoked when it changes. This induces banks to delay altering such rates until financial conditions have clearly shifted significantly. So when the authorities act to undertake open-market sales and to raise interest rates, rates on bank loans will lag behind somewhat. The resulting continued, or even enhanced, demand for bank loans will place further pressure on bank reserves, so that banks will be forced to bid even higher for certificates of deposit (C.D.s) and large time deposits in order to attract funds.

---

[1] *Federal Reserve Bank of New York Monthly Review*, vol. 54, no. 4 (April 1972) pp. 79–94.

[2] M. Hamburger has, however, demonstrated that the demand for money function remained quite stable over this period, see 'The Demand for Money in 1971: Was There a Shift?', *Journal of Money, Credit and Banking*, vol. 5, no. 2 (May 1973) pp. 720–5.

[3] T. Thomson and J. Pierce, 'A Monthly Money Market Model,' Federal Reserve Board, mimeo.

[4] Op. cit. pp. 90–4.

[5] For example, A. Wojnilower, in his talk on 'A New Monetary Environment' to the New York State Bankers Association, 16 November 1973 (The First Boston Corporation, New York, 1973), in the section on 'The Consequences of a Money Supply Policy'; and G. Pepper, *Monetary Bulletin*, no. 17 (Greenwell, London, October 1973).

As a result C.D. rates will rise relative to base rates. Indeed, there were several occasions in the United Kingdom, in 1972 and 1973, when for several months at a time there was a small potential turn to be made by a customer whose credit standing enabled him to borrow at the finest, blue-chip rate in borrowing money from his own bank to reinvest with another, in C.D.s! In this case the initial effect on the monetary aggregates of a restrictive policy can actually be perverse.[1] The same kind of problem has occurred in other countries also. For example in Canada, after the Porter Report recommendations encouraging the banks to compete had been promulgated, the keenness of the banks to bid ever higher for funds in order to satisfy borrowers led Governor Rasminsky to ask them to observe more self-restraint.[2]

D. Complications and Conclusions

Interpretation and analysis of monetary developments is never easy but it is, at least, facilitated by the frequency and promptness with which monetary data are available in the United States.[3] In most European countries, including the United Kingdom, data are

---

[1] Difficulties of this sort with the working of the new organisational form of the banking system in the United Kingdom, which had been unveiled in 1971 with the publication of the consultative document on 'Competition and Credit Control,' *Bank of England Quarterly Bulletin*, vol. 11, no. 2 (June 1971) pp. 189–93, were largely responsible for the adoption of the supplementary technique, involving calls for non-interest-bearing deposits to be placed with the Bank of England in relation to the growth of interest-bearing deposits above some allowable rate of expansion, which was introduced in December 1973. The purpose of this innovation was to reinforce the authorities' ability to control the pace of monetary expansion without reverting to the previous quantitative ceiling controls, see *The Bank of England Quarterly Bulletin*, vol. 14, no. 1 (March 1974).

[2] Thus in the *Bank of Canada Annual Report for 1967* (Bank of Canada, 1968) Governor Rasminsky commented (p. 9) as follows:

'The central bank's problem in deciding how much monetary expansion to permit in order to restrain the rise in interest rates was complicated by the structural changes which were occurring in the banking system as a result of the Bank Act revision which went into effect in May 1967. The general effect of this revision was to make the financial system more competitive by softening or removing most of the special restrictions under which the banks had been working. The banks naturally took advantage of these changes to compete more aggressively for an enlarged share of the total financial business of the community. Indeed, for a period in the autumn their competition for large blocks of short-term corporate funds was so aggressive that it appeared to be uneconomic, and I felt that it threatened to introduce some instability and distortions into the financial system. I informed the banks of my views and was gratified that a more normal relationship of rates came about soon thereafter.'

The same sequence of events was repeated in 1972. 'In the spring the process of escalation of Canadian short-term interest rates began to feed on itself and to distort financing patterns. Short-term interest rates – including those offered on bank deposits – rose further, while the banks' prime lending rates remained unchanged at 6 per cent. Thus it became increasingly attractive for those with funds to invest to place them on short-term deposit with the banks, and correspondingly attractive for large borrowers to use bank credit rather than to issue short-term paper in the market. The increase in bank loans accelerated. . . . The banks' fixed-term deposits (and those measures of the "money supply" that include such deposits) also rose dramatically. . . .

'These distortions in financial markets were discussed . . . with representatives of the chartered banks . . . [leading] to an agreement that rates of interest offered on deposits of $100,000 or more for terms up to 364 days would be limited to a maximum of $5\frac{1}{2}$ per cent.' *Bank of Canada Annual Report for 1972* (Bank of Canada, 1973). This agreement is generally known as the Winnipeg agreement.

[3] 'The daily average money supply series published by the Board is a constructed series based on member bank deposit data, weekly condition reports of large commercial banks, Federal Reserve Bank balance sheets, . . . [etc.]. This series is published weekly with an eight-day lag; that is, the first estimate published for a statement week ending Wednesday comes out a week from the subsequent Thursday. These estimates are usually revised to a degree over the weeks immediately following publication, as new or revised figures dribble in,' from S. Axilrod and D. Beck, 'Role of Projections and Data Evaluation with Monetary Aggregates as Policy Targets,' from *Controlling Monetary Aggregates II: The Implementation*, p. 95.

only available once a month, reporting the position as at the close of business on a single day. The monetary position on any one day is subject to a whole range of random factors, strikes, proximity to a movable holiday, e.g. Easter, large new issues on the Stock Exchange, foreign-exchange crises, etc., whose effects can only be roughly estimated. In addition the data are not entirely accurate: for example, banks may not always be in a position to tell whether they are dealing with another bank as agent for another party or as a principal. Thus the total of reported interbank claims on other banks differs from the total of reported interbank liabilities to other banks. The attribution of 'float' between deposits and over-drafts, and between sectors, represents an informed guess rather than a known statistic. There are other examples of weak points in the data, and there always remains residual human error.

With observations occurring once a month the expected size of the random variation can often be quite large relative to the systematic component. Data from the United Kingdom are shown below[1] for the percentage monthly changes in the seasonally-adjusted series for the narrowly-defined money stock, notes and coin and current accounts held by U.K. private-sector residents (M_1), and for the broadly-defined money stock (M_3), encompassing notes and coin plus all bank deposits (with a maturity of less than two years)

1

		Percentage change in M_1 on previous month	Percentage change in M_3 on previous month
1971	June	—	—
	July	+0·5	+0·6
	August	+1·9	+1·1
	September	+1·2	+0·6
	October	+0·4	+1·6
	November	+1·6	+1·5
	December	+2·3	+1·4
1972	January	−0·9	+2·1
	February	+0·4	−0·3
	March	+2·8	+2·4
	April	+1·9	+2·6
	May	+1·4	+1·6
	June	+2·5	+3·9
	July	−0·6	+2·1
	August	+0·4	+0·7
	September	+0·6	+2·0
	October	+1·4	+1·2
	November	+0·4	+1·3
	December	+1·8	+2·8
1973	January	−0·7	+2·1
	February	+0·6	+3·0
	March	+0·8	+1·5
	April	+2·3	+1·2
	May	+0·3	+0·5
	June	+1·1	+2·5
	July	+2·3	+3·9
	August	−0·3	+2·5
	September	−2·1	+2·4
	October	+0·2	+1·5

held by U.K. residents,[1] from June 1971 till October 1973. Fitting an equation of the form

$$\frac{M_t - M_{t-1}}{M_{t-1}} = \alpha + u$$

i.e. assuming that the rate of growth each month would be constant, subject to a stochastic error term (u), gave these results

for M_1, $\alpha = 0.9\%$, $\bar{R}^2 = 0.35$, SE (the standard error) $= 1.2\%$ DW $= 1.93$

for M_3, $\alpha = 1.8\%$, $\bar{R}^2 = 0.77$, SE $= 1.98\%$, DW $= 1.69$

Thus in both cases the standard error of the monthly observations was larger in size than the actual systematic trend rate of growth.[2]

The random fluctuations in these occasional data make it the more difficult to observe what the trends in the system really are at any time. If action is taken early on the basis of one or two months' figures there will be a danger of taking an unnecessary step, while if action is delayed until the need for it can be more firmly established there will be an opposite danger of the system diverging even further from its desired path (the more so since there will have been an additional lapse of time in compiling the statistics, a period requiring several weeks in the United Kingdom).

The authorities are uncertain what is really happening; they are uncertain of the precise effects on the system of the steps they may take to adjust it; they are uncertain of the timing of these effects. In this world a generous modicum of instability is inevitable. As already noted in Section B, and discussed further in Chapter 12, there is some choice over the form in which one may prefer to suffer such instability. If the authorities try to maintain some given rate of change in each period in the quantities, the monetary aggregates, by open-market operations irrespective of market conditions or of lagged reactions, they may be able to do so only at the expense of considerable price instability in such markets. Equally, the more price stability is maintained, the more severe will be the quantity instability.

To recapitulate, it is neither very helpful nor very informative, at least from the stand-point of the responsible authorities, to be told that, given stable/predictable ratios for banks' cash reserves and the public's currency/deposit holdings, the total money stock will – indeed must – vary in line with the high-powered money base. What matters are the problems that the authorities face in trying to alter the monetary base and the money stock, and the effect that actions to this end may have on other variables, e.g. interest rates. In this chapter we have tried to outline some of the main critical factors which do determine whether the authorities would have a simple, or at the other end of the scale a virtually impossible, task in trying to control monetary expansion.

There would seem to be four such main factors, which are:

(i) the size of the public-sector deficit;
(ii) the elasticity of substitution between foreign and domestic assets in an open economy with fixed exchange rates;
(iii) market reactions to the authorities' open-market operations; and
(iv) the interest elasticity of the demand for advances.

---

[1] For full details of the definitions involved, and an account of what happened to the abandoned M_2 series, see the *Bank of England Quarterly Bulletin* articles on 'The Stock of Money,' vol. 10, no. 3 (September 1970) pp. 320–6 and 'Changes in Banking Statistics,' vol. 12, no. 1 (March 1972) pp. 76–9.

[2] The correlation coefficient between these two series over this period was only $+0.17$, not sufficiently high for the null hypothesis of no relationship to be rejected at the 5 per cent significance level! Since M_1 is part of M_3, this implies that current accounts and deposit accounts with banks were often varying inversely, as was in fact the case during a period when the banks were aggressively bidding for funds by pushing up time deposit and C.D. rates, and thereby inducing people to switch out of zero-yielding current accounts into interest-bearing deposits.

Consequently the most useful statistical approach to the presentation of monetary data, for purposes of interpretation and analysis, is that which highlights these critical factors. Accordingly official monetary statistics in the United Kingdom, in the *Bank of England Quarterly Bulletin* and the C.S.O.'s *Financial Statistics*, contain tables of that accounting identity in which changes in the money stock are expressed in terms of the following components: the public-sector deficit, sales of public-sector debt to the non-bank public, bank advances to the private sector and external financing of the public sector.[1]

An example is given in Table 8.2, taken from the *Bank of England Quarterly Bulletin*, vol. 13, no. 4 (December 1973) Table 12.3, p. 511:

It is, of course, the case that no accounting identity by itself provides any theoretical explanation of the process of the determination of the money stock. But a well-chosen identity should lead the user of the statistics to go further to enquire the reasons for the fluctuations in debt sales, in international capital flows, etc. One cannot display the complete working of the monetary system in a single table, but one can, at least, encourage users to ask the right kind of questions about the more important behavioural relationships by one's choice of accounting identities.

---

[1] You may note that changes in the banks' cash reserve base are not separately distinguished in this presentation. The elements that are included show the volume of additional bank lending, in aggregate, to the central government, but not how this is split up among cash reserves, special deposits, Treasury bills, bonds, etc. Does this latter not matter? The banks generally do have a good deal of freedom in deciding the form in which they prefer to take-up, or to sell, government debt, to finance the authorities' residual borrowing requirement (i.e. that total not financed by the non-bank public or from overseas). Nevertheless, the authorities can seek to induce the banks to hold their public-sector debt in one or other way by varying the rates offered, or can force the banks by direct control to hold more of some particular asset, e.g. by varying reserve requirements or calling for special deposits. As these measures force the banks to wish to readjust their portfolios, they will change the rates they offer on deposits and advances and this step will alter, for example, the non-bank public's take-up of government debt and the demand for advances. A call for special deposits by itself need have no effect whatsoever on the total money stock, if it simply leads to a rearrangement of the banks' holdings of public-sector debt with no subsequent effect on relative interest rates (or on the non-price conditions that banks, particularly when operating under external constraints, may vary in order to influence the total of advances). The extent of the effect will depend on the adjustments in relative yields that ensue throughout the system.

(Changes in period £ millions)	Public-sector borrowing requirement (surplus −)		Purchases (−) of public-sector debt by private sector (other than banks)		Bank lending to private sector[c]	External finance			Money stock (M3)[f]	Domestic credit expansion[g]
	Central government[a]	Other public sector	Other public-sector debt	Central-government debt[b]		Public sector (increase−)[d]	Banking sector (increase−)[e]	Banks' net non-deposit liabilities (increase−)[c]		
	1	2	3	4	5	6	7	8	9	10
Financial years										
1969/70	−1118	+580	−149	−639	+718	+1239	−162	−95	+374	−541
1970/71	+13	+835	+2	−574	+1267	+1190	−618	−84	+2031	+1393
1971/72	+515	+509	+15	−1718	+3142	+1878	−1091	−439	+2811	+2249
1972/73	+1824	+699	−340	−576	+6288	−1419	+7	−748	+5735	+7280
Quarters (unadjusted)										
1973 1st qtr[h]	−439	+133	−156	+32	+1646	+49	−179	−190	+896	+917
2nd qtr[h]	+808	+598	−322	−630	+1217	+305	−446	−2	+1528	+1701
3rd qtr[h]	+676	{ +704	}	−403	+1679	−135	−199	+23	+2345	+2759
Quarters (seasonally adjusted)										
1973 1st qtr[h]	+471	+47	−158	+88	+1509	+47	−204	−297	+1503	+1658
2nd qtr[h]	+702	+572	−315	−647	+996	+299	−420	+104	+1291	+1338
3rd qtr[h]	+423	{ +718	}	−439	+2173	−137	−160	−132	+2446	+2978

[a] For further details, see table 1, ibid.
[b] Includes, as an offset, purchases of commercial bills by the Bank of England, Issue Department; see additional notes, ibid.
[c] See table 11(4), ibid.
[d] Equals the central government's 'total external transactions' in table 1 together with any overseas borrowing by the rest of the public sector.
[e] Bank deposits from overseas residents less lending to overseas residents – see table 11(4), ibid.
[f] Equals the total of columns 1 to 8 – see also Table 12(2), ibid.
[g] Domestic credit expansion equals the sum of columns 1 to 5 plus bank lending in sterling to overseas residents less bank lending in foreign currencies to U.K. residents for investment overseas.
[h] For treatment of new contributors see additional notes, ibid.

9

The Transmission Mechanism of Monetary Policy

SUMMARY

Monetary policy affects expenditure decisions by causing changes in relative asset yields and in wealth, thereby influencing the amount of assets which people want to hold. Such effects on expenditure can notionally be divided into the effect on the savings decision of the personal sector and on the investment decision of the 'productive' sector. Reductions in interest rates have offsetting substitution and income effects for savers, but they should be effective in stimulating the demand for real assets by the productive sector.

In the attempt to highlight this transmission mechanism in a complex world, economists have constructed simplified models, aggregating over most sectors and most assets. The Keynesian system, as simplified by Hicks, includes two sectors (the public and private sectors – and the actions of the public sector are treated as exogenous) and three assets (money, bonds, real assets); the IS/LM model can then be derived from the demand functions for these assets with the aid of some further assumptions. This model has dominated the analytical preconceptions of most economists for decades and for this reason its weaknesses should be probed. First, the paths along which substitution between assets is allowed to occur are unduly limited, being restricted to a single route from money to bonds and from bonds to real assets. Second, wealth effects are ignored; yet the positions of the IS/LM curves depend on the level of wealth, and changes in the variables in the model will alter wealth. Finally, the extent of aggregation is excessive. This is recognised in part in the Keynesian models actually used for forecasting and policy purposes, in which the expenditure decisions of several sectors are studied separately. But the appropriate degree of disaggregation, and the appropriate budget constraints, have not equally been applied on the financial side, with the result that most Keynesian models have unsatisfactory financial sectors.

Within the framework of the IS/LM model, the potency of monetary policy depends on the relative magnitudes of the interest elasticity of demand for money as compared with the interest elasticity of demand for goods. Empirical studies of the demand for money and of expenditure functions usually show low elasticities in both cases, with generally lower values in the expenditure functions, especially in the United Kingdom where few forms of expenditure, other than private-sector housing, seem sensitive to monetary factors at all. Yet both *a priori* theoretical reasoning and a study of economic history make one reluctant to accept such statistical findings unhesitatingly. There are so many reasons why these results may be biased and misleading. For example, the relationship between expenditures and financial factors may be discontinuous, only having a significant impact when financial conditions pass some threshold. The expenditure function should incorporate the differential between the prospective own yield and the alternative yield(s) on financial asset(s), but it is not possible to observe own yields. Since such prospective own yields vary systematically over the cycle, their omission may cause serious bias. Finally, financial factors will affect demand, but the functions tested generally make output the dependent variable. If there are supply limitations (and there frequently are in the real world), this too will be an incorrect specification.

None the less, the general conclusion obtained from studies of expenditure functions in Keynesian models, that financial factors had relatively little effect in the short run, of up to two or three years, would not be so subject to doubt if it were not for a further, and very different, set of empirical results showing, at least for the United States, a close relationship between money incomes and current and prior movements in the money stock. It is difficult to explain this in terms of reverse causation, with the money stock responding to current and prior changes in money incomes, because of the timing relationship whereby changes in the money stock appear to precede changes in money incomes. A further question, however, arises of how far the observed correlations in such single-equation exercises reflect the use (or lack of use) made of such control instruments to offset disturbances occurring elsewhere in the system.

In any case there remains some inconsistency between the statistical results of examining the direct relationship between money incomes and the money stock which, using U.S. data, suggest a rather quick, powerful monetary effect, and from examining the expenditure functions, when the monetary effect seems often weak and slow-acting. One can present reasons for scepticism about either set of results, but for the moment the question of the real strength of monetary policy remains subject to considerable doubt and disagreement.

A. The Keynesian (*IS/LM*) Framework

The proportionate amount of any asset, which people will wish to hold in their portfolios, depends on their total wealth and the relative yields (including prospective capital gains/losses) which they perceive on all the various available assets. This applies to the whole range of assets, both tangible and financial. Monetary policy affects expenditure decisions by causing changes in these relative yields and also by causing variations in people's wealth through altering the market value of outstanding assets. Such effects on real expenditures can notionally be divided into two parts. First, there is the effect on the savings decision of the personal sector to refrain from current expenditures on goods and services, in order to add to holdings of (financial) assets. Second, there is the effect on the investment decision of the productive sector to expand their real assets, in order to increase the current-flow output of goods and services.[1]

Taking the investment decision first, a reduction in yields on financial securities, including money (where the yield may be largely in the form of providing services of convenience), will open a gap between the yields available to investors on purchases of real assets and the reduced yield on financial securities, and therefore make it profitable for the members of the productive sector to run down their own holdings of financial assets, or issue new financial liabilities upon themselves, in order to obtain funds to purchase additional real assets. A fall in yields available on financial assets, relative to those on tangible

---

[1] The clarity of this division depends in part on the distinction, outlined in Chap. 5, between the productive sector, which can be regarded, in principle, as holding all real assets to produce flows of goods and services, and the personal sector, which is the residual holder of claims on all net wealth in the private sector and adds to that wealth by saving. In practice, of course, this division is blurred. The personal sector purchases real assets, e.g. houses, consumer durables, in order to provide flows of goods and services. The business manager may affect total private-sector savings by his decision on the proportion of net profits to pay out in dividends (though see M. Feldstein, 'Tax Incentives, Corporate Saving and Capital Accumulation in the United States,' *Journal of Public Economics*, vol. 2, no. 2 (April 1973) pp. 159–71, for a discussion whether changes in the retention ratio actually do affect the total of private-sector savings).

assets, should therefore lead to an increased demand for real assets. Asset prices will be bid up. The increase in the price of real assets relative to their cost of construction will encourage an expanded output of new assets, increased production in the investment-goods industry. Some may then try to avoid the rising price of buying new assets by hiring the services of existing assets. So the rise in prices of new tangible assets will be tempered by the elasticity of supply of the industry producing that good and by the existence of a pool of unutilised, or underutilised, assets which can be drawn back into full operation.

Second, changes in financial conditions may cause revisions to plans for adding to existing asset holdings by saving out of current incomes. A fall in yields will lessen the volume of consumption goods in future periods which can be obtained by giving up a unit of present consumption. This substitution effect will deter those members of the personal sector who are intending to add to their (financial) assets by saving, but would encourage those who want to run down accumulated financial assets or to borrow, i.e. to dissave. On the other hand, the reduction in interest rates will lessen future incomes from current savings, and thus reduce the available options for consumption over time – the budget constraint – to a prospective saver. In order to maintain consumption levels in future periods in the face of lower expected incomes, people may feel impelled to save more as interest rates fall. For net savers, therefore, the substitution and income effects of a change in interest rates pull in different directions.

The position of a prospective saver, with incomes preceding consumption, can be depicted as in Fig. 9.1, with all income, Y, in period 1, requiring saving to consume in period 2. With a given income $Y = 0A$ in period 1, and interest rate r, this individual faces the budget constraint curve AB, where $0B = Y(1 + r)$. A fall in interest rates to r' will shift the budget constraint curve to AC, where $0C = Y(1 + r')$. The new equilibrium point, X', may either be to the left, less consumption in period 1, or to the right of the initial equilibrium point, X, depending on the shape of the individual's indifference curves, drawn here to show a situation in which consumption/saving in period 1 is unchanged by the fall in interest rates.

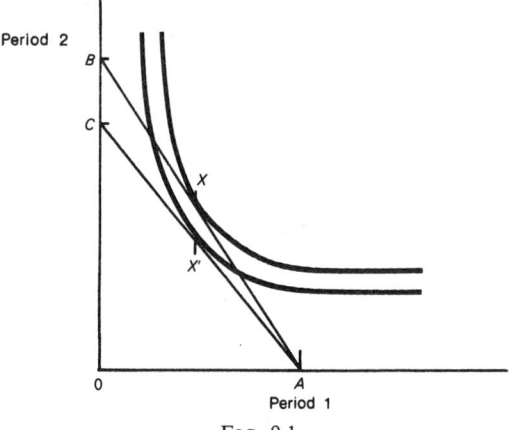

FIG. 9.1

A borrower, though, who wishes to consume initially in excess of his income and to pay off his debts subsequently, will find the income effect reinforcing the substitution effect, as interest rates vary. In practice, the standard life-cycle pattern of employment followed by retirement will lead those obtaining income from labour services to be, on balance, net savers. On the other hand, the productive investing sector is by nature a net borrower, since it has to issue financial liabilities (including equities) on itself to purchase the real assets which will subsequently provide the returns to meet the debt obligations. On these grounds one should expect the effect of reductions in interest rates to have a more expansive effect on the demand for real assets by the productive sector, including the demand for consumer durables and housing, than in stimulating a greater demand by persons for additional current consumption of goods and services. Indeed, even the sign of the response (more or less) of personal savings to changes in interest rates is uncertain.

Although a fall in interest rates raises the cost to a saver of obtaining a present command over a future stream of earnings, it equally raises the market value, wealth, of those assets already held. This increase in wealth, of existing asset holders, should also counter the depressing impact of the income effect – of lower interest rates – on the propensity to consume of the personal sector. Indeed, casual behavioural observation, for example that the prices of existing assets, such as houses, hardly ever enter into 'cost of living' indices[1], whereas people are extremely conscious of changes in the prices of assets which they already own, suggests that the 'wealth' effect may outweigh the 'income' effect for the personal sector. This asymmetry is plausible in a world of uncertainty and information costs. The assets currently held are there for sure; the prospect of buying other assets in the future is hypothetical and uncertain. When share prices rise, the share owner feels better off: the young person who will probably soon start to purchase shares is usually left completely unmoved. On such grounds there is further reason for expecting financial expansion to stimulate real expenditures.

The above analysis of the effects of monetary policy on expenditures rests on a number of implicit assumptions. Two of these, in particular, should be explicitly recognised. First, the analysis, confining itself to wealth and relative price effects, assumes perfect markets. If markets are imperfect, perhaps because of artificially-imposed constraints, the ability of investors to borrow will not just depend on posted rates of interest but also may be affected by a variety of non-price rationing devices. At the limit certain borrowers may be refused access altogether to credit channels. The apparent opportunities for borrowing, and somewhat less frequently for lending, at the stated interest rates may just not be available. Such availability effects, e.g. mortage rationing, bank-lending ceilings, etc., are emphasised by a number of economists as having in practice a stronger effect on expenditure plans than is imparted by the usual fairly mild variations in market interest rates.[2]

Second, the analysis has treated interest rates as externally determined parameters. This is valid in dealing with the response at the individual micro level. Once again, however, when one has aggregated to the macro level, the level of interest rates becomes itself affected by the myriad individual decisions. The previous analysis can, however, be justified on the grounds that we are here concerned with the effects brought about in the economy by an autonomous act of monetary policy undertaken by the authorities which is exogenous to the private sector. Nevertheless, over the longer run when the thrift of the personal sector and the productive opportunities in the business sector play a more dominating role in determining the (real, i.e. after adjusting for inflation) rate of interest, it must be treated as a jointly-determined, endogenous variable.[3]

---

[1] See on this subject A. A. Alchian and B. Klein, 'On a Correct Measure of Inflation,' *Journal of Money, Credit and Banking*, vol. 5, no. 1, pt 1 (February 1973) pp. 173–91.

[2] See, for example, D. K. Sheppard, *The Growth and Role of U.K. Financial Institutions 1880–1962* (Methuen, London, 1971) especially chap. 5 on 'Money, Encashable Assets, Private Institutional Credits and Private Expenditure in the U.K., 1880–1962,' pp. 68–101; also see the Radcliffe Report, *The Committee on the Working of the Monetary System Report*, Cmnd. 827 (H.M.S.O., London, 1959) especially paras 385–97.

[3] On this subject, see M. J. Bailey, *National Income and the Price Level* (McGraw-Hill, New York, 1962) especially chap. VII on 'The Effects of the Rate of Interest and Real Cash Balances on Consumption.'

The general forms of portfolio adjustment in response to changes in financial conditions are conceptually relatively simple. The difficulty has been rather to identify and to estimate the workings of these effects empirically, through observation of the real world. This task is made harder because the complete structure of the economic system, in which these transmission mechanisms are deemed to work, is extremely complex. As already noted, this leads analysts to try to reduce the scale of the problem by aggregating, both over different kinds of assets (Chapter 4) and over different members of the economic community (Chapter 5). Such aggregation both simplifies the exercise and focuses attention upon a chosen few critical relationships between the selected aggregates, but it does obscure differences in form and behaviour among the elements within each combined set, a drawback which will be serious if disparate elements are aggregated together. The initial selection of aggregates in any study can, indeed, exert a pervasive, and often unrealised, influence upon the way in which the analysis develops.[1]

Within the basic Keynesian model, as simplified by Hicks, the economy is aggregated into two groups, the private sector and the public sector (or government), with three forms of asset, real assets, public sector bonds and money, also a liability of the public sector. Attention is concentrated upon the adjustment process of the private sector. The government is generally assumed to hold no private-sector debt, so all private-sector debt is eliminated from consideration by the process of consolidation. Firms, financial intermediaries and persons are not separately distinguished.

The portfolio-adjustment matrix is therefore collapsed into a smaller size, as shown below:

	r_K	r_B	r_M	X	W_{t-1}	S
K	a_1	a_2	a_3	a_4	a_5	a_6
B	b_1	b_2	b_3	b_4	b_5	b_6
M	c_1	c_2	c_3	c_4	c_5	c_6

where K represents real assets, B government bonds, M government monetary liabilities, r_K, r_B, r_M the yields on each asset, X a vector of other variables, such as incomes, the expected rate of change of prices, etc., W_{t-1} the value of wealth at the start of the period, and S represents additions to wealth during the period. Moreover, the implicit assumption is usually made that $r_M = 0$ at all times (and/or that $a_3 = 0$) and that $c_1 = 0$. Thus, with X initially given, an increase in the monetary liabilities of the government (M) will have two effects on the demand for real assets by the private sector, a wealth effect and a substitution effect.[2] The substitution effect will then, by assumption, work entirely via the rate of interest on government bonds. If the impact of the wealth effect on the demand for real assets and on the propensity to save is thought to be relatively small, the effect of monetary changes upon the economy then depends only on the relative sizes of the elasticity of demand for money in response to changes in bond rates (c_2) in comparison with the elasticity of demand for

---

[1] Consult A. Leijonhufvud, *On Keynesian Economics and the Economics of Keynes*, sect. III, 'The Aggregative Structure of Alternative Models.'

[2] This example of an increase in governmental monetary liabilities, with other things being equal is, however, extremely artificial. Normally a change in the public sector's monetary liabilities will be the counterpart of a change in government expenditures, or taxes, which will change private-sector incomes, etc. (i.e. X not constant), or the counterpart of an open-market operation, which will change B and r_B. It is possible to imagine a government distributing additional money as a gift out of the blue to its citizens; indeed this has even formed part of the programme of a political party – the Social Credit party in Canada. Even so, it is probably best to regard such an example as an attempt to isolate the purely monetary effects of some transaction, in which the counterpart may also have some conceptually separable impacts upon economic activity.

goods in response to changes in the bond rate (a combination of (a_2) together with the elasticity of response, if any, of the propensity to consume to interest-rate changes).

On the assumption that r_K, r_M and B, the value of outstanding bonds, are given it is then possible to describe this system in a further reduced set of equations as follows:

$$I = f(Y, r_B)$$
$$S = f(Y, r_B)$$
$$I = S$$
$$M_d = f(Y, r_B)$$
$$M_d = M_s$$

where M_d is the demand and M_s the exogenously-determined supply of government monetary liabilities, and Y the level of money incomes. From this set of equations the standard diagram (Fig. 9.2) directly follows, where the IS curve traces out those combinations of r_B and Y which satisfy $I = S$, and the LM curve shows those combinations allowing $M_d = M_s$.

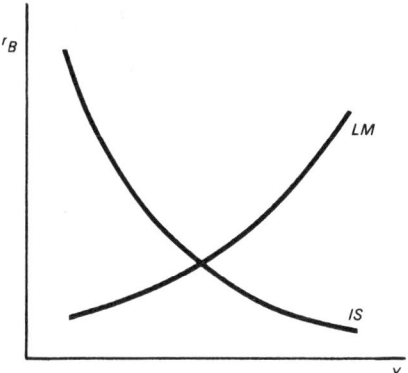

FIG. 9.2

The yield on (public-sector) bonds, r_B, thus enters as an argument into the IS/LM model, but the process of achieving equilibrium in the market for bonds does not overtly appear. This often confuses people. However, from the analysis in Chapter 3, Appendix A, we know that the coefficients in the portfolio-adjustment matrix have to satisfy certain constraints in order to maintain balance-sheet identities, etc. Because of these constraints, knowledge of the values of the coefficients in all the rows (individual asset-demand equations) except for one row allows one to deduce the coefficients in this omitted row. The equilibrium conditions for any one market, from a set of markets, can be derived from the equilibrium conditions in all other markets plus the various balance-sheet constraints. If these constraints are satisfied and all the markets, less one, are in equilibrium, then the final one must also be so. In this sense Walras's law allows one to eliminate one of the markets, here bonds, from specific attention in the model. As will be seen, however, this does *not* imply that the value of bond holdings should be treated as irrelevant to the determination of incomes or of interest rates.

The simplified IS/LM model of Keynesian analysis has achieved an unrivalled command over the analytical preconceptions of most Western economists; even Milton

Friedman now seems prepared to set his analysis within this framework.[1] For this very reason it is especially important to probe the weaknesses of this paradigm, which has formed the basis for much of the applied macro-economic work undertaken in recent decades. There are, perhaps, three main criticisms of this paradigm. These are,

(i) that the paths along which substitution is allowed to occur seem unduly restricted,
(ii) that wealth effects are ignored, and
(iii) that the aggregation of sectors and assets is taken to such extreme lengths (two sectors, only one of which is studied; three assets) that many vital features of the working of the real world are disregarded.

Indeed, in this model substitution occurs along only one single path from money to bonds and from bonds to real assets. There is apparently no substitution between money and real assets directly. The refusal of Keynesians to contemplate the possibility of other more direct channels of substitution has formed one of the main targets for 'monetarist' criticism. While the claim that there is no substitutability at all between real assets and money would be hardly defensible, there is nevertheless a real issue whether bonds are a relatively *much* closer substitute for money than real assets. Monetary assets are financial assets standing at one end of a continuous spectrum of such assets, at all points along which a relatively high degree of substitution can be expected. So, it may be argued, the degree of substitution between money (or liquid) financial assets and bonds (or longer-dated) (less-liquid) financial assets should be considerably greater than between money and tangible, real assets. Even if it is, perhaps, something of an exaggeration to assume, in the adjustment matrix, that $c_1 = 0$, at least $c_2 \gg c_1$.

There is another way of constructing the basic Keynesian system which provides, perhaps, more justification for concentrating on substitution via changes in r_B. In this version of the model the structure of aggregation is revised, and the scale of the model reduced still further. Long bonds are now aggregated with real assets (assumed to have relatively long lives), and all short financial assets aggregated with money. This leaves a two-asset model. The portfolio distribution between long and short assets, between risky assets and liquidity, then depends on the relative rates on the two blocs of assets, $r_B = r_K$ on the one hand, and r_M, which may be taken as fixed at zero in nominal terms on the other.

This is the approach adopted by Leijonhufvud[2] who claims, moreover, that this representation is closer to the real intentions of Keynes than so-called Keynesian models structured along different lines. Be that as it may as an exegetical issue, the practical question is what is the appropriate structure of aggregation for models of the economic system – a question that should obtain much more prominence in macro-economic theory than it is commonly allotted. In my opinion, Leijonhufvud's suggested two-asset (long, short) model is not acceptable. The empirical studies on the term structure of interest rates (Chapter 4), for example, reveal a greater degree of substitutability between long and short bonds

---

[1] See his articles, 'A Theoretical Framework for Monetary Analysis,' *Journal of Political Economy*, vol. 78, no. 2 (March/April 1970) pp. 193–238, and 'A Monetary Theory of Nominal Income,' *J.P.E.*, vol. 79, no. 2 (March/April 1971) pp. 232–7. Also note the resulting symposium commenting on Friedman's position, *J.P.E.*, vol. 80, no. 5 (September–October 1972) in the special issue on Monetary Theory, with contributions by Brunner and Meltzer, Tobin, Davidson, and Patinkin with a response by Friedman, pp. 837–950.

Indeed, in view of the potential weaknesses and flaws in the basic IS/LM paradigm there are surprisingly few economists engaged in fundamental criticism of it and reconstruction of alternative structural models. K. Brunner and A. Meltzer are among the few exceptions; see, for example, their paper on 'Money, Debt, and Economic Activity,' *J.P.E.*, vol. 80, no. 5 (September/October 1972) pp. 951–77.

[2] In his great book, *On Keynesian Economics and the Economics of Keynes*.

with less segmentation than I would have expected. A real asset has an uncertain running yield, and its future capital value is entirely conjectural, whereas a bond has a known nominal running yield and a fixed maturity value. In my view the analysis of the determination of investment expenditures (Chapter 5) requires explicit recognition of the significant distinctions between real assets and bonds.

Second, the IS/LM model is usually presented in such a way that wealth effects are omitted entirely, or are treated as of secondary importance. Yet the individual asset-demand functions, which are among the basic building blocks from which the IS/LM model should be constructed, must include the total of wealth as an argument. And the propensity to consume should also be a function of the level of wealth.[1] So the position of the curves in the IS/LM relationship at any point of time must depend on the level of wealth.

The omission of wealth effects causes certain problems in using the model. Variations in variables within the system, e.g. $\bar{M}_s$, r_B, cause changes in wealth, which should then result in shifts in the position of the IS and LM curves. A common example is the analysis of the effect of an increase in the money supply, with no counterpart in debt retirement or government expenditures.[2] This raises wealth, as well as changing relative prices, and the change in wealth should of itself lead to changes in desired asset holdings and desired consumption.

If there can be a distribution of money with no counterpart elsewhere in the system, equally there could be a free distribution of bonds. What would happen if a government, grateful for some act of its citizenry, should distribute additional bonds all around as largesse? This is, certainly, an unlikely act, but no more than a general distribution of money, which has entered surprisingly often into economic analysis. Now it may, or may not be, that this increase in the current value of their marketable financial assets will have a different effect on expenditure plans than, say, an increase in monetary liabilities, because people may fear future increases in taxes to pay for the interest and redemption of the bonds; this is discussed further in Chapter 10. Nevertheless, the current market value of the portfolio will have risen, and the ratio of bonds to money and of bonds to real goods will have altered, so that relative prices must surely adjust to allow portfolio equilibrium to be restored. Yet there is no room for such adjustments to take place within the IS/LM framework, since wealth (of which the value of bonds is one component) does not enter as an argument in any of the functions.

One line of reply to this criticism, for overlooking wealth effects, is to assert that this can be justified on 'de minimis' grounds, that such effects are in practice too small to worry about. The ratio of governmental monetary liabilities (currency and private-sector deposits with the Central Bank) to total private-sector wealth, net or gross, is so small that a large change in the value of such holdings will have a relatively small proportionate effect on total wealth. Holdings of other forms of public-sector financial debt, bonds etc., are considerably larger, especially in the United Kingdom where the national debt is comparatively much larger than in most other developed countries. There is, however, as already noted – and to be discussed further in Chapter 10 – a dispute about the true effect on wealth, and thus on expenditure decisions, of variations in the market value of such debt.

Finally, there is the question whether the IS/LM model, being so extremely aggregated, can be simply extended in its basic format to the more disaggregated multi-sectoral models which are actually used for forecasting and as a guide for policy. For when it comes to actual

---

[1] A survey of studies on this subject has recently been compiled by R. Ferber, 'Consumer Economics, A Survey,' *The Journal of Economic Literature*, vol. 11, no. 4 (December 1973) pp. 1303–42, especially pp. 1306–14.

[2] 'The analysis of the previous section applies to an economy in which there is no government debt, and money has to be created by some artificial construct such as throwing it out of airplanes. This is frequently the convention with textbook models,' R. Rasche, 'A Comparative Static Analysis of Some Monetarist Propositions,' *Federal Reserve Bank of St. Louis Review*, vol. 55, no. 12 (December 1973) p. 20. So much the worse for textbook models!

empirical estimation and forecasting, most economists believe it necessary to distinguish between various groups within the private sector, particularly between those groups which can be assigned to the 'productive' sector, i.e. companies, and those which form the 'personal' sector. In particular, the disaggregation of the system into several sectors should bring all the various private-sector financial assets/liabilities, previously eliminated by intra-sectoral consolidation, back into the model. The demand for money, and for goods, should then depend on the yields of a range of financial assets. Instead the tendency has been, as exemplified in the Federal Reserve Board model,[1] to develop models in which the demand and supply of money are equated by variations in one key short-term rate, e.g. the Treasury bill rate, and then other rates are determined recursively in response to movements in this short rate, and in other variables. This is not a satisfactory representation of a portfolio-adjustment process.[2]

In a more disaggregated model the inter-relationships between the yields on these financial assets and the balance-sheet (sources and uses of funds) constraints of each sector then become considerably more complex. In fact these constraints, even the government's Budget financing constraints, are rarely applied in empirical models. The implicit, or explicit, assumption appears to be that overall monetary conditions, essentially variations in the ratio of the money stock to money incomes, will determine *general* levels of interest rates in the economy and that relatively small differentials around this general level will cause sufficient flows of funds to allow the balance-sheet (sources and uses of funds) constraints for each sector, and the market constraints that purchases must exactly equal sales for each asset, to be satisfied.

From this it would follow that, given the forecast level of money incomes and a target level of the money stock, the expected interest rates on government bonds would be invariant to the size of the public-sector deficit. Whether a deficit occurs in the public sector, or in the company sector, whether the deficit needs to be large or small to achieve some forecast level of money incomes, it appears to make no difference (in the extended *IS/LM* model that is commonly used as a basis for econometric work) to the level of interest rates on government bonds. It may be so: if public-sector and private-sector debt are regarded as homogeneous, very close substitutes, then a large shift in relative outstanding quantities will only require a very small adjustment in relative prices to achieve equilibrium: so interest rates on bonds of a particular kind may, perhaps, prove to be unresponsive to a shift in the ratio of such bonds to other assets, given the existing ratio of money to incomes. Nevertheless, there must surely be doubts whether all assets are quite such close substitutes and whether shifts in relative quantities are so unimportant. The simple *IS/LM* model has taken economists a long way forward, but it may be time now to move on to more complete portfolio-adjustment models.

To investigate a large simultaneous system of considerable complexity the economist, and econometrician, need to be helped by theory and financial accounting to impose constraints on the system. Thus Frisch remarked that, 'If we are not to get lost in the overwhelming, bewildering mass of statistical data ..., we need the guidance and help of a powerful theoretical framework.' Yet when most model builders come to construct the financial part of their models, they throw away available constraints with insouciance, imposing instead certain arbitrary constraints on the demand for money function and some largely *ad hoc* statistical relationships between movements of prices (interest rates) among various kinds of financial asset.

---

[1] See, for example, R. H. Rasche and H. T. Shapiro, 'The F.R.B.–M.I.T. Econometric Model: Its Special Features,' *The American Economic Review*, vol. 58, no. 2 (May 1968) pp. 123–49, especially pt VII on the 'Financial Sector,' pp. 135–42.

[2] For a trenchant criticism of this approach, see G. Pierson, 'A Framework for Analysis of the Financial Sector,' *Harvard Institute of Economic Research, Discussion Paper, No. 124* (Harvard University, 1971).

There is a proper accounting framework available, the financial accounts, which require that all sectoral deficits/surpluses are financed and all financial markets balanced,[1] and a theoretical basis for analysis to hand in the theory of portfolio adjustment. The use of these tools should provide sufficient additional constraints upon the system to allow a better chance of observing the role of financial variables within the economic system. There has been a growing appreciation of the importance of imposing the appropriate financial constraints; not only have Tobin and the Yale school been expounding this general view, but also Brunner and Meltzer in their latest extension of monetarist theory[2] have inveighed against the weakness in this respect of the *IS/LM* model and have been careful to satisfy the government financing constraint and financial market equilibrium conditions in their analytical model. Indeed, a criticism of their work would be that they have not gone far enough along this road. Thus they disaggregate within the private sector between the banks and the rest, and they also see a distinction between producers' and purchasers' behavioural responses. This suggests a possible advantage from further disaggregation (including the appropriate disaggregation of the financial structure) of the private sector, possibly into companies and households. The expanded *IS/LM* model, as used in many Keynesian-type macro models, distinguishes sectoral behaviour in the income/expenditure accounts, but this is not then carried through to the financial accounts; even Brunner and Meltzer do not seem to have entirely purged themselves of this failing.

Monetary theorists ought now to be paying more attention to the desirability of applying the appropriate structure within the financial sector of economic models. That there is room for this can be gathered from the common statement that the Keynes of the Flow of Funds accounts has not yet appeared. No one can be sure that the resulting alterations to the models would in practice lead either to superior forecasting ability or to the capacity to give a more satisfactory explanation of the role of financial variables in the economy. Nevertheless, it would be nice to see economists having a go at it.

B. An Appeal to the Facts?

As already noted, within the *IS/LM* model the impact of monetary and financial developments upon expenditure decisions in the economy depends on the *relative* sizes of the interest elasticity of demand for money (c_2 in the matrix) and of demand for goods (a_2 in the matrix plus any effect of changes in bond rates on the propensity to save). Consider, for example, the effect of an open-market operation undertaken by the authorities in the bond market. The impact on the real economy will depend not so much on the *absolute* values of either the interest elasticity of the demand for money, reflecting the extent of substitution between money and bonds, or of the interest elasticity of the demand for goods, but on the *relative* values of these two elasticities. The higher the interest elasticity of demand for money *relative* to the interest elasticity of demand for goods, the less the impact of open-market operations on the demand for goods. It is the relativity between the two elasticities that determines the response, not the absolute level of either elasticity.

Although the *relative* values of these interest elasticities (reflecting the relative degree of substitution between these assets) would appear to be the main factor in determining the extent of monetary influence,[3] nevertheless a world in which there was in all cases a

---

[1] See A. D. Bain, 'Flow of Funds Analysis: A Survey,' *The Economic Journal*, vol. 83, no. 332 (December 1973) pp. 1055–93.

[2] 'Money, Debt, and Economic Activity,' *Journal of Political Economy* (September/October 1972) pp. 951–77.

[3] Another factor which is sometimes given prominence is 'credit availability.' Such 'credit availability' considerations can become of importance in conditions of imperfect markets, e.g. in the form of mortgage rationing. Although such imperfections may often exist, they may be regarded as pathological.

lesser *absolute* degree of substitution would be different in certain important respects from a world characterised by generally high elasticities. Changes in the quantities of assets would be accompanied by much larger changes in asset prices. Under such conditions wealth effects, such as they may be, would become rather more important in comparison with substitution effects.

If the question of the relative values of these two interest elasticities, of the demand for money and the demand for goods – or, if you prefer, of the relative slopes of the *IS/LM* curves – lies at the centre of dissension about the potency of monetary policy, then it would seem that the easiest way of resolving the issue would be to survey the empirical evidence obtained in reported research studies on the estimated values of these elasticities: then one might weigh up the evidence and announce a result, hedged about with a thicket of qualifications. Surveys of the empirical evidence have been made: Fisher and Sheppard have brought together a most useful collection of empirical studies on the effects of financial factors on expenditure in the United States;[1] Laidler and Goodhart and Crockett have reviewed the results of investigations of the factors affecting the demand for money. Even so, any assessment of the weight of the statistical findings remains subjective.

Nevertheless, some general assertions about the nature of the statistical findings in this field may be hazarded. First, almost all the evidence indicates that the interest elasticities of demand, for money and for goods, are quite low, well below unity for example, implying that the extent of substitution within the system, between money and bonds and between financial assets and goods, is rather limited. Such findings are difficult to reconcile with the *a priori* expectations of many, probably most, economists. Some would expect high elasticities in both cases; some would predicate a high degree of substitution between money and other financial assets (*vide* the Radcliffe Report – an extreme example); others, for example Leijonhufvud and the monetarists, would have expected a fairly high degree of substitution between bonds and real assets; few would have expected changes in relative prices to cause, apparently, little portfolio readjustment. To find very little response to relative price changes runs counter to the grain of economic analysis.

Much of the econometric evidence suggests that, while the interest elasticity of demand for money is quite low, the interest elasticity of the demand for goods is yet lower. The weight of the evidence from empirical estimation of the individual structural equations (i.e. the equations setting out the determinants of demand for the goods and assets which comprise the basic structure of the model), certainly among those presently estimated in the United Kingdom, would seem to imply that monetary policy was not of primary importance for the determination of money incomes, at least within a medium-term horizon of two or three years, even after making allowance for subsequent accelerator and multiplier effects. Probably the most careful effort to uncover, wherever possible, the effect of financial factors on expenditure along this 'Keynesian' route was undertaken by those involved in the construction of the F.R.B.–M.I.T. model for the United States. Their conclusions[2] were that monetary policy in that country was a powerful instrument of macro-economic policy, especially in the longer run, but they could not attribute to monetary policy the overriding influence on the determination of money incomes, especially in the short run, which certain adherents of monetarism have seemed to claim.

Certain features of their results are worth noting. A large proportion of the total effect, particularly in the short run, of monetary forces comes about through wealth effects upon personal consumption, mainly a result of monetary changes causing fluctuations in

---

[1] G. Fisher and D. Sheppard, *Effects of Monetary Policy on the United States Economy*, Organisation for Economic Co-operation and Development, Occasional Studies (O.E.C.D., Paris, December 1972).

[2] As reported by F. de Leeuw and E. Gramlich, 'The Channels of Monetary Policy,' a Staff Economic Study, *Federal Reserve Bulletin*, vol. 55, no. 6 (June 1969) pp. 472–91.

stock-market prices. The link between changes in monetary conditions and stock-market prices, while apparently significant in the United States at least, is not the most reliable of economic relationships for the policy-maker to depend upon.[1] Apart from this, the effect on company fixed-investment expenditure involves very long lags, while no discernible effect upon inventories was found. Moreover, it was one of the objectives of the exercise to identify, wherever possible, the effects of financial factors upon expenditure, and experience in applied economics suggests that research workers do tend to find what they set out to seek. Earlier multi-sectoral Keynesian models of the U.S. economy tended to find less evidence of financial factors influencing expenditure decisions.

In the United Kingdom the effect on the goods market of changes in financial factors has been even harder to discern. There is less firm evidence of changes in the propensity to consume resulting from variations in stock-market conditions,[2] as would seem to occur in the United States. The organisation in the United Kingdom of the nationalised industries and the local authorities, which are responsible for undertaking a considerable proportion of residential building, would also induce a lesser sensitivity to interest-rate variations than in the United States.[3] In some macro-economic models of the United Kingdom, for example that of the National Institute, monetary variables do not enter formally into the equations at all, though they may influence judgemental manipulations. In other macro-economic, income-expenditure models monetary variables enter, but only in a peripheral manner without strong effect. The limited weight placed on monetary variables in U.K. macro-economic models is not the result of a prejudiced obscurantism; it results from the fact that the addition of monetary variables to the structural equations determining expenditure functions in these models has not in general proved able to improve their explanatory power.

In economics, appeals to the facts, to the existence or absence of significant statistical relationships, can provide strong arguments for, or against, certain hypotheses, but given the impossibility of undertaking controlled experiments statistical inferences are rarely accepted by everyone as conclusive. There are so many reasons why it can be claimed that an unpalatable statistical result may be misleading. Under these circumstances some economists are prepared to give more weight to their *a priori* theoretical cogitations and less to statistical evidence. For example, Leijonhufvud has made out a powerful case for the existence of a high degree of substitutability between streams of returns of similar durations from bonds and from capital,[4] though see p. 177 earlier for a criticism of this case. This would imply that the interest elasticity of demand for long-lived goods, so long as the interest rate on long-lived bonds is used as the argument, should be high. Given a sufficiently strong *a priori* theoretical case it would be proper, Leijonhufvud appears to argue, to place less weight on apparently contradictory empirical findings (*vide* the passage on '*A priori* reasoning and time series evidence,' pp. 178–83).

Though not, perhaps, methodologically acceptable to all, this argument cannot be dismissed out of hand. However, it can equally well be applied by those who believe that

---

[1] A study by D. Gowland of the relationship between movements in the money stock and in stock-exchange prices in the United Kingdom, 'The Money Supply and Stock Market Prices,' given at the Conference of the Association of University Teachers of Economics (A.U.T.E.) at Manchester in April 1974, finds that no statistically significant relationship has been apparent in the United Kingdom in recent years.

[2] See, however, A. S. Deaton, 'Wealth Effects on Consumption in a Modified Life-Cycle Model,' *The Review of Economic Studies*, vol. 32, no. 120 (October 1972) pp. 443–53. In this paper Deaton reports finding a small, but long-lasting, effect of changes in stock-market values on consumption, p. 451 especially.

[3] Public-sector capital spending in the United Kingdom is largely unaffected by short-term changes in interest rates. Such investment is mostly centrally controlled and determined by other criteria.

[4] *On Keynesian Economics and the Economics of Keynes*, pp. 168–72 especially.

money and other financial assets are close substitutes. Thus the Radcliffe Report was, in effect, a detailed and brilliant exposition of the institutional basis for believing money, however defined, and other liquid financial assets to be close substitutes, culminating in that well-known sentence, 'There are many highly liquid assets which are close substitutes for money, as good to hold and only inferior when the actual moment for a payment arrives' (para. 392).[1] Instead the criticism, indeed virtual dismissal, of Radcliffe has been based on the grounds that the authors of the Report failed to take into account the econometric results, from the demand for money equations essentially, which showed evidence of a low and stable interest elasticity (though most of these econometric studies were not available until after the Report had been completed).

But what is sauce for the goose must be sauce for the gander. The authors of the Radcliffe Report may have utilised a priori reasoning, based on experience and institutional knowledge, to assert the high-interest elasticity of the demand for money, but empirical evidence, of a fashion, to support their view of a low interest elasticity of demand for goods. Monetarists, however, often appear to do exactly the reverse, basing their claims on a priori theoretical arguments to assert a high interest elasticity of demand for goods and on the econometric results to demonstrate a low elasticity of demand for money.[2] Theoretical reasoning may be used to cast doubt on the general empirical findings of rather low absolute elasticities, but it is less clear whether it can provide any guidance to suggest that the relativities between the interest elasticities, as calculated in the macro models, should be expected to shift in one direction rather than another.

Apart from such broad theoretical considerations, common observation makes it difficult to accept without hesitation the conclusion that the economic system is characterised by such generally low interest elasticities, such little response to relative price changes. A system of this kind would tend to exhibit large, erratic fluctuations in prices, interest rates and asset values, since relative prices would have to change very sharply to restore equilibrium. Moreover, if economic decisions were not responsive to relative price changes, one would not expect popular concern to be so sensitive, in the political arena, to such movements. In any case it seems doubtful whether financial and other markets do exhibit such large price variations as would be consistent with a system of very low interest elasticities. When any such large variations in interest rates and asset prices do occur, they often provoke considerable public concern about the possible effect upon the economy. Asset prices have barely to begin dropping before the financial editor of a newspaper will reach for the analogy to the 1929 Stock Market crash.

Reference to that infamous crisis suggests one way of reconciling theory, of adjustment to relative yields, with the statistical findings of limited response to changes in interest rates. This is that the relationship between expenditures and financial conditions may not

---

[1] It is, however, a justifiable complaint that the Radcliffe Committee never studied in any depth the question of how serious this final qualification might be.

[2] Leijonhufvud was very conscious of the danger of using differing forms of reasoning (applying separate standards) to different cases, depending on the conclusion that was desired (see, for example, pp. 180–1 where he castigates 'Keynesians' for this sin, though in my view 'monetarists' have been just as guilty). However, he did not criticise the Radcliffe Report on these grounds: indeed, he claimed that Professor Sayers and the Radcliffe Report were in the true Keynesian tradition (p. 203, footnote), a view which does seem a logical extension of his own general approach.

In place of the arguments on the relative values of the interest elasticities, Leijonhufvud's reinterpretation of Keynesian analysis concentrates rather on the possibility of difficulties arising from regressive expectations being especially prevalent in bond markets, thus preventing a transmission of monetary impulses to the demand for long-lived goods. But whereas this provided a most stimulating view of Keynes's theoretical position, the actual importance of regressive expectations in bond markets, as a limiting factor on the efficacy of monetary policy, is doubtful. Indeed, the worries of the authorities in the United Kingdom have tended to be the opposite, that the bond market was unstable because dealing was generally based on short-term extrapolative expectations.

exhibit the observed low elasticities over the whole schedule. The great bulk of the empirical evidence, which appears to demonstrate the interest inelasticity of expenditure functions, relates, for obvious reasons, to the period since 1945. Yet during this period the authorities have managed rather successfully to avoid major domestic financial disturbances by keeping the variations in financial conditions, in real interest rates, within limits.

A system of financial intermediation, dependent on trust and confidence and character-ised by borrowing short to lend long, is by nature liable, unless carefully guarded and pro-tected,[1] to the onset of sudden crises. At such times financial values are jeopardised, and credit only available at a very high cost, if at all. Such dramatic financial disturbances have happened on many occasions in the past, and when they occur they clearly do influence real-expenditure decisions. To look no further back than the 1930s, whatever the respon-sibility of financial factors, among them the Wall Street crash, for inducing the beginning of the Great Depression, few economists would now want to challenge the judgement that the wholesale failure of banks in the United States extended and deepened that slump very considerably.

Certainly the fear of discontinuities within the system, that growing financial pressure may seem to have little or no effect on the economy until at some unknown point some weak link collapses, transforming tightness into crisis, is rooted in banking history. A growing appreciation of the correct role of the Central Bank within the economy developed during the late nineteenth and early twentieth centuries. A primary objective was the prevention of financial and commercial crises, which littered these years like shipwrecks along the Dover Channel, in addition to the more general aims of maintaining the internal and external value of the currency. Indeed the very foundation of the Federal Reserve system in the United States was constructed specifically in order to counter the weaknesses of the national banking system which had allowed the financial crisis of October 1907 to develop, while the maturity of the Bank of England is generally acknowledged to have been rep-resented by its careful handling of the Baring crisis in 1891. Crises of this kind are not only of historical, antiquarian interest, as the Penn Central episode may have reminded central bankers everywhere; in the United Kingdom the collapse of the London and County in December 1973, and the subsequent run on other 'fringe banks,' acted as another reminder that crises of confidence are still possible. To argue then that econometric exercises, say on the determination of investment expenditures from 1956 to 1968, showing peradventure an insignificant interest elasticity of demand, demonstrate that monetary policy never matters, would be pure folly. The scope of economic history shows, about as conclusively as could be imagined, that monetary forces can matter a great deal.

It is possible, therefore, that the relationship between financial factors and expenditures is discontinuous, and that within the range of financial conditions which the authorities have maintained since 1945, monetary factors may, in the United Kingdom at least, have been of rather incidental importance, relative to other conditions. In this case so long as the monetary authorities maintain a cautious sensible policy, their world will appear to be a 'Keynesian' form, in which monetary actions are of minor significance. But any major jerk in monetary policy could push the economy over some threshold, past a discontinuity, beyond which the system takes on the attributes of a 'monetarist' model. This picture of minor cycles in the past not being strongly influenced by monetary phenomena, while major cycles often could be largely ascribed to monetary effects, fits in reasonably well with the historical analysis of experience in the United States undertaken by Cagan.[2] Such

---

[1] The potential dangers and instabilities inherent in the system can, however, be lessened by structural improvements, an example being the role of deposit insurance in the U.S. banking system.

[2] P. Cagan, *Determinants and Effects of Changes in the Stock of Money, 1875–1960*, Studies in Business Cycles, no. 13, National Bureau of Economic Research (Columbia University Press, New York, 1965) chap. 6, pp. 234–78 especially.

a view of the working of the system does, however, make it extremely hard to integrate monetary and real forecasts. There is no strong empirical basis on which to contest the view of the forecaster of income/expenditure flows that monetary factors can, apart from minor subjective adjustments, be largely disregarded, yet the financial forecaster will continually be warning that, if financial conditions are made too easy or too tight, beyond some unknown, uncertain threshold, then the reverberations of financial events could completely overturn the real forecasters' careful calculations. The financial forecaster feels rather like the little boy crying 'wolf', hoping that his cries will make his parents follow a path that will avoid a real wolf, but knowing that each time he cries 'wolf', and no wolf appears, his credibility diminishes.

There is no doubt about the historical reality of financial crises, and there may well be discontinuities in the relationship between financial conditions and expenditure decisions. This emphasis on the possible dangers of crossing some unseen threshold and exerting an excessive effect on certain expenditures, e.g. manufacturing investment and housing, however, imparts a negative, passive, accommodating influence on the conduct of monetary policy. Despite the fact that most statistical studies of the United Kingdom find virtually no evidence of monetary policy ever exerting more than a marginal influence on manufacturing investment, monetary policy has on certain occasions been restrained by the fear of what might happen to such expenditure if that policy were further tightened. Such fears have a debilitating effect. Even if discontinuities, triggered off, say, by the bankruptcy of some large company or financial intermediary, do lurk somewhere ahead, it may be better to brave them, trusting that the Central Bank can if necessary reverse the thrust of its policy flexibly, than to withdraw monetary policy into a continuously passive stance,[1] accommodating cyclical fluctuations within the economy.

The findings from the econometric studies of low interest elasticities in the expenditure functions and the historical experience of booms culminating in financial crises may also, perhaps, be reconciled and explained on the grounds of shifts in the expected return from real assets, as the economy passes through phases of optimism and pessimism. The demand for real assets depends on the relative yields on such assets and on alternative assets, government bonds in the IS/LM model. But the marginal efficiency of investment schedule is often treated as given for the purpose of analysis,[2] but in practice it is likely to vary systematically. Expectations of future quasi-rents, in nominal terms, from capital investment will vary with expectations of future movements in output, prices, wages, etc., and these expectations will depend on moods, confidence and states of mind (recall the analysis set out in Chapter 5, Section A). What we need to measure is the effect on the demand for real assets of a rise in financial interest rates (r_B) relative to the level of own yields (r_K). In practice we cannot easily observe movements in the expected yields on new investment, and thus

---

[1] A semantic dispute, about the use of adjectives to characterise the authorities' policy, should be noted. A Central Bank which does not raise interest rates sufficiently to choke off an acceleration in nominal incomes, and instead allows the money stock to rise in line with incomes, is here described as 'passive' and 'accommodating.' This is, perhaps, usual 'Keynesian' terminology. A 'monetarist,' however, would describe the Central Bank's action as 'expansionary' or 'inflationary.' But it is only a semantic issue; there is no implied approbation of being passive in the face of inflation or of accommodating excessive expansion.

[2] Moreover, the capital stock is treated as fixed in the normal IS/LM analysis. But if the stock of capital is fixed, the marginal productivity of capital should not decline as investment proceeds. Why then does the marginal efficiency of investment slope down? Probably the best answer to this is that as the pressure of demand increases on the investment goods industry, the price of capital goods rises relative to consumer goods, thus lowering the expected yield on such assets. If so, it may be noted that the IS/LM model does not generally distinguish between the markets for, and prices of, these two kinds of good. Another answer, however, could be that investors are aware of the likelihood that current investment expenditure will raise the stock of capital, and lower the marginal productivity of capital, in the next and future periods.

research workers often proxy the relative yield movement by the absolute change in bond interest rates. Yet, as Leijonhufvud noted, 'The hypothesis which is characteristic of all "Keynesian" theories of economic fluctuations is that it is typically and primarily shifts in the marginal efficiency of capital schedule which account for short-run movements in investment, income and the interest rate. In a typical Keynesian contraction, the observed values of these three endogenous variables will decline together as a consequence of an adverse shift in "opinions about prospective yields"' (p. 80).

Consider a possible sequence of events, beginning with an upwards shift in the marginal efficiency of investment schedule, which cyclical boom the authorities become determined to terminate by the use of monetary action. In stage 1, before the authorities respond, the marginal efficiency of investment will rise relatively to interest rates, though both will probably be rising in absolute terms as borrowers bid for funds, and investment will rise. In stage 2, the authorities will be consciously pushing interest rates up further, but there may be a fairly wide band over which entrepreneurs are rather insensitive to variations in interest rates. The desire of businessmen to maintain, or to increase, their share of an expanding market and the pervasive optimism engendered by a boom will tend to nullify over some range the disinflationary impact of rising interest rates. In retrospect such actions will be described as over-trading or speculation. Then at stage 3 rising rates might finally force some cut-back in expenditures. This stage may, on occasions, seem explosive if the cut-back accompanies some bankruptcies of firms which have 'over-traded.' Once stage 3 has begun to get under way, stage 4 supersedes it very rapidly indeed. In this stage the cut-back in expenditures occurring, say, from a stage-3 bankruptcy, diminishes the marginal efficiency of investment of others in the economy, as output and confidence in the future contract, so that the marginal efficiency of investment declines rapidly relative to interest rates. When this stage takes place, investment expenditures may contract very sharply. So long as stage 3 is short and/or explosive, the effect of financial conditions on the economy will appear to be discontinuous, initially having very little impact and then suddenly causing a drastic shift in business conditions. As Leijonhufvud points out, 'a very exact and reliable method of estimating the movements of the investment schedule would be required' (p. 180), in order to isolate the effects of interest rates upon expenditures in a system involving simultaneous inter-relationships of this kind.

So theory implies that the demand for real assets should be influenced by the relative expected rate of return on such real assets and on alternative (financial) assets over the appropriate planning period(s).[1] Yet most expenditure functions simply include as an argument the nominal yield to maturity on some financial asset. This probably represents a serious mis-specification. In order to provide a thorough test, one should have adequate proxies to represent expectations, e.g. of price and wage inflation,[2] of the rate of return (in real terms) expected on real assets, etc.

Clearly, a satisfactory specification of expenditure functions, which should include adequate proxies for expectations, is far from being realised in most models today. This

---

[1] We claimed in Chap. 5 that it was characteristic of many real assets to be specific in form, so that investment was irreversible. If this is the case, the investor cannot be myopic, i.e. concern himself only with current values of output, input costs, etc. The long life of investment goods, taking into consideration also their low second-hand value, if specific in form, might seem to imply a long planning period, over which the expected rate of return on the asset could be compared against some *long-term* financial yield(s). But one dimension of the investment expenditure decision will be to determine the timing of the initial expenditure, or at least the time profile of the financing arrangements, and this will require a *shorter* and more complex planning horizon.

[2] D. D. Hester has, however, warned that one-dimensional price and wage indices often fail to capture heterogeneous movements among prices and wages in different industries; see his paper on 'Inflation and the Recent American Happening,' Proceedings of the Association of University Teachers of Economics, Conference at Warwick 1973 (forthcoming).

judgement may be a little harsh, because one could argue that current expenditure functions represent in one equation a test of the joint hypotheses that relevant expectations are stably related to the included arguments and that decisions are stably related to the expectations thus generated. If, however, the theoretical basis of these expenditure functions is properly to be seen in such expectational terms, then it is often hard to see what are the links posited between the included observed variables and the expectations on which the decision must be made.

To be sure, it is not easy to construct functions based on expectations, particularly when there are so few reliable observations of expectations themselves. For example one could well ask how far the rise in nominal interest rates, since 1945, has been matched by a rise in inflationary expectations. Perhaps one reason for the slight estimated effect of changes in nominal interest rates on expenditures could be that they do not reflect changes in 'real'[1] interest rates, that is in nominal rates less expected rates of inflation.[2] One might, perhaps, expect to test this hypothesis by including as arguments in expenditure functions not only the nominal rate of interest but also a proxy variable intended to represent price expectations. This has been carried out in a number of exercises by making certain assumptions about the generation of expectations of price inflation, for example that expectations are some simple function of past and present experience, or alternatively that expectations always subsequently proved to be correct. Such tests have often failed to show evidence of any much more pronounced interest-rate effect. But one reason for this could well be that the assumptions about the generation of price expectations have been invalid. For example, in the immediate post-war years it is fairly well-documented that many people, basing their expectations on an analogy with the 1920/1 post-war period, expected a sharp boom to be followed by a future downturn in prices despite past, current and – as we now know – future continuation of inflation. Again, anyone who tries to estimate price expectations purely as some function of past experience is going to produce silly results on occasions when dramatic developments, such as devaluations, price freezes, wage explosions and energy shortages, force people to re-evaluate their expectations in very changed conditions.

In any case this approach, using expenditure functions to relate the quantities of various kinds of goods bought to various explanatory variables, e.g. incomes, etc. including interest rates – perhaps 'adjusted' for the current rate of inflation – may not serve to capture the full working of monetary forces. Monetary forces will, it is argued, cause changes in the strength of *demand* for certain goods and assets by shifting relative yields and overall wealth. But changes in *output* reflect both changes in demand and in the capacity of industry to *supply* additional goods. Supply conditions may alter, and it may take a long and variable time for an industry to meet additional demand. In those cases where the elasticity of supply in the short run is low and where a free, effective market in second-hand assets exists, the main initial effect of changes in monetary conditions may be to vary existing asset prices.

For example, the rapid growth in the money stock and fall in interest rates in the winter and spring of 1971/2 in the United Kingdom was accompanied by a sharp rise in house and land prices. The expansionary monetary policy had been intended to encourage additional expenditures and so bring about a reduction of unemployment. Yet there were few

---

[1] The word 'real' is something of a misnomer for a purely subjective variable which cannot be observed.

[2] Even if the rise in nominal interest rates is due to expectations of accelerating inflation, it may still cause immediate problems of servicing the initial repayments of interest (and principal) out of current incomes, particularly for young persons entering the mortgage and housing markets. If everyone was certain to have higher nominal incomes in future, in line with accelerating inflation, then one would be able to borrow against the security of such higher prospective earnings. But in practice uncertainty concerning future income from human capital makes it difficult to pledge as collateral for borrowing.

signs of much additional housing and construction expenditure. However, the failure of real expenditures to rise was not a sign that demand was unresponsive to monetary factors; instead it was the possibly short-term inelasticity of supply in the construction industry that prevented any larger quantitative response to financial encouragement.

Observation of demand effects becomes even more difficult where no effective second-hand market exists. In such cases a fluctuation in demand may lead only to a change in the length of order books and the backlog of unfinished work. Prices of new goods tend to be fixed administratively. A rise in demand may show itself fully neither in increased prices nor in increased output but in longer queues. It is one of the most unsatisfactory features of Keynesian-type models that supply constraints are broadly ignored, though casual observation suggests that they are prevalent. Of course, the existence of supply constraints can still mean that monetary policy may not have any reliable impact upon the volume of expenditure in the economy. Nevertheless, assessment of the situation, and even policy prescription, will differ if one should shift from believing statement A, that:

Monetary policy appears to have little effect on real demand in the economy,

to accepting statement B, that:

Monetary policy affects the demand for certain assets. This does not, however, entail any reliable or quick effect on output because of supply constraints.

The hypothesis here is that estimates of the responsiveness of *demand* to shifts in relative asset prices, in general terms the interest elasticity of demand for goods, have been severely biased downwards by calculating the effect on *output* of changes in interest rates without concern for *supply* conditions. There have been few studies of any depth to examine whether explicit consideration of supply constraints does raise estimated price elasticities. In one exercise to examine the determinants of U.K. exports, undertaken by H.M. Treasury (unpublished), the division of the data period into demand- and supply-constrained sub-periods did lead to a marked rise in the estimated price elasticity of demand for U.K. exports. And in a simulation exercise Brechling[1] demonstrated that supply constraints on the production of investment goods could lead to a considerable downwards bias on the estimated interest elasticity. Nevertheless, the evidence in support of this assertion is, as yet, rather limited.

C. Direct Statistical Links between Money Incomes and the Money Stock

In the last section a range of reasons was put forward to suggest why the statistical findings of very low interest elasticities of demand for goods (relative to the fairly low interest elasticity of demand for money), with the implication that monetary policy had little effect on the real economy, should be treated with a cautious reserve. Among such considerations were:

(i) possible discontinuities in the relationships;
(ii) inability to estimate own expected yields on real assets, particularly as these are likely to exhibit systematic fluctuations, with most variables tending to vary simultaneously;
(iii) the overlooking of supply limitations.

---

[1] F. Brechling, 'Monetary Policy and Neo-Classical Investment Analysis,' especially sect. 4 on 'Supply Factors in the Theory of Investment,' a paper presented at the Bournemouth Money Study Group Conference (February 1972) proceedings to be published by the Oxford University Press under the title, *Issues in Monetary Economics*, ed. R. Nobay and H. G. Johnson.

None the less, it seems doubtful whether the results of the empirical estimates of expenditure functions, showing relatively little impact of financial variables upon expenditures, would have been so questioned and challenged if it had not been for a further, and quite different, set of empirical results showing for the United States a close relationship between changes in money incomes and current and prior movements in the money stock, i.e.

$$\Delta Y_t = b_1 \, \Delta M_t + b_2 \, \Delta M_{t-1}, \dots, b_n \, \Delta M_{t-n} + cX$$

where X is a vector of other included explanatory variables and c is the associated vector of coefficients. It may, however, be noted that relationships of this kind are not equally good in all countries; in particular in the United Kingdom such relationships in general fit rather poorly.[1] Nevertheless, a statistically strong relationship has been found in the United States and in some other countries.[2]

The crucial point is that this finding appears to be inconsistent with the conclusion that financial variables do not strongly affect expenditures. To be sure, it does not follow that even where there are only weak monetary effects monetary changes would never be associated with changes in money incomes. If the changes in the money stock were associated with increases in budget deficits, with current-account surpluses (leading to foreign-exchange inflows), or with an increased demand to borrow for investment purposes from entrepreneurs, then both the rise in money incomes and in the money stock would be associated with additional income-creating expenditures. If, on the other hand, the rise in the money stock was the counterpart of some financial transaction – say, an open-market operation – then, with an interest elasticity of demand for money relatively greater than the demand for goods, the resulting effect on relative yields should exhaust itself mainly in causing re-adjustments in financial markets with little impact on real expenditures. Given that view of the relative elasticities, the relationship between changes in the money stock and in money incomes should be variable, as the economic developments associated with the changes in the money stock alter. In particular, the relationship between changes in the endogenous elements of expenditures, mainly consumption, and the 'exogenous' expenditures, e.g. government expenditures, exports, etc., should be expected to be closer than the relationship of these same endogenous expenditures with changes in money supply.

Friedman and Meiselman tested this relationship for the United States and found the opposite to be true, that the money multiplier was more stable than the 'Keynesian' multiplier.[3] Considerable further empirical digging[4] suggested that it was a moot point whether or not the one statistical relationship fitted better than the other. But in a sense such fine

---

[1] See among others M. Artis and A. R. Nobay, 'Two Aspects of the Monetary Debate,' *National Institute Economic Review*, no. 49 (August 1969) pp. 37–42, and C. Goodhart and A. Crockett, 'The Importance of Money,' *Bank of England Quarterly Bulletin*, vol. 10, no. 2 (June 1970) appendix II, pp. 197–8.

[2] Much of this work has been undertaken by the economists at the Federal Reserve Bank of St. Louis and published in their *Review*. The most influential of these papers being the study by L. Andersen and J. Jordan on the U.S. economy of 'Monetary and Fiscal Actions: A Test of Their Relative Importance in Economic Stabilization,' *Federal Reserve Bank of St. Louis Review*, vol. 50, no. 11 (November 1968) pp. 11–23. Further papers extending this approach to a wider selection of countries have been presented by M. W. Keran, 'Selecting a Monetary Indicator – Evidence from the United States and Other Developed Countries,' ibid. vol. 52, no. 9 (September 1970) pp. 8–19, and 'Monetary and Fiscal Influences on Economic Activity: The Foreign Experience,' ibid., vol. 52, no. 2 (February 1970) pp. 16–28.

[3] M. Friedman and D. Meiselman, 'The Relative Stability of Monetary Velocity and the Investment Multiplier in the United States, 1897–1958,' Research Study no. 2 in *Stabilization Policies: Commission on Money and Credit* (Prentice-Hall, Englewood Cliffs, N.J., 1963).

[4] See the paper by W. Poole and E. Kornblith, 'The Friedman–Meiselman CMC Paper: New Evidence on an Old Controversy,' *The American Economic Review*, vol. 63, no. 5 (December 1973) pp. 908–17.

comparisons were somewhat beside the point: even if the Keynesian multiplier fitted very well also, it was undeniable that in the United States – though not in the United Kingdom – there was a very good statistical fit between monetary changes and subsequent changes in money incomes.

How could that be, if the relative interest elasticities were such that monetary factors did not matter all that much? Examination of the simple statistical relationships between money incomes and the money stock reveals nothing directly of the mechanism relating the two variables. So at the first stage interpretation of these results is entirely inferential. The monetarists have had little doubt that the implication of these results is that, in reality, the response of expenditure decisions to relative yield changes must be quite large, compared with the interest elasticity of demand for money. Thus, for example, an increase in the fiscal deficit not matched by a monetary increase, i.e. financed by selling bonds, will lead to a rise in interest rates 'crowding out' an equivalent volume of other expenditures.[1] And a monetary expansion, even one without a direct association with extra expenditures, i.e. resulting from some financial re-arrangement, can so alter relative yields (and/or wealth) that there appears to be a large and predictable effect on expenditures within the next few quarters. In one model in this vein, by Laffer and Ranson,[2] the effect of the monetary change on money incomes was reckoned to be virtually immediate within the first quarter.

Indeed, one of the curious features of the results of these statistical exercises is the often rather quick apparent impact of monetary effects. This finding conflicts with other evidence which suggests a relatively slower response to changes in financial conditions, particularly where these take the form of changes in interest rates.[3] In the F.R.B.–M.I.T. model of the U.S. economy, constructed in a neo-Keynesian format, monetary changes also have a quick and quite large effect on consumption through their effect on stock-market prices. It is, however, difficult to believe that Wall Street fluctuations are sufficiently stable and predictable to act as a very firm link in the short run between money and money incomes in the United States. Apart from that in their model, as in most other Keynesian models, the effect of interest rates on housing, company fixed investment, etc., take quite a number of quarters to build up.

If there should be a tendency for any economy, even under conditions of uncertainty, to revert to some full-employment equilibrium, as the monetarists contend, then in the long run a proportionate rise in one kind of expenditure must 'crowd out' some other form of expenditure. Presumably these adjustments occur via relative price movements. In this sense, if we can accept the premise of long-run adjustment to equilibrium, the response to relative movements in prices and yields *must* be sufficiently elastic to achieve that result. However, there is very little evidence from the Keynesian models to suggest that the elasticity of that response is sufficiently large and reliable in the immediate future of usual policy relevance, say the next two years, to explain the large, quick and rather stable association between money and money incomes derived from the direct statistical relationship.

The common response of the monetarists has been to argue that the empirical results from the expenditure functions in the macro-economic models are biased and unreliable. In particular, Friedman claims that most macro-economic models, developed from the basic *IS/LM* cast, impose excessive restraints on the allowable links of substitution between the real and the financial system:

---

[1] See, for example, R. Spencer and W. Yohe, 'The "Crowding Out" of Private Expenditures by Fiscal Policy Actions,' *Federal Reserve Bank of St. Louis Review*, vol. 52, no. 10 (October 1970) pp. 12–24.

[2] A. B. Laffer and R. D. Ranson, 'A Formal Model of the Economy,' *Journal of Business*, vol. 44 (July 1971) pp. 247–70.

[3] See the study by G. Fisher and D. K. Sheppard, *Effects of Monetary Policy on the United States Economy*, O.E.C.D. Economic Outlook, Occasional Studies (O.E.C.D., Paris, 1972) *passim*.

The crucial issue that corresponds to the distinction between the 'credit' (Keynesian) and 'monetary' effects of monetary policy is not whether changes in the stock of money operate through interest rates but rather the range of interest rates considered. On the 'credit' view, monetary policy impinges on a narrow and well-defined range of capital assets and a correspondingly narrow range of associated expenditures. ... On the 'monetary' view, monetary policy impinges on a much broader range of associated expenditures.[1]

As was noted in Section A, this seems a reasonable criticism. However, there remains a very large gap between hypothesising that there may be certain features that could cause a bias in the established empirical estimates of the expenditure functions, and actually demonstrating that they do so. This latter step has not been taken. Indeed Friedman has, on occasion, suggested that the task was impossible because the relatively gentle, but pervasive, effect of monetary influences on any one asset would be obscured by more powerful but local factors, e.g. changes in tastes, affecting the market for that asset.

This is not a very satisfactory position. It is reasonable for monetarists to infer from the apparent inconsistencies between the statistical results obtained from a direct regression of the money stock on money incomes and the results obtained from studies of the various expenditure functions in the macro models that the latter could be seriously biased, and there are several plausible arguments why this might be so. As yet, however, they have provided no strong evidence of such bias in the macro models, nor even do they seem to be searching for such evidence: their attempted explanation of the conflicting results of the various statistical exercises therefore remains purely hypothetical.

In these circumstances the field has remained open to consider other hypothetical explanations of the time-series relationship between movements in the money stock and in money incomes. In particular, it has been suggested that in some part the strength of the correlation could be owing not to the 'causal' impact of monetary changes on incomes, but to the 'causal' effect of changes in incomes on the money stock. The demand for money is usually taken to be functionally related to the level of incomes and of interest rates. We may write then

$$M = f(Y, r)$$

If the monetary authorities' objectives include the pegging, or the support, of interest rates in the market, then the above demand for money relationship will lead them to allow the money stock to vary in line with the level of money incomes. Furthermore, it is widely accepted (see footnote 1, p. 135 in Chapter 6) that, until the last four or five years, the targets and objectives of the monetary authorities in the Anglo-Saxon countries, the United States, Canada and the United Kingdom, were generally expressed in terms of interest rates rather than in terms of monetary quantities. Indeed, it has been one of the major policy aims of 'monetarist' economists to wean the authorities away from what the monetarists argued was excessive concern with interest-rate levels and stability.

There is no denying that the situation has been such that 'reverse causation,' with cyclical and other variations in money incomes affecting the money stock, might have occurred.[2] But the actual form of the estimated statistical relationship between the two time series cannot easily be explained on these grounds. Essentially the evidence for a causal impact of monetary changes upon the level of money incomes rests on the time pattern of the relationship, and relies on the fact that a change in the money stock had a significant relationship with subsequent movements in money incomes whereas the reverse was not the case – or

---

[1] Friedman and Meiselman, op. cit. p. 217.

[2] See, for example, the paper by R. E. Lombra and R. G. Torto on 'Federal Reserve "Defensive" Behavior and the Reverse Causation Argument,' *Southern Economic Journal*, vol. 40, no. 1 (July 1973) pp. 47–55.

to a much weaker extent.[1] This is simply a *post hoc, propter hoc* argument, though none the worse for that. Once again, however, the relationships between these time series in the United Kingdom do not tally all that closely with the American findings.[2] Using the official quarterly national income and monetary series, the evidence in the United Kingdom even suggests opposite findings to those in the United States. But if certain other monetary and income series are used the results seem to swing around more into line with those in the United States. The difference between these findings may well be a reflection of the fact that the United Kingdom is an open economy, maintaining until 1972 a regime of fixed exchange rates, whereas the United States is virtually a closed economy. In an open economy with fixed exchange rates the private sector is in a stronger position to adjust its money balances to the current level of domestic expenditures, rather than vice versa, by transferring funds over the exchanges, e.g. in the form of international capital movements.

Certainly a finding that monetary changes have a significant relationship with subsequent income changes, but not vice versa, must imply a strong presumption that money changes cause the subsequent income changes.[3] Nevertheless, it is not clear exactly how strong this presumption is. For example, one can think of a number of examples where some variable appears to lead another without there being any causal relationship, Christmas cards and Christmas, swallows and summers. In almost all these cases, however, the key to the lead of the variable that precedes but does not cause the subsequent variable is the ability of the decision-maker who determines on the movements of the leading variable to predict the lagging variable. Swallows and Christmas-card buyers can predict, indeed know, the rotation of the seasons.

The lead of changes in money balances over money incomes could hardly, however, be explained on the grounds that money holders were seeking to adjust these in anticipation of changing future expected transaction requirements.[4] It would involve an opportunity cost in forgone interest receipts to build up money balances significantly in advance of anticipated requirements. Moreover, is it to be believed that households, who hold the bulk of the money stock, are likely to be good predictors of future changes in their incomes and expenditures?

A more interesting question, however, is whether the authorities are able to predict future developments. Assume that the authorities want to achieve some desired level for an economic variable, say national income Y. The level of national income will be affected by a number of disturbances, e.g. foreign developments and population trends, which they cannot control, which may be described by a vector Q. The authorities can command, more or less, a number of policy instruments, control tools, which they can influence, say $X_1, \ldots, X_n$. Let X_1 be a policy instrument which is known to have a positive but lagged effect on incomes, so that

$$\frac{dY_t}{dX_t} \simeq 0 \quad \text{but} \quad \frac{dY_{t+n}}{dX_t} > 0$$

---

[1] See, for example, M. J. Hamburger, 'Indicators of Monetary Policy: The Arguments and the Evidence,' *The American Economic Review*, vol. 60 (May 1970) papers and proceedings, pp. 32–9; and C. A. Sims, 'Money, Income, and Causality,' *The American Economic Review*, vol. 62, no. 4 (September 1972) pp. 540–52.

[2] Research along these lines has been conducted in the Bank of England, and a paper (mimeo, unpublished) by C. Goodhart, D. Gowland and D. Williams on 'Money, Income and Causality: The U.K. Experience' has been completed. Work along similar lines is also currently in process at Queen Mary College in London under the guidance of M. Peston.

[3] On this, see C. W. J. Granger, 'Investigating Causal Relations by Econometric Models and Cross-Spectral Methods,' *Econometrica*, vol. 37 (July 1969) pp. 424–38.

[4] This argument has, however, been recently put forward by P. Davidson and S. Weintraub, 'Money as Cause and Effect,' *The Economic Journal*, vol. 83, no. 332 (December 1973) pp. 1117–32, especially 1117–19.

Expressing the deviation of actual from desired incomes as a function of current disturbances, Q, and the lagged policy instrument, we can write

$$Y_t - Y^* = b_1 X_{t-n} + b_2 Q_t$$

Clearly, if the authorities are using that instrument X_1 for stabilisation purposes, then they
will aim to set

$$X_{1,t-n} = \frac{-b_2}{b_1} Q_t$$

In reality, of course, the authorities are uncertain of the lags in the system, the values of b_2
and b_1, and at times $t - n$ when they have to set the value of X they are uncertain about the
future values of Q. Under such circumstances they will be lucky to fix X just right to offset
all other disturbances, but they could over or under adjust.

If the authorities were accurate forecasters of future movements in Q, the sign of the
correlation between X_{t-n} and $Y - Y^*$ would depend only on whether they were able
exactly to offset movements in Q – which would bring about a zero correlation $r = 0$ – or
over-adjusted, $r > 0$, or under-adjusted, $r < 0$.[1] Thus if the authorities can forecast with
some accuracy future exogenous disturbances, the correlations between money incomes
and various alternative forms of control tool, say the growth in the money stock and/or
the fiscal deficit, cannot be simply interpreted as measuring their net effects on the economy.
Instead the results represent a combination of their direct economic impact plus their
systematic covariation with other economic factors, not included in this equation. Thus
one might even contend that the much stronger correlation in the United States between
the money stock and money incomes, than between fiscal variables and money incomes,
implied a more effective use of fiscal policy, than of monetary policy, as a contracyclical
stabilising device, rather than provided evidence of their direct economic effects. It should
be repeated, however, that this does depend on the possibility of accurate forecasting because, otherwise, there is unlikely to be any systematic covariation with excluded exogenous
disturbances.

Although it is possible on these, and other, grounds[2] to argue that the timing relationship between movements in the money stock and in money incomes, observed in past
decades in the United States, need not prove the existence of a causal chain running from
monetary changes to variations in money incomes, it does constitute a powerful presumption for this hypothesis. The onus really comes on those who do not believe in the implied
causal link to provide evidence of an alternative explanation of the relationship. To date a
number of hypotheses have been put forward to suggest possible explanations, but there
has been no hard evidence produced to support these hypotheses.

Thus analysis of the transmission mechanism of monetary policy stands at something
of an impasse.[3] Virtually all economists are agreed how the process works in theory, but

---

[1] On this subject see M. Peston, 'The Correlation between Targets and Instruments,' *Economica*,
vol. 39, no. 156 (November 1972) pp. 427–31; S. M. Goldfeld and A. S. Blinder, 'Some Implications
of Endogenous Stabilisation Policy,' *Brookings Papers on Economic Activity*, no. 3 (1972) pp.
585–640, with comments and discussion, pp. 641–4; Levis A. Kochin, 'Judging Stabilisation Policy'
(mimeo, Federal Reserve Bank of New York, 1972).

[2] See, for example, J. Tobin, 'Money and Income: Post Hoc Ergo Propter Hoc,' *Quarterly
Journal of Economics*, vol. 84, no. 2 (May 1970) pp. 301–17, and the subsequent 'Comment on
Tobin' by M. Friedman and 'Rejoinder' by Tobin, ibid. pp. 318–29.

[3] For an interesting survey of the present controversies in this area, written from a 'monetarist'
viewpoint, see K. M. Carlson, 'Monetary and Fiscal Actions in Macro-economic Models,' *Federal
Reserve Bank of St. Louis Review*, vol. 56, no. 1 (January 1974) pp. 8–18, especially the section on
'Research Methodology and the Controversy,' pp. 12–14.

there is a very wide range of disagreement about the strength of such effects in practice. Some point to the empirical findings of low interest elasticities in the expenditure functions in the macro models as evidence of slight monetary effects, but they are hard put to it to give convincing explanations, supported by factual evidence, to explain the results of the direct regressions (in the United States) of the money stock on money incomes. Others rely on this direct relationship as evidence of the importance of money, but they are equally at a loss to discredit the empirical results of fitting expenditure functions in the larger Keynesian macro models. In the United Kingdom, however, the evidence does tend to be rather more one-sided, because both the structural equations and the direct relationships imply a much lesser role for monetary forces here than in the United States. This, however, only raises the unanswered question of why there should be this difference between our two economies. Possibly the answer is that in an open economy there is more flexibility for monetary conditions to adjust to changes in the domestic economy, via international capital and monetary flows, than in a closed economy.

In time this conflict may be resolved, and we may look back on the debates about the importance, or otherwise, of monetary policy as a phenomenon peculiar to a certain period. But in the meantime the uncertainty and the debate adds a certain zest and edge to applied monetary analysis.

10

Money in an Uncertain World: Disequilibria and Wealth Effects

SUMMARY

In a world of certainty there would be no undesired unemployment, no disequilibria arising from incorrect and inconsistent decisions. In the real world there is neither the information nor the (marketing) mechanisms (e.g. a Walrasian auctioneer) available to allow equilibrium to be achieved. In a complex, decentralised economy, in which individual decision-makers can only conjecture about the likely actions of others in the economy, there is much scope for inconsistent decisions, e.g. of investors and savers, to lead to disequilibria. The institution of money provides the information network which enables a complex, decentralised economy to function at all. Because money is a necessary adjunct to such an economy, the disequilibria in the economy are sometimes regarded as monetary phenomena; it is, however, the inconsistency of decisions within the system, not the existence of the monetary framework, which is the proximate cause of disequilibria.

If the market mechanism should work perfectly, *with full information*, there would be no undesired unemployment. So the response of classical economists to the mass unemployment of the 1930s was to advocate the removal of frictions which restricted the flexible working of markets, *inter alia* to increase the downwards flexibility of wages and prices in response to insufficient demand. Keynes argued, in contrast, that general reductions in prices and wages, apart from their social and political consequences, might not be successful in restoring equilibrium. In particular, the fall in interest rates that should result, as the ratio of money balances to money incomes rises after a decline in prices, might be checked by regressive expectations about the future level of interest rates, resulting in a liquidity trap.

This implied that the price level might be indeterminate, despite there being a given nominal money stock. This was an unacceptable idea for most economists. The technical solution to this difficulty was found by realising that the net wealth of the private sector would be raised by falls in price, since the real value of their fixed-interest financial claims on other sectors (including monetary claims) would rise, even if interest rates remained sticky. So ultimately the 'wealth' effect should restore equilibrium, though the weakness of the effect and the continuing deflation and unemployment while it was working through did not lead economists to revise Keynes's policy prescriptions on this account.

Furthermore we shall argue that changes in the real value of the public sector's financial liabilities, including fiat money, which are held by the private sector do not represent any change in the net wealth of the community as a whole, as this should normally be defined. Yet these changes will have a real economic effect, not because the economy's wealth has changed, but because the public sector, being immune from bankruptcy, will not respond to an increase in the real value of its net liabilities in such a way as to offset the expansionary impact on private-sector behaviour of an increase in its net wealth. But such differential responses to changes in net wealth also exist within the private sector. In this case the depressing effect on company expenditures of increases in their net liability position possibly exceeds the expansionary effect of an accompanying increase in the real value of the personal sector's net assets. So a general decline in prices, raising the real value of all fixed-interest debt, may have either a reflationary or deflationary impact dependent on the initial pattern of the sectoral debt structure.

A. Uncertainty and Unemployment

Even if we knew exactly what was the relationship between changes in the money stock and subsequent changes in money incomes, there would still remain the question of the division of that change into price and output movements. It is not much help, for policy purposes, to be able to predict with reasonable accuracy that a 5 per cent increase in the money stock would lead, say, to a 4 per cent increase in money incomes, if it is not possible to forecast what proportion of that 4 per cent increase will reflect price inflation and what proportion a rise in the volume of output.

In the last chapter this subject of the division of expenditure changes into price and output responses was largely ducked, except that in Section B, on the empirical evidence about the relative size of the interest elasticities, there was some discussion of supply conditions affecting the response of the system to shifts in the demand for a good. The usual analysis of this subject is simple. The greater the margin of spare capacity in any industry or economy, the more the response to demand changes, expressed in nominal terms, is liable to be reflected in output changes; the nearer to full capacity, the more the response is likely to be reflected in price changes. Continuing stimulation of the economy is, therefore, likely to lead to a diminishing expansion of real output and growing inflation, as spare capacity is drawn back into use. Measuring the extent of spare capacity by the level of unemployment, this implies that the short-run[1] relationship between unemployment and inflation will be non-linear, probably tracing out a hyperbola as shown in Fig. 10.1, where $\dot{P}$ represents the rate of price inflation and UE the level of unemployment.

But this account presupposes the possible existence of spare capacity, and essentially describes the form of the commonly-observed relationships rather than explains the reasons for them. In particular, how can unemployed resources co-exist with unfulfilled wants, so long as there is an efficient price mechanism? In a world of certainty such maladjustments

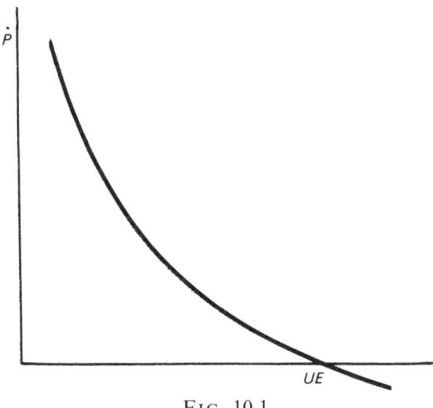

Fig. 10.1

---

[1] The short run is here defined as the period during which expectations about the future, particularly about the prospective rate of inflation, are taken as given. The implications, which are of major importance, of allowing for revisions in such expectations over time are considered later in Chap. 11.

would not occur. Everyone would know from the outset the underlying distribution of wants on the one hand and skills and resources on the other. Each individual would be able to select an optimal life plan of activity and expenditures consistent with equilibrium, which would entail working so long as the marginal utility, in the form of wage and work satisfaction, was greater than or equal to the marginal costs in leisure opportunities forgone. People might be 'resting', but they would be doing so by preference.

In a world of uncertainty there is neither the information nor the equilibrating mechanisms available to allow equilibrium to be achieved. Decision-makers have to respond as best as they can to very limited information. If sales should fall, producers have to guess whether it would be better for them to lower their offered prices or to cut back on output. Workers, combined into trade unions, have to decide whether to aim for a high wage/low employment industry, or seek to keep the industry more labour intensive by accepting lower wages.

In an atomistic free-enterprise economy the results of the decisions of one group will often depend on the reactions of another group.[1] If I cut my price, will my competitors follow my example? If we accept a lower wage settlement, what effect will that have on other union bargains? For this, and other reasons, the elasticities of response to a wage/price decision are a matter of pure conjecture. How much larger a volume of sales will be achieved by a price reduction, or how many jobs will be saved by accepting lower wages is virtually impossible to forecast. Moreover, in the short run habit and custom tend to keep price elasticities well below their long-run level. So it is difficult to point with clarity to obvious, immediate beneficial results of price reductions, even if the longer-run effects of certain relative price trends may be painfully clear. The disadvantageous effects of price/wage reductions are immediately obvious and certain: if the union leader accepts a lower wage, then this fact is immediately reflected in everyone's pay packets; if he holds out for a higher wage, then employment in the industry *may* be lower than would otherwise be the case and each worker faces a higher probability that his own job *might* be terminated; but these represent only hypothetical outcomes, in some cases with low subjective probabilities. Also, when the level of employment is cut back, there is often some other, more immediate cause acting as trigger to the decision, which can play the role of scapegoat.

If an individual worker cannot retain, or obtain, some particular job, which would provide him with greater prospective rewards than in other alternative jobs, why does he not offer his labour at a lower rate, so long as that still leaves him better off than in any alternative occupation? Clearly unions will strive to prevent this happening, since the possibility of competitive bidding down of wage rates by aspiring entrants would limit their own ability to select that combination of relative wage and size of industry that they prefer. But even in a non-unionised industry the transactions costs of dealing with each worker separately, and the information costs of assembling sufficient knowledge to bargain efficiently, suggest that wages will tend to be held at standardised, common, fixed levels

---

[1] The consequences of this atomistic, sequential process of decision making are far-reaching. Consider this quotation from R. W. Clower, 'The Keynesian Counterrevolution: A Theoretical Appraisal,' from *The Theory of Interest Rates*, ed. Hahn and Brechling, pp. 117–18, 'Established preference analysis tacitly presupposes that selling, buying and saving plans are all carried out simultaneously. . . . The notion that all household decisions are accomplished at a single stroke seems to be an analytically convenient and intuitively plausible procedure as long as we consider each household to be an isolated performer of conceptual experiments. When households are considered to be part of a connected market system, however, . . . what is then presupposed about planned sales and purchases cannot possibly be true of realised sales and purchases, unless the system as a whole is always in a state of equilibrium. . . . If we entertain the notion of developing market models that will have practical application to situations of chronic disequilibrium, however, we must surely question the universal relevance of the "unified decision" hypothesis and, by the same token, question whether the usual household supply and demand functions provide relevant market signals.'

with occasional quantum-jump readjustments, rather than being perfectly flexible. In such cases workers may well not be able to find jobs, even in non-unionised occupations, despite being prepared to accept wages below the going rate. Because of the learning process involved in becoming part of a productive team, the value to an employer of a long-standing, trained employee is considerably greater than is the case with a new entrant. Therefore a job seeker will be unlikely to replace an existing worker by offering to accept a slightly lower wage.

So in an uncertain world, with imperfections in the market, transactions costs, information costs, etc., people will often be unable to obtain the work of their choice,[1] even though they would be prepared to take that job at less than the going rate. This social problem is considerably accentuated by the specific nature of human capital. A worker is usually trained in some specific skill, with a considerable investment outlay in terms of time and money. The difference between the wage that a skilled worker would get if only he could obtain a job requiring that skill and his alternative prospects in the pool of unskilled workers may be very considerable. Again a worker will have developed specific attachments to his place of work, housing, schools, friends, etc. Even if a reasonable job can be found in some new area at a distance, an unemployed worker may prefer to risk his chances of finding one nearer home.

A distinction is often drawn between voluntary and involuntary unemployment. This is a dangerous use of words. As long as there are any job vacancies open, in the army, domestic service, etc., even if these are at a distance from home, the unemployed man is voluntarily deciding to refuse them and to wait for a better opportunity. In that sense virtually all unemployment is voluntary, since there are almost always some vacancies for jobs which the unemployed could accept. At the other extreme there would be some jobs in the economy, e.g. managing director, which virtually any unemployed worker would take if offered. In that sense all unemployment is involuntary, since he would prefer the nice, but unavailable, job to his present position.[2]

---

[1] What would happen if everyone wanted to be Prime Minister? In a certain world without information costs, the results of having Jones rather than Smith in that position would be known. The selection of Prime Minister, from among the contenders, would not go to the man offering to accept the lowest salary, but to the man who could provide the greatest additional value to the community in that job, i.e. productive output less factor cost. So the individual's choice of jobs in a certain world would be largely swayed by his comparative advantages in the skills required.

In an uncertain world employers (or selectors of a candidate for any job) have to rely on partial and inaccurate information about the abilities of aspiring candidates for the position. In this condition people look for information signals, e.g. qualifications, examination results, appearance at an interview. Such sorting processes have their distasteful aspects, but the correct inference could well be to improve the process, not to abandon it. In logic those who object to a system of grading through examinations, etc., should also advocate choosing Prime Ministers by random selection (or perhaps we should all get a five-minute turn at the job).

[2] In addition to the question whether an unemployed man *remains* in that state 'voluntarily' or 'involuntarily,' one can also ask whether an unemployed man *became* unemployed voluntarily by quitting his work, or was laid off, involuntarily on his part, by his employer. *Pace* much American analysis, which appears to treat unemployment as arising voluntarily through quits, in the United Kingdom the greater bulk of cyclical and structural unemployment appears to arise involuntarily through lay-offs. Indeed, it would be surprising if it were not so for, as Tobin noted in his presidential address to the American Economic Association, 'Inflation and Unemployment,' *The American Economic Review*, vol. 62, no. 1 (March 1972) pp. 1–18, workers can probably search for better jobs, as well or better, from the standpoint of holding an existing job, than from an unemployed position. In part, this is a problem of information costs, and the problem for prospective employers of spotting 'lemons' (bad workers); see G. Akerlof, 'The Market for "Lemons": Quality Uncertainty and the Market Mechanism,' *Quarterly Journal of Economics*, vol. 84, no. 3 (August 1970) pp. 488–500. The fact that the candidate for a job already has another one is some evidence that his current employer finds his work satisfactory. If the candidate is unemployed, it raises the possibility that he was let go because he was a relatively poor worker.

In place of this inappropriate dichotomy between voluntary and involuntary unemployment, Professor Phelps[1] likens the choice facing the unemployed man to an investment decision. By remaining unemployed and continuing to search for better jobs, the unemployed man forgoes current income, from the job vacancies currently available, in the hopes of enjoying a larger income in future from the job that he may secure by searching and waiting. He should continue to hold out so long as the present expected value of the returns to waiting, adjusted for risk, is greater than, or equal to, the costs involved.

In this sense unemployment is a chosen state, and the choice is subject to the process of rational decision-making. Yet the analogy with investment provides too comfortable a connotation, for the term investment is generally connected with growth and expansion. For the unemployed worker it will usually be a choice between evils, to accept now a worse job, perhaps in a distant community, or to wait in unpleasant straits for the uncertain possibility of getting a better job in due course; though both the economy and the unemployed worker may well be better off if he does not immediately accept the first job offered but assesses as well as possible the prospects of obtaining better jobs.

In an economy with perfect certainty foreseen changes in the pattern of wants would call forth smooth adjustments in the movements of factors of production between different uses. There would be no wastage of unemployed resources in the midst of want. But uncertainty will lead to error, particularly in the extent of specific capital investment in infrastructure, equipment and human skills, which remain dependent for full utilisation on the continued, uncertain prosperity of some particular activity.

A question next arises for monetary economists whether the institution of a monetary system exacerbates or alleviates the maladjustments, caused by lack of foresight, which give rise to unemployed workers and disused machinery. The institution of money is, as we have maintained throughout, a device for the provision and extension of additional information in a complex, decentralised economy. As the economy expands from a small tribal group, in which everyone knows everyone else, to a vast, *impersonal* industrial system, the increase in uncertainty is inevitable. In truth, the uncertainties in a modern, decentralised system are *so* great that it could not function unless institutions had developed to provide the additional information flows necessary.

The possibilities for disequilibria arise from lack of information within a decentralised economy. Uncertainty is inherent in the structure of this economic society; money is a device for mitigating that uncertainty. Without the information flows obtained by the use of money (or by some alternative or equivalent informational system), the system could not function. Even with the advantages accruing to the economy from the use of money, the uncertainties are still so pervasive that maladjustments and unemployment occur.

A monetary system is, therefore, a necessary adjunct for the development and expansion of a decentralised economy. But the institution of money, which allows such decentralisation within the economy, is then sometimes blamed for the disequilibria which subsequently arise.[2] Professor Shackle, for example, argues that disequilibrium is a *monetary* phenomenon. Thus he writes:[3]

---

[1] In his book on *Inflation Policy and Unemployment Theory: The Cost-Benefit Approach to Monetary Planning* (Macmillan, New York, 1972) especially pt 1 on 'Modern Unemployment Theory.' See also *Microeconomic Foundations of Employment and Inflation Theory*, ed. E. S. Phelps (Macmillan, New York, 1970) especially the paper by A. A. Alchian, 'Information Costs, Pricing, and Resource Unemployment,' pp. 27–52.

[2] A more centralised economy should be able to avoid certain forms of disequilibria which arise from the inconsistent decisions of independent decision-makers within a decentralised economy; thus a totalitarian state should manage to eradicate unemployment. But the more fundamental problem of obtaining, processing and reconciling information on the economic desires and capabilities of members of the economy remains. In a totalitarian, centralised economy individual wishes have less outlet. The centralised economy may, therefore, avoid certain forms of disequilibria but usually at the cost of functioning less efficiently to satisfy the real wants of its members.

[3] *The Years of High Theory: Invention and Tradition in Economic Thought 1926–1939* (Cambridge University Press, 1967) pp. 90–1.

Now when, instead of an equilibrium model, we suppose one where each producer must decide what size of output to produce and offer, of his own kind of product, on the basis of his mere *conjecture* of the demand curve facing him, there is nothing to ensure that the revenue (price times output) resulting from this offer will be, in the event, the amount which his decision assumed. Nonetheless if all today's conjectural income is intended, by those who expect it, to be spent on today's products, the total of revenue will necessarily, in the event, equal the total of these conjectural incomes, and a shortfall of one person's revenue below his expectation will be exactly compensated by an excess of others' revenue above their expectations. Thus in the model or assumed system where the only acceptable means of purchasing today's products is other of today's products, *total* demand and supply in value-unit terms are necessarily equal. It is only when we introduce a *substantive* means of purchase, one which does not merely *represent* today's products but exists or arises in its own right, *outside* the list of products, that total demand and total supply can be unequal. It is *money* which destroys the necessary, inevitable equality which they have in a· barter or virtual barter system. Money, of course, could not do so in the general *equilibrium* system, where indeed its independent existence would be meaningless and any role beyond that of unit of account non-existent. If we cared to construct a general equilibrium system where 'money' entered on the same footing as current products, the system of simultaneous equations determining this equilibrium would have to specify the conditional intentions in respect of spending or accepting money, and the enlarged system would still show an equality of that total of demand and supply which included offers and demands for money. For in a general equilibrium system we suppose that each action-chooser has full relevant knowledge, provided for him by the equilibrating mechanism whatever its precise nature and mode of working. Inequality of total demand and total supply, to be logically possible, requires the presence and the play of both *ignorance* and *money*. Ignorance, in the real world, there is indeed: ignorance of the future. And money is that institution which permits *deferment* of specialised, fully detailed choice. [Italics in original.]

In my opinion Professor Shackle is exaggerating the responsibility of the institution of money for the occurrence of disequilibria and unemployment. It is fair to argue that the existence of money, and other financial instruments, facilitates the separation of the decision to invest from the decision to save, and thus increases the likelihood of disequilibria in goods markets. Nevertheless, I would contend that it was the inconsistency of these decisions, and not the existence of a *monetary framework per se*, which made it easier for such decisions to be taken independently (with a resulting greater chance of inconsistencies occurring), which was responsible for the disequilibrium. Indeed, the maladjustments which occur in a monetary economy could also appear in a barter society, though probably in a much more muted form.

In a monetary economy people paid in money may choose to buy at existing prices fewer consumer goods than have been produced, leading to involuntary stock building. For various reasons the producers, faced with a (temporary?) fall in demand, may then choose to reduce output (and employment) rather than prices. But similarly in a barter society, a potter, for example, faced with a fall in the amount of corn or pigs, offered in return for his output of pots – perhaps because corn and pig producers were retaining more of their own output – has to decide whether to accept the lower price for his full output, or to withhold some of his pots from the market. If his reservation price is such that some of his current output goes into stock, he will probably decide to cut output in the subsequent period. He will then have spare time which he can fill with searching for an alternative, or secondary, occupation; or just waiting hopefully for demand to recover. If his training as a potter endows him with specific human capital, the return from alternative unskilled occupations may be far below his usual income in his profession. In such cases, if the price elasticity of demand for pots is (believed to be) low, the potter of this example will tend to respond to fluctuations in demand by varying his activity.

That such disequilibria could, and did, occur in atomistic, free-enterprise societies, resulting in unemployment, was an obvious and disturbing fact. The problem was how to cope with it, within the context of a democratic, pluralistic society. This was the key issue of debate between Keynes and the 'classical' economists during the Depression in the 1930s. The 'classical' economists argued, with apparent reasonableness, that the coexistence of unfulfilled wants and unemployed resources must be due to frictions and inefficiency within the market mechanism. The correct response should, therefore, be to improve that mechanism. If the problem was due to failure of market prices, especially wages, to adjust appropriately to fluctuations in demand, then surely the right response would be to try to increase the (downward) flexibility of wages and prices – in the interest of the unemployed, even though not to the advantage of those remaining in employment?

Keynes, however, argued[1] that, whereas price/wage flexibility might lead to a smooth adjustment to fluctuations in the *relative* pattern of demand, it was not a suitable approach to coping with an *aggregate* deficiency in demand, caused by an excess of *ex ante* saving over *ex ante* investment. In a general equilibrium model, where certainty is assumed, all hypothetical demand and supply functions are known, i.e. how much people want to buy and sell in each contingency. Then the existence of an excess supply of labour and unfulfilled wants (at a less than full employment position) could be easily cured by shifts in relative prices, in this case by a fall in wages relative to prices. In the real world the unemployed can only signal their demands subject to the constraint of their available funds, and producers only receive signals about realised demand, not about the notional demand that would result, say, in a full employment situation. In such circumstances the dynamic process of price/quantity adjustments need not be stabilising.[2]

If all wages and prices went down by X per cent, then real wages, real profits, etc., would remain unchanged. In the absence of money illusion, the functional relationship between the real levels of saving and investment desired and the level of real incomes would not then alter in response to a once-for-all proportionate shift in all prices. Moreover, the relationship between prices and wages, given the level of wages, presumably reflected the entrepreneur's view of his most favourable (profit maximising) trade-off between higher output with lower margins and a lower output with higher margins. So any attempt to cut wages more than prices might worsen the situation by causing a fall in consumption and output, more than offsetting the encouraging effect of any increase in margins; while a larger imposed fall in prices than in wages might temporarily encourage consumption and output, but only at the expense of further erosion in profit margins, confidence, investment and the continued viability of firms.

Even so, the reduction in money incomes, as prices and wages fell, would lead to a rise in the ratio of money balances to incomes. Moreover, the monetary authorities might seek to encourage expenditure by an expansionary monetary policy. In the standard *IS/LM* analysis, however, the transmission mechanism whereby financial factors affect the real economy is assumed to run entirely via changes in the yield on bonds. So any factors tending to prevent declines in bond yields would, therefore, frustrate the equilibrating influence of increases in real money balances, as prices fell. Keynes believed that the reduction in such interest rates, especially at the long end,[3] in response to increases in real money

[1] *The General Theory of Employment Interest and Money* (Macmillan, London, 1936) see especially chap. 19, 'Changes in Money-Wages.'

   On this point see R. W. Clower, 'The Keynesian Counterrevolution: A Theoretical Reappraisal,' from *The Theory of Interest Rates*, ed. Hahn and Brechling, pp. 103–25, also reprinted in *Monetary Theory*, ed. R. W. Clower (Penguin Modern Economic Readings, Baltimore, 1969) pp. 270–97.

[3] *The General Theory of Employment Interest and Money*, pp. 201–4, 266–7; for a detailed exegesis of Keynes's views on this issue, see A. Leijonhufvud, *On Keynesian Economics and the Economics of Keynes, passim*, e.g. pp. 202–3, 282–314, 354–85, 401–16.

balances, might be restrained and limited by speculation on some future rise in bond rates, based on regressive expectations of rates returning to normal levels. This implied that, at least in the short run until a longer historical experience of continuously low (short) rates led to a reassessment of the 'normal level' of rates, it might not be possible to depress the (long) rate of interest below some positive level, at which level the determinants of investment and saving might not allow full employment to be attained. This hypothetical situation is shown in Fig. 10.2.

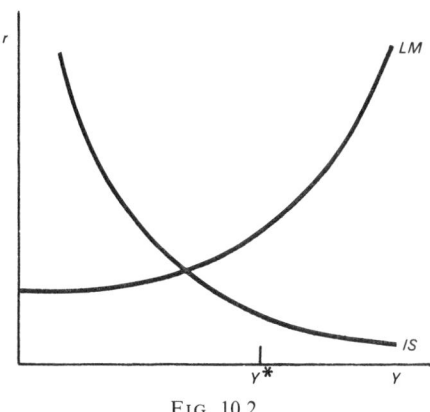

FIG. 10.2

In Fig. 10.2 the *IS* curve is depicted as consistent with full employment (Y^* being the full-employment level of incomes) at a nominal interest rate greater than zero, even though the liquidity trap – the horizontal section of the *LM* curve – in this example prevents that point being reached. Whereas empirical research has not produced much evidence in the historical periods examined of liquidity traps at low but positive interest rates,[1] it is undeniable that, so long as a monetary asset with a zero interest rate and no carrying costs exists, it will not be possible to force nominal interest rates below zero. So, if the *IS* curve should cut through the horizontal axis (where $r_b = 0$) before full employment was attained, it would not be necessary to appeal to speculative forces trapping interest rates at some positive level in order to show that full employment would not be restored by an expansionary monetary policy. Certainly it is possible to imagine depressed conditions with existing unutilised capacity where industrialists might not invest even if money could be borrowed at zero interest. But it is also true that as r_b approaches zero, so the value of a non-redeemable fixed-interest bond (e.g. Consols) approaches infinity. Even if changes in wealth should have a fairly weak effect on private-sector consumption (an issue to be discussed further in the next section), the enormous appreciation in value of public-sector bonds as the interest rate fell towards zero would surely engender consumption in excess of income, i.e. dis-saving. On these grounds it would seem fair to assume that the *IS* curve will always be consistent with full employment at a nominal rate greater than zero.

If the transmission mechanism of monetary stimuli was routed entirely via changes in the yield on government bonds, and variations in such yields were in turn restricted by speculative forces, leading to a liquidity trap, then it would be possible to envisage a stable

IS/LM equilibrium at less than full employment.[1] The excess of aggregate potential (full-employment) supply over demand in this state would continue to impose downwards pressure on wages and prices. But this fall in prices, in the initial Keynesian analysis, appeared to have no effect in increasing real demand. Therefore the fall could go on continuously, and the price level thus appeared to be indeterminate.

B. 'Inside' and 'Outside' Assets; and Wealth Effects

An indeterminate price level, despite a given stock of nominal money balances, was a concept which most economists with any appreciation for classical economic theory found hard to swallow, even if they accepted much, or all, of Keynes's other analytical reformulations. The way out of this difficulty was found by realising that the net financial wealth of the private sector would be raised by continuing falls in the price level, even if nominal interest rates remained sticky.[2] Even if a general reduction in wages and prices left real wages, real profits and real incomes unchanged, it would lead to an increase in the real value of public-sector fixed-interest financial liabilities, both monetary and bonds, whether marketable or non-marketable, held by the private sector (assuming unchanged interest rates).

It would, of course, also lead to a similar rise in the real value of monetary and other fixed-interest claims held by certain members of the private sector as claims on other members of the same sector. But by the assumption, implicit or explicit, of homogeneity of all the elements within the private sector, which allows their combination into a single aggregate, the effect on the behaviour of their holders of changes in the value of such intra-sector assets will be exactly matched and cancelled out by an equal and opposite effect on their issuers. We shall consider at more length in due course whether this postulate is acceptable, but for the moment it is sufficient to note that if the conditions for aggregation are met, then the behaviour of each aggregate sector depends on its holdings of real assets

---

[1] Conversely, speculative forces based on regressive expectations of a 'normal' level of rates might check upwards movements in interest rates; indeed at times markets seem unwilling to allow bond prices to fall below some support level. For example, in the United Kingdom for several years up till 1973 the approach of bond yields towards a 10 per cent level – on a number of occasions – seemed to call forth stronger demand. Yet there is no symmetrical possibility of a stable *IS/LM* equilibrium at greater than full employment, with a given nominal money supply, because speculative purchases of bonds are limited by the given size of the outstanding nominal stock of money, and within that by the need to maintain increasing transaction balances, as inflation raises the value of money incomes. One might, in turn, wonder whether the existence of a fixed stock of public-sector bonds would not equally set a limit to the persistence of a liquidity trap, but it should be remembered that this analysis was developed in the United Kingdom in the 1930s, at which time the size of the public-sector debt was historically – and on international comparisons – very large relative to the money supply or to the level of national income, so that debt sales by the private sector could continue on a very large scale over time without running into supply constraints.

[2] The principal architect of the reconstruction, to use a phrase coined by L. A. Metzler in his paper on 'Wealth, Saving and the Rate of Interest,' *Journal of Political Economy*, vol. 59 (April 1951) pp. 93–116, was A. C. Pigou, in particular in his book on *Employment and Equilibrium* (Macmillan, London, 1941) chap. 7; also see his paper on 'The Classical Stationary State,' *Economic Journal*, vol. 53 (December 1943) pp. 342–52. This whole subject, involving the integration of monetary and value theory, was further developed by D. Patinkin, in his book on *Money, Interest and Prices* (Row, Peterson, Evanston, Ill., 1956) and became the focus for much discussion in the 1950s and early 1960s; see, for example, H. G. Johnson's review article on 'Monetary Theory and Policy,' *The American Economic Review*, vol. 52, no. 3 (June 1962) pp. 335–84, reprinted in *Monetary Theory and Policy*, ed. R. S. Thorn (Random House, New York, 1966) especially the section on 'The Classical Dichotomy and the Neutrality of Money.'

and net financial claims on 'outside' sectors only. Claims on other elements within the same sector, 'inside' claims, cancel out. The terms *outside money* (i.e. monetary assets of the private sector in the form of claims on the public sector, or on a foreign country, or even holdings of real assets, e.g. gold) and *inside money* (i.e. monetary assets held within the private sector which are also liabilities of members of that same sector) follow taxonomically.

After a fall in the price level the ratio of outside monetary assets to incomes and expenditures and also to other assets, e.g. real capital, whose price will have fallen along with the general decline in prices, would rise. Even at the existing pattern of yields holders of money balances would want to switch into other assets, thus raising the demand for these other assets. The decline in prices would also raise the proportion of the net worth of the private sector held in the form of public-sector bonds, along with the increase in real money balances. The public would presumably then wish to make net sales of bonds at the initial set of relative yields, in order to purchase real assets. The process of portfolio readjustment should, therefore, lead to an increased demand for real assets, until the yield on such assets fell sufficiently to restore equilibrium (as the price of investment goods and the stock of capital rose), but conceivably could lead either to a rise or a fall in the yield on government bonds. The increased ratio of money balances to incomes might appear to presage a fall in bond yields, but the increased ratio of bonds to total wealth would suggest bond sales (increases in bond yields) in order to restore the desired portfolio balance.

Falling prices could, therefore, impart a financial stimulus directly, via the wealth effect, to private-sector demand for assets, without any need for reductions in interest rates. And at some point the increase in the value of 'outside' assets would lead, with a given level of real incomes, to an expansion of real consumption. So in time a decline in prices should expand real demand sufficiently to restore full employment. It is, however, widely accepted – as will be noted in greater detail subsequently – that in practice this real balance effect is weak,[1] and that a decline in prices may unleash other, possibly stronger, responses leading to further deflation.

One reason why an increase in the value of 'outside' assets may only have a relatively weak effect on expenditure is that an increase in the value of public-sector bonds may not leave the private sector feeling any better off. So the response to an increase in the real value of 'outside' financial assets, after a fall in the price level, may differ depending whether these outside assets are monetary balances or bonds. The point is that the future interest payments on the bonds, which are now more valuable in real terms, have to be financed somehow. If the interest payments are financed out of taxation or from higher charges on public goods, the present values of these future taxes, or charges, will rise in line with the present value of the bonds. On these grounds it can be argued that a rise in the present real value of 'outside' bonds does not represent a real increase in the 'wealth' of the private sector.

It is, however, presumably also open to the authorities to meet the future interest payments by printing money for the purpose, but if the economy is already at full employment the extra monetary expansion would cause inflationary pressures, effectively taxing existing holders of money balances and those who had not been able to anticipate the inflation. Perhaps it would be possible to argue analogously that even when the economy was underemployed, monetary expansion to pay the interest charges would reduce the rate of deflation and thus lower the return to holders of money balances, but this argument is thin.

---

[1] The omission of such real balance effects from early Keynesian analysis is generally regarded as lessening the rigorous tidiness of the theoretical construct rather than a major defect requiring revisions to be made to the practical policy implications of that analysis. The main attacks on Keynesian policy prescriptions, primarily from monetarist quarters, have not concentrated their fire so much on the omission of wealth effects from the basic (IS/LM) model, but much more on the restrictions in the paths of substitution, along which monetary stimuli can pass, which are imposed in the Keynesian model.

Of more importance as a counter-argument, the form of the future arrangements for financing the interest payments, and the incidence of the burden between individuals, even whether the present holder will be alive, remain uncertain. Even if the increase in the present value of the future financial imposts matches the rise in the present value of the bond, the latter is here and sure while the former represents an uncertain future contingent liability. An asset in the hand is worth more than a contingent future liability in the bush. Thus an expectation of future higher tax charges (in real terms) to meet the interest payments is likely to offset some, but not all, of the expansion resulting from a higher present value of 'outside' public-sector bonds.

Furthermore the same general argument, about future contingent liabilities acting as an offset to the value of existing assets, can be more widely applied, for example to property rights. Consider, for example, the grant of monopoly rights for the provision of a service, e.g. banking, or telephone communication, or the production of a good, which grant, we may assume, raises the value of the capital employed in that industry. Has real wealth increased? The present value of the capital stock may have risen, but that will be more than offset by the rise in the present discounted value of the costs to the public of the goods and services being provided, as the monopolist cuts output and raises price. Indeed, once one abandons simple accounting definitions of wealth to consider how future contingencies are affected in an uncertain world, or to search after consumer and producer surpluses, or to estimate areas under the hypothetical demand curve, it is dubious whether it is possible to arrive at any operationally practical and consistent definition of wealth. Nevertheless, it is worth keeping in mind the distinction between changes in the accounting value of balance sheets and changes in people's subjective opinions of how well off they feel themselves to be. The former may be used as a proxy for the latter, but may not be a very good proxy in all cases.

In my view, therefore, attempts to adjust the accounting value of a sector's present wealth position to take account of possible associated changes in future contingent costs or benefits leads only into a conceptual slough. Rough and ready though it may be, the private sector's wealth should be taken as the sum of the present value of its holdings of real assets and financial claims on other 'outside' sectors.

In a closed economy the 'outside' financial claims of the private sector are the liabilities of the public sector. Yet some economists[1] continue to reckon in their estimates of the wealth of the *whole economy*, i.e. aggregating over both the private and the public sector, the monetary and (more rarely) the other financial liabilities of the public sector to the private sector, which are intra-sector liabilities within the economy as a whole and, therefore, on accounting principles should cancel out.[2,3] The argument is advanced that the public

---

[1] 'Pesek and Saving start with three entirely correct propositions: Commodity money and fiat money are assets to their holders, but in no meaningful sense debts to anyone. Hence, they should be included in the consolidated net wealth of the community without any offsetting entries.' So commented M. Friedman and A. Schwartz in their paper on 'The Definition of Money: Net Wealth and Neutrality as Criteria,' *Journal of Money, Credit and Banking*, vol. 1, no. 1 (February 1969) p. 2, when reviewing the arguments of B. Pesek and T. Saving, *Money, Wealth and Economic Theory* (Macmillan, New York, 1967).

[2] As, indeed, happens in accounting estimates of national wealth, see, for example, J. Revell, *The Wealth of the Nation: The National Balance Sheet of the United Kingdom, 1957–1961* (Cambridge University Press, 1967) chaps 1 and 3; R. W. Goldsmith, *The National Wealth of the United States in the Postwar Period* (Princeton University Press, 1962); *The Measurement of National Wealth: Income and Wealth, Series VIII*, ed. R. W. Goldsmith and C. Saunders (Bowes & Bowes, London, 1959).

[3] There is a valid argument that, at any rate in a perfectly competitive system, the creation of any new form of financial asset/liability must leave people better off, otherwise they would not have voluntarily chosen to hold such assets in their portfolios. But this argument, of course, applies to all financial assets, e.g. unit-trust units, life-assurance policies, house mortgages, etc., and not just

(*Footnote* [3] *continued on p. 205*)

sector's monetary liabilities involve no interest burden and never have to be redeemed, and so do not represent any liability to anyone. They are, on the other hand, held as assets. If they rank as assets, without any corresponding liability, then they must add to net wealth.

Examine, however, the accounting relationships. Consider the case where real asset X is held by a private-sector entrepreneur financed by borrowing from a bank, which advances are balanced by private-sector holdings of deposits. Now assume that the industry and asset are nationalised, and that the purchase of the asset is financed by issuing currency which is used to buy the asset from the entrepreneur who pays back the bank advance. Certainly the portfolio balance of the bank has now changed, and there will be a subsequent readjustment resulting from the shift in the bank's reserve/deposit ratio, but that adjustment is logically quite separate from any changes in wealth arising up to this point from the rearrangement of asset holdings and financial indebtedness between the private and public sectors. If we examine this latter, the private sector has lost control over real assets of X and obtained instead monetary claims on the public sector of X. Thus the private sector's wealth has not changed,[1] nor similarly has the public sector's. Yet if we aggregate over the two sectors and continue to include the public sector's monetary liabilities, real assets remain the same, but the public sector's monetary liabilities have risen. Has the economy's real wealth actually increased by this rearrangement of asset holdings? Surely not!

If this increase in the private sector's holdings of outside money, in return for a sale of real assets to the public sector, subsequently led to an expansion of real output (but not of prices), as factors of production (labour and capital) already in being were more intensively used and new investment undertaken, then those who include the public sector's monetary liabilities in wealth would record this as a double increase in the value of wealth, the increase in the value of real capital (human and non-human) plus the increase in monetary liabilities. If, on the other hand, the increase in the private sector's monetary holdings led to inflation, rather than to an increase in real output, then there would be no increase in wealth from either source. An increase in the outside money holdings of the private sector may count as an increase in wealth (in a fully-employed economy) only in the interval between receiving the money and spending it, since such expenditures drive up prices thus restoring real balances to their initial level. Does this seem sensible?

Next assume that the public sector acquires real assets from the private sector, and then expends them in a war, e.g. tanks, aircraft and ships, or shoots them off to the moon, e.g. rockets. In this case the private sector has the same wealth as before, with more financial claims on the public sector – perhaps in monetary form – and fewer real assets, but the public sector now has dead-weight debt, liabilities not backed by assets. Has the wealth of the whole economy remained unchanged by the destruction of real assets, if these have been bought from the private sector by issuing money (this ignores though the possible

---

to money. The question is then whether the present market value of the institutions, including those within the public sector presumably, providing these financial intermediary services closely reflects the extent to which the economy has benefited by the existence of such institutions. I am very sceptical whether the relationship between calculated market values and real welfare is at all close, because of differences in market organisation (e.g. the degree of monopoly), institutional arrangements, etc. For example, in the United Kingdom in 1971 and 1972, following an institutional change and much increased profits, the market value of banks rose dramatically. Could anyone seriously argue that the benefit to the economy from the existence of a banking system had increased during this period to the same extent?

---

[1] According to B. Pesek and T. Saving, *Money, Wealth and Economic Theory*, if I have understood them correctly, this rearrangement would actually lead initially to a fall in private-sector wealth. Not only has the private sector lost X of real assets, but also the repayment of the bank advance, raising the reserve ratio, temporarily lowers the value of the banking system's power to create money (see chap. 4 especially). Their analysis seems extraordinarily convoluted to me.

returns – of various kinds – from being prepared to fight wars or go to the moon), or has it declined? Surely the latter.

In reality the great bulk of public-sector debt has been incurred to finance the acquisition of real assets, e.g. on nationalisation, or to fight wars, but the analysis of wealth effects is often done on the example of an issue of currency to finance the purchases of goods and services from one sector of the private sector for passing on as a transfer payment to another sector. In this case the real assets of the private sector remain unchanged (ignoring the second-round effects of the monetary expansion on prices or output) but their monetary claims on the public sector have risen, so their wealth has indubitably risen. Equally the monetary liabilities of the public sector have risen but, since they do not have to redeem these, is anyone worse off? If not, has not wealth increased?

Certainly the economic situation has now changed, but to describe this as a change in wealth runs counter to valid accounting principles. The essence of the situation is that the *behavioural* response of the two sectors to indebtedness between themselves is not identical, but it is desirable not to confuse such behavioural differences with statistical estimation of net-wealth positions. To take an analogy, if income is transferred from rich to poor, net consumption may increase because the behavioural response of the gainer and loser may differ, but this does not make a case for claiming that aggregate income is changed by the initial transfer. Similarly, an increase in the private sector's holdings of real financial claims on the public sector is likely to cause an increase in the private sector's expenditure, which need not be offset by a similar decrease in the public sector's expenditures as a result of its larger real outstanding liabilities. The public sector can never go bankrupt, despite having liabilities in excess of assets, though its executants can lose power. So the public sector does not have to worry about solvency when financing its deficits. Instead the main constraint is that the methods adopted, whether expropriation, charging, taxation or monetary creation, should not cause political dissent among the populace.

In short, the real balance effect, or more broadly the effect on total expenditures of an increase in the value of the private sector's financial claims on the public sector, is basically a distributional, or differential response, effect rather than a pure wealth effect. The question then arises whether such differential effects may not be more widespread. The disparate behavioural responses of the public and private sector are implicitly recognised by separating, disaggregating the two for purposes of analysis. The aggregation of the various elements within the private sector equally implies the assumption that their behaviour is similar, so that distributional 'wealth' effects will not occur. But is this latter assumption valid? It would seem very dubious.

There are surely systematic differences between companies and persons. For example, worries about bankruptcy must be generally of more immediate concern to companies, who are usually net financial debtors, than to persons, who are in the main net financial creditors; moreover, bankruptcy will tend to have just as, or more, disastrous an effect on the careers of company managers, who are unlikely to survive the ensuing liquidation or fundamental reorganisation of their bankrupt company with their careers unscathed, as on persons, the penalties for personal bankruptcy no longer being vindictive.

There might, therefore, be significant economic consequences resulting from shifts in the balance of financial indebtedness between groups within the private sector, especially between companies and persons. In particular, a decline in prices will raise the burden of the net fixed-interest liabilities of companies and raise the value of such assets held by persons. In contrast with the public sector's insouciance for the value of its outstanding liabilities – because it cannot be bankrupt – the company sector will become increasingly subject to the risk of bankruptcy, as its equity is eroded and interest payments take a larger share of the cash flow. Not only will this danger tend to restrict company expenditures, because the growing risk will raise the cost of finance even with a constant level of (riskless) interest rates (Chapter 5, Section B) and because fear is likely to depress initiative, but also the actual occurrence of bankruptcies will instantly check expenditures and reduce wealth. Indeed, as is well known, any large bankruptcy can have 'domino' effects on other companies as its failure reduces, or even eliminates, the value of other companies' claims upon it, imperilling their own solvency and liquidity.

When 'wealth' effects *within* the private sector are considered, the greater danger of bankruptcy to companies suggests that continuing price deflation would have deleterious effects on real expenditures, driving the economy further from equilibrium. Professor Minsky has often emphasised the potential danger of the debt/deflation spiral.[1] The deflationary impact on the economy of such 'wealth' effects within the private sector may very well exceed the expansionary influence of 'wealth' effects from 'outside' claims on the public sector. In part it may depend on the particular historical structure of debt within the system. Thus one contributory reason to explain why the great slump in the 1930s was much worse in the United States than in the United Kingdom may be that the higher ratio of company fixed-interest debt to public-sector fixed-interest debt in the United States imposed much more serious deflationary wealth effects in that country.

To summarise, we have been examining the behavioural response of certain distinguishable sectors to changes in their balance-sheet positions. When this change takes the form of an increase in the financial liabilities of one sector matched by a corresponding increase in the financial assets of another, with market yields, etc., remaining unchanged, the economic response of the two sectors need not be exactly offsetting. The main factor responsible for such differential responses is the relative concern about bankruptcy of the various sectors. This is greatest in the company sector and least in the public sector. A decline in prices raising the real value of all fixed-interest debt is likely to have deflationary or reflationary effects depending on the initial pattern of the debt structure.

---

[1] For example, in his articles in *The Bankers' Magazine*, vol. 214 (October, November and December 1972) and vol. 205 (February and March 1968) and in his paper 'Can "It" Happen Again' from *Banking and Monetary Studies*, ed. D. Carson (Irwin, Homewood, Ill., 1963) pp. 101–11.

11

Inflation

SUMMARY

Another reason why a general reduction in wages and prices might not stimulate a depressed economy is that it would be likely to generate expectations of further price falls. The process of sequential decision making in modern economies tends to produce autocorrelated price movements. It is more realistic to expect the rate of change (rather than the level) of prices to remain constant. In Chapter 10 a simple relationship between price inflation and the extent of spare capacity was postulated, which now has to be adjusted to take the anticipated rate of inflation $(E\dot{P})$ into account, as expressed in the following relationship

$$\dot{P}_t = b_0 + b_1 \frac{1}{UE_t} + b_2 E\dot{P}$$

In theory b_2 should equal unity. If, as suggested, $E\dot{P} = \dot{P}_{t-1}$, then the rate of inflation will accelerate, stabilise or decline, as the sum of

$$\left(b_0 + b_1 \frac{1}{UE_t} \right)$$

is greater, equal or less than zero. This formulation suggests that only in the short run can an advantage in higher real output and real incomes be obtained from running the economy at an inflationary pressure of demand. In the longer run inflation would accelerate without limit, the long-run Phillips curve being vertical, and no advantage at all in higher real output would remain to offset against the worsened rate of inflation. Most historical experience has, however, suggested that wage/price adjustments, even in the longer run, are rather less volatile than this analysis would suggest; the value of b_2, from the above relationship, calculated in empirical studies using data from the 1950s and 1960s was usually well below unity, often in the region of 0·5. But in recent years inflation has accelerated through the Western world, despite in some instances a higher average level of unemployment. This may reflect the evaporation of the last vestiges of money illusion, a growing consciousness of inflation.

How far are strictly monetary factors responsible for this dynamic process of inflation? Monetary expansion (deflation), if maintained with sufficient vigour over a number of quarters, should be *sufficient* to stimulate (deflate) the economy to a point (of capacity utilisation) where inflation begins to accelerate (to subside). The process of inflation will of itself reduce the level of real money balances. Unless the nominal stock of money is augmented, this reduction in real money balances should (in most circumstances) raise interest rates to a level high enough to deter expenditures and check the inflation. Thus an increase in the money stock is *necessary* for a *continuing* process of inflation to persist. Monetary expansion is not, however, necessary for the *initial* generation of inflation, which may be due to supply shortages, e.g. of energy and raw materials, war demands, wage-push (as in the United Kingdom in 1969), etc. Once inflation has begun, for whatever reason, the authorities are then left with the unpleasant choice between accommodating the going rate of inflation, by allowing monetary expansion, or of subjecting the economy to deflation and unemployment. But, when governments did steel themselves to take the second course, the resulting recessions were so politically unpopular that they felt forced to change course before they had much success in moderating inflation, which thus accelerated from cycle to cycle during the 1960s and 1970s. As inflation accelerates, strains within the economy develop.

Although there will be, at any point of time, some 'equilibrium' or 'natural' rate of unemployment, so defined that if the economy is run at a higher pressure of demand inflation will accelerate, the level of this natural rate is not exogenously fixed. One way of reducing the strains within the economy is to seek to lower the natural rate, so that the economy can be run at a higher, more acceptable pressure of demand without generating inflation. This is the purpose of prices and incomes policy. By restraining the sequential, independent process of wage bargaining, it might allow all workers to achieve together a higher level of real incomes with a lower rate of price inflation. The history of such policies is not, however, encouraging and such forms of direct intervention have increasingly damaging effects on resource allocation and efficiency over time.

A. Price Expectations

One reason, set out in the previous chapter, for doubting whether a general deflation of wages and prices would have a beneficial effect in restoring a depressed economy is that distributional 'wealth' effects within the private sector, as the debt/deflation process attacks the company sector, could overwhelm any expansionary wealth effect from private-sector holdings of 'outside' financial assets. An even more compelling argument is that a deflationary process is quite likely to lead to expectations of further falls in prices. So far in our analysis it has been implicitly assumed that at all times the best expectation of the price level in a future period would be that it would remain at the same level as now, that all changes in prices were believed to represent once-for-all changes, with no greater probability of a continuation of such price movements in future periods than of a reversal – back to some previous level.

It might be possible to envisage economies in which successive price movements were not correlated, i.e. when a fast rate of inflation in period t would give no indication of the probable rate of inflation in subsequent periods, $t + n$. In fact in our economies cyclical fluctuations in real demand and the atomistic nature of the economy, in which my price and wage decision will be influenced by your previous decision – without any mechanism to allow a simultaneous adjustment, and even perhaps a quasi-equilibrium, to be achieved – tends to lead to positive autocorrelation in price movements, so that if prices have fallen in the last period the best estimate of future price movements will be that they will fall again in the next. Indeed, a better forecast on historical experience is that the *rate of change*, rather than the level, of prices will remain constant, i.e. that the rate of inflation is as likely to increase as to decline in the future.

So a decline in prices is likely to give rise to expectations of future falls. Such prospective price movements will affect the expected relative yield on holding real capital as compared with fixed-interest financial debt. The expected rate of decline of prices would involve an equivalent expected advantage in holding fixed-interest financial debt rather than real assets whose market value is expected to fall over time. So relative yields have to be revised to take into account such expectations of future price movements. The prospective yield on an asset, after adjustment for these expectations of future price movements, is often described as the 'real' rate of interest: this 'real' rate is, however, a very impalpable construct depending on fleeting expectations.

Expectations of declining prices are, therefore, likely to cause a shift in demand from real to financial assets. *Ceteris paribus*, there would be a fall in the demand for real assets, and investment demand would decline. Furthermore, the propensity to save might rise, as the return on delaying expenditures until the expected future fall in prices had occurred became increasingly apparent. Expectations of future price falls, by raising 'real' interest rates, given the level of nominal rates could therefore depress real activity in the economy even further.

Similarly, expectations of future inflation should stimulate further expansion in demand. In practice, however, it has been remarkably hard to observe any strong response in investment demand or the propensity to consume, at least in the United Kingdom, to fluctuations in the rate of inflation. Indeed, at times businessmen have actually alleged that inflationary worries were the cause of *reductions* in investment plans. It may be, however, that uncertainties about the future response of the authorities to the worsening inflation raise the risks of proceeding with an investment and associated financing plan. In so far as accelerating inflation makes planning more difficult, so caution becomes the watchword.

Moreover, nominal interest rates have probably tended to vary quite closely with changing expectations of price inflation, presumably as both lenders and borrowers take the prospective rate of inflation into account in their calculations. So the real rate of interest in the economy has not been significantly reduced by inflation. For example, if it was assumed that real rates of interest, on Consols in this case, remained absolutely constant since 1945 at, say, 3 per cent,[1] the implied path of expectations of the rate of inflation (obtained by subtracting 3 per cent from the nominal Consol rate), shown as line A in Fig. 11.1, would look remarkably plausible. This may be compared with the actual rate of inflation, estimated as $(P_{t+12} - P_{t-12}/2P_t) \times 100$, where P_t is the retail price index, line B. The graph shows how in the immediate post-war period expectations, influenced by memories of the aftermath of the First World War, consistently underestimated the persistence of inflationary pressures. And the upsurge of (world) prices at the time of the Korean War was also treated as a temporary aberration, having little effect on nominal interest rates. From the late 1950s onwards, however, the course of nominal interest rates has accompanied changes in the pace of inflation very closely, which accords with the hypothesis that expectations of inflation are the main determinant of the level of nominal interest rates and that the current rate of inflation is, in 'normal' circumstances, taken as the best guide to the likely future rate of inflation.

Indeed, the rapidity of the response of nominal interest rates to changes in the pace of inflation, during the last fifteen or so years, is remarkable. The theory of the interaction of expected inflation and nominal rates of interest, derived from Irving Fisher,[2] usually has included a hypothesis of adaptive expectations, whereby expectations of inflation depend on some distributed lag of past inflationary experience. In general this formulation ensures that during periods of accelerating inflation, expectations and, therefore, nominal interest rates would lag behind actual inflationary experience. Furthermore, the higher nominal interest rates should reduce the demand for money (and private-sector wealth); with a given stock of nominal money balances (and bond holdings) there would then be some fall in real rates of interest. Therefore an acceleration in inflation would, on this

---

[1] Recent work by P. H. Hendershott and J. C. Van Horne, 'Expected Inflation Implied by Capital Market Rates,' *The Journal of Finance*, vol. xxviii, no. 2 (May 1973) pp. 301–13, p. 312 especially, suggests that during the 1960s the estimated real rate of interest on bonds in the United States fluctuated quite narrowly around the 3 per cent level. During the nineteenth century in Britain, a period of general price stability, the rate of interest on Consols remained close to 3 per cent. 'Among the economists who gave evidence to us Sir Roy Harrod and Professor J. R. Hicks gave particular attention to this concept of a normal rate of interest. Both of them regarded a yield on Consols of about 3 per cent as having historically some claim to be regarded as the norm, . . . Professor Hicks (in his paper on *The Future of the Rate of Interest*) bases his belief in the norm on a review of the last two hundred years,' *The Radcliffe Report*, paras 567–8.

[2] One statement of his theory can be found in his book on *The Theory of Interest* (Macmillan, London, 1930) pp. 399–451.

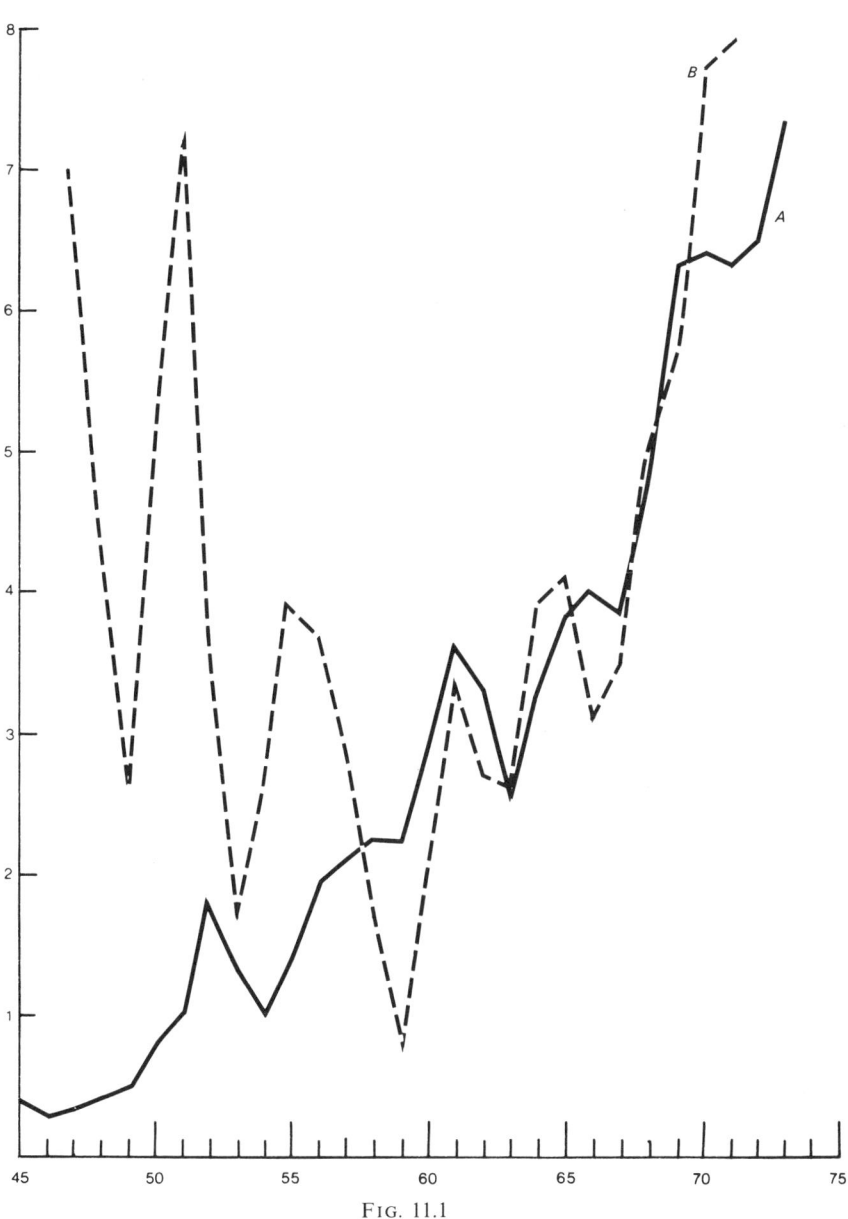

FIG. 11.1

account, be reflected partly in higher nominal rates of interest but also partly in lower real rates and greater output.[1]

But if people formulate their expectations rationally, these should not systematically diverge from actual experience. Indeed, their expectations should not be continuously worse than the predictions of economic models, the results of which are in any case often published. Furthermore, if one assumes an economic system without money illusion, where economic plans are all made in real terms, then foreseen changes in the rate of price inflation should become very quickly embodied in nominal interest terms, as Sargent (ibid.) has recently argued.

And it became increasingly obvious to people during these years that each time the rate of inflation went up another notch, whether owing to expansionary demand management, wage push or imported inflation, the government of the day had little stomach for imposing sufficient prolonged deflation and unemployment to reverse the previous jump in the rate of inflation. Whatever the going rate of inflation was, the authorities would validate it. Indeed, in these circumstances the surprising feature is, perhaps, the relatively slow rate of acceleration of inflation.

If the pressure of demand is sufficiently high in any period to generate an increase in the rate of inflation from some previous steady level – given that the best estimate of the future is for no change in the current rate of inflation – then the resulting real wage rate will be less than will have been expected and less than the bargaining strength of labour under conditions of high demand should provide. Other decision-makers, besides labour union leaders, taken unawares by the acceleration in the rate of inflation will incorporate this new information into their pricing decisions in the next period. At the start of Chapter 10 a simple relationship between the rate of inflation (price changes) and the pressure of demand (the extent of spare capacity) was posited. Now this relationship needs to be adjusted to take the anticipated rate of inflation into account. This may be expressed in an equation of the form

$$\dot{P}_t = b_0 + b_1 \frac{1}{UE_t} + b_2 E\dot{P}$$

where b_0 is a negative constant representing, *inter alia*, the trend growth in productivity, UE represents the level of unemployment, and enters the equation in this way in order to capture the non-linearity of the relationship, $\dot{P}$ represents the rate of price inflation and $E\dot{P}$ the anticipated rate of price inflation. In the absence of money illusion, one would expect decision-makers to attempt to achieve some desired *real* outcome for wages, profits, etc., and this implies that the coefficient b_2 on $E\dot{P}$ should be 1. Of course, we cannot observe exactly how expectations are formed, but people are likely to make efficient use of existing historical information on the time path of inflation. If in previous years changes in the rate of inflation have not exhibited autocorrelation, then the best expectation of the forthcoming rate of inflation would be that it would not change from its recent pace, except in so far as other current developments, whether political or economic, e.g. elections of a new government or devaluation, give grounds for revising forecasts. Under these circumstances the best expectation of current inflation should be for a continuation of the previous rate, so that

$$E\dot{P} = \dot{P}_{t-1}$$

Given the values of b_0 and b_1, there should be some value of UE such that

$$b_0 + b_1 \frac{1}{UE_t} = 0$$

---

[1] On this subject see T. J. Sargent, 'Rational Expectations, the Real Rate of Interest, and the Natural Rate of Unemployment,' *Brookings Papers on Economic Activity: 1973, 2* (The Brookings Institution, Washington, 1973) pp. 429–80.

In this case, from the previous argument, $\dot{P}_t = \dot{P}_{t-1}$, so that if the level of unemployment is at this 'equilibrium' level, then the current rate of inflation, whatever it may be, will persist. If

$$b_0 + b_1 \frac{1}{UE_t} \lessgtr 0$$

over time, then the rate of inflation must continually accelerate (>0) or decelerate (<0), as the faster (slower) inflation from each period becomes built into anticipations. In any short period the existence of a given set of expectations, and indeed of a given set of contractual arrangements, will, however, act as a check to price flexibility, and so a change in the pressure of monetary demand will bring about a (temporary) change in the utilisation of factors of production and in the rate of growth of output (and not just a readjustment in price levels). As discussed previously in Section A of Chapter 9, these (short-term) adjustments in capacity utilisation and output growth may be ascribed to errors in foresight in an uncertain world. In my view, however, miscalculation of the likely future rate of inflation is not the main feature in our economies causing quantitative disturbances, unemployment, inflation, etc. A greater difficulty is to be found in the fact that our large, complex, simultaneous economic system runs on the basis of a multitude of relatively small-scale sequential decisions.

Be that as it may, decision-makers will presumably learn from their past errors in predicting the rate of inflation, and adjust their expectations on the basis of unfolding historical experience. Thus in the longer period it will become increasingly hard to maintain a very high level of capacity utilisation – at a pressure of demand greater than that consistent with a constant rate of inflation – without incurring ever-accelerating inflation. In the short run, therefore, the relationship between capacity utilisation and inflation may allow a considerable gain in output to be had for a limited increase in inflationary pressures, but in the longer term it will be neither attainable nor desirable for the pressure of demand in the economy to diverge far from that level which will stabilise the rate of inflation.

Thus the short-run relationship between capacity utilisation and inflation, frequently termed the Phillips curve, is likely to look quite different from the long-run relationship, as shown in Fig. 11.2.

In practice, however, most historical experience has suggested that wage/price adjustments are rather less flexible – or perhaps volatile – than the preceding analysis would

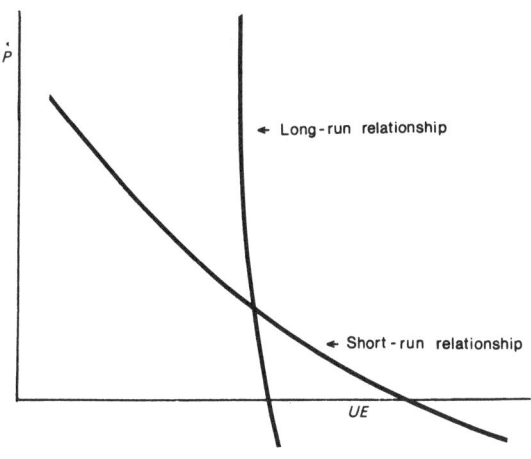

$\dot{P}$

← Long-run relationship

← Short-run relationship

UE

FIG. 11.2

suggest. For example, most econometric studies of a Phillips curve relationship of the form

$$\dot{P}_t = b_0 + b_1 \frac{1}{UE_t} + b_2 E\dot{P}$$

(where $E\dot{P}$ in turn is derived from a distributed lag on previous prices), in industrialised countries during the 1950s and 1960s found values of b_2 well below unity, often in the region of 0·5.[1] A number of reasons were advanced to account for this, for example that, so long as inflation remained below some threshold, it was easier and simpler – and approximately as good – to assume a zero rate of inflation as laboriously to incorporate some small and uncertain expectation into all calculations.

In any case in the last few years conditions have changed abruptly in several countries. The previous, relatively stable relationship, with $b_2 < 1$, seemed to break down, and inflation in several countries continued, or even accelerated, despite high levels of unemployment. Indeed, in the United Kingdom, assuming that the value of b_1 remained constant at its pre-1969 level, it would have required values of b_2 in excess of 1 in order to explain, in terms of this very simple relationship, the acceleration in wages and prices since 1969. It may be that recent experience reflects the evaporation of the last vestiges of money illusion, as inflationary pressures intensified during the latter years of the 1960s for a number of reasons (Vietnam, devaluation in the United Kingdom, etc.). It is still, however, too early to give any confident explanation for the general world-wide acceleration in inflation in the early 1970s. There were, no doubt, a number of contributory factors besides an increasing consciousness at all levels of the ravages of inflation.

B. Is Inflation a Monetary Phenomenon?

Monetary expansion will have a stimulating effect upon the economy, even though the exact transmission mechanism may be obscure and the process of uncertain strength and timing. Depending upon the existing availability of spare capacity, and current expectations, a general stimulus to money incomes will lead in part to a rise in real output and in part to a rise in prices. The less the availability of spare capacity and the more flexibly expectations of price inflation are revised upwards, the larger the relative effect upon inflation. Thus monetary expansion (contraction) if undertaken with enough vigour[2] over a reasonable length of time, say two or three years, should be sufficient to cause inflation (price deflation).

If there was an inflationary increase in prices and money incomes, without any matching increase in nominal money balances, say as a result of wage push by militant unions, then the ratio of money balances to incomes and to other (real) assets would be falling. The inflation, if expected to persist, would, however, also lower the real return on money, so it is conceivable that people would be content with their reduced real money balances, or even

---

[1] The sum of the coefficients on lagged price changes in the Phillips curve (wage equation) incorporated in the S.S.R.C.–M.I.T.–Penn (S.M.P.) model of the U.S. economy, at least in its 1971 form, was 0·57. Solow undertook special studies of this relationship in both the United States and the United Kingdom and also obtained values for b_2 of about 0·5; *Price Expectations and the Behaviour of the Price Level* (pamphlet) (Manchester University Press, Manchester, 1969), and 'Recent Controversy on the Theory of Inflation: An Eclectic View,' from *Inflation: Its Causes, Consequences and Control, A Symposium*, ed. S. W. Rousseas (New York University Press, 1968) pp. 1–16.

[2] In an open economy with a fixed exchange rate, domestic credit expansion (contraction) may lead to flows of funds out of (into) the country and thus cause changes in that country's international reserve holdings rather than have domestic monetary consequences, see Chap. 14.

find them excessive. In this latter case of a flight from money, inflation would make people unwilling to hold even such reduced real balances, and the attempt to purchase other assets with these excess balances would raise inflation further. This kind of reaction could set a hyperinflationary spiral into motion. In practice, however, empirical research into inflationary and hyperinflationary situations suggests that the system is not potentially explosive in this manner, except at extraordinarily high rates of inflation,[1] in part because expectations of future inflation may be slow to adjust to reality but mainly because the demand for money is not very elastic to relative yields. Indeed, hyperinflations have most often been due to a persistent attempt by the authorities to obtain command over a larger proportion of real output and real assets by continued monetary expansion than the economy, usually disrupted by war and/or political strife,[2] was able, or prepared, to support.

So, unless nominal money balances are increased, inflation will normally reduce real money balances below the level which, at the given relative real yields, people will desire. Nominal interest rates must therefore rise to restore portfolio equilibrium. If an inflationary situation develops in which prices, having been previously stable, now rise and are expected to go on rising by 5 per cent per annum, then this will lead to a *once-for-all* reduction of 5 per cent in real yields on financial assets with a given nominal interest rate. So long as nominal balances are held constant, the (assumed steady) inflationary process then reduces real money balances in each period, and therefore there must be a *continuing* rise in nominal and real interest rates in each period to restore equilibrium. It follows, therefore, that maintaining constant nominal money balances, in the face of a continuing inflation, must eventually – and probably not too long delayed – lead to a rise in both nominal and subsequently of real yields on financial, fixed-interest securities, sufficient to cut back on monetary demand for goods and assets and cause a decline in the pressure of demand and in the pace of price inflation.

Subject, therefore, to only a few minor qualifications, it is possible to claim that monetary expansion is both necessary and sufficient for continuing price inflation. If variable X is both necessary and sufficient for the achievement of variable Y, does it not follow that variable X can be described as the cause of variable Y, or in this context that inflation is a monetary phenomenon?

In my view it is possible, but not always helpful, to regard inflation as a purely monetary phenomenon, despite accepting that monetary expansion is both a sufficient and necessary condition for inflation. Three reasons will be adduced for this convoluted view. In the first place the fact that a monetary stimulus *can* be sufficient to cause the onset of inflation does not mean that such bouts are invariably generated by prior monetary excesses. For example, a major acceleration in inflation in the United Kingdom got under way in the final quarter of 1969. Yet monetary conditions, whether measured in terms of the rate of growth of the aggregates, e.g. money stock or domestic credit expansion, or in terms of nominal (or estimated 'real') interest rates, had been progressively tightened in the previous twelve months, until the stance of monetary policy by the autumn of 1969 had become severely restrictive, by post-war standards at any rate. To virtually all observers the recrudescence of inflation at this time was the immediate consequence of a sudden jump in the going rate at which wage negotiations were being settled following a successful, and much publicised, strike by local authority workers, and the complete collapse of the Government's

---

[1] See, for example, P. Cagan, 'The Monetary Dynamics of Hyperinflation,' in *Studies in the Quantity Theory of Money*, ed. M. Friedman (University of Chicago Press, 1956) pp. 25–117, and A. A. Shapiro, 'Inflation, Lags and the Demand for Money,' *International Economic Review*, vol. 14, no. 1 (February 1973) pp. 81–96.

[2] A recent example of an inflationary process of this kind is provided by the experience of Chile during Allende's government, and an earlier example by the experience of Indonesia during Soekarno's government.

policy of maintaining some control over prices and incomes earlier in the summer. This was a straightforward example of wage-push forces giving impetus to the inflationary spiral.[1,2,3]

Other developments, for example rising prices abroad, sudden shortages of raw materials and energy sources, wars and social disturbances, etc., can also unleash inflationary pressures. When such non-monetary factors are the initial cause of the inflationary condition, does it help to argue that the inflation remains none the less purely a monetary phenomenon? On the other side, it may be argued, whatever may – or may not have been – the original reasons for the acceleration of inflation, for example in the United Kingdom in 1969/70, it could have been checked by sufficiently restrictive policy, fiscal as well as monetary, capable of preventing any subsequent expansion in the money stock from accommodating the rise in money incomes. The authorities could, at least in principle, have used such policy to check inflation. They did not do so; *ergo* their handling (or mishandling) of policy is responsible for the inflation.

This argument is rather akin to blaming the medical authorities for the outbreak of an epidemic, whatever its proximate cause. The medical authorities could presumably have designed a system of quarantine, etc., to prevent the spread of the epidemic. They did not do so; therefore they are responsible. Whatever reasons the medical authorities may have for not isolating the community from the risks of an epidemic, the authorities do have a reason for not always stepping on the brakes, e.g. by raising taxes or pushing up interest rates, sufficiently hard to stop inflation in its tracks. The reason is that deflation is extremely painful and unpopular,[4] and in an uncertain world it is never clear how much

---

[1] The resurgence of inflationary pressures in early 1972, following the coal miners' successful strike, is a less clear-cut case, since demand management policy was being highly expansionary at exactly the same time.

[2] It is sometimes asserted that trades unions cannot use their monopoly power to generate wage-push inflation since their use of monopoly powers can only give them a once-for-all advantage, as monopolists *vis-à-vis* their less well-organised comrades. Thus M. Sumner in his note on 'The Current Inflation: A Programme for Control,' *The Bankers' Magazine*, vol. 215, no. 1550 (May 1973) pp. 231–6, commented, 'The logical flaws in the argument that inflation is caused by trade unions have often been stated. For example, monopoly is associated with prices higher than would otherwise obtain, not with prices rising more rapidly than they otherwise would. . . . Thus, to provide a convincing explanation of the wage explosion in terms of trade-union militancy, and to justify the associated policy prescription, it would be necessary to demonstrate a substantial growth in the power of the unions or a remarkable change in the attitude of their leaders, all within a period of five years or so.'

But this implies that the less well-organised unions, or pensioners, or whoever, are prepared to give up some of their relative share of real income, or cannot prevent it, in order to allow the strong unions to obtain more. If the strong are trying to improve their relative position, while everyone else is determined to maintain his relative position, there is bound to be pressure on the economy until the level of demand is brought down to that point at which so many people's positions are weakened that they can no longer in aggregate bid for income shares which exceed the total available output.

[3] Without controlled experiments no example can be entirely straightforward. Other economists, for example D. Laidler, would ascribe the developments in 1969 mainly to a lagged response to the earlier devaluation in 1967, and indeed to the previous monetary expansion that had necessitated that step. One may, however, ask why the lags in this case were so long, and whether their length was not affected by the Government's prices-and-incomes policy.

[4] For a contrary view, see the empirical evidence and analytical arguments set forth by G. J. Stigler, 'General Economic Conditions and National Elections,' *The American Economic Review*, papers and proceedings, vol. 63, no. 2 (May 1973) pp. 160–7, in which he denies that variations in unemployment or in real incomes have affected, or should affect, political popularity. Okun's

(*Footnote* [4] *continued on p. 217*)

deflation will actually be required, or over what time span, to achieve some given desired deceleration in inflation. Therefore the normal tendency is to shade policy so as to avoid the risk of further suffering in the form of unemployed resources even at the expense of greater risks in accelerating inflation, though this also causes suffering and injustice. Ultimately this is a political – not an economic – choice, depending on the preferences of the electorate and politically-powerful sub-groups, for inflation as compared with unemployment.

If the control of inflation by demand management, by monetary restriction sufficient to cause considerable unemployment and distress – even if only for some finite, but indefinite, period – is so unpopular, it does not really help to blame the authorities for responding to the general will of the public in being reluctant to take sufficiently strong measures to halt inflation. Moreover, if it is so painful to control inflation, once under way, it will be the more worthwhile to prevent conditions ever developing that will give it an initial impetus (though it is not easy to imagine how this could be done).

The second reason for baulking at acceptance of the view that inflation is a purely monetary phenomenon is that the relationship between monetary expansion and inflation runs via the effect of such expansion in stimulating demand, with the relationship between demand and inflation then depending on the level of spare capacity, expectations, etc. Neither link in this relationship is precise. In particular, as already noted in Chapter 9, the transmission mechanism between monetary changes and fluctuations in total demand is not clearly perceived, and of uncertain strength, particularly in the United Kingdom. The relationship between monetary expansion and inflation is therefore the less sure, because of the weakness of the link between monetary changes and variations in the pressure of demand.[1] It would, therefore, provide a more accurate representation of the fundamental relationships involved to state that inflation was a function of the pressure of demand in the economy, given the state of expectations, etc., and that monetary policy was an instrument, of uncertain but potentially considerable strength, which could be used to influence the pressure of demand. Moreover, monetary policy is neither the only nor in many cases the most predictable instrument of macro-economic demand management.

This reformulation would be especially helpful in illuminating the implications of the arguments of those who emphasise the direct relationship between the rate of growth of the money stock and inflation. Occasionally, and usually by the non-academic adherents of monetarism, the link between monetary changes and inflation is presented as a way of slowing the rate of inflation painlessly, as well as reasonably certainly. Presumably then the only reason why the authorities do not take it is because they are knaves or fools. The beguiling attraction of simple, painless solutions to difficult problems would evaporate if, instead, the analysis was presented to the public that inflation was mainly a function of the pressure of demand at which the economy is run and that monetary policy was a means, an uncertain means but perhaps one of the most powerful, for controlling that level.

---

comments, ibid. pp. 172–7, arguing the case for believing that fluctuations in real incomes would in some circumstances affect political popularity, seem in my opinion more realistic. For further empirical studies of the historical evidence of the relationship between economic conditions and political success, see C. Goodhart and R. Bhansali, 'Political Economy,' *Political Studies*, vol. 18, no. 1 (March 1970) pp. 43–106, and G. Kramer, 'Short-Term Fluctuations in U.S. Voting Behavior, 1896–1964,' *American Political Science Review*, vol. 66 (March 1971) pp. 131–43.

---

[1] For example, the previously calculated statistical relationships in the United Kingdom between the broad monetary aggregates and the level of money incomes completely broke down in 1972 and 1973, as reported by M. Artis and M. Lewis, 'The Demand for Money: Stable or Unstable,' *The Banker* (forthcoming), and G. Hacche, 'A Review of Demand for Money Relationships,' *Bank of England Quarterly Bulletin* (forthcoming).

Concentration on the direct long-run relationship between money and prices[1] serves to veil an underlying relationship of rather starker contours, between unemployment and inflation. As noted in the previous section, basic theory suggests that there will be some level of unemployment at which the rate of inflation will be stabilised; below that it will accelerate; above that it will decelerate. It is the level of utilisation of capacity, proxied by the level of unemployment, that is achieved and maintained that will determine whether inflation accelerates, stabilises or slows. It is hardly too simple to claim that those who press for slower monetary growth to halt inflation are really asking for a higher rate of unemployment to be maintained, at least for some indefinite period until inflationary expectations are diminished.

Most monetarists admit that a cure for inflation entails higher unemployment, and argue further that this has to be accepted as inevitable.[2] Moreover, they claim that soft-hearted reluctance to clutch this nettle simply allows inflation to accelerate further and will, therefore, make any subsequent correction more painful and of longer duration. This is essentially the crux of the problem. If their view is correct, the outlook for democratic industrialised capitalist societies in the West is bleak. The level of unemployment attained during periods of recession during the late 1960s and early 1970s in these economies was not sufficient in most cases to bring about any significant check to the rate of inflation, which tended to accelerate from cycle to cycle. Yet such recessions were usually sufficiently politically unpopular to force governments to limit both the extent and the duration of each recession before they had any tangible evidence of real success in dealing with inflation. In short, popular political pressure enforces a level of unemployment – on average over the cycle – at which inflation can only accelerate. As inflation does accelerate, economic, industrial and political strains are likely to mount; as Marx would note, there appear to be contradictions in capitalist economies and an unstable politico-economic dynamic, which could well lead to the adoption of a more centralised, controlled economy, whether the political colour of the regime was nominally left or right wing.

It is, however, just possible to take a more optimistic view. Essentially, the monetarist analysis views inflation as a response to variations in the pressure of demand around some 'natural' level of spare capacity (unemployment), at which market forces in the economy would lead to a stabilisation in the rate of change of prices. There is no denying the great importance of variations in the pressure of demand in the inflationary process. What can be challenged in this analysis is the acceptance of a *given* level of unemployment as the 'equilibrium' or 'natural' level at which inflation would stabilise. Professor Friedman argues that this 'equilibrium' level, which he has called the 'natural rate' of unemployment, is obtained from the grinding out of the various demand and supply functions within the general

---

[1] This relationship certainly exists. Over the longer run the variance in the inflation rate will be closely associated with the variance in money growth. Putting this proposition another way, if money growth had been observed to be constant, then one would expect to have observed a much lower variance in the rate of inflation. The relevant question is what one should deduce from this. Monetarists claim, on the basis of such propositions, that inflation is owing to the fault of the monetary authorities. The monetary authorities see themselves rather as constrained by short-run political imperatives. It is, indeed, not the province of the economist to animadvert on what may, or may not, be politically possible, but it is equally mistaken to ascribe the cause of a general political problem to technical, monetary developments which are themselves a function of the political milieu.

[2] Some, usually the non-academic publicists for monetarist policies, do not put their suggestions in this bare form, because they fear that such policies would then have little chance of general acceptance. In my view an emphasis on the direct links between money and inflation, without revealing the transmission mechanism via the pressure of demand and unemployment, is a form of subterfuge, promising the pleasure without mentioning the associated pain.

Walrasian system.[1] The theme of this book, however, is that modern monetary economies working under conditions of uncertainty do not approximate to a Walrasian general equilibrium system.

The forces that determine the level of unemployment (spare capacity) consistent with the stabilisation of inflation are probably many and various, several of them more social and structural[2] in character than purely economic. In this respect cost-push pressures can, perhaps, be defined as those forces pushing the equilibrium or natural rate of unemployment upwards. *There is no good reason for believing this rate to be stable;*[3] it might vary considerably in response to changing union militancy, differing institutional arrangements for negotiating wage settlements, unemployment benefits, labour re-training schemes, etc.

For example, after 1969 inflation in the United Kingdom shifted into a new higher range than in any recent peace-time period, despite a persistent higher level of unemployment from 1969 till 1972 than in any period since the depressed 1930s. Monetary expansion at the time was admittedly rapid, but why should a much larger proportion have been reflected in rising prices and a smaller proportion in rising output than would ever have been expected with that higher level of spare capacity on the basis of previous experience? A monetarist explanation tendered by Professor Walters[4] is that trade union leaders, and others, were by then looking to the rate of growth of the money stock as the best indicator of future rates of inflation, so that monetary expansion (and perhaps contraction?) had a more immediate, direct effect on inflation and a much reduced impact on output. This is a most ingenious hypothesis, but one would expect it to be supported by some institutional evidence to show that union leaders did behave in this way. None has been proffered.[5]

---

[1] In his presidential address to the American Economic Association on 29 December 1967, reprinted under the title 'The Role of Monetary Policy,' *The American Economic Review*, vol. 58, no. 1 (March 1968) pp. 1–17, especially pp. 7–11.

[2] For example, G. Perry has examined the effect of changes in the structure of labour markets, in the composition of the labour force (e.g. age–sex ratios) on the relationship between unemployment and inflation; see his paper on 'Changing Labor Markets and Inflation,' *Brookings Papers on Economic Activity: 1970, 3*, ed. A. Okun and G. Perry (The Brookings Institution, Washington, 1970) pp. 411–48.

[3] It is common ground among economists of most schools of thought that the natural rate can vary and could, in principle, be consciously altered by policy actions. The more difficult question is to find the best policies to achieve this in practice.

[4] Professor Walters's study of the relationship between monetary movements and fluctuations in incomes in the United Kingdom in 'Money in Boom and Slump,' *Hobart Paper*, 44, 2nd ed. (Institute of Economic Affairs, 1970) especially the postscript to this second edition, pp. 54–5, revealed some curious empirical relationships, which are difficult to interpret in the light of the theories discussed in this chapter. Thus in the 1920s and 1930s when there was considerable spare capacity, monetary changes appeared to be mainly associated with (subsequent) fluctuations in price levels, whereas in the post-war decades when the economy was near full capacity monetary movements tended to be more closely associated with swings in output. On *a priori* grounds one would have expected the opposite relationships, that monetary fluctuations would have a larger proportionate effect on real output when spare capacity was high.

[5] Sargent, 'Rational Expectations, the Real Rate of Interest, and the Natural Rate of Unemployment,' *Brookings Papers, 1973, 2*, has argued that systematic changes in the money supply should influence rational expectations of prospective inflation, and – in an economic system where the supply function took a form consistent with the assumption of a given natural rate of unemployment – would influence only price changes and not movements in real output.

His model, however, is of a closed economy with an exogenously-determined money supply. In an open economy, under a regime of fixed exchange rates, such as the United Kingdom up till 1972, the direction of causation is more likely to run from money incomes to the money stock. Results for the United Kingdom consistent with this view have been obtained in an exercise replicating Sims's exercise in the United States on 'Money, Income, and Causality,' *The American*

(*Footnote* [5] *continued on p. 220*)

An alternative, and on the evidence more plausible, hypothesis is that a combination of growing union militancy and the crumbling of the government's prices and incomes policy in the summer of 1969 shifted the equilibrium, natural rate of unemployment decisively upwards. Despite the use of macro-economic demand management instruments in such a way that actual unemployment rose to post-war record levels, and stayed there for several years, the previous wage explosion, and the further inflationary expectations thereby generated, prevented demand management from achieving much more than a stabilisation of the position in 1970 and 1971. Then in 1972, despite the high level of unemployment, the successful breakthrough to a new high in wage increases by the miners, consolidated by the railwaymen, builders, engineers, etc., combined with the authorities imparting a strong stimulus to demand for the purpose of reducing the level of spare capacity in the economy, led to the imminent danger of a further jump in the rate of inflation. Meanwhile, the money supply was growing relatively fast in order to prevent actual unemployment from increasing any more. In this story, therefore, the active force was the shift in the equilibrium, natural rate of unemployment. Once the government had decided on the appropriate actual pressure of demand to aim for, in order to manage the economy under such circumstances, the growth in the money stock had to be such as to accommodate this objective. The rate of monetary growth became the passive element.

In this context, of course, a prices and incomes policy can be seen as a method of trying to reduce the equilibrium, natural rate of unemployment, in order to allow the rate of inflation to be checked without having to run the economy at a politically unacceptable low level of demand. The hope is that by intervening to influence the institutional arrangements for determining wages and prices it may be possible to reduce the 'equilibrium' rate of unemployment, and also that the policy may into the bargain have some favourable impact on expectations. This may not work very well. Such intervention is bound to have increasingly deleterious effects over time on the allocation of resources. By reducing efficiency and productivity it could thereby even exacerbate cost-push inflationary pressures and have, in the end, a perverse effect. The evidence of previous attempts to follow such a policy is not very encouraging. The institutional, social and political factors that help to determine the equilibrium, natural rate of unemployment are often deep-rooted and slow changing, so that Government attempts at intervention may only exacerbate industrial relations or do no more than impose a temporary and inefficient camouflage upon underlying conditions.

It is sometimes, wishfully, suggested that if only workers would learn, from experience or from propaganda, that higher wage demands and cost inflation lead to unemployment, then they would voluntarily reduce their demands in order to avoid such a painful outcome. Unfortunately this overlooks the problems caused by the decentralisation of decision-making, already noted in Chapter 10. A union leader, or wage bargainer, is uncertain of the behaviour (partly in response to his own initial actions) of other union leaders and wage bargainers. He might prefer the price stability and lower unemployment that could result if *all* wage demands were simultaneously restrained. But if he should unilaterally hold back his own demands to a greater extent than other union leaders/wage bargainers, his own members will have suffered a certain loss in relative real incomes, for which he is clearly to blame, for very little apparent advantage in aggregate employment and real expenditure. The loss in relative real incomes would be concentrated among his own

---

Economic Review, vol. 62, no. 4 (September 1972) pp. 540–52; this note on Sims's results by Goodhart, Gowland and Williams, 'Money, Income and Causality: the U.K. Experience' (Bank of England, mimeo). It suggests that in the United Kingdom movements of incomes tended to cause subsequent monetary changes.

There are, therefore, two separable points, first whether a rational man in the United Kingdom would have looked at current monetary data as a guide to future inflation, and second whether, rational or not, union leaders actually did behave this way. In both cases the answer would seem to be no.

members. Any gain in higher-aggregate real expenditures, as the result of the slackening of inflation and the easier position for macro-economic demand management arising from his individual restraint, would be spread thinly over the whole economy. Just as it is not worth any consumer offering to pay for public goods, it is not worth any union leader voluntarily holding back his own members' wage demands in the public interest. One aspect of a prices-and-incomes policy is that it may, therefore, provide a surrogate form of centralisation of wage demands, allowing *all* workers to achieve a preferred higher level of employment and real incomes (with lower price inflation).

Direct intervention in the process of determining prices and wages is a policy of doubtful efficacy and with shaky intellectual credentials (though the basis for assuming a fixed 'natural' rate of unemployment is even more evanescent). Nevertheless, what is the alternative? Monetarists might, perhaps, hope to convince the populace that they should, in their own long-run benefit, accept whatever rate of unemployment is consistent with (first reducing and then) maintaining the rate of inflation at some acceptable level. In the meantime a political platform based on the theme that more unemployment would be good for us, and that they also serve who only stand and wait and suffer (and if they do not suffer it will not help, since the natural rate of unemployment would rise if unemployment was made a more comfortable condition), is unlikely to make much headway.

If we cannot shift the natural rate of unemployment down to a more acceptable level by a prices-and-incomes policy, nor make the existing, possibly fixed, natural rate more acceptable, the economies of the West will remain faced with an internal contradiction which may well serve to destroy the atomistic, democratic, capitalist structure of their existing system.

12

Monetary Policy

SUMMARY

In a world of certainty the authorities know the exact effect of varying their control instruments, e.g. through monetary or fiscal policy actions, upon the various objectives of policy, such as full employment, stable prices, etc. Difficulties will be encountered, however, whenever there are more objectives than instruments. In such cases not all objectives can be fully met, and the most that can be done is to achieve the best possible compromise (or trade-off) between the various objectives. An alternative, and apparently more attractive, approach is to search for further (independent) instruments. But it is a common experience to find that the employment of another instrument can reveal a threat to some further objective. Thus if demand management seems incapable of maintaining both a reasonable level of employment and price stability, the introduction of a prices and incomes policy to help in containing inflation may endanger, *inter alia*, the allocative function of the price mechanism.

The most common conflict is between jam today and jam tomorrow. Policy decisions taken with the intention of affecting the economy now are likely, in many cases, to influence outcomes in future periods because of the dynamic properties of the system. Thus in the short run, with given expectations, there can be scope for expanding the level of employment without a large acceleration of inflation. But the acceleration of inflation, small though it may be initially, then gets built into the system, thereby worsening future policy options. Similarly, Mundell's proposals for achieving short-term balance, both internally and externally, under a fixed exchange rate, can in some cases lead to a longer-run worsening state of affairs. Since the objectives of our society outnumber the instruments for their achievement, the most that policy can strive to attain even in a world of certainty is a fair compromise.

In the next section (B), uncertainty is introduced, but only in a limited form. The authorities are assumed still to know the structure of the system exactly, but not to be able to foresee the stochastic shocks that may perturb it. Despite the unreality of the assumption of perfect knowledge of the structure, much of economic forecasting, and policy choices that derive from these forecasts, proceed as if the deterministic models used were an accurate representation of the underlying system. The main subject of this section is how to cope with the random shocks that cannot be foreseen, even assuming the structural form of the deterministic model to be correct. Put simply, the answer is to identify where the main source of disturbance is likely to occur and to arrange a policy response, in the intervals between periodic reviews of the economy, which will provide an automatic stabilisation against shocks from this source. In the IS/LM context, if the main source of disturbance comes from shocks in the goods market (to the IS schedule), then the authorities should maintain a stable rate of monetary growth; if the shocks predominantly come in the money market (to the LM schedule), then it would be better to stabilise interest rates. Although theoretical explorations of optimal stabilisation policies along such lines have been much in vogue recently, their practical significance has probably been overstated. Given the assumption of a structurally-correct model, the analysis only has relevance over those periods during which the source and forms of shocks to the economy *cannot* be identified (and thus exactly offset) while reliable data on both the monetary aggregates and interest rates *can* be obtained. In fact, in the United Kingdom and in many other countries where monetary data are obtained only once a month, information about the development of the economy as a whole, e.g. industrial production, trade figures, etc., is available just about as soon and with the same (lack of) reliability as the monetary data. The concept of steering the ship by observing monetary signals, while waiting for the fog to clear from the economic landscape is, perhaps, peculiar to the North American scene. In other countries the monetary signals are also fogged out.

In any case the real problem for policy, raised in Section C, is that the forecasting models used are, to be sure, not accurate representations of the underlying world. Many economists ignore this problem, because each believes that his own preferred model is correct, but the policy-maker faced with a plethora of models and advice cannot. This difficulty is most acute when there is a widespread belief that existing models do not capture some important aspects of reality. This has been the situation in the United Kingdom in recent years; policy-makers and commentators generally have been persuaded, largely on the basis of reports and work emanating from the United States, that monetary factors have a significant impact on the domestic economy, but all the existing (extended Keynesian) forecasting models showed this impact to be negligible. So there has been a sharp dichotomy in the United Kingdom between expressions of beliefs about the working of the economy and the estimated structure of the forecasting models. In these circumstances it is difficult to choose an 'optimal' monetary policy, and the tendency, when faced with a policy instrument which is believed to be powerful but whose effects may not have been clearly measured, is to play for safety. This final section ends by reviewing exactly what playing for safety may entail in an inflationary world.

A. Objectives and Instruments

In the simple IS/LM model the level of incomes (Y) depends on autonomous factors, e.g. foreign demand for exports, affecting expenditure decisions and on the level of the money stock. If such autonomous factors (X) are taken as given, then the model can be easily transformed into a money multiplier of the standard form

$$\Delta Y = f(\Delta M \mid X)$$

where Y represents nominal incomes and M the money stock. Indeed, in the IS/LM model the policy instrument, which is always specifically mentioned, is the money stock, while the variable which policy-makers are presumably seeking to control is the level of incomes, by setting the level of the policy instrument (M) at that value which will bring the objective, i.e. incomes (Y), to its desired level (Y^*). The structural IS/LM model depicts the transmission mechanism whereby this occurs, and the parameters of the structural relationships show the size of variation in the control instrument necessary to achieve the desired objective. Of course, it was thought possible that in some circumstances, when a liquidity trap existed, changes in this control instrument might have no effect upon the objective. But this was always regarded as an unlikely, indeed pathological condition, and, as noted in Chapter 10, consideration of net wealth effects offered an alternative route whereby monetary stimuli could, theoretically, affect income levels even when nominal interest rates were held in a liquidity trap.

But the level of money incomes, Y, the apparent objective in the IS/LM model, is not in practice a true objective of economic management. Instead, policy-makers are concerned with the *composition* of any change in money incomes, applauding generally any increase in real incomes and output ($\dot{y}$) but deploring usually any (upwards) change in the level of prices ($\dot{p}$). Two consequences follow. The first is that it becomes necessary to consider how a change in money incomes becomes divided into a change in real incomes and prices respectively. This problem is not tackled in the *IS/LM* model or by the money multiplier approach, and the assumption that either prices or real output can be treated as autonomously given is obviously invalid. This subject was discussed in the previous two chapters. Without suggesting that the matter is solved, we may perhaps postulate for the purpose of this chapter that the relationships between changes in real income and prices can be reasonably described by equations[1] of the form:

$$\dot{y}_t = f(\dot{m}_t, \ldots, \dot{m}_{t-n}, \dot{p}_t, \ldots, \dot{p}_{t-n}, y_{t-1} - y_{t-1}^*, \ldots, y_{t-n} - y_{t-n}^*) \tag{1}$$

where y^* is full employment income, and

$$\dot{p}_t = f(\dot{p}_{t-1}, \ldots, \dot{p}_{t-n}, y_t - y_t^*, \ldots, y_{t-n} - y_{t-n}^*) \tag{2}$$

So there are now two objectives, $\dot{y}$ and $\dot{p}$, and only one instrument, $\dot{m}$. Indeed, we can simplify the structure of the above equations into a reduced form to describe the immediate choice set available of the kind

$$\dot{y} = a_1 \dot{m} + a_2 \dot{p}$$
$$\dot{p} = b\dot{y}$$

We can only obtain instantaneous values for the two objectives in combinations depending on the coefficients in the structural equations

$$\dot{y} = \frac{a_1}{(1 - a_2 b)} \dot{m}$$

and

$$\dot{p} = \frac{a_1 \cdot b}{(1 - a_2 b)} \dot{m}$$

The values of these coefficients will not, however, be constant over time, but will depend at each point of time on current conditions, i.e. they are dependent on the past history of the system, the previous lagged values of the endogenous variables (and the current and previous values of omitted exogenous variables, here y^*).

As set down, monetary measures directly affect only output, depending on the rate of price inflation and the level of spare capacity, while the rate of inflation, given previous inflationary experience, depends on the pressure of demand. Monetary developments would influence the rate of inflation directly if they were taken as signals of prospective future inflation and thus entered immediately into the formation of current inflationary expectations. We argued in Chapter 11 that this was not the case, in the United Kingdom at least, and have therefore excluded monetary variables from equation (2) (pp. 219–20).

A graphical example of such a relationship is shown in Fig. 12.1, with the line *MM'* showing the combination of $\dot{y}$ and $\dot{p}$ attainable as $\dot{m}$ increases. Although the simple algebraic example above made the relationship between $\dot{y}$ and $\dot{p}$ linear, Fig. 12.1 presents the relationship as curvilinear, in view of the full capacity constraint on y, and therefore on $\dot{y}$, given the

---

[1] Which, it may be noted, are quite similar in format to those contained in the St. Louis model of the economy developed by L. Andersen and K. Carlson in their paper on 'A Monetarist Model for Economic Stabilization,' *Federal Reserve Bank of St. Louis Review*, vol. 52, no. 4 (April 1970) pp. 7–25.

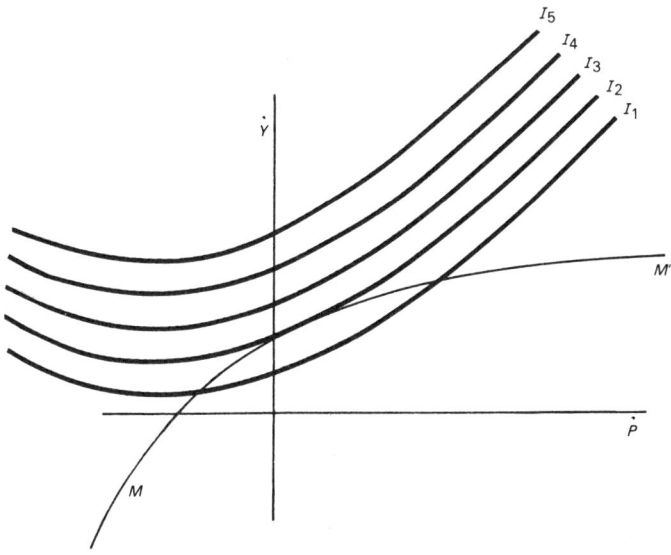

FIG. 12.1

initial level of real incomes,[1] y_{t-1}, and also of the downwards inflexibility of wages and prices during periods of unemployment and depression. Next we may imagine the shape of the community's indifference curves, derived from their utility function(s); they prefer larger real incomes and less inflation.[2] Given the initial level of real incomes, people may find the attractions of higher real incomes declining, and the possible disadvantages of accelerated change mounting as growth becomes faster, while on the other hand inflation may become an increasing nuisance as it rises to a level where it has to be continually borne in mind in all economic decisions. Thus the indifference curves must slope upwards to the right and will be convex to the origin. The optimal position, where the highest indifference curve is tangential to MM', must always occur before that level of full capacity where all additional monetary stimulus is translated into price inflation.

A more common representation of the same basic relationship is provided by the standard Phillips curve relationship, showing how general demand management can be used

---

[1] Given the initial level of real incomes, y_{t-1}, the higher the current *level* of incomes, y_t, is pushed, the higher is the current *rate of growth* of incomes, $y_t - y_{t-1}$. Thus if we are only concerned with the immediate short-term future, it does not matter greatly whether the real income objective is specified in terms of levels or rates of growth (though as noted subsequently the process of change itself may involve tensions). Over the longer term there can, however, be conflict between these two objectives. Running the economy at a persistently lower level of demand might possibly force fiercer competition and thus induce a more efficient economy with a faster rate of growth of productivity and innovation. Alternatively, it might be desired to slow down the rate of growth of the economy, e.g. to conserve scarce resources, but (especially with a continuing growth of productivity) this might make it difficult to sustain a full-employment level of incomes. Thus one should distinguish clearly between the two alternative real income objectives, relating to the level on the one hand and the rate of growth on the other, but while dealing only with short-term considerations, as above, the distinction can, perhaps, be left blurred.

[2] Experience of falling prices, if at all pronounced, may also prove to be unwelcome and unpleasant, as depicted in the indifference curves in Fig. 12.1, which turn slightly upwards in the upper left-hand quadrant.

to provide various short-run combinations of employment levels and price inflation. Again one can imagine, or even try to estimate,[1] the likely shape of the community's indifference curves and show what the hypothetical (short-run) optimum would be (see Fig. 12.2).

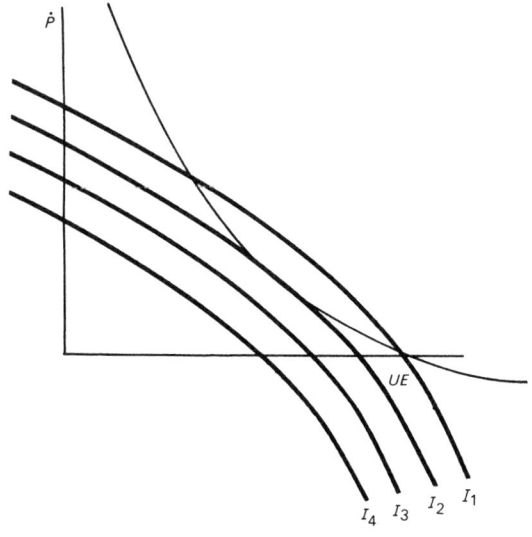

FIG. 12.2

So if there are two, or more, objectives (in this case current rates of output and inflation) and only one instrument, it is not usually possible to achieve the desired levels of both variables simultaneously. The best that can be done is to reach the preferred available *combination* of outcomes for the objectives. The natural response to such limitations on our ability to reach our desired targets is to search for another instrument. Thus if we have two objectives, X and Y, and two instruments, Q and R, so that

$$X = a_1 Q + a_2 R$$
$$Y = b_1 Q + b_2 R$$

we can achieve any desired values of X and Y simultaneously, so long as each of the instruments does have an effect on, at least, one of the objectives and also that $a_2/a_1 \neq b_2/b_1$ (i.e. that the two instruments are not simple linear transforms of each other in effect, having precisely similar relative impacts on the two objectives, but instead are independent).

It can be more difficult to satisfy these conditions than it may look at first sight. In the present example we have been considering ways of achieving certain output and price objectives through the use of monetary policy. Well, if monetary policy is not sufficient by itself to achieve the desired outcomes for both objectives simultaneously, why not appeal to that common alternative standby, fiscal policy? In the first place some economists

---

[1] M. Chossudovsky, 'Optimal Policy Configurations under Alternative Community Group Preferences,' *Kyklos*, vol. 25, no. 4 (1972) pp. 754–70, attempted to do this by questionnaire. Goodhart and Bhansali, 'Political Economy,' *Political Studies*, vol. 18, no. 1 (March 1970) pp. 43–106, tried to do it by observing the response of political popularity, as measured in the opinion polls, to changes in unemployment and inflation. Both methods have obvious flaws.

argue, and offer supporting evidence from the United States[1] that, given the level of the money stock, variations in the size of the budget deficit, financed by bond sales, will have little or no impact on the total of real output or on the rate of inflation, except in the very short run within the first few quarters. The argument is that the rising interest rates required to sell the additional bonds will 'crowd out'[2] in a relatively short space of time an equivalent value of other expenditures. Again, however, the supporting evidence in the United States comes from quasi-reduced form equations, money multipliers with additional fiscal variables, and the results, once more, seem inconsistent with the coefficients estimated in structural equations.[3] Moreover, there is no evidence from any source, including replications of quasi-reduced form equations, of strong crowding-out effects in the United Kingdom.[4]

So the first question is whether fiscal policy can affect the aggregate level of demand at all, or just the allocation of expenditure between different purposes (e.g. between expenditure on public or private goods). The majority of economists believe that fiscal policy can have a significant impact on the level of aggregate demand – indeed it is the instrument of demand management on which the greatest reliance is placed in many countries, including the United Kingdom. This does not, however, necessarily solve our instrument/objective problem, because the question remains whether fiscal policy affects output and inflation in a significantly different way than does monetary policy. Monetary expansion affects money incomes by stimulating the general level of demand, and so does fiscal policy; they are both instruments of demand management. As such they can hardly be expected to have significantly differentiated effects on the split of nominal incomes between real incomes and inflation. If so, fiscal policy is not in this context a separate, distinguishable instrument from monetary policy, so there would still be two objectives and one basic instrument, demand management.

Perhaps fiscal policy can be used in different ways – apart from its aggregate demand-management role – to influence inflation. Certain taxes, e.g. indirect taxes, and subsidies have a direct impact on price levels. Why not, therefore, reduce indirect taxes and raise subsidies to control inflation, and impose other taxes, say on incomes and profits, or raise interest rates and cut back on monetary growth in order to maintain aggregate demand at the desired level? But such policies will affect the allocation of expenditure between the subsidised goods and other output which must be cut back commensurately, and may affect the distribution of incomes and the returns to working, risk taking, etc. If we are also concerned with these outcomes, because they affect such objectives as growth, equity, etc., then the use of fiscal policy to affect inflation directly via taxes and subsidies may prevent the achievement of these other objectives. So it seems that we *could* find another, distinguishable instrument to influence inflation by varying the pattern of taxes, subsidies, etc., via fiscal policy, but it would then be necessary to recognise these additional fiscal objectives; so we would still be left with more objectives than instruments, and must continue to accept some compromises in the attainment of economic objectives.

If fiscal policy, as a demand-management instrument, is too akin to monetary policy in its effects on the economy to have a significantly different impact, clearly prices and incomes policy comes from a very different stable, so there is no question of similar effects.

---

[1] See, for example, L. Andersen and J. Jordan, 'Monetary and Fiscal Actions: A Test of Their Relative Importance in Economic Stabilization,' *Federal Reserve Bank of St. Louis Review*, vol. 50, no. 11 (November 1968) pp. 11–23.

[2] R. Spencer and W. Yohe, 'The "Crowding Out" of Private Expenditures by Fiscal Policy Actions,' *Federal Reserve Bank of St. Louis Review*, vol. 52, no. 10 (October 1970) pp. 12–24.

[3] See G. Fisher and D. Sheppard, *Effects of Monetary Policy on the United States Economy* (O.E.C.D. Occasional Studies, 1972) especially chap. 4.

[4] See, for example, M. Artis and A. R. Nobay, 'Two Aspects of the Monetary Debate,' *National Institute Economic Review*, no. 49 (August 1969) pp. 33–51, especially pp. 37–42.

Once again, however, there are those who doubt whether an incomes policy is an effective instrument. Do attempts to intervene directly in the process of wage negotiation and price fixing, for example, really have any significant effect on the rate of inflation?[1] Moreover, such intervention will tend to prevent relative adjustments of prices and wages from signalling the changing pattern of requirements and scarcities. The imposition of a policy of direct control will, therefore, progressively erode the allocative efficiency of the economic system,[2] with consequential effects upon other objectives such as growth. Moreover, the resulting changes to the institutional structure of decision-making within the economy may trespass upon certain political objectives, for example 'the participatory democracy of collective bargaining'. So in this case also the introduction of another instrument to control a recalcitrant objective only serves to draw attention to certain further objectives, which will be affected or even endangered by manipulation of the instrument in single-minded pursuit of one objective. For every possible cure, there seem to be two complications; for every possible instrument, more objectives appear in view; compromise is also the art of political economy.

A nice example of this discouraging phenomenon can be provided by reviewing the thesis, attributed to Mundell,[3] for using monetary and fiscal policy for the joint maintenance of internal equilibrium, i.e. some desired level of capacity utilisation, and external equilibrium, i.e. no pressure on reserves, under a regime of fixed exchange rates. Both monetary and fiscal policy affect the domestic economy as demand-management instruments, and also influence the balance of payments via changes in the pressure of demand domestically. In addition to this, monetary policy – but not fiscal policy – also affects the balance of payments directly by encouraging capital flows in response to changing international interest-rate differentials.

One can show graphically those combinations of monetary policy and fiscal policy, tightening monetary policy and easing fiscal policy,[4] or vice versa, that might achieve the same level of *domestic* demand, line AA' in Fig. 12.3. Since monetary policy has an extra bite, beyond influencing the level of domestic demand, in affecting external equilibrium, a relatively smaller change in monetary policy, compared to a given change in fiscal policy, would be necessary to achieve the same balance in external equilibrium. Therefore the line BB' in Fig. 12.3 showing those combinations of the two instruments giving the same external balance is steeper than line AA'. So with two instruments, separable and effective, monetary and fiscal policy, it would seem possible to achieve two objectives, internal and external balance.

Indeed, it is generally possible to achieve a desired *immediate* balance, both internally and externally under these circumstances by an appropriate combination of monetary

---

[1] See, for example, R. Lipsey and M. Parkin, 'Incomes Policy: A Re-appraisal,' *Economica*, vol. 37, no. 146 (May 1970) pp. 115–38.

[2] These deleterious effects are usually thought to be relatively slight in the short run, but to become increasingly severe as the controls are prolonged. The conclusion is then often drawn that a prices-and-incomes policy is only suitable as a short, sharp crisis measure, after which it would be put aside again. But this raises the empirical question whether a temporary policy of this kind would not lead only to an accumulation of repressed price and wage adjustments, which would break through with such a surge when the barrier was lifted as to undo any benefit from the previous restraint.

[3] R. A. Mundell, 'The Appropriate Use of Monetary and Fiscal Policy for Internal and External Stability,' *International Monetary Fund Staff Papers*, vol. 9 (March 1962) pp. 70–7, reprinted as chap. 26 in *Monetary Theory and Policy*, ed. R. S. Thorn (Random House, New York, 1966).

[4] This bland phrase, however, can hide an unattractive situation for the monetary authorities, who might have to sell very large quantities of bonds in a fashion that would raise rates sufficiently to choke off excess demand generated by fiscal ease; and to do this without causing a financial crisis, which would bring the whole pack of cards down, and without imposing such severe distributional effects, e.g. a crunch in the housing market, that there would be revulsion from the direction of policy.

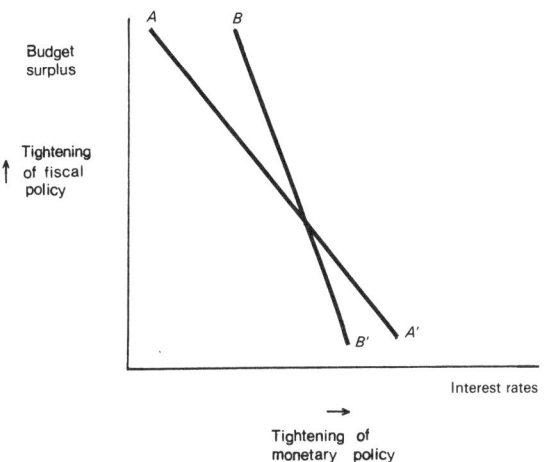

FIG. 12.3

and fiscal policy, but the result of this policy stance will also have implications for *future* values of real incomes, wealth, etc., which are also objectives of policy. The chosen combination of fiscal and monetary policy is likely to influence the allocation of expenditure, e.g. as interest rates rise those forms of expenditure especially sensitive to higher rates will tend to decline. Shifts in the pattern of expenditure, between investment and consumption, are likely to influence the rate of growth of productivity, the time path of consumption, etc. If a balance-of-payments deficit is to be met by raising interest rates, investment and productivity may fall off, leading to worse inflation at any given level of demand, and thus to a steady worsening in the basic balance-of-payments deficit to be financed.[1]

Furthermore, a rise in interest rates when there is a current-account deficit maintains temporary external balance by sucking in capital inflows which have to be serviced. A current-account deficit financed by attracting additional capital will lead inexorably to a growing deficit on interest and dividends within the current account. Only if the additional capital inflows go to finance domestic investment, the return from which in increased output can service the extra interest payments, as occurred for example during the nineteenth century when British capital helped to finance U.S. and Canadian expansion, is this policy viable in the longer run. Moreover, the long-term continuing flow of capital between any two countries in response to a given interest differential, as wealth increases, is likely to be quite small in comparison with the flow resulting from a portfolio readjustment, as interest differentials alter. Therefore the finance of any given basic deficit by the attraction of capital is likely to require continuously rising interest rates with cumulative effects on domestic expenditures and the overseas debt burden. So in the short run internal and external balance may be achieved by some combination of fiscal and monetary policies; but

---

[1] Some economists, for example J. Williamson, ascribe some of the blame for the relatively slow growth of the British economy over the last two decades to a policy mix of relaxing fiscal policy, i.e. offering politically-popular tax cuts, to counter periods of high unemployment, while jacking up interest rates in face of balance-of-payments crises during time of high employment. This argument would be more persuasive, if it did not seem that inflation has probably kept real rates of interest at such very low levels throughout the whole period. Williamson's theoretical attack on Mundell's theorem is to be found in his paper 'On the Normative Theory of Balance-of-Payments Adjustment,' chap. VII in *Monetary Theory and Monetary Policy in the 1970s*, ed. G. Clayton, J. Gilbert and R. Sedgwick (Oxford University Press, 1971).

in the longer run this may only be a viable policy under restrictive conditions. Otherwise it may be a prescription for disaster, meeting current objectives only at the risk of imperilling future ones.

Many of these policy problems arise because of the dynamic nature of the economic system, in which the current achieved levels of the objective variables, and also of the control instruments, may affect subsequent values of the objective variables. Incorporating such dynamic relationships into the analysis often raises a whole range of additional problems and difficulties. You may have noted that in the first example in this section, of the interplay between demand management, real incomes and inflation, there were also such dynamic relationships, as shown for example in equations (1) and (2) (p. 224) which were ignored and suppressed in the earlier analysis, which only considered the immediate, instantaneous choice set available. In particular, as noted in the previous chapter, previous inflationary experience will influence current expectations and thus will affect at any moment of time the possible combinations, or trade-off, between inflation and unemployment. So the current choice of available options between growth and output on the one hand and inflation on the other will circumscribe the form of future available options. When such dynamic inter-relationships occur, one should not aim for immediate results without paying attention to the future consequences of present decisions. In principle each objective variable, for example real incomes, could be treated as a vector of dated elements stretching into the distant future, each element weighted by some discount factor, with the decision-maker developing a plan to deploy his policy instruments over time so as to maximise the expected utility attainable from the present values of the discounted future streams of the various objective variables. This represents a highly idealised picture of what might be possible under conditions of certainty; in the real world, where life is uncertain and short, simpler *ad hoc* rule of thumb decision processes are, indeed have to be, adopted instead. Nevertheless, it is possible to argue the case for or against, say, having more output and income now, even at the expense of having to accept a higher level of inflation in future (for any given level of demand), on rational grounds, even in actual conditions of real-life uncertainty.[1]

A further example of the kind of problem arising from such dynamic relationships was touched on previously in Chapter 8, referring to the problem of instrument instability. Even if there is only one objective variable, say incomes, and one instrument, say the money supply, the lagged relationship between incomes and current and prior values of the money stock might be such as to prevent the maintenance of incomes along some desired growth path without forcing movements in the money stock to follow some unstable path.[2]

---

[1] See, for example, E. S. Phelps, *Inflation Policy and Unemployment Theory, The Cost–Benefit Approach to Monetary Planning* (Macmillan, London, 1972); and also the presidential address to the American Economic Association, 28 December 1971, by J. Tobin, 'Inflation and Unemployment,' *The American Economic Review*, vol. 62, no. 1 (March 1972) pp. 1–18.

[2] Several recent papers have reported and analysed the problem of instrument instability. In particular, see R. Holbrook, 'Optimal Economic Policy and the Problem of Instrument Instability,' *The American Economic Review*, vol. 62, no. 1 (March 1972) pp. 57–65, but also note the papers by W. Poole, 'Alternative Paths to a Stable Full Employment Economy,' *Brookings Papers on Economic Activity, 1971, 3* (The Brookings Institution, Washington, 1971) pp. 579–614, and E. Gramlich, 'The Usefulness of Monetary and Fiscal Policy as Discretionary Stabilization Tools,' *Journal of Money, Credit and Banking*, vol. 3, no. 2 (May 1971) pt 2, pp. 506–32, especially 524–30.

If the instrument, X, affects the objective, Y, with a distributed lag so that $Y_t = a_1 X_t + a_2 X_{t-1} + a_3 X_{t-2}, \ldots, + a_n X_{t-n}$ the values of the a_i coefficients may be such that it will be impossible to bring about a smooth rate of change in Y without causing instability in the time path of X. Thus if the posited relationship was

$$Y_t = 0 \cdot 2 X_t + 0 \cdot 6 X_{t-1} + 0 \cdot 2 X_{t-2}$$

an increase in Y of one per period would require the following sequence of values of X: $+5$, -5, $+25$, -50, $+150$, -370, $+995$, -2575, $+6775$, $\ldots$

This instability in the instrument variable may be disliked for its own sake, perhaps involving real operational costs, and might also be such as to make the variations in the instrument required for complete stabilisation of the path of the objective variable in practice incapable of actual achievement.

To summarise, the desires and objectives of man are virtually limitless, while the instruments for achieving those objectives are few. Compromise in the achievement of objectives is inevitable. Moreover, the choice of policy is complicated by the fact that current decisions will affect the system not only now, but also in the future, so that consideration has to be paid not only to our present concerns but to the future prospects for the system. This would be a difficult enough task, at least technically, if the authorities had perfect foresight; in a world of uncertainty, high expectations will only lead to disillusionment.

B. Policy Under Uncertainty, I: Random Disturbances

In the discussion in the previous section on the use of control instruments for the achievement of economic objectives, it was by and large assumed that the authorities knew what they were doing; that they knew exactly how the economic system worked, so that basically their main problem was to compromise between a multiplicity of objectives by the use of a limited number of instruments in a system complicated by inter-temporal relationships. In reality this is still hopelessly idealised. The authorities do not know the full consequences of their actions; they struggle along in a thick fog of uncertainty.

The simplest form of uncertainty to introduce is to postulate a system in which the authorities are presumed to know the exact form of the structural relationships within that system, but that these functional relationships are subject to stochastic, random errors, which cannot be predicted. The implications of such an assumption have usually been explored within the context of an IS/LM model, ranging from studies of the simplest basic model to stochastic simulations of full-scale macro-economic extended versions of the IS/LM framework. For heuristic purposes it is probably easiest to stick to the simplest IS/LM construction.

In this basic model there are three main behavioural equations, which assuming linearity and no uncertainty, may be written

$$I = a_1 Y + b_1 r \quad \text{Investment function}$$
$$S = a_2 Y + b_2 r \quad \text{Savings function}$$
$$Md = a_3 Y + b_3 r \quad \text{Demand for money function}$$

Given these relationships, and assuming that the authorities have fixed the nominal supply of money, the slopes and positions of both the IS and LM curves are determinate. By varying the quantity of money the authorities can shift the LM curve in order to achieve their desired value of Y.

It may, however, be the case that the authorities know the structure of the system well enough, i.e. the values of the structural coefficients are known with certainty, but that there are unforeseeable random factors, such as strikes, political events, technological discoveries and changes in the weather, which enter to disturb these known relationships. Then these equations must be rewritten

$$I = a_1 Y + b_1 r + e_1$$
$$S = a_2 Y + b_2 r + e_2$$
$$Md = a_3 Y + b_3 r + e_3$$

where e_1, e_2, e_3 are each separate random variables with an expected mean value of zero.

So the authorities still know exactly what the slopes of the two curves are, but they cannot now be sure exactly of their position, since both the IS and the LM curve can be shifted, in an unforeseeable manner, from their predicted position. Thus, as shown in

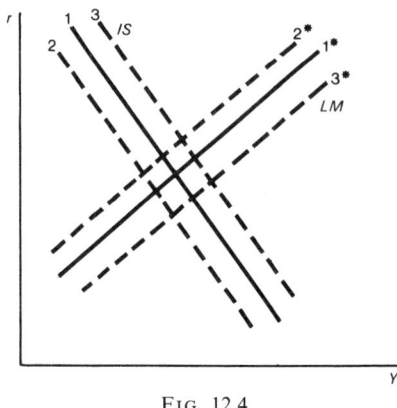

FIG. 12.4

Fig. 12.4, the authorities may predict that the *IS* and *LM* curves will have positions 1 and 1*, but random forces may shift the curves (though maintaining the slopes) say to 2 or 3, or to 2* or 3* in the case of the *LM* curve.

Why should this matter? As the authorities observe each shift in the behavioural relationships, in response to these random factors, can they not – in the context of this postulated *IS/LM* model – readjust the stock of money in order to offset these stochastic shifts and maintain the level of income at the desired value? One problem is that they may not be able to observe the occurrence of these stochastic forces, or at least they may find is difficult to estimate the extent of their effect upon the system, perhaps until some time has passed. The length of time, which may have to pass before the authorities can tell whether unforeseen developments have pushed the economy off target, will depend on the speed of collection and the reliability of data measuring the course of the economy. If such data are gathered infrequently, far in arrears of current developments, and are inaccurate, then there could be a long delay between a disturbance affecting the economy and the information reaching the authorities to enable them to counter the shock.

When the authorities are deciding on their policy they will use the latest available information about the economy to try to estimate the positions of the curves. On this basis, in a world adequately described by the *IS/LM* model, they would then set their instrument, the money stock, to achieve that level of interest rates and incomes which they desire. But new information is only available at discrete intervals and the process of forecasting and policy review is time consuming. So revisions to policy only occur at occasional intervals, say once every few months. In the meantime there will be these disturbances affecting the structural relationships in the system. This leads on to the question of how policy, based on forecasts which have to take the expected value of random shocks as zero (the forecasting model being treated as deterministic, since the values of all coefficients are assumed to be known), should be handled during periods between policy reviews when the system is responding, in a manner that cannot be clearly observed, to random shocks.

If the money stock is held constant at the level that was initially estimated to give the optimal results, then the interest rate will be forced by these shocks away from the value predicted to be consistent with the desired level of money incomes. If, on the other hand, the interest rate is held constant at this initial level, then the money stock will have to adjust away from the value which seemed optimal at the time of the forecast. In these conditions of uncertainty, owing to limited information, should the authorities choose to maintain the money supply or interest rates nearer to the initial chosen, optimal without disturbance, value?

If the shocks only affect the *IS* curve, assuming normal conditions in which this slopes downwards[1], the economy will fluctuate less in response to such shocks if the authorities

---

[1] There is, however, also the possibility that the *IS* curve could slope upwards, if a higher *level* of incomes should encourage investment more than savings, perhaps via some form of accelerator-type mechanism. This obviously will cause some difficulties, because at any point *off* the *IS* curve the non-equilibrium interest rate assuming $dI/dr < 0$ and $ds/dr > 0$ will be tending to force the system even further away from equilibrium, as shown in Fig. 12.5, where *A* and *B* are two dis-equilibrium points and, it is assumed, the normal assumption, that the initial response to disequilibria in the goods market is changes in money incomes, while the initial response to disequilibria in the money market is changes in interest rates. If, however, the *LM* curve is steeper than the *IS* curve, then a stable equilibrium will still be attained, as shown diagrammatically in Fig. 12.6. If the *IS*

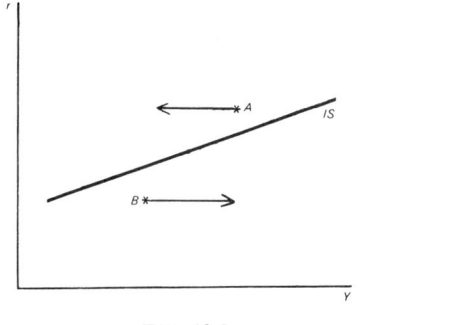

Fig. 12.5

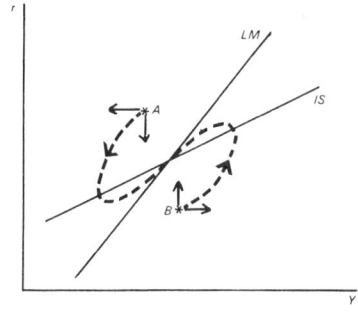

Fig. 12.6

curve were steeper, equilibrium in the money market would be attained at the expense of con-tinuously exploding incomes, as shown in Fig. 12.7. In the first, stable case with *LM* steeper, random fluctuations in the *IS* schedule will necessitate changes in interest rates if an equilibrium is to be restored. Consider a policy of holding interest rates constant in the face of random disturbances, say a fall, in the *IS* schedule, from *IS*1 to *IS*2. It might seem, see Fig. 12.8, as if point *C*, with a higher level of incomes (after a fall in the *IS* schedule!) would be a possible equilibrium, but the economy could never get there: instead incomes would steadily decline along the line *DD'*. If, on the other hand, the money stock was held constant, equilibrium would be restored at point *E*.

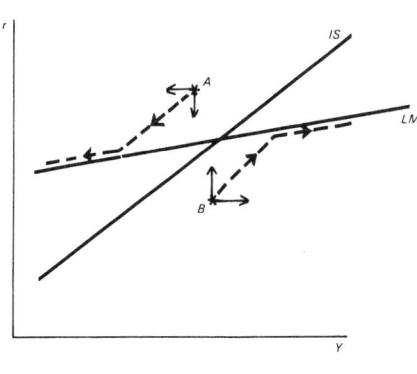

Fig. 12.7

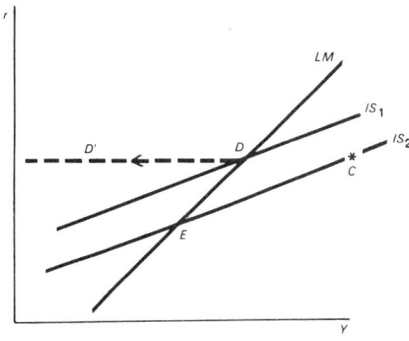

Fig. 12.8
(*Footnote* [1] *continued on p. 234*)

stick to their initial money-stock target. This is shown graphically in Fig. 12.9. A shift in the *IS* curve, say from *IS*1 to *IS*2 or 3, will change incomes by amounts 0*Q* and 0*R* respectively if the money stock is held constant, but by the larger amounts 0*P* and 0*S* if interest rates are held fixed.

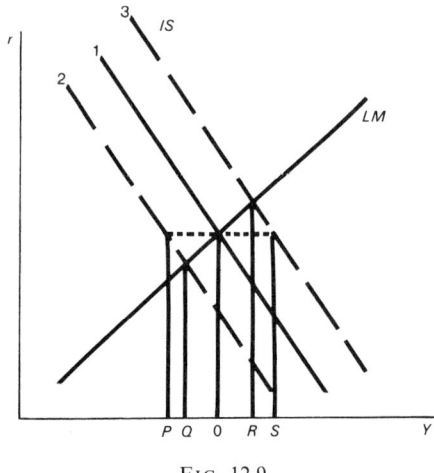

FIG. 12.9

If, on the other hand, random disturbances only impinge upon the position of the *LM* curve (that is if these disturbances have their entire effect upon the demand for money function), then the economy, i.e. the level of nominal incomes, would be subject to less disturbance if interest rates were held constant. In this situation, in order to hold interest rates constant the authorities have to offset shifts in the demand for money by a change in the supply of money. The *LM* curve would not appear to move, and the initial *IS/LM* curves and (desired) values of *Y* and r_b would be unaltered by the random disturbance in the demand for money, compensated exactly by a change in the money supply. If, however,

---

Thus the same conclusion holds, with respect to the appropriate monetary operations in the face of shifts in the *IS* (or the *LM*) curve, whether the *IS* curve is downwards or upwards sloping, assuming, however, that the structure is basically stable with the *IS* curve cutting the *LM* curve from above.

On the other hand when the *IS* curve is upward sloping, monetary policy appears to be more powerful when the interest elasticity of demand for money is high (with a flatter *LM* curve slope – so long as this remains consistent with the stability conditions). This reverses one of the standard results of the traditional model, which assumes a downward sloping *IS* curve. See W. Silber, 'Monetary Policy Effectiveness: The Case of a Positively Sloped *IS* Curve,' *The Journal of Finance*, vol. 26, no. 5 (December 1971) pp. 1077–82.

the authorities maintain the money supply at its initial level, interest rates and thus money incomes must alter in response to this random shift in demand, forcing the economy away from its intended course.

This analysis has had some influence in recent years, partly because of the lucidity and elegance with which it has been developed by W. Poole,[1] in providing a theoretical basis and guide for the short-run operations of the monetary authorities, *in the intervals between forecasting rounds and policy reviews.* If the extent of random variation within this interval is much higher in the goods markets (*IS* curve) than in the money market (*LM* curve), the implication is that it would be better for the authorities to stick to the planned rate of monetary growth. If the demand for money, and financial markets generally, exhibit greater instability, then the authorities should stabilise interest rates in these intervals between policy reviews.

On the whole, demand for money functions with quarterly or annual observations, i.e. with the individual periodicity of observation being fairly long, have appeared to be relatively stable, though there have been some examples of large, unforeseen shifts in the relationships.[2] Over intervals of this length, of say six months to a year, there are opportunities for considerable, unpredictable shifts in conditions in good markets, owing to changes in world demand, wars, strikes, political factors, technological changes and shifts in moods, with such initial disturbances exaggerated over time by multiplier/accelerator mechanisms. So in the medium-term run, of say six months, according to this view of the relative size of the disturbances to be expected, it might be better to put more emphasis on maintaining the planned rate of growth of the money supply.

In the very short run, however, financial markets can be notably volatile, with prices shifting sharply in response to the wayward play of expectations. On the other hand, expenditures and output, abstracting from strikes and natural disasters, roll forward with stolid inertia from day to day and week to week since revisions to planned expenditure patterns, and *a fortiori* to production programmes, are costly in time and often in money. So during shorter intervals, e.g. day by day and week by week, the random variance in money markets will probably be large relative to that in goods markets, with the implication that the shorter the time period the greater the emphasis that the monetary authorities should place on stabilising interest rates in money markets.[3] If the time interval between

---

[1] See, for example, his paper on 'Optimal Choice of Monetary Policy Instruments in a Simple Stochastic Macro Model,' *Quarterly Journal of Economics*, vol. 84, no. 2 (May 1970) pp. 197–216.

[2] Thus in 1972 the demand for money, broadly defined to include time deposits, of companies in the United Kingdom suddenly jumped to a much higher level, given the circumstances of that year, than their previous behaviour would have indicated. Subsequent research may explain why this occurred, but it will remain true that at the time this development came as a surprise.

[3] On the other hand short-period fluctuations in the demand for money function will not matter much if, in the short run, the *IS* curve is steep. It is only as the *IS* curve becomes shallower in the longer run that monetary instability would be important, and this is the time horizon over which, we have suggested, monetary instability tends to be less marked. I am indebted to David Laidler for pointing this out to me.

policy reviews is long enough, this could leave the authorities with a problem of reconciling short-term, day-to-day stabilisation of money markets with the medium-term, quarter-by-quarter objective of obtaining steady monetary growth. For example, if short-term stabilisation of rates allows a faster growth of the money stock over, say, the first few weeks of any quarter than had been intended would it be desirable to offset that excess by a period of slower growth (than the initially planned rate) and, if so, how soon need, or should, growth be reduced, i.e. over what period is it desirable to maintain a planned, average rate? Or should bygones be bygones, and is the best policy to operate in financial markets so as to bring the rate of monetary expansion back to the initial target rate, but no further? If bygones are not forgotten, how far back should one look to adjust future policy to offset past diversions from path?

Such issues arising from this analysis on the appropriate conduct of monetary policy have stimulated considerable interest among economists and even among practitioners, especially in the United States.[1] But in my view the importance of this analysis as a guide to monetary operations has been overstated.[2] In the first place the analytical exposition has usually been based on the simplest possible *IS/LM* model. It is dangerous to generalise from the conclusions based on a very simple, and as argued in Chapter 9 a seriously mis-specified, model to proposals for the conduct of monetary policy in the real world.

Consider, for example, a simple extension of the model to encompass the possibility that there may be lags before the public adjusts its desired money holdings to variations, say in interest rates.[3] Then it may be virtually impossible to control the rate of growth of the money stock in the short run except at the expense of extreme variations in interest rates. Moreover, if the lag is underestimated, and commentators and politicians are inherently impatient for quick results from policy actions, then it may seem to them that not enough has been done, and the dose will be repeated. If public expenditures do not rise immediately in response to decisions to spend more, if the money stock does not fall significantly in response to rises in interest rates, the tendency is often to press even harder on the same lever, or even to deduce that there is no effect and look for some other instrument of control, e.g. direct limitations on bank advances.[4]

On the other hand it can be argued that if there are also lags in expenditure functions, in the *IS* relationship, with delays before decision-makers adjust their expenditure/output

---

[1] See, in particular, *Open Market Policies and Operating Procedures – Staff Studies*, including papers by Axilrod, Davis, Andersen, Pierce, Friedman, Poole, and Kareken (Federal Reserve Board, Washington, 1971).

[2] Its importance perhaps lies, as yet, more in clarifying the proper analytical approach to policy issues than as a detailed guide to actual policy. Uncertainty is obviously the key to policy, but until the late 1960s economists studied policy almost entirely within the context of certainty models. The need was to incorporate uncertainty directly in the formal models so that the real policy issues could be studied analytically, and this is what Poole did, purposely setting up the simplest possible model for this exercise.

[3] The most searching studies of the lag structure of the demand for money function have been those undertaken by the staff of the Federal Reserve Board; for example T. Thomson and J. Pierce, 'A Monthly Econometric Model of the Financial Sector,' unpublished.

[4] Many of the actions undertaken by policy-makers, which commentators have claimed, with the benefit of hindsight, to have been errors, can be attributed to this syndrome. An example in the fiscal field may be the enormous fluctuations in the size of the fiscal deficit/surplus in the United Kingdom during the financial years 1968/69–1973/74. An example in the monetary field might be the fluctuations in interest rates and the money stock in the United States during 1971. During that year the money stock grew faster than intended during the first half of the year, so interest rates were continuously pushed upwards. Then when the money stock growth receded from July onwards, partly as a lagged response to previous high interest rates, its growth rate fell below course for the next six or so months, despite large reductions in interest rates, which in turn could have been sowing the seeds for a subsequent re-acceleration, and so on. This latter example was also discussed in Chap. 8, pp. 163–4.

plans in response to interest-rate changes (and this is generally believed to be the case), then it would require extreme variations in interest rates to have much immediate significant impact on nominal incomes. In such circumstances the lag in the demand for money function could offset the lag in the expenditure function, in the sense that the lag in the demand for money function would initially cause a large change in interest rates, but the lag in the expenditure functions would dampen its effect on current demand. As time passed, there could be a fall back in interest rates from their initial peak, but the effect on expenditures would contrariwise be building up. So, despite lags, maintenance of steady monetary growth in the face of shifts in the *IS* curve could allow fairly stable growth in money incomes, though at the expense of very large, and possibly increasing, oscillations in interest rates.[1]

---

[1] The formal mathematics of the analysis, nicely developed by D. P. Tucker, 'Dynamic Income Adjustment to Money-Supply Changes,' *The American Economic Review*, vol. 56, no. 3 (June 1966) pp. 433–49, go as follows:

The basic (Keynesian) model is

$$I_t = (1 - j)(a_1 + b_1 Y_t + dr_t) + jI_{t-1} \qquad \text{(1) Investment}$$
$$C_t = (1 - j)(a_2 + b_2 Y_t) + jC_{t-1} \qquad \text{(2) Consumption}$$
$$Y_t = C_t + I_t \qquad \text{(3) Income identity}$$
$$Md_t = (1 - m)(e + f Y_t + gr_t) + mMd_{t-1} \qquad \text{(4) Demand for money}$$
$$Md_t = Ms_t \qquad \text{(5) Money market identity}$$

where j and m, $0 < j, m < 1$, are the lag parameters b_1, b_2, $f > 0$, $d, g < 0$, and it is assumed (a stability condition) that

$$b_1 + b_2 < 1 + \frac{df}{g}$$

These equations, when solved for Y in terms of M, yield the following first-order linear difference equation

$$Y_t - A Y_{t-1} = B + D(M_t - mM_{t-1})$$

where

$$A = \frac{j}{1 - (1 - j)[b_1 + b_2 - df/g]}$$

$$D = \frac{Ad(1 - j)}{gj(1 - m)}$$

and B is a constant of no importance.

The shift in the time path of income in response to a unit permanent change in M at $t = 1$ is

$$Y_t' = \frac{D(1 - m)}{(1 - A)} + D\frac{(m - A)}{(1 - A)} A^{t-1}$$

This is the shift in the path that income would follow if there were no disturbances. The second term depends on the difference between A and m, i.e. between a term depending largely on the expenditure lag and the demand for money lag. Tucker notes (p. 440), 'In a general sense, then, it is the *difference* between product-demand lags and money-demand lags, as much as it is the inherent characteristics of the lags themselves, that determines the speed of income adjustment.' In particular, if $m = A$, $Y_t' = D$, and the response of income to a change in the money stock is complete in the first period, whatever the values of m and j.

The analysis of the effects of lags in the system has been taken further by several economists, see for example J. E. Tanner, 'Lags in the Effects of Monetary Policy: A Statistical Investigation,' *The American Economic Review*, vol. 59, no. 5 (December 1969) pp. 794–805, and D. Laidler, 'Expectations, Adjustment, and the Dynamic Response of Income to Policy Changes,' *Journal of Money, Credit and Banking*, vol. 5, no. 1, pt 1 (February 1973) pp. 157–72. For a survey of work in this field see B. J. Moore, 'Optimal Monetary Policy,' *The Economic Journal*, vol. 82, no. 325 (March 1972) pp. 116–39.

Thus it is not necessarily the case that the very large variations in interest rates that would generally be required to stabilise the rate of growth of the money supply in the short run, given lags in the demand for money function, would destabilise the path of money incomes. Nevertheless, the risks of introducing major disturbances in the economy by insisting upon a policy of continuously-fixed monetary growth under such circumstances would increase if, for example, there were discontinuities, caused say by bankruptcies,[1] in the response of the system to variations in interest rates, or if the lag patterns were themselves changing and not accurately estimated.[2]

Another reason for scepticism of the practical value of this analysis as a guide to policy action is that it usually abstracts from consideration of the actual availability and adequacy of statistics. The exercise usually proceeds on the implicit assumption that the authorities have sufficient data to monitor the growth of the money stock over very short intervals, say week by week, as well as observing the variations in interest rates, but do *not* have an accurate or up-to-date estimate of current movements in expenditures and incomes. It needs to be remembered that in this analysis the structure of the system, i.e. the slopes of the *IS/LM* curves, is assumed to be known exactly to the authorities, so if they could observe a divergence between actual and desired incomes they could prevent it. In practice there are, of course, a large number of indicators, of varying reliability, of the current level of demand in the economy which come out with only a short delay, e.g. unemployment, industrial production, price indices, etc. It is usually possible to get some inkling fairly quickly of whether the current pace of the economy is above, near or below the target.

On the other hand in many countries, other than the United States, monetary data are only available once a month.[3] Although they are published quite soon after the date of

---

[1] A good example of this occurred in the United Kingdom in December 1973 when a sharp upward jab in interest rates helped to push a fringe banking institution into failure. This led to an immediate reconsideration of the safety of deposits in all similar institutions and precipitated a general run on these banks. If this had not been staunched (by a re-cycling of deposits), the effects could have been calamitous.

[2] The claim here that sticking to a policy of maintaining some pre-ordained rate of monetary expansion at all times may in certain cases have deleterious consequences should *not* be taken as implying that it would be better to stick instead to a policy of fixing interest rates. Indeed, a continuous policy of interest-rate stabilisation may well have perverse longer-term effects on interest rates, and on the stability of the financial system itself. Persistent efforts by the monetary authorities to cushion interest-rate movements can allow excessive fluctuations in money incomes to develop. The resulting changes in economic activity and in the inflation rate could well produce larger differences between the longer-run peaks and troughs in interest rates than would otherwise occur. The argument is *not* that the maintenance of stable nominal interest rates is always preferable to the maintenance of a stable rate of monetary expansion (the reverse is probably nearer the truth), but rather that a judicious assessment of the complexities of the actual conjuncture should allow a better selection of policy than sticking to any pre-determined posture.

[3] W. Poole has reminded me that it is not necessary to assume that the money stock can be continuously observed and controlled, if some other monetary variable, e.g. the stock of high-powered money, to which the money supply is closely related can be continuously observed and controlled. The supply of money is then a stochastic function of this monetary base, and this equation combined with the stochastic demand for money function would yield the stochastic *LM* function. The absence of accurate observation (*a fortiori* of precise control) of the money stock in this case increases the variance of the *LM* function, but does not affect the formal analysis in any way.

Unfortunately, this does not help to overcome the actual data problem, at least in the United Kingdom. Without current observations of actual bank deposits, banks can only be required to maintain reserves in relation to their last reported deposit totals. So in the United Kingdom the clearing banks maintain cash reserves related to their last previously reported monthly position, until in the last day or so before the new make-up date they attempt to anticipate the required position at the coming make-up date. Under this system it is *not* possible for the Bank of England to estimate from movements in its own liabilities in the monthly intervals between make-up dates how the monetary aggregates are growing.

collection, the interval now being about four or five weeks in the United Kingdom, each individual observation is subject to a large random fluctuation, owing to factors such as the timing of large loans, strikes, the dates of large new issues in capital markets, errors in the data, etc. These random factors, as noted in Chapter 8, can easily cause changes of $\pm\frac{1}{2}$ per cent in the figures for the monthly aggregates at any one date. Thus from month to month, unless the money stock is growing very fast, the random variation can easily swamp the systematic element. Imagine that there is an underlying acceleration in the rate of monetary growth during December, with say the first figures to show this collected in mid-January. These will become available in mid-February. Such data, showing a larger than usual jump in the figures between a single date in mid-December and a single date in mid-January will, however, hardly provide reliable or compelling evidence on the underlying systematic acceleration. It is likely to be mid-March at the earliest before the authorities accept the evidence of a change in trend that began three months before. By then they ought to have some indication whether this faster monetary growth than initially planned has, or has not, been accompanied by a divergence of the economy from its intended path.

There are two separable points here. The first is that in circumstances where the monetary series are erratic and infrequently observed, and where the response of the public in adjusting their demand for bank credit and bank deposits to interest-rate variations is lagged,[1] it is not possible to obtain a stable rate of monetary growth, even quarter by quarter let alone month by month, whatever the objective of the monetary authorities may be. Moreover, and more important, the authorities will usually have some information on the nature of the shocks, unforeseen at the time of the previous forecast and policy review, which are currently hitting the economy. They can observe, by and large, how the economy is going just about as well, at least in many countries, as they can observe monetary trends. They can see situations when there is a danger of sizeable shifts in liquidity preference, for example in the aftermath of the Penn Central or the Rolls Royce bankruptcies, and act to alleviate these. Thus the extent of information available ought to allow the authorities to do better than they could by simple reliance on rules of thumb for the stabilisation of interest rates or of the money stock over some time interval.

The real weakness of this approach in my view is, however, that it emphasises one area of uncertainty, the possibility of random disturbances in the structural relationships, a rather secondary problem for economic management, at the expense of ignoring a far more serious difficulty, our uncertainty about the basic form of the structural relationships themselves within the system. Thus the standard analysis of this topic usually contains the

---

[1] In some circumstances the initial response can even be perverse. Thus on occasions in the United Kingdom, and also in Canada, the response of the banks to pressures on their reserve base has been to raise the rates they bid for additional funds in the C.D. and inter-bank markets (the wholesale markets), both absolutely and relatively to the rates at which they lend, largely because these latter rates, base rates or prime rates, being administered rates are costly to change – for a number of reasons – and politically visible, so banks are unwilling to bear the odium of raising them, unless they are convinced of the necessity. The result is that not only may bank advances temporarily become relatively cheaper than other sources of funds, but even that in certain circumstances, as pertained in the United Kingdom in June–July 1972 and January–February 1973, a turn may be made by borrowing from a bank to redeposit with the banking system via the C.D. market. During these occasions, when the authorities were trying to restrain monetary expansion, this merry-go-round undoubtedly inflated the totals both of bank lending and of bank deposits, at least on a broad definition.

After a further prolonged period during which the pattern of interest rates encouraged such arbitrage, July–December 1973, thereby reinvigorating an unwelcome surge in bank lending and in interest-bearing deposits, the authorities introduced a new supplementary deposits scheme. This imposed a penalty on banks whose interest-bearing deposits, time deposits and C.D.s were growing too fast (i.e. above an allowed rate of increase). The intention was to force a wedge between rates charged on bank loans and offered on interest-bearing deposits, and thus to ensure that interest-rate relativities did not get out of kilter.

(implicit) assumptions that the slopes of the IS/LM curves are accurately known, and that this system is an accurate representation of the real world. If this was the case it would be possible at each forecast and policy review to reset the policy instruments in such a way as to obtain with complete certainty the best expected results for the objective variable(s). In practice, in most industrialised countries forecasts and policy reviews are undertaken several times a year, and the use of computers virtually allows any comprehensive, coherent forecast to be updated and revised as each new item of information comes in. Thus the time interval between policy reviews, which allow objectives for both monetary growth rates and interest rates to be reset, is now quite short and, if the effort were worthwhile, could be made shorter yet. So if we really knew how the system worked, if our only uncertainties related to the occurrence of stochastic disturbances to that system, then we could easily reset the controls often enough to make the problem of how to operate in the short intervals between reviews of very minor importance.[1]

C. Policy under Uncertainty, II: When the Structure of the System is Not Known

The main problem for monetary management does not lie in our inability to predict the disturbances that will agitate the economic system, but in our ignorance of how that system actually works. This latter problem has a number of dimensions. In order to comprehend the working of the real, complex economy, we may try to capture the important features of the system in a simplified model, in which the inter-relationships between the variables can be empirically estimated. These econometric calculations not only provide an estimate of the mean, average, coefficient of the value of each specified relationship, but also give the standard error of that coefficient; this provides a first, and simple, measure of the accuracy with which the relationship is defined.[2] These estimates, however, are obtained from models of a particular specification, estimated over a particular data period, during which there was a given institutional and political structure. Models with different specifications, even if estimated over the same data period, often give very different results for economic relationships, well beyond the range of their respective standard errors.

---

[1] While it seems intuitively plausible that the choice of instruments should make less difference as the frequency of policy decisions increases, it has been formally shown, by J. Kareken and N. Wallace, 'The Monetary Instrument Variable Choice: How Important?', *Journal of Money, Credit and Banking*, vol. 4, no. 3 (August 1972) pp. 723–9, that under some conditions the instrument variable choice 'does not of necessity make less difference, or become less important, as the frequency with which policy is decided increases.' As I understand their analysis, there are some circumstances in which the relative autocorrelations in the error terms in the IS and LM functions are such that the *difference* in expected outcomes between choosing to fix the rate for monetary growth or nominal interest rates over some long-term period is less than the *difference* in expected outcome from the choice in the short run. Kareken and Wallace, however, present no evidence that the economic structure is such as to make such circumstances likely. In any case the *actual* expected loss from running either policy will be less if policy decisions are more frequent; in this sense it will not matter which instrument is chosen. When policy decisions are less frequent, the expected loss will be much larger; in some cases it may be true that the *expected* loss may be much the same whichever instrument is picked, but the potential scope for *actual* large losses, if the authorities pick wrong, perhaps by chance, will be much greater.

[2] A common, and often justified, complaint of economists providing advice to policy-makers is that the latter turn away from, and find difficult to absorb, forecasts expressed in terms of bands of probability, confidence limits. Instead they want to be given, and work on the basis of, the 'best' mean estimates. Too little attention is paid to available measurements of the errors in estimation. Then when the point forecasts go wrong – as they must – the quantitative economist is blamed for promising more than he can provide!

For example, the St. Louis reduced-form money multiplier,[1] or the Laffer–Ranson model,[2] can give quite different implications from one of the extended Keynesian macro-models for the impact over time of changes in, say, the monetary base.[3] Moreover, there may be significant changes in the estimated values of the relationships in similarly specified models over differing data periods.

The policy-maker is then generally faced with a gallimaufry of empirical estimates of any economic relationship. Moreover he is concerned with a time period, the future, which in certain respects, some predictable some not, will be very different from any past period during which the relationships were estimated. At this point qualitative considerations, or judgement, have to guide the policy-maker in deciding how much weight to place upon the various alternative quantitative estimates. Indeed, in some cases the policy-maker may feel extremely suspicious, on *a priori* grounds, of all the quantitative estimates.

An apposite example can be found in the quantitative estimates of the impact of monetary changes upon expenditures contained in the extended *IS/LM* macro-economic models of the United Kingdom. In these models, for example of the National Institute for Economic and Social Research (N.I.E.S.R.) and of the London Business School (L.B.S.), the effect of financial factors, mainly specified as transmitted via changes in a few financial yields, is estimated to be extremely slight. The Treasury economic model is known to be closely akin, in this respect as in others, to these other two models. Thus the answer to the question from the policy-maker of what would be the effect of changing the rate of growth of the money supply, say by ± 5 per cent per annum, or varying interest rates, say by ± 3 per cent per annum, obtained from examination of these models is that the impact on domestic expenditures would be extremely slight, with the exception of a significant but lagged effect on the private housing market.

Nor have more direct attempts to estimate the relationship between monetary aggregates and money incomes in the United Kingdom yet yielded evidence of a sufficiently close relationship to provide an alternative basis for deciding on an appropriate rate of growth of the money supply. Money multipliers, relating the change in money incomes to current and past changes in the money stock, estimated with U.K. data have tended to show relatively weak relationships,[4] though somewhat stronger relationships have been found between certain credit aggregates (lending totals) and forms of expenditure, e.g. between bank lending and stockbuilding, than between monetary aggregates and nominal incomes.[5]

---

[1] Andersen and Jordan, 'Monetary and Fiscal Actions: A Test of Their Relative Importance in Economic Stabilization,' *Federal Reserve Bank of St. Louis Review* (November 1968).

[2] A. B. Laffer and R. D. Ranson, 'A Formal Model of the Economy,' *Journal of Business*, vol. 44 (July 1971) pp. 247–70.

[3] On this subject see M. J. Hamburger, 'The Lag in the Effect of Monetary Policy: A Survey of Recent Literature,' *The Federal Reserve Bank of New York Monthly Review*, vol. 53, no. 12 (December 1971) pp. 289–98. He concludes that 'estimates of the length of the lag differ considerably.' On the other hand, 'the type of statistical estimating model (structural versus reduced form equations)' was 'found to be less important' as a factor causing such differences.

[4] For instance: A. A. Walters, 'Money in Boom and Slump,' *Hobart Papers No. 44*, 2nd ed. (Institute of Economic Affairs, London, 1970); M. W. Keran, 'Monetary and Fiscal Influences on Economic Activity: The Foreign Experience,' *Federal Reserve Bank of St. Louis Review*, vol. 52, no. 2 (February 1970) pp. 16–28, especially pp. 27–8; C. Goodhart and A. D. Crockett, 'The Importance of Money,' *Bank of England Quarterly Bulletin*, vol. 10, no. 2 (June 1970) pp. 197–8; M. Artis and A. R. Nobay, 'Two Aspects of the Monetary Debate,' *National Institute Economic Review*, no. 49 (August 1969) pp. 33–42.

[5] See, for example, D. K. Sheppard, *The Growth and Role of U.K. Financial Institutions, 1880–1962* (Methuen, London, 1971) chap. 5 especially, and A. D. Crockett, 'Timing Relationships between Movements of Monetary and National Income Variables,' *Bank of England Quarterly Bulletin*, vol. 10, no. 4 (December 1970) pp. 459–72.

In short the quantitative evidence from the various models does not suggest in this country any strong and reliable relationship between monetary variables and domestic expenditures. The Keynesian models seem to show that the relationship is very weak, while the money multipliers imply that the relationship is unreliable, if on average somewhat stronger. Thus the answer that might be given to the policy-maker enquiring about the effect of monetary policy on the domestic economy is, 'We cannot tell at all accurately what the effect is. The evidence of our models used for forecasting purposes, both official and private, suggests, however, that its impact is negligible – at least so long as the variables remain within the ranges observed during the data period in which the models were estimated.' Such an answer hardly helps the policy-maker to select an 'optimal' monetary policy for the domestic economy! This uncertainty over the effect of monetary policy may be contrasted with the apparent confidence exhibited by the forecasters in being able to track the resulting effects on expenditures of fiscal changes. For example, the National Institute has published papers giving rules-of-thumb for estimating the quarter-by-quarter results of certain fiscal changes calculated virtually down to the nearest £ million[1] – with, incidentally, no attention whatsoever being paid to the method of financing the resulting fiscal deficit/surplus! In this state of the art of model construction in the United Kingdom, a Chancellor of the Exchequer wishing, say, to achieve some given change in aggregate incomes and expenditures can be provided by his advisers with a menu of alternative fiscal changes (tax changes, subsidies, public expenditures), each of which can be calculated to achieve the desired aggregate objective fairly closely. But if he should ask what change in his monetary instruments would achieve this same objective, or have the equivalent effect on aggregate expenditures of some fiscal change, he will get an embarrassed silence; no quantitative, precise answer can be provided.

In these circumstances it is not surprising that the main instrument used for contra-cyclical demand management in the United Kingdom has been fiscal policy, with monetary policy being cast in an accommodating, passive role. Throughout most of the 1960s, indeed, interest rates were varied mainly in response to external conditions, being raised whenever there was a need to support the fixed exchange rate, which was often under pressure, and lowered – in a spirit of general benevolence towards the encouragement of investment – as each balance-of-payments crisis temporarily receded.[2] With interest-rate policy mainly determined by external considerations, the money supply was allowed to vary passively. Meanwhile direct controls, on the terms of instalment (hire-purchase) credit (i.e. minimum downpayments and maximum repayment periods) and ceilings on bank advances, were increasingly used to affect direct expenditures, though in the latter case of ceilings on bank advances there was no quantitative evidence of their effects either, so that the choice of level was an entirely arbitrary, *ad hoc* procedure.

It should be recognised that this use of instruments *did* accord with the available quantitative evidence on the structure of the economy. Fiscal policy did appear to have an accurately measurable effect on the domestic economy, the general instruments of monetary policy, i.e. changes in interest rates and/or in the money stock, did not. Restrictions on hire-purchase credit did have a measurable effect on consumption. Increases in interest rates, unless offset by an accompanying worsening of confidence,[3] would shift international arbi-

---

[1] See, for example, J. R. Shepherd and M. J. Surrey, 'The Short-Term Effects of Tax Changes,' *National Institute Economic Review*, no. 46 (November 1968) pp. 36–41, and W. A. B. Hopkin and W. A. H. Godley, 'An Analysis of Tax Changes,' ibid. (May 1965).

[2] See D. Fisher, 'The Instruments of Monetary Policy and the Generalised Trade-off Function for Britain, 1955–1968,' *Manchester School of Economic and Social Studies*, vol. 38, no. 3 (September 1970) pp. 209–22, and 'The Objectives of British Monetary Policy, 1951–1964,' *The Journal of Finance*, vol. 23, no. 5 (December 1968) pp. 821–31; also the chapter on 'Monetary Policy in the United Kingdom,' by C. Goodhart from *Monetary Policy in Twelve Industrial Countries*, ed. K. Holbik (Federal Reserve Bank of Boston, 1973) especially pp. 521–3.

[3] As occurred in November 1964.

trage margins in favour of the United Kingdom and, though it was difficult to measure, it was thought that this did lead to some capital inflows (or a prevention of capital outflows), and thus strengthen sterling. So the use of monetary policy to provide temporary support for sterling during crises and of fiscal policy to achieve internal domestic equilibrium appeared to be a sensible and appropriate assignment of instruments (remember, however, the criticism of this policy stance outlined previously in Section A of this chapter).

By the end of the 1960s, however, confidence that these (extended Keynesian) models really gave an accurate representation of the effects of monetary variables on the domestic economy ebbed away, largely as a result of the evolution of economic thinking in the United States rather than from any new developments in domestic circumstances and experience within the United Kingdom. The theoretical work of Friedman, Tobin and Leijonhufvud gave a basis for belief that changes in financial conditions *should* affect expenditure decisions, whatever the 'Keynesian' models might show. The empirical results of Friedman and Meiselman, and Andersen and Jordan showed a strong positive correlation between income movements and synchronous and prior changes in the money stock in the United States. Even the latest 'Keynesian' model developed by the Federal Reserve Board, in association with several universities (the F.R.B. – M.I.T. – Penn model), incorporated a number of channels whereby monetary changes affected the real economy significantly.[1]

Although most of these empirical results could not be easily replicated in the United Kingdom,[2] the belief that monetary factors had a considerable influence on the course of the economy tended to be translated from the United States, where there was supporting evidence – though the weight of the evidence there, of course, remains a matter of dispute – to the United Kingdom, where there was much less supporting quantitative, empirical evidence for this thesis.[3]

This has resulted in an unhappy dichotomy between commonly-held beliefs about the importance of monetary policy, as a demand-management instrument, and the available empirically-estimated models of the economy. The view has been widely expressed, by ministers and politicians of both main political parties, by eminent commentators, and by many academics, that control over the monetary aggregates is a very important, perhaps the most important, element of demand management. Yet no available model of the U.K. economy gives any clear indication what effect on the level of aggregate demand a change in the rate of growth of one of the monetary series, say $M1$, might be expected to have and the forecasting models actually used, e.g. by the National Institute, imply that the effect would be negligible. How do you select an 'optimal' monetary policy under such conditions?

About the only stable empirical relationship in this field for the United Kingdom seemed at one time to be that relating the money stock to current and previous levels of incomes and interest rates, a demand for money function of the form

$$M = P \cdot f(y, r)$$

where P is the price level, y real output and r is some set of interest rates. Even in this case

---

[1] F. de Leeuw and E. Gramlich, 'The Channels of Monetary Policy,' a Staff Economic Study, *Federal Reserve Bulletin*, vol. 55, no. 6 (June 1969) pp. 472–91.

[2] For example, it is not easy to find traces in the United Kingdom of any sizeable effect on consumption of changes in stock-market values, which is the route through which monetary policy is estimated in the F.R.B. model to have its main quick-acting influence on expenditures. Nor indeed is it possible to find any close relationship in this country between movements in the monetary aggregates and fluctuations in equity prices, as reported in a paper by D. Gowland, 'The Money Supply and Stock Market Prices,' presented at the Association of University Teachers of Economics Conference in Manchester, April 1974.

[3] Though there is less evidence in the United Kingdom of a close link between movements in the money stock and in money incomes, the link between certain credit flows and private expenditures may be somewhat stronger. This was the conclusion reached by D. K. Sheppard, *The Growth and Role of U.K. Financial Institutions, 1880–1962* (Methuen, London, 1971) esp. chap. 5.

some versions of the demand for money function, those using a broad definition as the dependent variable, gave extremely bad predictions, indeed collapsed, in the years following the structural changes introduced in 1971.[1] The banks had then been allowed and encouraged to bid more aggressively for deposits – both externally-imposed constraints and internal cartel arrangements being removed – and they did so with sufficient vigour to induce a significant shift in portfolio distributions, particularly of the liquid asset holdings of companies.

At least the demand for money function, to the extent that it proved reliable, should indicate what growth in the money stock would be consistent with any planned level of real incomes, prices and interest rates; nevertheless it gave, of itself, no indication how the effects on the system of any change in the money stock brought about, say, by open-market operations or changes in the fiscal deficit, might be distributed between changes in interest rates, output or prices. The negligible impact of interest-rate changes on expenditures in the 'Keynesian' models implied that most of the effect might become expended on changing interest rates[2] and asset prices[3] with little impact on output. Nevertheless, this relationship could be used to estimate what monetary growth would accommodate some planned level of incomes and interest rates,[4] and indicated very roughly what kind

---

[1] As reported by M. Artis and M. Lewis, 'The Demand for Money: Stable or Unstable?', *The Banker*, vol. 124, no. 577 (March 1974) pp. 239–47; and G. Hacche, 'A Review of Demand for Money Relationships' (mimeo, Bank of England, 1974).

[2] In an open economy with fixed exchange rates such variations in domestic interest rates, *vis-à-vis* foreign rates, could lead to very large-scale capital flows. These flows not only offset and dampen the internal thrust of domestic monetary policy, but may have unwelcome and disruptive effects upon reserve holdings and the stability of the international monetary system. External considerations, in a system of fixed exchange rates, serve therefore to limit each country's autonomy in varying monetary conditions to achieve domestic objectives.

[3] It is possible for an expansionary monetary policy to raise the price of existing real assets, e.g. capital goods and houses, without having much stimulating impact on the output of new assets if the supplying industry responds slowly. Moreover, if prices of these new capital goods are administratively set, the immediate response may be a lengthening of order books, etc., with very little noticeable effect on nominal expenditures and output. There was some evidence that in the United Kingdom in early 1972 a monetary policy, which was intentionally expansionary, was exhausting itself in higher prices for existing housing and land, with very little noticeable effect on expenditures on new housing, etc. Whether this could be described as a weakness of monetary policy or of the structure of the construction industry, whose reponses are delayed, *inter alia*, by planning procedures and land shortages, is debatable.

[4] A slight extension to the model can be introduced to establish what rate of expansion of domestic credit would accommodate and be consistent with some planned surplus in the balance of payments.

Assume that the balance of payments surplus (S) is a function of the trade balance between exports (X), an exogenously-determined variable, and imports (W), and also of the level of domestic interest rates, r, which assuming foreign rates to be given influences international capital flows, so that

$$S = f(X - W, r) \qquad (1)$$

The level of imports is a function of incomes

$$W = f(Y) \qquad (2)$$

The level of incomes is a function of exports, fiscal policy (F) and perhaps of monetary policy (M or r), so that

$$Y = f(X, F, M \text{ or } r) \qquad (3)$$

(*Footnote* [4] *continued on p. 245*)

of monetary growth rate might be appropriate if the authorities wanted to 'aim off', to make monetary policy on the restrictive or easy side.

Given this uncertainty about the effects of changes in monetary conditions on the economy, the temptation has been to continue to use fiscal policy to adjust actual to desired incomes and then to set monetary growth at its calculated 'accommodating' value. Having done this on the basis of an assumed level of interest rates selected, perhaps, in the light of prospective financial developments abroad, e.g. in the euro-dollar market or in monetary policy in Washington, one then, and only then, comes to the question of whether to maintain the forecast monetary growth rate, obtained in this fashion, or the selected level of nominal interest rates, in the intervening period up till the next policy review.

At this stage one returns to the issues already discussed in Section B, though with the difference that in reality no one has much confidence that either the forecast monetary growth or interest-rate level would, in the absence of unforeseen random disturbances, prove optimal anyhow. In practice, in the United Kingdom current monitoring of developments, between forecasts and policy reviews, takes place with a reasonable approximation to the approach sketched out in Section B. In the short run, day to day and week to week, most attention is paid to movements of prices and interest rates in financial markets, inevitably so since quantitative data on the monetary aggregates are only available monthly. Over longer time periods, monthly and quarterly, attention is increasingly drawn to the developments in the monetary aggregates. This accords with *a priori* expectations about the relative variability of the goods markets and financial markets in the short and longer time intervals.

Greater emphasis on the development of the monetary aggregates has also followed as a result of the increasing inflation, with its implications for financial markets. If one is uncertain what to do, there is a tendency to do as little as possible. Earlier central bankers often tended to construe a passive policy as one of maintaining nominal interest rates constant. This stance gave no help in stabilising cyclical variations in expenditures in the economy *even* when prices were and could be expected to remain constant. Allowance for adaptive expectations of price inflation implies further that a policy of stabilising nominal interest rates will be destabilising for the economy, since it will tend to cause procyclical

---

Then with a demand for money function

$$Md = f(Y, r) \tag{4}$$

we can close the system with a supply of money accounting identity, relating the money supply to current domestic credit creation, inflows of money through the balance of payments, plus the money supply in the previous period, so that

$$Ms = DCE + S + Ms_{t-1} \tag{5}$$

which together with a money-market equilibrium condition

$$Ms = Md \tag{6}$$

gives a system with six equations and six unknowns, M_s, M_d, W, Y, r, S. DCE, like F, is a policy instrument, not an endogenous variable.

Given X, the achievement of the desired level of S (S^*) will require some combination of Y and r, from equations (1) and (2). Given the chosen Y and r satisfying S^*, equations (4), (5) and (6) determine the level of DCE consistent with this policy choice. If an unforeseen disturbance somewhere in the system forces S from S^* then, with a given DCE, Ms will be forced from its planned value in such a way as to cause changes in Y or r of a kind that will automatically tend to cause S to return towards S^*.

variations in real interest rates.[1] Acceptance of this distinction between nominal and real interest rates, arising from expectations of non-zero future rates of change of prices, led to the realisation that the stabilisation of nominal rates in an increasingly inflationary world was not in any conceivable sense 'passive', but a positively expansionary policy. So in a system with varying, and possibly volatile, expectations of future price inflation – and, indeed, with fluctuating general moods of confidence and depression about the future of the economy – maintenance of nominal rates at some chosen level will not represent a neutral or passive policy, nor will it be possible to calibrate the overall effect of monetary policy by measuring variations in nominal interest rates.

Under circumstances of unobservable variations in price expectations, and of unforeseen fluctuations in the pressure of demand (shifts in the *IS* curve), the maintenance of the initially-chosen, 'optimal', rate of growth of the money stock might appear to be the most 'neutral', stabilising policy: this indeed is the line advocated by monetarists. There are, however, some complications with this approach. In the first place, as already noted, a policy of holding monetary growth constant will be destabilising in circumstances where there are unforeseen shifts in the demand for money function. Certainly in the short run volatile swings in expectations can disturb financial markets, so that in week-to-week operations some stabilisation of prices in financial markets may be appropriate, and still consistent with steady monetary growth over the medium-term horizon.[2] But the advantages to be obtained from adherence to this latter medium-term target will still depend on the relative stability of the demand for money function over longer intervals, say on a quarter-by-quarter basis.

The experience of the United Kingdom in 1972/3 provides, however, one example when such stability was lacking. In these years demand for money relationships, especially those for the broader definition including time deposits and C.D.s, estimated in the United Kingdom over the previous decade, consistently and significantly underpredicted the quantity of money which the private sector, and especially companies, decided to hold.[3] How was one to interpret the situation? Did the large excess in money holdings (mainly

---

[1] If demand is a function of a vector of exogenous variables, X, and real interest rates (nominal interest rates less the expected rate of price inflation), $r - E\dot{p}$, so that

$$y = f(X, r - E\dot{p}), \quad \text{where} \quad \frac{dy}{d(r - E\dot{p})} < 0,$$

and the rate of change of prices is a function of variations in y around its normal, 'equilibrium,' value

$$\dot{p} = f(y - y^*), \quad \text{where} \quad \frac{dp}{d(y - y^*)} > 0$$

with expectations depending on current and recent developments, so that

$$E\dot{p} = f(\dot{p}_t, \dot{p}_{t-1}, \ldots, \dot{p}_{t-n}), \quad \text{where} \quad \frac{dE\dot{p}}{d\dot{p}_{t-i}} > 0$$

then the maintenance of nominal interest rates r at a fixed value will tend to exaggerate a disturbance to the system and may cause it to explode.

[2] See, for example, R. G. Davis, 'Short-run Targets for Open Market Operations,' from *Open Market Policies and Operating Procedures – Staff Studies* (Federal Reserve Board, 1971) pp. 38–69, and by the same author, 'Implementing Open Market Policy with Monetary Aggregate Objectives,' *Federal Reserve Bank of New York Monthly Review*, vol. 55, no. 7 (July 1973) pp. 170–82.

[3] A new institutional system to control credit and to encourage competition had been introduced in September 1971. It could be foreseen that the accompanying structural change might cause certain consequential adjustments in the behavioural relationships, but there was no good way of predicting the extent of such perturbations.

in the form of interest-bearing time deposits and C.D.s) above the level predicted, given the development of the economy, prices, interest rates, output, simply imply that the demand for money relationship had shifted, so that from now on the private sector, companies especially, would maintain a continuously higher ratio of money balances to nominal incomes? Was the surge in money holdings, above the predicted level, perhaps a temporary phenomenon, which would unleash a great expansion in demand at some future point of time, or at the least prevent any contractionary policy from working effectively? And if the authorities should take steps, on precautionary grounds, to lower the rate of growth of the money stock, might not the increased interest rates stifle any hoped for renaissance in investment?

It is easy enough to determine the appropriate adjustment for monetary policy, if both the rate of growth of the money stock and the pressure of demand in the economy are above desired levels simultaneously. But virtually throughout 1972, especially at the start, diminishing at the end, the growth of real output and real expenditures in the economy was below the government's expressed intentions. Wages, and subsequently prices, were accelerating during 1972 in the aftermath of the coal miners' strike, with prices being further spurred on by the fall in the external value of sterling after the abandonment of fixed exchange rates in June 1972 and by the world-wide rise in raw material prices. But would a reduction in the rate of growth of the money supply have its initial effect, such as it might be, on output or wages/prices, and when would this effect come through? One could hold a view on such matters, but the available quantitative information on the structure of the U.K. economy has been too slight to permit anyone to express a confident opinion.

How should policy-makers and advisers respond when there is only limited information available on the underlying workings of the economy? In practice the authorities use the available information to make a judgemental selection of the appropriate policy response. But even if they search diligently for information, and use it intelligently when obtained, the existence of uncertainty is bound to lead to error. Professor Friedman has queried whether under these circumstances better results might not be obtained by adherence to some rule. He proposes adherence to a constant growth in the money stock.[1] The attractions of this rule, however, depend largely on three postulates – that the demand for money is relatively stable, that there is a unique natural rate of unemployment, at which the rate of inflation will stabilise, and that the real economy is basically stable. The first would ensure that shifts in the *LM* curve would not destabilise the economy; the second suggests that discretionary use of demand-management instruments to maintain the economy at any position other than this given natural equilibrium level of demand will ultimately be futile; the third implies that if the authorities do not intervene to disrupt the course of the economy it will move back to its equilibrium level of demand, from any disequilibrium of excess or insufficient demand, relatively quickly.

All these propositions are debatable, perhaps the most important being the last of these. As noted in Chapter 10, inconsistent decisions, taken under conditions of great uncertainty and little information, can cause the economy to move to a disequilibrium position, and further mechanisms within the system (accelerator/multiplier responses for example) can aggravate this disequilibrium. Professor Friedman, however, argues that many of the periods of serious disequilibria in the economic history of the United States (and by inference more generally) can be ascribed to the monetary authorities' maladroit intervention, in the great slump in the 1930s, in inflationary war finance, etc.[2] Even so,

---

[1] 'I have favoured increasing the quantity of money at a steady rate designed to keep final product prices constant, a rate that I have estimated to be something like 4 to 5 per cent per year for the U.S. . . . ,' from 'The Optimum Quantity of Money,' chap. 1 in *The Optimum Quantity of Money and Other Essays* (Macmillan, London, 1969) p. 47.

[2] M. Friedman and A. Schwartz, *A Monetary History of the United States, 1867–1960*, National Bureau of Economic Research (Princeton University Press, 1963) especially the section on 'Independence of Monetary Changes' from chap. 13, 'A Summing Up,' pp. 686–95.

there does not seem strong evidence to suggest that the economy is sufficiently resilient to recover an equilibrium position from serious shocks without a delay of several years, perhaps even decades. If the 'automatic' response of the economy from disequilibria is slow and painful, there will be intense political pressure on the authorities to take steps to accelerate the recovery.

In general, the available models on the working of the economic system do not suggest that there is a very strong automatic tendency towards reversion to equilibrium within the normal time horizon of most forecasts, say up to three years ahead. In the meantime the authorities have, and are known by the public to have, control over instruments which can be used to move the economy within a shorter time horizon towards a more preferred position, and thus to alleviate rapidly some of the pains of disequilibrium. Given uncertainty about the longer-term effects of the use of such policy instruments, together with the short time span between political elections, there is virtually bound to be a myopic concern with short-term economic considerations. Political pressures will force the authorities to respond flexibly, and to be seen to respond, to economic distress; they cannot sit on their hands and wait for Adam Smith's invisible hand to restore equilibrium at some unknown future date. Perhaps economists, who doubt the value of discretionary policies, may be able to educate the public on the necessity of taking the long view. It will be a difficult task.

13

The Structural Objectives of Monetary Policy

SUMMARY

The primary emphasis of monetary policy is usually placed on its role as an instrument of macro-economic demand management, as already discussed in Chapter 12. There are, however, other longer-term structural objectives which the monetary authorities should also pursue. Thus the authorities should seek to ensure that the financial system, in common with other industries, works efficiently. In this context it has been argued that the provision of bank deposits (though not of financial services such as the transmission of payments) is costless, so that it would be desirable to pay interest on deposits at a rate equal to the rate of return available on other assets, e.g. real capital. This proposal ignores the risks (e.g. of unforeseen cash withdrawals) which private-sector intermediaries assume in their business. The public sector may be better placed to bear such risk, but a system of financial intermediation dominated by the public sector would be unlikely to exhibit much initiative: public-sector insurance of private-sector intermediation may be the best course.

In the meantime the pricing policy and portfolio selection of financial intermediaries, especially of the banks, is constrained by various monopolistic, or cartelised, practices and, to an even greater extent, by direct controls imposed on them by the authorities. Such restrictions tend to reduce the volume and raise the price of intermediation, causing welfare losses to the community. The competitive position of the intermediaries is thereby weakened; except to the extent that the intermediaries can rearrange their practices to avoid the bite of such constraints, there will be a tendency for financial flows to be diverted to other unconstrained channels.

Even if financial intermediaries were to be encouraged to pay a competitive rate for deposits, the authorities have a monopoly over the issue of legal tender and need pay no interest on currency. This distinction may cause certain, probably slight, distortions within the monetary system, e.g. by encouraging the use of bank deposits – if these bear interest – rather than currency as a means of payment. But currency is a lure for crime and, by providing an anonymous means of payment, facilitates anti-social activities. Furthermore, the non-payment of interest on currency can be regarded as a very broadly based and acceptable tax. So there are valid reasons for doubting whether it is right, even in principle, to pay interest on currency.

In any case it is difficult to devise a method for making nominal interest payments on currency holdings. It would, however, be possible to provide a positive 'real' rate of return on currency, if there was a steady rate of price deflation in the economy. Trying to manipulate the rate of inflation in order to obtain some desired real rate of return on currency seems, however, like taking a sledgehammer to deal with a nut of an issue, at least in any real world, practical context. There are much more important considerations, such as trying to minimise information and transactions costs, which should determine that rate of inflation in an economy which the authorities should aim to achieve in the long run.

A. Financial Efficiency

The main subject of discussion in the preceding chapter was the use of monetary instruments for the attainment of mainly short-run, macro-economic objectives. In conditions of uncertainty, which obscure our vision of future developments and allow for the development of current disequilibria, the primary emphasis of monetary policy will usually be placed on its role in achieving short-run stabilisation. Nevertheless, there are other, subsidiary objectives, besides short-term stabilisation, which monetary policy can be designed to attain. In order to highlight these further objectives, one may imagine a long-term context in which, by assumption, there is sufficient information and wage/price flexibility to allow the full employment of resources, in which experience has eliminated money illusion, in which, in short, conditions approximate to those postulated for a neo-classical, Walrasian equilibrium. In these circumstances, in which we abstract from the continuously pressing short-run objectives of monetary policy, what would be left to achieve?

First, the authorities should see that the context is such that financial intermediation services (along with all other goods and services) are provided as efficiently as possible, thus making optimal use of scarce resources. Second, with full employment being given by assumption, a faster monetary growth will be reflected in fast inflation. In the absence of disequilibria, money illusion, distribution effects, caused by uncertainty, there is a question of exactly what rate of price inflation would be best for the economy. The former issue of structural efficiency is clearly a practical matter, even if treated as secondary in importance to stabilisation policy. The latter question of the optimal rate of price change under neo-classical conditions of continuous full employment is much more abstract. It is dubious whether there is much value, except perhaps as a mental exercise, in examining the 'optimal' rate of inflation in a long-run neo-classical context – in which as Keynes noted we are all dead – when this long-run is formed from a succession of short-run periods with very different assumed conditions. Nevertheless, the two issues have been linked together, particularly in the paper by Professor Friedman on 'The Optimum Quantity of Money.'[1]

That title is, perhaps, a misnomer, since it brings to mind issues of short-term contra-cyclical policy, e.g. the appropriate rate of monetary expansion for the authorities to select, rather than longer-term, structural matters. But as Professor Johnson noted, 'The question [of the optimum quantity of money] has nothing to do with the optimal conduct of short-run stabilization policy. Instead it belongs to the pure theorist's world of continuous full employment of resources; as such, its policy relevance is to the framework of monetary organisation and the long-run environmental objectives of monetary policy.'[2]

The first of the two main issues in this area, the achievement of productive efficiency, is a subject of economic analysis common to all industries. In this instance analysis has tended to concentrate on two main points, banks' pricing policy (i.e. the way they charge for their services and pay interest on their borrowed funds), and the effects on the efficiency of financial intermediation of the authorities' interventions, e.g. in fixing interest-rate ceilings, required reserve ratios, etc. Study of banks' pricing policy has not, however, been advanced by their treatment in much of this literature as a special intermediary, whose liabilities are 'costless to produce', and whose size is apparently not dependent on adjustment towards an equilibrium position of profit maximisation where marginal revenue equals marginal cost.

In one sense, of course, all financial liabilities are costless to produce. Anyone – a bank, an insurance company, a manufacturing company, a person – can write out an

---

[1] Chap. 1, pp. 1–50 in *The Optimum Quantity of Money and Other Essays* (Aldine, Chicago, 1969).

[2] H. G. Johnson, 'Is There An Optimal Money Supply?,' *Journal of Finance*, vol. 25, no. 2 (May 1970) p. 435.

I.O.U. at zero cost. The cost in each case to the issuer of the financial liability instead lies in the inducements which he has to offer the lender, in order to persuade the lender to transfer funds to himself. Only when someone is in a position to issue legal tender can he obtain command over goods and services without having to meet this cost (see Chapter 7). The inducements which financial intermediaries, including banks, offer usually represent some mixture of services, e.g. safe-keeping, book-keeping, running the payments-transmission system, brokerage, provision of information, etc., and of purely financial inducements, e.g. interest payments. These latter financial (i.e. non-service) inducements can also take various forms – interest payments, insurance provisions, equity participation, etc. – as noted in Chapter 6. The form and terms upon which these liabilities were issued will be a major factor determining the risks of unforeseen withdrawals of funds; while the dangers of illiquidity and/or insolvency resulting from such withdrawals will be conditioned by the deployment among alternative assets of the funds thus obtained.

The argument is sometimes made that, since it is 'costless' to produce money, bank deposits, it would be optimal to make the cost of holding money, instead of capital or other assets, zero, i.e. to 'satiate' people's desire for money by making interest payments on money equal to the rate of return on bonds, or on capital. But this ignores the role of risk, uncertainty, in causing differences between the mean expected yields at which people will hold alternative assets. So long as the risks involved in holding bonds or capital were greater than the risks of holding money (which will be the normal case; though the existence of widows and orphans, wishing to avert the income risk of the variance of money interest rates, and a general fear of inflation will lead to some continuing demand for bonds and capital), everyone would prefer to hold money, when mean expected yields were equalised. Money balances would dominate these other assets (i.e. same yield, lower risk). People would go on selling these other assets, when an attempt was made to establish a common expected yield, until the money issuer had bought up most of these other assets in exchange for money.

Of course no private-sector intermediary could possibly do such a thing. To issue liquid liabilities at the same yield as it was buying riskier assets could lead any intermediary directly into both illiquidity and insolvency. It is possible, however, as noted earlier in Chapter 6, to envisage the authorities taking over all intermediation services and tailoring the pattern of their liabilities exactly to the preferences of the public, with a common expected yield, since they have the position, the power, to ignore risks of both illiquidity and insolvency. So the proposal for paying interest on money balances equal to the rate of return on capital either involves the assumption of certainty, in which context there is no role for money as a separate asset anyhow, or else in a world of uncertainty represents a somewhat disguised plea for the authorities to act as the main provider of all intermediary services. And there is an argument for this. The risk–return combinations available from a public-sector 'intermediary' should be superior to those that the private sector could offer because the public sector is better placed to assume risk. There could, therefore, be an advantage in the public sector taking over all financial intermediation operations, including the provision of bank-type deposits. In practice, however, the monopoly position of the public sector would tend to dampen energy and innovation, and would often be used as an easy means of levying taxes (monopoly profits) rather than of achieving a wider portfolio opportunity set. Furthermore, the authorities can pass on their special advantages in risk reduction quite widely to private-sector intermediaries, while maintaining the benefits of competition, by such means as providing deposit insurance, for example the Federal Deposit Insurance Corporation (F.D.I.C.) in the United States, and through Central Bank support of the financial system.

In the meantime, given the present institutional structure of financial intermediation, private-sector intermediaries are offering certain services, which involve real costs to the community, and also issuing liabilities of various risk classes. In order to achieve an efficient allocation of resources, in a perfectly competitive system, the price of these financial services should be equal to the marginal cost of providing them, while the interest paid, or financial inducement offered, for the deposit of funds should provide a combination of expected yield and risk that would leave the intermediary with no more than a 'normal' expected profit from his subsequent employment of these funds in purchasing assets.

If the financial intermediary, say a bank, is selling services at a higher price than their marginal cost, or offering financial inducements to depositors which *after due allowance for risk factors* are lower than the rate on real capital, it will be enjoying a super-normal profit margin on its operations. If the industry is competitive new entrants to it should compete any monopoly profit away. Restrictions and barriers to entry of various kinds may, however, allow the continuation of monopolistic practices among financial intermediaries; the analysis of the welfare cost of this follows the same lines as the normal analysis of the welfare loss from monopoly pricing, where marginal revenue equals marginal cost but price is greater than marginal cost.

Under monopoly, output will be $0Q$, price $0A$ (see Fig. 13.1). Under perfect competition, which will cause each of the atomistic separate producers to feel that they face a horizontal demand curve ($AR = MR$), despite the downward-sloping industry demand curve shown above, output will be $0R$, price $0B$. The welfare gain of competition to the community will be represented by the area TUV, covering the area where the demand curve, showing the amount people were prepared to pay, remains above the additional cost of providing the extra services.[1]

Such a change in pricing policy would also have distributional effects, since the monopoly profits accruing to the shareholders of financial intermediaries would decline,[2] though

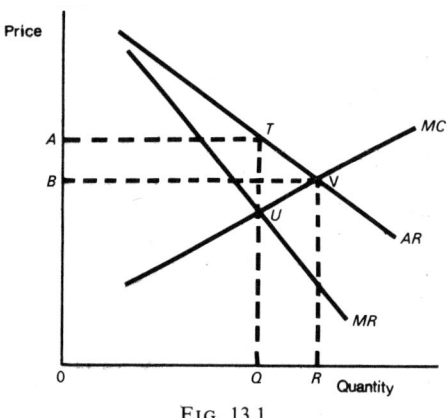

FIG. 13.1

---

[1] The extent of this welfare gain depends on the elasticities of demand and of supply. If the demand for money balances is extremely inelastic to relative price changes, then the welfare gain from shifting to an optimal pricing policy will be negligible (e.g. the area TUV will disappear if the AR curve is vertical). This poses some difficulty for Professor Friedman, for he has tended to argue both that the interest elasticity of demand for money is very low, which implies a very inelastic AR curve, and that the welfare implications of pricing policy for the monetary system are worthy of consideration. I am grateful to M. H. Miller for pointing this out to me. The same point has also been noted by W. D. Nordhaus in his paper on 'The Effects of Inflation on the Distribution of Economic Welfare,' *Journal of Money, Credit and Banking*, vol. 5, no. 1 (February 1973) pt II, pp. 465–504, especially pp. 492–3.

[2] The stock-market value of bank capital would decline. This represents a fall in non-human wealth in an accounting sense, and if we are sticking to accounting principles, probably the easiest course, see Chap. 10, Sect. B, is properly so measured. If, however, the analyst is trying to capitalise all future benefits and costs, then this can *not* be treated as a fall in wealth.

more than offset by an improvement in benefits to depositors and, perhaps, to borrowers. Furthermore, the additional holdings of financial intermediary deposits as their return, after allowance for risk, is brought into line with the return on real capital, will induce a rise in the proportion of the portfolio held in this form, since there is assumed to be always a positive response to own yields. This will cause an adjustment in asset holdings, given wealth, away from bond holdings and from holdings of real capital, e.g. stocks of real goods. Under certain plausible assumptions about payment periods, etc., this portfolio readjustment is likely to lead to fewer transactions, transfers between bank deposits and bonds (trips to the broker), but rather more transactions, transfers between bank deposits and real assets, goods (trips to the supermarket). If bank deposits yield a higher return, the individual is less likely to place a proportion of his assets earmarked against short-term future contingent requirements (transactions and precautionary balances) in bonds, but, if he decides to hold fewer stocks of goods, real assets, in order to maintain larger balances with financial intermediaries, he will have to go shopping more often. The incorporation of these transactions costs into the analysis of the optimum quantity of money has, perhaps, received more attention in the last few years than its importance warrants.[1] Nevertheless, assessment of alternative asset portfolios should cover not only return and risk but also another dimension, that is the associated transaction (and information) costs associated with the maintenance of that portfolio over time.

Often the inducements to hold the liabilities of financial intermediaries, in the form of services and interest payments, are provided jointly, for example safe-keeping of funds together with interest payments on such deposits. The provision of services involves real costs, e.g. buildings, vaults, armoured transport vehicles for safe-keeping, while the interest payment does not, except for accounting, book-keeping, management, etc. Financial intermediaries can be regarded as multi-product firms. Frequently, however, they do not charge separately for the individual different services, but instead offer a lower interest payment to the depositor, with the margin between the fully competitive rate and the offered rate sufficient to cover the (average) costs of providing the joint services. This means that users of financial services are generally *not* being charged the marginal costs for the provision of such services, while on the other hand the depositors are not getting the full return for transferring the use of their funds to the intermediary. This common charging may induce depositors to make more use of expensive services, e.g. the payments transmission mechanism and financial advisory services, and to hold fewer balances than would be desirable in order to make most efficient use of scarce resources.

Although, in principle, separate charges for separate services and full competitive interest payments will achieve greatest efficiency, the principle can be taken too far. For example, it was announced in the English press in 1972 that one of the main deposit banks might in future charge for consultations with the bank manager. This certainly follows the precept of charging specifically for separate services; but it will also involve the need to set up a whole additional accounting system. One could well imagine that for every thirty minutes' interview, an additional three minutes of somebody's time would be taken up in processing the consequential accounting. It may hardly be sensible to charge separately for individual transactions in banking; the cost might be too high.

Thus, in principle, it might seem correct to make a specific charge for giving a current-account depositor the option of making instantaneous withdrawals (up to some limit), rather along the lines of payment for arranged, but unused, facilities, and then to make a separate calculated charge for actual turn-over. Apart from these charges, credit and debit

---

[1] See the various papers on 'The Roles of Money in an Economy and the Optimum Quantity of Money,' by M. Perlman, *Economica*, vol. 38, no. 151 (August 1971) pp. 233–52; E. Feige and M. Parkin, *American Economic Review*, vol. 61, no. 3 (June 1971) pt. 1, pp. 335–49; E. Feige, M. Parkin, R. Avery and C. Stones, *Economica*, vol. 40, no. 160 (November 1973) pp. 416–31; M. Perlman, *Economica*, vol. 40, no. 160 (November 1973) pp. 432–41.

balances could receive the full market rate of interest and other services could be separately charged. In practice the additional accounting costs involved might outweigh any benefits in additional choice from the use of separate charging. It may be more economical to adopt a simpler form of charging for banking services, which would avoid the chore of having separate payments for each individual transaction. Moreover, so long as there was sufficient competition, it should pay institutions to differentiate their offered mix of services and interest yield, despite maintaining in each case simplified accounting and low transactions costs. Some institutions would offer more services and lower yields, others would offer fewer services and higher yields.

If banks are prevented, by internal cartel or external regulation, from offering competitive yields, say on current accounts, then they will compete by offering additional services, say in the form of free transmission services, free cheque books, neighbourhood branches, etc., until marginal costs rise to equal marginal revenues. The demand for bank deposits, and for other financial intermediary liabilities, may well respond more elastically to variations in relative yields than to variations in services offered. So restricting competition to the provision of services, and limiting interest-rate competition, may represent a form of market discrimination leading to higher profits. It has been argued, in the United States mainly, that competition between banks in the offer of interest payments on demand deposits could make them shift to riskier asset portfolios in order to raise the revenue to service these higher payments. It is not clear, however, why the cost of providing competitive financial services to depositors would not have the same effect. Perhaps it is the higher profit margins, given some restriction on entry, resulting from the limitation of interest payments on demand deposits that is seen as offering the additional safety to banks.

Be that as it may, banks in the United States are prevented from paying interest on demand deposits by regulation.[1] Control over rates which financial intermediaries may offer on deposits or charge on loans is but one of the several forms of direct controls which the authorities have imposed on financial intermediaries in general, and the banking system in particular. Since controls, almost by definition, are forcing the affected intermediaries into a less preferred position, their imposition will reduce the size of such intermediaries and lower the rate of return offered by them to depositors. Except for lump-sum taxes or subsidies, which are not really controls in this sense anyhow, direct intervention will result in some distortion to the business of the intermediary. For example, the imposition of required liquid assets and reserve ratios will force the banks to adjust their asset portfolios in order to avoid the penalties incurred from an infringement of the regulations. In general the banks will be induced to hold more of the prescribed reserve assets than they would wish to do voluntarily. This tends to benefit issuers of reserve assets, usually the central government, at the expense of the financial intermediaries and other borrowers.

The imposition of controls, direct intervention, will also have the effect of diverting financial flows from their normal channels. In part this will occur as the controlled intermediaries seek to readjust their business to escape the constraints of such controls.[2] Thus the imposition of Regulation Q on rates offered on C.D.s in the United States led to the development by banks there of alternative means of attracting funds through issues of commercial paper and euro-dollar borrowing. In part such diversions of financial flows will occur because the competitive position of the controlled intermediary is weakened relative to uncontrolled intermediaries, and this will normally lead to a shift of business

---

[1] See, on this subject, G. Benston, 'Interest Payments on Demand Deposits and Bank Investment Behavior,' *Journal of Political Economy*, vol. 72, no. 5 (October 1964) pp. 431–49.

[2] If controls, for example in the form of a required reserve ratio, were to be placed on the international (euro-dollar) business of banks in certain financial centres, the banks would seek to avoid such controls by shifting the locus of their international business to a place of business where fewer constraints were imposed upon them.

to the latter. Official intervention generally forces a wedge between borrowing and lending rates in the intermediaries concerned. The extent to which this can be avoided by some rearrangement of business practices by that intermediary, or evaded by a transfer of business through other financial channels is unknown. The net resulting effect on expenditure decisions, e.g. investment and saving, arising from such direct control is thus incalculable in the absence of much greater information about the working of the system than anyone now possesses. Certainly the economic effect of, say, ceilings on bank lending cannot be observed by monitoring the subsequent movements in bank lending because the relationships between, say, bank advances and company or personal expenditures will have been so distorted by the control itself that the constrained variations in bank advances will tell the enquirer virtually nothing about the net economic impact of the measure. If circumstances have been such as to encourage expenditures financed by bank borrowing, the imposition of ceilings on bank lending will be somewhat akin to breaking the thermometer in the hopes that the patient's fever will then go away. It is, possibly, a fair retort to remark that in our present state of knowledge, or ignorance, the movements in financial variables, say the monetary aggregates or interest rates, do not contain all that much clear, useful information either, even in the absence of direct controls. Whereas the imposition of direct controls do not make the selection of an optimal short-term stabilisation policy any easier nor so much worse, they do, however, have the added disadvantage of causing structural inefficiency.[1,2]

In those circumstances, though, when inordinate public attention is being paid to some proximate indicator of monetary policy, say the volume of bank lending, or the monetary aggregates, or some interest rate, in place of any fully-worked-out analysis of the effect of such financial variables on the ultimate objectives of policy, e.g. incomes, inflation, etc., direct controls may have some presentational, cosmetic effect in persuading people that the proximate indicator in the public eye is being 'brought under control.' However, the full effect of this step on the economy is virtually incalculable, and the presentational advantage has been gained at the expense of structural inefficiency. Nevertheless, the world being what it is, the presentational advantages can often appear politically desirable.

B. The Payment of Interest on Currency and the Optimal Rate of Inflation

A distinction has been made, a line drawn, between official government institutions with the power to offer liabilities which are legal tender, and all other sectors and financial intermediaries (including banks) whose liabilities are not legal tender. These intermediaries cannot force people to hold their liabilities; instead they have to induce the public to place funds with them by offering them inducements in the form of services and financial return. Those with the right to issue legal tender can use this power to obtain command over

---

[1] It is sometimes claimed that the use of direct controls entails the further possibility of allowing the authorities to select the direction of funds between competing recipients. Whether or not such selection can be justified on general economic grounds, the development of secondary financial markets, e.g. the inter-company market, makes it difficult to sustain such selectivity, or again to measure its net effect.

[2] In so far as constraints on the freedom of financial intermediaries to determine their own pricing policy or to pick their preferred asset portfolio cause structural inefficiency without greatly improving the ability of the authorities to conduct contracyclical stabilisation policy, why then are such constraints so commonly imposed? Why, for example, is the banking sector in most countries so strictly regulated, whereas there is considerable diversity among countries in the extent of control over other industries? The cynical may believe that the main function of such controls is to provide the government with cheap finance. To be sure, this has sometimes been one of the considerations, but only rarely has this been a main, or even a major, element in the introduction of such controls. The main justification for controls, on prudential grounds, was set out in Chap. 7. Essentially the aim is to limit the extent of risk taken on by financial intermediaries, especially by banks, since the social costs of failures may be much greater than the private costs to the entrepreneur involved.

assets, goods and services, without offering anything in return. People cannot legally refuse to accept legal tender in payment.

Whereas competition should lead financial intermediaries, including banks, to offer services and competitive interest rates to depositors until monopoly profit is eliminated, the authorities have a monopoly based on power over the issue of currency, do not need to pay interest on currency, and can therefore enjoy a monopoly profit, or seignorage. Ignoring possible distributional effects which may follow, since the return from the currency issue enables the authorities to hold taxes elsewhere at a lower level, this distinction (in the provision of interest payments) between legal-tender currency and other assets, such as bank deposits, is sometimes held to have a deleterious structural effect on the monetary system. It encourages people to hold and to use bank deposits, on which a return may be obtained, as a means of payment in place of currency. As noted before, there are considerable real costs involved in processing cheque payments. If an interest payment was made on currency, the additional use of currency would lessen the burden on the banking system of processing payments. This would represent a real resource gain to the economy. In addition larger average inventories of currency would reduce the number of trips to the banks undertaken in order to adjust actual to desired currency holdings. Furthermore, the non-payment of interest on legal-tender currency raises the costs to financial intermediaries, especially banks, and others of holding such assets. This 'tax' on currency holding will, in some part, be avoided by attempts by banks to economise on currency holdings, which will entail the use of real resources in currency transportation and management. The 'tax' on currency will, therefore, represent a disadvantage to large-scale currency users, who have to tie up a lot of their funds in zero-yielding assets, but will benefit the rest of the community who would have to make up in higher taxes any interest payments on currency.

In practice, the scale of this factor is not very large. A rough estimate of the value of seignorage, paid over to the Treasury in the United Kingdom, arising from the non-payment of interest on currency can be obtained from the annual report and accounts of the Bank of England. Thus in its accounts for the year ended 28 February 1973 were the following figures for the Issue Department,[1] shown in Table 13.1.

This total of £204 million may, perhaps, be compared with the revenue flowing from taxes on incomes, which amounted to £11,477 million in 1972, and from taxes on consumers' expenditure which came to £7290 million in 1972.[2] Moreover, this seignorage on currency represents an extremely broadly based tax, except for its relatively heavy impact

TABLE 13.1

Income and Profits:	
Securities of, or guaranteed by, the British Government	179,662
Other securities	34,113
	213,775
Expenses:	
Cost of production of Bank notes	6059
Cost of issue, custody and payment of Bank notes	3336
Other expenses	131
	9526
Payable to H.M. Treasury	204,249

---

[1] *Bank of England, Report and Accounts for the Year ended 28th February 1973* (Bank of England Printing Works, Loughton, Essex, 1973) p. 40.

[2] *National Income and Expenditure, 1973* (Blue Book) Central Statistical Office (H.M.S.O., London, 1973) pp. 54–5, tables 46–7.

on the banking system,[1] arousing less disaffection than income or expenditure taxes. Any proposal to pay out the seignorage in interest to currency holders, and to recoup the loss by raising taxes (or cutting public expenditures) elsewhere, in the hopes of causing some (minor) improvement in the efficiency of the monetary system, is likely to prove unpopular and might cause an even worse allocation of resources elsewhere. And if such interest payments were financed by a faster rate of monetary expansion, then in the long run the rate of inflation would rise equivalently and leave the 'real' long-run rate of interest on currency unchanged.[2]

In any case the proposal to pay interest on currency often founders at the first obstacle, that of devising a practical and cheap way of paying interest on currency which is proof against fraud.[3] There have been suggestions, for example by Professor Friedman, that this problem might be solved by 'giving banks permission to compete in the issuance of notes – as they used to do before the Bank Charter Act of 1844 in the United Kingdom and the National Banking Act of 1863 in the United States – and leaving them to figure out the technicalities of how to pay interest on such notes'.[4] As the references to these two acts surely suggest, this must raise the question of whether the authorities would be able to control this new system adequately for the purpose of short-term stabilisation. How would the note issue be backed? Would these notes be legal tender – surely not, or the system would become entirely unstable! Would this not lead to the possibility of large swings in the public's preferred legal-tender currency/bank note ratio? Would the authorities and the banks compete in the provision of notes to the public? Would the authorities be able to ensure that the volume of currency under this new system would respond flexibly to seasonal and other variations in demand?[5] Would the authorities be able to control the rate of growth of the money supply as easily under such a system?

Thus seignorage on currency acts as a relatively painless tax, and it would be difficult to devise a practical method of paying interest on currency. Furthermore, the holding and use of currency may involve large costs to society, beyond the costs of production, which are not borne by the currency holder or user (external costs). In this respect a tax on currency is appropriate; indeed, there may be a case for an even larger tax than is occasioned by non-payment of interest. In particular, the existence of anonymous means of payment provides a central lure for crime. The authorities have the responsibility for maintaining law and order, but do not make specific charges to those in particular need of protection. There is a whole security industry, police, Securicor, armoured cars, safes, vaults, etc., much of whose existence is made necessary by the existence of large-scale holdings, movements[6] and use of currency.

---

[1] In the United Kingdom, however, the reserve ratio, to which all banks must adhere, does *not* require them to hold a large volume of zero-yielding reserve assets. To this extent ratio control in the United Kingdom represents much less of an interest burden, or tax, on the banking system than in many other countries, such as for example the United States.

[2] J. Grandmont and Y. Younes, 'On the Efficiency of a Monetary Equilibrium,' *Review of Economic Studies*, vol. 40, no. 122 (April 1973) pp. 149–65, especially pp. 161–2.

[3] The real difficulty would be policing the system. Otherwise everyone could simply report their average currency balances to the authorities and receive payment. But would such reports be honest?

[4] As reported by H. G. Johnson, in his paper, 'Is there An Optimal Money Supply?,' *Journal of Finance* (May 1970) p. 437.

[5] One of the main functions of a Central Bank in its role as note issuer, which is unsung precisely because it usually works so efficiently and flexibly as to be unnoticed, is to adjust the available currency supply to accommodate the sizeable fluctuations in demand for currency over holidays and the changing seasons of the year. The lack of such flexibility was regarded as the main deficiency of the National Banking System prior to 1913.

[6] A tax on currency would, however, lead to more trips to the bank or between the banks and the Central Bank, as everyone tried harder to economise on cash balances. In so far as movements of currency are particularly susceptible, and conducive, to criminal attack, the protection costs might be increased by a tax on currency.

Moreover, the existence of currency, providing an anonymous means of payment, facilitates those shady or illegal activities which flourish in obscurity: tax evasion, gambling, prostitution, crime, all tend to run on the basis of currency payments. The diffusion of personal information, which is an inherent part of credit transactions, tends to blight those activities which do not meet with the approval of society, as currently organised. At a rather more mundane level, a reason often advanced to explain why some workers like to be paid in cash rather than by cheque is that they do not want the wife to know exactly how much they earn.

It is a curious phenomenon that some groups of self-styled radical anarchists wish to abolish money. The abolition of money – means of payment – requires that all transactions must be undertaken on a multilateral credit basis.[1] This can only be achieved in circumstances requiring an extremely high level of personal behavioural information. It would become much more difficult to work for the radical alteration of society in such a system. The abolition of money is, in reality, an extremely reactionary and authoritarian programme. It would limit the freedom of the individual to undertake transactions of which society may disapprove, and it would tend to force behaviour to conform under sanction to the rules of the game as laid down by the authorities, whoever these may be.[2]

If the balance of the arguments still suggests that it would be desirable in principle to pay interest on currency, but no practical method of making such payments can be found, then an alternative way of achieving a desired *real* rate of interest on currency holdings can be found by bringing about, via changes in the rate of expansion of the nominal money supply, the appropriate rate of change of prices. Since the real rate equals the nominal rate less the expected rate of inflation, a fixed nominal rate does not prevent the achievement of a given real rate, if the rate of inflation can be manipulated. If the intention is to establish positive real rates of return on currency, the rate of change of prices should be negative. It does, however, seem a vast and indiscriminate sledgehammer of an in-

---

[1] Unless the anarchists are proposing a return to a barter society. But even there information costs and transaction difficulties would tend to make the resulting economies much more narrow, rigid and probably authoritarian in organisation than a monetary economy would be.

[2] Indeed the real issue in this field lies between (economic) efficiency and freedom. In order to raise the efficiency and rate of growth of the modern state, it might be desirable to phase out currency (anonymous means of payment) altogether, perhaps initially by imposing a tax on its use. Instead one would require, possibly by subsidies supported by sanctions, the provision of additional accurate personal information by all members of the community. The availability of additional personal information, stored for easy access in data banks, would lead, of course, to the substitution of bilateral credit – possibly in some cases even multilateral credit arrangements – for physical exchange of means of payment as media of exchange.

That such developments are not only technologically possible, but would also prove a cheaper and more efficient method of running the payment (and credit-giving) system in the economy seems almost beyond question. David Peretz, in his paper on 'Thirty-five Years of Change for the Financial System,' *Futures* (December 1971) p. 353, stated that, 'It is already quite clear that the technologies most appropriate to this information-handling task will be computers and data communications; the costs of paper handling associated with cash and cheques are becoming prohibitive.' Yet it remains arguable how far it is desirable to move in this direction. Increased access to personal information is the *sine qua non* of a 'more efficient' exchange technology, but also represents a loss of privacy; this is the more blatant when this access is not agreed or not revealed to the individual, but it will be a loss of privacy even if volunteered.

The question of the way personal information is to be gathered, to be stored, and to be used is going to remain a central issue of general political–social–economic debate for years to come. Indeed it has already surfaced in the letter columns of *The Times*, viz. the letter from Sir Jeremy Mostyn on 24 January 1972 on the 'Obsolescence of Money': 'Sir, Mr. M. Macmillan (18 January) expresses concern that the gradual obsolescence of money is leading to a huge central credit control system. But what, in heaven's name, does he think that money is but a credit control system of an extremely clumsy and inconvenient, not to say unhygienic, nature.'

strument, changing the rate of inflation, to deal with a tiny nut of an issue, efficiency within the monetary system. But it must be remembered that this analysis usually takes place within an extremely artificial context, involving assumptions of continuous full employment of resources, no money illusion, no distribution effects, etc.

Certainly this kind of exercise gives no guidance for the conduct of immediate short-term policy, but it does raise the pertinent question of what rates of inflation the authorities might aim for in the long run. In the short run expectations will be based on recent historical experience. An attempt to enforce a sudden large change in the rate of price inflation in the system, especially to reduce it sharply at a stroke, is likely to disrupt the basis on which plans in the community will have been formulated, and thus runs the danger of provoking conflicts between groups on the basis of inconsistent expectations, with resulting disequilibria, unexpected distribution shifts[1] and resentment.

In the long run, however, it is possible at any rate to imagine a situation in which the rate of inflation has been at X per cent for years and is universally expected to go on being at X per cent in future. This is built into everyone's plans. There are no unintended distributional effects, no incorrect plans, no disequilibria. Does it matter then what value X takes? One answer, with which one must sympathise, is that these assumptions are such fantasy that the question is irrelevant. If you can hypothesise such a world, why not hypothesise that everyone is honest, so there would be no problem in paying interest on currency? Indeed why have any money in a system in which the crucial ingredient of uncertainty has been largely suppressed?

Even though the long run is approached through a series of short runs, in which more realistic assumptions apply, there still remains the question of the long-term rate of inflation to aim for, even though the speed with which one should adjust towards that in any short period should be constrained by the historical context of plans, expectations, experience, etc. Given these short-term constraints, a forceful set of arguments suggests that a zero rate of change of prices would be desirable to minimise information and transaction costs. Keeping informed on current rates of price change and trying to predict future rates involves a cost in time and effort. Those who do not make the effort will probably make the null assumption that prices will remain unchanged, which suggests that the dispersion of expectations may widen, and planning errors become more serious, as the rate of change of prices becomes greater. The attempt to work out what the rate of change of prices has been and to estimate how price levels may be expected to alter in future involves arithmetical exercises, compound interest: so long as the rate of change is non-zero this will involve a cost to all and an impossibility for some. Furthermore, there are considerable transactions costs involved in altering price and wage levels. The faster the rate of inflation (or of deflation), the greater the shift in the relative position of a given wage or price during the period in which it remains fixed. Faster rates of change of prices either imply greater disturbances to relativities or greater transactions costs. Indeed, it has been argued that it is precisely this constant see-saw in relative prices and relative incomes and wages that makes very rapid inflation so intolerable,[2] rather than any permanent distributive effects.

---

[1] It is often asserted that the unintended distribution effects of inflation are bad, with the weakest sections of the community faring worst. Studies, however, of income distribution in recent inflationary periods give very little support for this thesis, see, for example, E. Phelps, *Inflation Policy and Unemployment Theory* (Macmillan, New York, 1972) chap. 5, 'Distributional Effects of Employment and of Unexpected Inflation'; and also W. D. Nordhaus, 'The Effects of Inflation on the Distribution of Economic Welfare,' *Journal of Money, Credit and Banking* (February 1973) pp. 465–504. But even when such distribution effects are broadly regarded as beneficial, on balance, they were not achieved through any political process of discussion and negotiation and their arbitrary impact will be resented.

[2] See the paper 'Do Trade Unions Cause Inflation?' by H. Turner, D. Jackson and F. Wilkinson, *University of Cambridge Department of Applied Economics, Occasional Paper 36* (Cambridge University Press, 1972) especially pp. 38–9.

In comparison with these considerations, the possible advantages for the structure of the monetary system from a steady rate of price deflation, sufficient to raise the real rate on currency into line with the yield offered on capital, seem in my opinion to be relatively trivial. Nevertheless, with rising productivity, shifting tastes, etc., individual wages and prices are never going to be constant. It may be a reasonable approximation to a system where information and transactions costs are minimised to have nominal wages and money incomes remaining roughly constant and goods prices slowly declining, which would offer some real return on cash balances. In practice, though, such regimes may run into greater difficulties and rigidities than those with constant goods prices and rising nominal wages.

A more radical approach to this matter has been adopted by Professor Phelps, who argues that the seignorage received on currency is a relatively efficient tax, and that an increase in the proportion of taxes raised in this manner 'would improve the approximation of the tax system to its various objectives.' On these grounds Professor Phelps argues not only against deflation but for some positive rate of inflation: '"An inflation tax" is a useful addition to the armoury of fiscal tools.'[1]

Certainly the main alternative to the objective of maintaining stable prices canvassed in the literature has been to propose a positive average rate of inflation. The usual grounds for this are not the above, but that a positive rate of inflation is likely to stimulate the demand for real assets (by reducing outside financial wealth while raising the return on capital relative to that on financial assets), thus leading to a higher capital/output ratio and at least temporarily to faster growth. A number of economists have examined this argument,[2] often in the context of rather formal growth models. But it would take us rather too far afield to pursue that further here. Although positive price inflation may have some stimulating effect on capital accumulation and growth even in the long run, this will be at the expense of worsening allocative and structural inefficiencies and rising information and transactions costs. My own subjective view is that the long-run stimulation of capital accumulation from *anticipated* inflation is quite slight, whereas the costs of inflation mount quite rapidly once it accelerates beyond a rate of 2 to 3 per cent per annum.

---

[1] *Inflation Policy and Unemployment Theory*, pp. 210–20. He argues, further, pp. 202–10, that the larger desired holdings of real cash balances at low rates of inflation, and accompanying low nominal interest rates, will provide the system with the liquidity that could feed any increase in demand for real goods, and make the authorities' stabilisation policies more difficult. 'At low rates of inflation the trials of the stabilisers are made harder and their tools made blunter and less reliable. In a world of uncertainty, a policy of moderately high inflation in order to contain liquidity somewhere below the otherwise ideal level imposes a cost which can be viewed as the premium charged for (limited!) insurance against economic instability.' This is a curious argument. To encourage higher average rates of price inflation in order to prevent unforeseen surges in real demand is a paradox that is too eccentric to accept.

[2] See, for example, H. Johnson, 'Money in a Neo-Classical One-Sector Growth Model,' chap. 4 in his *Essays in Monetary Economics*, 2nd ed. (Allen & Unwin, London, 1969) pp. 143–78, and J. Tobin, 'Money and Economic Growth,' *Econometrica*, vol. 33, no. 4 (October 1965) pp. 671–84.

14

The Regional Adjustment Process

SUMMARY

In previous chapters we were concerned with the process of adjustment over time of various groups in the economy, but these groups were not given a geographical location. In the final two chapters we shall examine how adjustment is achieved spatially, between different areas. For ease of analysis this subject will be divided into two parts. In the first part, in Chapter 14, we shall examine the process of adjustment between regions in a single country where there is a single common currency: then in Chapter 15 we shall move on to consider the process of adjustment between countries with separate monetary systems and individual monetary policies.

The main emphasis in this study of inter-regional adjustment is that it involves an inter-linked process of the achievement of both flow and stock equilibria. A formal model illustrating the nature of the linkages between flow and stock relationships is set out in Appendix A; this model provides much of the analytical basis for the description of the adjustment process in the rest of the chapter. The dichotomy between expenditure-flow relationships and asset-stock adjustments is mirrored in the distinction between the analysis of the determination of the current-account balance and the analysis of how this balance is financed. Reversing the usual procedure, we consider first in Section A how regional current-account imbalances are financed.

In general, the existence of an integrated financial system and capital market shared by regions within a country allow regional current-account imbalances to be very easily financed, so much so that there is no analogue at the regional level to the recurring concern at national levels about the adequacy of their foreign-exchange reserves. Given the high degree of substitution between financial claims of similar kinds issued in different regions, a region does not face the same immediate financial pressure to correct a current-account imbalance as does an individual country, with a lower international elasticity of substitution between financial assets. Even so, financial pressures will develop in regions if appropriate adjustment to current-account imbalance is long delayed. If a current-account deficit is not a reflection of local investment opportunities, it will involve a growing burden of debt servicing, rising invisible account deficits, and falling incomes and wealth. Financial pressures to adjust will not appear in the guise of exhausted reserves but of an increasing unwillingness to provide further loans to the borrowers in the indebted area.

Then in Section B we turn back to an examination of the determinants of the current-account balance. We start with the simplest case, in which all prices, including factor prices, interest rates, etc., are determined nationally. In this case an external shock, causing say a rise in the region's exports, will cause a multiple increase in incomes and wealth, with the ultimate adjustment required depending on the size of the marginal propensity to import. The time path to that equilibrium, explored in Appendix A, is functionally more complex, and the system may well experience oscillations in the process of adjustment. These changes in incomes and output, with wage levels given, would cause fluctuations in the level of employment or migration. These labour market developments can be painful, and there may alternatively be some flexibility in movements of relative wage rates between regions, though such flexibility is reduced by concern over parity of treatment.

Such flexibility in wage rates would restore employment in depressed regions either through a substitution of labour for capital or by raising the return to capital (and therefore new investment) in the region, even if final prices of goods remained nationally fixed. But this latter is a strong assumption, and we next examine how the current account of a region responds to changes in the prices of its goods relative to the prices of goods produced elsewhere in the country. Given the supply elasticities of production in the regions involved, and the initial trade balance, this depends on the price elasticities of demand in each region for the exports of the other regions. The higher these elasticities, the more favourable the effect on the balance of a relative reduction in prices. This concept of the price elasticity of demand is not, however, an easy one, since changes in relative prices affect incomes and supply conditions, as well as having pure substitution effects. So the increase of sales of exports and fall in imports, following a fall in relative prices, depends on an amalgam of different and even offsetting factors. In particular, if a region (country) is relatively small it ought, by lowering the prices of its products, to be able to displace goods of a similar kind produced by other regions (countries). Thus, whatever the aggregate price elasticity of demand for such goods, the price elasticity of demand facing any one region (country) should be high. In practice, however, the apparent response of trade flows to devaluations in recent years has often seemed sluggish, but I attribute this more to slow supply response than to low demand elasticities.

A. Financing Current-Account Imbalances: The Capital Account

So far we have been concerned with the process of adjustment over time, in response to changes in the parameters of the system, of various groups in the economy. These groups were not, however, given any location in geographical space; as far as the analysis indicated up till this point, they all lived together at the same spot. In fact, of course, people spread out over regions and countries, and it is therefore also necessary to study how adjustment to shocks and changes is achieved spatially, involving the economic inter-relationships of one area with another.

Sometimes this subject appears even more complicated than it need, because two separable issues are taken together in a complex mixture, rather than distinguished and discussed consecutively. These two issues are, first, the process of regional adjustment between regions who share a single currency (and monetary authority) and, secondly, the question of the effects of alternative possible monetary relationships between individual countries with their own separate distinct currencies. Frequently analysis of the effects of various forms of *inter-national* monetary relationships, e.g. flexible exchange rates, fixed but adjustable rates, the gold standard, etc., is pressed forward before the process of *intra-national* regional adjustment has been fully explained. Yet if you do not understand how balance between Manchester and London, or Chicago and New York, is maintained, how will it be possible to comprehend clearly economic relationships between London and New York, where the existence of separate currencies introduces a further layer of complexity.

So in this chapter the intention is to discuss adjustment between regions in a single country with one common currency: indeed we shall generally assume that the total money supply in this single country is given. Then having discussed the intra-national adjustment process, the analysis is broadened in the next chapter to encompass the additional problems introduced by the existence of several autonomous countries with their separate monetary systems and individual monetary policies.

The first stage, therefore, is to examine the process of adjustment between separate regions within the same country. Many writers dealing with this subject, at least in the post-Keynesian period, focused their attention mainly on the determination of inter-regional trade flows and their inter-relationship with income-expenditure flows: the analysis dealt mostly with the effects of the foreign trade multiplier on the one hand, and of changes in the relative prices of tradable goods on the other.[1] While such flow relationships form a major part of the story, it has more recently been realised that this overlooked the inter-related and equally important question of the achievement of asset-stock balance, with financial assets and money, as well as goods moving from one region to another.[2] In this account we shall try to give a description of the inter-linked process of the achievement of both flow and stock equilibrium, with both expenditure flows and shifts in asset holdings responding to relative prices (and interest rates), as well as to changes in incomes and wealth. The basic framework of our approach is an extended portfolio adjustment model.

A model of this kind is set out in Appendix A. It provides a formalised picture of the structure and workings of one region within a large country which is intended to be an aid to understanding the process of inter-regional adjustment. The background to the analysis in the remainder of the chapter may become clearer if the appendix is read first, and there are several references in the text to it. Nevertheless, any formal model can give only a limited

---

[1] An early example is to be found in F. Machlup, *International Trade and the National Income Multiplier* (The Blakiston Company, Philadelphia, 1943, reprinted 1950).

[2] There have been several strands in this development. The simplest, but nevertheless useful, model which incorporates consideration of asset balance concentrates on the achievement of equilibrium between the demand and supply of money in any region. In this model the demand for money depends, mainly, on domestic incomes, while the supply comes from domestic credit (money) creation and monetary flows via the balance of payments. This analysis was initially developed within the I.M.F. as a guide to policy recommendations in the international sphere, see for example, J. J. Polak, 'Monetary Analysis of Income Formation and Payments Problems,' *International Monetary Fund Staff Papers*, vol. 6 (1957/58) pp. 1–50, and V. Argy and J. J. Polak, 'Credit Policy and the Balance of Payments', *I.M.F. Staff Papers*, vol. 18 (1971) pp. 1–24. This approach was subsequently taken up by certain monetary economists who brought it into the main stream of monetarist analysis, for instance R. A. Mundell, H. G. Johnson and A. K. Swoboda (with their main centre at the International Economics Workshop at the University of Chicago). They em-phasised those aspects of the model which reach back to Hume's (1752) classic analysis 'Of the Balance of Trade,' from *Essays, Moral, Political and Literary*, vol. 1 (Longmans Green, London, 1898) pp. 330–41, 343–5, reprinted in *International Finance*, ed. R. N. Cooper (Penguin Books, Harmondsworth, Middlesex, 1969) pp. 25–37. Examples of their analysis can be found in H. G. Johnson, 'The Monetary Approach to Balance-of-Payments Theory,' chap. 9 in *Further Essays in Monetary Economics* (Allen & Unwin, London, 1972), also reproduced as chap. 11 in *International Trade and Money*, ed. M. B. Connolly and A. K. Swoboda (Allen & Unwin, London, 1973). The latter also contains contributions on the same subject by K. Brunner, 'Money Supply Process and Monetary Policy in an Open Economy,' chap. 8, and by A. K. Swoboda and R. Dornbusch, 'Adjustment, Policy, and Monetary Equilibrium in a Two-Country Model,' chap. 12. A further paper on 'The Monetary Theory of Balance of Payments Policies' by H. G. Johnson is to be included in a book on *The Monetary Approach to the Balance of Payments*, ed. J. Frenkel and H. G. Johnson (Allen & Unwin, London, 1974).

Their analysis concentrates, however, on the achievement of asset balance for only one asset, namely money, and tends to ignore the need to describe and to demonstrate how asset balance is obtained for all assets, in each region, including real capital and non-monetary financial assets. It is, of course, true that in a three-asset world, goods, money and bonds, if the markets for two assets are in equilibrium, the third must also be. This appeal to Walras's law as a justification for omitting specific consideration of the market in non-monetary financial assets fails in those cases when we are interested in the process of adjustment in non-Walrasian systems. In this respect more com-plete and more satisfactory accounts of the achievement of stock-flow equilibrium for a wider range of assets have been developed by J. E. Floyd, 'Monetary and Fiscal Policy in a World of Capital Mobility,' *The Review of Economic Studies*, vol. 86, no. 108 (October 1969) pp. 503–17, and E. Tower, 'Monetary and Fiscal Policy in a World of Capital Mobility: a Respecification,' ibid. vol. 39, no. 119 (July 1972) pp. 251–62, with finally 'A Reply' from J. E. Floyd, ibid. vol. 40, no. 122 (April 1973) pp. 299–303.

and partial representation of the real world, and some may find it indigestible; so it can be skipped, if preferred.

The dichotomy between expenditure-flow relationships and asset-stock adjustments is mirrored in the distinction, in studying the balance of payments, between the analysis of the determination of the current-account balance and the analysis showing how this balance (surplus or deficit) will be financed by flows of financial assets, in the capital account plus reserve movements. Because it seems relatively easier to do so, and accords with our emphasis on asset equilibrium and financial flows, we shall consider these two parts of the balance of payments in reverse order, discussing first the ways in which a (regional) current-account imbalance will be financed.

Nobody doubts that regions do run current-account surpluses (or deficits) in trade with each other; that some regions find it becoming relatively easier or more difficult to sell their goods and services in inter-regional (national) markets; that marked regional disparities in wealth, incomes and unemployment develop between regions and that large net regional migrations take place. Yet despite such signs of balance-of-payments problems, it is often claimed[1] that in inter-regional transactions – as compared and contrasted with international transactions – there are no balance-of-payments problems, or at least that these are of a qualitatively different kind. What this actually means is that the portfolio adjustments required *to finance* a current-account surplus/deficit can be much more smoothly and easily arranged in inter-regional transactions, indeed so simply facilitated that they may pass virtually unnoticed.

To the inhabitants of, say, Manchester a fall in the demand for their goods and services from the rest of the country does not evidence itself in newspaper headlines about exports and imports, but initially in a fall in their monetary balances (see equation (v) of the model in Appendix A) and in the local banks' cash reserves (see equation (vi) of the model). In fact in a branch bank system, in which cash reserves are centralised at Head Office in the main money-market centres, the deficit of the Manchester area (with other areas) at the clearing will not even be settled by reserve flows. Instead the Manchester banks would increase their (book) liabilities at Head Office, with an increasingly deficit position (i.e. local loans becoming larger than local deposits). In a branch banking system the initial financial counterpart of a current-account imbalance occurs virtually automatically. In a unit bank system, in which each area bank maintains its own reserves, the initial financing of an imbalance may have a more noticeable impact, since the clearing will provide some areas with surplus reserve funds and lead to pressures on the reserves of deficit areas. Hence the pressures on the area banks to readjust their portfolios in order to restore their desired balance-sheet position may well be more acute and immediate than in a branch bank system.

In any case, whatever the form of the banking system, the inhabitants of Manchester will feel the need to readjust their asset portfolios. Thus an initial fall in exports to, say, London, probably results in a local accretion of stocks of goods. So at the end of the initial period wealth (and incomes) have not yet been changed, but the asset balance has been disturbed with excessive capital (unsold stocks) and insufficient money. In the next period people will want to invest less – to restore their desired holdings of real capital: this will reduce incomes and (the rate of growth of) wealth. This reduction in incomes and wealth will serve to lessen the current-account deficit by holding down imports, but that forms the next part of the story, to come in Section B. When an undesired reduction in money balances takes place, reinforced by a reduction in wealth, people will attempt to restore their asset balance by running down their holdings of other assets, particularly financial assets which can be relatively easily realised.

---

[1] See J. C. Ingram, 'Some Implications of Puerto Rican Experience,' from *Regional Payments Mechanism: The Case of Puerto Rico* (University of North Carolina Press, Chapel Hill, 1962) pp. 113–33, reprinted in *International Finance*, ed. R. N. Cooper, chap. 4, pp. 87–104.

Mancunians, at least by the second round of the process,[1] will then be selling financial non-monetary assets and, perhaps, trying to borrow more in order to restore their monetary balances. In some part their attempts to redeem their non-monetary financial assets may put further pressure on financial intermediaries in the area, through a withdrawal of time deposits with local banks, deposits with local building societies, deposits with local Trustee Savings Banks, etc. But a large, very possibly even preponderant, part of their reduction in non-monetary financial assets will take the form of reductions of claims on inhabitants of other regions. This induces a capital flow to finance the current-account deficit; furthermore, in so far as Mancunians borrow outside the region, this also finances the deficit.

Nevertheless, to the extent that Mancunians seek to realise claims on, or to increase liabilities to, local financial intermediaries more pressure will be placed on the latter's balance-sheet position. In round 1 there was a reduction in local money balances (current accounts with banks) balanced (see equation (iv) in the model) by a reduction in the local banks' cash reserves – or by building up a larger deficit position with Head Office. In round 2 the local people are running down their non-monetary financial assets, e.g. time deposits with various financial intermediaries, and seeking to borrow more in the form of loans from them; meanwhile the reduction in imports (via the reduction in incomes) and the sale of non-monetary financial assets abroad may not yet have stemmed the decline in the money stock. So the local financial intermediaries, including of course the banks, are likely to observe a continued (but more broadly spread over different kinds of liability) decrease in their liabilities at the same time as they are faced with a growing demand for credit. To some extent, especially in a unit banking system, this pressure can be met by the intermediaries running down their second line of reserve, their claims on other regions, e.g. by unit banks in deficit areas in the United States running down their balances with correspondents or by selling their holdings, say, of U.S. government debt. Perhaps to an even greater extent, without any apparent commotion at all, such pressures can be absorbed in a branch banking system simply by allowing some areas to become deficit areas (i.e. loans large relative to deposits) financed in effect by other areas becoming, *per contra*, surplus areas.

Furthermore, it may be possible for some financial intermediaries to raise the rates of interest which they offer on their liabilities (or charge on their advances) relative to the general, national rate. Since, we may assume, financial intermediaries in all the regions of this one country are treated as essentially alike in credit standing and attractions (except for the convenience pull of the local banks) a relatively small shift in relative rates should induce a large inter-regional capital flow. Thus intermediaries in, say, the Southern States of the United States, subject to any severe local pressure on their reserves with falling local liabilities and rising loan demands, might be able to deal with this situation fairly easily by raising the rates offered on deposits and charged on loans very slightly above the general national level.

The ease of inter-regional financial adjustment results from the high degree of substitution between financial claims issued in the different regions. This may be contrasted with a significantly lower degree of substitution between financial claims issued in different countries, e.g. because of unfamiliarity with each other's laws and customs, because of the possibility of conflict between autonomous governments, because of concern over exchange rates, etc. At the limit one might assume that there was no substitution at all between the

---

[1] The initial first-round position was one in which the capital stock was £X higher than desired and money balances £X lower. Thus it might be thought that the first-round readjustment would simply be to cut back planned investment by £X, leaving other financial assets untouched. Even at this first round, however, people know that it takes time to restore cash balances by reducing orders for goods, so some liquid financial assets, which are relatively close substitutes for money, will be realised to restore the cash position.

non-monetary financial assets of different countries.[1] In this case a country, suffering a current-account deficit, could not restore its reserves (of internationally accepted cash, e.g. gold, or wampum, or S.D.R.s, or whatever) by selling its non-monetary financial assets to foreigners, or by borrowing from them.

In this international case the inbuilt deflationary effect of a current-account deficit, via the foreign-trade multiplier, is thus further reinforced by financial contraction, taking the guise of sharply rising interest rates and domestic monetary contraction. This contrasts with inter-regional conditions where interest rates do not need to rise much, relatively to other areas, to finance a current-account imbalance and the regional money stock can adjust smoothly to people's preferences. In reality, however, this contrast between international and inter-regional adjustment processes is much too stark, precisely because the assumption that there is little substitution between the financial assets of the different countries (though there is – it will be noted – substitution between their goods) may often be invalid. The higher the degree of substitution between countries' financial assets (e.g. via an integration of capital markets), the greater the ease of financing current-account imbalances without provoking sharp interest-rate fluctuations and monetary disturbances.[2] Still, the degree of substitution between financial assets internationally should generally be lower than inter-regionally, and to this extent the finance of current-account imbalances will require more noticeable increases in interest rates and monetary contraction in deficit countries relative to surplus countries. Unfortunately for quantitatively-minded economists, the degree of substitution between financial assets in different countries does depend on such qualitative factors as people's expectations of future exchange-rate conditions, changes in tax regimes, institutions and laws, the possibility of expropriation, etc.; so the subjective elasticity of substitution may vary quite sharply, even in the short run as 'confidence' fluctuates. A current-account deficit may be easily financed one year and only with considerable difficulty the next.

A region, with high inter-regional elasticity of substitution among financial assets, does not therefore face the same immediate financial pressures to correct a current-account imbalance as does an individual country with a lower elasticity of substitution. Even so, financial pressures will develop if appropriate adjustment to current-account imbalances is long delayed. A current-account imbalance does, however, automatically set in motion changes in incomes, and wealth, and also possibly of relative prices that should serve to improve the position.[3] Moreover, by definition, the local authorities in a single region are

---

[1] Monetarists, from Hume onwards, have tended to make this assumption in the process of demonstrating how current-account imbalances bring about international monetary flows.

[2] The relatively smooth balance of payments adjustments of countries during the gold-standard period, 1890–1914, used to be attributed largely to the flexibility of national price levels in response to monetary movements. A new view has now developed giving much more prominence to the role of London, the integrated major world capital market, in providing the capital movements necessary to finance imbalances. On this view substitution between financial assets (largely taking place on London markets), in conditions of minimal exchange risk because of the assumed permanence of the mint par exchanges, allowed adjustments to take place with a *minimum* of monetary disturbances. For examples of this reassessment of the way in which balance of payments adjustments took place during the gold-standard period, see D. McCloskey and R. Zecher, *How the Gold Standard Worked, 1880–1913* (forthcoming); J. G. Williamson, *American Growth and the Balance of Payments* (University of North Carolina Press, Chapel Hill, 1964); and C. Goodhart, *The Business of Banking, 1891–1914*, L.S.E. research monograph (Weidenfeld & Nicolson, London, 1972).

[3] As financial assets are sold to residents of other regions, or local inhabitants borrow from outsiders, so the net flow of interest payments will become increasingly adverse. If the adjustment of incomes and/or relative prices is slow, the current account could, at least for a time, worsen.

not in a position to use *monetary policy* to counter any reductions in incomes, employment and wealth, arising from falling inter-regional competitiveness, that may occur in their locality.

Nevertheless, one can think of situations in which a current-account imbalance would persist. If entrepreneurs see future possible profitable opportunities (profits to be obtained from sales in all regions) from current investment, then a current-account deficit could well develop as a probable accompaniment of the present higher investment. This is not really a situation of imbalance, however, so long as the expectations of future profitable sales provide a reasonable expectation of paying off the presently incurred debts. Essentially a region (or country) running a current-account deficit is getting into debt, and the ultimate creditors of the region have to assess whether expectations of its meeting that debt are good. If a region is running a deficit, not because new profitable investment opportunities are springing up, but because its industries have become uncompetitive, then views of the credit worthiness of the area will be jaundiced. If the shipyards of the north become unprofitable, or its coal mines run down, the region will find it less than easy to meet the cash drain, as sales to other regions fall, by borrowing from the local banks, forcing them into increasing deficit positions within the branch banking system. The financial pressure on a region to adjust its current account will be felt most keenly as the bank manager, under pressure from Head Office, seeks to restrict credit to those industries in the region whose commercial future looks unpromising. Asset sales, perhaps even of real assets at knock-down prices because of their specific nature (see Chapter 5), and reductions in wealth must follow, reinforcing other factors causing the current account to come back into balance. It is even possible in extreme cases to envisage the collapse of local financial intermediaries, whose fortunes have become too closely linked to the regional industries going through bad times, thus exaggerating the local debt–deflation cycle.

Even though local authorities cannot use *monetary* policy to protect their own people from depression, they can often use *fiscal* policy. They can borrow money in national financial markets to be spent, either directly or via grants and transfers to local inhabitants, in maintaining income and employment levels in their area. But unless their expenditure leads to an improvement in local competitiveness, say by improvements in local transport facilities, the level of income can only be maintained by running up an increasing burden of external debt. This debt has to be serviced; so the maintenance of income levels by borrowing from other regions – after a fall in the competitiveness of local industry – must lead to an increasing net interest outflow, worsening the current account and making the ultimate required adjustment even more severe.[1] At some point the external debt burden would become large relative to the capacity of the local population to meet these debt obligations through higher taxes. At this point, unless the central government steps in with guarantees, etc., which represent an actual, or hypothetical, inter-regional aid transfer, the rate of interest which the local government would have to pay to borrow in the national market would rise as its credit standing became impaired. So in this case also financial pressures would eventually mount up, to enforce a return to balance in inter-regional transactions.[2]

---

[1] If the rate of time discount is sufficiently high, it may nevertheless appear desirable to take this path.

[2] Ingram, op. cit. tends to underestimate the inherent limitations on financing continuing deficits, even for regions within an integrated country. This has been pointed out by several economists, including R. N. Cooper in his editorial introduction to *International Finance*, p. 12. See, for example, Ingram's 'Comment' on P. B. Kenen's paper on 'The Theory of Optimum Currency Areas: An Eclectic View,' in *Monetary Problems of the International Economy*, ed. R. A. Mundell and A. K. Swoboda (University of Chicago Press, 1969) p. 99, 'It would seem that capital movements could continue to equilibrate the balance of payments for as long a run as it seems reasonable to be concerned about.'

Unless supported by a continuing transfer of funds from the central government, a region cannot, therefore, continue to run a chronic imbalance on its current account indefinitely without running up against financial pressures and constraints. Nevertheless, the high elasticity of substitution between financial liabilities of the same class issued in different regions enables regions to finance current-account imbalances with a minimum of difficulty and financial disruption. Clearly the ease with which imbalances between regions can be financed copes with one form in which balance of payments problems are manifest. The concern in each individual country over the adequacy of its stock of international reserves simply has no counterpart in inter-regional transactions.

B. Adjustment to a Current-Account Imbalance

Having considered how a current-account imbalance will be financed by flows of financial assets, it is time to revert to an examination of the determination of the current-account position itself. The simplest case to study, with which we shall begin, is one in which all prices of goods, labour, etc., and all interest rates are set on national markets and are fixed independently of conditions in region A, say because A is so small relative to the country as a whole. With all prices constant, by assumption, exports, imports and consumption in A become functions of local incomes, Y_A, local wealth W_A, and incomes in other regions, Y_B. While most expenditure *flows* are thus functions of the *levels* of income and wealth, it is the desired *stock* of capital which is a function of local incomes (output) and wealth, and so the *flow* of investment expenditure is a function of the *change* in incomes and wealth. In turn the level of incomes is the sum of expenditure flows on investment, exports and consumption, less imports, while the increase in wealth (prices and interest rates remaining constant) is the sum of net new investment plus the current-account surplus (all this is formally set out in Appendix A). So the current levels of incomes and wealth in A depend in part on the previous path of incomes and wealth in that region.

In this case, ignoring the effect on the invisibles component of the current account of financing trade imbalances (as being too small to matter), the system reduces to a couple of simultaneous difference equations determining Y_{At} and W_{At} in terms of Y_{At-1} and W_{At-1} with Y_B treated as exogenously given and all prices taken as constant. This is demonstrated in Appendix A, and a numerical example is given. In that example (after an upwards shift in Y_B), the system does converge ultimately to a stable equilibrium, though income oscillates during the process of adjustment around an upwards trend. This oscillation is due to the specification of the investment function, which is in a form akin to the accelerator of standard trade-cycle models. Wealth, however, converges in the example smoothly and monotonically towards the new equilibrium, since the fluctuations in investment are offset by swings in the trade balance – i.e. as investment rises, the trade balance deteriorates and vice versa. The structure of the model is such that it would become dynamically unstable with slightly different, and still plausible, values for the coefficients, but it would in my view be misleading to place much weight on the particular dynamic properties of this extremely simplified model.[1]

---

[1] For instance the investment function incorporated in the model takes, under the assumed conditions, a simple accelerator form, and this undoubtedly exaggerates the degree of instability in the system. Not only are there likely to be practical limitations to prevent negative investment, but also the model implies that expectations (assuming capital to be both specific and long lived, as argued in Chap. 5) are formed on an incredibly naive basis, i.e. that the current level of output will continue henceforth. It is likely that entrepreneurs will take into consideration a much longer run of past experience in formulating their views on the probable trends in output to be expected over

(*Footnote* [1] *continued on p. 269*)

Even though a more complex model might be needed to simulate a more realistic time path of adjustment, the ultimate changes in incomes (and wealth) necessary in these circumstances to restore full equilibrium after some external shock can be easily found. When prices are fixed, the demand for imports depends on the level of output. If exports change by £X, and the marginal propensity to import is, say, 0·2, then output must change by 5X to restore the same balance between exports and imports. So when exports rise by 20, incomes have to rise by 100 to restore equilibrium;[1] all the rest of the coefficients in the model merely serve to determine the time path of the economy towards that equilibrium.

The value of the marginal propensity to import is, therefore, critical in determining the size of the multiple change in incomes and wealth in response to an external shock, in conditions where relative prices are assumed to be fixed. In this respect the above value (of 0·2) is probably fairly realistic for middle-sized industrial *countries* (it is lower than this for giant countries such as the United States, Russia or China), but it is almost certainly much higher in relatively small regions such as Manchester in the United Kingdom, or Rhode Island in the United States. In general the smaller the region the higher the marginal propensity to import will be – an unsurprising proposition. But from this it follows that the smaller the region the easier it will be for that region to adjust to external shocks by relatively acceptable changes in real incomes and wealth, without having to rely on relative price changes: whereas large, self-sufficient regions would have to undertake massive shifts in incomes (wealth) to maintain external equilibrium, in the absence of relative price changes.

To digress for a moment, we have been considering (here and in the example in Appendix A) alternative positions of stationary equilibrium, and whether the time path of the economy would allow a smooth transition from one such equilibrium to another. In practice, of course, there has been in recent centuries continuous growth of both population and technological innovations. Either of these features would prevent the attainment of a stationary equilibrium. With growing knowledge and a growing labour force any equilibrium must be dynamic, with all the various stocks and flows increasing at a fairly steady rate over time. If the stock of capital in a region is growing, and with it the level of money incomes, then the stock of money and other financial assets must also grow, in order to maintain asset equilibrium over time. In order to sustain a growing level of monetary deposits, each region needs a continuing inflow of cash reserves. This inflow of reserves may, possibly, be satisfied by continuing net sales of financial claims on the region to outsiders, with the reserve inflow financed therefore by a capital-account surplus. But in order for equilibrium to be maintained, these net sales must not disturb the asset balance in the region between capital, money and other financial assets, nor the current-account balance between exports, imports and net interest payments. A more likely method for a region to satisfy its growing demand for money is for it to run a steady current-account surplus over time.

---

the prospective lifetime of the capital equipment which they are thinking of installing. There will also, in general, be longer lags in the response of expenditure to changes in incomes than postulated in this simple model. These lags should serve to dampen the oscillations of the economy as it moves from one (stationary) equilibrium to another after some external shock has hit the system: nevertheless, economies in the real world continue to exhibit some minor cyclical features (e.g. stock cycles) which may be described in terms of dampened models of this kind.

---

[1] So long as exports ≠ imports, there is a current-account imbalance, since we are in this exercise abstracting from the balance on invisible trade. This imbalance will cause a change in wealth in the region, unless it is offset by a contrary movement in the value of domestic real capital (via investment flows); either way, whether the value of wealth or of the capital stock is changing, there will be continuing adjustments in the economy. A full static equilibrium cannot be achieved until the current account is in balance.

This, however, raises a more general problem of how to make it possible for all the growing regions, taken in aggregate, to be simultaneously running current-account surpluses in order to satisfy their needs for money.[1] One standard solution for this has been for the monetary reserve to be some real object, e.g. gold or pigs or red feathers, produced in one region but used as a monetary reserve throughout the country. In this case the producing region can treat the monetary object as an export, while the other regions can treat it as an addition to monetary reserves. In this fashion all regions *can* simultaneously run a current-account surplus. Nowadays, with the replacement of real objects serving as money by fiat money, the requirement for cash reserves is probably more largely filled by capital-account transactions, with the monetary authorities undertaking open-market purchases of financial assets offered by those (whether intermediaries or not) in any region wishing to add to their monetary balances. But some part of regional cash requirements may also be met by the governmental centre (e.g. London, Washington, Canberra), with its attendant army of bureaucrats, running a continual current-account deficit with the rest of the country, financed in part by printing money, which the rest of the country is keen to absorb. In this sense the government centre (or centres) may be running, in its geographical dimension, a chronic deficit with other areas.[2]

To revert to the main thread of the analysis, when all prices are fixed an imbalance in the current account has to be corrected by a movement of incomes and wealth, the size of which depends on the marginal propensity to import. When the marginal propensity to import is low, the requisite shift in incomes could be very large indeed. With the level of wage rates in the region given (as well as all other prices), the demand for labour will vary with the level of output, resulting in a surplus of labour when demand for the region's output falls off, or a deficiency when there is a surge in the demand for the output of local industries. Such fluctuations in the demand for labour may be met either by variations in employment levels or by inter-regional migration. Both unemployment and migration are painful for those who are forced by circumstances into such a position. These fluctuations in labour markets could be ameliorated by variations in the relative wage rate in each region,[3] whether or not final prices on local goods responded flexibly to shifts in local wage costs.

A reduction in local wage rates *vis-à-vis* the price of capital goods would lead to some substitution of labour for capital, depending on the elasticity of substitution between the factors of production; and, depending on the form of the production function, the return to capital would be affected by the change in wage rates, either encouraging or dampening further investment. The short-term elasticity of substitution of labour for capital is probably quite low, and the fall in wage rates would in these circumstances raise the return on capital employed, given the level of demand, so that a small substitution to labour in existing plants should be reinforced by a significant increase in investment in new plants, in order to increase output for sale both at home and in other regions. Either way, whether by substitution in place of capital or by encouragement of a larger domestic output (or some combination of the two), persistent unemployment in a region should be capable of solution by a reduction in local wage rates relative to wage rates elsewhere.

---

[1] The problem of ensuring an adequate growth of monetary reserves is usually treated as an aspect of *international* monetary relations. Indeed, the problems are more difficult in that context. Analytically, however, there is an analogue in the inter-regional case.

[2] As an exception to our previous comments, there will be no ultimate financial pressure on the government centre to remedy such a chronic deficit because, as explained in Chaps 1 and 6, it always has the power to create legal tender to pay off any debts and cannot become bankrupt economically.

[3] Migration will still be stimulated by regional wage differentials, but voluntary moves to higher-paid jobs elsewhere are quite different in character from migrations forced by lack of job opportunities at home.

Why then do we observe continuing higher unemployment in some regions than in others? Why do relative wage levels not adjust to eliminate such maldistribution? In part we need only rehearse the answers which we have already offered to a similar question in Chapter 10. A reduction in wages has a direct, obvious, general, and immediate depressing effect on the income of every worker in that job; its beneficial effect on employment opportunities is hypothetical, tangential, of benefit only to those unknown few who would otherwise have lost their job. Given the decentralised basis of decision-making, and the information available to each worker, it is unlikely that any trade union or group of organised workers would accept a wage cut in some locality because unemployment there was relatively high.

This line of argument, which was used in Chapter 10 to explain the incidence of unemployment, extends even further in this context to incorporate the concept of *parity*. If a worker in a car plant in Coventry is paid £X per week, why should a worker in a car plant in Glasgow be paid any less? People tend to measure their worth, or to feel that they are measured, in terms of their income: is a Scot working in a car plant in Glasgow working any less hard or less intelligently than an Englishman in Coventry? Why should wages for similar kinds of work differ between regions? One answer often is that at the existing wage rates there is relatively high unemployment among Scots, in part because in Scotland, through no fault of the Scots, there may be a historically determined high incidence of declining industries, because transport costs are higher, because the land is more rugged and less conducive to economic exploitation. If, then, people insist on parity of pay for Scots in most industries, more Scots will either be thrown into unemployment, or be forced to migrate to more prosperous regions, or find that the only job opportunities open to them are in those industries which offer relatively low wages.

This desire for parity of pay in similar types of jobs, irrespective of different economic conditions in the regions where the jobs are offered, is a curious phenomenon. It often operates with very considerable strength between regions of the same country, especially in unionised industries and where information on regional relativities is easily available to the workers, but seems to dissolve almost entirely in international comparisons. A worker at an engine factory in Peterborough may be prepared to strike for months to get the same wage as a worker in an engine factory in Coventry, but will pay virtually no attention to the pay, or increases in pay, obtained by a worker in an engine factory in Germany, Italy or the United States. It will be interesting to see whether this distinction between the concern for parity within each country and the lack of interest in the same question between countries will survive the increasing links of communication, tourism and, perhaps, even of political ties between countries. Anyhow, inflexibility in adjusting relative (real) wage rates between regions perpetuates differences in regional activity rates and hinders the process of regional balance-of-payments adjustment.

Flexible wage rates should suffice on their own to restore full employment in a depressed region, even where the prices of all traded goods (and services) are assumed to be nationally fixed. This latter assumption is, however, a strong one, and we shall now relax it in order to examine the relationship between price and wage movements and the process of balance-of-payments adjustment more closely. We may start by assuming that the goods of region A (call them A goods) are sold on perfectly competitive national markets. On such markets the aggregate (all-region) demand and supply functions are initially as shown in schedule D_1 and S_1 in Fig. 14.1 with an equilibrium price at P_1 and output at Q_1. To the individual producer, perhaps in region A, the demand schedule will appear horizontal, d_1, and his individual supply function will depend on his marginal cost schedule s_1, as shown in Fig. 14.2, where $p_1 = P_1$.

Now let us assume that there is a fall off (a shift) in the aggregate demand schedule for these goods, perhaps because of a fall in real incomes in other regions or a shift in tastes; demand declines to schedule D_2 (as shown in Fig. 14.1). Unless producers have foreseen this fall in prices their production will have continued at the previous pace, and at the point

K

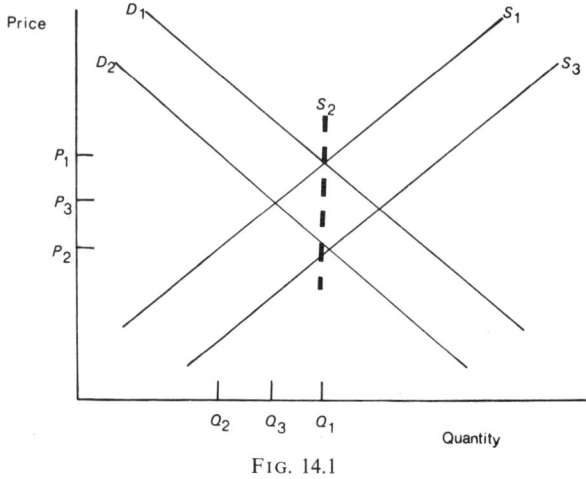

FIG. 14.1

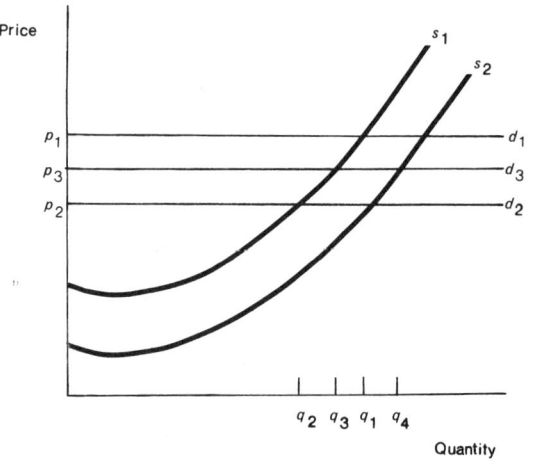

FIG. 14.2

of time when demand shifts there will be an existing stock of goods (all of which are to be sold on the competitive market) just sufficient to meet prior demand at the old equilibrium price: thus the short-run supply function will be the dashed vertical line S_2, which will now be sold at price P_2.

The individual producer then observes a decline in his horizontal demand curve to d_2 (Fig. 14.2) at prices $p_2 = P_2$, so he now decides to reduce output to q_2. With all producers behaving alike, this would cause a move along the aggregate (medium-run) supply curve S_1 to point Q_2. Clearly this is not an equilibrium either, since at this point there is now an excess demand in the market. Assuming (reasonably enough) that the dynamics of market responses allow convergence to equilibrium, a new quasi-equilibrium will be obtained at price P_3 with output Q_3. The individual producer will then face a steady horizontal demand function d_3 at price $p_3 = P_3$, where he produces q_3 ($\sum_1^n q_3 = Q_3$).

We have, however, described this as only a point of quasi-equilibrium. The reason for this is that, at the assumed given level of wages, employment in A production will have declined (and incomes from A production will have gone down). In this case in regions, such as region A, where production of type A goods provides a relatively large proportion of total employment, unemployment will increase. Unless the movement is prevented, for example by nationally-determined wage bargaining, wage rates should fall in jobs in A production, and particularly in areas concentrating in A production, as in region A. If wage rates fall in A production, there will be a shift in the marginal cost schedule to s_2, encouraging the producer to increase his output to q_4.

If all producers of type A goods, irrespective of region, experienced the same reduction in wage rates, aggregate (medium-term) supply would shift to S_3. Whether or not income receipts from sales of A goods would then rise or fall depends on the *aggregate* price elasticity of demand for that good. If it was less than unity, incomes would fall; if greater than unity, they would rise. The assumption, however, that wage rates in A industries fall by a uniform amount is, perhaps, somewhat extreme. In regions such as A, concentrating on the production of A goods, there will be a much larger excess supply of labour than in regions with only a small A production, where labour conditions may be buoyed up by a stronger demand for other goods. So wage rates in region A may fall relative to wage rates elsewhere. Then as A expands production of A goods (after a relative decline in local wage rates) and forces prices down in the competitive market, the supply of A goods from B regions will shrink, as the decline in prices which they face forces them back down along their marginal cost curves. At the limit, when A is a very small producer of A goods, a fall in wage rates in A may allow it to expand its output almost entirely by displacing production from other regions, without requiring any significant fall in prices.

Whereas the concepts of the price elasticity of demand facing individual producers of A goods (here assumed to be infinitely elastic) and in the market for A goods as a whole are straightforward, the concept of the price elasticity of demand for all A goods marketed by producers in region A (or region i for that matter) is more complicated. Their sales, as their offered price changes, do *not* depend just on an independently-determined *demand* curve, but also on the supply response of other producers to changes in price. Their sales, as their prices change, derive from the combined effect of the price elasticity of the aggregate market demand curve and the extent to which their sales displace sales from other regions, where the reductions in prices no longer make it worthwhile producing goods for this market. So the degree of competitiveness between producers in different regions will be a factor determining the price elasticity of demand for the products of any one region. If producers in region i can induce, by a small reduction in prices, producers in all other regions to cut back their market sales, then the price elasticity of demand for goods from region i will be high, even if the price elasticity of demand in the market as a whole is low.

If we consider instead markets where the individual producers are imperfectly competitive, the analysis of the effects of shifts in the demand for certain goods on inter-regional trade flows remains essentially much the same. Under imperfect competition, producers try to fix a price that will – given the expected reactions of their competitors – maximise profits. They maintain that price, in the face of random variations in demand, by allowing stocks of final goods to expand or to contract. If aggregate demand for their goods falls off (e.g. if the demand curve shifts downwards because of a change in tastes or a reduction in real incomes), initially their stocks pile up. A persistent increase in stocks of unsold goods forces them either to cut prices (in the hopes of selling more) or to cut output. If they cut prices, their revenue (per item sold) will fall relative to their costs, so the plants working with the lowest margins will make losses, and will presumably be closed. If they cut output, then the surplus of revenue over cost will be rising as they close their least profitable plants, inducing a greater willingness to shade prices in order to expand business. The path that the adjustment process actually follows will depend on the particular business milieu in which the entrepreneurs find themselves, but it should lead to the establishment of a new quasi-equilibrium in the overall market for these goods, involving some reduction in output and some reduction in price.

Again this will only be a quasi-equilibrium, because employment and incomes in the production of such goods will have declined, and this may induce a secondary effect on wage rates in these industries and in regions heavily dependent on such industries. If labour costs fall in region A relative to other regions, the substitution of production from other regions to region A may be even greater and more rapid (than in the case of perfect competition) as oligopolistic multi-regional companies reorganise and concentrate production in the more profitable areas. Again this demonstrates the complexity of the concept of the price elasticity of demand for a region's goods. Even though the price elasticity of demand for the individual producer of, say, cars may be less than for, say, sweaters, and the aggregate price elasticity of demand in the market as a whole may be less for cars than for sweaters, nevertheless the response of output, and sales, of cars to shifts in relative costs (and of prices) between regions may be significantly greater than with sweaters. With cars, Mr Ford or Lord Stokes may reallocate production between alternative plants in different regions with considerable sensitivity to relative profitability, while each local sweater-maker may strive to his utmost to maintain his own individual sales, and be prepared to absorb reductions in profit margins in the process.[1]

The immediate effect, therefore, of a downwards shift in the demand for the output of a particular region, say region A, will be an initial decline in prices and output (and therefore in incomes) in that region. This, particularly the fall in output and the rise in unemployment, may induce a secondary response of reductions in wage rates and, perhaps, of certain other costs, relative to those in other regions. This would induce a recovery in output in A, and with a relative fall in costs and a revived output of A goods prices of A goods would tend to be lowered relative to other goods. If the price elasticity of demand for goods produced in region A, reflecting both the shift of demand to A goods from other goods as relative prices change in the overall market and also the displacement of production of A goods from other regions to A, was low then only few additional sales of A goods could be made without driving prices down to levels at which it was no longer profitable to expand output. Output in A will rise,[2] following the relative decline in A prices but real incomes may rise or fall depending whether Y_A (output of region A) rose faster than

$$\frac{P_A}{(1 - b)P_A + bP_B}$$

(the ratio of the prices of goods produced in A to the cost of living in A)[3] was falling.

The conditions under which a shift in relative prices will improve the current-account balance have been extensively documented in the literature. The conditions most commonly

---

[1] R. Masera, in correspondence with me, has put forward a counter-argument. Oligopolistic multi-regional companies are most common in manufacturing industries subject to economies of scale. Such industries, for example the car industry, are usually fully unionised, and concern about parity of pay will be strong, quite irrespective of productivity/unemployment conditions. This feature will tend to reverse the conclusions in the main text. Suppose that production in A is heavily dependent on the car industry and is specialised, say, more particularly in big cars. Now the demand for such cars falls. Hence unemployment in A rises, but this need not be accompanied by a general fall in relative wage rates paid in the car industry in region A. In these conditions Masera argues that it is more likely that, in A, production of alternative products, say textiles, will be stepped up, because the excess supply of labour will tend to be absorbed at declining wage rates by those industries where 'parity' with other regions is not directly and immediately called for by trade unions.

[2] Ignoring the possibility that A goods are Giffen goods, the demand for which falls as their prices fall.

[3] P_B is the price index of goods imported into region A, and b is the average propensity to import. The notation is taken from the formal model set out in Appendix A. Region B stands for the rest of the country, in which A is a (small) region.

cited[1] require that, on the assumption that the elasticity of supply of both A and B goods is infinite, and that initially $P_A X_A$ (exports) $= P_B \cdot {}_A X_B$ (imports), the sum of the price elasticities of demand for imports (into A from B and into B from A, where B is the rest of the country (world) in which A is a region) shall be greater than unity.[2]

From the point of view of the inhabitants of region A, the concept of the price elasticity of B's demands for imports from A as P_A alters seems perfectly straightforward. On the other hand, the concept of the price elasticity of A's demands for imports from B as P_A shifts relative to P_B is more complicated because it incorporates not only the substitution effect, but also some more complex income effects. Via the substitution effect, the propensity to import into A will decline as P_A falls relative to P_B, to an extent depending on the elasticity of substitution. The rise in export volumes (X_A) in A will lead to an increase in incomes there (Y_A) which, *ceteris paribus*, will increase investment (I_A), and via the multiplier consumption (C_A), and thus will serve to buoy up the demand for imports. On the other hand, as P_A falls relative to P_B the real value of incomes derived from A output falls (owing to the worsening in the terms of trade, as

$$\frac{P_A}{(1-b)P_A + bP_B}$$

declines), and this may lead to a cut back in consumption. In short, the effects on the demand for imports (in region A) arising from a change in the relative prices of P_B and P_A are quite complex, and simply wrapping them all up in the single concept of the price elasticity of demand in A for imports from B may possibly serve to obscure the several different effects upon the level of imports. The problem is that price changes do have effects on incomes, etc., but definitions of price elasticities which incorporate income effects are not very satisfactory. One response has been to try notionally to separate the various effects over time. We might envisage an initial impact of price changes on expenditure flows, with real incomes in the various regions being treated as unchanged, followed by subsequent changes in incomes as the foreign-trade multiplier works through, on the basis of the new given set of prices. In practice, however, the adjustments of prices and quantities cannot be simply disentangled in this or any other fashion. Possibly the proper conclusion is that one can only analyse adjustment to a new equilibrium within the context of a general equilibrium model.

But we may, perhaps, identify four main channels of response arising from a decline in P_A relative to P_B. First, there is the substitution effect, switching expenditure in both A and B to A goods and from B goods. Second, there is the terms of trade effect reducing domestic expenditures in A (as real incomes fall) and raising them in B. Both these serve to increase the volume of A exports and to reduce the volume of B exports, but may not do so sufficiently to improve the current account if the elasticity of substitution in response to relative price changes is low. Thirdly, the increase in export volume in A (decrease in B) will raise investment and consumption expenditures in A (reducing them in B) via the normal accelerator/multiplier mechanism. Fourth, the rise in output in A (fall in B) will

---

[1] These conditions were first formulated by Alfred Marshall, *The Pure Theory of Foreign Trade; The Pure Theory of Domestic Values* (London School of Economics Reprints of Scarce Tracts in Economics and Political Science, no. 1: London, 1930), and subsequently by A. P. Lerner, *The Economics of Control* (Macmillan, New York, 1944) chap. 28. The conditions are, therefore, generally known as the Marshall–Lerner conditions.

[2] For a more general statement of the requisite conditions, and a more elaborate model of trade adjustment, see, *inter alios*, S. C. Tsiang, 'The Role of Money in Trade-Balance Stability: Synthesis of the Elasticity and Absorption Approaches,' *The American Economic Review*, vol. 51, no. 5 (December 1961) pp. 912–36, reproduced in *International Finance*, ed. R. N. Cooper, chap. 6, pp. 135–64.

reduce the excess supply of labour in A (excess demand in B) and thus lead to a relatively faster increase in costs (and thus prices) in A (vice versa in B). These last two factors will act to brake an improvement in A's current account resulting from an initial decline in P_A relative to P_B.

In practice these factors act as a sort of counterpoise. If the elasticity of substitution leads to a large improvement in the current-account balance, the braking forces come into operation more quickly. If the elasticity of substitution, in response to relative price changes, is low, then exports (and import substitutes) will not increase much in volume, so domestic expenditures and employment will remain weak, and there will be continuing downward pressure on wages and prices in the depressed region. This pressure, at some stage, will be further reinforced by financial pressures (discussed already in Section A). So long as relative price movements do not suffice to restore current-account balance, there will be a continuing drain of financial assets from the area (an increasing indebtedness to other areas). This outflow of financial assets, to finance the current-account imbalance, leads to a reduction in (the rate of growth of) wealth in the area and to a growing indebtedness that ultimately will cause additional deflationary pressure. The lower the elasticity of substitution in response to shifts in relative prices, the greater the decline, at least temporarily, in employment in the disadvantaged region and the greater the long-term adjustments in incomes and wealth, if current-account balance is to be achieved.

Even where the elasticity of substitution of goods between regions is high it may, however, not happen that a decline in the demand for the products of region A and the emergence of regional unemployment would lead to a restorative shift in relative costs and thence in prices. No single group of workers will accede, without a determined struggle, to a collective bargaining agreement which is directly seen to cut their own real wages, particularly since its effect on local employment seems indirect and very likely to the benefit of others unknown.[1] There will, therefore, be resistance to any direct downward pressure on wages, despite any depression in the local economy. Furthermore, concern with parity may impel union leaders to aim for much the same kind of wage increases as have been obtained in other areas. Indeed, this concern with parity in nominal wages could even induce disequilibrating trends in unit labour costs, if productivity in the more prosperous regions was rising relative to that in less prosperous regions.

It is under these conditions, when falls in the demand for the products of an area have not brought about an equilibrating response in relative costs and prices, that countries adopt the expedient of devaluing (regions, of course, do not have this option). The effect of devaluation is to cause a reduction in real wage rates in the devaluing country relative to the price (and cost) levels ruling in other countries. It represents, therefore, an artificial way of introducing an equilibrating adjustment in relative wage costs.

But if the workers, e.g. through their unions, had refused to accept a reduction in (relative) real wages through collective bargaining, why should they accept it when imposed through administrative action? There are several reasons for this. Collective wage bargains affect individual groups of workers who have little information and no guarantee on the outcome of other wage bargains. Devaluation centralises and makes uniform the effect on

---

[1] Andrew Crockett has posed the question to me why then unions often encourage short-time working during slumps, in order to spread the reduction in real incomes more evenly among the labour force. In large part the reason for the acceptance of short-time working as contrasted with the refusal to accept wage cuts during slumps depends on differences in information and in the power relationships. If a union accepts a wage cut, it has no power to ensure that the final price is shaded commensurably; the profit margin might be raised instead. And even if final prices are reduced, the union may have little idea what improvement in sales may result from this step; whereas meeting a given reduction in output by short-time working involves little need for additional information and may give the union negotiators more control over the fate of their members than leaving management to declare redundancies.

all workers in the country concerned: but the success of this does depend on labour being prepared to accept some reduction, albeit perhaps temporary, in (the rate of growth of)real wages relative to that in other countries. Otherwise devaluation would only lead to an immediate catch-up in nominal wages and prices restoring the *status quo ante*,[1] except that the pace of inflation would have now accelerated.

Where regions are relatively small, so that the cost of living mainly depends on price fluctuations in imported goods, and social, cultural and political ties with contiguous regions are strong, so that individuals regularly compare their position against their opposite numbers in other regions, devaluation – even should institutional conditions, requiring the existence of separate monetary authorities, permit – would be much less likely to provide a successful and satisfactory adjustment procedure. It may, however, prove possible to overcome such obstacles to regional adjustment, even under these circumstances where variations in exchange rates are not possible (because it is a single-currency system) or impractical (because local wages and prices will rapidly adjust to restore the *status quo ante*), by taking appropriate fiscal action. Among the many fiscal innovations suggested by Professor Kaldor was the idea of regionally varying taxes and subsidies on labour, i.e. the regional employment premium.[2] As has been frequently pointed out, the effect of devaluation on prices of goods being traded is equivalent to the imposition of a set of taxes and subsidies. The regional employment premia and taxes can therefore be adjusted to have the effect of a change in relative parities. It does this, however, without having an immediately disturbing impact effect on the observed relativities of real wage rates between workers in the same industry in different areas.[3] In this respect it could be an *even more* effective adjustment mechanism than allowing each region to maintain a separate currency and vary its exchange rate against its neighbours. Furthermore, the payment of taxes in more active and prosperous regions and subsidies to the less prosperous regions should, in general, act to improve the distribution of incomes and wealth over the whole community. Indeed, the chances of success in achieving larger politico-economic groupings among states (as in the E.E.C.) may well depend vitally and urgently upon the further extension of such fiscal techniques.

So far we have been considering cases where, owing for example to a fall off in the demand for products of region *A*, the region has been suffering simultaneously an adverse current-account balance and a depression of domestic incomes and output. To be sure, current-account imbalance can be caused not only by such external shocks but also by domestic developments. A faster rate of domestic expansion, fuelled say by fiscal or monetary stimuli, will worsen the current-account balance in three ways: the higher level of domestic expenditure and output will pull in more imports; the greater pressure on domestic capacity will raise domestic costs and prices relative to those in other regions; the greater pressure on capacity may lead to some rationing (delivery delays) of sales to customers in other regions and at home, who may turn instead to importers. In such cases the effect of devaluation, in switching demand to local producers, will be ineffective in improving the

---

[1] Some monetarists would argue that this could only occur if the authorities were prepared to validate these higher wage levels by increasing the domestic money supply. If not, the claims for higher nominal wages to restore previous real wage rates would lead initially to unemployment and, thereafter at some point, to a moderation in wage demands.

[2] See, for example, N. Kaldor, 'The Case for Regional Policies,' *Scottish Journal of Political Economy*, vol. 17, no. 3 (November 1970) pp. 337–48, especially pp. 346–7. Kaldor, however, notes that since the cost of the premia are borne not by the region but by the tax-paying community as a whole, 'it would be politically very difficult to introduce it on a scale that could make it really effective.'

[3] G. E. Wood pointed out to me, in correspondence, that, whereas there need be no impact effect on relative wages, the demand for labour in the various regions would, as indeed intended, alter and this would lead over time to some readjustments in observed relativities.

current account, without accompanying steps to reduce total domestic expenditures. Devaluation by itself would place even more pressure on capacity, redoubling inflationary pressure and supply constraints; it could, at best, only improve the current account temporarily at the expense of worsening the diverging trends in regional inflation.

Indeed, *supply* conditions, both in the devaluing country and also in the rest of the world, play a most important role in determining whether devaluation is to be successful in restoring current-account balance. Of course, the overall price elasticity of demand in the markets for the goods traded is an important factor, but if the goods from a devaluing country can reasonably easily displace goods from other countries in these markets, then the price elasticity of demand for that one country's goods should be high irrespective of the aggregate price elasticity of demand. On these grounds, theorists have argued that the price elasticity of demand for the exports of any one country *must* be pretty large (at least greater than unity), unless that country is virtually the sole producer of a good with a price inelastic demand.[1]

On the other hand, the supply response to devaluation, the response of businessmen to the changing opportunities occasioned by devaluation, may be quite slow. Devaluation may make exports to some additional markets notionally more profitable and imports less profitable (to the foreign exporter), but many goods are only traded through established commercial channels. It takes time, effort and confidence in the future to set up such channels, and once established they will not be easily abandoned in the face of a temporary decline in profitability. Such set-up costs reduce supply elasticities, even when there is spare capacity in the devaluing country. So the supply response may for a number of reasons be quite slow.

In my view it is this that helps to explain the experience of apparently sluggish response – upon the current-account balance – to several recent devaluations and revaluations, e.g. the U.K. devaluation of 1967 and the exchange-rate adjustments of 1971. Given the strong *a priori* arguments that the price elasticities of demand for exports should be high, I believe that this experience reflected slow supply responses rather than low price elasticities.[2]

APPENDIX A

A Framework for the Analysis of Inter-Regional Adjustment

The approach adopted here is to concentrate upon the adjustment process in one particular region, region A, treating the rest of the country as region B. The purpose of this appendix is to set out a model of the structure of region A as a guide to examining the inter-regional adjustment process. Presumably both regions could be producing a wide assortment of goods, both consumption and capital goods, which could be traded with the other region, and offering a wide variety of services which could be used by inhabitants of both regions. For simplicity, however, it will be assumed that it is possible to aggregate the goods produced in each region into a composite A good and B good respectively, each with its

---

[1] See, for example, A. C. Harberger, 'Some Evidence on the International Price Mechanism,' *Journal of Political Economy*, vol. 65, pp. 506–21 (1957), reprinted in *International Finance*, ed. R. N. Cooper (Penguin Modern Economics, 1969) pp. 165–90.

[2] Though see H. S. Houthakker and S. P. Magee, 'Income and Price Elasticities in World Trade,' *The Review of Economics and Statistics*, vol. 51, no. 2 (May 1969) pp. 111–25. They found that, 'The price variables do not perform nearly so well [as the income variables], with many insignificant estimates and a few incorrect signs. . . . Even where the estimated price elasticities are significant and negative their standard errors were usually too large to permit a definite stand in the "elasticity pessimism" controversy' (pp. 113–14). However, their study takes no account of possible lags in response from the supply side.

accompanying price level. Although the goods (services) are thus distinguished by the region producing them into A or B goods, this does not exclude the possibility that the bulk of the goods being produced and traded either may be, or could be with relative ease, produced in both regions. With a single currency and (assumed) low transport costs the price of both A goods, P_A, and B goods, P_B, are determined nationally rather than regionally. As a simplifying device it will be assumed that the import content (in both A and B) of all goods whatever their end use, whether for inter-regional export, investment or consumption is the same, and furthermore that the expenditure propensities with respect to all forms of income, whether in the form of returns to capital or to labour, are also the same. This allows the demand for imports, and for consumption, etc., to be expressed as a simple function of income levels without worrying about the distribution of incomes between differing kinds of expenditures or of factor incomes.

In the model five separate assets are identified. Individuals (persons and companies) hold real capital (K), non-monetary financial assets (F), and monetary deposits (M),[1] and borrow from intermediaries on loans (L). Financial intermediaries issue as liabilities both non-monetary financial claims (F) and monetary deposits (M) and hold as per contra assets loans to individuals (L), non-monetary financial claims on other intermediaries, and cash reserves $(H$, high-powered money). The non-monetary financial claims are assumed, for simplicity, to have a fixed nominal value. Monetary deposits have – again by assumption – a zero nominal yield. For the purposes of this exercise it is assumed that all real capital in any region is entirely owned by the inhabitants of that region, who also maintain all their monetary deposits with local intermediaries (banks); a possible justification for this latter assumption would be on grounds of convenience. Again on grounds of convenience, inhabitants of a region will presumably go first to their local financial intermediary to discuss the terms of loan financing, but will shift to more distant external intermediaries if there is a difference in terms offered. Non-monetary financial assets, F, issued in one region are, however, regarded as effectively identical with those issued in another, e.g. a security issued in London is considered to be essentially the same as one issued in Manchester by anyone living in the United Kingdom. Inhabitants (and intermediaries) of both regions $(A$ and $B)$ hold non-monetary financial claims on both A and B intermediaries and buy and sell these in the open market to adjust their asset positions.[2] In the notation used here $_AF_B$ represents a claim issued in B and held in A. Since these assets are regarded as identical, irrespective of issuing region, there will be one nationally-determined interest rate at which these assets are traded. If A is very small relative to the rest of the country, the rate of interest on both financial claims, r_F, and on loans, r_L, will be determined independently of the demand for such instruments by A inhabitants or the supply of them by A intermediaries. Finally, the net balance of the current and capital account of inter-regional transactions results in a positive (surplus) or negative (deficit) balance in monetary clearings between the intermediaries of each region, and these clearing balances are met by transfers of cash reserves (H) by the intermediaries from the deficit to the surplus region.

---

[1] In this model people do not hold cash; all their money balances are held in the form of demand deposits with financial intermediaries. This assumption helps to simplify the analysis without omitting any vital element of the system.

[2] In this model there is, therefore, portfolio investment – but no direct investment – in the capital account of the inter-regional balance of payments. This treatment differs somewhat from that of Floyd, 'Monetary and Fiscal Policy in a World of Capital Mobility,' *The Review of Economic Studies* (October 1969), who emphasises the role of direct investment in the Canadian capital account. The reason for giving more prominence to portfolio investment here is in order to highlight the role of transactions in financial instruments and the role of financial intermediaries in the adjustment process. In reality direct investment flows can also be very important, but to include them also would further complicate the model.

Having given a brief description of the system, the next stage is to set down the formal structure of the model, starting with certain accounting identities.

(i) Output equals expenditure

$$P_A \cdot Y_A = P_A \cdot X_A - P_B \cdot {}_AX_B + [(1 - b)P_A + bP_b](I_A + C_A) - r_F({}_BF_A - {}_AF_B)$$

P_A represents the price of A goods, b is the average propensity to import into A so that $(1 - b)P_A + bP_B$ represents a general price index of goods bought in A. Y_A is the production of A goods in A, X_A the export of A goods, excluding interest payments, ${}_AX_B$ the import of B goods and services into A, I_A investment in additional capital in A,[1] C_A consumption in A, r_F is the national interest rate on non-monetary financial assets, ${}_BF_A$ are such assets issued by A intermediaries held by B residents, while ${}_AF_B$ are assets issued in B and held in A,[2] so the final term shows the size and direction of net interest flow between the regions.

(ii) Output equals income

$$P_A \cdot Y_A = \pi_A. \quad [(1 - b)P_A + bP_B]K_A + w \cdot Z_A$$

π_A is the rate of return paid to capital in A and K_A the real capital stock in A. The wage rate paid is w; for the moment it will be assumed that the wage rate paid in region A is determined nationally, say by collective bargaining fixing a single national rate. If region A is small, the state of the labour market in A will have a relatively small impact on the wage rate determined nationally. Z_A gives the total number of workers employed at wage rate w in A. The demand for workers at this wage rate is always satisfied, either by variations in local unemployment or by inter-regional migration.

(iii) Private-sector wealth is composed of existing assets

$$W_A = M_A + {}_AF_A + {}_AF_B + [(1 - b)P_A + bP_B]K_A - L_A$$

W_A is the level of wealth of private-sector residents in A (in nominal terms), M_A is the money stock (bank deposits) held by A residents, ${}_AF_A$ and ${}_AF_B$ are the non-monetary financial claims held by A residents, K_A the real capital stock in A, and L_A are the loans obtained by A residents from their local intermediaries.[3]

(iv) The assets of intermediaries balance their liabilities

$$L_A + {}_{IA}F_B + H_A = M_A + {}_AF_A + {}_BF_A$$

H_A are the intermediaries' cash reserves; ${}_{IA}F_B$ represent the holdings by A intermediaries of non-monetary claims on B intermediaries; ${}_BF_A$ represent non-monetary liabilities issued by A intermediaries to B residents (including intermediaries in B).

---

[1] Capital is assumed not to depreciate. Existing capital and new capital equipment are perfect substitutes and sell at the same price.

[2] There may also be a flow of interest payments on loans made by intermediaries in one region to inhabitants of the other. This term could be easily added also, but would just make the accounting identities even more unwieldy.

[3] In order to limit the number of terms in the accounting identities, it is assumed here that all loans to inhabitants of a region are made by intermediaries situated in that region. There would be no difficulty in relaxing that assumption to take account of borrowing from intermediaries in other regions.

The ex-post conditions determining the flow of money into, or out of, region A can now easily be worked out from equations (i) and (iii). Taking the assumption that P_A and P_B are constant, in order to avoid dealing with changes in the current value of existing capital goods, equation (iii) can be written in first-difference form, as

$$\Delta M_A \quad = \quad \Delta W_A \qquad -\Delta_A F_A - \Delta_A F_B \qquad -\Delta K_A \qquad +\Delta L_A$$

| (increase in money stock) | (increase in wealth) | (less purchase of non-monetary financial assets) | (less investment in real assets) | (plus increase in intermediary loans) |

but

$$\Delta W_A \quad = \quad P_A \cdot Y_A \qquad -[(1-b)P_A + bP_B]C_A$$

| (increase in wealth) | (income) | (less consumption) |

(i.e. the change in wealth is equal to the value of new savings when there is no change in price levels to produce capital gains.) From equation (i) we have

$$P_A \cdot Y_A - [(1-b)P_A + bP_B]C_A = [(1-b)P_A + bP_B]I_A$$

| (new saving) | (new investment) |

$$+ P_A X_A - P_B \cdot {}_A X_B + r_F({}_A F_B - {}_B F_A)$$

| (current-account surplus) |

Then collecting terms, and noting that if $P_{At} = P_{At-1}$ and $P_{Bt} = P_{Bt-1}$ then $I_A = \Delta K_A$, we have

(v) Factors associated with regional monetary expansion

$$\Delta M_A \quad = P_A X_A - P_B \cdot {}_A X_B + r_F({}_A F_B - {}_B F_A)$$

| (increase in money stock) | (current-account surplus) |

$$- \Delta_A F_A - \Delta_A F_B \qquad + \Delta L_A$$

| (less purchase of non-monetary financial assets) | (plus increase in loans) |

In short, the inhabitants of A can obtain more money either by running a current-account surplus with their neighbours, or by (net) sales of their holdings of non-monetary financial assets, or by borrowing from their local financial intermediaries.

From equations (iv) and (v), it is next easy to set out the conditions determining the flow of the intermediaries' cash reserves (ΔH_A) into, or out of, the region. Putting equation (iv) in first difference form, we have

$$\Delta H_A \quad = \quad \Delta M_A \qquad + \Delta_A F_A + \Delta_B F_A \qquad - \Delta L_A \qquad - \Delta_{IA} F_B$$

| (increase in reserves) | (increase in deposits) | (increase in non-monetary liabilities of A intermediaries taken up by A, B residents) | (less increase in loans) | (less increase in A intermediaries' claims on B intermediaries) |

Then collecting terms and substituting into (v), equation (vi) is obtained:

(vi) Factors associated with inter-regional cash reserve transfers

$$\Delta H_A = [P_A X_A - P_B \cdot {}_A X_B + r_F({}_A F_B - {}_B F_A)]$$

(increase in   (current-account surplus)
reserves)

$$-\Delta_A F_B - \Delta_{IA} F_B \qquad\qquad\qquad + \Delta_B F_A$$

(less A purchases of B's assets)   (plus B's purchases of A assets)
(capital account)

So by manipulation of the basic accounting identities one can show that the flow of reserves into, out of, any region has to be exactly that necessary to clear the balance on the current and capital account with neighbouring regions.

All this, however, remains purely definitional. Given the assumptions of the model, these equations are accounting identities that must hold at all times, both in and out of equilibrium. In order to examine the process of adjustment, it is necessary to supplement the accounting identities with sets of relationships, showing the desired relationships between income and expenditure flows, and between wealth and asset holdings, all as functions of relative prices and the relevant budget constraints.

The analysis is complicated by the need to show the connections between the achievement of flow equilibrium and stock equilibrium. Income and expenditure flows, whether or not they are equilibrium flows, may cause changes in quantities and/or prices that disturb the asset equilibrium and, similarly, asset adjustments may disturb expenditure flows. The main, and most obvious, linkage between flow and stock relationships, at least in this model, comes in the treatment of real capital. Investment, a change in the stock of real capital, enters the income account as an expenditure *flow*, yet the production function relates the demand for a *stock* of capital to the flow of output (income), and as an element of wealth the demand for capital must be a function of the net wealth of the community, together with the prospective yields and risks on alternative assets.

Following our previous procedure we shall once again set down the behavioural relationships in matrix form, making the normal simplifying assumption of linearity, starting with the adjustment matrix for the inhabitants of region A (other than intermediaries).

	Y_A	W_A	Y_B	P_A	P_B	r_F	r_L	w
$P_B \cdot {}_A X_B$	a_{11}	/	/	a_{14}	a_{15}	/	/	/
$[(1-b)P_A + bP_B]C_A$	a_{21}	a_{22}	/	a_{24}	a_{25}	a_{26}	a_{27}	/
$P_A X_A$	/	/	a_{33}	a_{34}	a_{35}	/	/	/
$[(1-b)P_A + bP_B]K_A$	a_{41}	a_{42}	/	a_{44}	a_{45}	a_{46}	a_{47}	a_{48}
${}_A F_A$	a_{51}	a_{52}	/	a_{54}	a_{55}	a_{56}^*	a_{57}	a_{58}
${}_A F_B$	a_{61}	a_{62}	/	a_{64}	a_{65}	a_{66}	a_{67}	a_{68}
L_A	a_{71}	a_{72}	/	a_{74}	a_{75}	a_{76}	a_{77}	a_{78}
M_A	a_{81}	a_{82}	/	a_{84}	a_{85}	a_{86}	a_{87}	a_{88}

The sub-matrix below the broken line represents simply another version of our standard asset-portfolio adjustment model, set out previously, in which the demand for the ith asset is expressed in terms of wealth, the budget constraint, relative prices, and other independent variables (which the inhabitants regard as parameters to which they respond) such as incomes. As before, the sum of column 2 from row 4–8 must add to unity, and – to preserve the balance-sheet identity – the coefficients of rows 4–8 in all other columns must add to zero.

The sub-matrix above the broken line describes the demand for A's exports, imports and consumption flows as a function of incomes, wealth (affecting consumption), incomes in region B (affecting the demand for A's exports), relative prices, and interest rates (affecting consumption). The wage level does *not* affect expenditure flows, since it was assumed that the distribution of income (given the level of income) between returns to capital and to labour had no effect on expenditure propensities.

Considering this matrix in more detail the /s represent coefficients whose value is expected to be zero. Going through the matrix column by column, first taking column 1, a_{11} and a_{21} set out the standard expenditure propensities (marginal assumed to equal average) as a function of incomes. The coefficients $a_{41}-a_{81}$ in column 1 are more interesting, since they show how the inhabitants would want to readjust their assets if income was, say, higher but total wealth was unchanged. Clearly if people hold more of one asset, e.g. real capital, their holdings of some other assets, e.g. financial claims, would, with a given total of wealth, have to be less. The need to produce additional goods and to finance a higher level of transactions suggests that $a_{41}, a_{81} > 0$ and that $a_{51}, a_{61}, a_{71} < 0$, i.e. that the inhabitants of A will borrow more from banks and run down their other financial claims to finance larger holdings of real capital and of money.

In column 2, a_{22} represents the wealth effect on consumption, $a_{22} > 0$. The coefficients $a_{42}-a_{82}$ sum to unity. All these coefficients will be > 0, except for a_{72} which will possibly be less than zero, as people might increase their financial indebtedness – in order to achieve their preferred time path of consumption – *pari passu* with growing wealth. An increase in income levels in B will raise A's exports, but should have no other effect on A's expenditure propensities or preferred asset balance. An increase in the price of A goods, other prices and wages being constant (by assumption),[1] will cause inhabitants in both A and B to substitute B goods in place of A goods, the extent of the shift depending on the elasticity of substitution between them. In addition the change in P_A will change real incomes in both A and B. If P_A rises, then

$$\frac{P_A}{(1 - b)P_A + bP_B}$$

rises, so long as $1 > b > 0$, i.e. incomes obtained from the production of A goods can now buy more of the desired consumption basket of A and B goods. Similarly, real incomes in B decline. The change in real incomes (for a given Y_A, Y_B) will have an effect on the demand for imports, consumption and exports.

The increase in P_A will have two main effects[2] on the desired asset balance in A. First, by raising the general price level it will raise the general level of money incomes and expenditures, and thus the demand for transactions balances. Second, the increase in P_A will raise the price of capital equipment in A (thus providing capital gains to existing owners of capital) and, with the level of wages (w) held constant, will shift the price of capital relative to the price of labour. With labour becoming relatively cheaper, there would be some substitution of labour for capital. The rate of return on capital in A may either rise or fall, depending on the elasticity of substitution between labour and capital in the production function. The short-run elasticity of substitution is probably quite low, and the return to capital should

---

[1] Since other prices, and wages, are assumed to be constant, the increase in P_A must reflect either increased demand for A goods or attempts by their producers to obtain a larger profit margin.

[2] Abstracting from the possible effect of a change in price levels in influencing expectations of future changes in price levels.

rise. If the rate of return on capital rises, following a rise in P_A, then the demand for capital (at a given level of wealth) would be greater.[1]

The effect of a change in P_A, *ceteris paribus*, on the demand for money balances will, therefore, be positive, $a_{84} > 0$, but the sign of the effect on the demand for other assets in the portfolio is uncertain without further information about the form of the production function in A (though our expectation would be that $a_{44} > 0$ and $a_{54}, a_{64}, a_{74} < 0$). A rise in P_B will similarly have substitution and income effects on the flow demand for exports, imports and consumption, with substitution effects leading inhabitants in A and B to purchase A goods instead of B goods when P_B rises, and income effects resulting in a fall in real incomes (and expenditures) among A inhabitants as the price of B goods rises. The substitution effect of an increase in P_A relative to P_B must be the same whether the differential occurs as a result of a change in P_A or P_B, but the income effect will vary depending on the weight of A and B goods in the overall consumption basket. Therefore the submatrix

$$\begin{bmatrix} a_{14} & a_{15} \\ a_{34} & a_{35} \end{bmatrix}$$

will not in general be symmetrical. Nevertheless, the effect of a rise in P_B on these expenditure flows (exports, imports, consumption) will be of the opposite sign to that of a rise in P_A. The effect of a rise of P_B on asset demands (with Y_A and W_A given) is, however, more like a similar, but slighter,[2] reflection of a change in P_A. A rise in P_B raises the average price level of transactions, and with w constant raises the price of capital relative to that of labour. In this case, however, the rate of profit on the production of A goods must fall, since revenue $(P_A \cdot Y_A)$ remains, by assumption, unchanged, while the price of a capital import has risen; so $a_{45} < 0$, $a_{85} > 0$ and the sign of the other asset coefficients is ambiguous.

An increase in the rate on non-monetary financial assets, r_F, or loans, r_L, raises the yield on that asset relative to the yield on all other assets. On the usual assumption that all assets are substitutes in a sector's portfolio, a rise in the yield on the ith asset will have a positive effect on the demand for that asset and a negative effect on the demand for other assets. Thus $a_{56}, a_{66} > 0$, and $a_{46}, a_{76}, a_{86} < 0$; similarly $a_{77} > 0$ and $a_{47}, a_{57}, a_{67}, a_{87} < 0$ (i.e. in this latter case where loans are a liability – a negative asset – a rise in bank loan rate will make people want to diminish their liability on bank loans, $a_{77} > 0$, and they will obtain the finance to do so by running down their holdings of real capital, non-monetary financial assets and money, $a_{47}, a_{57}, a_{67}, a_{87} < 0$). As noted previously in Chapter 9, a change in interest rates may make people revise their consumption plans. A rise in interest rates will cause a substitution effect in favour of future consumption (current saving), which will generally be supported by a wealth effect (as market values of existing assets fall), but may be offset by an income effect as the rise in rates allows current incomes to have a greater

---

[1] If the shift in relative factor prices should cause a divergence between rates of return on capital in A and B, then one would also expect to see inter-regional capital flows for direct investment in real assets, but for simplicity this model excludes such capital flows. An increase in rates of return in A (relative to B) should raise investment and thus incomes and imports in A and so worsen A's current account in the short run. This may be to some extent offset, even within the context of the present model, by the rise in returns on real capital in A causing portfolio-investment flows into A, as A inhabitants and intermediaries sell financial assets to B residents in order to take up more real capital. None the less, the capital account offset to the worsening current account in such circumstances is likely to be considerably less in the absence of direct inter-regional investment flows. In the longer run, however, the investment in A should help to make A's products more competitive and thereby generate a sufficient export surplus to redeem the indebtedness previously incurred.

[2] Assuming $0 < b < 0.5$.

command over the desired consumption basket of current and future goods. Theoretically, therefore, the sign of the coefficients a_{26}, a_{27} is ambiguous, but it would probably command general assent to treat them as mildly negative.

With Y_A, W_A, P_A and P_B given, and on the assumption that the distribution of incomes between labour and capital has no effect on expenditure propensities, a change in wage rates would have no effect on ${}_A X_B$, C_A or X_A. Nor with Y_A, P_A and P_B given, would money incomes change in response to the shift in wage rates, so the demand for money balances would be unaltered. The main effect – under these circumstances – of a fall in w would be to alter the price of capital relative to the price of labour but, as noted already, the effect of this on the demand for real capital (with a consequential effect on other assets, to retain the wealth constraint) is not certain, though we would expect in practice to see at least an initial increase in demand for capital. In reality, of course, a change in wage rates would probably bring forth an accompanying change in the prices of goods, including capital equipment, i.e. the assumption of P_A constant in the face of a change in w is implausible. How far a change in wage rates would be reflected in a general shift in all prices, leaving relative factor prices as before, and how far a change in wage rates would lead to a shift in relative factor prices is a matter outside the scope of this appendix.

Having discussed the likely response of the inhabitants in A to shifts in the economic parameters facing them, we may set out the signs of these responses in the coefficients of the previous matrix: a double sign ($++$ or $--$) suggests a relatively large response, a (?) implies a weak and/or uncertain response.

	Y_A	W_A	Y_B	P_A	P_B	r_F	r_L	w
$P_B \cdot {}_A X_B$	+	/	/	+	−	/	/	/
$[(1-b)P_A + bP_B]C_A$	+	+	/	+	−	−?	−?	/
$P_A X_A$	/	/	+	−	+	/	/	/
$[(1-b)P_A + bP_B]K_A$	+	+	/	+?	−	−	−	?
${}_A F_A$	−	+	/	−?	?	++	−	?
${}_A F_B$	−	+	/	−?	?	++	−	?
L_A	−	−	/	−?	?	−	++	?
M_A	+	+	/	++	+	−	−	?

The range of choice open to intermediaries is relatively circumscribed in comparison with the much wider range available to individuals. On our assumptions, the interest rate offered on monetary deposits is fixed at zero, and the rates to be offered on non-monetary financial instruments (F) and loans (L) are determined nationally, and are treated by the intermediaries in each region as parameters. The intermediaries may have some leeway to deter, or to encourage, loan business at the going rate by varying non-rate terms, e.g. the requirements for collateral, but basically they have to accept all deposits, both monetary and non-monetary, and undertake all reasonable, credit-worthy loan business at the going rates. The only margin of freedom which this leaves them, with the volume of their liabilities and of their loans and advances exogenously determined, is the ability to adjust their liquid assets (in this case cash reserves, H, and claims on financial intermediaries in other regions) in such a way as best to distribute the balance of the portfolio between liquidity and earning assets.[1] The available choice set open to intermediaries in A can then be

---

[1] On this, see W. White, 'Models of Deposit Bank Portfolio Behaviour,' part of the Proceedings of the London Business School Conference of June 1972 on *Modelling the U.K. Economy* (forthcoming).

described in terms of the following simple matrix

$$
\begin{array}{c|cc}
 & r_F & M_A + F_A - L_A \\
\hline
H_A & b_{11} & b_{12} \\
{}_{IA}F_B & b_{21} & b_{22}
\end{array}
$$

Here $M_A + F_A - L_A$ represents total available liquid assets, that is the budget constraint, which is exogenously determined; b_{12} and b_{22} are both > 0 and must together add to unity. The rate of interest on financial intermediary claims, r_F, determines the relative yield obtained on the two alternative liquid assets, since the rate of interest on reserves is assumed equal to zero, so $b_{21} = -b_{11}$.

Possibly the condition that the levels of interest rates, particularly on rates for non-monetary deposits, is nationally determined may be excessively restrictive, especially in a large country. If intermediaries in one region are short of liquidity they may be in a position to respond by raising the rates which they bid for funds above the level bid in other areas, thus opening up an inter-regional differential. In a single country, where the liabilities of intermediaries in different regions are treated as effectively identical, the establishment of a small differential should cause a large shift in desired holdings of that asset by inhabitants of all regions towards those liabilities issued by the region now offering the higher return. In this case it becomes necessary to distinguish between r_{FA} and r_{FB}. The choice matrix for the intermediary then becomes

$$
\begin{array}{c|ccc}
 & r_L & r_{FB} & M_A + F_A - L \\
\hline
H_A & b_{11} & b_{12} & b_{13} \\
{}_{IA}F_B & b_{21} & b_{22} & b_{23} \\
r_{FA} & b_{31} & b_{32} & b_{33}
\end{array}
$$

and the probable nature (sign) of the responses are as shown below

$$
\begin{array}{c|ccc}
 & r_L & r_{FB} & M_A + F_A - L \\
\hline
H_A & + & - & + \\
{}_{IA}F_B & - & + & + \\
r_{FA} & + & + & -
\end{array}
$$

If the loan rate rises, with a given volume of liquid assets, the intermediary will probably respond by raising rates offered on liabilities in order to obtain additional funds to make the higher earning loans. With higher earnings on the loan portfolio, the intermediary is likely to seek additional liquidity, at the expense of earnings, in the liquid-assets portfolio, so $b_{11} > 0$ and $b_{21} < 0$.

Furthermore, if r_{FA} can differ from r_{FB}, this will introduce an additional price in response to which private-sector individuals will have to adjust their asset holdings. Generally a rise in r_{Fi} relative to r_{Fj} $(i \neq j)$ will cause a large increase in the demand for non-monetary claims on i intermediaries, financed largely by running down similar claims on j intermediaries, but also partly by running down other assets.

At this stage it would be possible to give some numerical examples of the adjustment of the system in response to disturbances, along the lines already followed in Chapters 6 and 7. However, I shall restrict myself to illustrating the simple case set out at the start of Section B, in which all prices and interest rates are taken as constant: for it seems hardly worthwhile to put much weight on such limited models, especially when one does not give empirical content to the coefficients, and where the dynamic process in conditions of limited information is difficult to discern and to specify. In the case of this model, apart from these drawbacks, the model as set out does not allow one to study the interaction between regions A

and B, since the economic position of region B is taken as given, and even certain important elements in region A, viz. a separate company sector, or a regional fiscal authority able to vary local taxes and expenditures are lacking. Rather, the model in this appendix should be regarded basically as a prolegomenon to the analysis in the text, showing in a more formal and compressed way how the main elements in the system fit in together.

Anyhow, in the case posited at the start of Section B all prices, interest rates, etc., are taken as constant, and the effects of financial asset readjustments on inter-regional interest payments – and thus on the regional current-account balance – are ignored; that is to say P_A, P_B, b, w, r_F, r_L are all taken as constant and $r_F(_BF_A - {_A}F_B)$ is assumed to equal zero throughout. So from equation (i)

$$Y_A = X_A + I_A + C_A - {_A}X_B$$

Then substituting from the private sector's adjustment matrix

$$Y_{At} = a_1 + a_{33}Y_{Bt} + a_{41}(Y_{At} - Y_{At-1}) + a_{42}(W_{At} - W_{At-1})$$
$$+ a_{21}Y_{At} + a_{22}W_{At} - a_{11}Y_{At}$$

Collecting terms,

$$(1 - a_{41} - a_{21} + a_{11})Y_{At} = a_1 + a_{33}Y_{Bt} - a_{41}Y_{At-1} + (a_{42} + a_{22})W_{At} - a_{42}W_{At-1} \quad \text{(vii)}$$

Similarly, from the previous accounting identities (with prices constant)

$$W_{At} - W_{At-1} = X_A - {_A}X_B + I_A$$

Substituting from the adjustment matrix gives

$$W_{At} = a_2 + a_{33}Y_{Bt} - a_{11}Y_{At} + a_{41}(Y_{At} - Y_{At-1}) + a_{42}(W_{At} - W_{At-1}) - W_{At-1}$$

Collecting terms again,

$$(1 - a_{42})W_{At} = a_2 + a_{33}Y_{Bt} + (a_{41} - a_{11})Y_{At} - a_{41}Y_{At-1} + (1 - a_{42})W_{At-1} \quad \text{(viii)}$$

In a stationary equilibrium $W_{At} = W_{At-1}$ and $Y_{At} = Y_{At-1}$: assuming that $a_1 = a_2 = 0$, then from equation (viii) above it follows that in such an equilibrium it is necessary that $a_{33}Y_{Bt} = a_{11}Y_{At}$, i.e. that exports equal imports; otherwise, even when $Y_{At} = Y_{At-1}$ there would be changes in wealth. Then from equation (vii) it follows that, with $a_{33}Y_{Bt} = a_{11}Y_{At}$, and wealth constant, it is necessary for $Y_{At} = a_{21}Y_{At} + a_{22}W_{At}$, i.e. that domestic income is exactly matched by domestic consumption, in order to maintain incomes at a constant level.

Given the values of the coefficients in the adjustment matrix and the value of Y_B, it is then possible to calculate the equilibrium stationary values for the variables in region A and the time paths of these variables. Let us take a numerical example, with $a_1 = a_2 = 0$, and the coefficients in the remaining, reduced-size adjustment matrix having the following values

	Y_A	W_A	Y_B
$_AX_B$	0·2	/	/
C_A	0·60	0·05	/
X_A	/	/	0·1
K_A	0·2	0·35	/

and let the initial value of Y_B be 4000. Then the stationary equilibrium requires that $a_{33}Y_{Bt} = 0·1 \times 4000 = a_{11}Y_{At} = 0·2 \times Y_{At}$; so $Y_{At} = Y_{At-1} = 2000$, and $X_A = {_A}X_B = 400$. Similarly, domestic income must be exhausted by domestic consumption in stationary equilibrium, so $Y_{At} = 0·6 \times Y_{At} + 0·05 \times W_{At}$; with $Y_{At} = 2000$, $W_t = W_{t-1} = 16,000$, and $C_t = 2000$. The constant capital stock (there being no depreciation) equals 6000.

If Y_B should increase from 4000 to 4200, then in order to restore a stationary equilibrium Y_A should rise to 2100 and W_A to 16,800. However, in this postulated system the variables will not adjust monotonically from one equilibrium state to another. Equations (vii) and (viii) represent a couple of simultaneous difference equations,[1] which in this case have the following numerical coefficients

$$0.4Y_{At} = 420 - 0.2Y_{At-1} + 0.40W_{At} - 0.35W_{At-1}$$
$$0.65W_{At} = 420 - 0.2Y_{At-1} + 0.65W_{At-1}$$

Starting from the previous equilibrium position with $W_{At-1} = 16,000$ and $Y_{At-1} = 2000$ the time paths of the variables, following a rise in Y_B in period 1, are as shown in Table 14.1.

TABLE 14.1

	W	Y	$_AX_B$	C	I	X
$t = 0$	16,000	2000	400	2000	0·0	400
1	16,031	2081	416	2050	26·92	420
2	16,037	2019	404	2013	−10·21	420
3	16,061	2070	414	2045	18·75	420
4	16,071	2032	406	2023	−4·25	420
5	16,092	2064	413	2043	13·60	420
6	16,103	2041	408	2030	−0·65	420
7	16,121	2061	412	2042	10·34	420
8	16,133	2047	409	2035	1·48	420
9	16,150	2060	412	2043	8·24	420
10	16,162	2051	410	2039	2·73	420
11	16,177	2060	412	2045	6·86	420
12	16,189	2055	411	2042	3·42	420
13	16,203	2060	412	2046	5·94	420
14	16,216	2058	412	2045	3·77	420
15	16,229	2061	412	2048	5·29	420
16	16,241	2060	412	2048	3·92	420
17	16,253	2062	412	2050	4·82	420
18	16,264	2062	412	2050	3·95	420
19	16,276	2064	413	2052	4·46	420
20	16,287	2064	413	2053	3·89	420

[1] The system has the general form

$$Y_{At} = a_1 u_t + a_2 Y_{At-1} + a_3 W_{At} + a_4 W_{At-1}$$
$$W_{At} = b_1 v_t + b_2 W_{At-1} + b_3 Y_{At} + b_4 Y_{At-1}$$

where u and v are (vectors of) exogenous variables.

In this case the conditions for stability are

$$-1 < \frac{a_4 b_4 - a_2 b_2}{1 - a_3 b_3} < 1$$

and

$$-1 < \frac{a_2 + b_2 + a_3 b_4 + a_4 b_3}{1 + a_2 b_2 - a_3 b_3 - a_4 b_4} < 1$$

I am grateful to J. P. Burman and D. Williams for help with the mathematics of this system.

In the first round when Y_B increases, the increase in exports causes an increase in Y_A and thus, through the accelerator mechanism, an increase in investment. In the next round, however, with Y_B constant, there is no further stimulus to incomes from rising exports. Without a continuing stimulus, however, investment and incomes must fall back from previous levels; wealth, however, continues to rise, since the cut back in investment is offset by the improved current-account balance. Given these values for the coefficients, Y_A oscillates in an increasingly damped manner from one period to the next under the influence of the investment accelerator; wealth, however, converges steadily and mono-tonically to the new equilibrium position, since the fluctuations in investment and in the trade balance offset each other.

15

International Monetary Relations

SUMMARY

There are two main factors determining whether the balance of payments adjustments of some geographic area would be more easily handled as a region within a common currency area or as an independent country with a separate currency and a potentially variable exchange rate. The first of these is size. The smaller the size of the region, the easier it is for it to adjust within a common currency area and the greater the difficulty of making an independent command over monetary and exchange-rate policies effective. Larger countries may enjoy certain economies of scale (for example in government itself) and the existence of large currency areas does eliminate the need for continuous currency exchanges within the area. On the other hand, a region which cannot adjust its exchange rate in response to external shocks will have to bear additional adjustment costs in terms of disturbances to labour markets (e.g. migration and unemployment) and large shifts in incomes and wealth. If the prime goal is internal stability, it would seem that the greater the number of separate currencies the better. However, simple observation shows that single currency areas range from huge countries down to very small states. This diversity suggests that the costs of diverging from the optimally-sized currency area are not sufficient to outweigh other more powerful forces shaping political boundaries.

Indeed the second, and more important, factor determining the optimal extent of currency areas is the existence of social and political unity between the regions of the area. If this exists, fiscal transfers (and migration) will ease, and possibly resolve, regional disparities, and allow the burden of adjustment to disturbances to be amicably shared. It is, however, possible to find counter-examples of countries linked together in a single currency area without the support of a (partially) centralised fiscal authority. One such example is provided by the fixed relationship between the Irish and U.K. currencies. Another more famous example is provided by the Gold Standard.

The maintenance of permanently-fixed exchange rates virtually implies the abandonment of autonomous control over domestic monetary policy. Otherwise the more inflationary country, within a fixed exchange-rate system, would not only obtain command over additional goods and services, but would also pass on unwanted inflation to its partners. No such system can, therefore, persist without some discipline over the monetary policies of the countries involved. But, in the modern world, powerful, independent nations are not likely to submit themselves to the external constraints of automatic rules. The discipline and decisions necessary to run a fixed exchange-rate system will nowadays have to depend on political harmony.

The political scene today gives few grounds for optimism on the prospects for establishing a permanently-fixed exchange-rate system over the Atlantic community. The world system will continue to contain a number of countries (currency areas) with separate currencies whose value in exchange can, and will, vary. The question, addressed in Section B, is how such adjustments are best carried out; in particular we examine whether the exchange rate should be allowed to float entirely freely or whether its movements should be managed by the authorities; and if the decision is to manage the exchange rate, whether this should be by maintaining (temporarily) fixed but adjustable parities or by intervening to moderate the rate of change of the exchange rate.

I doubt whether it would be desirable to leave the exchange rate entirely at the mercy of market forces. In the short run devaluations often seem to worsen the trade account, probably because of lags in adjustment to price changes (the J-curve syndrome), while speculation is also usually on too short run a basis to provide a stabilising influence. So a regime of freely floating rates may lead to considerable 'overshooting' and unnecessary instability. Moreover, when external balance is disturbed, not by an external shock, but by some impulse from domestic conditions, reliance on flexible exchange rates to restore external balance will tend to exaggerate the initial divergence from internal balance. Supporters of flexible exchange rates have a liberal optimism in the perfectability of domestic policy making.

On the other hand, once an exchange rate is pegged it ceases to insulate the economy from external shocks. If the authorities are not driven from their internal objectives – and the whole idea is to prevent that happening – an external imbalance will develop over time. The existence and direction of this imbalance will generally become obvious, opening up one-way options to speculators. If the authorities try to peg the rate for any length of time, the change in the rate ultimately necessary to restore equilibrium will become larger. Large, abrupt, occasional changes in market conditions tend to impose greater adjustment costs than small, continuous changes. Furthermore, the longer a rate is forcibly held at some disequilibrium level the harder it may be to see what the appropriate level at which to re-fix might be.

For all these reasons my own conclusion is that the authorities should intervene in exchange markets, but that their concern should not be to pick and to defend any particular level of rates, but to control the *rate of change* of parities, managing this rate of change to see that it never becomes too large (e.g. under the influence of low short-run elasticities and destabilising market speculation) to become a disruptive force.

A. Optimal Currency Areas

From the analysis of the previous chapter we should now be able to extract and to identify the main features which differentiate the international from the inter-regional adjustment process. The most obvious difference, of course, is that regions share a single common currency, whereas each nation maintains a separate currency, autonomously controlled, which can in principle vary in value against the currencies of other independent states.

In certain ways the adjustment problem for the region is easier than for the larger state which contains it. Being smaller, and also producing a smaller range of goods, its marginal propensity to import will be higher. So, in those cases when there are no equilibrating relative price/cost movements, it would take a lesser variation in incomes and wealth to restore equilibrium in the region, as compared with the country. In any case the region will be part of a single currency area with, presumably, an integrated capital market; in this market there should be a high degree of substitution between financial assets of similar kinds issued in the various regions. So each region should be able to finance fluctuations in its current account with considerable ease; so much so that the financial problems that do arise will appear rather in the guise of concern over the future viability of local industries than in the forms which concern separate nations, with their recurring worries over the level of official reserves and their persistent efforts to identify and to influence the channels of international capital flows.

Finally, and perhaps most important, social unity between regions provides the popular support for fiscal centralisation which should, given the usual schedules of benefits and taxes, provide a flow of funds from the more active and the more prosperous regions to the depressed and poorer parts of each country; this should ameliorate imbalances and disparities. Furthermore, sympathy with the plight of the less fortunate regions may cause the central government to act directly to improve the competitiveness of the depressed regions by encouraging the development of new industries there, by improving the capital infrastructure (transport, communications, etc.), by special efforts to train and to educate the local labour force, etc. And, as has been already noted, the central government does also have at hand the fiscal tools, in the form of regional employment premia and taxes, to cause divergences between final prices and wage costs in the various areas, which can act as a surrogate for exchange-rate changes. Finally, even if the government does not, or cannot, act effectively to prevent disparities between prosperous and depressed regions developing and persisting, social unity between the regions of the country, encompassing and depending on such matters as language and accent, common legal institutions, etc., would facilitate easier migration between regions, which would also serve to ease the situation.[1]

The main difficulty confronting regions in their attempts to adjust to imbalances, which usually show themselves in a decline in the demand for local products, is their comparative inability to induce an equilibrating movement in relative costs and prices. Moreover, a fairly small region often concentrates upon the production of a few goods, coal say, or textiles, or cars, so that its balance is bound to be frequently disturbed by minor variations in taste, in technology or in foreign competitiveness, while the larger country should find some of these somewhat random developments offsetting each other.[2] It is not only that regions cannot formally devalue, or revalue, against other regions; the very social unity between one region and another leads to concern over parity of (real) incomes, with wage negotiations undertaken on a national basis, so that market-based wage changes in response to local excess-supply conditions may be suppressed. In these circumstances a decline in activity in some region is less likely to lead to a relative reduction in wages and prices there. On the other hand, social cohesion should limit the emergence and development of disequilibrating movements in wages and prices in the first place.[3]

Even if a very small area did obtain monetary autonomy, and was able to vary its exchange rate, it is dubious whether this would be nearly as successful as in the case of a larger country. To be sure the elasticity of demand for a small region's exports should be usually higher; despite a greater concentration on a few products it will provide a smaller proportion of world supply and should, therefore, find it easier to displace other suppliers.[4]

---

[1] Migrants tend to be young adult males. So emigration may worsen the dependency ratio of the home region and push its rate of growth of productivity down further. It is far from clear whether the longer-term regional problems of areas which have experienced large-scale emigration, e.g. Ireland, Southern Italy, have been greatly eased by such migration. On this see Dr T. K. Whitaker, 'Monetary Integration: Reflections on Irish Experience,' *Moorgate and Wall Street* (autumn 1973) pp. 4–21, especially p. 16.

[2] A point emphasised by P. B. Kenen in his paper on 'The Theory of Optimum Currency Areas: An Eclectic View,' contained in the book *Monetary Problems of the International Economy*, ed. R. A. Mundell and A. Swoboda (University of Chicago Press, 1969) pp. 41–60.

[3] I am indebted to John Williamson for reminding me of this point.

[4] If this were not so, the high propensity to import of a small area might make deflation a cheaper method – in terms of the absorption of goods given up – of adjustment to a deficit than a devaluation, *assuming* for the moment that such a devaluation could succeed in reducing real wages in the small region. Formally, on the assumption also of completely elastic supplies of goods, though this is implausible particularly for the small region, deflation would be preferable to devaluation if

$$1 + \frac{1}{m} < \frac{\eta_x + \eta_m}{\eta_x + \eta_m - 1}$$

where m is the marginal propensity to import, η_x the external elasticity of demand for the small region's exports, and η_m its elasticity of demand for imports. I am grateful to W. A. Allen for pointing this out to me. Although m will be higher in a small region, so also will η_x normally be. The value of m is bounded, but η_x can rise to infinity: the higher external elasticity of demand for the exports of a small region should, in my view, normally outweigh the effect of the greater propensity to import, thus making devaluation, *on these assumptions*, the more preferable option for the very small region.

On the other hand, the high propensity to import of a small region, its openness,[1] will cause any variation in exchange rates to be rapidly reflected in a nearly equivalent (inverse) shift in prices. Such a larger and more obvious effect of devaluation on real wage rates and living standards may call forth greater resistance on the part of labour. This will be greater the more that social unity between contiguous areas encourages a comparison between living standards and prompts people in similar occupations in differing regions to demand similar real living standards. Furthermore, the large weight of imported goods in consumption, and therefore the crucial significance of the terms of trade between local wages and import prices, may make labour and others prefer to have their receipts specified, and their assets denominated, in terms of foreign prices.[2] In these circumstances the ability of the local monetary authorities to undertake an independent monetary policy or to vary the rate of exchange with the stronger foreign currency may be severely curtailed.[3]

There appear to be two common factors here determining whether the balance-of-payments adjustments of some geographical area would be more easily solved as a region within a common-currency area or as an independent country with a separate currency and a potentially-variable exchange rate. These are size, and social unity with surrounding, contiguous regions. The smaller the size of the region, the easier it is for it to adjust within a common currency area and the greater difficulty it will have, as a small, open economy, in making its supposed independent command over monetary policy and exchange rates effective. One can point to examples of independent countries which are too small to maintain an effective independent monetary policy; nevertheless, even tiny countries by the standards of the giants, e.g. Russia, the United States, do operate independent monetary policies.[4] The more important factor is social unity: if this exists, fiscal transfers (and migration) will on the one hand ease and even possibly solve regional disparities, while on the other hand concern for parity may suppress equilibrating movements in relative costs and prices, whether market-based or induced by exchange-rate variations.

Frankly it is difficult to believe that size is the most crucial variable determining the boundaries of the 'optimal' currency area, or even a particularly important variable once the minimum size necessary to support effective independence has been attained. Simple observation shows that the basic single-currency areas, i.e. the independent nation states, vary from vast giants, e.g. China, Russia, the United States, whose administrative regions, e.g. the States of California, New York, Texas, etc., are much larger on any criterion than the majority of independent nations, right down to relatively tiny nation states. If size were so very important, surely economic pressure would encourage separatist movements in the larger countries and attempts at mergers and unification among groupings of smaller countries, with a convergence towards some common size for each single national-currency

---

[1] R. I. McKinnon emphasised the importance of this factor in determining whether it would or would not be advantageous for a region to become part of a wider single-currency area, in his paper on 'Optimum Currency Areas,' *American Economic Review*, vol. 53, no. 4 (September 1963) pp. 717–25.

[2] W. M. Corden, in his pamphlet on 'Monetary Integration,' *Essays in International Finance*, no. 93 (April 1972) (International Finance Section of the Department of Economics of Princeton University), criticises the choice of the extent of 'openness' of an economy as an indicator of the likely advantages of monetary union on the grounds that exchange-rate movements can still allow even a small open economy to be insulated from variations in external prices feeding through into import prices. This is so, but living standards can also be protected from imported inflation by relating domestic wage rates to import prices. Relating local wages to wages and prices in neighbouring areas may give the inhabitants of a small, open region a greater feeling of certainty than reliance on the vagaries of the foreign-exchange market, which in the case of a small country would be a narrow market.

[3] See also Chap. 1, pp. 10–12.

[4] Practical experience suggests that Luxembourg may be too small, but Denmark is large enough, to operate an effective independent monetary policy. Eire appears to be on the border-line.

area. There is little evidence of this occurring, or of its having occurred in the past. The economic advantages of a larger grouping of small principalities (and among these economic considerations the ease of balance-of-payments adjustments was itself a minor issue) played some role in the unification of Germany and possibly of other countries also, but historical experience suggests that if there are adjustment costs involved in maintaining single-currency areas greater or less than some 'optimum' size, these costs are too slight[1] to affect seriously the historical process determining their size. This great diversity in the size of existing common-currency areas should cause a certain hesitance in putting forward the thesis that there is a well-defined optimally-sized currency area, or that adjustment costs increase significantly as the size of the area diverges markedly from the optimal (i.e. that size is, or should be, an important determinant of the boundaries of a common currency area).

The additional adjustment costs (in terms of extra unemployment, forced migration and reduced incomes and wealth) that may arise when a region cannot adjust its exchange rate, in order to shift relative (wage) costs and prices, seem clear and obvious; the offsetting gains of having a larger currency area seem generally more nebulous.[2] As a result several authors on this topic have found themselves virtually forced into the position of arguing in favour of currency regions which are as small as feasible (i.e. just large enough still to allow for effective independence of monetary policy and for variable exchange rates to be a useful instrument). Mundell, for example, argued:

> If then, the goals of internal stability are to be rigidly pursued, it follows that the greater is the number of separate currency areas in the world, the more successfully will these goals be attained.... But this seems to imply that regions ought to be defined so narrowly as to count every minor pocket of unemployment arising from labour immobility as a separate region, each of which should apparently have a separate currency.[3]

He went on to note, however, that besides the stabilisation argument, which pointed to having a plethora of currency areas, there were costs associated with the maintenance of many currency areas. These were that it reduced the usefulness of each independent money as a medium of exchange, that it would lead to excessively narrow exchange-rate markets, and that in small regions with high import propensities the community might not accept the changes in real incomes brought about by exchange-rate variations for the reasons we have already mentioned. Nevertheless, these costs cannot have bulked high with him, since he concluded,[4] 'If the world can be divided into regions within each of which there is factor mobility and between which there is factor immobility, then each of these regions should have a separate currency which fluctuates relative to all other currencies.'

Again Kenen[5] argues that the less diversified are a region's products, the more necessary it is for that region to maintain a flexible exchange rate. '*Ex ante*, diversification serves to average out external shocks and, incidentally, to stabilise domestic capital formation. *Ex post*, it serves to minimise the damage done when averaging is incomplete.'[6] But the

---

[1] This is not to say that these costs are in fact negligible. It is rather that they are hard to visualise and are outweighed by other stronger political forces.

[2] See, for example, the assessment of the 'pros' and 'cons' of monetary unification within the European Economic Community by J. Marcus Fleming, 'On Exchange Rate Unification,' *The Economic Journal*, vol. 81, no. 323 (September 1971) pp. 467–88.

[3] R. A. Mundell, 'A Theory of Optimum Currency Areas,' *American Economic Review*, vol. 60, no. 4 (September 1961) p. 662.

[4] Ibid. p. 663.

[5] In 'The Theory of Optimum Currency Areas: An Eclectic View,' in *Monetary Problems of the International Economy*, ed. R. A. Mundell and A. Swoboda (University of Chicago Press, 1969) pp. 41–60.

[6] Ibid. p. 54.

smaller the area, the more likely that it will be concentrating on the production of a limited number of goods. This principle appears to lead to the curious conclusion that the smaller the region, the greater the need for an independent monetary policy and flexible exchange rates.

There must be something wrong with that. In my view these authors are placing too much weight on the effects of size, with its implications for openness and diversity, as a determinant of the costs of adjustment within a single-currency area and too little on the role of social unity. If there is social unity throughout a country, irrespective of size, the authorities could, and should, introduce fiscal measures that will ease adjustment costs as, or perhaps even more, effectively as exchange-rate changes. Moreover, in such conditions labour migration will be easier, and relative wage/price adjustments harder to bring about under any exchange-rate regime.

If people in the prosperous regions of a single-currency area, say in the south-east of England, feel that everyone in the country deserves the same treatment as them, they will not resent a continuing transfer of funds, through the fiscal mechanism,[1] to the less prosperous regions, say in Scotland or the north-east.[2] Equally the fiscal redistribution should soften the impact of current-account imbalances on activity and incomes in the lagging regions and, perhaps, lessen the attraction of political separatism. On the other hand, any attempt to impose an exchange-rate union on a set of areas without an underlying social unity can lead rapidly to disaster. If the members of the more prosperous regions (e.g. Germany and Holland in the E.E.C.) should object to providing a potentially very large flow of funds for an indefinite time period to the less prosperous regions (e.g. Ireland and Italy), on the grounds that these foreigners are different and should be content with different treatment, then the adjustment costs and separatist pressures within the single-currency area could easily become intense. The 'optimal' currency area is a function not so much of geography but rather of social psychology.

Indeed, as far as one can observe, the problems of maintaining balance between regions in a single-currency area do not seem qualitatively that much harder in vast countries such as the United States or Russia than in much smaller countries such as the United Kingdom, Italy or Sweden. The disparity between economic conditions in West Virginia and, say, New York does not seem qualitatively so much worse than, say, the difference between parts of Scotland and the south of England, or between the south and north of Italy. The extent, severity and persistence of regional disparities do not seem to be very closely correlated with the size of the currency area.

The costs of maintaining a common-currency area (due to the prevention of the use of exchange-rate variations among the constituent regions as an instrument of adjustment to imbalances) are not – we have argued – particularly closely related to the size, the extent, of that area. Are there, perhaps, any gains, any advantages, on the other hand, to be obtained from having larger currency areas? If so, with no significant additional costs but real advantages, one would advocate having common-currency areas among all those regional groups with sufficient social unity to make them work well.

The most obvious benefit from having a larger currency area is that it eliminates the need for currency exchanges within the area and also uncertainty about likely future exchange rates. Consider the additional time and effort that would have to be devoted to currency exchanges by all travellers and businessmen, as well as the further employment

---

[1] They will, no doubt, complain about the level of taxation, but they are not likely to resent the fact that there are net fiscal transfers to other regions.

[2] Within most industrialised countries the fiscal mechanism transfers considerable sums from the more to the less prosperous regions without there being much fuss or bother about it. Yet the provision of development aid to very much poorer people in foreign countries runs into much political opposition and resentment. One of the few cases of really large-scale transfers beyond political frontiers was Marshall Aid, but that was in special circumstances and is continuously cited as an exceptional case.

of specialised exchange brokers with their attendant equipment, if every state among the fifty United States had its separate currency and exchange rate. Even worse, there would be a multiplication of Central Banks and Central Bankers, each with its staff of bureaucrats and its printing press, churning out fifty different currencies. Or think of the extra bother if each county in the United Kingdom tried to run an independent monetary system. Alternatively, imagine the advantages, in ease and simplicity, of having a single currency all over the world.[1]

These exchange costs are largely incurred because of uncertainty about the future relative values of the separate currencies. If everyone knew exactly what the exchange rate of the pound and franc was going to be at every point of time, people would accept either currency equally readily.[2] In part this uncertainty can be reduced, at a cost, by obtaining extra information, e.g. reading the newspaper to see what current exchange rates are, or by hedging future foreign-exchange commitments in the forward market. But there are limits to the extent that uncertainty can be overcome, whether by the acquisition of extra information or by operations in forward markets.

This uncertainty about exchange rates is one of the major factors, alongside difficulties of communication over long distances, separate languages, differing legal institutions, etc., which raise barriers to trade in goods and assets. A single common-currency area aids the integration of markets, which should improve allocative efficiency, allowing capital to move with greater flexibility to those areas where it can offer the highest return. For example, one of the major benefits of a move towards a common European currency should be the impetus this would give to the development of an integrated capital market.[3,4]

It is, however, unrealistic to discuss 'optimal' currency areas without giving explicit consideration to the close links between control of the currency and national sovereignty. As noted in Chapter 1, the right to issue legal-tender currency is one of the most important, and prized, aspects of independent, sovereign power. Monetary independence entails the power also to change the exchange rate of the country vis-à-vis the currencies of other areas. If, say, British Columbia, or Florida, or Scotland, was given a separate Central Bank, a separate currency and the power to vary its exchange rate vis-à-vis the Canadian dollar, or U.S. dollar or English pound, how much would be, or could be, left of national union between the two areas? Not only monetary policy, common currencies and integrated markets would have gone, but it is also extremely difficult to see how it would be possible to maintain any coherent common fiscal policy between the two areas.[5]

---

[1] On this subject see G. E. Wood, 'European Monetary Union and the U.K. – A Cost–Benefit Analysis,' *Surrey Economic Papers*, no. 9 (July 1973).

[2] Or almost so. The payment of money generally leaves the recipient's asset balance out of equilibrium, i.e. he will want to use most of these monetary receipts to buy goods or services or financial assets. If there is a lag between the receipt of the money and his ability to redistribute it, he will prefer to receive the currency which will appreciate in this interval.

[3] In their pamphlet on *European Monetary Integration* (A Federal Trust Report, 1972), G. Magnifico and J. H. Williamson see one of the main advantages of establishing a new European currency (the 'Europa') that it could 'fill the role that the Euro-dollar has performed for the past decade in acting as an instrument for the creation of unified European money and capital markets,' p. 9; see also pp. 7–10 and 20.

[4] There is always, however, a possibility of conflict between efficiency and equity. It could well be that, at the moment, the marginal return to capital is higher in Germany than in Italy. An integrated capital market would then direct investment even more towards Germany, thus raising total E.E.C. output obtainable from a given total of factor inputs, but at the expense of exaggerating intra-E.E.C. disparities. This provides a further indication of the vital importance of an appropriate fiscal and regional policy in the E.E.C. if it is to become generally acceptable.

[5] Many of the arguments here resemble the question of precedence of the chicken or the egg. The establishment of a successful monetary union may well require support from a strong, centralised, or at least inter-regionally co-ordinated, fiscal (and regional) policy to ease the complications of regional adjustment. Yet it is very difficult to establish a centralised fiscal authority unless

(*Footnote* [5] *continued on p. 297*)

Thus Kenen asked:[1]

How would taxes be collected if a single fiscal system were to span a number of currency areas, each of them entitled to alter its exchange rate? How would a treasury maintain the desired distribution of total tax collections? Suppose that the treasury levied an income tax to be paid in each resident's regional currency and that the West was printing money faster than the East, causing a more rapid rise in prices and incomes. Unless the West's currency were to depreciate pari passu with the faster rise in money incomes, the West would come to pay a larger fraction of the tax (and if the tax were graduated, might also have to furnish a larger share of the goods and services absorbed by the government, as its tax payments would rise faster than its prices). The same problem would arise even more dramatically if the treasury relied on property taxation. Property values and property assessments might not keep pace with money incomes, and even if the difference in rates of inflation were exactly matched by the change in the exchange rate, there could be a significant redistribution of the tax burden. In which currency, moreover, would the central government pay for goods and services? Which one would it use to pay its civil servants? And what may be the thorniest practical problem in which currency should the central government issue its own debt instruments?

Neither he, nor Corden,[2] were prepared to go so far as to claim that these problems were insurmountable, but they are clearly very difficult. If social and political unity is sufficient to solve amicably the problems of fiscal redistribution when a central budget is disturbed by exchange-rate variations, the necessary conditions surely also exist for the successful establishment of a single-currency area. Alternatively, if pressures within an area are such as to require the establishment, or maintenance, of separate currency areas, there is unlikely to be much agreement forthcoming on the transfer to a central authority of local fiscal powers, or on how such powers as it has been granted should be exercised. Fiscal and monetary harmonisation will march together, or not at all.

If separate currency areas do entail separate fiscal areas, then all the main economic powers have been devolved. Groupings of such areas, each with its own independent fiscal policy, monetary policy and exchange rate, may form a confederation or an alliance, but hardly a union, much less a united country. It is extremely difficult, perhaps impossible, for a unified country to extend over more than one currency area. If so, possible economies of scale that may appertain to larger countries, e.g. in defence, administration, etc., require the establishment of large currency areas. To put it bluntly, if each state in the Union had retained its own independent currency after the War of Independence it is doubtful whether they would now form part of a set of United States.

I have argued both that a single-currency area requires a strong, centralised fiscal authority,[3] ready and able to ease regional adjustment problems, and also that it will be

---

there is a monetary union, a single currency, throughout the area. In order to establish conditions conducive to the successful working of a single-currency area the constituent regions need to exhibit social unity, but the existence of different currencies is one of the factors tending to divide and separate groups of people. The problems involved in moving, through a process of political agreement, from a system consisting of several independent currencies to a single-currency area are extremely difficult and delicate. In my view the Werner Report, on the attainment of economic and monetary union within the E.E.C., failed to give adequate attention to the complexities of the course which it was charting.

---

[1] Op. cit. p. 46.

[2] 'Monetary Integration,' p. 38.

[3] Simple inspection shows that it is not necessary for *all* fiscal operations to be centralised within a single-currency area. Within sovereign countries there is often a considerable devolution of the right to levy taxes and to determine expenditures to the local, State, county, township level. How much fiscal centralisation is necessary to keep a single-currency area working smoothly is a matter for conjecture.

difficult to establish any effective centralised fiscal authority covering areas with independent, separate currencies; i.e. both that a single-currency area cannot cover several, independent, unco-ordinated fiscal areas, and the converse that an integrated fiscal area cannot extend over several independent currency areas. There are no doubt exceptions to both rules but the weaker claim, on historical experience, seems to be that a currency area requires strong centralised fiscal support. Without reaching too far back in time, the success of the Gold Standard in the period from 1890 to 1914 shows that it has been possible for countries to establish virtually a common-currency area, an apparently permanent, fixed exchange-rate system, without the support of fiscal policy.[1]

How then did the Gold Standard system work so well in these years, while nowadays, we have argued, any system of permanently-fixed exchange rates would need help from fiscal measures to ease regional adjustments? Of course, the countries on the Gold Standard did enjoy several of the benefits of a single-currency area. The establishment of an integrated capital market in London, together with confidence in the maintenance of the parity of the major industrial countries,[2] did allow large-scale accommodating (short-term) capital flows. As discussed in the previous chapter (Section A), a high elasticity of substitution among financial assets enables current-account imbalances to be settled with little monetary disturbance. Furthermore, the continued strong balance-of-payments position of the United Kingdom (with a large surplus on invisibles more than offsetting a trade deficit) prevented the growth of short-term sterling liabilities, claims on London, relative to the stock of U.K. gold reserves from becoming a serious problem.[3] But this only helps to explain how the system was able to finance current-account imbalances;[4] it still leaves unanswered

---

[1] A second, more up-to-date, counter-example is to be found in the case of the fixed exchange rate between sterling and the Irish pound. Irish fiscal policy is certainly independent; yet there do not seem to be any serious strains in maintaining the fixed parity. The factors responsible for this state of affairs were analysed by Dr T. K. Whitaker, the Governor of the Central Bank of Ireland, in his paper on 'Monetary Integration: Reflections on Irish Experience,' *Moorgate and Wall Street* (autumn 1973) pp. 4–21. These include a very open economy, with a high proportion of trade conducted with the United Kingdom; free and easy migration between Ireland and the United Kingdom; considerable integration of the financial system, and indeed many of the other economic institutions, between the two countries; the continued ability of the Irish to use tariffs, export subsidies, etc., in lieu of exchange-rate variations, which, as Dr Whitaker notes (p. 20), calls into question the association often posited in the E.E.C. context between establishing a customs union and a monetary union.

[2] This confidence developed in the particular historical circumstances of the period. It is not, however, producible by design; certainly not by assertions of intent from political leaders.

[3] Gold does not offer an interest rate; sterling balances did, and were also exchangeable for gold. Apart from the atavistic desires of certain Central European Central Banks to build up 'war chests' of gold in their own vaults, sterling balances were a relatively more attractive investment. Foreign holdings of claims on London almost certainly increased over these years, 1890–1914, far more than U.K. gold reserves. This did cause London bankers a lot of worry at the time, particularly in the foreseen context of an outbreak of hostilities, with 'enemy' countries possibly making a financial raid on London by withdrawing all their funds and thus endeavouring to bring about a financial collapse there. There were several papers on this subject delivered by prominent London bankers at the time, see for example Sir Felix Schuster, 'Our Gold Reserves,' *Journal of the Institute of Bankers* (January 1907); see also the discussion on the gold holdings of the London banks in C. Goodhart, *The Business of Banking*, pp. 100–7.

Nevertheless, the growth of foreign claims on London, relative to U.K. reserves, never caused the same instability in the system, as did the growth of foreign claims on the United States during the 1950s and 1960s, see R. Triffin, *Gold and the Dollar Crisis* (Yale University Press, 1960), because the underlying balance-of-payments position of the United Kingdom in the 1900s was much stronger than that of the United States in the 1960s.

[4] Another factor was the willingness of Central Banks to bend the rules of the Gold Standard system in order to ease financial adjustments; on this see A. I. Bloomfield, *Monetary Policy Under The International Gold Standard, 1880–1914* (monograph, Federal Reserve Bank of New York, 1959).

the central question of how these imbalances themselves were resolved, in a fixed-rate system, without apparently causing unacceptably large-scale fluctuations in employment, incomes and wealth.[1] What makes the Gold Standard period particularly interesting is the puzzle of trying to decipher its adjustment mechanism. A partial explanation may be found in the fact that the nineteenth century, including the years up till 1914, was characterised by enormous, cyclic migration flows;[2] standard analysis suggests that migration should mitigate some of the economic effects of regional imbalance. Other economists have suggested that prices (and wages) responded sufficiently flexibly to regional conditions of excess or insufficient demand (whether induced by a monetary multiplier mechanism or by a Keynesian foreign-trade multiplier)[3] to restore equilibrium. It may, therefore, have been the greater stickiness of (real) wage rates and prices since 1914 which is partially to blame for the subsequent failings of fixed exchange-rate systems.[4] Certainly if all wages/ prices were completely flexible, the only (weak) economic argument for abandoning a one-world single-currency system would be that different countries (regions) had preferences for different rates of price inflation (an issue touched on again in the next section).

The maintenance of fixed exchange rates does, however, practically imply the abandonment of independent control over the domestic money supply,[5] a step with major political connotations. To illustrate why this is so, consider a counter-example, in which two countries agree to accept each other's currencies in payment at par (fixed exchange rates) but both retain their freedom to expand, or to contract, their own money stock. The country that has the faster monetary expansion will experience a relative increase in domestic expenditures and prices, sucking in imports and non-monetary financial assets from abroad, paid for by exports of money balances accepted in the other country, by assumption, at par. So the more inflationary country not only obtains command over additional assets (or the services of assets),[6] but also passes on much of the additional inflation to its partner. Clearly no fixed exchange-rate system can persist without some discipline over the monetary policies of the countries involved.[7] One way of maintaining

---

[1] In that period people had less faith in the ability of governments to manage the economy; so they did not attach quite so much blame to governments for economic misfortunes, nor expect them to find answers to all economic problems. To that extent the fluctuations in incomes, prices, etc., that were politically acceptable then may have been larger than they are now.

[2] See Brinley Thomas, *Migration and Economic Growth* (Cambridge University Press, 1954).

[3] Monetarists tend to emphasise the importance of monetary flows as a factor causing price adjustments, see for example M. Friedman and A. Schwartz, *A Monetary History of the United States, 1867–1960*, p. 141. Keynesians, on the other hand, often argue that accommodating capital flows allowed the money stock in the major countries to adjust to demand, and that it was the variations in foreign demand for the domestic products that led directly to price changes, via the foreign-trade multiplier.

[4] The turmoil and disruptions caused by the First World War and the subsequent erratic plunges of government policies in the 1920s and 1930s threw far more pressure on the adjustment mechanism than it had had to cope with before 1914. Whether the mechanism really had become significantly less responsive after 1914 remains doubtful.

[5] Ignoring the theoretical possibility of using variable exchange controls to reconcile fixed exchange rates with an independently-determined money supply.

[6] In so far as interest is paid on money balances, the additional command over current output enjoyed by the more inflationary country will involve a subsequent offset in transfers required to service the interest payments.

[7] The tenor of much European criticism of U.S. international economic policy has basically been that the United States has played the role of the more inflationary country in the above example, because it accepted no external discipline over its domestic monetary policy. The U.S. reply appears to have been that the system of fixed exchange rates, at existing parities, was maintained at the behest of the Europeans, not of themselves; so they saw no need to accept a discipline to maintain a system which they did not particularly wish to preserve. They argued that the Europeans could always have revalued to avoid any inflationary pressures emanating from U.S. monetary expansion. Indeed, they claimed that the Europeans wanted to have their cake, of an undervalued exchange rate making

(*Footnote* [7] *continued on p. 300*)

such a discipline is for the monetary authorities in each country to commit themselves to relate their domestic monetary creation to their international reserve holdings, and to settle international deficits (surpluses) by transferring (titles to) such reserves. Then the more inflationary country loses reserves as it expands, and this forces it to check its monetary expansion.

Any asset which is in fairly inelastic supply and of sufficient uniformity to serve as 'money' without requiring extensive investigation in transfer (see Chapter 1, Section B) could do in principle as the international reserve base – gold, oil, corn, cows, S.D.R.s. The use of a commodity reserve money, such as gold or oil or cows, suffers certain serious disadvantages. The growth of such reserves, affecting the overall rate of change of prices in the system, is largely dependent on erratic shifts in supply technology and on changes in the nature of demand for purposes other than monetary reserves for the commodity. The increased demand for these objects, to add to monetary reserves, encourages the use of scarce resources in their production[1] but the stocks amassed for such reserve purposes sit unused and unhelpfully, say in the vaults of the Federal Reserve Bank of New York.[2] Anyone observing the settlement of international imbalances by the transfer of a gold bar from a pile marked, say, Germany and placing it on a pile marked, say, Japan in a vault under a bank in New York, cannot be other than struck by the ridiculous nature of the whole proceedings.

There are better ways to maintain monetary discipline within a fixed exchange-rate area. One method is to replace commodity money as the international reserve by a financial asset (e.g. S.D.R. or Bancor), thus avoiding the waste of scarce resources, supply uncertainties, etc. This does require political agreement on the distribution and creation of international reserves – perhaps more than is required to adhere to a commodity standard – but under modern conditions it seems unlikely that, unless there is sufficient political harmony to agree on the methods of providing the international financial reserve base, there would be sufficient social unity to devise means of overcoming adjustment strains (e.g. by inter-area transfers) within a (permanently) fixed exchange-rate area. Large individual countries cannot, in the modern world, be forced willy-nilly into particular forms of balance-of-payments adjustment by the scarcity of some selected international reserve asset.

Although a financial asset base, instead of a commodity base, to international reserves should allow a planned overall rate of growth of reserves,[3] the monetary authorities must still abide by certain rules (of the game) if a (permanently) fixed exchange-rate

---

their exports competitive, and eat it, by escaping the inflationary consequences of the resulting export surpluses and monetary inflows.

In turn the various European countries would argue that their own individual exchange rates were not out of line with those of other countries, except for the United States. Thus no individual European country would wish to revalue unilaterally. The main imbalance was between the United States and the rest, and that could be most easily cured by action by the United States.

And so the argument went on.

---

[1] The additional demand for such commodities in their role as monetary reserves also affects the terms of trade between areas with a comparative advantage in their production and those without.

[2] In some respects it would be much more sensible to use cows rather than gold as monetary reserves. The cows, unlike the gold bars, need not be barren and could provide milk to thirsty bankers while acting as reserves. If everything King Midas touched had turned to beef he would have been a much happier man.

[3] Problems with the *composition* of international reserves may arise under either a commodity or a financial asset reserve-base system. If a country, especially one whose currency is much used in international transactions, offers a liquid asset with a more attractive yield than the basic reserve asset, e.g. bills on London, U.S. Treasury bills, other countries may prefer to hold these rather than the basic reserve assets, treating them as the equivalent of reserves. Thus a very slight increase

(*Footnote* [3] *continued on p. 301*)

system is to work. Adherence to these rules may often involve stress. It is dubious whether independent countries, especially large powerful ones, are likely to submit to the external constraints of automatic rules. It seems unlikely then that a fixed exchange-rate system can be maintained on any permanent basis until political harmony and social agreement allow the division of burdens within the area and the direction of policy in each major part of the system to be decided by an accepted central *political* process. Once that stage has been reached the next step, to a more efficient single-currency area, eliminating the need for separate currencies, exchange transactions, etc., should be simple.

B. Monetary Relationships between Currency Areas

There are a number of benefits, therefore, that can be obtained from the establishment of a large-scale currency area; it facilitates the development of more efficient integrated markets, eliminates the costs and uncertainties connected with internal exchange transactions, and allows the establishment of larger governmental units in those fields where there may be considerable economies of scale. But except in circumstances, now probably rare, where local wage rates and prices vary sufficiently flexibly, relatively to each other, to maintain activity and employment in each region, the maintenance of a system of completely fixed exchange rates, as in a single-currency area, may well impose considerable strains of adjustment in the face of trade imbalances among the constituent regions.[1,2] Even when confidence in the permanence of the fixed-rate system allows imbalances to be *financed* with the minimum of fuss and difficulty, inability to induce an equilibrating move in relative costs and prices can allow marked disparities in incomes and wealth to develop, and lead to significant differences in regional unemployment rates and/or large-scale 'forced' migration.

(or even a fall) in basic reserves may be consistent with a very rapid increase in perceived reserves. But in that case the ratio of claims on this reserve-centre country to its own holdings of basic reserves may reach a point which raises doubts about the fundamental international liquidity of its liabilities. At this stage attempts by holders to cash in the claims, exercising their convertibility rights, only precipitates the crisis. On this see R. Triffin, *Gold and the Dollar Crisis: The Future of Convertibility*.

Nevertheless, even disregarding the possibility of political agreement to limit the use of claims on other countries as part of official reserves, the adoption of a financial asset base reserve should, in principle, help to solve this problem, since it should prove possible to devise means of paying, and varying, interest on the base financial asset in order to influence the composition as well as the total of official reserve assets.

---

[1] Even if wages/prices were sufficiently flexible to cope with all problems of adjustment – though this is not the case in reality – it might still be argued that a single-currency area would impose a single rate of price change over its whole extent, whereas differing groups within the area might have differing 'tastes for inflation.' And it is true that some countries have in the last decade or so experienced significantly differing rates of inflation. The differences in inflation rates that have been observed, e.g. between the United Kingdom and Germany, may owe something to a differing weighting (trade-off) among the populace in each country with respect to the relative pain of unemployment and inflation, though other factors, e.g. the elasticity of supply of foreign workers in Germany, have no doubt also been responsible. Indeed the Germans have consistently had both lower inflation and lower unemployment than the British. But whatever the cause of the faster inflation in the United Kingdom, it is hardly due to an *absolute* preference among the British for a higher rate of inflation. It is not clear to me why geographical groupings of people, which will include all kinds, creditors and debtors, young and old, rich and poor, should hold significantly different views about the most desirable long-run rate of inflation.

[2] Strains on both the deficit and surplus countries. The deficit country experiences a fall in real output and employment; the surplus country will be providing more goods and services in trade than it receives in return, and will suffer additional inflationary pressures.

These adjustment problems can, in my view, be overcome within the confines of a fixed exchange-rate system, even under conditions where relative real wages are slow to adjust. To do so, however, requires the adoption of 'appropriate' fiscal policy, which would probably involve a large-scale, and often long-continued, transfer of real resources from the more prosperous to the disadvantaged regions, e.g. through the provision of unemployment benefits, direct expenditure, regional employment premia for the disadvantaged regions, financed through the collection of income (or property) taxes imposed centrally at rates harmonised over the whole area. The decision to provide such transfers of resources between regions is essentially political; whether people will accept such inter-regional transfers depends on their feelings of social unity.

The political scene today gives few grounds for believing that there is sufficient harmony among peoples to establish a permanently-fixed exchange-rate system, or even better a single-currency area, on such a basis over the Western world, or even among the industrialised countries of the Atlantic community. It is not possible to establish a 'one-world' system, or solution, to international monetary relationships, in a world effectively divided among independent powers. Indeed, it is difficult enough to forge a monetary union between a small number of like-minded neighbouring countries. So the international monetary system is likely to remain fissile. Independent countries, or perhaps wider currency areas, will seek to retain control over their own domestic monetary policies and exchange rates in order to follow their perceived self-interests.

Thus, whether or not the next decade sees a growing trend towards the successful emergence of currency areas embracing several countries, the world system will still contain a number of countries (currency areas) maintaining separate currencies whose value can vary in exchange, i.e. can be adjusted in relation to those of other countries. The question then becomes to decide how these exchange-rate adjustments can best be carried out in order to maintain prosperity and stability for the countries involved.

Should the exchange rates between these separate areas be freely determined in the market place, i.e. flexible or 'floating' rates, or should they be managed, controlled, by the respective monetary authorities? And if the exchange rates are to be managed, how should the authorities seek to do this, by *ad hoc* interventions to influence an otherwise freely-determined exchange rate (i.e. managed floating), by setting limits to the extent that the free market price can move from day to day, but allowing the rate to vary freely (or almost so) within these limits (i.e. gliding or crawling parities), by pegging the rate but allowing frequent small moves or occasional large moves (pegged but adjustable rates)?

The basic reason why countries feel the need to retain the ability to vary their exchange rate is because external developments, e.g. a fall in foreign demand for domestic products or increasing inflation abroad, threaten the maintenance of internal balance. For example, an attempt to prevent the domestic economy inflating in response to foreign-generated inflation by domestic deflationary measures will under a fixed-rate system only serve to worsen the external imbalance and draw in more money from abroad, with probably only very limited success on the home front. Expressions of preference among alternative exchange-rate regimes are likely, therefore, to hang mainly on the issue of which allows the smoothest domestic adjustment to external shocks.

In this respect adoption of a regime of freely-floating exchange rates has a number of apparent advantages. If the authorities maintain some particular level of domestic demand (i.e. if the volume of domestic output and the level of domestic prices are fixed) then, with a given set of external, foreign economic conditions,[1] there will be, in general,[2] one, and

---

[1] Including among such prior conditions the existing set of restrictions (tariffs, quotas, exchange controls, etc.) on international transactions.

[2] Though not in all cases. As Professor Hahn has noted, in his review article on J. Kornai's book *Anti-Equilibrium: On Economic Systems Theory and the Tasks of Research* (North-Holland, Amsterdam and London, 1971) entitled 'The Winter of our Discontent,' *Economica*, vol. 40,

(*Footnote* [2] *continued on p. 303*)

only one, exchange rate that will allow the maintenance of external balance consistent with the chosen internal balance. The authorities do not have the information, indeed no one has, to enable them to tell what this rate may turn out to be. If they try to pick a rate to support, it will turn out to be more or less far from the 'equilibrium' rate as defined above, and this will cause problems of varying severity – depending on how far out the selection was – in maintaining both internal and external balance. If the chosen rate differs sufficiently from this 'equilibrium,' so that the external imbalance becomes too severe and/or persistent to finance by an acceptable variation in reserve levels or in interest rates[1] (relative to those abroad), then either domestic demand may have to be varied from the desired level in order to maintain external balance, or controls of one kind or another placed on international transactions (e.g. import quotas or exchange controls) to buttress the exchange rate, or the rate itself abandoned.

In theory at least, the acceptance of market-determined, flexible exchange rates should allow the authorities to concentrate on the exercise of achieving a proper level of internal balance, allowing the exchange rate to act as a buffer to absorb external shocks. And, again in theory at least, adoption of flexible exchange rates should lessen the incentive to resort to direct controls over international transactions, which interfere with allocative efficiency, and should reduce the need for, and public and political concerns with, international reserve holdings. Finally, if the domestic monetary authorities are not trying to manipulate their exchange rate with another country, but are responding passively to market developments, a direct conflict of objectives between governments is somewhat less likely to arise than if both sets of authorities are seeking directly to manage their exchange rates.

At the end of Chapter 14 it was argued, on *a priori* grounds, that the *long-term* price elasticity of demand for any one country's exports should be significantly greater than unity. The long-run change in the exchange rate required to adjust to an external shock – given the level of domestic demand – should, therefore, be quite small. But for a number of reasons, many of them depending on lags and rigidities in the response of suppliers (even when there is 'spare capacity' in the devaluing country) to relative price changes, the short-run price elasticity of demand for a country's exports may seem much lower; indeed so much so that in the short run, for a few quarters, the effect of a devaluation may be to worsen the trade balance. This has now been termed the J-curve effect, since the shape of the capital letter J mimics the initial decline in the balance followed, after an elapse of time, by an even larger improvement.

If the elasticities are so low in the short run that the trade balance may even temporarily deteriorate after a devaluation, complete reliance on movements in exchange rates to maintain external balance, while keeping a constant level of internal demand, would not be viable, *unless* the fall in the exchange rate should induce a capital inflow. If there was no sustaining capital inflow, and no action by the authorities to support the rate in one way or another, then over any short period the exchange rate would be unstable; a reduction in the sterling exchange rate would lower the demand for pounds.

Even if the situation does not actually become unstable because the elasticities are not that low, or because there are countervailing capital flows, the lower short-run price elasticities could, in an exchange market without official intervention, force the exchange rate to overshoot the long-term equilibrium level. Excessive short-run variations in exchange rates, in relation to the adjustment needed in the longer term, would have a

---

no. 159 (August 1973) p. 324, the student of Arrow–Debreu general equilibrium theory 'would note at once not only that there may be no equilibrium level, but also that if there is one such level there may be very many.'

---

[1] Recall the criticism in Chapter 12 of Mundell's ingenious suggestion for using monetary and fiscal policy in tandem to maintain external and internal balance under fixed exchange-rate regimes.

L

number of serious consequences. In the first place large fluctuations in exchange rates complicate the authorities' task of maintaining internal balance. A large fall in the exchange rate will raise domestic prices and shift incomes, at least in the short run, quite sharply towards profits and away from wages. This is bound to make the efforts of the authorities to restrain inflation that much harder. If the devaluation was caused by an external shock (say a decline in foreign demand for domestic products), so that in the absence of the devaluation domestic incomes and output would have declined from the desired level, this effect of the overshoot – if not too exaggerated – might be tolerable. But if the devaluation was caused by a perhaps unforeseen expansion of domestic demand, any such overshoot would seriously intensify the problems of domestic demand management.

Secondly, exaggerated fluctuations in exchange rates, again in the sense that they exceeded the long-run adjustment required, could cause large swings in the profit margins obtainable in the production of tradeable goods. Profits would be more variable, uncertainty would be increased, it would be more difficult to plan ahead and there would be less stability in industrial activities. The greater instability would, one may assume, lead to more planning errors. Specific investment in human and non-human capital would be more likely to be wasted.

It is admitted by most proponents of completely flexible exchange rates that the price elasticities may be fairly low in the short run: they would have us put our trust then in countervailing capital flows to stabilise the exchange rate in the short run and prevent any large-scale 'overshooting'.[1] The argument runs as follows: suppose a country's exchange rate is depreciating. The price elasticities are larger in the long run; *ergo* the exchange rate should not need to depreciate very far in the longer term to achieve the required adjustment. If the (long-term) forward rate should fall below the actual rate expected to rule at this time, then speculators, acting on their expectations about the appropriate, or 'equilibrium,' rate in the longer-term future, should buy forward. A fall in current spot rates, relative to these forward rates, pegged by speculators' expectations, opens up a profit on covered inward interest arbitrage; that is an investor switching funds into temporary investment in the depreciating country can buy the currency spot cheaper than he can sell it forward, and so will enjoy an additional safe return on the switch. The demand for spot currency to undertake such interest arbitrage (i.e. the capital inflow) should prevent its price falling far from its expected longer-term future level.

There are a number of reasons for entertaining doubts about this suggested story. First, the estimation, indeed the concept, of an appropriate, or 'equilibrium,' level of exchange rates at some future date does depend on making some assumption about the expected future level of domestic output and prices. If these are taken as given, or at least as predictable, then speculators have some basis for working out their expectations of future equilibrium rates. But, as has already been noted, a devaluation may complicate the task of internal demand management, especially when it was itself caused by internal expansion. How is the speculator to be reasonably sure that internal demand management will be conducted well enough over the long run in order to feel confident about the maintenance of any 'long-run equilibrium' exchange rate?[2]

---

[1] See, for example, M. Friedman, 'The Case for Flexible Exchange Rates,' in *Essays in Positive Economics* (University of Chicago Press, 1953) especially pt II, sect. C on 'Flexible Exchange Rates and the Timing of Adjustment,' pp. 182–6; also S. Brittan, *The Price of Economic Freedom: A Guide to Flexible Rates* (Macmillan, London, 1970) pp. 67–8.

[2] One way of giving speculators the necessary confidence is for the authorities to signal their determination not to allow domestic conditions, especially inflation, to deteriorate by accompanying any depreciation with overt steps to reduce domestic claims on resources. This can, however, cause difficulties, because the authorities – as for example in the immediate aftermath of the 1967 devaluation – may feel that any such steps are unnecessary or even damaging domestically. Yet in such cases, without such signals of intent, it would hardly be surprising to find speculators uncertain about the long-term future of the exchange rate.

The second reason for doubting whether such 'stabilising' speculation will materialise is that the time scale is too long. No one has any clear idea exactly how long it takes for the major part of the adjustment to an exchange-rate variation to work through the system, but eighteen months to two years would not be regarded as excessive.[1] That is a long period of time in a market context. In that period there may be economic and political crises or wars involving any number of countries. Uncertainty about the state of the world in two years' time will discourage people from trying to visualise a state of long-term equilibrium (a condition which is never achieved), or from backing their predictions with money. In any case the long-term forward market is very thin. Much more action takes place in the one- and three-month forward exchange market. Here, at least, speculators may feel that they have more hard information to bite on. But, given the low short-term elasticities, the short-term information that speculators will receive, and act on, is that a depreciating currency is likely to depreciate more in the coming quarter, unless the authorities do something to check the short-term worsening of the trade balance.[2] If this is so, the inherent problems of short-run instability in a freely-floating exchange-rate system may well be exacerbated by the action of speculators with short planning horizons.

Experience in this respect has been mixed. The Canadian experiment with floating exchange rates during the years 1950–62 has been assessed by several observers[3] as broadly

---

[1] 'As to the timing of trade effects, collective wisdom, based mainly on intuition rather than empirical study, put the time it would take for most of the effects of the Smithsonian realignment to work through at somewhere between eighteen months and two years. However, there are reasons why one might expect the adjustment to take longer than that.' H. B. Junz and R. R. Rhomberg, 'Price Competitiveness in Export Trade among Industrialised Countries,' *The American Economic Review*, vol. 63, no. 2 (May 1973) p. 412. Indeed, they conclude (p. 418), 'The response of trade flows to relative price changes quite clearly seems to stretch out over a rather longer period than has generally been assumed, perhaps around four to five years.'

There have been other research studies of the lags in adjustment (e.g. by P. Minford for the United Kingdom, unpublished, and by P. W. Clark, 'Some Early Estimates of the Price and Quantity Effects of the Smithsonian Agreement on the U.S. Trade Account,' presented to the annual meeting of the Econometric Society, 28–30 December 1973, New York, mimeo) which go to support the findings of Junz and Rhomberg of even longer lags than 'collective wisdom' had·appreciated.

[2] 'Those who rely on market forces fail to recognise that most foreign exchange operators are concerned with the future only over a short interval of time – very few with more than six or nine months. On the other hand, an exchange rate depreciation frequently begins by exercising a perverse influence on the basic balance of payments. . . . It usually takes quite a long time for the volume effects to outweigh the price effects. . . . The foreign exchange operators are therefore right to exercise a downward pressure on the value of the currency. If they are so perspicacious as to realise that, within the short space of time that concerns them, this depreciation will worsen the balance of payments, they will carry the depreciation far further than would have been called for to restore the competitive position.' R. Kahn, 'The International Monetary System,' *The American Economic Review*, vol. 63, no. 2 (May 1973) p. 182.

[3] 'The general conclusion of the research efforts into the Canadian experience of 1950–62 is that a flexible exchange rate system can be made to operate successfully if those setting monetary and other economic policies understand its implications. . . . The potential benefits of a flexible exchange rate for the Canadian economy as a whole and for policy makers in particular, are sizable.' R. M. Dunn Jr, *Canada's Experience with Fixed and Flexible Exchange Rates in a North American Capital Market* (Canadian-American Committee, sponsored by National Planning Association [U.S.A.] and Private Planning Association of Canada, 1971) pp. 67 and 74.

Dunn gives a list of economists who studied the Canadian experience (p. 60), including Wonnacott, Mundell, Marsh, Plumptre and Yeager and concludes, 'Virtually all of the students of Canada's history with a flexible rate conclude that the difficulties of 1958–62 were not the fault of the system, but instead grew out of a series of unfortunate or perhaps disastrous policy decisions in Ottawa.'

successful. There were few signs of serious short-term instability or of destabilising speculation.[1] On the other hand, recent experience in 1971–3 of a more general system of floating rates has been less happy. During the years 1972–3 there were continuous bouts of speculation driving the exchange rate of the \$ down and that of certain European currencies (especially the DM) upwards. It is difficult ever to make a sure judgement about what the 'long-term equilibrium' relativities might be, but many observers felt that some of these movements in exchange rates did represent considerable 'overshooting'.[2] There are a number of qualifications that may be made about the role of speculation in this period, e.g. that the initial starting point for exchange rates in 1971 was so badly out of line that it was harder to estimate appropriate relativities, that some of the fluctuations in rates were due to the authorities' actions, e.g. the tight German monetary policy, not to speculation, and that anyhow the speculators were largely concerned with trying to predict the authorities' short-run policy moves. But, however you may qualify it, the conclusion of many observers[3] remains that speculation during this period did not assist, on balance, in stabilising the international monetary system.

Basically there seem to be two main arguments emerging from this discussion that militate against complete acceptance of freely-floating exchange rates. The first is that if external balance is disturbed not by an external shock but by some change in domestic *internal* conditions, then reliance on flexible exchange rates to restore external balance will exaggerate the initial divergence from internal balance. Internal deflation will raise the exchange rate, thus depressing domestic activity even more. Flexible rates, therefore, buffer the economy from external shocks, but exaggerate internal shocks. Following the same line of analysis as outlined in Chapter 12 (Section B) in the discussion on stabilisation policy under uncertainty, the extent to which one should wish to keep exchange rates fixed, or flexible, depends on the relative likelihood of domestic or foreign disturbances.[4] Given

---

[1] For models of the working of the Canadian economy under the two exchange-rate regimes, see R. R. Rhomberg, 'Canada's Foreign Exchange Market: A Quarterly Model,' *International Monetary Fund Staff Papers*, vol. 7 (1959–60) pp. 439–56, and his later paper, 'A Model of the Canadian Economy under Fixed and Fluctuating Exchange Rates,' *Journal of Political Economy*, vol. 72, no. 1 (February 1964) pp. 1–31.

[2] 'The exchange market is apt to push a weak floating currency too far down, and a strong floating currency too far up.' *National Institute Economic Review*, no. 67 (February 1974) 'Appraisal,' p. 5.

[3] Take, for example, the remarks of H. J. Witteveen, Managing Director of the International Monetary Fund, at the World Banking Conference in London, 15 January 1974.

Experience has shown us, however, that floating rates can be subject to wide fluctuations, and rate movements can be exaggerated beyond what is consistent with underlying adjustment needs. When this happens, countries may with good reason wish to engage in intervention to prevent rates diverging unduly from a pattern considered to be conducive to the achievement of equilibrium (*Press Release*, pp. 1 and 2).

Private markets sometimes over-react to changes in underlying conditions, whether because of a failure to appreciate fully the lags involved in the adjustment process, or because of purely speculative factors (*Press Release*, p. 3).

Also see the statement of the Managing Director, in presenting the 28th Annual Report of the Executive Directors to the Board of Governors of the International Monetary Fund, in Nairobi, on 24 September 1973, *Press Release No. 3*, final paragraph.

[4] So in a sense support for a system of flexible exchange rates can be construed as a vote of confidence in the authorities' ability to handle domestic policy effectively, and preference for fixed exchange rates as a vote of no confidence. Seen in this light the usual line-up of supporters and opposers of a move to more flexible exchange rates often has an ironic appearance. Though to be fair, supporters of flexible exchange rates usually add the caveat that the domestic economy should at the same time be run according to their own precepts.

On this general point see S. Brittan, *The Price of Economic Freedom: A Guide to Flexible Exchange Rate* (Macmillan, London, 1970) chap. 7, 'Objections to Floating Rates,' especially pp. 61–7.

that the possibility of internal economic disturbances is greater than zero, there is on these grounds a case for some limits to the complete market-determined flexibility of rates.

The second argument, which has been outlined in more detail, is that a regime of freely-flexible exchange rates may involve greater short-term variations in rates, a tendency towards 'overshooting,' than is necessary for long-term adjustment of the external balance. On these grounds as well there is a case for some limitations to be imposed on the extent of short-run movements in rates.

There are, therefore, reasons for trying to temper the extent of short-run movements in exchange rates, for managing the exchange market to avoid unfavourable internal repercussions and unnecessary instability.[1] But how far along this road should one go? Remember that we claimed that the basic reason why countries retained the right to vary their exchange rate (and to maintain an independent monetary policy) was to be able to insulate their domestic economy from external shocks. The objective is to allow variations in the exchange rate to maintain external balance, while the authorities concentrate on achieving the desired level of domestic demand.

If the exchange rate is pegged it is not going to be doing this job. If the authorities are not driven to abandon their internal objectives – and the whole idea was to prevent this happening – then an external imbalance will develop, and often grow over time, as the 'equilibrium' rate diverges from the pegged rate (e.g. under the influence of differing trend rates of inflation among the various countries). For a time such imbalances may, perhaps, be financed by acceptable fluctuations in reserve holdings or by relatively small variations in interest rates *vis-à-vis* other countries. There are, however, fairly narrow bounds to the extent that this is possible, particularly in support of a rate that appears to be overvalued.[2] Reserves are limited[3] and there can be difficulties in arranging large-scale international borrowing on acceptable terms. The main problem, however, is that such financing of itself does nothing to correct the imbalance caused by the divergence between the pegged and the 'equilibrium' exchange rate. At some point of time there will, therefore, be pressures on the authorities to correct the external imbalance by adjusting the exchange rate. It will generally be obvious under such conditions which way the exchange rate must move, if it moves at all: there is only a 'one-way option.' This 'one-way option' encourages speculation against the pegged currency, and such speculation will cause large-scale flows of capital out of the country which is seen as a devaluation candidate into the country which

---

[1] Moreover, whether or not you accept these reasons for official intervention in the exchange market, most countries will in practice seek to manage their rates, whenever exchange-rate movements seem to threaten their objectives. If some countries do this, others will feel defensively compelled to follow, and this provides a case for establishing certain 'rules of the game.'

[2] This asymmetry between the problems of financing a large deficit, as compared with a large surplus, in the balance of payments may account for the bias towards devaluations which some observers have claimed to discern in the working of the Bretton Woods system of fixed but adjustable rates.

[3] The widespread feeling of shortages of reserves is often regarded as the consequence of an insufficient supply of new reserves. Conferences are arranged to discuss the process of creating an adequate flow of additional international reserves. Such fluctuations in supply do affect the *short-term* adequacy of reserves, but over the *longer term* the 'adequacy' of reserves will be determined by the relative incentive to hold reserve assets compared with the return on other assets. If the reserve asset offers a low yield, governments will economise on their holdings of reserve assets, in order to allow the economy to enjoy a current greater command over goods and higher-yielding assets. A faster growth in the supply of gold, or S.D.R.s, would then simply encourage more expenditure and higher prices, ultimately leaving the 'shortage' of reserves exactly as it was. Our discussion in Chap. 13 on the optimal quantity of money revealed that the key issue was not how many notes should be printed, but what was the appropriate rate of interest to offer on money. Exactly analogously, in the international field it is only now beginning to be realised that the key issue is not how many S.D.R.s to create but what rate of return they should bear (and how this can be financed). On this subject see H. G. Johnson, *Inflation and the Monetarist Controversy* (North-Holland, Amsterdam, 1972) pp. 86–8.

is seen as a revaluation candidate.[1] The volume of such flows has probably been much increased, but *not caused*, by the development of an efficient, large-scale, international money market[2] in the shape of the euro-dollar market.

During the course of the last decade the volume of mobile private capital that could, and would, move in response to the emergence of an apparent imbalance – a divergence between the pegged and 'equilibrium' rate – seems to have expanded enormously. The size of short-term capital flows now can swamp the reserve positions of most countries in a flash, as was seen in June 1972 when sterling was forced to float after a speculative flurry lasting only about a week. Thus, even if it should be a sensible policy in the first place, the scope open to a country to finance an imbalance, without taking other steps to correct it, is becoming increasingly attenuated.

If the authorities are willing neither to sacrifice internal balance to the dictates of the external position, nor to allow the exchange rate to vary in response to external pressures, and they are not in a position to finance an external imbalance for long, what instruments have they got left to control their external position? The answer, of course, is to be found in direct controls on external transactions, controls on both trade flows and flows of financial assets, capital flows. As Corden, for example, points out,[3] the likely concomitant of the establishment of a system of firmly pegged, but ultimately adjustable, exchange rates (in his terms, a 'pseudo-monetary union') is a growing proliferation of controls over international transactions, a result hardly in keeping with endeavours of statesmen in other areas to ensure freer movement of goods and capital from country to country.

Even such controls are palliatives, to disguise and to cloak the existence of imbalance rather than to cure it. Apart from the increasing allocative inefficiency that such controls are likely (but not certain) to cause, direct controls over trade flows are liable to cause international antagonism and, perhaps, retaliation, while controls over capital flows, though less unpopular, are equally less easy to enforce. In a world of multi-national companies there are many loopholes open through which capital can be transmitted from country to country. Controls may work for a time, but in the longer run they cannot prevent the need for a more fundamental adjustment.

Thus a persistent current-account imbalance must ultimately force a country to readjust its exchange rate. Can one claim that a longer retention of a fixed parity, *vis-à-vis* other currencies, a less frequent occurrence of parity changes imparts a net benefit to the community? It would seem doubtful. The less frequent are the parity changes, the larger they are likely to be. The larger the parity changes, the more disruptive they will probably be, causing sharp changes in relative profitability between industries, sharp changes in price levels and in income distribution.[4] Moreover, the uncertainty engendered by a system of occasional large changes in parity would seem likely to be greater than that of a system involving more frequent small steps. Markets, especially forward markets, ought to be able to adjust to coping with regular, small price movements, but the prospect of a really major change may paralyse them. Finally, the longer a parity has been pegged, the more difficult it probably becomes to see how great the underlying imbalance really is. The occasional large parity change is likely to leave the country still some way from a position of long-run balance. Although the situation is bedevilled by slow, lagged adjustments to relative price changes, at least more frequent exchange-rate revisions provide an opportunity for correcting obvious mistakes, in a situation where lack

---

[1] The volume of such flows would no doubt redouble if countries were *required* to devalue or to revalue in response to some presumptive indicator which speculators could anticipate and observe.

[2] The efficiency of this market increases the response to a given incentive to redistribute funds, but is not itself responsible for the emergence of such an incentive.

[3] In his pamphlet on 'Monetary Integration,' especially pp. 21–4.

[4] Moreover, in the intervening period larger distortions in the allocation of resources build up, so there will be both static and dynamic costs.

of information is virtually bound to make the authorities pick a more or less inappropriate level of rates.

The conclusion, to which we are drawn by this discussion, is that the authorities charged with running the international monetary system, as set up at Bretton Woods, have heretofore kept their eye fixed on the wrong measure. They have usually been concerned with parity *levels* and controlling, pegging, or adjusting these levels. But they do not, and cannot, know what levels are correct; their attempts to maintain such levels lead to the imposition of distortions on the world economy (e.g. via direct controls); and the occasional large-scale jumps in exchange rates to rectify an impossible situation are disruptive. Instead their concern ought to be with the *rate of change* of parities, and controlling and managing this rate of change to see that it is never too large (e.g. under the influence of low short-run elasticities) to represent a disruptive force.

On this issue my sympathies are closely in line with the band of international monetary economists[1] who have proposed various schemes for 'gliding' or 'crawling' parities, for these are in essence methods for imposing some control over the rate of change of parities rather than over their level. It may be, however, that such intervention to limit the rate of change of parities is better done on a discretionary than on any automatic basis. Central Banks have lost so much of their power to control rates, given the development of the international money markets, etc., that they could, perhaps, be knocked off even more modest targets for limiting the rate of change of rates. For example, could a system of 'crawling' or 'gliding' rates have been maintained in the face of a severe disruption such as the energy crisis of 1973–4? Discretionary Central Bank intervention does have a role, since they are (or should be) better informed of economic prospects and more capable of taking a long view than are private speculators; Central Banks should have the opportunity to stabilise exchange rates and make a profit in so doing.

Nevertheless, it is not the details of these schemes to manage the rate of change of parities that matter yet (e.g. whether the authorities' intervention should be automatic, determined by the rules of the game, or discretionary), but the basic principle. There is still dissension between those who believe in absolutely free exchange markets, those who want to peg exchange-rate levels, and those who want to manage the rate of change of exchange rates, and the aim of this section is to try to convince you that the last of these alternatives is the best.

---

[1] The general idea of a moving parity of this kind was first put forward by J. Black of Merton College, Oxford, in an unsigned note in *The Economist* of 4 November 1961, and was then taken up with various refinements by several other economists, notably R. N. Cooper, 'Flexing the International Monetary System: The Case for Gliding Parities,' in *The International Adjustment Mechanism* (Federal Reserve Bank of Boston, Proceedings of a Conference held in October 1969, Conference Series No. 2, 1970); J. E. Meade, 'Exchange-Rate Flexibility,' *The Three Banks Review*, no. 70 (June 1966) pp. 3–27; J. H. Williamson, 'The Crawling Peg,' *Essays in International Finance*, no. 50 (December 1965) (International Finance Section, Department of Economics, Princeton University).

Bibliography

I Books

S. Axilrod *et al.*, *Open Market Policies and Operating Procedures – Staff Studies* (Federal Reserve Board, Washington, 1971).

M. J. Bailey, *National Income and the Price Level* (McGraw-Hill, New York, 1962).

Bank of Canada, *Annual Report for 1967* (Bank of Canada, 1968).

—, *Annual Report for 1972* (Bank of Canada, 1973).

Bank of England, *Report and Accounts for the Year Ended 28th February 1973* (Bank of England Printing Works, Loughton, Essex, 1973).

A. I. Bloomfield, *Monetary Policy under the International Gold Standard, 1880–1914* (Federal Reserve Bank of New York, monograph, 1959).

S. Brittan, *The Price of Economic Freedom: A Guide to Flexible Exchange Rates* (Macmillan, London, 1970).

P. Cagan, *The Demand for Currency Relative to the Total Money Supply*, National Bureau of Economic Research, Occasional Paper 62 (New York, 1958).

—, *Determinants and Effects of Changes in the Stock of Money, 1875–1960*, National Bureau of Economic Research, Studies in Business Cycles, no. 13 (Columbia University Press, 1965).

R. Cameron, *Banking in the Early Stages of Industrialisation* (Oxford University Press, London, 1967).

Central Statistical Office (C.S.O.), *Financial Statistics* (H.M.S.O., London).

—, *National Income and Expenditure, 1972* (Blue Book) (H.M.S.O., London, 1973).

R. N. Cooper (ed.), *International Finance* (Penguin Books, Harmondsworth, Middlesex, 1969).

P. Cootner (ed.), *The Random Character of Stock Market Prices* (M.I.T. Press, Cambridge, Mass., 1967).

R. M. Dunn Jr, *Canada's Experience with Fixed and Flexible Exchange Rates in a North American Capital Market* (Canadian-American Committee, sponsored by National Planning Association (U.S.A.) and Private Planning Association of Canada, 1971).

E. Feige, *The Demand for Liquid Assets: A Temporal Cross Section Analysis* (Prentice-Hall, Englewood Cliffs, N.J., 1964).

G. Fisher and D. Sheppard, *Effects of Monetary Policy on the United States Economy*, Organisation for Economic Co-operation and Development, Occasional Studies (O.E.C.D., Paris, December 1972).

I. Fisher, *The Theory of Interest* (Macmillan, London, 1930).

M. Friedman (ed.), *Studies in the Quantity Theory of Money* (University of Chicago Press, 1956).

M. Friedman, *The Optimum Quantity of Money and Other Essays* (Aldine, Chicago, 1969).

M. Friedman and A. J. Schwartz, *A Monetary History of the United States, 1867–1960*, National Bureau of Economic Research (Princeton University Press, 1963).

G. Garvy and M. Blyn, *The Velocity of Money* (Federal Reserve Bank of New York, New York, 1969).

R. W. Goldsmith and C. Saunders (eds), *The Measurement of National Wealth: Income and Wealth, Series VIII* (Bowes & Bowes, London, 1959).

R. W. Goldsmith, *The National Wealth of the United States in the Postwar Period* (Princeton University Press, 1962).

C. Goodhart, *The Business of Banking, 1891–1914* (Weidenfeld & Nicolson, London, 1972).

—, *The New York Money Market and the Finance of Trade, 1900–1913* (Harvard University Press, 1969).

311

J. Gurley and E. Shaw, *Money in a Theory of Finance* (The Brookings Institution, Washington, 1960).

J. Hirshleifer, *Investment, Interest and Capital* (Prentice-Hall, Englewood Cliffs, N.J., 1970).

D. Hodgman, *Commercial Bank Loan and Investment Policy* (University of Illinois Bureau of Economic and Business Research, 1963).

House of Representatives' sub-committee on banking and currency, *Investigation of the Financial and Monetary Conditions in the United States*, otherwise known as the *Money Trust Investigation* or *Pujo Investigation*, under House Resolutions nos 429 and 504, 2 vols, 29 parts (Government Printing Office, Washington, 1912/13).

D. M. Jaffee, *Credit Rationing and the Commercial Loan Market* (John Wiley, New York, 1971).

H. G. Johnson, *Inflation and the Monetarist Controversy* (North-Holland, Amsterdam, 1972).

—, *Essays in Monetary Economics*, 2nd ed. (Allen & Unwin, London, 1969).

R. Kessel, *The Cyclical Behavior of the Term Structure of Interest Rates*, Occasional Paper 91, National Bureau of Economic Research (New York, 1965).

J. M. Keynes, *The General Theory of Employment Interest and Money* (Macmillan, London, 1936).

J. Kornai, *Anti-Equilibrium: On Economic Systems Theory and the Task of Research* (North-Holland, Amsterdam and London, 1971).

D. Laidler, *The Demand for Money: Theories and Evidence* (International Textbook Company, Scranton, 1970).

A. Leijonhufvud, *On Keynesian Economics and the Economics of Keynes* (Oxford University Press, New York, 1968).

A. P. Lerner, *The Economics of Control* (Macmillan, New York, 1944).

I. M. D. Little and A. C. Rayner, *Higgledy Piggledy Growth Again* (Blackwell, Oxford, 1966).

F. Macaulay, *Some Theoretical Problems Suggested by the Movements of Interest Rates, Bond Yields, and Stock Prices in the United States since 1856* (National Bureau of Economic Research, New York, 1938).

F. Machlup, *International Trade and the National Income Multiplier* (Blakiston, Philadelphia, 1943; reprinted 1950).

G. Magnifico and J. H. Williamson, *European Monetary Integration* (Federal Trust Report, 1972).

B. G. Malkiel, *The Term Structure of Interest Rates* (Princeton University Press, Princeton, N.J., 1966).

R. Marris and A. Wood (eds), *The Corporate Economy* (Macmillan, London, 1971).

A. Marshall, *The Pure Theory of Foreign Trade; The Pure Theory of Domestic Values* (London School of Economics, Reprints of Scarce Tracts in Economics and Political Science, no. 1, London, 1930).

R. S. Masera, *The Term Structure of Interest Rates* (Clarendon Press, Oxford, 1972).

D. McCloskey and R. Zecher, *How the Gold Standard Worked, 1880–1913* (forthcoming).

D. Meiselman, *The Term Structure of Interest Rates* (Prentice-Hall, Englewood Cliffs, N.J., 1962).

B. J. Moore, *An Introduction to the Theory of Finance* (The Free Press, New York, 1968).

G. R. Morrison, *Liquidity Preferences of Commercial Banks* (University of Chicago Press, 1966).

W. T. Newlyn, *The Theory of Money* (Clarendon Press, Oxford, 1962).

D. Orr, *Cash Management and the Demand for Money* (Praeger, New York, 1970).

D. Patinkin, *Money, Interest and Prices* (Row, Peterson, Evanston, Ill., 1956).

B. Pesek and T. Saving, *Money, Wealth and Economic Theory* (Macmillan, New York, 1967).

E. S. Phelps, *Inflation Policy and Unemployment Theory: The Cost-Benefit Approach to Monetary Planning* (Macmillan, New York, 1972).

E. S. Phelps (ed.), *Microeconomic Foundations of Employment and Inflation Theory* (Macmillan, New York, 1970).

A. C. Pigou, *Employment and Equilibrium* (Macmillan, London, 1941).

Radcliffe Report, *The Committee on the Working of the Monetary System, Report*, Cmnd. 827 (H.M.S.O., London, 1954).

J. Revell, *The Wealth of the Nation: The National Balance Sheet of the United Kingdom, 1957–1961* (Cambridge University Press, 1967).

G. L. S. Shackle, *Expectation in Economics* (Cambridge University Press, 1949).

—, *Uncertainty in Economics* (Cambridge University Press, 1955).

—, *The Years of High Theory: Invention and Tradition in Economic Thought 1926–1939* (Cambridge University Press, 1967).

—, *A Scheme of Economic Theory* (Cambridge University Press, 1968).

D. K. Sheppard, *The Growth and Role of U.K. Financial Institutions, 1880–1962* (Methuen, London, 1971).

C. Sprenkle, *Effects of Large Firm and Bank Behavior on the Demand for Money of Large Firms* (American Bankers Association, mimeo, 1971).

R. Solow, *Price Expectations and the Behavior of the Price Level*, pamphlet (Manchester University Press, 1969).

B. Thomas, *Migration and Economic Growth* (Cambridge University Press, 1954).

N. Thygesen, *The Sources and the Impact of Monetary Changes, an Empirical Study of Danish Experiences, 1951–68* (Studies from the Copenhagen University Economic Institute, no. 17, Copenhagen, 1971).

R. Triffin, *Gold and the Dollar Crisis: The Future of Convertibility* (Yale University Press, 1960).

J. G. Williamson, *American Growth and the Balance of Payments* (University of North Carolina Press, Chapel Hill, 1964).

II Articles

S. Ahmad, 'Is Money Net Wealth?', *Oxford Economic Papers*, vol. 22, no. 3 (November 1970).

A. A. Alchian, 'Information Costs, Pricing, and Resource Unemployment,' in *Microeconomic Foundations of Employment and Inflation Theory*, ed. E. S. Phelps (Macmillan, New York, 1970).

A. A. Alchian and H. Demsetz, 'Production, Information Costs and Economic Organisation,' *American Economic Review*, vol. 62, no. 5 (December 1972).

A. A. Alchian and B. Klein, 'On a Correct Measure of Inflation,' *Journal of Money, Credit and Banking*, vol. 5, no. 1, pt 1 (February 1973).

L. Andersen and J. Jordan, 'Monetary and Fiscal Actions: A Test of Their Relative Importance in Economic Stabilization,' *Federal Reserve Bank of St. Louis Review*, vol. 50, no. 11 (November 1968).

L. Andersen and K. Carlson, 'A Monetarist Model for Economic Stabilization,' *Federal Reserve Bank of St. Louis Review*, vol. 52, no. 4 (April 1970).

A. P. Andrew, 'Substitutes for Cash in the Panic of 1907,' *Quarterly Journal of Economics*, vol. 22, no. 4 (August 1908).

V. Argy and J. J. Polak, 'Credit Policy and the Balance of Payments,' *International Monetary Fund Staff Papers*, vol. 18 (1971).

J. R. Aronson, 'The Idle Cash Balances of State and Local Governments: An Economic Problem of National Concern,' *Journal of Finance*, vol. 23, no. 3 (June 1968).

K. Arrow, 'Optimal Capital Policy, the Cost of Capital and Myopic Decision Rules,' *Annals of the Institute of Statistical Mathematics*, vol. 16, nos 1–2 (Tokyo, 1964).

M. Artis and A. R. Nobay, 'Two Aspects of the Monetary Debate,' *National Institute Economic Review*, no. 49 (August 1969).

M. Artis and M. Lewis, 'The Demand for Money: Stable or Unstable?,' *The Banker*, vol. 124, no. 577 (March 1974).

S. Axilrod and D. Beck, 'Role of Projections and Data Evaluation with Monetary Aggregates as Policy Targets,' *Controlling Monetary Aggregates II: The Implementation* (Federal Reserve Bank of Boston, 1973).

A. D. Bain, 'Flow of Funds Analysis: A Survey,' *The Economic Journal*, vol. 83, no. 332 (December 1973).

Bank of England, 'Changes in Banking Statistics,' *Bank of England Quarterly Bulletin*, vol. 12, no. 1 (March 1972).

—, 'Competition and Credit Control,' *Bank of England Quarterly Bulletin*, vol. 11, no. 2 (June 1971).

—, 'The Stock of Money,' *Bank of England Quarterly Bulletin*, vol. 10, no. 3 (September 1970).

—, 'Analyses of Financial Statistics,' *Bank of England Quarterly Bulletin* (included in all issues).

R. J. Barro and A. M. Santomero, 'Household Money Holdings and the Demand Deposit Rate,' *Journal of Money, Credit and Banking*, vol. 4, no. 2 (May 1972).

R. J. Barro, 'Inflation, the Payments Period, and the Demand for Money,' *Journal of Political Economy*, vol. 78, no. 6 (November/December 1970).

—, abstract of doctoral dissertation, *Journal of Finance*, vol. 26, no. 3 (June 1971).

W. J. Baumol, 'The Transactions Demand for Cash: an Inventory Theoretic Approach,' *Quarterly Journal of Economics*, vol. 66 (November 1952).

W. J. Baumol and B. G. Malkiel, 'The Firm's Optimal Debt-Equity Combination and the Cost of Capital,' *Quarterly Journal of Economics*, vol. 81, no. 4 (November 1967).

G. Benston, 'Interest Payments on Demand Deposits and Bank Investment Behavior,' *Journal of Political Economy*, vol. 72, no. 5 (October 1964).

J. Bispham (ed.), 'Appraisal,' *National Institute Economic Review*, no. 67 (February 1974).

J. Black, 'Note on a Moving Parity,' *The Economist* (4 November 1961).

K. Borch, 'A Note on Uncertainty and Indifference Curves,' *Review of Economic Studies*, vol. 36 (1), no. 165 (January 1967).

F. Brechling, 'Monetary Policy and Neo-Classical Investment Analysis,' in *Issues in Monetary Economics*, ed. R. Nobay and H. G. Johnson (Oxford University Press, 1974).

M. Bronfenbrenner and T. Mayer, 'Liquidity Functions in the American Economy,' *Econometrica*, vol. 28, no. 4 (October 1960).

K. Brunner, 'Money Supply Process and Monetary Policy in an Open Economy,' in *International Trade and Money*, ed. M. B. Connolly and A. K. Swoboda (Allen & Unwin, London, 1973).

—, 'A Survey of Selected Issues in Monetary Theory,' Reprint no. 2 of the Research Project in Monetary Theory and Monetary Policy at the University of Konstanz (University of Konstanz, 1971).

K. Brunner and A. Meltzer, 'Some Further Investigations of Demand and Supply Functions for Money,' *The Journal of Finance*, vol. 19, no. 2, pt 1 (May 1964).

—, 'Economies of Scale in Cash Balances Reconsidered,' *Quarterly Journal of Economics*, vol. 81, no. 8 (August 1967).

—, 'Friedman's Monetary Theory,' *Journal of Political Economy*, vol. 80, no. 5 (September/October 1972).

—, 'Money, Debt, and Economic Activity,' *Journal of Political Economy*, vol. 80, no. 5 (September/October 1972).

—, 'The Uses of Money: Money in the Theory of an Exchange Economy,' *American Economic Review*, vol. 61, no. 5 (December 1971).

J. P. Burman, 'Yield Curves for Gilt-edged Stocks: Further Investigation,' *Bank of England Quarterly Bulletin*, vol. 13, no. 3 (September 1973).

J. P. Burman and W. R. White, 'Yield Curves for Gilt-edged Stocks,' *Bank of England Quarterly Bulletin*, vol. 12, no. 4 (December 1972).

A. Buse, 'The Structure of Interest Rates and Recent British Experience: A Comment,' *Economica*, vol. 34, no. 135 (August 1967).

P. Cagan, 'The Monetary Dynamics of Hyperinflation,' in *Studies in the Quantity Theory of Money*, ed. M. Friedman (University of Chicago Press, 1956).

T. Cargill and R. Meyer, 'A Spectral Approach to Estimating the Distributed Lag Relationship Between Long and Short Term Interest Rates,' *International Economic Review*, vol. 13, no. 2 (June 1972).

K. M. Carlson, 'Monetary and Fiscal Actions in Macro-economic Models,' *Federal Reserve Bank of St. Louis Review*, vol. 56, no. 1 (January 1974).

M. Chossudovsky, 'Optimal Policy Configurations under Alternative Community Group Preferences,' *Kyklos*, vol. 25, no. 4 (1972).

G. C. Chow, 'On the Long-Run and Short-Run Demand for Money,' *The Journal of Political Economy*, vol. 74, no. 2 (April 1966).

C. F. Christ, 'A Short-Run Aggregate-Demand Model of the Inter-dependence and Effects of Monetary and Fiscal Policies with Keynesian and Classical Interest Elasticities,' *The American Economic Review*, vol. 57 (May 1967) papers and proceedings.

—, 'A Simple Macroeconomic Model with a Government Budget Restraint,' *Journal of Political Economy*, vol. 76, no. 1 (January/February 1968).

P. W. Clark, 'Some Early Estimates of the Price and Quantity Effects of the Smithsonian Agreement on the U.S. Trade Account,' presented to the annual meeting of the Econometric Society, 28–30 December 1973, New York, mimeo.

R. W. Clower, 'The Keynesian Counterrevolution: a Theoretical Reappraisal,' in *The Theory of Interest Rates*, ed. F. Hahn and F. Brechling (Macmillan, London, 1965), also reprinted in *Monetary Theory*, ed. R. W. Clower (Penguin Modern Economic Readings, Baltimore, 1969).

—, 'Theoretical Foundations of Monetary Policy,' *Monetary Theory and Monetary Policy in the 1970s, Proceedings of the 1970 Sheffield Money Seminar*, ed. G. Clayton, J. C. Gilbert and R. Sedgwick (Oxford University Press, 1971).

R. H. Coase, 'The Nature of the Firm,' *Economica*, new series, vol. 4 (November 1937), reprinted in *Readings in Price Theory*, American Economic Association Series (Allen & Unwin, London, 1953).

B. C. Cohen, 'The Demand for Money by Ownership Category,' *National Banking Review*, vol. 4, no. 3 (March 1967).

R. N. Cooper, 'Flexing the International Monetary System: The Case for Gliding Parities,' *The International Adjustment Mechanism* (Federal Reserve Bank of Boston, Proceedings of a Conference held in October 1969, Conference Series no. 2, 1970).

W. M. Corden, 'Monetary Integration,' *Essays in International Finance*, no. 93 (April 1972: International Finance Section of the Department of Economics of Princeton University).

A. B. Cramp, 'The Control of Bank Deposits,' *Lloyds Bank Review*, no. 86 (October 1967).

A. D. Crockett, 'Timing Relationships, between Movements of Monetary and National Income Variables,' *Bank of England Quarterly Bulletin*, vol. 10, no. 4 (December 1970).

J. M. Culbertson, 'The Term Structure of Interest Rates,' *Quarterly Journal of Economics*, vol. 71 (November 1957).

—, 'The Interest Rate Structure: Towards Completion of the Classical System,' in *The Theory of Interest Rates*, ed. F. Hahn and F. Brechling (Macmillan, London, 1965).

P. Davidson, 'A Keynesian View of Friedman's Theoretical Framework for Monetary Analysis,' *Journal of Political Economy*, vol. 80, no. 5 (September/October 1972).

P. Davidson and S. Weintraub, 'Money as Cause and Effect,' *The Economic Journal*, vol. 83, no. 332 (December 1973).

R. G. Davis, 'Short-run Targets for Open Market Operations,' from *Open Market Policies and Operating Procedures – Staff Studies* (Federal Reserve Board, 1971).

—, 'Implementing Open Market Policy with Monetary Aggregate Objectives,' *Federal Reserve Bank of New York Monthly Review*, vol. 55, no. 7 (July 1973).

A. S. Deaton, 'Wealth Effects on Consumption in a Modified Life-Cycle Model,' *The Review of Economic Studies*, vol. 32, no. 120 (October 1972).

F. de Leeuw and E. Gramlich, 'The Channels of Monetary Policy,' a Staff Economic Study, *Federal Reserve Bulletin*, vol. 55, no. 6 (June 1969).

D. S. Dutton and W. P. Gramm, 'Transactions Costs, the Wage Rate and the Demand for Money,' *The American Economic Review*, vol. 63, no. 4 (September 1973).

E. F. Fama, 'Risk, Return, and Equilibrium,' *Journal of Political Economy*, vol. 79, no. 1 (January/February 1971).

D. I. Fand, 'Some Implications of Money Supply Analysis,' *The American Economic Review*, vol. 57 (May 1967) papers and proceedings.

E. Feige, M. Parkin, R. Avery, and C. Stones, 'The Roles of Money in an Economy and the Optimum Quantity of Money,' *Economica*, vol. 40, no. 160 (November 1973).

E. Feige and M. Parkin, 'The Optimal Quantity of Money, Bonds, Commodity Inventories, and Capital,' *The American Economic Review*, vol. 61, no. 3, pt 1 (June 1971).

M. S. Feldstein, 'Mean-Variance Analysis in the Theory of Liquidity Preference and Portfolio Selection,' *Review of Economic Studies*, vol. 36 (1), no. 105 (January 1969).

—, 'Tax Incentives, Corporate Saving and Capital Accumulation in the United States,' *Journal of Public Economics*, vol. 2, no. 2 (April 1973).

R. Ferber, 'Consumer Economics, A Survey,' *The Journal of Economic Literature*, vol. 11, no. 4 (December 1973).

D. Fisher, 'The Structure of Interest Rates: A Comment,' *Economica*, vol. 31, no. 124 (November 1964).

—, 'Expectations, the Term Structure of Interest Rates, and Recent British Experience,' *Economica*, vol. 33, no. 131 (August 1966).

—, 'The Objectives of British Monetary Policy, 1951–1964,' *The Journal of Finance*, vol. 23, no. 5 (December 1968).

—, 'The Demand for Money in Britain: Quarterly Results 1951 to 1967,' *The Manchester School of Economic and Social Studies*, vol. 36, no. 4 (December 1968).

—, 'The Instruments of Monetary Policy and the Generalised Trade-off Function for Britain, 1955–1968,' *Manchester School of Economic and Social Studies*, vol. 38, no. 3 (September 1970).

J. M. Fleming, 'On Exchange Rate Unification,' *The Economic Journal*, vol. 81, no. 323 (September 1971).

J. E. Floyd, 'Monetary and Fiscal Policy in a World of Capital Mobility,' *The Review of Economic Studies*, vol. 86, no. 108 (October 1969).

—, 'A Reply,' *The Review of Economic Studies*, vol. 40, no. 122 (April 1973).

M. Friedman, 'The Case for Flexible Exchange Rates,' *Essays in Positive Economics* (University of Chicago Press, 1953).

—, 'The Quantity Theory of Money – A Restatement,' in *Studies in the Quantity Theory of Money*, ed. M. Friedman (University of Chicago Press, 1956).

—, 'The Demand for Money: Some Theoretical and Empirical Results,' *Journal of Political Economy*, vol. 67, no. 4 (August 1959).

—, 'The Role of Monetary Policy,' *The American Economic Review*, vol. 58, no. 1 (March 1968).

—, 'A Theoretical Framework for Monetary Analysis,' *Journal of Political Economy*, vol. 78, no. 2 (March/April 1970).

—, 'Comment on Tobin,' *Quarterly Journal of Economics*, vol. 84 (May 1970).

—, 'A Monetary Theory of Nominal Income,' *Journal of Political Economy*, vol. 79, no. 2 (March/April 1971).

—, 'Government Revenue from Inflation,' *Journal of Political Economy*, vol. 79, no. 4 (July/August 1971).

—, 'Comments on the Critics,' *Journal of Political Economy*, vol. 80, no. 5 (September/October 1972).

M. Friedman and D. Meiselman, 'The Relative Stability of Monetary Velocity and the Investment Multiplier in the United States, 1897–1958,' *Research Study Two in Stabilization Policies*, prepared by E. Cary Brown and others for the Commission on Money and Credit (Prentice-Hall, Englewood Cliffs, N.J., 1964).

M. Friedman and A. J. Schwartz, 'Money and Business Cycles,' *Review of Economics and Statistics*, vol. 45, supplement (February 1963).

—, 'The Definition of Money,' *Journal of Money, Credit and Banking*, vol. 1, no. 1 (February 1969).

I. Friend, 'Mythodology in Finance,' *The Journal of Finance*, vol. 28, no. 2 (May 1973).

A. Glyn, 'The Stock Market Valuation of British Companies and the Cost of Capital, 1955–69,' *Oxford Economic Papers*, vol. 25, no. 2 (July 1973).

S. M. Goldfeld and A. S. Blinder, 'Some Implications of Endogenous Stabilisation Policy,' *Brookings Papers on Economic Activity*, no. 3 (1972).

C. Goodhart, 'Monetary Policy in the United Kingdom,' from *Monetary Policy in Twelve Industrial Countries*, ed. K. Holbik (Federal Reserve Bank of Boston, 1973).

C. Goodhart and R. Bhansali, 'Political Economy,' *Political Studies*, vol. 18, no. 1 (March 1970).

G. Goodhart and A. Crockett, 'The Importance of Money,' *Bank of England Quarterly Bulletin*, vol. 10, no. 2 (June 1970).

C. Goodhart and D. Gowland, 'Rational Expectations and the U.K. Gilt Market' (Bank of England, mimeo, 1974).

C. Goodhart, D. Gowland and D. Williams, 'Money, Income and Causality: the U.K. Experience' (Bank of England, mimeo, 1974).

J. P. Gould, 'Adjustment Costs in the Theory of Investment of the Firm,' *Review of Economic Studies*, vol. 35 (1), no. 101 (January 1968).

D. Gowland, 'The Money Supply and Stock Market Prices,' paper presented at the A.U.T.E. Conference at Manchester in April 1974, mimeo.

E. Gramlich, 'The Usefulness of Monetary and Fiscal Policy as Discretionary Stabilization Tools,' *Journal of Money, Credit and Banking*, vol. 3, no. 2 (May 1971) pt 2.

E. Gramlich and J. Kalchbrenner, 'A Constrained Estimation Approach to the Demand for Liquid Assets,' presented at the Federal Reserve Committee on Financial Analysis (April 1969) mimeo.

J. Grandmont and Y. Younes, 'On the Efficiency of a Monetary Equilibrium,' *Review of Economic Studies*, vol. 40, no. 122 (April 1973).

C. W. J. Granger, 'Investigating Causal Relations by Econometric Models and Cross-Spectral Methods,' *Econometrica*, vol. 37 (July 1969).

J. Grant, 'Meiselman on the Structure of Interest Rates: A British Test,' *Economica*, vol. 31, no. 121 (February 1964).

G. Hacche, 'A Review of Demand for Money Relationships,' *Bank of England Quarterly Bulletin*, vol. 14, no. 3 (September 1974).

F. H. Hahn, 'On the Foundations of Monetary Theory,' *Essays in Modern Economics*, ed. M. Parkin (Longman, London, 1973).

—, 'The Winter of our Discontent,' *Economica*, vol. 40, no. 159 (August 1973).

C. W. Haley, 'Taxes, the Cost of Capital, and the Firm's Investment Decision,' *The Journal of Finance*, vol. 26, no. 4 (September 1971).

M. J. Hamburger, 'Indicators of Monetary Policy: The Arguments and the Evidence,' *The American Economic Review*, vol. 60 (May 1970) papers and proceedings.

—, 'The Lag in the Effect of Monetary Policy: A Survey of Recent Literature,' *The Federal Reserve Bank of New York Monthly Review*, vol. 53, no. 12 (December 1971).

—, 'Expectations, Long-Term Interest Rates and Monetary Policy in the United Kingdom,' *Bank of England Quarterly Bulletin*, vol. 11, no. 3 (September 1971).

—, 'The Demand for Money in 1971: Was there a Shift?,' *Journal of Money, Credit and Banking*, vol. 5, no. 2 (May 1973).

M. Hamburger and E. Platt, 'The Expectations Hypothesis and the Efficiency of the Treasury Bill Market' (Federal Reserve Bank of New York, mimeo, 1973).

B. Hansen, 'On the Effects of Fiscal and Monetary Policy: A Taxonomic Discussion,' *The American Economic Review*, vol. 63, no. 4 (September 1973).

A. C. Harberger, 'Some Evidence on the International Price Mechanism,' *Journal of Political Economy*, vol. 65 (1957) reprinted in *International Finance*, ed. R. N. Cooper (Penguin Modern Economics, 1969).

H. R. Heller, 'The Demand for Money: The Evidence from the Short-Run Data,' *The Quarterly Journal of Economics*, vol. 79, no. 2 (May 1965).

P. H. Hendershott and J. C. Van Horne, 'Expected Inflation Implied by Capital Market Rates,' *The Journal of Finance*, vol. 28, no. 2 (May 1973).

D. D. Hester, 'Inflation and the Recent American Happening,' Proceedings of the Association of University Teachers of Economics, Conference at Warwick 1973 (to be published).

D. Hester and D. Britto, 'Stability and Control of the Money Supply,' *Quarterly Journal of Economics*, vol. 88, no. 2 (May 1974).

J. Hicks, 'The Future of the Rate of Interest,' a paper read before the Manchester Statistical Society on 12 March 1958, and published by the Society: also presented as a Memorandum to the Radcliffe Committee, *Memoranda of Evidence*, vol. 3 (H.M.S.O., London, 1960).

K. Hilton and D. Crossfield, 'Short-run Consumption Functions for the U.K., 1955–66,' in *The Econometric Study of the United Kingdom*, ed. K. Hilton and D. Heathfield (Macmillan, London, 1970).

R. Holbrook, 'Optimal Economic Policy and the Problem of Instrument Instability,' *The American Economic Review*, vol. 62, no. 1 (March 1972).

A. Holmes and P. Meek, 'Open Market Operations and the Monetary and Credit Aggregates – 1971,' *Federal Reserve Bank of New York Monthly Review*, vol. 54, no. 4 (April 1972).

W. Hopkin and W. Godley, 'An Analysis of Tax Changes,' *National Institute Economic Review*, no. 32 (May 1965).

H. S. Houthakker and S. P. Magee, 'Income and Price Elasticities in World Trade,' *The Review of Economics and Statistics*, vol. 51, no. 2 (May 1969).

D. Hume, 'Of the Balance of Trade,' from *Essays, Moral, Political and Literary*, vol. 1 (Longmans Green, London, 1898), reprinted in *International Finance*, ed. R. N. Cooper (Penguin Books, Harmondsworth, Middlesex, 1969).

J. C. Ingram, 'Some Implications of Puerto Rican Experience,' *Regional Payments Mechanism: The Case of Puerto Rico* (University of North Carolina Press, Chapel Hill, 1962), reprinted in *International Finance*, ed. R. N. Cooper.

—, 'Comment on Kenen,' *Monetary Problems of the International Economy*, ed. R. A. Mundell and A. K. Swoboda (University of Chicago Press, 1969).

M. C. Jensen, 'Capital Markets: Theory and Evidence,' *The Bell Journal of Economics and Management Science*, vol. 3, no. 2 (autumn 1972).

H. G. Johnson, 'Monetary Theory and Policy,' *The American Economic Review*, vol. 52, no. 3 (June 1962), also reproduced in *Monetary Theory and Policy*, ed. R. S. Thorn (Random House, New York, 1966).

—, 'Inside Money, Outside Money, Income, Wealth and Welfare in Monetary Theory,' *Journal of Money, Credit and Banking*, vol. 1, no. 1 (February 1969).

—, 'Is There An Optimal Money Supply?,' *Journal of Finance*, vol. 25, no. 2 (May 1970).

—, 'The Monetary Approach to Balance-of-Payments Theory,' in *Further Essays in Monetary Economics* (Allen & Unwin, London, 1972), also produced in *International Trade and Money*, ed. M. B. Connolly and A. K. Swoboda (Allen & Unwin, London, 1973).

—, 'The Monetary Theory of Balance of Payments Policies,' in *The Monetary Approach to the Balance of Payments*, ed. J. Frenkel and H. G. Johnson (Allen & Unwin, London, 1974).

H. B. Junz and R. R. Rhomberg, 'Price Competitiveness in Export Trade Among Industrialised Countries,' *The American Economic Review*, vol. 63, no. 2 (May 1973).

R. Kahn, 'The International Monetary System,' *The American Economic Review*, vol. 63, no. 2 (May 1973).

N. Kaldor, 'Alternative Theories of Distribution,' *Review of Economic Studies*, vol. 23 (1955) (reprinted in *Essays on Value and Distribution*).

—, 'The Case for Regional Policies,' *Scottish Journal of Political Economy*, vol. 17, no. 3 (November 1970).

J. Kareken and N. Wallace, 'The Monetary Instrument Variable Choice: How Important?,' *Journal of Money, Credit and Banking*, vol. 4, no. 3 (August 1972).

E. Karni, 'The Transactions Demand for Cash: Incorporation of the Value of Time into the Inventory Approach,' *Journal of Political Economy*, vol. 81, no. 5 (September/October 1973).

N. J. Kavanagh and A. A. Walters, 'Demand for Money in the U.K., 1877–1961: Some Preliminary Findings,' *Bulletin of the Oxford University Institute of Economics and Statistics*, vol. 28, no. 2 (May 1966).

P. B. Kenen, 'The Theory of Optimum Currency Areas: An Eclectic View,' in *Monetary Problems of the International Economy*, ed. R. A. Mundell and A. K. Swoboda (University of Chicago Press,1969).

M. W. Keran, 'Monetary and Fiscal Influences on Economic Activity: The Foreign Experience,' *Federal Reserve Bank of St. Louis Review*, vol. 52, no. 2 (February 1970).

—, 'Selecting a Monetary Indicator – Evidence from the United States and Other Developed Countries,' *Federal Reserve Bank of St. Louis Review*, vol. 52, no. 9 (September 1970).

M. S. Khan, 'A Note on the Secular Behaviour of Velocity within the Context of the Inventory– Theoretic Model of Demand for Money,' *The Manchester School Journal*, no. 2 (June 1973).

M. A. King, 'Announcements of Tax Changes and Optimal Investment Behaviour,' presented to the European Meeting of the Econometric Society (Budapest, September 1972) mimeo.

D. Kinley, 'Credit – Currency and Population,' *Journal of Political Economy*, vol. 10, no. 1 (December 1901).

J. J. Klein, Discussion of Fand's paper on 'A Monetarist Model of the Monetary Process,' *The Journal of Finance*, vol. 25, no. 2 (May 1970).

L. A. Kochin, 'Judging Stabilisation Policy' (Federal Reserve Bank of New York, mimeo, 1972).

G. Kramer, 'Short-Term Fluctuations in U.S. Voting Behavior, 1896–1964,' *American Political Science Review*, vol. 66 (March 1971).

A. B. Laffer, 'Trade Credit and the Money Market,' *Journal of Political Economy*, vol. 78, no. 2 (March/April 1970).

A. B. Laffer and R. D. Ranson, 'Formal Model of the Economy,' *Journal of Business*, vol. 44 (July 1971).

D. Laidler, 'The Rate of Interest and the Demand for Money – Some Empirical Evidence,' *The Journal of Political Economy*, vol. 74, no. 6 (December 1966).

—, 'The Definition of Money,' *Journal of Money, Credit and Banking*, vol. 1, no. 3 (August 1969).

—, 'The Influence of Money on Economic Activity – A Survey of Some Current Problems,' in *Monetary Theory and Monetary Policy in the 1970s*, ed. G. Clayton, J. C. Gilbert and R. Sedgwick (Oxford University Press, London, 1971).

—, 'Thomas Tooke on Monetary Reform,' in *Essays in Honour of Lord Robbins*, ed. M. Peston and B. Corry (Weidenfeld & Nicolson, London, 1972).

—, Review of D. Orr's *Cash Management and the Demand for Money*, in *Economica*, vol. 39, no. 156 (November 1972).

—, 'Expectations, Adjustment, and the Dynamic Response of Income to Policy Changes,' *Journal of Money, Credit and Banking*, vol. 5, no. 1, pt. 1 (February 1973).

D. Laidler and J. M. Parkin, 'The Demand for Money in the United Kingdom, 1955–67: Preliminary Estimates,' *The Manchester School of Economic and Social Studies*, vol. 38, no. 3 (September 1970).

T. H. Lee, 'Substitutability of Non-Bank Intermediary Liabilities for Money: The Empirical Evidence,' *The Journal of Finance*, vol. 21, no. 3 (September 1966).

—, 'Alternative Interest Rates and the Demand for Money: The Empirical Evidence,' *The American Economic Review*, vol. 57, no. 5 (December 1967).

D. Levhari and D. Patinkin, 'The Role of Money in a Simple Growth Model,' *The American Economic Review*, vol. 58, no. 4 (September 1968).

R. Lipsey and M. Parkin, 'Incomes Policy: A Re-appraisal,' *Economica*, vol. 37, no. 146 (May 1970).

R. E. Lombra and R. C. Torto, 'Federal Reserve "Defensive" Behavior and the Reverse Causation Argument,' *Southern Economic Journal*, vol. 40, no. 1 (July 1973).

D. Luckett, 'Multi-Period Expectations and the Term Structure of Interest Rates,' *Quarterly Journal of Economics*, vol. 81, no. 2 (May 1967).

R. I. McKinnon, 'Optimum Currency Areas,' *The American Economic Review*, vol. 53, no. 4 (September 1963).

A. N. McLeod, 'Credit Expansion in an Open Economy,' *The Economic Journal*, vol. 72, no. 287 (September 1962).

B. Malkiel and E. Kane, 'The Term Structure of Interest Rates: An Analysis of a Survey of Interest-Rate Expectations,' *The Review of Economics and Statistics*, vol. 49, no. 3 (August 1967).

R. Marris, 'Why Economics Needs a Theory of the Firm,' *The Economic Journal*, vol. 82, no. 325s (March 1972, supplement).

A. L. Marty, 'Inside Money, Outside Money and the Wealth Effect,' *Journal of Money, Credit and Banking*, vol. 1, no. 1 (February 1969).

R. Masera, 'Properties of a Monetarist Model for Economic Stabilisation: Comment on Andersen,' Proceedings of the First Konstanzer Seminar, Supplement to *Kredit und Kapital*, ed. K. Brunner (Duncker & Humblot, Berlin, 1972).

J. E. Meade, 'Exchange-Rate Flexibility,' *The Three Banks Review*, no. 70 (June 1966).

L. A. Metzler, 'Wealth, Saving and the Rate of Interest,' *Journal of Political Economy*, vol. 59 (April 1951).

A. H. Meltzer, 'The Demand for Money: The Evidence from the Time Series,' *The Journal of Political Economy*, vol. 71, no. 3 (June 1963).

—, in a discussion on the question 'Is There an Optimal Money Supply?,' *The Journal of Finance*, vol. 25, no. 2 (May 1970).

M. H. Miller and D. Orr, 'A Model of the Demand for Money by Firms,' *Quarterly Journal of Economics*, vol. 80, no. 3 (August 1966).

—, 'The Demand for Money by Firms: Extensions of Analytic Results,' *The Journal of Finance*, vol. 23, no. 5 (December 1968).

H. Minsky, 'Can "It" Happen Again?,' in *Banking and Monetary Studies*, ed. D. Carson (Irwin, Homewood, Ill., 1963).

—, 'An Evaluation of Recent U.S. Monetary Policy, Monetary Control and Economic Stability,' *The Bankers' Magazine*, vol. 214, no. 1544 (November 1972).

F. Modigliani and F. Cotula, 'An Empirical Analysis of Financial Flows and the Composition of the Financial Wealth of the Economy,' *Banca Nazionale del Lavoro* (forthcoming).

F. Modigliani and M. H. Miller, 'The Cost of Capital, Corporation Finance and the Theory of Investment,' *The American Economic Review*, vol. 48, no. 3 (June 1958).

F. Modigliani and R. J. Shiller, 'Inflation, Rational Expectations and the Term Structure of Interest Rates,' *Economica*, vol. 40, no. 157 (February 1973).

F. Modigliani and R. C. Sutch, 'Innovations in Interest Rate Policy,' *The American Economic Review*, vol. 56, no. 2 (May 1966).

—, 'Debt Management and the Term Structure of Interest Rates: An Empirical Analysis of Recent Experience,' *Journal of Political Economy*, vol. 75, no. 4, pt II (August 1967) supplement.

M. Monti, 'A Theoretical Model of Bank Behaviour and its Implications for Monetary Policy,' *L'Industria Revista di Economia Politica*, no. 2 (1971).

B. J. Moore, 'Optimal Monetary Policy,' *The Economic Journal*, vol. 82, no. 325 (March 1972).

B. Motley, 'A Demand for Money Function for the Household Sector–Some Preliminary Findings,' *The Journal of Finance*, vol. 22, no. 3 (September 1967).

R. A. Mundell, 'A Theory of Optimum Currency Areas,' *The American Economic Review*, vol. 60, no. 4 (September 1961).

—, 'The Appropriate Use of Monetary and Fiscal Policy for Internal and External Stability,' *International Monetary Fund Staff Papers*, vol. 9 (March 1962), reprinted in *Monetary Theory and Policy*, ed. R. S. Thorn (Random House, New York, 1966).

A. E. Murphy, 'The Nature of Money–with Particular Reference to the Irish Bank Closure' (mimeo, Trinity College, Dublin, 1972).

J. F. Muth, 'Rational Expectations and the Theory of Price Movements,' *Econometrica*, vol. 29 (July 1961).

W. T. Newlyn, 'The Supply of Money and its Control,' *The Economic Journal*, vol. 74, no. 214 (June 1964).

S. Nickell, 'On the Role of Expectations in the Pure Theory of Investment,' *Review of Economic Studies*, vol. 41 (1), no. 125 (January 1974).

J. Niehans, 'Money in a Static Theory of Optimal Payments Arrangements,' *Journal of Money, Credit and Banking*, vol. 1, no. 4 (November 1969).

—, 'Money and Barter in General Equilibrium with Transactions Costs,' *The American Economic Review*, vol. 61, no. 5 (December 1971).

W. D. Nordhaus, 'The Effects of Inflation on the Distribution of Economic Welfare,' *Journal of Money, Credit and Banking*, vol. 5, no. 1 (February 1973) pt. II.

W. Nordhaus and H. Wallich, 'Alternatives for Debt Management,' *Federal Reserve Bank of Boston Conference on Issues in Federal Debt Management*, June 1973 (Federal Reserve Bank of Boston, 1974).

W. E. Norton, 'Debt Management and Monetary Policy in the United Kingdom,' *The Economic Journal*, vol. 79, no. 315 (September 1969).

D. Orr and W. G. Mellon, 'Stochastic Reserve Losses and Expansion of Bank Credit,' *The American Economic Review*, vol. 51, no. 4 (September 1961).

J. M. Ostroy, 'The Informational Efficiency of Monetary Exchange,' *The American Economic Review*, vol. 63, no. 4 (September 1973).

M. Parkin, 'The Portfolio Behaviour of Commercial Banks,' in *The Econometric Study of the United Kingdom*, ed. K. Hilton and D. Heathfield (Macmillan, London, 1970).

—, 'The Portfolio and Interest Rate Behaviour of Building Societies,' *The Manchester School of Economic and Social Studies* (December 1972).

—, 'Discount House Portfolio and Debt Selection,' *Review of Economic Studies*, vol. 37 (4), no. 112 (October 1970).

M. Parkin and M. Gray, 'Portfolio Diversification as Optimal Precautionary Behaviour,' in *Theory of Demand: Real and Monetary*, by M. Morishima *et al.* (Clarendon Press, Oxford, 1973).

M. Parkin, R. Barrett and M. Gray, 'The Demand for Financial Assets by the Personal Sector of the U.K. Economy,' Proceedings of the London Business School Conference of June 1972 on *Modelling the U.K. Economy* (forthcoming).

D. Patinkin, 'Friedman on the Quantity Theory and Keynesian Economics,' *Journal of Political Economy*, vol. 80, no. 5 (September/October 1972).

G. Pepper, *Monetary Bulletin*, no. 17 (Greenwell, London, October 1973).

D. Peretz, 'Thirty-five Years of Change for the Financial System,' *Futures*, vol. 3, no. 4 (December 1971).

M. Perlman, 'The Roles of Money in an Economy and the Optimum Quantity of Money,' *Economica*, vol. 38, no. 151 (August 1971).

—, 'The Roles of Money in an Economy and the Optimum Quantity of Money: Reply,' *Economica*, vol. 40, no. 160 (November 1973).

G. Perry, 'Changing Labor Markets and Inflation,' in *Brookings Papers on Economic Activity: 1970, 3*, ed. A. Okun and G. Perry (The Brookings Institution, Washington, 1970).

M. Peston, 'The Correlation between Targets and Instruments,' *Economica*, vol. 39, no. 156 (November 1972).

J. Pierce and T. Thomson, 'A Monthly Econometric Model of the Financial Sector' (Federal Reserve Board Staff Studies, mimeo).

J. Pierce and T. Thomson, 'Some Issues in Controlling the Stock of Money,' *Controlling Monetary Aggregates II: The Implementation*, proceedings of a Conference held in September 1972, sponsored by the Federal Reserve Bank of Boston (Federal Reserve Bank of Boston, 1973).

G. Pierson, 'A Framework for Analysis of the Financial Sector,' *Harvard Institute of Economic Research, Discussion Paper, No. 124* (Harvard University, 1971).

A. C. Pigou, 'The Classical Stationary State,' *The Economic Journal*, vol. 53 (December 1943).

J. J. Polak, 'Monetary Analysis of Income Formation and Payments Problems,' *International Monetary Fund Staff Papers*, vol. 6 (1957/58).

W. Poole, 'Commercial Bank Reserve Management in a Stochastic Model: Implications for Monetary Policy,' *The Journal of Finance*, vol. 23, no. 5 (December 1968).

—, 'Optimal Choice of Monetary Policy Instruments in a Simple Stochastic Macro Model,' *Quarterly Journal of Economics*, vol. 84, no. 2 (May 1970).

—, 'Alternative Paths to a Stable Full Employment Economy,' *Brookings Papers on Economic Activity, 1971:3* (The Brookings Institution, Washington, 1971).

W. Poole and E. Kornblith, 'The Friedman–Meiselman CMC Paper: New Evidence on an Old Controversy,' *The American Economic Review*, vol. 63, no. 5 (December 1973).

L. D. Price, 'The Demand for Money in the United Kingdom: A Further Investigation,' *Bank of England Quarterly Bulletin*, vol. 12, no. 1 (March 1972).

R. Rasche, 'A Comparative Static Analysis of Some Monetarist Propositions,' *Federal Reserve Bank of St. Louis Review*, vol. 55, no. 12 (December 1973).

R. Rasche and H. Shapiro, 'The F.R.B.–M.I.T. Econometric Model: Its Special Features,' *The American Economic Review*, vol. 58, no. 2 (May 1968).

A. C. Rayner, 'Premium Bonds – The Effect of the Prize Structure,' *Bulletin of the Oxford University Institute of Economics and Statistics*, vol. 31, no. 4 (November 1969).

R. R. Rhomberg, 'Canada's Foreign Exchange Market: A Quarterly Model,' *International Monetary Fund Staff Papers*, vol. 7 (1959/60).

—, 'A Model of the Canadian Economy under Fixed and Fluctuating Exchange Rates,' *Journal of Political Economy*, vol. 72, no. 1 (February 1964).

J. Robinson, 'The Rate of Interest,' *Econometrica*, vol. 19 (1951).

P. A. Samuelson, 'The Fundamental Approximation Theorem of Portfolio Analysis in terms of Means Variances and Higher Moments,' *Review of Economic Studies*, vol. 37 (4), no. 112 (October 1970).

T. J. Sargent, 'Rational Expectations and the Term Structure of Interest Rates,' *Journal of Money, Credit and Banking*, vol. 4, no. 1 (February 1972).

—, 'Rational Expectations, the Real Rate of Interest, and the Natural Rate of Unemployment,' *Brookings Papers on Economic Activity: 1973, 2* (The Brookings Institution, Washington, 1973).

F. Schuster, 'Our Gold Reserves,' *Journal of the Institute of Bankers* (January 1907).

G. L. Shackle, Comments on Clower's paper on 'Theoretical Foundations of Monetary Policy,' in *Monetary Theory and Monetary Policy in the 1970s, Proceedings of the 1970 Sheffield Money Seminar*, ed. G. Clayton, J. C. Gilbert, and R. Sedgwick (Oxford University Press, 1971).

A. A. Shapiro, 'Inflation, Lags and the Demand for Money,' *International Economic Review*, vol. 14, no. 1 (February 1973).

D. K. Sheppard and C. R. Barrett, 'Financial Credit Multipliers and the Availability of Funds,' *Economica*, vol. 32, no. 126 (May 1965).

J. R. Shepherd and M. J. Surrey, 'The Short-term Effects of Tax Changes,' *National Institute Economic Review*, no. 46 (November 1968).

M. Shubik, 'Commodity Money, Oligopoly, Credit and Bankruptcy in a General Equilibrium Model,' *Western Economic Journal*, vol. 11, no. 1 (March 1973).

W. Silber, 'Monetary Policy Effectiveness: The Case of a Positively Sloped IS Curve,' *The Journal of Finance*, vol. 26, no. 5 (December 1971).

C. A. Sims, 'Money, Income and Causality,' *The American Economic Review*, vol. 62, no. 4 (September 1972).

A. Sinai and H. Stokes, 'Real Money Balances: An Omitted Variable from the Production Function?,' *The Review of Economics and Statistics*, vol. 54, no. 3 (August 1972).

V. Smith and R. Marcis, 'A Time Series Analysis of Post Accord Interest Rates,' *The Journal of Finance*, vol. 27, no. 3 (June 1972).

R. Solow, 'Recent Controversy on the Theory of Inflation: An Eclectic View,' *Inflation: Its Causes, Consequences and Control, A Symposium*, ed. S. W. Rousseas (New York University, New York, 1968).

R. Spencer and W. Yohe, 'The "Crowding Out" of Private Expenditures by Fiscal Policy Actions,' *Federal Reserve Bank of St. Louis Review*, vol. 52, no. 10 (October 1970).

C. Sprenkle, 'The Uselessness of Transactions Demand Models,' *The Journal of Finance*, vol. 24, no. 5 (December 1969).

—, 'On the Observed Transactions Demand for Money,' *The Manchester School of Economic and Social Studies*, no. 3 (September 1972).

D. A. Starrett, 'Inefficiency and the Demand for "Money" in a Sequence Economy,' *The Review of Economic Studies*, vol. 40 (4), no. 124 (October 1973).

G. Stevens, 'On Tobin's Multiperiod Portfolio Theorem,' *Review of Economic Studies*, vol. 39, no. 120 (October 1972).

K. Stewart, 'Government Debt, Money and Economic Activity,' *Federal Reserve Bank of St. Louis Review*, vol. 54, no. 1 (January 1972).

G. J. Stigler, 'General Economic Conditions and National Elections,' *The American Economic Review*, Papers and Proceedings, vol. 63, no. 2 (May 1973).

J. Stiglitz, 'A Re-examination of the Modigliani–Miller Theorem,' *The American Economic Review*, vol. 59, no. 5 (December 1969).

—, 'Some Aspects of the Pure Theory of Corporate Finance: Bankruptcies and Take-overs,' *The Bell Journal of Economics and Management Science*, vol. 3, no. 2 (autumn 1972).

J. Stiglitz, 'Taxation, Corporate Financial Policy, and the Cost of Capital,' *Journal of Public Economics*, vol. 2, no. 1 (February 1973).

M. Sumner, 'The Current Inflation: A Programme for Control,' *The Bankers' Magazine*, vol. 215, no. 1550 (May 1973).

A. K. Swoboda and R. Dornbusch, 'Adjustment, Policy and Monetary Equilibrium in a Two-Country Model,' in *International Trade and Money*, ed. M. B. Connolly and A. K. Swoboda (Allen & Unwin, London, 1973).

J. E. Tanner, 'Lags in the Effects of Monetary Policy: A Statistical Investigation,' *The American Economic Review*, vol. 59, no. 5 (December 1969).

R. L. Teigen, 'Demand and Supply Functions for Money in the United States: Some Structural Estimates,' *Econometrica*, vol. 32, no. 4 (October 1964).

B. Tew, 'The Implications of Milton Friedman for Britain,' *The Banker*, vol. 119, no. 522 (August 1969).

T. Thomson and J. Pierce, 'A Monthly Money Market Model' (Federal Reserve Board, mimeo).

J. Tobin, 'Liquidity Preference and Monetary Policy,' *Review of Economics and Statistics*, vol. 21 (May 1947).

—, 'Liquidity Preference as Behavior Towards Risk,' *Review of Economic Studies*, vol. 25 (February 1958).

—, 'Commercial Banks as Creators of "Money",' in *Banking and Monetary Studies*, ed. D. Carson (Irwin, Homewood, Ill., 1963).

—, 'Comments on Borch and Feldstein,' *Review of Economic Studies*, vol. 36 (1), no. 105 (January 1969).

—, 'Money and Economic Growth,' *Econometrica*, vol. 33, no. 4 (October 1965).

—, 'The Theory of Portfolio Selection,' in *The Theory of Interest Rates*, ed. F. Hahn and F. Brechling (Macmillan, London, 1965).

—, 'Money and Income: Post Hoc Ergo Propter Hoc,' *Quarterly Journal of Economics*, vol. 84, no. 2 (May 1970).

—, 'Inflation and Unemployment,' *The American Economic Review*, vol. 62, no. 1 (March 1972).

—, 'Friedman's Theoretical Framework,' *Journal of Political Economy*, vol. 80, no. 5 (September/October 1972).

E. Tower, 'Monetary and Fiscal Policy in a World of Capital Mobility: a Respecification,' *The Review of Economic Studies*, vol. 39, no. 119 (July 1972).

J. Townend, 'Substitution among Capital-Certain Assets in the Personal Sector of the U.K. Economy, 1963–71,' *The Bank of England Quarterly Bulletin*, vol. 12, no. 4 (December 1972).

S. C. Tsiang, 'The Rationale of the Mean-Standard Deviation Analysis, Skewness Preference, and the Demand for Money,' *The American Economic Review*, vol. 62, no. 3 (June 1972).

—, 'The Role of Money in Trade-Balance Stability: Synthesis of the Elasticity and Absorption Approaches,' *The American Economic Review*, vol. 51, no. 5 (December 1961), reproduced in *International Finance*, ed. R. N. Cooper.

D. P. Tucker, 'Dynamic Income Adjustment to Money-Supply Changes,' *The American Economic Review*, vol. 56, no. 3 (June 1966).

H. Turner, D. Jackson, and F. Wilkinson, 'Do Trade Unions Cause Inflation,' *University of Cambridge Department of Applied Economics, Occasional Paper 36* (Cambridge University Press, 1972).

A. Walters, 'Professor Friedman on the Demand for Money,' *Journal of Political Economy*, vol. 73, no. 5 (October 1965).

—, 'Money in Boom and Slump,' *Hobart Paper, 44*, 2nd ed. (Institute of Economic Affairs, 1970).

T. K. Whitaker, 'Monetary Integration: Reflections on Irish Experience,' *Moorgate and Wall Street* (autumn 1973).

W. R. White, 'The Term Structure of Interest Rates – A Cross-Section Test of a Mean-Variance Model,' in *Issues in Monetary Economics*, ed. R. Nobay and H. G. Johnson (Oxford University Press, 1974).

—, 'Models of Deposit Bank Portfolio Behaviour,' Proceedings of the London Business School Conference of June 1972 on *Modelling the U.K. Economy* (forthcoming).

—, 'Expectations, Investment and the U.K. Gilt-Edged Market – Some Evidence from Market Participants,' *The Manchester School of Economic and Social Studies*, no. 4 (December 1971).

H. J. Witteveen, 'Statement of the Managing Director,' presenting the 28th Annual Report of the

Executive Directors to the Board of Governors of the International Monetary Fund (Nairobi, September 1973).

—, Press Release, World Banking Conference in London, 15 January, 1974.

J. H. Williamson, 'On the Normative Theory of Balance-of-Payments Adjustment,' in *Monetary Theory and Monetary Policy in the 1970s*, ed. G. Clayton, J. Gilbert, and R. Sedgwick (Oxford University Press, 1971).

—, 'The Crawling Peg,' *Essays in International Finance* (International Finance Section, Department of Economics, Princeton University, December 1965).

O. Williamson, 'Managerial Discretion, Organisation Form, and the Multi-division Hypothesis,' in *The Corporate Economy*, ed. R. Marris and A. Wood (Macmillan, London, 1971).

A. Wojnilower, 'A New Monetary Environment' (The First Boston Corporation, New York, 1973).

G. E. Wood, 'European Monetary Union and the U.K. – A Cost–Benefit Analysis,' *Surrey Economic Papers*, no. 9 (July 1973).

J. Wood, 'Expectations, Errors, and the Term Structure of Interest Rates,' *Journal of Political Economy*, vol. 71, no. 2 (April 1963).

Index